DISTRIBUTED, CLUSTER AND GRID COMPUTING

DATA MANAGEMENT IN THE SEMANTIC WEB

DISTRIBUTED, CLUSTER AND GRID COMPUTING

Yi Pan (Series Editor)

(Georgia State University, GA, U. S.)

Advanced Parallel and Distributed Computing: Evaluation, Improvement and Practice
Yuan-Shun Dai, Yi Pan and Rajeev Raje (Editors)
2006. ISBN: 1-60021-202-6

Parallel and Distributed Systems: Evaluation and Improvement
Yuan-Shun Dai, Yi Pan and Rajeev Raje (Editors)
2006. ISBN: 1-60021-276-X

Performance Evaluation of Parallel, Distributed and Emergent Systems.
Mohamed Ould-Khaoua and Geyong Min (Editors)
2007. ISBN: 1-59454-817-X

From Problem Toward Solution: Wireless Sensor Networks Security
Zhen Jiang and Yi Pan (Editors)
2009. ISBN: 978-1-60456-457-0

Congestion Control in Computer Networks: Theory, Protocols and Applications
Jianxin Wang
2010. ISBN: 978-1-61728-698-8

Data Management in the Semantic Web
Hal Jin (Editor)
2012. ISBN: 978-1-61122-862-5

DISTRIBUTED, CLUSTER AND GRID COMPUTING

DATA MANAGEMENT IN THE SEMANTIC WEB

HAL JIN
EDITOR

Nova Science Publishers, Inc

New York

For permission to use material from this book please contact us:
Telephone 631-231-7269; Fax 631-231-8175
Web Site: http://www.novapublishers.com

Additional color graphics may be available in the e-book version of this book.

LIBRARY OF CONGRESS CATALOGING-IN-PUBLICATION DATA

Data management in the semantic web / editor, Hal Jin.
p. cm.
Includes bibliographical references and index.
ISBN 978-1-61122-862-5 (hardcover)
1. Web databases. 2. Internet searching. 3. Semantic Web. I. Jin, Hal.
QA76.9.W43D38 2011
025.042'7--dc22
2010048369

Published by Nova Science Publishers, Inc. † New York

CONTENTS

PREFACE

Effective and efficient data management is vital to today's applications. Traditional data management mainly focuses on information procession involving data within a single organization. Data are unified according to the same schema and there exists an agreement between the interacting units as to the correct mapping between these concepts. Nowadays, data management systems have to handle a variety of data sources, from proprietary ones to data publicly available. Investigating the relevance between data for information sharing has become an essential challenge for data management. This book explores the technology and application of semantic data management by bringing together various research studies in different subfields.

As discussed in Chapter 1, the emerging Web of Data utilizes the web infrastructure to represent and interrelate data. The foundational standards of the Web of Data include the Uniform Resource Identifier (URI) and the Resource Description Framework (RDF). URIs are used to identify resources and RDF is used to relate resources. While RDF has been posited as a logic language designed specifically for knowledge representation and reasoning, it is more generally useful if it can conveniently support other models of computing. In order to realize the Web of Data as a general-purpose medium for storing and processing the world's data, it is necessary to separate RDF from its logic language legacy and frame it simply as a data model. Moreover, there is significant advantage in seeing the Semantic Web as a particular interpretation of the Web of Data that is focused specifically on knowledge representation and reasoning. By doing so, other interpretations of the Web of Data are exposed that realize RDF in different capacities and in support of different computing models.

The rapid growth of the web imposes scaling challenges to general-purpose web crawlers that attempt to download plentiful web pages so that these are made available to the search engine users. Perhaps the greatest challenge associated with harvesting the web content is how to ensure that the crawlers will not waste resources trying to download pages that are of no or little interest to web users. One way to go about downloading useful web data is to build crawlers that can optimize the priority of the unvisited URLs so that pages of interest are downloaded earlier. In this respect, many attempts have been proposed towards focusing web crawls on topic-specific content. In Chapter 2, the authors build upon existing studies and they introduce a novel focused crawling approach that relies on the web pages' semantic orientation in order to determine their crawling priority. The contribution of the authors'approach lies on the fact that the authors integrate a topical ontology and a passage extraction algorithm into a common framework against which the crawler is trained, so as to be able to detect pages of interest and determine their crawling priority. The evaluation of the authors'proposed approach demonstrates that semantics-aware focused crawling yields both accurate and complete web crawls.

The semi-structured document format, such as the XML format, is used in data-management to efficiently structure, store and share the information between different users. Although the information can efficiently be accessed within a semi-structured document, automatically retrieving the relevant information from a corpus still remains a complex problem, especially when the documents are semi-structured text documents. To tackle this, the corpus can be partitioned according to the content of each document in order to make the search efficient. In document categorization, a predefined partition is given and the problem is to automatically assign the documents of the corpus to the relevant categories. The quality of the categorization highly depends on the data representation and on the similarity measure, especially when dealing with complex data such as natural language text. In Chapter 3, the authors present a semantic tree to semantically represent an XML text document and the authors propose a semantic kernel, which can be used with the semantic tree, to compute a similarity measure. The semantic meanings of words are extracted using an ontology. The authors use a text categorization problem in the biomedical field to illustrate the authors'method. The UMLS framework is used to extract the semantic information related to the biomedical field. The authors have applied this kernel with a SVM classifier to a real-world medical free-text categorization problem. The results have shown that the authors'method outperforms other common methods such as the linear kernel.

To understand the reuse process, the authors have analyzed the feasibility of ontology reuse based on which they discuss its economic aspects. In analogy to methods in the field of software engineering the authors relate costs of ontology development to the level of ontology reuse and to the costs of developing and maintaining reusable ontologies. Subsequently the authors propose a cost model focusing on activities in ontology reuse whose goal is to support a trade-off analysis of reusable ontology development costs vs. the costs of the development from scratch. The research leading to this model aims to address the following questions:

1. *Which factors influence the costs for reusing ontologies?*
2. *How can the benefits of ontology reuse be shown in monetary terms?*
3. *Which general statement can be made about the financial feasibility of ontology reuse in specific settings?*

In order to answer these questions the authors elaborate on an extension of the ONTOCOM model for cost estimation of ontologies for reuse. The authors'aim is to isolate the costs of reuse of different artifacts on different levels of the ontology engineering process, that is, reuse on the requirements, the conceptual, or the implementation level. Secondly, following work by others on economic models for software reuse, the authors intend to show the monetary value of ontology reuse in different reuse scenarios on these levels.

The remainder of Chapter 4 is organized as follows: Section 2. gives an overview of ontology reuse including the reuse process, the current state of practice, and existing methodologies for ontology reuse. Section 3. analyzes economic aspects of ontology development and reuse, presents an economic analysis, and a cost estimation model whose aim is to predict ontology reuse costs. Finally, Section 4. concludes the chapter.

In Chapter 5, the relationships between the logical and representational features on ontologies are analysed. Through several questions, this chapter restates the use of Computational logic in Ontology Engineering.

Current research in biology heavily depends on the availability and efficient use of information. In order to build new knowledge, various sources of biological data must often be combined. Semantic Web technologies, which provide a common framework allowing data to be shared and reused between applications, can be applied to the management of disseminated biological data. However, due to some specificities of biological data, applying these technologies to life science is a real challenge. Chapter 6 shows that current Semantic Web technologies start to become mature and can be used to develop large applications. However, in order to get the best from these technologies, improvements are needed both at the level of tool performance and knowledge modeling.

The next generation Internet has the potential ability to be a ubiquitous and pervasive medium communication carrier for all types of information. The World Wide Web is emerging with a broader variety of resources that include both data and services. Yet, a lot of research work focused on either service discovery or data discovery although they cannot be separated from each other. In addition, the current Network, due to its decentralized nature and weak support for semantic, is still chaotic and lacks of the ability to allow users to discover, extract and integrate information of interest from heterogeneous sources. In Chapter 7, the authors present a scalable, high performance system for data and service unified discovery, and to increase the success rate, an ontology-based approach is used to describe data and services. As for service, the authors add quality of service (QoS) information to OWL-S files to get more accurate results for users. Moreover, the authors also bring JXTA, which is a suitable foundation to build future computer systems on, to the authors'system.

Most nations in the world are currently committed to provide advanced services for their citizens. The development of a software support capable of meeting the needs for this context requires to engage in a long term bet. The success for this kind of projects is deeply related to the provision of a solid back office support for services and the use of open technologies for the interconnection and interchange of information. In Chapter 8, it is presented a formal description of the business model involved in the provision of such solution using semantics as a tool to share this conceptualization. This characterization of the problem to be solved is derived from artifacts identified in the domain and described in relation with the interaction required to fulfill the citizen's needs. On the top of this description, an entire software platform is described. Also, some useful conclusions are presented for its consideration on further projects.

In Chapter 9, the authors discuss utility of semantic topic modeling with the latent Dirichlet allocation model (LDA) and its application in bioinformatics domain. Through capturing the statistical structure of word usage patterns, LDA is capable of identifying semantic topics from a collection of text documents in an unsupervised manner. The authors show that semantic topic modeling with LDA can be used to automatically identify biological concepts from corpora of biomedical literature, thus providing more concise representation of the biomedical knowledge. The authors further demonstrate that representing text documents in semantic topic space facilitates classification of text documents. Finally, the authors show that connecting proteins in the semantic topic space enables efficient evaluation of the functional coherence of a group of proteins.

In Chapter 10 the authors present a new approach to supporting users to annotate and browse resources referred by a folksonomy. The authors'approach proposes two hierarchical structures and two related algorithms to arrange groups of semantically related tags in a hierarchy; this allows users to visualize tags of their interests according to desired semantic granularities and, then, helps them to find those tags best expressing their information needs. In this chapter the authors first illustrate the technical characteristics of the authors'approach; then the authors describe the prototype implementing it; after this, they illustrate various experiments allowing its performance to be tested; finally, the authors compare it with other related approaches already proposed in the literature.

The increasing availability of small-size sensor devices during the last few years and the large amount of data that they generate has led to the necessity for more efficient methods regarding data management. In Chapter 11, the authors review the techniques that are being used for data gathering and information management in sensor networks and the advantages that are provided through the proliferation of Semantic Web technologies. The authors present the current trends in the field of data management in sensor networks and propose a three-layer flexible architecture which intends to help developers as well as end users to take advantage of the full potential that modern sensor networks can offer. This architecture deals with issues regarding data aggregation, data enrichment and finally, data management and querying using Semantic Web technologies. Semantics are used in order to extract meaningful information from the sensor's raw data and thus facilitate smart applications development over large-scale sensor networks.

The first and overwhelmingly major challenge of the Semantic Web is annotating semantic information in text. Semantic analysis is often used to combat this problem by automatically creating the semantic metadata that is needed. However, semantic analysis has been proven difficult to get ideal results, because of two controversial problems; semantic scheme and classification. Chapter 12 presents an answer to these two problems. For semantic scheme, semantic dependency is chosen and for classification a number of machine learning approaches are examined and compared. Semantic dependency is chosen as it gives a deeper structure and better describes the richness of semantics in natural language. The classification approaches encompass standard machine learning algorithms, such as Naive Bayes, Decision Tree and Maximum Entropy, as well as multiple classification and rule-based correction approaches. The best results receive a state-of-the-art accuracy of 85.1%. In addition, an integrated system called SEEN (Semantic dEpendency parsEr for chiNese) is introduced, which combines research presented in this chapter as well as segmentation, part-of-speech, and syntactic parsing modules that are freely available from other researchers.

The amount of multimedia resources that is created and needs to be managed is increasing considerably. Additionally, a significant increase of metadata, either structured (metadata fields of standardized metadata formats) or unstructured (free tagging or annotations) is noticed. This increasing amount of data and metadata, combined with the substantial diversity in terms of used metadata fields and constructs, results in severe problems to manage and retrieve these multimedia resources. Standardized metadata schemes can be used but the plethora of these schemes results in interoperability issues. In Chapter 13, we propose a metadata model suited for personal content management systems. The authors create a layered metadata service that implements the presented model as an upper layer and combines different metadata schemes in the lower layers. Semantic web technologies are used to define and link formal representations of these schemes. Specifically, the authors create an ontology for the DIG35 metadata standard and elaborate on how it is used within this metadata service. To illustrate the service, the authors present a representative use case scenario consisting of the upload, annotation, and retrieval of multimedia content within a personal content management system.

Increasing heterogeneous Open Content is an ongoing trend in the current Social Semantic Web (S2W). Generic concepts and how-tos for higher-layered reuse of the arbitrary information overload for interactive knowledge transfer and learning - mentioning the Internet of Services (IoS) - are not covered very well yet. For further directed use of distributed services and sources, inquiry, interlinking, analysis, machine- and human-interpretable representation is as essential as lightweight user-oriented interoperation and competence in handling. In the following, the authors introduce the qKAI application framework (qualifying Knowledge Acquisition and Inquiry) [3]- a service-oriented, generic and hybrid approach combining knowledge related offers for convenient reuse. qKAI aims at closing some residual gaps between the "*sophisticated*" Semantic Web and "*hands-on*" Web 2.0 enabling loose-coupled knowledge and information services focused on knowledge life cycles, learning aspects and handy user interaction. Accomplishing user interoperation and standardized web techniques is a promising mixture to build a next generation of web applications. The focus of Chapter 14 lies on the qKAI data layer as part of the application framework and basic prerequisite to build user interaction scenarios on top of it. The qKAI data layer utilizes available, distributed semantic data sets in a practically manner using an affordable Quadcore hardware platform and preselected data dumps. Overall, the authors boost Open Content as an inherent part of higher-layered, lightweight applications in knowledge and information transfer via standard tasks of knowledge engineering and augmented user interaction. Beyond giving an overview of research background and periphery assumption, this chapter introduces the hybrid data concept - a minimalistic data model with maximized depth - implementation results and lessoned learned. The authors discuss the Semantic Web query language SPARQL and the Resource Description Format (RDF) critically to enlighten their limitations in current web application practice. qKAI implements search space restriction (Points of Interests) by smart enabled RDF representation and restriction to SQL as internally used query language. Acquiring resources and discovering the Web of Data is a massively multithreading part of the qKAI application framework that serves as basis for further knowledge based tasks.

Classical approaches of data integration, based on schemas mediation, are not suitable for the World Wide Web (WWW) environment where data is frequently modified or deleted. This chapter describes a new approach of heterogeneous data source fusion called Multi-data source Fusion Approach (MFA). Data sources are either static or active: static data sources can be structured or semi-structured, whereas active sources are services. The aim of MFA is to facilitate data sources fusion in dynamic contexts such as the Web. The authors introduce an XML-based Multi-data source Fusion Language (MFL). MFL provides two sub-languages: the Multi-data source Definition Language (MDL) - used to define the multi-data source - and the Multi-data source Retrieval Language (MRL) - that aims to retrieve conflicting data from multiple data sources.

In Chapter 15, the authors also study how to reconciliate semantically data sources. This study is based on OWL/RDF technologies. The authors' main objective is to combine data sources with a minimal effort required from the user. This objective is crucial because, in the authors'context, the authors suppose that the user is not an expert in the domain of data fusion, but he/she understands the meaning of data being integrated. The results of semantic reconciliation between data sources are used to improve the problem of rewriting MRL semantic queries into a set of equivalent sub-queries over the data sources. The authors show the design of the Multi-Data Source Management System called MDSManager. Finally, the authors give an evaluation of the authors' MRL language. The results show that our language improves significantly the XQuery language especially considering its expressiveness power and its performances.

The recent proliferation of high-level and domain-specific ontologies has necessitated the development of prudent integration strategies. Visualization techniques are an important tool to support the data and knowledge integration initiative. Chapter 16 reviews a methodology to visualize clusters of relations from ontologies specified using the Web Ontology Language (OWL). The relations, which in OWL are referred to as object properties, from various ontologies are organized into clusters based upon their intrinsic semantics. The intrinsic semantics of every relation from an input ontology is explicitly specified by a framework of 32 common elements; each element captures a specific aspect of the relationship between a relation's domain and range. Using this framework, each relation can be represented in a 32-dimensional "relation space." Relation clusters in 32 dimensions are projected to 3 dimensions using an automated 3-dimensional (3D) star coordinate-based visualization technique. Results from applying an algorithm to create and subsequently visualize relation clusters formed from the IEEE Suggested Upper Merged Ontology (SUMO) are presented in this chapter and discussed in the context of their potential utility for knowledge reuse and interoperability on the Semantic Web.

Semantic annotation of digital engineering resources is attributed as an enabling technology for knowledge sharing in sustainable manufacturing, where the economic, environmental and social objectives are incorporated into technical solutions to achieve competitive product advantages. The emerging needs for sustainability require seamless sharing of product lifecycle information and machine-understandable semantics across design and manufacturing networks. Towards this end, Chapter 17 proposes an ontology-driven approach to semantic annotation of multidisciplinary engineering resources. The targeted application is for product knowledge sharing in sustainable manufacturing of consumer electronics. The proposed approach is based on two mechanisms: 1) ontology modeling – how to specify the meaning of annotations with ontological representations to enhance sharability of the annotation content; and 2) ontology implementation – how to effectively apply the meaning of annotations to heterogeneous computer-aided tools and lifecycle processes on the basis of ontology. These semantic knowledge sharing mechanisms are validated through annotation scenarios. Two use scenarios are illustrated in the chapter for semantics sharing based on annotations in sustainable manufacturing of consumer products.

In: Data Management in the Semantic Web
Editor: Hal Jin, pp. 1-38
ISBN: 978-1-61122-862-5

Chapter 1

INTERPRETATIONS OF THE WEB OF DATA

Marko A. Rodriguez*
T-5, Center for Nonlinear Studies
Los Alamos National Laboratory
Los Alamos, New Mexico, U. S.

Abstract

The emerging Web of Data utilizes the web infrastructure to represent and interrelate data. The foundational standards of the Web of Data include the Uniform Resource Identifier (URI) and the Resource Description Framework (RDF). URIs are used to identify resources and RDF is used to relate resources. While RDF has been posited as a logic language designed specifically for knowledge representation and reasoning, it is more generally useful if it can conveniently support other models of computing. In order to realize the Web of Data as a general-purpose medium for storing and processing the world's data, it is necessary to separate RDF from its logic language legacy and frame it simply as a data model. Moreover, there is significant advantage in seeing the Semantic Web as a particular interpretation of the Web of Data that is focused specifically on knowledge representation and reasoning. By doing so, other interpretations of the Web of Data are exposed that realize RDF in different capacities and in support of different computing models.

1. Introduction

The common conception of the World Wide Web is that of a large-scale, distributed file repository [6]. The typical files found on the World Wide Web are Hyper-Text Markup Language (HTML) documents and other media such as image, video, and audio files. The "World Wide" aspect of the World Wide Web pertains to the fact that all of these files have an accessible location that is denoted by a Uniform Resource Locator (URL) [56]; a URL denotes what physical machine is hosting the file (i.e. what domain name/IP address), where in that physical machine the file is located (i.e. what directory), and finally, which protocol to use to retrieve that file from that machine (e.g. `http`, `ftp`, etc.). The "Web"

*E-mail address: marko@lanl.gov

aspect of the World Wide Web pertains to the fact that a file (typically an HTML document) can make reference (typically an `href` citation) to another file. In this way, a file on machine A can link to a file on machine B and in doing so, a network/graph/web of files emerges. The ingenuity of the World Wide Web is that it combines remote file access protocols and hypermedia and as such, has fostered a revolution in the way in which information is disseminated and retrieved—in an open, distributed manner. From this relatively simple foundation, a rich variety of uses emerges: from the homepage, to the blog, to the online store.

The World Wide Web is primarily for human consumption. While HTML documents are structured according to a machine understandable syntax, the content of the documents are written in human readable/writable language (i.e. natural human language). It is only through computationally expensive and relatively inaccurate text analysis algorithms that a machine can determine the meaning of such documents. For this reason, computationally inexpensive keyword extraction and keyword-based search engines are the most prevalent means by which the World Wide Web is machine processed. However, the human-readable World Wide Web is evolving to support a machine-readable Web of Data. The emerging Web of Data utilizes the same referencing paradigm as the World Wide Web, but instead of being focused primarily on URLs and files, it is focused on Uniform Resource Identifiers (URI) [7] and data.[1] The "Data" aspect of the Web of Data pertains to the fact that a URI can denote anything that can be assigned an identifier: a physical entity, a virtual entity, an abstract concept, etc. The "Web" aspect of the Web of Data pertains to the fact that identified resources can be related to other resources by means of the Resource Description Framework (RDF). Among other things, RDF is an abstract data model that specifies the syntactic rules by which resources are connected. If U is the set of all URIs, B the set of all blank or anonymous nodes, and L the set of all literals, then the Web of Data is defined as

$$\mathcal{W} \subseteq ((U \cup B) \times U \times (U \cup B \cup L)).$$

A single statement (or triple) in $\mathcal{W}$ is denoted (s, p, o), where s is called the subject, p the predicate, and o the object. On the Web of Data

> "[any man or machine can] start with one data source and then move through a potentially endless Web of data sources connected by RDF links. Just as the traditional document Web can be crawled by following hypertext links, the Web of Data can be crawled by following RDF links. Working on the crawled data, search engines can provide sophisticated query capabilities, similar to those provided by conventional relational databases. Because the query results themselves are structured data, not just links to HTML pages, they can be immediately processed, thus enabling a new class of applications based on the Web of Data." [9]

As a data model, RDF can conveniently represent commonly used data structures. From the knowledge representation and reasoning perspective, RDF provides the means to make assertions about the world and infer new statements given existing statements. From the network/graph analysis perspective, RDF supports the representation of various network

[1]The URI is the parent class of both the URL and the Uniform Resource Name (URN) [56].

data structures. From the programming and systems engineering perspective, RDF can be used to encode objects, instructions, stacks, etc. The Web of Data, with its general-purpose data model and supporting technological infrastructure, provides various computing models a shared, global, distributed space. Unfortunately, this general-purpose, multi-model vision was not the original intention of the designers of RDF. RDF was created for the domain of knowledge representation and reasoning. Moreover, it caters to a particular monotonic subset of this domain [29]. RDF is not generally understood as supporting different computing models. However, if the Web of Data is to be used as just that, a "web of data," then it is up to the applications leveraging this data to interpret what that data means and what it can be used for.

The URI address space is an address space. It is analogous, in many ways, to the address space that exists in the local memory of the physical machines that support the representation of the Web of Data. With physical memory, information is contained at an address. For a 64-bit machine, that information is a 64-bit word. That 64-bit word can be interpreted as a literal primitive (e.g. a byte, an integer, a floating point value) or yet another 64-bit address (i.e. a pointer). This is how address locations denote data and link to each other, respectively. On the Web of Data, a URI is simply an address as it does not contain content.[2] It is through RDF that a URI address has content. For instance, with RDF, a URI can reference a literal (i.e. `xsd:byte`, `xsd:integer`, `xsd:float`) or another URI. Thus, RDF, as a data model, has many similarities to typical local memory. However, the benefit of URIs and RDF is that they create an inherently distributed and theoretically infinite space. Thus, the Web of Data can be interpreted as a large-scale, distributed memory structure. What is encoded and processed in that memory structure should not be dictated at the level of RDF, but instead dictated by the domains that leverage this medium for various application scenarios. The Web of Data should be realized as an application agnostic memory structure that supports a rich variety of uses: from Semantic Web reasoning, to Giant Global Graph analysis, to Web of Objects execution.

The intention of this article is to create a conceptual splinter that separates RDF from its legacy use as a logic language and demonstrate that it is more generally applicable when realized as only a data model. In this way, RDF as the foundational standard for the Web of Data makes the Web of Data useful to anyone wishing to represent information and compute in a global, distributed space. Three specific interpretations of the Web of Data are presented in order to elucidate the many ways in which the Web of Data is currently being used. Moreover, within these different presentations, various standards and technologies are discussed. These presentations are provided as summaries, not full descriptions. In short, this article is more of a survey of a very large and multi-domained landscape. The three interpretations that will be discussed are enumerated below.

1. The Web of Data as a knowledge base (see §2.).
    - The Semantic Web is an interpretation of the Web of Data.
    - RDF is the means by which a model of a world is created.
    - There are many types of logic: logics of truth and logics of thought.

[2]This is not completely true. Given that a URL is a subtype of a URI, and a URL can "contain" a file, it is possible for a URI to "contain" information.

- Scalable solutions exist for reasoning on the Web of Data.

2. The Web of Data as a multi-relational network (see §3.).

   - The Giant Global Graph is an interpretation of the Web of Data.[3]
   - RDF is the means by which vertices are connected together by labeled edges.
   - Single-relational network analysis algorithms can be applied to multi-relational networks.
   - Scalable solutions exist for network analysis on the Web of Data.

3. The Web of Data as an object repository (see §4.).

   - The Web of Objects is an interpretation of the Web of Data.
   - RDF is the means by which objects are represented and related to other objects.
   - An object's representation can include both its fields and its methods.
   - Scalable solutions exist for object-oriented computing on the Web of Data.

The landscape presented in this article is by no means complete and only provides a glimpse into these different areas. Moreover, within each of these three presented interpretations, applications and use-cases are not provided. What is provided is a presentation of common computing models that have been mapped to the Web of Data in order to take unique advantage of the Web as a computing infrastructure.

2. A Distributed Knowledge Base

The Web of Data can be interpreted as a distributed knowledge base—a Semantic Web. A knowledge base is composed of a set of statements about some "world." These statements are written in some language. Inference rules designed for that language can be used to derive new statements from existing statements. In other words, inference rules can be used to make explicit what is implicit. This process is called reasoning. The Semantic Web initiative is primarily concerned with this interpretation of the Web of Data.

> "For the Semantic Web to function, computers must have access to structured collections of information and sets of inference rules that they can use to conduct automated reasoning." [8]

Currently, the Semantic Web interpretation of the Web of Data forces strict semantics on RDF. That is, RDF is not simply a data model, but a logic language. As a data model, it specifies how a statement τ is constructed (i.e. $\tau \in ((U \cup B) \times U \times (U \cup B \cup L))$). As a logic language is species specific language constructs and semantics—a way of interpreting what statements mean. Because RDF was developed in concert with requirements provided by the knowledge representation and reasoning community, RDF and the Semantic Web have been very strongly aligned for many years. This is perhaps the largest conceptual stronghold that exists as various W3C documents make this point explicit.

[3]The term "Giant Global Graph" was popularized by Tim Berners-Lee on his personal blog at this URL `http://dig.csail.mit.edu/breadcrumbs/node/215`.

> "RDF is an assertional logic, in which each triple expresses a simple proposition. This imposes a fairly strict monotonic discipline on the language, so that it cannot express closed-world assumptions, local default preferences, and several other commonly used non-monotonic constructs." [29]

RDF is monotonic in that any asserted statement $\tau \in \mathcal{W}$ can not be made "false" by future assertions. In other words, the truth-value of a statement, once stated, does not change. RDF makes use of the open-world assumption in that if a statement is not asserted, this does not entail that it is "false." The open-world assumption is contrasted to the closed-world assumption found in many systems, where the lack of data is usually interpreted as that data being "false."

From this semantic foundation, extended semantics for RDF have been defined. The two most prevalent language extensions are the RDF Schema (RDFS) [14] and the Web Ontology Language (OWL) [39]. It is perhaps this stack of standards that forms the most common conception of what the Semantic Web is. However, if the Semantic Web is to be just that, a "semantic web," then there should be a way to represent other languages with different semantics. If RDF is forced to be a monotonic, open-world language, then this immediately pigeonholes what can be represented on the Semantic Web. If RDF is interpreted strictly as a data model, devoid of semantics, then any other knowledge representation language can be represented in RDF and thus, contribute to the Semantic Web. This section will discuss three logic languages: RDFS, OWL, and the Non-Axiomatic Logic (NAL) [59]. RDFS and OWL are generally understood in the Semantic Web community as these are the primary logic languages used. However, NAL is a multi-valent, non-monotonic language that, if to be implemented in the Semantic Web, requires that RDF be interpreted as a data model, not as a logic language. Moreover, NAL is an attractive language for the Semantic Web because its reasoning process is inherently distributed, can handle conflicting inconsistent data, and was designed on the assumption of insufficient knowledge and computing resources.

2.1. RDF Schema

RDFS is a simple language with a small set of inference rules [14]. In RDF, resources (e.g. URIs and blank nodes) maintain properties (i.e. `rdf:Property`). These properties are used to relate resources to other resources and literals. In RDFS, classes and properties can be formally defined. Class definitions organize resources into abstract categories. Property definitions specify the way in which these resources are related to one another. For example, it is possible to state there exist people and dogs (i.e. classes) and people have dogs as pets (i.e. a property). This is represented in RDFS in Figure 1.

RDFS inference rules are used to derive new statements given existing statements that use the RDFS langauge. RDFS inference rules make use of statements with the following URIs:

- `rdfs:Class`: denotes a class as opposed to an instance.
- `rdf:Property`: denotes a property/role.
- `rdfs:domain`: denotes what a property projects from.
- `rdfs:range`: denotes what a property projects to.

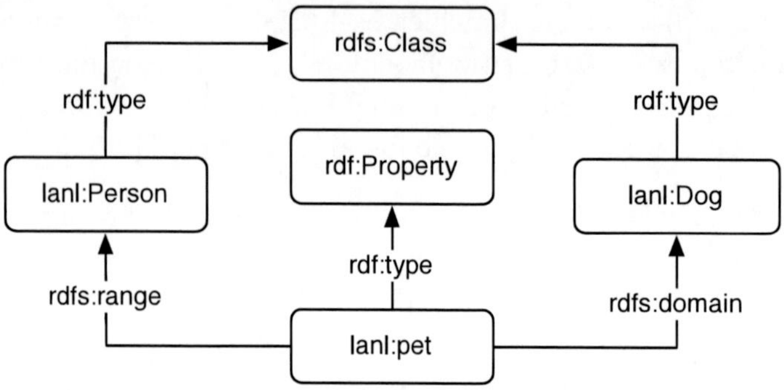

Figure 1. An RDFS ontology that states that a person has a dog as a pet.

- `rdf:type`: denotes that an instance is a type of class.
- `rdfs:subClassOf`: denotes that a class is a subclass of another.
- `rdfs:subPropertyOf`: denotes that a property is a sub-property of another.
- `rdfs:Resource`: denotes a generic resource.
- `rdfs:Datatype`: denotes a literal primitive class.
- `rdfs:Literal`: denotes a generic literal class.

RDFS supports two general types of inference: subsumption and realization. Subsumption determines which classes are a subclass of another. The RDFS inference rules that support subsumption are

$$(?x, \texttt{rdf:type}, \texttt{rdfs:Class}) \implies (?x, \texttt{rdfs:subClassOf}, \texttt{rdfs:Resource}),$$

$$(?x, \texttt{rdf:type}, \texttt{rdfs:Datatype}) \implies (?x, \texttt{rdfs:subClassOf}, \texttt{rdfs:Literal}),$$

$$(?x, \texttt{rdfs:subPropertyOf}, ?y) \wedge (?y, \texttt{rdfs:subPropertyOf}, ?z) \implies (?x, \texttt{rdfs:subPropertyOf}, ?z).$$

and finally,

$$(?x, \texttt{rdfs:subClassOf}, ?y) \wedge (?y, \texttt{rdfs:subClassOf}, ?z) \implies (?x, \texttt{rdfs:subClassOf}, ?z).$$

Thus, if both

```
(lanl:Chihuahua, rdfs:subClassOf, lanl:Dog)
(lanl:Dog, rdfs:subClassOf, lanl:Mammal)
```

are asserted, then it can be inferred that

```
(lanl:Chihuahua, rdfs:subClassOf, lanl:Mammal).
```

Next, realization is used to determine if a resource is an instance of a class. The RDFS inference rules that support realization are

$$(?x, ?y, ?z) \implies (?x, \texttt{rdf:type}, \texttt{rdfs:Resource}),$$

$$(?x, ?y, ?z) \implies (?y, \texttt{rdf:type}, \texttt{rdf:Property}),$$

$$(?x, ?y, ?z) \implies (?z, \texttt{rdf:type}, \texttt{rdfs:Resource}),$$

$$(?x, \texttt{rdf:type}, ?y) \wedge (?y, \texttt{rdfs:subClassOf}, ?z) \implies (?x, \texttt{rdf:type}, ?z),$$

$$(?w, \texttt{rdfs:domain}, ?x) \wedge (?y, ?w, ?z) \implies (?y, \texttt{rdf:type}, ?x),$$

and finally,

$$(?w, \texttt{rdfs:domain}, ?x) \wedge (?y, ?w, ?z) \implies (?z, \texttt{rdf:type}, ?x).$$

Thus if, along with the statements in Figure 1,

```
(lanl:marko, lanl:pet, lanl:fluffy)
```

is asserted, then it can be inferred that

```
(lanl:marko, rdf:type, lanl:Person)
(lanl:fluffy, rdf:type, lanl:Dog).
```

Given a knowledge base containing statements, these inference rules continue to execute until they no longer produce novel statements. It is the purpose of an RDFS reasoner to efficiently execute these rules. There are two primary ways in which inference rules are executed: at insert time and at query time. With respect to insert time, if a statement is inserted (i.e. asserted) into the knowledge base, then the RDFS inference rules execute to determine what is entailed by this new statement. These newly entailed statements are then inserted in the knowledge base and the process continues. While this approach ensures fast query times (as all entailments are guaranteed to exist at query time), it greatly increases the number of statements generated. For instance, given a deep class hierarchy, if a resource is a type of one of the leaf classes, then it asserted that it is a type of all the super classes of that leaf class. In order to alleviate the issue of "statement bloat," inference can instead occur at query time. When a query is executed, the reasoner determines what other implicit statements should be returned with the query. The benefits and drawbacks of each approach are benchmarked, like much of computing, according to space vs. time.

2.2. Web Ontology Language

The Web Ontology Language (OWL) is a more complicated language which extends RDFS by providing more expressive constructs for defining classes [39]. Moreover, beyond subsumption and realization, OWL provides inference rules to determine class and instance equivalence. There are many OWL specific inference rules. In order to give the flavor of OWL, without going into the many specifics, this subsection will only present some examples of the more commonly used constructs. For a fine, in depth review of OWL, please refer to [36].

Perhaps the most widely used language URI in OWL is `owl:Restriction`. In RDFS, a property can only have a domain and a range. In OWL, a class can apply the following restrictions to a property:

- `owl:cardinality`
- `owl:minCardinality`
- `owl:maxCardinality`
- `owl:hasValue`
- `owl:allValuesFrom`
- `owl:someValuesFrom`

Cardinality restrictions are used to determine equivalence and inconsistency. For example, in an OWL ontology, it is possible to state that a country can only have one president. This is expressed in OWL as diagrammed in Figure 2. The `_:1234` resource is a blank node that denotes a restriction on the country class's `lanl:president` property.

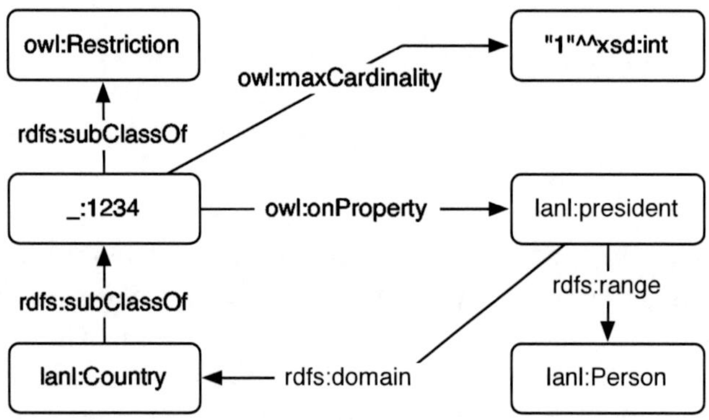

Figure 2. An OWL ontology that states that the president of a country is a person and there can be at most one president for a country.

Next, if `usa:barack` and `usa:obama` are both asserted to be the president of the United States with the statements

```
(usa:barack, lanl:president, usa:United_States)
(usa:obama, lanl:president, usa:United_States),
```

then it can be inferred (according to OWL inference rules) that these resources are equivalent. This equivalence relationship is made possible because the maximum cardinality of the `lanl:president` property of a country is 1. Therefore, if there are "two" people that are president, then they must be the same person. This is made explicit when the reasoner asserts the statements

```
(usa:barack, owl:sameAs, usa:obama)
(usa:obama, owl:sameAs, usa:barack).
```

Next, if `lanl:herbertv` is asserted to be different from `usa:barack` (which, from previous, was asserted to be the same as `usa:obama`) and `lanl:herbertv` is also asserted to be the president of the United States, then an inconsistency is detected. Thus, given the ontology asserted in Figure 2 and the previous assertions, asserting

```
(lanl:herbertv, owl:differentFrom, usa:barack)
(lanl:herbertv, lanl:president, usa:United_States)
```

causes an inconsistency. This inconsistency is due to the fact that a country can only have one president and `lanl:herbertv` is not `usa:barack`.

Two other useful language URIs for properties in OWL are

- `owl:SymmetricProperty`
- `owl:TransitiveProperty`

In short, if y is symmetric, then if (x, y, z) is asserted, then (z, y, x) can be inferred. Next, if the property y is transitive, then if (w, y, x) and (x, y, z) are asserted then, (w, y, z) can be inferred.

There are various reasoners that exist for the OWL language. A popular OWL reasoner is Pellet [44]. The purpose of Pellet is to execute the OWL rules given existing statements in the knowledge base. For many large-scale knowledge base applications (i.e. triple- or quad-stores), the application provides its own reasoner. Popular knowledge bases that make use of the OWL language are OWLim [34], Oracle Spatial [3], and AllegroGraph [1]. It is noted that due to the complexity (in terms of implementation and running times), many knowledge base reasoners only execute subsets of the OWL language. For instance, AllegroGraph's reasoner is called RDFS++ as it implements all of the RDFS rules and only some of the OWL rules. However, it is also noted that RacerPro [26] can be used with AllegroGraph to accomplish complete OWL reasoning. Finally, OpenSesame [16] can be used for RDFS reasoning. Because OpenSesame is both a knowledge base and an API, knowledge base applications that implement the OpenSesame interfaces can automatically leverage the OpenSesame RDFS reasoner; though there may be speed issues as the reasoner is not natively designed for that knowledge base application.

2.3. Non-Axiomatic Logic

If RDF is strictly considered a monotonic, open-world logic language, then the Semantic Web is solidified as an open-world, monotonic logic environment. If reasoning is restricted to the legacy semantics of RDF, then it will become more difficult to reason on the Semantic Web as it grows in size and as more inconsistent knowledge is introduced. With the number of statements of the Semantic Web, computational hurdles are met when reasoning with RDFS and OWL. With inconsistent statements on the Semantic Web, it is difficult to reason as inconsistencies are not handled gracefully in RDFS or OWL. In general, sound and complete reasoning will not be feasible as the Semantic Web continues to grow. In order to meet these challenges, the Large Knowledge Collider project (LarKC) is focused on developing a reasoning platform to handle incomplete and inconsistent data [21].

> "Researchers have developed methods for reasoning in rather small, closed, trustworthy, consistent, and static domains. They usually provide a small set of axioms and facts. [OWL] reasoners can deal with 10^5 axioms (concept definitions), but they scale poorly for large instance sets. [...] There is a deep mismatch between reasoning on a Web scale and efficient reasoning algorithms over restricted subsets of first-order logic. This is rooted in underlying assumptions of current systems for computational logic: small set of axioms, small number of facts, completeness of inference, correctness of inference rules and consistency, and static domains." [21]

There is a need for practical methods to reason on the Semantic Web. One promising logic was founded on the assumption of insufficient knowledge and resources. This logic is called the Non-Axiomatic Logic (NAL) [58]. Unfortunately for the Semantic Web as it is now, NAL breaks the assumptions of RDF semantics as NAL is multi-valent, non-monotonic, and makes use of statements with a subject-predicate form. However, if RDF is considered simply a data model, then it is possible to represent NAL statements and make use of its efficient, distributed reasoning system. Again, for the massive-scale, inconsistent world of the Semantic Web, sound and complete approaches are simply becoming more unreasonable.

2.3.1. The Non-Axiomatic Language

There are currently 8 NAL languages. Each language, from NAL-0 to NAL-8, builds on the constructs of the previous in order to support more complex statements. The following list itemizes the various languages and what can be expressed in each.

- NAL-0: binary inheritance.
- NAL-1: inference rules.
- NAL-2: sets and variants of inheritance.
- NAL-3: intersections and differences
- NAL-4: products, images, and ordinary relations.
- NAL-5: statement reification.
- NAL-6: variables.
- NAL-7: temporal statements.
- NAL-8: procedural statements.

Every NAL language is based on a simple inheritance relationship. For example, in NAL-0, which assumes all statements are binary,

$$\texttt{lanl:marko} \rightarrow \texttt{lanl:Person}$$

states that Marko (subject) inherits (→) from person (predicate). Given that all subjects and predicates are joined by inheritance, there is no need to represent the copula when formally representing a statement.[4]. If RDF, as a data model, is to represent NAL, then one possible representation for the above statement is

```
(lanl:marko, lanl:1234, lanl:Person),
```

where `lanl:1234` serves as a statement pointer. This pointer could be, for example, a 128-bit Universally Unique Identifier (UUID) [37]. It is important to maintain a statement pointer as beyond NAL-0, statements are not simply "true" or "false." A statement's truth is not defined by its existence, but instead by extra numeric metadata associated with the statement. NAL maintains an

> "experience-grounded semantics [where] the truth value of a judgment indicates the degree to which the judgment is supported by the system's experience. Defined in this way, truth value is system-dependent and time-dependent. Different systems may have conflicting opinions, due to their different experiences." [59]

A statement has a particular truth value associated with it that is defined as the frequency of supporting evidence (denoted $f \in [0, 1]$) and the confidence in the stability of that frequency (denoted $c \in [0, 1]$). For example, beyond NAL-0, the statement "Marko is a person" is not "100% true" simply because it exists. Instead, every time that aspects of Marko coincide with aspects of person, then f increases. Likewise, every time aspects of Marko do not coincide with aspects of person, f decreases.[5] Thus, NAL is non-monotonic as its statement evidence can increase and decrease. To demonstrate f and c, the above "Marko is a person" statement can be represented in NAL-1 as

$$\texttt{lanl:marko} \rightarrow \texttt{lanl:Person} < 0.9, 0.8 >,$$

where, for the sake of this example, $f = 0.9$ and $c = 0.8$. In an RDF representation, this can be denoted

```
(lanl:marko, lanl:1234, lanl:Person)
(lanl:1234, nal:frequency, "0.9"^^xsd:float)
(lanl:1234, nal:confidence, "0.8"^^xsd:float),
```

where the `lanl:1234` serves as a statement pointer allowing NAL's `nal:frequency` and `nal:confidence` constructs to reference the inheritance statement.

NAL-4 supports statements that are more analogous to the subject-object-predicate form of RDF. If Marko is denoted by the URI `lanl:marko`, Alberto by the URI `ucla:apepe`, and friendship by the URI `lanl:friend`, then in NAL-4, the statement "Alberto is a friend of Marko" is denoted in RDF as

---

[4]This is not completely true as different types of inheritance are defined in NAL-2 such as instance $\circ\!\!\rightarrow$, property $\rightarrow\!\!\circ$, and instance-property $\circ\!\!\rightarrow\!\!\circ$ inheritance. However, these 3 types of inheritance can also be represented using the basic $\rightarrow$ inheritance. Moreover, the RDF representation presented can support the explicit representation of other inheritance relationships if desired.

[5]The idea of "aspects coinciding" is formally defined in NAL, but is not discussed here for the sake of brevity. In short, a statement's f is modulated by both the system's "external" experiences and "internal" reasoning—both create new evidence. See [61] for an in depth explanation.

```
(ucla:apepe, lanl:friend, lanl:marko).
```

In NAL-4 this is represented as

$$(\texttt{ucla:apepe} \times \texttt{lanl:marko}) \rightarrow \texttt{lanl:friend} < 0.8, 0.5 >,$$

where $f = 0.8$ and $c = 0.5$ are provided for the sake of the example. This statement states that the set $(\texttt{ucla:apepe}, \texttt{lanl:marko})$ inherits the property of friendship to a certain degree and stability as defined by f and c, respectively. The RDF representation of this NAL-4 construct can be denoted

```
(lanl:2345, nal:_1, ucla:pepe)
(lanl:2345, nal:_2, lanl:marko)
(lanl:2345, lanl:3456, lanl:friend)
(lanl:3456, nal:frequency, "0.8"^^xsd:float)
(lanl:3456, nal:confidence, "0.5"^^xsd:float).
```

In the triples above, `lanl:2345` serves as a set and thus, this set inherits from friendship. That is, Alberto and Marko inherit the property of friendship.

2.3.2. The Non-Axiomatic Reasoner

> "In traditional logic, a 'valid' or 'sound' inference rule is one that never derives a *false* conclusion (that is, it will be contradicted by the future experience of the system) from *true* premises [19]. [In NAL], a 'valid conclusion' is one that is most consistent with the evidence in the past experience, and a 'valid inference rule' is one whose conclusions are supported by the premises used to derive them." [61]

Given that NAL is predicated on insufficient knowledge, there is no guarantee that reasoning will produce "true" knowledge with respect to the world that the statements are modeling as only a subset of that world is ever known. However, this does not mean that NAL reasoning is random, instead, it is consistent with respect to what the system knows. In other words,

> "the traditional definition of validity of inference rules—that is to get true conclusions from true premises—no longer makes sense in [NAL]. With insufficient knowledge and resources, even if the premises are true with respect to the past experience of the system there is no way to get infallible predictions about the future experience of the system even though the premises themselves may be challenged by new evidence." [59]

The inference rules in NAL are all syllogistic in that they are based on statements sharing similar terms (i.e. URIs) [45]. The typical inference rule in NAL has the following form

$$(\tau_1 < f_1, c_1 > \ \wedge \tau_2 < f_2, c_2 >) \ \vdash \ \tau_3 < f_3, c_3 >,$$

where τ_1 and τ_2 are statements that share a common term. There are four standard syllogisms used in NAL reasoning. These are enumerated below.

1. deduction: $(x \rightarrow y < f_1, c_1 > \wedge y \rightarrow z < f_2, c_2 >) \vdash x \rightarrow z < f_3, c_3 >$.
2. induction: $(x \rightarrow y < f_1, c_1 > \wedge z \rightarrow y < f_2, c_2 >) \vdash x \rightarrow z < f_3, c_3 >$.
3. abduction: $(x \rightarrow y < f_1, c_1 > \wedge x \rightarrow z < f_2, c_2 >) \vdash y \rightarrow z < f_3, c_3 >$.
4. exemplification: $(x \rightarrow y < f_1, c_1 > \wedge y \rightarrow z < f_2, c_2 >) \vdash z \rightarrow x < f_3, c_3 >$.

Two other important inference rule not discussed here are choice (i.e. what to do with contradictory evidence) and revision (i.e. how to update existing evidence with new evidence). Each of the inference rules have a different formulas for deriving $< f_3, c_3 >$ from $< f_1, c_1 >$ and $< f_2, c_2 >$.[6] These formulas are enumerated below.

1. deduction: $f_3 = f_1 f_2$ and $c_3 = f_1 c_1 f_2 c_2$.
2. induction: $f_3 = f_1$ and $c_3 = \frac{f_1 c_1 c_2}{f_1 c_1 c_2 + k}$.
3. abduction: $f_3 = f_2$ and $c_3 = \frac{f_2 c_1 c_2}{f_2 c_1 c_2 + k}$.
4. exemplification: $f_3 = 1$ and $c_3 = \frac{f_2 c_1 f_2 c_2}{f_1 c_1 f_2 c_2 + k}$.

The variable $k \in \mathbb{N}^+$ is a system specific parameter used in the determination of confidence.

To demonstrate deduction, suppose the two statements

$$\texttt{lanl:marko} \rightarrow \texttt{lanl:Person} < 0.5, 0.5 >$$

$$\texttt{lanl:Person} \rightarrow \texttt{lanl:Mammal} < 0.9, 0.9 > .$$

Given these two statements and the inference rule for deduction, it is possible to infer

$$\texttt{lanl:marko} \rightarrow \texttt{lanl:Mammal} < 0.45, 0.2025 > .$$

Next suppose the statement

$$\texttt{lanl:Dog} \rightarrow \texttt{lanl:Mammal} < 0.9, 0.9 > .$$

Given the existing statements, induction, and a $k = 1$, it is possible to infer

$$\texttt{lanl:marko} \rightarrow \texttt{lanl:Dog} < 0.45, 0.0758 > .$$

Thus, while the system is not confident, according to all that the system knows, Marko is a type of dog. This is because there are aspects of Marko that coincide with aspects of dog—they are both mammals. However, future evidence, such as fur, four legs, sloppy tongue, etc. will be further evidence that Marko and dog do not coincide and thus, the f of `lanl:marko` $\rightarrow$ `lanl:Dog` will decrease.

The significance of NAL reasoning is that all inference is based on local areas of the knowledge base. That is, all inference requires only two degrees of separation from the resource being inferred on. Moreover, reasoning is constrained by available computational resources, not by a requirement for logical completeness. Because of these two properties, the implemented reasoning system is inherently distributed and when computational resources are not available, the system does not break, it simply yields less conclusions. For

[6]Note that when the entailed statement already exists, its $< f_3, c_3 >$ component is revised according to the revision rule. Revision is not discussed in this article.

the Semantic Web, it may be best to adopt a logic that is better able to take advantage of its size and inconsistency. With a reasoner that is distributable and functions under variable computational resources, and makes use of a language that is non-monotonic and supports degrees of "truth," NAL may serve as a more practical logic for the Semantic Web. However, this is only possible if the RDF data model is separated from the RDF semantics and NAL's subject-predicate form can be legally represented.

There are many other language constructs in NAL that are not discussed here. For an in depth review of NAL, please refer to the *defacto* reference at [61]. Moreover, for a fine discussion of the difference between logics of truth (i.e. mathematical logic—modern predicate logic) and logics of thought (i.e. cognitive logic—NAL), see [60].

3. A Distributed Multi-Relational Network

The Web of Data can be interpreted as a distributed multi-relational network—a Giant Global Graph.[7] A mutli-relational network denotes a set of vertices (i.e. nodes) that are connected to one another by set of labeled edges (i.e. typed links).[8] In the graph and network theory community, the multi-relational network is less prevalent. The more commonly used network data structure is the single-relational network, where all edges are of the same type and thus, there is no need to label edges. Unfortunately, most network algorithms have been developed for the single-relational network data structure. However, it is possible to port all known single-relational network algorithms over to the multi-relational domain. In doing so, it is possible to leverage these algorithms on the Giant Global Graph. The purpose of this section is to

1. formalize the single-relational network (see §3.1.),
2. formalize the multi-relational network (see §3.2.),
3. present a collection of common single-relational network algorithms (see §3.3.), and then finally,
4. present a method for porting all known single-relational network algorithms over to the multi-relational domain (see §3.4.).

Network algorithms are useful in many respects and have been generally applied to analysis and querying. If the network models an aspect of the world, then network analysis techniques can be used to elucidate general structural properties of the network and thus, the world. Moreover, network query algorithms have been developed for searching and ranking. When these algorithms can be effectively and efficiently applied to the Giant Global Graph, the Giant Global Graph can serve as a medium for network analysis and query.

[7]The term "graph" is used in the mathematical domain of graph theory and the term "network" is used primarily in the physics and computer science domain of network theory. In this chapter, both terms are used depending on their source. Moreover, with regard to this article, these two terms are deemed synonymous with each other.

[8]A multi-relational network is also known as a directed labeled graph or semantic network.

3.1. Single-Relational Networks

The single-relational network represents a set of vertices that are related to one another by a homogenous set of edges. For instance, in a single-relational coauthorship network, all vertices denote authors and all edges denote a coauthoring relationship. Coauthorship exists between two authors if they have both written an article together. Moreover, coauthorship is symmetric—if person x coauthored with person y, then person y has coauthored with person x. In general, these types of symmetric networks are known as undirected, single-relational networks and can be denoted

$$G' = (V, E \subseteq \{V \times V\}),$$

where V is the set of vertices and E is the set of undirected edges. The edge $\{i, j\} \in E$ states that vertex i and j are connected to each other. Figure 3 diagrams an undirected coauthorship edge between two author vertices.

Figure 3. An undirected edge between two authors in an undirected single-relational network.

Single-relational networks can also be directed. For instance, in a single-relational citation network, the set of vertices denote articles and the set of edges denote citations between the articles. In this scenario, the edges are not symmetric as one article citing another does not imply that the cited article cites the citing article. Directed single-relational networks can be denoted

$$G = (V, E \subseteq (V \times V)),$$

where $(i, j) \in E$ states that vertex i is connected to vertex j. Figure 4 diagrams a directed citation edge between two article vertices.

Figure 4. A directed edge between two articles in a directed single-relational network.

Both undirected and directed single-relational networks have a convenient matrix representation. This matrix is known as an adjacency matrix and is denoted

$$\mathbf{A}_{i,j} = \begin{cases} 1 & \text{if } (i,j) \in E \\ 0 & \text{otherwise,} \end{cases}$$

where $\mathbf{A} \in \{0, 1\}^{|V| \times |V|}$. If $\mathbf{A}_{i,j} = 1$, then vertex i is adjacent (i.e. connected) to vertex j. It is important to note that there exists an information-preserving, bijective mapping between the set-theoretic and matrix representations of a network. Throughout the remainder of this section, depending on the algorithm presented, one or the other form of a network is used. Finally, note that the remainder of this section is primarily concerned with directed networks as a directed network can model an undirected network. In other words, the undirected edge $\{i, j\}$ can be represented as the two directed edges (i, j) and (j, i).

3.2. Multi-Relational Networks

The multi-relational network is a more complicated structure that can be used to represent multiple types of relationships between vertices. For instance, it is possible to not only represent researchers, but also their articles in a network of edges that represent authorship, citation, etc. A directed multi-relational network can be denoted

$$M = (V, \mathbb{E} = \{E_0, E_1, \ldots, E_m \subseteq (V \times V)\}),$$

where $\mathbb{E}$ is a family of edge sets such that any $E_k \in \mathbb{E} : 1 \leq k \leq m$ is a set of edges with a particular meaning (e.g. authorship, citation, etc.). A multi-relational network can be interpreted as a collection of single-relational networks that all share the same vertex set. Another representation of a multi-relational network is similar to the one commonly employed to define an RDF graph. This representation is denoted

$$M' \subseteq (V \times \Omega \times V),$$

where Ω is the set of edge labels. In this representation if $i, j \in V$ and $k \in \Omega$, then the triple (i, k, j) states that vertex i is connected to vertex j by the relationship type k.

Figure 5 diagrams multiple relationship types between scholars and articles in a multi-relational network.

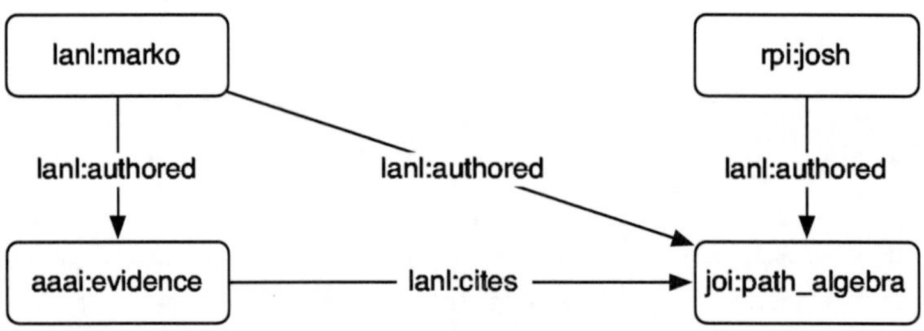

Figure 5. Multiple types of edges between articles and scholars in a directed multi-relational network.

Like the single-relational network and its accompanying adjacency matrix, the multi-relational network has a convenient 3-way tensor representation. This 3-way tensor is denoted

$$\mathcal{A}^k_{i,j} = \begin{cases} 1 & \text{if } (i,j) \in E_k : 1 \leq k \leq m \\ 0 & \text{otherwise.} \end{cases}$$

This representation can be interpreted as a collection of adjacency matrix "slices," where each slice is a particular edge type. In other words, if $\mathcal{A}^k_{i,j} = 1$, then $(i, k, j) \in M'$. Like the relationship between the set-theoretic and matrix forms of a single-relational network, M,

M', and $\mathcal{A}$ can all be mapped onto one another without loss of information. In this article, each representation will be used depending on the usefulness of its form with respect to the idea being expressed.

On the Giant Global Graph, RDF serves as the specification for graphing resources. Vertices are denoted by URIs, blank nodes, and literals and the edge labels are denoted by URIs. Multi-relational network algorithms can be used to exploit the Giant Global Graph. However, there are few algorithms dedicated specifically to multi-relational networks. Most network algorithms have been designed for single-relational networks. The remainder of this section will discuss some of the more popular single-relational network algorithms and then present a method for porting these algorithms (as well as other single-relational network algorithms) over to the multi-relational domain. This section concludes with a distributable and scalable method for executing network algorithms on the Giant Global Graph.

3.3. Single-Relational Network Algorithms

The design and study of graph and network algorithms is conducted primarily by mathematicians (graph theory) [17], physicists and computer scientists (network theory) [12], and social scientists (social network analysis) [62]. Many of the algorithms developed in these domains can be used together and form the general-purpose "toolkit" for researchers doing network analysis and for engineers developing network-based services. The following itemized list presents a collection of the single-relational network algorithms that will be reviewed in this subsection. As denoted with its name in the itemization, each algorithm can be used to identify properties of vertices, paths, or the network. Vertex metrics assign a real value to a vertex. Path metrics assign a real value to a path (i.e. an ordered set of vertices). And finally, network metrics assign a real value to the network as a whole.

- shortest path: path metric (§3.3.1.)
- eccentricity: vertex metric (§3.3.2.)
- radius: network metric (§3.3.2.)
- diameter: network metric (§3.3.2.)
- closeness: vertex metric (§3.3.3.)
- betweenness: vertex metric (§3.3.3.)
- stationary probability distribution: vertex metric (§3.3.4.)
- PageRank: vertex metric (§3.3.5.)
- spreading activation: vertex metric (§3.3.6.)
- assortative mixing: network metric (§3.3.7.)

A simple intuitive approach to determine the appropriate algorithm to use for an application scenario is presented in [35]. In short, various factors come into play when selecting a network algorithm such as the topological features of the network (e.g. its connectivity and its size), the computational requirements of the algorithms (e.g. its complexity), the type of results that are desired (e.g. personalized or global), and the meaning of the algorithm's result (e.g. geodesic-based, flow-based, etc.). The following sections will point out which features describe the presented algorithms.

3.3.1. Shortest Path

The shortest path metric is the foundation of all other geodesic metrics. The other geodesic metrics discussed are eccentricity, radius, diameter, closeness, and betweenness. A shortest path is defined for any two vertices $i, j \in V$ such that the sink vertex j is reachable from the source vertex i. If j is unreachable from i, then the shortest path between i and j is undefined. Thus, for geodesic metrics, it is important to only considered strongly connected networks, or strongly connected components of a network.[9] The shortest path between any two vertices i and j in a single-relational network is the smallest of the set of all paths between i and j. If $\rho : V \times V \to Q$ is a function that takes two vertices and returns the set of all paths Q where for any $q \in Q$, $q = (i, \ldots, j)$, then the length of the shortest path between i and j is $min(\bigcup_{q \in Q} |q| - 1)$, where min returns the smallest value of its domain. The shortest path function is denoted $s : V \times V \to \mathbb{N}$ with the function rule

$$s(i,j) = min\left(\bigcup_{q \in \rho(i,j)} |q| - 1\right).$$

There are many algorithms to determine the shortest path between vertices in a network. Dijkstra's method is perhaps the most popular as it is the typical algorithm taught in introductory algorithms classes [20]. However, if the network is unweighted, then a simple breadth-first search is a more efficient way to determine the shortest path between i and j. Starting from i a "fan-out" search for j is executed where at each time step, adjacent vertices are traversed to. The first path that reaches j is the shortest path from i to j.

3.3.2. Eccentricity, Radius, and Diameter

The radius and diameter of a network require the determination of the eccentricity of every vertex in V. The eccentricity of a vertex i is the largest shortest path between i and all other vertices in V such that the eccentricity function $e : V \to \mathbb{N}$ has the rule

$$e(i) = max\left(\bigcup_{j \in V} s(i,j) : i \neq j\right),$$

where max returns the largest value of its domain [28]. In terms of algorithmic complexity, the eccentricity metric calculates $|V| - 1$ shortest paths for a particular vertex.

The radius of the network is the minimum eccentricity of all vertices in V [62]. The function $r : G \to \mathbb{N}$ has the rule

$$r(G) = min\left(\bigcup_{i \in V} e(i)\right).$$

[9] Do not confuse a strongly connected network with a fully connected network. A fully connected network is where every vertex is connected to every other vertex directly. A strongly connected network is where every vertex is connected to every other vertex indirectly (i.e. there exists a path from any i to any j).

Finally, the diameter of a network is the maximum eccentricity of the vertices in V [62]. The function $d : G \rightarrow \mathbb{N}$ has the rule

$$d(G) = max\left(\bigcup_{i \in V} e(i)\right).$$

Both radius and diameter required $V^2 - V$ shortest path calculations.

The diameter of a network is, in some cases, telling of the growth properties of the network (i.e. the general principle by which new vertices and edges are added). For instance, if the network is randomly generated (edges are randomly assigned between vertices), then the diameter of the network is much larger then if the network is generated according to a more "natural growth" function such as a preferential attachment model, where highly connected vertices tend to get more edges (colloquially captured by the phrase "the rich get richer") [11]. Thus, in general, natural networks tend to have a much smaller diameter. This was evinced by an empirical study of the World Wide Web citation network, where the diameter of the network was concluded to be only 19 [2].

3.3.3. Closeness and Betweenness Centrality

Closeness and betweenness centrality are popular network metrics for determining the "centralness" of a vertex and have been used in sociology [62], bioinformatics [43], and bibliometrics [10]. Centrality is a loose term that describes the intuitive notion that some vertices are more connected/integral/central/influential within the network than others. Closeness centrality is one such centrality measure and is defined as the mean shortest path between some vertex i and all the other vertices in V [5, 38, 53]. The function $c : V \rightarrow \mathbb{R}$ has the rule

$$c(i) = \frac{1}{\sum_{j \in V} s(i, j)}.$$

Betweenness centrality is defined for a vertex in V [13, 23]. The betweenness of $i \in V$ is the number of shortest paths that exist between all vertices $j, k \in V$ that have i in their path divided by the total number of shortest paths between j and k, where $i \neq j \neq k$. If $\sigma : V \times V \rightarrow Q$ is the function that returns the set of shortest paths between any two vertices j and k such that

$$\sigma(j, k) = \bigcup_{q \in p(j,k)} q : |q| - 1 = s(j, k)$$

and $\hat{\sigma} : V \times V \times V \rightarrow Q$ is the set of shortest paths between two vertices j and k that have i in the path, where

$$\hat{\sigma}(j, k, i) = \bigcup_{q \in p(j,k)} q : (|q| - 1 = s(j, k) \; \wedge \; i \in q),$$

then the betweenness function $b : V \rightarrow \mathbb{R}$ has the rule

$$b(i) = \sum_{i \neq j \neq k \in V} \frac{|\hat{\sigma}(j, k, i)|}{|\sigma(j, k)|}.$$

There are many variations to the standard representations presented above. For a more in depth review on these metrics, see [62] and [12]. Finally, centrality is not restricted only to geodesic metrics. The next three algorithms are centrality metrics based on random walks or "flows" through a network.

3.3.4. Stationary Probability Distribution

A Markov chain is used to model the states of a system and the probability of transition between states [27]. A Markov chain is best represented by a probabilistic, single-relational network where the states are vertices, the edges are transitions, and the edge weights denote the probability of transition. A probabilistic, single-relational network can be denoted

$$G'' = (V, E \subseteq (V \times V), \omega : E \rightarrow [0, 1])$$

where ω is a function that maps each edge in E to a probability value. The outgoing edges of any vertex form a probability distribution that sums to 1.0. In this section, all outgoing probabilities from a particular vertex are assumed to be equal. Thus, $\forall j, k \in \Gamma^+(i) : \omega(i, j) = \omega(i, k)$, where $\Gamma^+(i) \subseteq V$ is the set of vertices adjacent to i.

A random walker is a useful way to visualize the transitioning between vertices. A random walker is a discrete element that exists at a particular $i \in V$ at a particular point in time $t \in \mathbb{N}^+$. If the vertex at time t is i then the next vertex at time $t + 1$ will be one of the vertices adjacent to i in $\Gamma^+(i)$. In this manner, the random walker makes a probabilistic jump to a new vertex at every time step. As time t goes to infinity a unique stationary probability distribution emerges if and only if the network is aperiodic and strongly connected. The stationary probability distribution expresses the probability that the random walker will be at a particular vertex in the network. In matrix form, the stationary probability distribution is represented by a row vector $\pi \in [0, 1]^{|V|}$, where π_i is the probability that the random walker is at i and $\sum_{i \in V} \pi_i = 1.0$. If the network is represented by the row-stochastic adjacency matrix

$$\mathbf{A}_{i,j} = \begin{cases} \frac{1}{|\Gamma^+(i)|} & \text{if } (i, j) \in E \\ 0 & \text{otherwise} \end{cases}$$

and if the network is aperiodic and strongly connected, then there exists some π such that $\pi\mathbf{A} = \pi$. Thus, the stationary probability distribution is the primary eigenvector of $\mathbf{A}$. The primary eigenvector of a network is useful in ranking its vertices as those vertices that are more central are those that have a higher probability in π. Thus, intuitively, where the random walker is likely to be is a indicator of how central the vertex is. However, if the network is not strongly connected (very likely for most natural networks), then a stationary probability distribution does not exist.

3.3.5. PageRank

PageRank makes use of the random walker model previously presented [15]. However, in PageRank, the random walker does not simply traverse the single-relational network by moving between adjacent vertices, but instead has a probability of jumping, or "teleporting," to some random vertex in the network. In some instances, the random walker will follow an outgoing edge from its current vertex location. In other instances, the random walker will jump to some other random vertex in the network that is not necessarily adjacent to it. The benefit of this model is that it ensures that the network is strongly connected and aperiodic and thus, there exists a stationary probability distribution. In order to calculate PageRank, two networks are used. The standard single-relational network is represented as the row-stochastic adjacency matrix

$$\mathbf{A}_{i,j} = \begin{cases} \frac{1}{|\Gamma^+(i)|} & \text{if } (i,j) \in E \\ \frac{1}{|V|} & \text{otherwise.} \end{cases}$$

Any $i \in V$ where $\Gamma^+(i) = \emptyset$ is called a "rank-sink." Rank-sinks ensure that the network is not strongly connected. To rectify this connectivity problem, all vertices that are rank-sinks are connected to every other vertex with probability $\frac{1}{|V|}$. Next, for teleportation, a fully connected network is created that is denoted $\mathbf{B}_{i,j} = \frac{1}{|V|}$.

The random walker will choose to use $\mathbf{A}$ or $\mathbf{B}$ at time step t as its transition network depending on the probability value $\alpha \in (0, 1]$, where in practice, $\alpha = 0.85$. This means that 85% of the time the random walker will use the edges in $\mathbf{A}$ to traverse, and the other 15% of the time, the random walker will use the edges in $\mathbf{B}$. The α-biased union of the networks $\mathbf{A}$ and $\mathbf{B}$ guarantees that the random walker is traversing an strongly connected and aperiodic network. The random walker's traversal network can be expressed by the matrix

$$\mathbf{C} = \alpha\mathbf{A} + (1 - \alpha)\mathbf{B}.$$

The PageRank row vector $\pi \in [0, 1]^{|V|}$ has the property $\pi\mathbf{C} = \pi$. Thus, the PageRank vector is the primary eigenvector of the modified single-relational network. Moreover, π is the stationary probability distribution of $\mathbf{C}$. From a certain perspective, the primary contribution of the PageRank algorithm is not in the way it is calculated, but in how the network is modified to support a convergence to a stationary probability distribution. PageRank has been popularized by the Google search engine and has been used as a ranking algorithm in various domains. Relative to the geodesic centrality algorithms presented previous, PageRank is a more efficient way to determine a centrality score for all vertices in a network. However, calculating the stationary probability distribution of a network is not cheap and for large networks, can not be accomplished in real-time. Local rank algorithms are more useful for real-time results in large-scale networks such as the Giant Global Graph.

3.3.6. Spreading Activation

Both the stationary probability distribution and PageRank are global rank metrics. That is, they rank all vertices relative to all vertices and as such, require a full network perspective. However, for many applications, a local rank metric is desired. Local rank metrics rank a subset of the set of all vertices in the network relative to some set of source vertices. Local rank metrics have the benefit of being faster to compute and being relative to a particular area of the network. For large-scale networks, local rank metrics are generally more practical for real-time queries.

Perhaps the most popular local rank metric is spreading activation. Spreading activation is a network analysis technique that was inspired by the spreading activation potential found in biological neural networks [4, 18, 30]. This algorithm (and its many variants) has been used extensively in semantic network reasoning and recommender systems. The purpose of the algorithm is to expose, in a computationally efficient manner, those vertices which are closest (in terms of a flow distance) to a particular set of vertices. For example, given $i, j, k \in V$, if there exists many short recurrent paths between vertex i and vertex j and not so between i and k, then it can be assumed that vertex i is more "similar" to vertex j than k. Thus, the returned ranking will rank j higher than k relative to i. In order to calculate this distance, "energy" is assigned to vertex i. Let $x \in [0, 1]^{|V|}$ denote the energy vector, where at the first time step all energy is at i such that $x_i^1 = 1.0$. The energy vector is propagated over $\mathbf{A}$ for $\hat{t} \in \mathbb{N}^+$ number of steps by the equation $x^{t+1} = x^t\mathbf{A} : t + 1 \leq \hat{t}$. Moreover, at every time step, x is decayed some amount by $\delta \in [0, 1]$. At the end of the process, the vertex that had the most energy flow through it (as recorded by $\pi \in \mathbb{R}^{|V|}$) is considered the vertex that is most related to vertex i. Algorithm 1 presents this spreading activation algorithm. The resultant π provides a ranking of all vertices at most $\hat{t}$ steps away from i.

```
begin
    t = 1
    while t ≤ t̂ do
        π = π + x
        x = (δx)A
        t = t + 1
    end
    return π
end
```

Algorithm 1: A spreading activation algorithm.

A class of algorithms known as "priors" algorithms perform computations similar to the local rank spreading activation algorithm, but do so using a stationary probability distribution [63]. Much like the PageRank algorithm distorts the original network, priors algorithms distort the local neighborhood of the graph and require at every time step, with some probability, that all random walkers return to their source vertex. The long run behavior of such systems yield a ranking biased towards (or relative to) the source vertices and thus, can be characterized as local rank metrics.

3.3.7. Assortative Mixing

The final single-relational network algorithm discussed is assortative mixing. Assortative mixing is a network metric that determines if a network is assortative (colloquially captured by the phrase "birds of a feather flock together"), disassortative (colloquially captured by the phrase "opposites attract"), or uncorrelated. An assortative mixing algorithm returns values in $[-1, 1]$, where 1 is assortative, -1 is disassortative, and 0 is uncorrelated. Given a collection of vertices and metadata about each vertex, it is possible to determine the assortative mixing of the network. There are two assortative mixing algorithms: one for scalar or numeric metadata (e.g. age, weight, etc.) and one for nominal or categorical metadata (e.g. occupation, sex, etc.). In general, an assortative mixing algorithm can be used to answer questions such as:

- Do friends in a social network tend to be the same age?
- Do colleagues in a coauthorship network tend to be from the same university?
- Do relatives in a kinship network tend to like the same foods?

Note that to calculate the assortative mixing of a network, vertices must have metadata properties. The typical single-relational network $G = (V, E)$ does not capture this information. Therefore, assume some other data structure that stores metadata about each vertex.

The original publication defining the assortative mixing metric for scalar properties used the parametric Pearson correlation of two vectors [40].[10] One vector is the scalar value of the vertex property for the vertices on the tail of all edges. The other vector is the scalar value of the vertex property for the vertices on the head of all the edges. Thus, the length of both vectors is $|E|$ (i.e. the total number of edges in the network). Formally, the Pearson correlation-based assortativity is defined as

$$r = \frac{|E| \sum_i j_i k_i - \sum_i j_i \sum_i k_i}{\sqrt{\left[|E| \sum_i j_i^2 - (\sum_i j_i)^2\right] \left[|E| \sum_i k_i^2 - (\sum_i k_i)^2\right]}},$$

where j_i is the scalar value of the vertex on the tail of edge i, and k_i is the scalar value of the vertex on the head of edge i. For nominal metadata, the equation

$$r = \frac{\sum_p e_{pp} - \sum_p a_p b_p}{1 - \sum_p a_p b_p}$$

yields a value in $[-1, 1]$ as well, where e_{pp} is the number of edges in the network that have property value p on both ends, a_p is the number of edges in the network that have property value p on their tail vertex, and b_p is the number of edges that have property value p on their head vertex [41].

3.4. Porting Single-Relational Algorithms to the Multi-Relational Domain

All the aforementioned algorithms are intended for single-relational networks. However, it is possible to map these algorithms over to the multi-relational domain and thus, apply them to the Giant Global Graph. In the most simple method, it is possible to ignore edge labels and simply treat all edges in a multi-relational network as being "equal." This method represents a multi-relational network as a single-relational network and then uses the aforementioned single-relational network analysis algorithm on it. This method, of course, does not take advantage of the rich structured data that multi-relational networks offer. Another method is to only make use of a particular edge label of a multi-relational network. If only a particular single-relational slice of the multi-relational network is desired (e.g. a citation network, `lanl:cites`), then this single-relational component can be isolated and subjected the previously presented single-relational network algorithms. This method is limited in that it ignores much of the information that is present in the original multi-relational network.

[10] Note that for metadata property distributions that are not normally distributed, a non-parametric correlation such as the Spearman ρ or Kendall τ may be the more useful correlation coefficient.

If a multi-relational network is to be generally useful, then a method that takes advantage of the various types of edges in the network is desired. The methods presented next define abstract/implicit paths through a network. By doing so, a multi-relational network can be redefined as a "semantically rich" single-relational network. For example, in Figure 5, there does not exist `lanl:authorCites` edges (i.e. if person i wrote an article that cites the article of person j, then it is true that i `lanl:authorCites` j). However, this edge can be generated/inferred by making use of both the `lanl:authored` and `lanl:cites` edges. In this way, a breadth-first search or a random walk can use these generated edges to yield "semantically-rich" network analysis results. The remainder of this section will discuss this idea in more depth.

3.4.1. A Multi-Relational Path Algebra

A path algebra is presented to map a multi-relational network to a single-relational network in order to expose the multi-relational network to single-relational network algorithms. The multi-relational path algebra summarized is discussed at length in [51]. In short, the path algebra manipulates a multi-relational tensor, $\mathcal{A} \in \{0,1\}^{|V|\times|V|\times|\mathbb{E}|}$, in order to derive a semantically-rich, weighted single-relational adjacency matrix, $\mathbf{A} \in \mathbb{R}^{|V|\times|V|}$. Uses of the algebra can be generally defined as

$$\Delta : \{0,1\}^{|V|\times|V|\times|\mathbb{E}|} \rightarrow \mathbb{R}^{|V|\times|V|},$$

where Δ is the user-defined path operation.

There are two primary operations used in the path algebra: traverse and filter.[11] These operations are composed to create a more complex operation. The traverse operation is denoted $\cdot : \mathbb{R}^{|V|\times|V|} \times \mathbb{R}^{|V|\times|V|}$ and uses standard matrix multiplication as its function rule. Traverse is used to "walk" the multi-relational network. The idea behind traverse is first described using a single-relational network example. If a single-relational adjacency matrix is raised to the second power (i.e. multiplied with itself) then the resultant matrix denotes how many paths of length 2 exist between vertices [17]. That is, $\mathbf{A}^{(2)}_{i,j}$ (i.e. $(\mathbf{A} \cdot \mathbf{A})_{i,j}$) denotes how many paths of length 2 go from vertex i to vertex j. In general, for any power p,

$$\mathbf{A}^{(p)}_{i,j} = \sum_{l \in V} \mathbf{A}^{(p-1)}_{i,l} \cdot \mathbf{A}_{l,j} : p \geq 2.$$

This property can be applied to a multi-relational tensor. If $\mathcal{A}^1$ and $\mathcal{A}^2$ are multiplied together then the result adjacency matrix denotes the number of paths of type $1 \rightarrow 2$ that exist between vertices. For example, if $\mathcal{A}^1$ is the coauthorship adjacency matrix, then the adjacency matrix $\mathbf{Z} = \mathcal{A}^1 \cdot {\mathcal{A}^1}^\top$ denotes how many coauthorship paths exist between vertices, where $\top$ transposes the matrix (i.e. inverts the edge directionality). In other words if Marko (vertex i) and Johan (vertex j) have written 19 papers together, then $\mathbf{Z}_{i,j} = 19$. However, given that the identity element $\mathbf{Z}_{i,i}$ may be greater than 0 (i.e. a person has coauthored with their self), it is important to remove all such reflexive coauthoring paths back to the original

[11] Other operations not discussed in this section are merge and weight. For a in depth presentation of the multi-relational path algebra, see [51].

author (as a person can not coauthor with their self). In order to do this, the filter operation is used. Given the identify matrix $\mathbf{I}$ and the all 1 matrix $\mathbf{1}$,

$$\mathbf{Z} = \left(\mathcal{A}^1 \cdot \mathcal{A}^{1^\top}\right) \circ (\mathbf{1} - \mathbf{I}),$$

yields a true coauthorship adjacency matrix, where $\circ : \mathbb{R}^{|V|\times|V|} \times \mathbb{R}^{|V|\times|V|}$ is the entry-wise Hadamard matrix multiplication operation [31]. Hadamard matrix multiplication is defined as

$$\mathbf{A} \circ \mathbf{B} = \begin{bmatrix} \mathbf{A}_{1,1} \cdot \mathbf{B}_{1,1} & \cdots & \mathbf{A}_{1,j} \cdot \mathbf{B}_{1,m} \\ \vdots & \ddots & \vdots \\ \mathbf{A}_{n,1} \cdot \mathbf{B}_{n,1} & \cdots & \mathbf{A}_{n,m} \cdot \mathbf{B}_{n,m} \end{bmatrix}.$$

In this example, the Hadamard entry-wise multiplication operation applies an "identify filter" to $\left(\mathcal{A}^1 \cdot \mathcal{A}^{1^\top}\right)$ that removes all paths back to the source vertices (i.e. back to the identity vertices) as it sets $\mathbf{Z}_{i,i} = 0$. Filters are generally useful when particular paths through a multi-relational network should be excluded from a computation. The presented example demonstrates that a multi-relational network can be mapped to a semantically-rich, single-relational network. In the original multi-relational network, there exists no coauthoring relationship (e.g. no self-loops). However, this relation exists implicitly by means of traversing and filtering particular paths.[12]

The benefit of the summarized path algebra is that is can express various abstract paths through a multi-relational tensor in an algebraic form. Thus, given the theorems of the algebra, it is possible to simplify expressions in order to derive more computationally efficient paths for deriving the same information. The primary drawback of the algebra is that it is a matrix algebra that globally operates on adjacency matrix slices of the multi-relational tensor $\mathcal{A}$. Given that size of the Giant Global Graph, it is not practical to execute global matrix operations. However, these path expressions can be used as an abstract path that a discrete "walker" can take when traversing local areas of the graph. This idea is presented next.

3.4.2. Multi-Relational Grammar Walkers

Previously, both the stationary probability distribution, PageRank, and spreading activation were defined as matrix operations. However, it is possible to represent these algorithms using discrete random walkers. In fact, in many cases, this is the more natural representation both in terms of intelligibility and scalability. For many, it is more intuitive to think of these algorithms as being executed by a discrete random walker moving from vertex to vertex recording the number of times it has traversed each vertex. In terms of scalability, all of these algorithms can be approximated by using less walkers and thus, less computational resources. Moreover, when represented as a swarm of discrete walkers, the algorithm is inherently distributed as a walker is only aware of its current vertex and those vertices adjacent to it.

---

[12]While not explored in [51], it is possible to use the path algebra to create inference rules in a manner analogous to the Semantic Web Rule Language (SWRL) [32]. Moreover, as explored in [51], it is possible to perform any arbitrary SPARQL query [46] using the path algebra (save for greater-than/less-than comparisons of and regular expressions on literals).

For multi-relational networks, this same principle applies. However, instead of randomly choosing an adjacent vertex to traverse to, the walker chooses a vertex that is dependent upon an abstract path description defined for the walker. Walkers of this form are called grammar-based random walkers [48]. A path for a walker can be defined using any language such as the path algebra presented previous or SPARQL [46]. The following examples are provided in SPARQL as it is the *defacto* query language for the Web of Data. Given the coauthorship path description from previous,

$$\left(\mathcal{A}^1 \cdot \mathcal{A}^{1^\top}\right) \circ (\mathbf{1} - \mathbf{I}),$$

it is possible to denote this as a local walker computation in SPARQL as

```
SELECT ?dest WHERE {
  @ lanl:authored ?x .
  ?dest lanl:authored ?x .
  FILTER (@ != ?dest)
}
```

where the symbol `@` denotes the current location of the walker (i.e. a parameter to the query) and `?dest` is a collection of potential locations for the walker to move to (i.e. the return set of the query). It is important to note that the path algebra expression performs a global computation while the SPARQL query representation distributes the computation to individual walkers. Given the set of resources that bind to `?dest`, the walker selects a single resource from that set and traverses to it. At which point, `@` is updated to that selected resource value. This process continues indefinitely and, in the long run behavior, the walker's location probability over V denotes the stationary distribution of the walker in the Giant Global Graph according to the abstract coauthorship path description. The SPARQL query redefines what is meant by an adjacent vertex by allowing longer paths to be represented as single edges. Again, this is why it is stated that such mechanisms yield semantically rich, single-relational networks.

In the previous coauthorship example, the grammar walker, at every vertex it encounters, executes the same SPARQL query to locate "adjacent" vertices. In more complex grammars, it is possible to chain together SPARQL queries into a graph of expressions such that the walker moves not only through the Giant Global Graph, but also through a web of SPARQL queries. Each SPARQL query defines a different abstract edge to be traversed. This idea is diagrammed in Figure 6, where the grammar walker "walks" both the grammar and the Giant Global Graph.

To demonstrate a multiple SPARQL query grammar, a PageRank coauthorship grammar is defined using two queries. The first query was defined above and the second query is

```
SELECT ?dest WHERE {
  ?dest rdf:type lanl:Person
}
```

This rule serves as the "teleportation" function utilized in PageRank to ensure a strongly connected network. Thus, if there is a α probability that the first query will be executed and

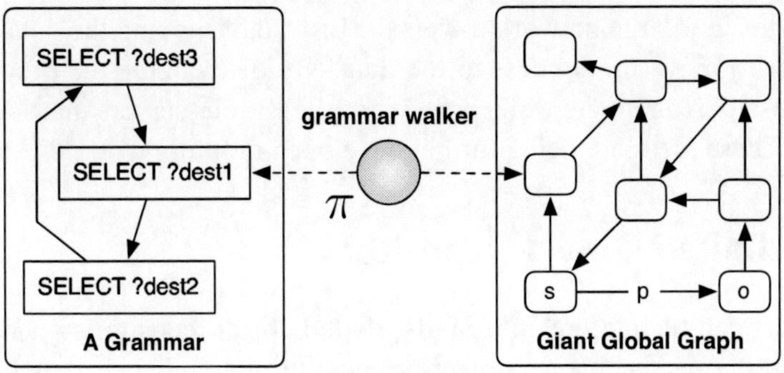

Figure 6. A grammar walker maintains its state in the Giant Global Graph (its current vertex location) and its state in the grammar (its current grammar location—SPARQL query). After executing its current SPARQL query, the walker moves to a new vertex in the Giant Global Graph as well as to a new grammar location in the grammar.

a $(1 - \alpha)$ probability that the second rule will be executed, then coauthorship PageRank in the Giant Global Graph is computed. Of course, the second rule can be computationally expensive, but it serves to elucidate the idea.[13] It is noted that the stationary probability distribution and the PageRank of the Giant Global Graph can be very expensive to compute if the grammar does not reduce the traverse space to some small subset of the full Giant Global Graph. Thus, in many cases, grammar walkers are more useful for calculating semantically meaningful spreading activations. In this form, the Giant Global Graph can be searched efficiently from a set of seed resources and a set of walkers that do not iterate indefinitely, but instead, for some finite number of steps.

The geodesic algorithms previously defined in §3.3. can be executed in an analogous fashion using grammar-based geodesic walkers [52]. The difference between a geodesic walker and a random walker is that the geodesic walker creates a "clone" walker each time it is adjacent to multiple vertices. This is contrasted to the random walker, where the random walker randomly chooses a single adjacent vertex. This cloning process implements a breadth-first search. It is noted that geodesic algorithms have high algorithmic complexity and thus, unless the grammar can be defined such that only a small subset of the Giant Global Graph is traversed, then such algorithms should be avoided. In general, the computational requirements of the algorithms in single-relational networks also apply to multi-relational networks. However, in multi-relational networks, given that adjacency is determined through queries, multi-relational versions of these algorithms are more costly. Given that the Giant Global Graph will soon grow to become the largest network instantiation in existence, being aware of such computational requirements is a necessary.

Finally, a major concern with the Web of Data as it is right now is that data is pulled to a machine for processing [50]. That is, by resolving an `http`-based URI, an RDF subgraph is returned to the retrieving machine. This is the method advocated by the Linked Data community [9]. Thus, walking the Giant Global Graph requires pulling large amounts of

[13]Note that this description is not completely accurate as "rank sinks" in the first query (when `?dest` $= \emptyset$) will halt the process. Thus, in such cases, when the process halts, the second query should be executed. At which point, rank sinks are alleviated and PageRank is calculated.

data over the wire. For large network traversals, instead of moving the data to the process, it may be better to move the process to the data. By discretizing the process (e.g. using walkers) it is possible to migrate walkers between the various servers that support the Giant Global Graph. These ideas are being further developed in future work.[14]

4. A Distributed Object Repository

The Web of Data can be interpreted as a distributed object repository—a Web of Objects. An object, from the perspective of object-oriented programming, is defined as a discrete entity that maintains

- fields: properties associated with the object. These may be pointers to literal primitives such as characters, integers, etc. or pointers to other objects.
- methods: behaviors associated with the object. These are the instructions that an object executes in order to change its state and the state of the objects it references.

Objects are abstractly defined in source code. Source code is written in a human readable/writeable language. An example `Person` class defined in the Java programming language is presented below. This particular class has two fields (i.e. `age` and `friends`) and one method (i.e. `makeFriend`).

```
public class Person {
  int age;
  Collection<Person> friends;

  public void makeFriend(Person p) {
    this.friends.add(p);
  }
}
```

There is an important distinction between a class and an object. A class is an abstract description of an object. Classes are written in source code. Object's are created during the run-time of the executed code and embody the properties of their abstract class. In this way, objects instantiate (or realize) classes. Before objects can be created, a class described in source code must be compiled so that the machine can more efficiently process the code. In other words, the underlying machine has a very specific instruction set (or language) that it uses. It is the role of the compiler to translate source code into machine-readable instructions. Instructions can be represented in the native language of the hardware processor (i.e. according to its instruction set) or it can be represented in an intermediate language that can be processed by a virtual machine (i.e. software that simulates the behavior of a hardware machine). If a virtual machine language is used, it is ultimately the role of the virtual machine to translate the instructions it is processing into the instruction set used by

[14] A protocol to support this model of distributed computing on the Web of Data has been developed and implemented. This protocol is called Linked Process. More information about Linked Process can be found at `http://linkedprocess.org`.

the underlying hardware machine. However, the computing stack does not end there. It is ultimately up to the "laws of physics" to alter the state of the hardware machine. As the hardware machine changes states, its alters the state of all the layers of abstractions built atop it.

Object-oriented programming is perhaps the most widely used software development paradigm and is part of the general knowledge of most computer scientists and engineers. Examples of the more popular object-oriented languages include C++, Java, and Python. Some of the benefits of object-oriented programming are itemized below.

- abstraction: representing a problem intuitively as a set of interacting objects.
- encapsulation: methods and fields are "bundled" with particular objects.
- inheritance: subclasses inherit the fields and methods of their parent classes.

In general, as systems scale, the management of large bodies of code is made easier through the use of object-oriented programming.

There exist many similarities between the RDFS and OWL Semantic Web ontology languages discussed in §2. and the typical object-oriented programming languages previously mentioned. For example, in the ontology languages, there exist the notion of classes, their instances (i.e. objects), and instance properties (i.e. fields).[15] However, the biggest differentiator is that objects in object-oriented environments maintain methods. The only computations that occur in RDFS and OWL are through the inference rules of the logic they implement and as such are not specific to particular classes. Even if rules are implemented for particular classes (for example, in SWRL [32]), such rule languages are not typically Turing-complete [55] and thus, do not support general-purpose computing.

In order to bring general-purpose, object-oriented computing to the Web of Data, various object-oriented languages have been developed that represent their classes and their objects in RDF. Much like rule languages such as SWRL have an RDF encoding, these object-oriented languages do as well. However, they are general-purpose imperative languages that can be used to perform any type of computation. Moreover, they are object-oriented so that they have the benefits associated with object-oriented systems itemized previously. When human readable-writeable source code written in an RDF programming language is compiled, it is compiled into RDF. By explicitly encoding methods in RDF—their instruction-level data—the Web of Data becomes an object-oriented repository.[16] The remainder of this section will discuss three computing models on the Web of Objects:

1. partial object repository: where typical object-oriented languages utilize the Web of Objects to store object field data, not class descriptions and methods.
2. full object repository: where RDF-based object-oriented languages encode classes, object fields, and object methods in RDF.

[15]It is noted that the semantics of inheritance and properties in object-oriented languages are different than those of RDFS and OWL. Object-oriented languages are frame-based and tend to assume a closed world [57]. Also, there does not exist the notion of sub-properties in object-oriented languages as fields are not "first-class citizens."

[16]It is noted that other non-object-oriented RDF computer languages exist. For example, the Ripple programming language is a relational language where computing instructions are stored in `rdf:Lists` [54]. Ripple is generally useful for performing complex query and insert operations on the Web of Data. Moreover, because programs are denoted by URIs, it is easy to link programs together by referencing URIs.

3. virtual machine repository: where RDF-based classes, objects, and virtual machines are represented in the Web of Objects.

4.1. Partial Object Repository

The Web of Objects can be used as a partial object repository. In this sense, objects represented in the Web of Objects only maintain their fields, not their methods. It is the purpose of some application represented external to the Web of Objects to store and retrieve object data from the Web of Objects. In many ways, this model is analogous to a "black board" tuple-space [24].[17] By converting the data that is encoded in the Web of Objects to an object instance, the Web of Objects serves as a database for populating the objects of an application. It is the role of this application to provide a mapping from the RDF encoded object to its object representation in the application (and vice versa for storage). A simple mapping is that a URI can denote a pointer to a particular object. The predicates of the statements that have the URI as a subject are seen as the field names. The objects of those statements are the values of those fields. For example, given the `Person` class previously defined, an instance in RDF can be represented as

```
(lanl:1234, rdf:type, lanl:Person)
(lanl:1234, lanl:age, "29"^^xsd:int)
(lanl:1234, lanl:friend, lanl:2345)
(lanl:1234, lanl:friend, lanl:3456)
(lanl:1234, lanl:friend, lanl:4567),
```

where `lanl:1234` represents the `Person` object and the `lanl:friend` properties points to three different `Person` instances. This simple mapping can be useful for many types of applications. However, it is important to note that there exists a mismatch between the semantics of RDF, RDFS, and OWL and typical object-oriented languages. In order to align both languages it is possible either to 1.) ignore RDF/RDFS/OWL semantics and interpret RDF as simply a data model for representing an object or 2.) make use of complicated mechanisms to ensure that the external object-oriented environment is faithful to such semantics [33].

Various RDF-to-object mappers exists. Examples include Schemagen[18], Elmo[19], and ActiveRDF [42]. RDF-to-object mappers usually provide support to 1.) automatically generate class definitions in the non-RDF language, 2.) automatically populate these objects using RDF data, and 3.) automatically write these objects to the Web of Objects. With RDF-to-object mapping, what is preserved in the Web of Objects is the description of the data contained in an object (i.e. its fields), not an explicit representation of the object's process information (i.e. its methods). However, there exists RDF object-oriented programming languages that represent methods and their underlying instructions in RDF.

[17]Object-spaces such as JavaSpaces is a modern object-oriented use of a tuple-space [22].

[18]Schemagen is currently available at `http://jena.sourceforge.net/`.

[19]Elmo is currently available at `http://www.openrdf.org/`.

4.2. Full Object Repository

The following object-oriented languages compile human readable/writeable source code into RDF: Adenine [47], Adenosine, FABL [25], and Neno [49]. The compilation process creates a full RDF representation of the classes defined. The instantiated objects of these classes are also represented in RDF. Thus, the object fields and their methods are stored in the Web of Objects. Each aforementioned RDF programming language has an accompanying virtual machine. It is the role of the respective virtual machine to query the Web of Objects for objects, execute their methods, and store any changes to the objects back into the Web of Objects.

Given that these languages are designed specifically for an RDF environment and in many cases, make use of the semantics defined for RDFS and OWL, the object-oriented nature of these languages tend to be different than typical languages such as C++ and Java. Multiple inheritance, properties as classes, methods as classes, unique SPARQL-based language constructs, etc. can be found in these languages. To demonstrate methods as classes and unique SPARQL-based language constructs, two examples are provided from Adenosine and Neno, respectively. In Adenosine, methods are declared irrespective of a class and can be assigned to classes as needed.

```
(lanl:makeFriend, rdf:type, std:Method)
(lanl:makeFriend, std:onClass, lanl:Person)
(lanl:makeFriend, std:onClass, lanl:Dog).
```

Next, in Neno, it is possible to make use of the inverse query capabilities of SPARQL. The Neno statement

```
rpi:josh.lanl:friend.lanl:age;
```

is typical in many object-oriented languages: the age of the friends of Josh.[20] However, the statement

```
rpi:josh..lanl:friend.lanl:age;
```

is not. This statement makes use of "dot dot" notation and is called inverse field referencing. This particular example returns the age of all the people that are friends with Josh. That is, it determines all the `lanl:Person` objects that are a `lanl:friend` of `lanl:josh` and then returns the `xsd:int` of their `lanl:age`. This expression resolves to the SPARQL query

```
SELECT ?y WHERE {
  ?x <lanl:friend> <rpi:josh> .
  ?x <lanl:age> ?y }.
```

[20] Actually, this is not that typical as fields cannot denote multiple objects in most object-oriented langauges. In order to reference multiple objects, fields tend to reference an abstract "collection" object that contains multiple objects within it (e.g. an array).

In RDF programming languages, there does not exist the impedance mismatch that occurs when integrating typical object-oriented languages with the Web of Objects. Moreover, such languages can leverage many of the standards and technologies associated with the Web of Data in general. In typical object-oriented languages, the local memory serves as the object storage environment. In RDF object-oriented languages, the Web of Objects serves this purpose. An interesting consequence of this model is that because compiled classes and instantiated objects are stored in the Web of Objects, RDF software can easily reference other RDF software in the Web of Objects. Instead of pointers being 32- or 64-bit addresses in local memory, pointers are URIs. In this medium, the Web of Objects is a shared memory structure by which all the world's software and data can be represented, interlinked, and executed.

> "The formalization of computation within RDF allows active content to be integrated seamlessly into RDF repositories, and provides a programming environment which simplifies the manipulation of RDF when compared to use of a conventional language via an API." [25]

A collection of the previously mentioned benefits of RDF programming are itemized below.

- the language and RDF are strongly aligned: there is a more direct mapping of the language constructs and the underlying RDF representation.
- compile time type checking: RDF APIs will not guarantee the validity of an RDF object at compile time.
- unique language constructs: Web of Data technology and standards are more easily adopted into RDF programming languages.
- reflection: language reflection is made easier because everything is represented in RDF.
- reuse: software can reference other software by means of URIs.

There are many issues with this model that are not discussed here. For example, issues surrounding security, data integrity, and computational resource consumption make themselves immediately apparent. Many of these issues are discussed, to varying degrees of detail, in the publications describing these languages.

4.3. Virtual Machine Repository

In the virtual machine repository model, the Web of Objects is made to behave like a general-purpose computer. In this model, software, data, and virtual machines are all encoded in the Web of Objects. The Fhat RDF virtual machine (RVM) is a virtual machine that is represented in RDF [49]. The Fhat RVM has an architecture that is similar to other high-level virtual machines such as the Java virtual machine (JVM). For example, it maintains a program counter (e.g. a pointer to the current instruction being executed), various stacks (e.g. operand stack, return stack, etc.), variable frames (e.g. memory for declared variables), etc. However, while the Fhat RVM is represented in the Web of Objects, it does not have the ability to alter its state without the support of some external process. An external process that has a reference to a Fhat RVM can alter it by moving its program location through a collection of instructions, by updating its stacks, by altering the objects in its heap, etc. Again, the Web of Objects (and more generally, the Web of Data) is simply a data structure. While it can represent process information, it is up to machines external to the Web of Objects to manipulate it and thus, alter its state.

In this computing model, a full computational stack is represented in the Web of Objects. Computing, at this level, is agnostic to the physical machines that support its representation. The lowest-levels of access are URIs and their RDF relations. There is no pointer to physical memory, disks, network cards, video cards, etc. Such RDF software and RVMs exist completely in an abstract URI and RDF address space—in the Web of Objects. In this way, if an external process that is executing an RVM stops, the RVM simply "freezes" at its current instruction location. The state of the RVM halts. Any other process with a reference to that RVM can continue to execute it.[21] Similarly, an RVM represented on one physical machine can compute an object represented on another physical machine. However, for the sake of efficiency, given that RDF subgraphs can be easily downloaded by a physical machine, the RVMs can be migrated between data stores—the process is moved to the data, not the data to the process. Many issues surrounding security, data integrity, and computational resource consumption are discussed in [49]. Currently there exists the concept, the consequences, and a prototype of an RVM. Future work in this area will hope to transform the Web of Objects (and more generally, the Web of Data) into massive-scale, distributed, general-purpose computer.

5. Conclusion

A URI can denote anything. It can denote a term, a vertex, an instruction. However, by itself, a single URI is not descriptive. When a URI is interpreted within the context of other URIs and literals, it takes on a richer meaning and is more generally useful. RDF is the means of creating this context. Both the URI and RDF form the foundational standards of the Web of Data. From the perspective of the domain of knowledge representation and reasoning, the Web of Data is a distributed knowledge base—a Semantic Web. In this interpretation, according to which ever logic is used, existing knowledge can be used to infer new knowledge. From the perspective of the domain of network analysis, the Web of Data is a distributed multi-relational network—a Giant Global Graph. In this interpretation, network algorithms provide structural statistics and can support network-based information retrieval systems. From the perspective of the domain of object-oriented programming, the Web of Data is a distribute object repository—a Web of Objects. In this interpretation, a complete computing environment exists that yields a general-purpose, Web-based, distributed computer. For other domains, other interpretations of the Web of Data can exist. Ultimately, the Web of Data can serve as a general-purpose medium for storing and relating all the world's data. As such, machines can usher in a new era of global-scale data management and processing.

[21] In analogy, if the laws of physics stopped "executing" the world, the state of the world would "freeze" awaiting the process to continue.

Acknowledgments

Joshua Shinavier of the Rensselaer Polytechnic Institute and Joe Geldart of the University of Durham both contributed through thoughtful discussions and review of the article.

References

[1] Jans Aasman. Allegro graph. *Technical Report* **1**, Franz Incorporated, 2006.

[2] Reka Albert and Albert-Laszlo Barabasi. Diameter of the world wide web. *Nature*, **401**:130–131, September 1999.

[3] Nicole Alexander and Siva Ravada. RDF object type and reification in the database. In *Proceedings of the International Conference on Data Engineering*, pages 93–103, Washington, DC, 2006. IEEE.

[4] John R. Anderson. A spreading activation theory of memory. *Journal of Verbal Learning and Verbal Behaviour*, 22:261–295, 1983.

[5] Alex Bavelas. Communication patterns in task oriented groups. *The Journal of the Acoustical Society of America*, **22**:271–282, 1950.

[6] Tim Berners-Lee, Robert Cailliau, Ari Luotonen, Henrik F. Nielsen, and Arthur Secret. The World-Wide Web. *Communications of the ACM*, **37**:76–82, 1994.

[7] Tim Berners-Lee, Roy T. Fielding, Day Software, Larry Masinter, and Adobe Systems. Uniform Resource Identifier (URI): Generic Syntax, January 2005.

[8] Tim Berners-Lee, James A. Hendler, and Ora Lassila. The Semantic Web. *Scientific American*, pages 34–43, May 2001.

[9] Christian Bizer, Tom Heath, Kingsley Idehen, and Tim Berners-Lee. Linked data on the web. In *Proceedings of the International World Wide Web Conference*, Linked Data Workshop, Beijing, China, April 2008.

[10] Johan Bollen, Herbert Van de Sompel, and Marko A. Rodriguez. Towards usage-based impact metrics: first results from the MESUR project. In *Proceedings of the Joint Conference on Digital Libraries*, pages 231–240, New York, NY, 2008. IEEE/ACM.

[11] Bélaa Bollobás and Oliver Riordan. The diameter of a scale-free random graph. *Combinatorica*, **24**(1):5–34, 2004.

[12] Ulrick Brandes and Thomas Erlebach, editors. *Network Analysis: Methodolgical Foundations*. Springer, Berling, DE, 2005.

[13] Ulrik Brandes. A faster algorithm for betweeness centrality. *Journal of Mathematical Sociology*, **25**(2):163–177, 2001.

[14] Dan Brickley and Ramanathan V. Guha. RDF vocabulary description language 1.0: RDF schema. *Technical report*, World Wide Web Consortium, 2004.

[15] Sergey Brin and Lawrence Page. The anatomy of a large-scale hypertextual web search engine. *Computer Networks and ISDN Systems*, **30**(1–7):107–117, 1998.

[16] Jeen Broekstra, Arjohn Kampman, and Frank van Harmelen. Sesame: A generic architecture for storing and querying RDF. In *Proceedings of the International Semantic Web Conference*, Sardinia, Italy, June 2002.

[17] Gary Chartrand. *Introductory Graph Theory*. Dover, 1977.

[18] Allan M. Collins and Elizabeth F. Loftus. A spreading activation theory of semantic processing. *Psychological Review*, **82**:407–428, 1975.

[19] Irving M. Copi. *Introduction to Logic*. Macmillan Publishing Company, New York, NY, 1982.

[20] Edsger W. Dijkstra. A note on two problems in connexion with graphs. *Numerische Mathematik*, 1:269–271, 1959.

[21] Dieter Fensel, Frank van Harmelen, Bo Andersson, Paul Brennan, Hamish Cunningham, Emanuele Della Valle, Florian Fischer, Zhisheng Huang, Atanas Kiryakov, Tony Kyung il Lee, Lael School, Volker Tresp, Stefan Wesner, Michael Witbrock, and Ning Zhong. Towards larkc: a platform for web-scale reasoning. In *Proceedings of the IEEE International Conference on Semantic Computing*, Los Alamitos, CA, 2008. IEEE.

[22] Eric Freeman, Susanne Hupfer, and Ken Arnold. *JavaSpaces: Principles, Patterns, and Practice*. Prentice Hall, 2008.

[23] Linton C. Freeman. A set of measures of centrality based on betweenness. *Sociometry*, **40**(35–41), 1977.

[24] David Gelernter and Nicholas Carriero. Coordination languages and their significance. *Communications of the ACM*, **35**(2):97–107, 1992.

[25] Chris Goad. Describing computation within RDF. In *Proceedings of the International Semantic Web Working Symposium*, 2004.

[26] Volker Haarslev and Ralf Möller. Racer: A core inference engine for the Semantic Web. In *Proceedings of the 2nd International Workshop on Evaluation of Ontology-based Tools*, pages 27–36, 2003.

[27] Olle Häggström. *Finite Markov Chains and Algorithmic Applications*. Cambridge University Press, 2002.

[28] Frank Harary and Per Hage. Eccentricity and centrality in networks. *Social Networks*, **17**:57–63, 1995.

[29] Patrick Hayes and Brian McBride. RDF semantics. Technical report, World Wide Web Consortium, February 2004.

[30] Simon Haykin. *Neural Networks. A Comprehensive Foundation*. Prentice Hall, New Jersey, USA, 1999.

[31] Roger Horn and Charles Johnson. *Topics in Matrix Analysis*. Cambridge University Press, 1994.

[32] Ian Horrocks, Peter F. Patel-Schneider, Harold Boley, Said Tabet, Benjamin Grosof, and Mike Dean. SWRL: A Semantic Web rule language combining OWL and RuleML. Technical report, World Wide Web Consortium, May 2004.

[33] A. Kalyanpur, D. Pastor, S. Battle, and J. Padget. Automatic mapping of OWL ontologies into java. In *Proceedings of Software Engineering. - Knowledge Engineering*, Banff, Canada, 2004.

[34] Atanas Kiryakov, Damyan Ognyanov, and Dimitar Manov. OWLIM – a pragmatic semantic repository for OWL. In *International Workshop on Scalable Semantic Web Knowledge Base Systems*, volume LNCS 3807, pages 182–192, New York, NY, November 2005. Spring-Verlag.

[35] Dirk Koschützki, Katharina Anna Lehmann, Dagmar Tenfelde-Podehl, and Oliver Zlotowski. *Network Analysis: Methodolgical Foundations*, volume 3418 of *Lecture Notes in Computer Science*, chapter Advanced Centrality Concepts, pages 83–111. Spring-Verlag, 2004.

[36] Lee W. Lacy. *OWL: Representing Information Using the Web Ontology Language*. Trafford Publishing, 2005.

[37] Paul J. Leach. A Universally Unique IDentifier (UUID) URN Namespace. Technical report, Network Working Group, 2005.

[38] Harold J. Leavitt. Some effects of communication patterns on group performance. *Journal of Abnornal and Social Psychology*, **46**:38–50, 1951.

[39] Deborah L. McGuinness and Frank van Harmelen. OWL web ontology language overview, February 2004.

[40] Mark E. J. Newman. Assortative mixing in networks. *Physical Review Letters*, **89**(20):208701, 2002.

[41] Mark E. J. Newman. Mixing patterns in networks. *Physical Review E*, **67**(2):026126, Feb 2003.

[42] Eyal Oren, Benjamin Heitmann, and Stefan Decker. ActiveRDF: Embedding semantic web data into object-oriented languages. *Web Semantics: Science, Services and Agents on the World Wide Web*, **6**(3):191–202, 2008.

[43] Arzucan Ozgur, Thuy Vu, Gunes Erkan, and Dragomir R. Radev. Identifying gene-disease associations using centrality on a literature mined gene-interaction network. *Bioinformatics*, **24**(13):277–285, July 2008.

[44] Bijan Parsia and Evren Sirin. Pellet: An OWL DL reasoner. In *Proceedings of the International Semantic Web Conference*, volume 3298 of *Lecture Notes in Computer Science*, Hiroshima, Japan, November 2004. Springer-Verlag.

[45] Gunther Patzig. *Aristotle's Theory of The Syllogism.* D. Reidel Publishing Company, Boston, Massachusetts, 1968.

[46] Eric Prud'hommeaux and Andy Seaborne. SPARQL query language for RDF. *Technical report,* World Wide Web Consortium, October 2004.

[47] Dennis Quan, David F. Huynh, Vineet Sinha, and David Karger. Adenine: A metadata programming language. *Technical report*, Massachusetts Institute of Technology, February 2003.

[48] Marko A. Rodriguez. Grammar-based random walkers in semantic networks. *Knowledge-Based Systems*, **21**(7):727–739, 2008.

[49] Marko A. Rodriguez. *Emergent Web Intelligence*, chapter General-Purpose Computing on a Semantic Network Substrate. Advanced Information and Knowledge Processing. Springer-Verlag, Berlin, DE, 2009.

[50] Marko A. Rodriguez. A reflection on the structure and process of the Web of Data. *Bulletin of the American Society for Information Science and Technology*, **35**(6):38–43, August 2009.

[51] Marko A. Rodriguez and Joshua Shinavier. Exposing multi-relational networks to single-relational network analysis algorithms. *Journal of Informetrics*, in press, 2009.

[52] Marko A. Rodriguez and Jennifer H. Watkins. Grammar-based geodesics in semantic networks. Technical Report LA-UR-07-4042, Los Alamos National Laboratory, 2007.

[53] Gert Sabidussi. The centrality index of a graph. *Psychometrika*, **31**:581–603, 1966.

[54] Joshua Shinavier. Functional programs as Linked Data. In *3rd Workshop on Scripting for the Semantic Web*, Innsbruck, Austria, 2007.

[55] Alan M. Turing. On computable numbers, with an application to the entscheidungsproblem. *Proceedings of the London Mathematical Society*, **42**(2):230–265, 1937.

[56] W3C/IETF. URIs, URLs, and URNs: Clarifications and recommendations 1.0, September 2001.

[57] Hai H. Wang, Natasha Noy, Alan Rector, Mark Musen, Timothy Redmond, Daniel Rubin, Samson Tu, Tania Tudorache, Nick Drummond, Matthew Horridge, and Julian Sedenberg. Frames and OWL side by side. In *10th International Protégé Conference*, Budapest, Hungary, July 2007.

[58] Pei Wang. Non-axiomatic reasoning system (version 2.2). Technical Report 75, Center for Research on Concepts and Cognition at Indiana University, 1993.

[59] Pei Wang. From inheritance relation to non-axiomatic logic. *International Journal of Approximate Reasoning*, **11**:281–319, 1994.

[60] Pei Wang. Cognitive logic versus mathematical logic. In *Proceedings of the Third International Seminar on Logic and Cognition*, May 2004.

[61] Pei Wang. *Rigid Flexibility: The Logic Of Intelligence*. Springer, 2006.

[62] Stanley Wasserman and Katherine Faust. *Social Network Analysis: Methods and Applications*. Cambridge University Press, Cambridge, UK, 1994.

[63] Scott White and Padhraic Smyth. Algorithms for estimating relative importance in networks. In *Proceedings of the International Conference on Knowledge Discovery and Data Mining*, pages 266–275, New York, NY, 2003. ACM Press.

In: Data Management in the Semantic Web
Editor: Hal Jin, pp. 39-56
ISBN: 978-1-61122-862-5

Chapter 2

TOWARD SEMANTICS-AWARE WEB CRAWLING

Lefteris Kozanidis[1,a]***, Sofia Stamou***[1,b]
and Vasilis Megalooikonomou[1,2,c]
[1] Computer Engineering and Informatics Department,
Patras University, Rio, Greece
[2] Data Engineering Lab, Temple University, Philadelphia, PA, U. S.

Abstract

The rapid growth of the web imposes scaling challenges to general-purpose web crawlers that attempt to download plentiful web pages so that these are made available to the search engine users. Perhaps the greatest challenge associated with harvesting the web content is how to ensure that the crawlers will not waste resources trying to download pages that are of no or little interest to web users. One way to go about downloading useful web data is to build crawlers that can optimize the priority of the unvisited URLs so that pages of interest are downloaded earlier. In this respect, many attempts have been proposed towards focusing web crawls on topic-specific content. In this chapter, we build upon existing studies and we introduce a novel focused crawling approach that relies on the web pages' semantic orientation in order to determine their crawling priority. The contribution of our approach lies on the fact that we integrate a topical ontology and a passage extraction algorithm into a common framework against which the crawler is trained, so as to be able to detect pages of interest and determine their crawling priority. The evaluation of our proposed approach demonstrates that semantics-aware focused crawling yields both accurate and complete web crawls.

1. Introduction

The most prominent way for harvesting the proliferating data that is available on the web is to build a web crawler that navigates on the web graph and downloads the pages it comes across. In the simplest implementation, a web crawler is a program that given a seed list of

[a] E-mail address: kozanid@ceid.upatras.gr
[b] E-mail address: stamou@ceid.upatras.gr
[c] E-mail address: vasilis@ceid.upatras.gr

URLs it starts its web visits and retrieves web data sources simply by following their internal links. Link-based crawling is very effective towards building a complete search engine index, but it is generally insufficient for discriminating between pages that deal with specific topics. To overcome such inefficiencies, researchers have proposed several methods towards focusing web crawls on topically-specific web content in an attempt to ensure that the downloaded web resources meet certain quality standards, such as the pages' relevance to specific topics or user needs.

Here, we introduce an approach towards building a focused web crawler, by giving emphasis on the encapsulation of semantic knowledge into the crawling process. To build our crawler there are three main challenges that we need to address. Firstly, we need to make the crawler understand the semantic orientation of the pages it comes across during its web navigations. Secondly, we need to build a well-balanced set of training examples that the crawler will regularly consult in its web visits. Finally, we need a method for organizing the unvisited URLs in the crawler's frontier so that the pages of great relatedness to the concerned topics are retrieved first. For the first challenge, we describe how to equip a general-purpose web crawler with a decision support mechanism that relies on the semantics of the pages the crawler comes across and judges their usefulness with respect to a set of pre-defined topics. For the second challenge, we explore a semantics-aware web data classifier that automatically generates and updates training examples that will guide the crawler's decision making algorithm towards semantics-aware web crawls. Finally, for the third challenge, we introduce a novel downloading policy that the crawler follows while setting the retrieval priority of the queued URLs.

The rest of the chapter is organized as follows. We begin our discussion with an overview of relevant works. In Section 3, we introduce our focused crawler and we describe how it operates for populating a search engine index with topic-specific web pages. In particular, we describe the distinct modules that our crawler integrates in order to be able to identify the semantic orientation of the pages it comes across and we present our approach towards building topical-focused training examples that the crawler consults in its web visits. We also discuss the crawler's downloading policy. In Section 4, we describe the experiments we carried out for assessing our focused crawler's performance in detecting topic-specific web pages and we present the experimental results. In Section 5, we discuss in detail the main implications of our crawling method, we outline the advantages and disadvantages that our crawler entails compared to other focused crawling methods and we empirically assess the contribution of our technique. We conclude the chapter in Section 6 where we summarize the main findings of our work and outline avenues for future work..

2. Related Work

A significant amount of work has been devoted towards focusing web crawls on specific web content and a number of algorithms have been proposed for supporting the crawler's decisions concerning which pages to download first. FishSearch is a well-known focused crawling algorithm, proposed in [9] that treats every URL as a *fish* whose survivability depends on the visited pages' relevance to specific topics and the server's speed. Among its positive points are its simplicity and dynamic nature. Unfortunately the discrete scoring mechanism that is used offers very low differentiation to enqueued webpages An extension of the FishSearch algorithm is SharkSearch, introduced in [15]. SharkSearch relies on the vector space model via which it estimates the degree of similarity that a visited page has to a given query by exploiting meta-information found in the page anchor text or the query surrounding text.

In addition to the above methods, researchers (cf. [7] [21]) have studied a number of learning techniques that they incorporate in a crawler so that it retrieves the maximum number of pages relating to a particular subject by using the minimum bandwidth. Moreover, Chakrabarti et al. [5] suggest the exploitation of a document taxonomy for building classification models that the crawler periodically consults and they propose two different rules for link expansion, namely the Hard Focus and the Soft Focus rules. In a subsequent study Chakrabarti et al. [6] introduced two separate models for computing the pages' relevance and the URLs' visiting order, i.e. the online training examples for the URL ranking and the source page features for deriving the pages' relevance.

Ehrig and Maedche [11] suggested a new focused crawling approach based on a graph–oriented knowledge representation model and showed that their method outperforms typical breadth–first keyword or taxonomic-based approaches. In [13] a link analysis algorithm is used in combination with an ontology based metric association to define the downloading priority of the candidate URLs before the process of crawling. In a different approach, Altingovde and Ulusoy [3] developed a rule-based crawler which uses simple rules derived from inter-class linkage patterns to decide its next move. Their suggested crawler supports tunnelling, i.e. the ability to identify on-topic pages via off-topic web resources and tries to learn which off-topic pages can eventually lead to high quality on-topic ones.

Another focused crawling approach is introduced in [2]. This approach utilizes Latent Semantic Indexing and combines link analysis with text content in order to retrieve domain specific web documents. A strong point of this approach is that training is only dependent on unlabeled text samples. A problem addressed is that the insertion of new pages in the collection means that the index has to be regenerated and that the computational complexity increases as more documents are added in the frontier. As a solution, it is proposed to discard less authoritative documents at the bottom of the queue. The authors in [21] propose a novel scheme, named RLwCS, for assigning scores to a URL, based on Reinforcement Learning (RL) framework. In their approach a Reinforcement learning method chooses the best classifier from a variety of classification schemes encapsulated in the WEKA [28] machine learning library. They evaluate their method online on a number of topics and they compare it with another RL approach (named TD-FC) and a classifier-based crawler (Best-first Focused Crawler). The proposed approach outperforms both TD-FC and BF-FC.

A large number of existing focused crawling systems incorporate classification algorithms that rely on both positive and negative training examples to build the page classification model. A model is built either via the use of a Naïve Bayes classifier (cf. the work of [10]) or through the data encoded in standard topical taxonomies such as the Dmoz or the Yahoo subject hierarchies (cf. [5] and [6]). To overcome the difficulties associated with building and maintaining training examples, [27] proposed a new focused crawling paradigm, namely the *iSurfer* crawler that uses an incremental method to learn a page classification model and a link prediction model. With the incremental learning capability, the crawler can start from a few positive samples and gain more integrated knowledge about the target topic over time, so that the precision and robustness of the page classifier and the link predictor are improved.

In addition, [16] proposed a *relevancy context-graph* focused crawling approach. Their method uses both general word and topic-specific word distributions in order to collect web samples of topic relevance and create a general-purpose language model. Such data is utilized for the construction of a context graph for a given topic. This context graph is employed for calculating the ranking priority of every page in the crawler's queue. A simulation-based experimental study showed that the context-graph crawler can effectively estimate the proper order of unvisited pages and performs better than pure context-graph and breadth-first spiders for a topic.

Besides utilizing classification methods and link structure analysis techniques, [19] proposed the exploitation of anchor text for determining the priority of the URLs in a focused crawler's frontier. Their method relies on the assumption that anchor texts are good summaries for the target pages' contents. Therefore, they explore the pages' anchor texts in order to build sets of positive and negative anchor examples, which they supply to a decision tree algorithm. Based on the set of examples, the algorithm decides the crawling priority of every web page. The experimental evaluation of this approach demonstrated that there are only 3% pages needed in order to download 50% of the topic-specific pages.

A relevant field of study is the implementation of hidden web crawlers. Given the plethora of web data that is available in online databases, it is imperative to build crawlers that focus their web visits on content that is hidden behind search interfaces. In this respect, researchers have studied ways of learning the crawler how to interact with a hidden web interface so that it can have access to the online data sources that are stored in database systems. In this direction, [8] studied ways of enabling the crawler detect whether a particular page contains a search form, while [1] and [20], investigated methods for assisting the crawler in selecting queries that will retrieve most of the hidden web content in a cost-effective manner.

Finally, in [12] it is introduced an effective Deep Web Discovery crawler technique which utilizes both a predefined domain ontology and the link structure of the Deep Web, so as to improve the crawler's decision accuracy. The crawler avoids visiting irrelevant pages by learning features of links and paths that lead to pages that contain searchable forms, it employs appropriate stopping criteria and computes the topic similarity. Three classification modules are involved in the classification process. The first module classifies the pages towards a specific topic of the taxonomy, the second module is used to identify forms that can lead to useful information and the third one discovers links that are likely to lead to pages that contain searchable form interfaces.

Based on the existing focused crawling techniques, we have designed and implemented a novel crawling module that aims at automatically identifying the topical orientation of the web pages it comes across in its web visits so as to determine which pages are of interest and thus they should be downloaded. Our focused crawling module is complementary to existing tools that try to capture the focus of web pages. However, the novelty of our approach lies on the integration of a semantic hierarchy and a number of heuristics in the crawler's downloading policy that ensure the proper encapsulation of a page's focus before these are actually downloaded in the engine's index.

3. Semantics-Aware Crawler

To build a topical-focused web crawler there are three main challenges we need to address: (i) how to make the crawler identify web sources of specific topic orientation, (ii) how to provide the crawler with training examples that will serve as a reference source throughout its web visits and (iii) how to organize the unvisited URLs in the crawler's frontier so that pages of great relatedness to the concerned topics are downloaded first. In Section 3.1, we describe the process that the crawler follows for automatically determining whether an unvisited URL points to topic-specific content or not. In Section 3.2, we discuss the process we follow for specifying a small set of training examples that the crawler consults before making a retrieval decision. Finally, in Section 3.3, we present the downloading policy that our crawler assigns to every unvisited topic-specific URL so as to ensure that it will not waste resources trying to download pages of little topical relevance. Before delving into the details of our topical-focused crawling approach, we schematically illustrate the crawler's architecture, in Figure 1.

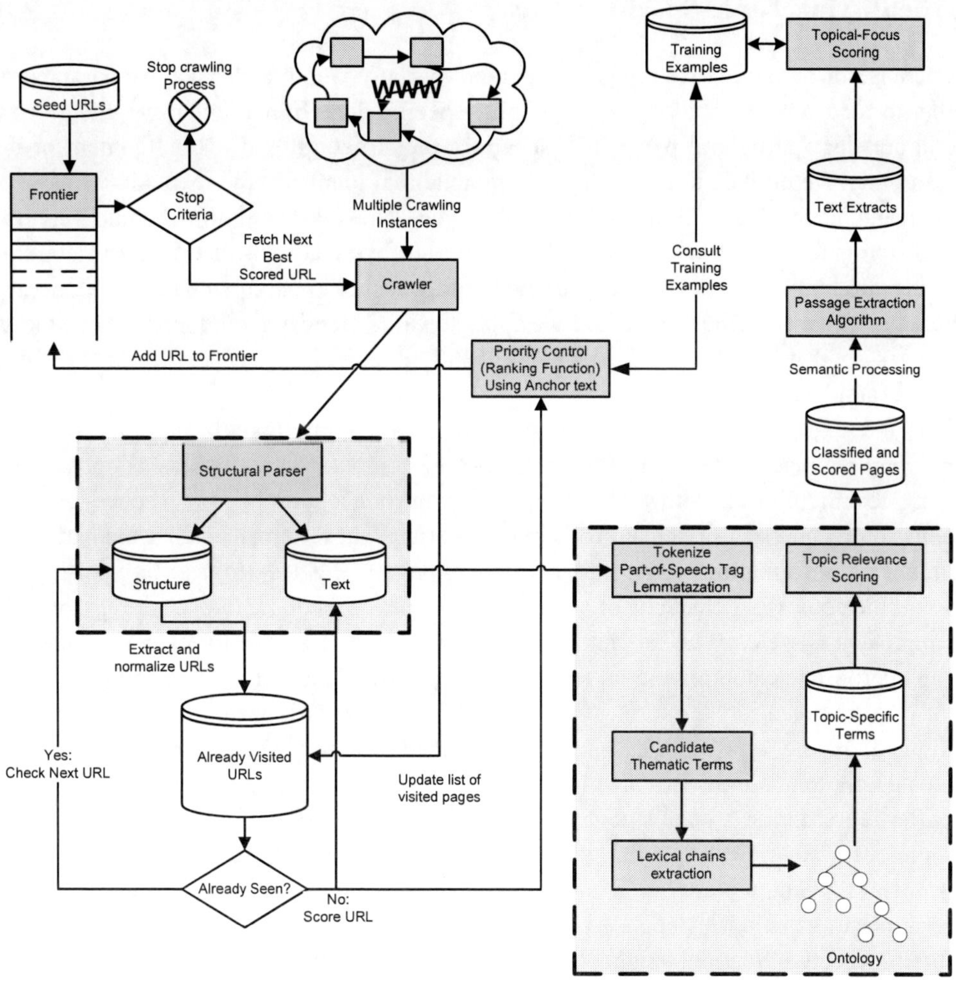

Figure 1. Focused Crawler Architecture.

As the figure shows, the main components that our crawler integrates are: (i) a term extraction module that extracts thematic terms from the pages' content and anchor text, (ii) a topical ontology against which thematic terms that represent specific topics are identified, (iii) a classification module that associates keywords to topics and scores the topical relevance of every page, (iv) a passage extraction algorithm that relies on the classified web pages, it semantically processes their contents and extracts from every page a text nugget (i.e., training example) that is semantically closest to the page's semantic orientation and (v) a ranking function (cf. priority control module) that organizes the topical-focused URLs in the crawler's frontier according to their probability of guiding the crawler to highly focused topic-specific pages.

Having presented the general architecture of our focused crawling module, we now turn our attention to the detailed description of each and every module and we also discuss how these are put together in order to turn a generic crawler into a topical focused one.

3.1. Identifying Topic-Specific URLs

In the course of our study, we relied on a general-purpose web crawler that we parameterized in order to focus its web walkthroughs on topic-specific data. In particular, we integrated to a generic crawler a structural parser that separates the structural and textual content of every page and then we utilized a term extraction module that identifies the thematic terms in both the text and anchor text of the considered pages. The main intuition behind relying on thematic terms for identifying the topical orientation of web pages is that the pages containing terms that are highly representative of particular topics should be downloaded by the crawler. In this section we describe the method we apply towards identifying the topical orientation of web pages so that this knowledge is subsequently supplied to the crawler in the form of training examples.

For the extraction of thematic terms, we firstly apply tokenization, Part-of-Speech tagging and lemmatization to the considered pages' content. Thereafter, we adopt the lexical chaining technique and following the approach introduced in [4], we reduce the pages' contents into sequences of semantically related terms. These terms[1], called thematic words, communicate information about the respective pages' themes (topics). In particular, to represent the contextual elements of a web page as a set of thematic terms, we rely on a three-step approach: (i) select a set of candidate terms from the page, (ii) for each candidate term, find an appropriate chain relying on a relatedness criterion among members of the chains, and (iii) if it is found, insert the term in the chain. The relatedness factor in the second step is determined by the type of the links that are used in WordNet [25] for connecting the candidate term to the terms that are already stored in existing lexical chains.

After representing a page's contents as lexical chains, we disambiguate the sense of the words in every chain by employing the scoring function *f* introduced in [23], which indicates the probability that a word relation is a correct one. Given two words, w_1 and w_2, their scoring function *f* via a relation *r*, depends on the words' association score, their depth in WordNet and their respective relation weight. The association score (*Assoc*) of the word pair (w_1, w_2) is determined by the words' co-occurrence frequency in a corpus that has been previously

[1] From all the terms appearing in a page, we examine only the nouns and the proper nouns as candidate words for participating in the page's chain, because these convey most of the thematic information in texts [14].

collected. In practice, the greater the association score between a word pair w_1 and w_2 is, the greater the likelihood that w_1 and w_2 refer to the same topic. Formally, the (*Assoc*) score of the word pair (w_1, w_2) is given by:

$$Assoc\,(w_1, w_2) = \frac{\log\,(p\,(w_1, w_2) + 1)}{N_s(w_1) \times N_s(w_2)} \tag{1}$$

where $p(w_1,w_2)$ is the corpus co-occurrence probability of the word pair (w_1,w_2) and $N_s(w)$ is a normalization factor, which indicates the number of WordNet senses that a word w has. Given a word pair (w_1, w_2) their *DepthScore* expresses the words' position in WordNet hierarchy and is defined as:

$$DepthScore\,(w_1, w_2) = Depth\,(w_1) \times Depth(w_2) \tag{2}$$

where *Depth* (w) is the depth of word w in WordNet and indicates that the deeper a word is in the WordNet hierarchy, the more specific meaning it has.

Within the WordNet lexical network two words w_1 and w_2 are connected through one or more semantic relations, e.g. hypernmy, synonymy, meronymy, etc. In our framework, we value the strength of every semantic relation depending on how much their connected concepts share common semantics. In our work, we have experimentally set the relation weights (*RelationWeight*) to: 1 for reiteration, 0.2 for synonymy and hyper/ hyponymy and 0.4 for mero/holonymy. *RelationWeight* values contribute to the disambiguation of the chain word senses by communicating the degree to which selected word meanings are related to each other. Formally, the scoring function *f* of w_1 and w_2 is defined as:

$$f_s(w_1, w_2, r) = Assoc(w_1, w_2) \times DepthScore\,(w_1, w_2) \times RelationWeight\,(r) \tag{3}$$

The value of the function *f* represents the probability that the relation type r is the correct one between words w_1 and w_2. In order to disambiguate the senses of the words within lexical chain C_i we calculate its score, by summing up the f_s scores of all the words w_{j1} w_{j2} (where w_{j1} and w_{j2} are successive words) within the chain C_i. Formally, the score of lexical chain C_i, is expressed as the sum of the score of each relation r_j in C_i.

$$Score\,(C_i) = \sum_{r_j \, in \, C_j} f_S\left(w_{j1}, w_{j2}, r_j \right) \tag{4}$$

Eventually, in order to disambiguate we pick the relations and senses that maximize the *Score* (C_i) for that particular chain, given by:

$$Score\,(C_i) = \max_{C_i \in C} Score\,(C) \tag{5}$$

To find the topic(s) that a page discusses, we follow the TODE categorization scheme, presented in [24] and we map the pages' thematic words to the ontology's concepts. For thematic words that match the ontology's concepts we follow their hypernymy (generalization) links until we reach a top level topic.

Then, we rely on the page thematic terms that match some ontology nodes in order to compute the degree to which a page relates to each of the identified topics. Specifically, we apply the Relatedness Score (*RScore*) function, which indicates the expressiveness of every ontology topic in describing the Web pages' contents. Formally, the relatedness score of a page p_i (represented by the lexical chain C_i) to the ontology's topic T_k is defined as the product of the page's chain Score (C_i) and the fraction of words in the page's chain that are descendants (i.e., specializations) of T_k. Formally, the *RScore* of a page to each of the ontology's matching topics is given by:

$$RScore_k(i) = \frac{Score(C_i) \times \#\,of\ \ C_i\ elements\ of\ D_k\ matched}{\left|\#\,of\ \ C_i\ elements\right|} \tag{6}$$

The denominator is used to remove any effect the length of a lexical chain might have on *RScore* and ensures that the final score is normalized so that all values are between zero and one, with 0 corresponding to no relatedness at all and 1 indicating the topic that is highly expressive of the page's thematic content. Based on the above formula we estimate the degree to which every page relates to each of the ontology topics. At the end of this process, we assign to every web page its corresponding topical labels and their respective *RScore* values.

Having identified the topical category-(ies) to which a given page belongs, the next step is to determine a set of training examples that the crawler can use for learning to discriminate between on-topic and off-topic pages. In other words, we need a method for deriving topic-descriptive phrases from the pages' contents, in order to associate every ontology topic with a focused example phrase. In the following section, we describe our approach towards extracting topic-expressive text nuggets from the pages' textual content and we present the contribution of those examples in the crawler's decision making downloading policy.

3.2. Building Training Examples

Having determined a set of pages that are classified under our ontology topics and having also computed the degree to which every page relates to each of the considered topics, we now describe how we can use the above *knowledge* for selecting within the contents of a topical-focused page the text fragment that is the most representative of the page topic. This is in order to determine for every topic a set of example sentences that are descriptive of the topic semantics. Based on these examples, we believe that the crawler will be able to make informed decisions about whether a new (unclassified) page belongs to a given topic and thus it should be downloaded, or not. The details of our method are presented below.

For extracting topic descriptive sentences from a topical-focused page, we have designed and implemented a passage selection algorithm that given our topical ontology and a set of pages classified under each of the ontology topics; it selects for every topic the most descriptive topical sentences. By descriptive, we refer to the sentences whose semantics are very similar to the topic semantics.

Before running our algorithm, we segment the contents of the classified pages into passages of 50 consecutive terms, which formulate the candidate training phrases. Then, given an ontology topic and a set of candidate training phrases that have been extracted from the pages listed under that topic, we explore the semantic correlation between the ontology topic and each of the candidate phrases in order to identify which of the phrases are the most descriptive of the topic semantics. In this respect, we start by mapping the thematic terms in each of the candidate phrases to their corresponding ontology nodes. Then, we apply the Wu and Palmer [26] similarity metric in order to compute the degree to which every thematic term semantically relates to the given ontology topic. Formally, the semantic similarity between a topical term c_i and a thematic term c_j is given by:

$$Similarity\ (c_i, c_k) = \frac{2 \times Depth\ \left(LCS\ (c_i, c_k)\right)}{Depth(c_i) + Depth(c_k)} \quad \textbf{(7)}$$

where LCS is the least common subsumer that connects two concepts together. Having computed paired similarity values between passage terms and the ontology topic we take the average similarity values between a topic and the thematic terms in a candidate phrase in order to quantify the semantic similarity that every candidate sentence has to the considered topic, formally given by:

$$Topic\text{-}Sentence\,Terms\ Similarity\ (T,S) = \frac{1}{s}\sum_{j=1}^{s} Similarity\,(T_i, S_j) \quad \textbf{(8)}$$

where S is the candidate sentence, T_i is the term representing the ontology topic T_i, S_j is the corresponding ontology node of the sentence term j ($s_j \in s$) and s is the total number of thematic terms in sentence S. Finally, we pick from each topical page, the sentence that exhibits the maximum Topic-Sentence Terms Similarity value as the phrase that is the most descriptive of the topic semantics from all the page sentences.

Based on the above steps, we identify within a topic specific page the sentence that is the most descriptive of the topic semantics. Given that there are several pages listed under each of the ontology topics, we essentially need to retain for every topic a set of sentences that are the most correlated to the topic semantics. To enable that, we apply the following formula:

$$Topic\text{-}Sentence\,Similarity\,(T,S) = \underset{k}{\arg\max}\, Topic\text{-}Sentence\,Terms\ Similarity\,(T,\ S_k) \quad \textbf{(9)}$$

where T represents an ontology topic and S_k denotes the set of thematic terms in a candidate sentence S in such way that maximizes similarity. The average similarity between the topic and the sentence items indicates the ***semantic correlation*** between the two. Thus, from all the page passages that are similar to the topic semantics, we retain the top *k* passages as the example topical sentences against which the crawler will be trained to discriminate between on-topic and off-topic pages. By applying the above process to the pages classified under each of the ontology topics, we end up with *k* descriptive sentences for each of the considered topics. These sentences are given as input to a core crawling module together with a list of URLs to be downloaded.

Every time the crawler reaches a page URL that is not already included in the frontier, it examines the page anchor text in which it looks for patterns that match the crawler's training examples. If there are matching patterns found, the crawler adds the URL in its crawling queue and makes a download decision. On the other hand, in case there are no matching patterns between the sampled page contents and the crawler's focused training examples, the respective page URL is not considered in the subsequent crawler's web visitations.

By following the above process, we build a set of training topic-specific examples that the crawler consults for deciding whether a page URL points to topic specific content or not. The last issue we need to consider before the actual deployment of our focused crawler is to design a method that helps the crawler determine the crawling priority that should be given to every topic specific URL in the crawler's frontier.

3.3. Ordering URLs in the Crawler's Frontier

A key element in all focused crawling applications is ordering the unvisited URLs in the crawler's frontier in a way that reduces the probability that the crawler will visit irrelevant sources. To account for that, we have integrated into our focused crawler a probabilistic algorithm that estimates for every URL in the frontier the probability that it will guide the crawler to topic-specific pages. In addition, our algorithm operates upon the intuition that the links contained in a page, which highly relate to a given topic, have increased probability of guiding the crawler to other pages that deal with the same topic. To derive such probabilities, we designed our algorithm based on the following dual assumption. The stronger the topical relevance is between the thematic terms identified in the anchor text of a link, the increased the probability that the link points to some topical focused page. Moreover, the more thematic terms are identified in the anchor text of a link, the greater the probability that the link's visitation will guide the crawler to other topic-specific web pages.

To deduce the degree of topical relevance between the thematic terms that surround the anchor text of a link, we rely on our ontology against which we compute the amount of information that thematic terms share in common. Formally, we estimate the topical relevance between pairs of thematic terms in the anchor text of a link (u) as:

$$Relevance\left(u,\ T\right) = \frac{\left|topic - specific\ \ anchor\ \ terms\right|}{\left|anchor\ \ terms\right|} \quad \textbf{(10)}$$

where T denotes an ontology topic, and u denotes the anchor text of a url. Based on the above formula, we derive the degree to which the anchor terms of a link pertain to some specific topic. That is, if the anchor text of a link contains many topic specific terms then there is some probability that the link points to some topic specific page. Depending on the number of topics to which anchor terms match, we derive the probability with which the link points to any of the identified topics. However, topical correlation is not sufficient per se for ordering URLs in the crawler's frontier since it does not account the probability that the visitation of a topical focused URL will lead the crawler to other topical focused pages.

To fill this gap, we take a step further and we introduce a metric that computes the probability with which every topical-focused URL points to other topic-specific pages. For our computations, we rely on the distribution of thematic terms in the anchor text of the links that the page URL contains. Recall that while processing anchor text, we have already derived the thematic terms that are contained in it. Our intuition is that the more thematic terms the anchor text of a link contains, the more likely it is that following this link will guide the crawler to other topic-specific pages. Formally, to quantify the probability that a link (u) in a topical-focused page points to a page of the same topical focus, we estimate the fraction of thematic terms in the anchor text of (u) that correspond to a given topic T and we derive the topical focus of (u) as:

$$Topical\ Focus\,(u,T) \;=\; \frac{|thematic\ anchor\ terms\ (u,T)|}{|thematic\ anchor\ terms\,(u)|} \qquad \textbf{(11)}$$

Where Topical Focus (u, T) indicates the probability that the visitation of (u) will result into the retrieval of a page about T. Topical Focus scores are normalized, taking values between 0 and 1; with 0 indicating that the visitation of (u) is improbable to guide the crawler to a page about T and 1 indicating that the visitation of (u) is highly probable to guide the crawler to a page relevant to T. In simple words, the higher the fraction of topic-specific terms in the anchor text of a link, the greater the probability that this link points to a topic-specific page.

For far, we have presented a metric for quantifying the probability with which a URL has a topical orientation (cf. Relevance) and we have also introduced a measure for estimating the probability that the visitation of a topical-focused URL will guide the crawler to other topical-focused pages (cf. Topical Focus). Now we turn our attention on how we can combine the two metrics in order to rank the URLs in the crawler's frontier so that the URL with the highest topical orientation and the highest probability of pointing to other topical-focused pages is visited earlier. To rank the URLs in the crawler's frontier according to their probability of focusing web visits to highly topic-specific content, we rely on the URLs' topical relevance and Topical Focus values and we compute their downloading priority as:

$$Rank\,(u) \;=\; Avg.Relevance\ (u,T) + Topical\ \ Focus\,(u,T) \qquad \textbf{(12)}$$

where Rank (u) indicates the priority score assigned to every queued URL, so that the higher the Rank value of a URL (u) the greater downloading priority it has. Based on the above formula, we estimate for every URL in the crawler's frontier its download priority and we order them in descending priority values. This way, the crawler starts its web visits from the URL with the highest priority.

4. Experimental Evaluation

In this section, we validate the effectiveness of our proposed topical focused crawler. For our evaluation, we carried out an experiment in order to assess our crawler's performance in effectively discovering and downloading pages dealing with the topic of geography. For our purpose, we utilized a subset of our topical ontology that contains only geography-specific concepts. For fast computations of the lexical chains, we stored the ontology topics in main memory, while WordNet hierarchies were stored on disk and were accessed through a hash-table whenever necessary. Moreover, words' co-occurrence statistics were pre-computed in the corpus and stored in inverted lists, which were again made accessible upon demand. Of course, the execution time for training the crawler depends on both the number of pages considered and the ontology's coverage. In our experimental setup it took only a few hours to build an average set of 10,000 training examples for a single ontology topic, namely geography. With respect to the crawler's complexity, we need to stress that the crawler is only trained once for a topic; therefore any time overheads associated with building the training examples is diminished by the fact that the entire process is executed offline and prior to the crawler's initialization.

To begin with our experiments, we compiled a seed list of URLs from which the crawler would start its web walkthroughs. In selecting the seed URLs, we relied on the pages organized under the Dmoz categories [*Regional*: *North America*: *United States*]. Note that the respective Dmoz topics are also represented in the concepts of our topical ontology. Therefore, by picking URLs listed under those topics we ensure that the crawler's first visit will pertain to geographic content. Having decided on the topical categories to which the crawler would focus its web visits and having also selected the set of pages that are classified under those categories and from the contents of which we would obtain the crawler's training data, we applied the method presented in Section 3 in order to firstly estimate the topical relevance between every categorized page and its corresponding ontology topic and thereafter extract from the highly relevant topical pages a set of phrases whose semantics are expressive of their topical orientation.

Having built for the examined topic a set of training examples to be utilized as the reference sources that the crawler would consult in its web visits, we compiled the crawler's list of seed URLs and we run the crawler for a time period of one week. We then relied on the URLs that the crawler downloaded for the considered topic in order to evaluate its crawling accuracy.

4.1. Semantics-Aware Crawling Performance

To evaluate the performance of our focused crawler, we rely on the following measures: accuracy and quality of crawls. Specifically, to assess the crawler's accuracy we measure the absolute acquisition rate of topic-specific pages in order to see how effective our crawler is in targeting its web visits on specific content. In addition, to estimate the quality of crawls we compared the performance of our focused crawler to the performance of other focused crawling strategies and we comparatively analyze the obtained results.

To begin with our experiments, we compiled a seed list of URLs from which the crawler would start its web walkthroughs. In selecting the seed URLs, we relied on the pages organized under the Dmoz category *Regional* from which we picked 100 URLs and used them for compiling the crawler's seed list. Recall that we had previously processed pages listed under the above category in order to build the crawler's training examples. Therefore, by picking the above page URLs as the crawler's seed data, we ensure that the crawler's first visit will pertain to on-topic contents. Based on these 100 seed topical focused URLs, we run our crawler for a period of one week during which the crawler downloaded a total set of 2.5 million pages as geography-specific data sources. Note that the crawler's visits adhere to the depth-fist paradigm, which implies that the crawler follows all the links from the first link of the starting page before proceeding with the next seed URL. However, in the course of our experiment we limited the depth of the crawler's visits to level 5, i.e. starting form a page the crawler examined its internal links up to 5 levels down in their connectivity graph. This limitation was imposed in order not to waste the crawler's resources before the latter exhausts the list of seed URLs.

To estimate our crawler's accuracy in focusing its visits on topical-focused pages, we essentially measured the fraction of pages that the crawler downloaded as relevant for the topic of geography from all the pages that relate to geography and which the crawler came across in its web walkthroughs. Specifically, to be able to judge which of the pages that the crawler visited are indeed topic-specific, we built a utility index in which the crawler directed the URLs it encountered but did not download, because it considered them as off-topic pages. In simple words, every URL that the crawler examined but not downloaded was recorded in the utility index, whereas every URL that the crawler downloaded was recorded in the geography index. We then relied on the two sets of URLs, namely visited-but-not-downloaded and visited-and-downloaded and we supplied them as input to a generic crawler in order to retrieve their contents. Thereafter, we processed their contents (as previously described) in order to identify topical concepts among their contextual elements. Page URLs containing thematic terms relevant to the topic of geography were deemed as topic specific pages, while page URLs with thematic terms not corresponding to the topic of geography were deemed as off-topic pages. Thereafter, we relied on the set of pages that the crawler downloaded as geography relevant (i.e., pages stored in the geographic index) and set of pages that deal with geography but were not downloaded by the crawler, although visited, and we estimated our crawler's accuracy in retrieving topic-specific data, based on the following metric:

$$Accuracy\,(t_i) = \frac{|P\,(t_i)\,downloaded\,|}{|P\,(t_i)\,visited|} \tag{13}$$

where the numerator represents the number of pages that the crawler identified and thus downloaded as relevant to topic t_i (t_i = geography) and the denominator represents the number of all pages that the crawler visited for topic t_i (i.e. both downloaded and not-downloaded topic specific pages). Formally, we quantify the crawler's accuracy as the fraction of topic-specific pages that it downloaded from all the topical focused pages that it visited. Based on the above formula, we quantified the crawler's accuracy for the considered topic. Obtained results summarize to the following: our focused crawler visited a total set of 14.1 million pages of which 2.8 million are geography-relevant. From those 2.8 million geography pages, the crawler managed to correctly identify and thus download 2.5 million pages. Results, reported in Table 1, indicate that our crawler has overall 89.28% accuracy in identifying geographically-relevant data in its web visits. This finding suggests that given a geographic ontology and simple parsing techniques, our method in quite effective in focusing web crawls on location specific content.

Table 1. Topical-focused crawling accuracy.

Geography visited pages	2.8 million
Geography downloaded pages	2.5 million
Geo-focused crawling accuracy	89.28%

Another factor that we assessed during our crawling experiment concerns the quality of crawls performed by our focused crawler in comparison to the quality of crawls performed by another focused crawling technique. For this experiment, we implemented a Naïve Bayes classifier (Duda and Hart, 1973) and we integrated it into a generic web crawler so as to assist the latter in focusing its web visits on specific web content. The reason for selecting to integrate a Bayesian classifier into a generic crawler is because Naïve Bayes classifiers are both effective and accurate for web scale processing. To build the classifier, we relied on the set of 10,000 URLs listed under the Dmoz topic *Regional* that were used to compile the training data in our previous experiments. For the topic URLs we extracted a set of keywords based on the TF*IDF formula in order to supply them to the classifier as training examples. Based on the above data, we estimated the topical focus of every page URL based on Equation 11. Topical Focus values indicate the fraction of topic-specific entities among the pages' contextual elements, so that the more topical terms a page contains the higher its Topical Focus value is. Topical Focus scores are normalized, ranging between 0 and 1; with zero values indicating the absence of elements about a topic T in the page's content and values close to one indicating the presence of many entities about T in the page's contents. Pages of Topical Focus values for topic T above threshold h (h=0.5) are deemed as on-topic documents, whereas pages with Topical Focus values for T below h are deemed as off-topic documents. After creating the set of on-topic and off-topic pages for the category of geography, we trained the classifier so that it is able to judge for a new page it comes across whether it is geography-specific or not.

Having trained the classifier, we integrated it in a crawling module, which we call baseline focused crawler. To perform our comparative evaluation, we run the baseline focused crawler using the same seed list of 100 URLs that our semantics-aware focused crawler explored in the previous experiment. Note that the execution period for the baseline focused crawler was again set to one week and the depth of the crawling path was again limited to five levels down the internal links' hierarchy. For every page visited by the baseline crawler, we recorded in the utility index the page URL and its classification label, i.e. geography or non-geography. Based on the set of geography-specific pages that the baseline crawler visited and the set of geography-specific pages that the baseline focused crawler downloaded, we employed our accuracy metric (cf. formula 13) in order to estimate the harvest rate of the baseline focused crawler. Table 2 reports the accuracy rate of the baseline focused crawler and compares it to the accuracy of our focused crawler for the same topic and seed topic URLs.

Table 2. Comparison of crawling accuracy between the semantics-aware and the baseline focused crawlers.

Geo-ficused crawling accuracy	89.28%
Classification-aware crawling accuracy	71/25%

Results indicate that our semantics-aware focused crawler clearly outperforms the baseline focused crawler. In particular, we observe that from all the topical-relevant pages that each of the crawlers' visited, our module managed to accurately identify and thus download more pages than the baseline focused crawler did. Although we are aware of the fact that we cannot directly compare the performance of two crawlers, since we cannot guarantee that their visits will concentrate on the exact same set of pages, nevertheless by exploring the fraction of relevant documents downloaded from all the relevant documents visited, we believe that we can derive some valuable conclusions concerning the quality of crawls, where the latter is defined as the ability of the crawler to locate pages of interest (i.e. topic-specific).

5. Discussion

In this chapter, we have presented a novel focused crawling technique that relies on the semantic orientation of the pages before making a decision about whether a page should be retrieved or not. Like any other focused crawling method, our proposed technique relies upon the intuition that for some web applications it is desirable to consider pages of specific content rather than try to download them all. Thus, the advantage that focused crawlers have over general-purpose ones is that they can discriminate between interesting and uninteresting pages. However, such discrimination is not always straightforward and most of the times it is associated with additional computational overheard. Therefore, the obvious tradeoff between general-purpose and focused crawling approaches is that the former require a significant amount of resources and may sometimes retrieve pages that are of no real interest to any user (e.g. spam pages) whereas the latter require additional programming efforts and external resources that the crawler will utilize for learning the features of interesting pages.

Motivated by the desire to implement a focused crawler that can *understand* the semantic orientation of the pages it comes across in its web visits we have presented a novel crawling method. In brief, our proposed crawler incorporates a topical ontology and employs a number of techniques that are leveraged from the NLP community in order to determine from a set of pre-classified pages which page features are descriptive of the respective topic semantics. The utilization of a topical ontology while training the crawler entails a significant advantage and some minor disadvantages. The apparent advantage is that a topical ontology is an extremely rich semantic resource that can be readily explored by any computational application since it structures the data it stores hierarchically; making thus transparent the semantic associations between terms and senses. Of course, picking the correct ontology to use for training a crawler is a difficult task since it requires good knowledge for the domain of interest, i.e. the domain on which the crawler should focus its web visitations. A disadvantage of using the ontology to train the crawler is that training time is proportional to the number of topics on which we would like our crawler to focus. In simple words, if we want to learn our crawler to recognize pages that span across many topics, we would need a certain amount of time for training the crawler for each of the topics separately. However, considering on the one hand that there are currently plenty of domain ontologies available, and on the other hand that the crawler needs to be trained only once for each of the topics, we believe that the above disadvantages are somewhat diminished and that both the effort and the resources put in this respect are worth.

Additionally, via the use of the topical ontology our method extends beyond data classification tasks and challenges issues pertaining to the URLs organization within the crawler's frontier. As already mentioned deciding the crawling priority of the unvisited URLs is of paramount importance for all crawling applications; both general-purpose and focused ones. This is essentially because we would not like to waste resources trying to fetch pages that take excessive amounts of access times. In addition, we would not like to allocate resources toward downloading pages that have already been visited and retrieved by the crawler in its previous web visits. With the above in mind, the determination of the crawler's downloading policy is of paramount importance in all applications and tools. In our proposed focused crawler approach, we have introduced a novel ranking formula that differs from existing ones in that it determines the order in which every URL in the frontier should be visited based on a dual probability: (i) the URL's relevance to the topic of interest and (ii) the URL's probability of containing links to other interesting pages. The advantage of our downloading policy is that it relies on a small amount of data for ranking the unvisited URLs and that it runs fast and scales well with the dynamic web data. Another advantage is that it updates the URLs ranking scores every time the frontier gets updated with new elements to be considered.

In previous works we have conducted, the technical details which can be found in [17] and [18], and we have experimentally studied our crawler's performance. Obtained results demonstrated that our crawler is both accurate and effective in correctly identifying and thus retrieving pages of interest. The comparative evaluation between our focused crawler and other focused crawling approaches revealed that our method outperforms existing ones with respect to both the crawling accuracy and the topical coverage of the considered pages. Overall, we deem our focused crawling method to be complementary to existing techniques that are more concerned with data classification issues for learning web crawlers to identify and maintain their visitation foci. Given that a topical ontology can substitute or complement the supervised classification process, we believe that our proposed method can be fruitfully explored by other researchers in an attempt to build more content-aware web applications and services.

6. Conclusion

In this chapter we presented a novel focused crawling method that explores the semantic orientation of the page text and anchor text in order to infer whether a given URL points to a page of interest and thus it should be downloaded. The novelty of our approach lies on the fact that we utilize a topical ontology for learning the crawler to recognize the topical features of the web pages it comes across and that we rely on a passage selection algorithm for building training examples that the crawler regularly consults throughout its web visits. In addition, we have presented a novel ranking algorithm that orders the unvisited URLs in the crawler's frontier in terms of their probability of guiding the crawler to the desired data sources. Building a focused crawler is a challenging task since it requires a number of external resources to be considered in order to train the crawler towards making informed decisions. The resources that we utilized in the course of our study (e.g., WordNet) are freely available and they can be easily integrated in different applications. Therefore, we believe that our method can be fruitfully explored by others.

Related Terms

Focused Crawler: a focused crawler is a web robot that attempts to download only web pages that are relevant to a pre-defined topic or set of topics.

Topical Ontology: A topical ontology is concerned with a set of topics identified to represent the knowledge structure of the domain expert. It reflects the specific scope, perspectives and granularity of conceptualization about the considered topics.

Lexical Chain: a sequence of semantically related terms, which provides context for the resolution of an ambiguous term and enables the identification of the concept that the term represents.

Passage Selection algorithm: an algorithm that given an input topic, it runs over a text in order to select the most topic-describe extract.

Semantic Similarity: concept whereby a set of documents or terms within term lists are assigned a metric based on the likeness of their meaning/semantic content.

Frontier: As a web crawler visits URLs, it identifies all the web links in a visited page and adds them to the list of URLs to visit, called the crawl frontier.

Supervised classification: the task of assigning a document to one or more categories based on its content and by using external mechanisms to provide information on the correct classification of the document.

References

[1] Agichtein, E., Ipeirotis, P. & Gravano, L. (2003). Modeling query-based access to text databases. In *Proceedings of the Web and DataBases (WebDB) Workshop*.

[2] Almanidis, G., Kotropoulos, C &Pitas, I. (2007). Combining text and link analysis for focused crawling- An application for vertical search engines. In *Information Systems,* vol.32, no.6, pp. 886-908.

[3] Altingovde, I.S. & Ulusoy, O. (2004). Exploiting interclass rules for focused crawling. In the *IEEE Intelligent Systems*, pp. 66- 73.

[4] Barzilay R. (1997). *Lexical chains for summarization*. Master's Thesis. Ben-Gurion University, Beer-Sheva, Israel.

[5] Chakrabarti, S., van den Berg, M. & Dom, B. (1999). Focused crawling: a new approach to topic-specific web resource discovery. In *Computer Networks* 31, pp. 11–16.

[6] Chakrabarti, S., Punera, K., & Subramanyam, M. (2002). Accelerated focused crawling through online relevance feedback. In *Proceedings of the ACM World Wide Web Conference* (WWW), Honolulu, Hawaii USA.

[7] Cho, J., Garcia-Molina, H. & Page, L. (1998). Efficient crawling through url ordering. In *Proceedings of the 17th International ACM World Wide Web Conference* (WWW)..

[8] Cope, J., Craswell, N. & Hawking, D. (2003). Automated discovery of search interfaces on the web. In *Proceedings of the 14th Australasian Conference on Database Technologies*.

[9] De Bra, P., Houben, G., Kornatzky, Y., & Post, R. (1994). Information retrieval in distributed hypertexts. In *Proceedings of the 4th RIAO Conference*, New York, pp. 481–491.

[10] Dilligenti, M., Coetze, F.M., Lawrence, S., Giles, C.L. & Gori M. (2000), Focused crawling using context graphs. In *Proceedings of the 26th International Conference on Very Large Databases (VLDB).*

[11] Ehrig, M. & Maedche, A. (2003). Ontology-focused crawling of web documents. In *Proceedings of the the ACM Symposium on Applied Computing.*

[12] Fang, W., Cui, Z. &Zhao, P. (2007). Ontology-based focused crawling of deep web sources. In *Knowledge Science, Engineering and Management*, pp. 514-519.

[13] Ganesh, S. (2005). Ontology-based web crawling – a novel approach. In Advances in Web Intelligence, pp. 140-149, Spinger.

[14] Gliozzo, A., Strapparava, C. & Dagan, I. (2004). Unsupervised and supervised exploitation of semantic domains in lexical disambiguation. In *Computer Speech and Language*, 18(3), pp. 275-299.

[15] Hersovici, M., Jacovi, M., Maarek, Y., Pelleg, D., Shtalhaim, M., & Ur, S. (1998). The shark-search algorithm - An application: tailored web site mapping. In *Proceedings of the 7th International World Wide Web Conference* (WWW), Brisbane, Australia.

[16] Hsu, C.C. & Wu, F. (2006). Topic-specific crawling on the web with the measurements of the relevancy context graph. In *Information Systems* 31(4), pp. 232-246.

[17] Kozanidis, L., Stamou, S. & Spiros, G. (2009). Focusing web crawls on location-specific contents. In *Proceedings of the 5th International Conference on Web Information Systems (WebIST).*

[18] Kozanidis, L. & Stamou, S. (2009). Towards a geo-referenced search engine index. In the *International Journal of Web Applications*, vol.1, no.1.

[19] Li, J., Furuse, K. & Yamaguchi, K. (2005). Focused crawling by exploiting anchor text using decision trees. In *the Special Interest Tracks and Posters of the 14th International World Wide Web Conference*, (WWW).

[20] Ntoulas, A., Zefros, P. &Cho, J. (2005). Downloading textual hidden web content through keyword queries. In *Proceedings of the 5th ACM Joint Conference on Digital Libraries*, (JCDL).

[21] Partalas, I., Paliouras, G. Vlahavas, I. (2008). Reinforcement learning with classifier selection for focused crawling. In *Proceedings of the European Conference of Artificial Intelligence*. Pp. 759-760.

[22] Rennie, J. & McCallum, A. (1999). Using reinforcement learning to spider the web efficiently. In *Proceedings of the International Conference on Machine Learning*.

[23] Song, Y.I., Han, K.S. & Rim, H.C. (2004). A term weighting method based on lexical chain for automatic summarization. In *Proceedings of the 5th International Conferece on Intelligent Text Processing and Computational Linguistics*, (CICLing), pp. 636-639.

[24] Stamou, S., Krikos, V., Kokosis, P., Ntoulas, A. & Christodoulakis, D. (2005). Web directory construction using lexical chains. In *Proceedings of the 10th International Conference on Applications of Natural Language to Application Systems (NLDB),* pp. 138-149.

[25] WordNet (1998). Available form: http://www.cogsci.princeton.edu/~wn

[26] Wu, X. & Palmer, M. (1994). Web semantics and lexical selection. In *Proceedings of the 32nd Meeting of the Association on for Computational Linguistics.*

[27] Ye, Y., Ma, F., Lu, Y., Chiu, M. & Huang, J. (2004). iSurfer: a focused web crawler based on incremental learning from positive samples. In *Proceedings of the Asian-Pacific Web Conference (APWeb),* pp. 122-134.

[28] WEKA available from: http://www.cs.waikato.ac.nz/ml/weka/

In: Data Management in the Semantic Web
Editor: Hal Jin, pp. 57-80
ISBN: 978-1-61122-862-5

Chapter 3

A SEMANTIC TREE REPRESENTATION FOR DOCUMENT CATEGORIZATION WITH A COMPOSITE KERNEL

***Sujeevan Aseervatham*[1,2,*] *and Younès Bennani*[2,†]**
[1]Yakaz Lab, 34, Rue de Cléry
F-75002 Paris, France
[2]LIPN - UMR 7030 CNRS, Université Paris 13
99, Av. J.B. Clément, F-93430 Villetaneuse, France

Abstract

The semi-structured document format, such as the XML format, is used in data-management to efficiently structure, store and share the information between different users. Although the information can efficiently be accessed within a semi-structured document, automatically retrieving the relevant information from a corpus still remains a complex problem, especially when the documents are semi-structured text documents. To tackle this, the corpus can be partitioned according to the content of each document in order to make the search efficient. In document categorization, a predefined partition is given and the problem is to automatically assign the documents of the corpus to the relevant categories. The quality of the categorization highly depends on the data representation and on the similarity measure, especially when dealing with complex data such as natural language text. In this chapter, we present a semantic tree to semantically represent an XML text document and we propose a semantic kernel, which can be used with the semantic tree, to compute a similarity measure. The semantic meanings of words are extracted using an ontology. We use a text categorization problem in the biomedical field to illustrate our method. The UMLS framework is used to extract the semantic information related to the biomedical field. We have applied this kernel with a SVM classifier to a real-world medical free-text categorization problem. The results have shown that our method outperforms other common methods such as the linear kernel.

*E-mail addresses: sujeevan@lipn.univ-paris13.fr
†E-mail addresses: younes@lipn.univ-paris13.fr

1. Introduction

The use of semi-structured document format has became an important aspect of data management. Indeed, the information is shared and used between many different users and thus it needs to be formatted in a way that can easily be understood. The XML file format has emerged as a practical and efficient solution to structure, store and distribute the information and it is now widely used. Although the information can efficiently be accessed within the XML file thanks to its structure, retrieving the relevant information from a corpus of XML files is still a complex problem due to the size of the corpus. Dividing a large corpus into partitions makes the information retrieval easier. Nevertheless, defining a relevant partition and assigning each document to a category of the partition is also a time-consuming problem which often needs to be done by an expert. However, the use of experts being costly, automatic text categorization has become an active field of research[28]. In the supervised machine learning approach [27], an expert defines a set of categories (labels) and assigns a small sample of documents to the relevant categories. This labeled sample is called the training data. A machine learning algorithm can then be used on the training set to induce a classification function which maps a document to a category. This function can be used to classify the rest of the corpus, i.e., the unlabeled documents.

Since a decade, research in the field of machine learning applied to Natural Language Processing (NLP) has focused on kernel-based methods and especially on Support Vector Machines (SVM) [32]. The SVM is a supervised discriminative binary classification algorithm based on the Optimal Hyperplane Algorithm (OHA) [32]. Given a training data, the OHA linearly divides the input space into two subspaces such that one subspace contains, only, the training data of a given category (the positive instances) and the other one contains the rest of the training data (the negative instances). The OHA can be extended to a non-linear classification algorithm, i.e. the SVM algorithm, by using the kernel trick [3, 32, 29]. A kernel is an inner-product in a Hilbert space (called the feature space or the linearization space), which uses a mapping from the input space to the Hilbert space. The kernel trick consists in expressing the dot product in the feature space in terms of a kernel evaluated on input patterns. In other words, kernel functions are similarity measures of data points in the input space, and they correspond to the dot product in the feature space to which the input space data patterns are mapped. Hence, by replacing all dot products of an algorithm (such as the OHA) with a kernel, the algorithm will implicitly be used in the feature space. With a non-linear kernel mapping, the SVM constructs a separating hyperplane with maximum margin in the feature space. This yields a non-linear decision boundary in the input space. Moreover, even if the SVM is a binary classification algorithm, it can be used for multi-category classification, e.g., with the "one-against-the-rest" strategy [14].

Not only SVMs have given promising results [16, 17] but also, thanks to the kernel functions [29], SVMs can be used on complex input data such as textual data, graphs and trees. Furthermore, kernels can be used to define a cosine-based similarity measure in an implicit feature space with an implicit mapping. This property allows to define complex similarity measures according to the nature of the input data. Defining a good kernel is crucial since the performance of classification algorithms is largely affected by the kernel (the similarity measure).

In this chapter, we focus on biomedical semi-structured documents composed of different medical observation parts such as the patient records. We propose to use the Unified Medical Language System (UMLS)[1] as a biomedical ontology to define a new semantic kernel that can be used as a similarity measure for a semantic features representation of such documents. We show how a document can be modeled as a semantic tree structure using the UMLS framework. Such trees will be used as inputs to the Semantic Kernel. This kernel is defined using the kernel convolution framework [13]. Moreover, it incorporates UMLS-based semantic similarity measures for a smooth similarity computation. We illustrate the use of this semantic kernel on a text categorization task in the biomedical domain.

After discussing the related work in the next section, we briefly present the UMLS framework in section 3. In section 4, the document modeling with a tree structure is presented. This is followed by the definition of the UMLS-based Semantic Kernel in section 5. Then, we present the experimental performance of the kernel in section 6. The chapter concludes in section 7.

2. Related Work

In kernel methods for NLP tasks, the Vector Space Model (VSM) [26], also called the *bag-of-words* model, is commonly used. Given a dictionary of n words, the VSM defines a n-dimensional space over $\mathbb{R}$ where each dimension i of the space is associated with the ith word of the dictionary. The dictionary is composed of the words which appear in the training corpus. In this model, a document is represented by a vector in which each component represents the occurrence frequency of a given word in the document. It has been shown that kernels, such as the simple Linear Kernel which is the standard inner product, i.e., the dot product, defined for this model have a good level of performance [16, 17]. In fact, these kernels require an important amount of words in each document and in the training corpus to capture the discriminative information. In real life, training corpora are often small as the expert annotation is costly. Moreover, the document size in words can also be small, for example, in the case of free texts, documents can be composed of only two or three sentences. In order to capture the relevant information within small corpora, the semantic approach has been proposed and has become an active field of research since a few years. This approach can be divided in two main categories. The first one uses statistical information to extract semantic features and the second one relies on external sources of information such as linguistic concept taxonomies.

The Latent Semantic Analysis (LSA) [8] belongs to the first category. LSA uses the Singular Value Decomposition (SVD) on the term-by-document matrix M to extract latent concepts. Each column i of M is the vector representation, in the VSM, of the document i. The SVD of M gives three matrices such that $M = U\Sigma V^T$ where U is the change-of-coordinate matrix from the VSM to the Latent Semantic Space (LSS), Σ the square matrix of singular values and V the change-of-coordinate matrix from the document space to the LSS. The LSS is defined by the left eigenvectors of M given by the columns of U. Each eigenvector defines a latent concept which is a linear relation between the words of the VSM dictionary. The LSS has two main advantages. Firstly, it can be a dimension reduction method by defining a low-dimensional space composed of the k concepts associated

[1]http://www.nlm.nih.gov/research/umls

with the k highest singular values. Secondly, the LSS captures second-order co-occurrence frequencies between the words. Thus, it efficiently handles polysemous and synonymous words. The LSA-based kernels [7, 11], compute the dot product of two documents in the LSS after mapping them from the VSM to the LSS with the change-of-coordinate matrix U. The LSA kernels slightly outperform the linear VSM kernel. Nevertheless, the extracted semantic features, i.e., the latent concepts are difficult to interpret.

The second category of semantic kernels uses linguistic knowledge sources to extract semantic information from the words of a document. These kernels are, usually, defined as similarity measures in an implicit feature space. In [30], the WordNet taxonomy was used as an external source of information. A semantic similarity is computed using the inverse path length in the taxonomy and then smoothed using a Gaussian kernel. This kernel was improved in [23] by replacing the path-length by the conceptual density similarity measure and by removing the Gaussian smoothing. In [2], several similarity measures were tested and the Lin measure [19] achieved the best performance. These kernels were, mainly, evaluated on the Reuters corpus in which documents are "flat texts" and have a standard length. Nowadays, many textual documents are semi-structured in sections. The most common text format is now the XML format. Semantic kernels should then be defined to take account of the different kinds of information.

3. The UMLS Framework

The UMLS is a free[2] knowledge framework for the biomedical domain. It contains knowledge data as well as software tools to facilitate their use. The UMLS was especially developed for NLP tasks. It is composed of three parts:

The Specialist Lexicon is an English lexicon including many biomedical terms. It is provided with many NLP tools such as lexical tools and part of speech taggers.

The Metathesaurus is a vocabulary database containing information about biomedical concepts such as their names and the relationships between them. It can incorporate vocabularies from various sources and various languages. Each source defines an ontology e.g. MeSH, SNOMED-CT. The Metathesaurus can be installed with the MetamorphoSys installation program. MetamorphoSys allows the user to select the vocabulary sources. For our purpose, we just make a typical installation (all free sources+SNOMED-CT). The installation creates many text files such as *MRREL*, *MRSTY*, *MRXNS* and *MRXNW* which, respectively, define the relationships among concepts, the mapping between concepts and semantic classes, the mapping between normalized strings and concepts and the mapping between normalized single words and concepts.

The Semantic Network defines 135 semantic classes with 54 different relationships between them. The semantic classes are used to categorize the whole concepts of the Metathesaurus.

[2]Some parts require specific license agreements

4. Document Modeling

In this chapter, we consider semi-structured medical documents. By semi-structured, we mean data that do not have a "strict" relational model e.g. XML documents. Moreover, we restrict our work to documents with the following properties: (1) a document is composed of one or more parts and (2) all the parts should be textual data (non textual elements can simply be ignored). For example, we can consider medical records where each record, for a patient, is composed of multiple parts, each part being a medical observation from a specific service e.g. a clinical observation, radiology impressions. With such documents, the computation of the similarity between two documents, for categorization or clustering tasks, needs to correctly handle each part according to the source. Indeed, it can be irrelevant to compare, for example, a radiology impression with a psychological observation.

For each part of a document, the following preprocessing stages are performed:

1. Document cleaning: All words that can introduce noises are eliminated. Hence, all numbers, either in numerical or textual format, and non textual symbols, i.e., non-alphabetical symbols are removed. For example, the characters such as '@', '#' and '*' are removed from the documents.

2. Text segmentation: The segmentation is used to divide the whole text into meaningful units. The simplest method is to cut the text into words separated by punctuation marks or white spaces. However, with such a segmentation, we can deteriorate or even completely lose the right meaning of a group of words. This is especially true in the medical domain where words are often combined together to form expressions with new meanings. To handle this problem, one method is to divide the text into lexical units (lexical items). A lexical unit can either be a single word or a group of words. Contrary to words, the lexical units are difficult to identify and require prior knowledge of the domain, i.e., a lexicon.. Given a lexicon, a naive way to segment the text is to use an algorithm that splits the text into groups of words, each group being the longest group that matches a lexical unit of the lexicon. For example, there are two different ways to segment "*Political campaigns*". It can either be segmented into two lexical units: "*Political*" and "*campaigns*" or into one lexical unit: "*Political campaigns*". This is due to the fact that "*Political*", "*campaigns*" and "*Political campaigns*" are all defined in English lexicons. However, the longest group of words is "*Political campaigns*" which has a more specific meaning than the two other lexical units. Nevertheless, this method ignores the grammatical forms of the words so it may merge words that belong to different grammatical categories. Some lexical units can then be irrelevant and they can lead to, both, a loss of information and noises. Hence, the segmentation of the sentence "*He has written materials for the university*" will give the following set of lexical units: {"*he*","*has*","*written materials*", "*for*", "*the*", "*university*"}. A better solution is to use a part-of-speech (POS) tagger and then use the previous matching algorithm to find the longest groups of words with the same grammatical category. For the above example, the use of a POS tagger will give [*He(personal pronoun) has(verb) written(verb) materials(noun)for(preposition) the(determiner) university(noun)*]. By using the previous matching algorithm on the POS tagged sentence will give the following lexical units {"*he*","*has written*","*materials*", "*for*", "*the*", "*university*"}. For our research, we used the dTagger software [9] provided with the UMLS SPECIALIST lexicon. dTagger is able to segment a text into lexical units according to the POS.

3. Stopword removal: A stopword is a common term with a high occurrence frequency and with no relevant meaning. Moreover, stopwords provide no discriminative information. They are useless in most of the NLP tasks such as text categorization and document indexing. For example, among others, stopwords include articles, case particles, conjunctions, pronouns and auxiliary verbs. Stopword lists for different languages can be found on the Internet [3]. Thus, from the set of lexical units, we remove the lexical units that are in fact stopwords.

4. Text normalization: Words can have different inflections, thus providing a grammatical information. This information induces a high-dimensional sparse space which makes it difficult to use them in a machine learning process. To reduce the space dimension, each lexical unit is normalized, i.e., words are reduced to their root forms. For example, the words "*writing*", "*written*" and "*write*" have approximately the same meaning, so they can be reduced, with a small loss of information, to the root form "*write*". However, some words may have many root forms, for example the normalized strings of "*left*" are "*left*" (if it means a direction) and *leave* (if it means the action of leaving). Consequently, each lexical unit will be associated to a set of normalized strings. In the UMLS, the SPECIALIST lexicon is provided with the *Lexical Variant Generation (lvg)* java program which can be used to normalize lexical items. The normalization is done in 6 main stages as illustrated by figure 1.

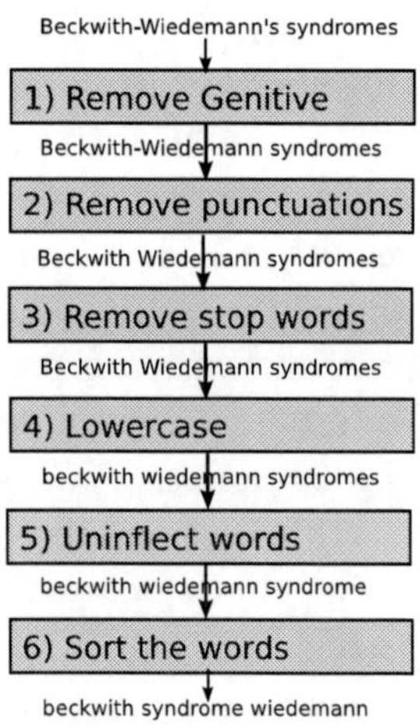

Figure 1. The lexical unit normalization process.

5. Semantic annotation: Morphological information is not sufficient to efficiently compare the similarity between two words. Indeed, it is usually better to compare the meanings of the words than the words themselves, e.g., two synonyms, "*car*" and "*automobile*", are similar in meaning but different in morphology. For this, we need to define a meaning to each normalized string. In the UMLS Metathesaurus, words are defined with their concepts (a word can have multiple concepts). A concept can be seen as a class of words where the words have, approximately, the same meaning, i.e., they are synonyms. A concept is labeled

[3] http://snowball.tartarus.org

by an ID or by a string describing its meaning. For example, the concept "*heart(body)*" is a class that includes the following words: "*heart*", "*pump*", and "*ticker*". Moreover, concepts are linked to each other by various relationships. Concepts, with their relationships, can be used to compute a semantic similarity. Therefore, a set of concepts will be affected to each normalized strings. The semantic annotation algorithm, we developed, is described in algorithm 1.

The algorithm iterates through all the documents; for each document it iterates through the document parts and for each part it iterates through its lexical units (line 1). For each lexical unit *lu*, the algorithm tries to map each normalized string *ns* to a set of UMLS concepts. It, first, looks for the concepts in the UMLS MRXNS file which contains a set of normalized strings with their UMLS concepts (line 3). If the normalized string *ns* has not been found in the MRXNS file, the algorithm looks in the UMLS MRXNW file which contains a set of normalized words with their concepts (line 5). The algorithm then continues by processing the next normalized string of *lu*. In the special case where none of the normalized strings of *lu* have been found in both MRXNS and MRXNW files, the algorithm splits the lexical unit into individual words because there are more chances to find a single word than a multi-word string in UMLS[4]. The lexical unit *lu* is then removed from the document part (line 9) and a lexical unit (along with its set of normalized strings) is created for each new individual word and added to the document part (line 10). Thus, the newly created lexical units will be processed in the next iterations. However, if a lexical unit is a single word, it cannot be split. In this case, the lexical unit is kept as it is (i.e. with normalized strings *ns* without concepts: *ns.concepts*= $\emptyset$) in the document part. Nevertheless, one may wonder if it is better to simply remove such lexical units from the document part. In fact, it will depend on the quantity of information provided by such strings. The quantity of information provided by a string depends on its occurrence frequency in the corpus. The more a string occurs in documents, the more the string will be important for document classification. Moreover, there are mainly two reasons why a string has no UMLS concept: firstly because it contains spelling mistakes (in this case, the information provided is noise) and, secondly because it contains words, such as abbreviation, that are specific to the author (in this last case, the information provided can be very important). The best compromise is to remove only the strings (with no concepts) that have a low occurrence frequency in the training corpus.

At the end of each iteration (line 12-14), empty lexical unit nodes, empty document part nodes and empty document nodes are removed.

Finally, after all these preprocessing stages, each document has a tree structure as shown in figure 2.

5. The Semantic Kernel

5.1. The Mercer Kernel Framework

Given two data points $\mathbf{x}, \mathbf{y} \in \mathcal{X}$ and a map function $\Phi : \mathcal{X} \times \mathcal{X} \rightarrow \mathcal{H}$, a Mercer kernel (also known as positive semi-definite kernel) is a symmetric function that computes the inner

[4]Though, single words are more ambiguous than multi-words (strings).

Algorithm 1 The Semantic annotation algorithm

for all document d **and** part $p \in d.parts$ **and** lexical unit $lu \in p.LU$ **do**
  for all normalized strings $ns \in lu.NS$ **do**
    $ns.concepts \leftarrow$ find_concepts(ns) from UMLS MRXNS
    if $ns.concepts$ is empty **then**
      $ns.concepts \leftarrow$ find_concepts(ns) from UMLS MRXNW
    end if
  end for
  if $\forall ns \in lu.NS,\ ns.concepts$ is empty **and** lu is a multi-words string **then**
    remove lu from $p.LU$
    $p.LU \leftarrow p.LU \cup$ {break lu into single words}
  end if
  $lu.NS = \emptyset \Rightarrow$ remove lu from $p.LU$
  $p.LU = \emptyset \Rightarrow$ remove p from $d.parts$
  $d.parts = \emptyset \Rightarrow$ remove d
end for

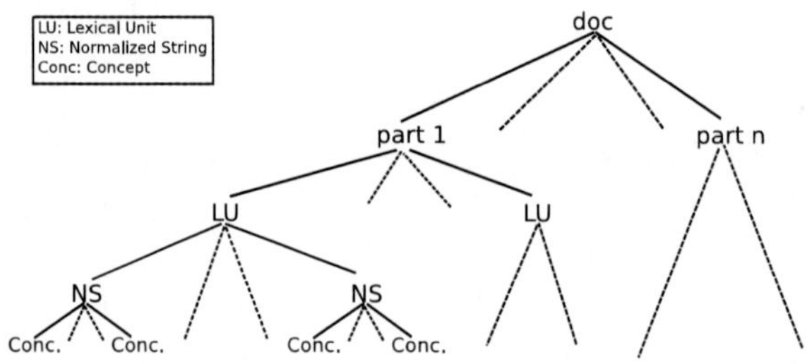

Figure 2. The tree model of a document.

product between two vectors in a Hilbert space $\mathcal{H}$, called the feature space, such that :

$$K(\mathbf{x}, \mathbf{y}) = \langle \Phi(\mathbf{x}), \Phi(\mathbf{y}) \rangle \tag{1}$$

Mercer kernels are used in inner product-based algorithms such as the Support Vector Machine [32, 29]. Thus, by defining a Mercer kernel with a non-linear map function, a linear algorithm can be turned into a non-linear one. This is called the kernel trick because, thanks to its embedding map, the linear algorithm will be, implicitly, used in the feature space. Furthermore, according to the definition 5.1: 1) it is not necessary to explicitly define/compute the map function and 2) the input space does not need to be a vector space.

Definition 5.1 (Mercer Kernel [1]) Let $\mathcal{X}$ be a non emptyset. A function $K : \mathcal{X} \times \mathcal{X} \rightarrow \mathbb{R}$ is called a positive semi-definite kernel (or Mercer kernel) if and only if K is symmetric (i.e. $K(x, y) = K(y, x)$ for all $x, y \in \mathcal{X}$) and

$$\sum_{i,j=1}^{n} c_i c_j K(x_i, x_j) \geq 0 \tag{2}$$

for all $n \in \mathbb{N}$, $\{x_1, \ldots, x_n\} \subseteq \mathcal{X}$ and $\{c_1, \ldots, c_n\} \subseteq \mathbb{R}$. K can be represented as an inner-product in a feature space, as defined in equation 1.

Using this definition, we can define an appropriate cosine-based similarity function between two semi-structured documents and prove that it is a Mercer kernel by ensuring the function to be symmetric and positive semi-definite. Moreover, using a matrix notation, equation 2 can be rewritten as: $\mathbf{c}^T M \mathbf{c} \geq 0$ where $\mathbf{c}$ is any real-valued n-column vector and M a $n \times n$ symmetric matrix such that $M_{ij} = K(x_i, x_j)$ (M is said to be the Gram matrix of K). Thus, equation 2 holds true if and only if M is a positive semi-definite matrix.

However, when the input data are not vectors but discrete composite structures like strings, trees, and graphs, defining a Mercer kernel becomes a difficult task. To face this problem, a general framework named the convolution kernel was developed in [13]. The idea is to decompose the input structure into primitive parts and use different Mercer kernels on the primitives according to their data types. More formally, let $\mathcal{X}_1, \ldots, \mathcal{X}_n$ be n different spaces such that $\forall x \in \mathcal{X}$ the input space, x can be decomposed into $\mathbf{x} = x_1, \ldots, x_n$ with $x_i \in \mathcal{X}_i$. Let R be a relation such that $R(\mathbf{x}, x)$ holds iff $\mathbf{x}$ are the parts of x, we can define the inverse relation $R^{-1}(x) = \{\mathbf{x} : R(\mathbf{x}, x)\}$. Given x and $y \in \mathcal{X}$, the convolution kernel is defined as:

$$K(x, y) = \sum_{\mathbf{x} \in R^{-1}(x)} \sum_{\mathbf{y} \in R^{-1}(y)} K_{composite}(\mathbf{x}, \mathbf{y}) \tag{3}$$

Although the composite kernel is defined in [13] as:

$$K_{composite}(\mathbf{x}, \mathbf{y}) = \prod_{i=1}^{n} K_i(x_i, y_i) \tag{4}$$

we prefer to give a more general definition as follows:

$$K_{composite}(\mathbf{x}, \mathbf{y}) = F(K_1(x_1, y_1), \ldots, K_n(x_n, y_n)) \tag{5}$$

with F a mixing function.

The convolution kernel is a Mercer kernel if the composite kernel is a Mercer kernel because the sum of Mercer kernels is a Mercer kernel [29].

5.2. The UMLS-based Kernel

Given the tree structure shown in figure 2, we define $\mathcal{D}$ as being the space of trees rooted at node *doc* and $\mathcal{P}_1, \ldots, \mathcal{P}_n$ as being subspaces of $\mathcal{D}$ where $\mathcal{P}_i$ is the space of trees rooted at node $part_i$. The UMLS-based Kernel is, then, defined by the formula 3 where $\mathcal{X} = \mathcal{D}$ and $\mathcal{X}_i = \mathcal{P}_i$. The expression of the composite kernel (formula 5) still holds. However, we process the different parts of the documents in a same manner so we simplify equation 5 by setting $K_i(x_i, y_i) = K_p(x_i, y_i)$. Moreover, we define a weighted polynomial mixing function:

$$F(a_1, \ldots, a_n) = \left(\frac{\sum_{i=1}^{n} w_i a_i}{\sum_{i=1}^{n} w_i} \right)^l \tag{6}$$

with $a_i, w_i \in \mathbb{R}^+$ and $l \in \mathbb{N}$. The composite function is then:

$$K_{composite}(\mathbf{x}, \mathbf{y}) = \left(\frac{1}{\sum_{i=1}^{n} w_i} \sum_{i=1}^{n} w_i K_p(x_i, y_i) \right)^l \tag{7}$$

By setting $l = 1$, $K_{composite}$ becomes the expected value of the similarity between parts of the same space and for $l > 1$, $K_{composite}$ uses a much richer feature space i.e. a higher dimension feature space. It can be shown that if K_p is a Mercer kernel then $K_{composite}$ is also a Mercer kernel for $l \in \mathbb{N}$ and $w_i \in \mathbb{R}^+$.

Using the convolution framework, we define the following kernels:

$$\begin{aligned}
K_p(x_i, y_i) &= \sum_{u_1 \in \Gamma(x_i)} \sum_{u_2 \in \Gamma(y_i)} \sigma(u_1)\sigma(u_2) K_l(u_1, u_2) \\
K_l(u_1, u_2) &= \sum_{n_1 \in \Gamma(u_1)} \sum_{n_2 \in \Gamma(u_2)} K_n(n_1, n_2) \\
K_n(n_1, n_2) &= \begin{cases} \delta_{n_1, n_2} \\ \quad \text{if } \Gamma(n_i) = \emptyset \text{ or } |\Gamma(n_i)| > \tau, i = 1, 2 \\ \sum_{c_1 \in \Gamma(n_1)} \sum_{c_2 \in \Gamma(n_2)} K_c(c_1, c_2) \\ \quad \text{otherwise} \end{cases}
\end{aligned} \tag{8}$$

where $\sigma(u)$ is the frequency of the lexical unit u in the document, δ_{n_1,n_2} the Kronecker delta function, $\Gamma(t)$ the set of children of the node t, τ a natural number defining a threshold and K_c the concept similarity kernel defined in subsection 5.3..

K_p computes the similarity between two document parts by comparing each pair of lexical units. In a same way, K_l compares each pair of normalized strings and K_n compares each pair of concepts. However, for K_n, if a normalized string of a lexical unit contains too much concepts (above a fixed threshold τ) then the string becomes too ambiguous and using the concept similarity will add noise. Thus, it is better to fix the concept set $\Gamma(n)$ of a normalized string n to the empty set if the string n is too ambiguous (i.e. $|\Gamma(n)| > \tau$). To simplify equation 8, the test $|\Gamma(n)| > \tau$ (in eq. 8) is done once during the preprocessing stage in algorithm 1 by adding, between line 11 and 12, the following line: $\forall ns \in lu.NS,\ |ns.concepts| > \tau \Rightarrow ns.concepts \leftarrow \emptyset$.

Furthermore, the concept similarity cannot be computed if a normalized string has no concept. Hence, in these two cases, K_n will just use the Kronecker delta function (δ_{n_1,n_2}) to compare the normalized strings.

It is straightforward to show that if K_n is a Mercer kernel then K_l and K_p are Mercer kernels.

Proposition 5.1 *Let K_c be a Mercer kernel, K_n is then a Mercer kernel.*

Proof. For this proof, we suppose that the test $|\Gamma(n)| > \tau$ (in eq. 8) is done in the preprocessing stage (see the paragraph above). Hence, $K_n(n_1, n_2)$ has two expressions depending on whether $\Gamma(n_i)$ is empty or not for $i = 1, 2$. We define K'_n as follows:

$$K'_n(n_1, n_2) = K_{nc}(n_1, n_2) + K_{nid}(n_1, n_2)$$

$$
\begin{aligned}
K_{nc}(n_1,n_2) &= \sum_{c_1 \in \Gamma(n_1)} \sum_{c_2 \in \Gamma(n_2)} K_c(c_1,c_2) \\
K_{nid}(n_1,n_2) &= (1-g(n_1)g(n_2))K_{id}(n_1,n_2) \\
K_{id}(n_1,n_2) &= \delta_{n_1,n_2} \quad (i.e, 1 \text{ if } n_1 = n_2 \text{ otherwise } 0) \\
g(n) &= 1 \text{ if } |\Gamma(n)| > 0 \text{ otherwise } 0
\end{aligned}
$$

To show that $K'_n(n_1,n_2)$ is equivalent to $K_n(n_1,n_2)$, we consider two cases:

1. $\exists i \in \{1,2\}, \Gamma(n_i) = \emptyset$: according to eq. 8, we have $K_n(n_1,n_2) = \delta_{n_1,n_2}$ and $K'_n(n_1,n_2) = K_{nid}(n_1,n_2)$ since the summation over an empty set is zero ($K_{nc}(n_1,n_2) = 0$). $g(n_1)g(n_2)$ being equal to zero, $K_{nid}(n_1,n_2)$ is equal to $K_{id}(n_1,n_2) = \delta_{n_1,n_2}$. In this case, we can conclude that K_n is equivalent to K'_n.

2. $\forall i \in \{1,2\}, \Gamma(n_i) \neq \emptyset$: according to eq. 8, we have $K_n(n_1,n_2) = \sum_{c_1 \in \Gamma(n_1)} \sum_{c_2 \in \Gamma(n_2)} K_c(c_1,c_2)$ and $K'_n(n_1,n_2) = K_{nc}(n_1,n_2)$ because $K_{nid}(n_1,n_2) = 0$ since $g(n_1)g(n_2) = 1$. Thus, in this case, K_n is also equivalent to K'_n.

We can then conclude that K_n is equivalent to K'_n.

Now, we conclude the proof by showing that K'_n is a Mercer kernel. K_{nc} is a convolution kernel so if K_c is a Mercer kernel, K_{nc} is also a Mercer kernel. For K_{nid}, the gram matrix $\bar{K}_{nid}$ associated to it, for any finite subset, is a diagonal matrix where each entry of the diagonal is 0 or 1. The eigenvalues of $\bar{K}_{nid}$ being positives, the matrix is positive semi-definite. And, according to the definition 5.1, K_{nid} is a Mercer kernel. Hence, K'_n is a Mercer kernel.

Moreover, all the kernels K_p, K_l and K_n are normalized to give equal weights to each nodes. Thus, nodes of different length (in terms of the number of children) can be compared on the same scale. The normalization is done according to the following formula:

$$\hat{K}(x,y) = \frac{K(x,y)}{\sqrt{K(x,x)}\sqrt{K(y,y)}} \tag{9}$$

5.3. The Concept Kernel

The concept kernel, K_c, is used to compute the similarity between two concepts. It uses a taxonomy of "is-a" relations between concepts. The taxonomy can be represented by a directed acyclic graph in which a child can have multiple parents. From the UMLS Metathesaurus, we can build such a taxonomy by 1) merging all the ontologies by simply ignoring the source field, 2) removing, from the ontology, all relations that are not "is-a" relations and 3) removing residual relations[5] that introduce cycles. Given the concept taxonomy, K_c relies on two measures of concept similarity:

The conceptual similarity: This similarity is based on the conceptual distance. The idea is that the more similar two concepts are, the nearer they will be in the taxonomy. The distance metric between two concepts c_1 and c_2 can be expressed as the minimum number

[5]These relations often come from the naive merge of multiple ontologies.

of concepts (p) separating c_1 from c_2 i.e. the number of concepts in the shortest path from c_1 to c_2. The similarity is, then, given by the inverse of the distance. Leacock and Chodorow [18, 20] have proposed to normalize this similarity by the maximum length of a path (2× the taxonomy's depth) and to use a logarithm on the result. We take the Leacock and Chodorow measure, after normalization, as the conceptual similarity :

$$sim_{lch}(c_1, c_2) = -\frac{\log\left(\frac{p}{2.depth}\right)}{\log\left(2.depth\right)} \tag{10}$$

This similarity measure is clearly insufficient to correctly express the relatedness of two concepts. Firstly, it gives equal weight to each concept of the taxonomy whereas the specific concepts provide much more information than the general ones. Secondly, it doesn't take account of how much a parent and his child are related to each other.

The information content similarity: We use the Lin measure [19], which, given two concepts c_1 and c_2, gives a higher similarity value when 1) the nearest common ancestor of c_1 and c_2 ($nca(c_1, c_2)$) is the most specific and 2) c_1 and c_2 are the most nearer and related to $nca(c_1, c_2)$. The Lin measure uses the information content (IC) [24] as a measure of specificity. Indeed, the specific concepts have higher IC values than the general concepts.

$$sim_{lin} = \frac{2.IC(nca(c_1, c_2))}{IC(c_1) + IC(c_2)} \tag{11}$$

$$IC(c) = -\log\left(\frac{freq(c)}{freq(root)}\right) \tag{12}$$

$$freq(c) = freq(c, \mathcal{C}) + \sum_{s \in \Gamma(c)} freq(s)$$

where $\Gamma(c)$ is the set of concepts that have c for parent and $freq(c, \mathcal{C})$ the number of lexical units in a relevant corpus $\mathcal{C}$ that can be mapped to the concept c. In our setup, we used the learning and the test corpus as a relevant corpus. This setup can be seen as a semi-supervised method.

Given the above similarity measures, the Concept Kernel is then defined by:

$$K_c(c_1, c_2) = sim_{lch}(c_1, c_2) \times sim_{lin}(c_1, c_2) \tag{13}$$

Theorem 5.1 *K_c is a Mercer kernel.*

Proof. For any finite subset of the concept space, the gram matrix $\bar{K}_c$ associated to K_c is a symmetric matrix with positive entries since the similarity measures are positive functions. $\bar{K}_c$ can be diagonalized and all his eigenvalues are positives so $\bar{K}_c$ is positive semi-definite. According to the definition 5.1, K_c is a Mercer kernel.

6. Experimental Evaluation

With the aim of showing the benefit of the UMLS-based Semantic Kernel, for text categorization, we compared it with the *bag-of-words* Linear Kernel [16] and with the multinomial Naive Bayes classifier [15] on a text categorization problem. The kernels were used with the SVM classifier [32].

6.1. The SVM Classifier

We have described the basic ideas of the SVM in the introduction, we now give a much more detailed description of this machine learning method. The SVM is an extension of the OHA classifier which is, in fact, a linear separator that divides the space into two subspaces. Given a data $\mathbf{x} \in \mathcal{X}$, a label $y \in \mathcal{Y} = \{-1, 1\}$ is given to $\mathbf{x}$ according to the subspace where $\mathbf{x}$ lies. This can be stated as:

$$y = sign(\langle \mathbf{w}, \mathbf{x} \rangle + b) \tag{14}$$

where $\mathbf{w}$ is a weight vector, normal to the separating hyperplane, and b the intercept.

Given a training set $\{(\mathbf{x_i}, y_i) \in \mathcal{X} \times \mathcal{Y}\}_{i=1}^{N}$, $\mathbf{w}$ is chosen to maximize the margin, i.e., twice the shortest distance from the separating hyperplane to the closest training data. $\mathbf{w}$ and b can be found by solving the following quadratic problem:

$$\begin{aligned} \text{minimize} \quad & \frac{1}{2}\langle \mathbf{w}, \mathbf{w} \rangle + C \sum_{i=1}^{N} \xi_i \\ \text{subject to:} \quad & \forall_{i=1}^{N}\ y_i(\langle \mathbf{w}, \mathbf{x_i} \rangle + b) \geq 1 - \xi_i \\ & \forall_{i=1}^{N}\ \xi_i \geq 0 \end{aligned} \tag{15}$$

where C is a trade-off parameter between error and margin (a small value of C increase the number of training errors).

The SVM algorithm is obtained by replacing, in the OHA, the Euclidean inner-product $(\langle \cdot, \cdot \rangle)$ with a Mercer kernel $(K(\cdot, \cdot) = \langle \cdot, \cdot \rangle_{\mathcal{H}})$. We recall that a Mercer kernel is an inner-product in a feature space $\mathcal{H}$ (which is also an Hilbert space). Hence, by using a kernel, the SVM will implicitly map the input data to the feature space corresponding to the kernel and then it will use the OHA to linearly separate the data in the feature space. This is called the kernel trick [3, 32]. By using a non-linear kernel, the data will be linearly separated in the feature space thanks to the OHA, but the separation will be non-linear in the input space. Hence, the OHA is a special case of the SVM. Indeed, the SVM with a linear kernel (i.e. the Euclidean inner-product) is equivalent to the OHA since the feature space of the linear kernel is an Euclidean space.

6.2. The Multinomial Naive Bayes Classifier

In this section, we briefly present the Multinomial Naive Bayes Classifier we used for our experiments. Given a set of classes $\mathcal{C}$, a feature space $\mathcal{F}$, the probability that a document d belongs to a class $c \in \mathcal{C}$ is given by the Bayes conditional probability:

$$P(c|d) = \frac{P(c,d)}{P(d)} = \frac{P(d|c)P(c)}{\sum_{c_i} P(d|c_i)P(c_i)} \tag{16}$$

with $P(c)$ empirically given by the number of training documents of class c divided by the total number of training documents. The conditional probability to have a document d given a class c is given by:

$$P(d|c) = \prod_{w_i \in \mathcal{F}} P(w_i|c)^{freq_d(w_i)} \tag{17}$$

with $freq_d(w_i)$ the number of occurrences of the word w_i in the document d. The posterior probability that a word w_i occurs given a class c is given by the following formula:

$$P(w_i|c) = \frac{1 + freq_c(w_i)}{|\mathcal{F}| + \sum_{w \in \mathcal{F}} freq_c(w)} \tag{18}$$

with $freq_c(w)$ the overall number of occurrences of the word w in the training documents of the class c.

6.3. The Corpus

We used, for our experiments, the CMC medical corpus [21] released by the Computational Medicine Center (CMC) of the Cincinnati Children's Hospital Medical Center (CCHMC) for the CMC's 2007 Medical NLP challenge [6]. The corpus is composed of a labeled set for training and an unlabeled set for classification purpose. Each set contains almost 1000 "anonymized" documents. A document is composed of two parts of short natural language free texts. The first section is the clinical observation and the second one is the radiology impression. Figure 3 shows an example of documents from the corpus. In the training set, each document has been assigned to, at least, one ICD-9-CM category by three different companies. The final codes are assigned to the documents using the majority vote between the companies. The ICD-9-CM codes are used to justify specific medical procedures to be performed for a patient. Moreover, these codes are used by insurance companies for reimbursements. Figure 4 shows a small sample of the ICD-9-CM hierarchical codes.

The training set contains 45 different ICD-9-CM codes and 94 distinct combinations from these codes were used to label the training documents. The purpose of the challenge was to assign one or more codes to each document of the test set.


```
<doc id="97636670" type="RADIOLOGY_REPORT">
    <codes>
        <code origin="CMC_MAJORITY" type="ICD-9-CM">786.2</code>
        <code origin="COMPANY3" type="ICD-9-CM">786.2</code>
        <code origin="COMPANY1" type="ICD-9-CM">204.0</code>
        <code origin="COMPANY1" type="ICD-9-CM">786.2</code>
        <code origin="COMPANY1" type="ICD-9-CM">V42.81</code>
        <code origin="COMPANY2" type="ICD-9-CM">204.00</code>
        <code origin="COMPANY2" type="ICD-9-CM">786.2</code>
    </codes>
    <texts>
        <text origin="CCHMC_RADIOLOGY" type="CLINICAL_HISTORY">
            Eleven year old with ALL, bone marrow transplant on Jan. 2,
            now with three day history of cough.
        </text>
        <text origin="CCHMC_RADIOLOGY" type="IMPRESSION">
            1. No focal pneumonia. Likely chronic changes at the left
            lung base.  2. Mild anterior wedging of the thoracic
            vertebral bodies.
        </text>
    </texts>
</doc>
```


Figure 3. An example of a semi-structured document from the CMC free text corpus.

6 www.computationalmedicine.org/challenge

-- ...
-- DISEASES OF THE CIRCULATORY SYSTEM
    -- DISEASES OF PULMONARY CIRCULATION
        -- 415 Acute pulmonary heart disease
        -- 416 Chronic pulmonary heart disease
        -- 417 Other diseases of pulmonary circulation
    -- ...
-- DISEASES OF THE RESPIRATORY SYSTEM
    -- ACUTE RESPIRATORY INFECTIONS
        -- 460 Acute nasopharyngitis
        -- 461 Acute sinusitis
        -- ...
-- CONGENITAL ANOMALIES
    -- Spina bifida
        -- 741.0 With hydrocephalus
        -- 741.9 Without mention of hydrocephalus
    -- ...
-- ...

Figure 4. A small sample of the ICD-9-CM codes.

6.4. Experimental Setup

The unlabeled set was only used in the UMLS-Based Semantic Kernel, for the Lin similarity measure.

All experiments were led on the training set using a ten folds cross-validation repeated 10 times. The results were then expressed as the means, with the standard deviations, of the 100 runs.

For the Semantic Kernel, the weights w_i were set to one in equation 7. Indeed, we want to give an equal weight to each part of the document.

For the Linear Kernel and the Naive Bayes methods, the parts of each document were merged. A simple bag-of-words representation was used. The stopwords were removed and the dimension of the space was reduced by performing a stemming on each word with the Porter stemming algorithm [7]. Moreover, for the Linear Kernel, each word was weighted with the TF-IDF weighting scheme. The document vectors were, then, normalized to give an equal length to each document.

This classification problem being a multi-class problem, we used, for the SVM classifier, for both the semantic and the Linear Kernel, a one-against-the-rest strategy [14]. For each class, a classifier was learned with documents of this class as positive instances and the others as negative instances. Thus, 45 classifiers per run were learned for this text categorization.

To assign more than one code to a document, we used the SCut strategy [33]. The training set was split into a training set and a validation set. the new training set was, then, used to learn a classifier model. The model was used to score the documents of the validation set. 45 scores per document were assigned to the validation set. For each class c, a threshold t_c was defined and a document d was assigned the label c iff the score of d for c was above the threshold t_c. Each threshold was then tuned on the validation set to optimize the F_1 score. In our setting, 20% of the initial training data was used for the validation and only 80% was really used for training.

We recall that, given a confusion matrix for a category c such as the one in table 1, the

[7] www.snowball.tartarus.org

precision of a classifier, for the class c, is the number of documents correctly assigned to c over the total number of documents assigned to c. The recall is the number of documents correctly assigned to c over the total number of documents belonging to c. The F_1 score is then the harmonic mean of the precision and the recall. The formal definition is:

$$\text{precision}(c) = \frac{\text{TP}_c}{\text{TP}_c + \text{FP}_c} \tag{19}$$

$$\text{recall}(c) = \frac{\text{TP}_c}{\text{TP}_c + \text{FN}_c} \tag{20}$$

$$F_1(c) = \frac{2 * \text{precision}(c) * \text{recall}(c)}{\text{precision}(c) + \text{recall}(c)} \tag{21}$$

Table 1. The confusion matrix for a class c.

	Positive	**Negative**
Predicted Positive	TP_c	FP_c
Predicted Negative	FN_c	TN_c

In a multi-category classifier, the micro-average and the macro-average are used to evaluate the system. In the micro-averaging, documents are given an equal weight whereas in the macro-averaging, an equal weight is given to categories. Table 2 gives the formulas for the precision and recall. The global F_1 score is then: $F_1 = \frac{2*\text{precision}*\text{recall}}{\text{precision}+\text{recall}}$ according to the kind of average used.

Table 2. Micro and macro averaging for N categories.

	Micro	**Macro**
Precision	$\frac{\sum_c \text{TP}_c}{\sum_c (\text{TP}_c + \text{FP}_c)}$	$\frac{1}{N} \sum_c \text{precision}(c)$
Recall	$\frac{\sum_c \text{TP}_c}{\sum_c (\text{TP}_c + \text{FN}_c)}$	$\frac{1}{N} \sum_c \text{recall}(c)$

6.5. Experimental Results

Figure 5 shows how the F_1 performance of the Semantic Kernel vary according to the polynomial order l of the mixing function with $\tau = 10$. The best score, micro-F_1=84%, is obtained for $l = 2$ then the performance decrease when l increase. Nevertheless, the F_1 becomes stable for $l > 30$. These results show that, for this corpus, mixing similarities between different parts doesn't provide any information. Indeed, a high similarity for one type of part doesn't necessarily induce a high similarity for the second one. Thus, different types of parts shouldn't be linked together. A simple weighted average performs well for this data. In fact, a polynomial of degree 2 is a good tradeoff.

Figure 6 shows that the variation of the concept threshold τ doesn't affect the performance of the Semantic Kernel. Our main assumption about concepts was that a normalized

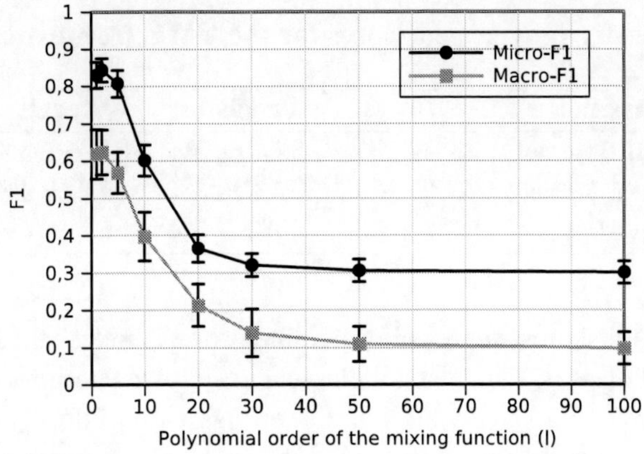

Figure 5. F_1 variation according to the polynomial order (l) of the mixing function (eq. 6) on the CMC free text corpus (with $\tau = 10$).

string, that has too much concepts, is probably too much ambiguous to provide a clear meaning. Whereas this assumption seems to be relevant, we used a specialized taxonomy that suits well to this corpus. Thus, 1) a normalized string has, generally, less than 15 concepts and 2) all concepts for the same string have nearly the same meaning. However, a value of 10 for τ gives a slightly better result.

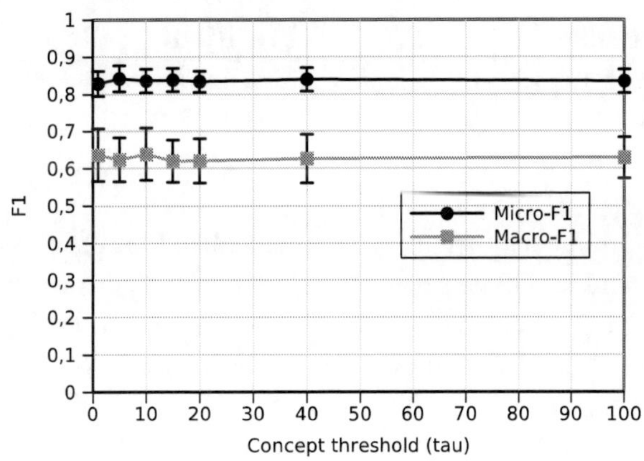

Figure 6. F_1 variation according to the concept threshold τ (eq. 8) on the CMC free text corpus (with $l = 2$).

The performances of the Semantic Kernel (with $\tau = 10$ and $l = 2$), the Linear Kernel and the Naive Bayes classifier are reported in tables 3 and 4. As we can seen, the Semantic Kernel, clearly, outperforms by 7% the Linear Kernel and by 26% the Naive Bayes classifier for the micro-averaged F_1 score. The good performance of the Linear Kernel shows that the words used within the documents of the same class have the same morphological form. Thus, after stemming, same-class documents share, generally, the same words.

Nevertheless, according to table 4, although the macro-averaged F_1 score of the Semantic Kernel is better than the Linear Kernel by 2%, they have almost the same performance.

Table 3. Micro-averaged scores for the CMC free text corpus.

Classifier	F_1	Precision	Recall
UMLS Kernel	$83\% \pm 3\%$	$82\% \pm 3\%$	$84\% \pm 3\%$
Linear Kernel	$76\% \pm 3\%$	$77\% \pm 3\%$	$75\% \pm 4\%$
Naive Bayes	$57\% \pm 4\%$	$59\% \pm 5\%$	$55\% \pm 4\%$

For the macro-averaged scores, scores are calculated for each class then averaged. A same weight is given to all classes. Thus, small classes, i.e. classes with fewer documents, will affect the overall scores in a same way than larger classes will do. The ICD-9-CM being an hierarchical coding system, some classes belong to the same hierarchical branch. Therefore, such classes are semantically similar. The Semantic Kernel affects the documents of a smaller class to a larger class that is semantically similar. Recall that we used the one-against-all strategy. The macro-recall for the smaller class will be low and the macro-precision for the larger class will, also, be low. This will result in a low F_1 score. The Linear Kernel reacts in a different way. Indeed, it looks for common stemmed words. So, if the smaller class have specific words that don't appear in the larger class, the performance of the Linear Kernel won't be affected by this problem.

Table 4. Macro-averaged scores for the CMC free text corpus.

Classifier	F_1	Precision	Recall
UMLS Kernel	$62\% \pm 4\%$	$63\% \pm 5\%$	$63 \pm 4\%$
Linear Kernel	$60\% \pm 6\%$	$62\% \pm 6\%$	$61\% \pm 6\%$
Naive Bayes	$36\% \pm 5\%$	$40\% \pm 7\%$	$38\% \pm 6\%$

The impact of the number of training documents used on the classifier's performance is shown in figures 7 and 8. The experiment shows that the performance, in terms of both micro and macro F_1, of the Naive Bayes classifier scales linearly according to the number of training data. This result was quite expected as the Naive Bayes is a probabilist method based on the occurrence frequency. Thus, it needs a large amount of training data to efficiently estimate the word distribution of the data. The Semantic Kernel needs only 40% of the training data to nearly reach his optimal micro-F_1 score and 70% to reach the optimal macro-F_1 measure. The difference between the two percentages can be explained by the fact that the corpus contains categories with a very few documents. A large fraction of the training documents is then needed to capture the discriminative information. The micro-F_1 gives an equal weight to all documents so it won't be affected by the small categories. However, the macro-F_1 is an average over the categories thus small categories will drastically affect the score. The F_1 variation of the Linear Kernel is quite the same as the Semantic Kernel but with a much more linear shape. The optimal micro-F_1 score of the linear kernel is reached by the Semantic Kernel with only 20% of the training data. This result shows that the use of the semantic information significantly improves the categorization.

Another interesting point is shown in figure 8. For a small amount of training documents, the macro-F_1 value of the Linear Kernel is higher than the one of the Semantic

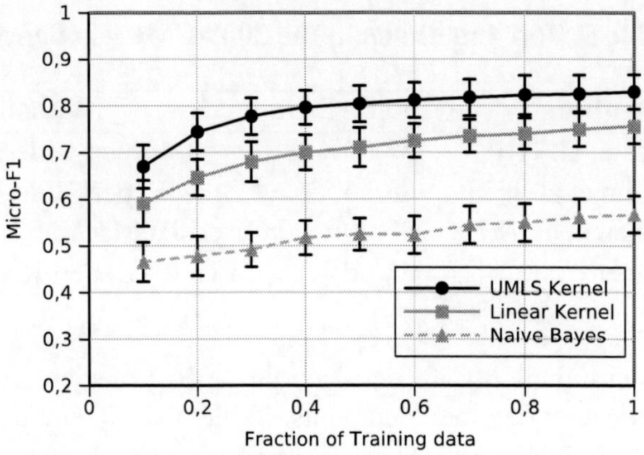

Figure 7. Micro-F_1 variation according to the fraction of training data used.

Kernel. As we said above, this is mainly due to small categories. The meanings of these categories extracted by the Semantic Kernel are too ambiguous and correlated with the meanings of the large categories. The classification is then done in favor of the large categories. The Linear Kernel is based on the term frequency. By finding discriminant words for the small categories, the macro-F_1 of the Linear kernel is less affected by this problem.

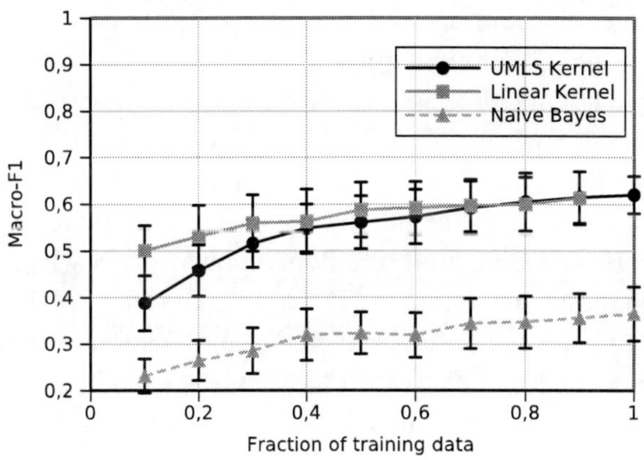

Figure 8. Macro-F_1 variation according to the fraction of training data used.

6.6. Discussion about the 2007 CMC Medical NLP Challenge

As a final evaluation, we trained a SVM classifier, with the semantic kernel, on the whole training set (20% was used as a validation set). The classifier was, then, used to categorize the unlabeled test set. We sent the categorized test set to the CMC for the 2007 Medical NLP International Challenge. Our algorithm has obtained a micro-F_1 score of 85%. The Semantic Kernel was ranked in the top ten of the best algorithms among the 44 algorithms used in the challenge.

The algorithms that performed the best in this challenge were those that were especially

Table 5. Top 4 methods in the 2007 CMC challenge.

Rank	Authors	micro-F_1	Method
1	Farkas et al. [10]	89.08%	Expert Rule-based
2	Goldstein et al. [12]	88.55%	Expert Rule-based
3	Suominen et al. [31]	87.69%	Cascaded Machine Learning (ML)
4	Crammer et al. [6]	87.60%	Cascaded Expert Rule-based+ML

designed to be used with the CMC free text corpus. Most of them use manually defined rules to automatically categorize the documents. Table 5 shows the top 4 methods. Three of the top 4 methods are expert rule-based method. In [10], Farkas et al. use the ICD-9-CM coding guide to generate expert rules. The rules were enriched by examining and extracting rules from the training dataset. Although, the system used for the challenge was manually defined, the authors have proposed two statistical systems to automatically extract rules from the training set. The first method use a C4.5 decision tree[22] to predict the false negative of the manually defined rule-based system. The rules of the decision tree are then used to enrich the expert system. The second method use the maximum entropy method to calculate the probability of a false negative prediction for each token. The relevant words and phrases are then added to the expert system. These two methods reach the same performance on the CMC corpus than the manually enriched system.

In [12], Goldstein et al. have a proposed an expert rule-base model. The model was constructed by analyzing the training corpus.

Suominen et al. [31] have proposed a fully automatic cascaded system. The system use the Regularized Least Squares (RLS) learning algorithm [25]. The documents are represented by binary vectors. The features are composed of words and UMLS concepts. Moreover, the vectors are enriched by adding features expressing negation and uncertainty for words and concepts, and by adding the hypernyms of the UMLS concepts. The RLS model is then used to predict one or more ICD-9-CM codes for each document. If the model has been unable to predict a code or has predicted a combination of codes that is not present in the training set, a second model is used to predict the final code. The second model is constructed with the RIPPER rule induction-based learning method [4]. The use of the RIPPER model in the case of a wrong prediction by the RLS model significantly improves the performance of the system compared to the performance of the stand-alone RLS model.

In [6], Crammer et al. have proposed a cascaded system composed of an expert rule-based model and a machine learning model. The expert rules are manually extracted from the ICD-9-CM coding guide and the training set. The prediction of the rule-based model is then used as a feature for the MIRA algorithm [5].

7. Conclusion

In this chapter, we have presented a Semantic Mercer Kernel that uses the UMLS framework to incorporate semantic meanings during the similarity estimation between textual documents. The kernel was designed to process semi-structured medical documents. We have described a preprocessing method to represent such documents by concept trees. The

Semantic Kernel uses a taxonomy of concepts build from the *UMLS Metathesaurus* to compute a similarity value between two concept trees.

The performances of the Semantic Kernel were, experimentally, evaluated on a text categorization task with a medical corpus of free text documents, the CMC ICD-9-CM corpus. The results have shown that this kernel significantly outperforms the Linear Kernel and the multinomial Naive Bayes classifier. Moreover, the kernel was evaluated at the 2007 medical NLP international challenge(*Classifying Clinical Free Text Using Natural Language Processing*)[8] organized by the CMC and it was ranked in the top ten of the best algorithms among 44 classification methods. However, the performance of this kernel on the ICD-9-CM corpus provided for the challenge can be improved, for example, by ensuring that the combination of ICD-9-CM codes predicted by our system is relevant with the set of codes used in the training set. In case that a combination does not appear in the training set, one method to correct is to use the largest subset of the combination such that the subset appears in the training set.

Although the proposed Semantic Kernel was primarily designed for the biomedical domain, it can, easily, be adapted for other domains by using the appropriate concept taxonomy. In the future, we plan to use this kernel on general corpora such as the Reuters corpus using the WordNet taxonomy. Furthermore, there are two points that need to be improved. Firstly, a disambiguation process should be introduced when normalizing lexical units and when assigning concepts to these lexical units. Secondly, a some kind of orders or links should be used to organize the lexical units in a document part.

Acknowledgments

This work was carried out within the Cap Digital Infomagic project [9]. We are very grateful to Tsiriniaina Andriamampianina for fruitful discussions and advices.

References

[1] C. Berg, J. P. R. Christensen, and P. Ressel, Harmonic Analysis on Semigroups: Theory of Positive Definite and Related Functions, Springer-Verlag, Berlin, 1984.

[2] S. Bloehdorn, R. Basili, M. Cammisa, and A. Moschitti, Semantic Kernels for Text Classification Based on Topological measures of feature similarity., *Proceedings of the 2006 IEEE International Conference on Data Mining (ICDM'06)*, 2006, pp. 808–812.

[3] B. E. Boser, I. M. Guyon, and V. N. Vapnik, A training algorithm for optimal margin classifiers, *COLT '92: Proceedings of the fifth annual workshop on Computational learning theory* (New York, NY, USA), ACM, 1992, pp. 144–152.

[4] W. W. Cohen, Fast Effective Rule Induction, *International Conference on Machine Learning*, 1995, pp. 115–123.

[8] http://www.computationalmedicine.org/challenge/res.php

[9] http://www.capdigital.com

[5] K. Crammer, Online Learning of Complex Categorial Problems, Ph.D. thesis, Hebrew University of Jerusalem, 2004.

[6] K. Crammer, M. Dredze, K. Ganchev, P. Talukdar, and S. Carroll, Automatic Code Assignment to Medical Text, *Biological, translational, and clinical language processing* (Prague, Czech Republic), Association for Computational Linguistics, June 2007, pp. 129–136.

[7] N. Cristianini, J. Shawe-Taylor, and H. Lodhi, Latent Semantic Kernels., *Journal of Intelligent Information Systems* **18** (2002), no. 2-3, 127–152.

[8] S. C. Deerwester, S. T. Dumais, T. K. Landauer, G. W. Furnas, and R. A. Harshman, Indexing by Latent Semantic Analysis, *Journal of the American Society of Information Science* **41** (1990), no. 6, 391–407.

[9] G. Divita, A. C. Browne, and R. Loanne, dtagger: A POS Tagger, *Proceedings AMIA Fall Symposium*, 2006, pp. 201–203.

[10] R. Farkas and G. Szarvas, Automatic construction of rule-based icd-9-cm coding systems, *BMC Bioinformatics* **9** (2008), no. 3.

[11] A. Gliozzo and C. Strapparava, Domain Kernels for Text Categorization, *Proceedings of the Ninth Conference on Computational Natural Language Learning (CoNLL-2005)* (Ann Arbor, Michigan), Association for Computational Linguistics, June 2005, pp. 56–63.

[12] I. Goldstein, A. Arzumtsyan, and O. Uzuner, Three Approaches to Automatic Assignment of ICD-9-CM Codes to Radiology Reports, *Proceedings of the Fall Symposium of the American Medical Informatics Association* (Chicago, Illinois, USA), November 2007, pp. 279–283.

[13] D. Haussler, Convolution Kernels on Discrete Structures, Tech. Report UCS-CRL-99-10, UC Santa Cruz, 1999.

[14] C.-W. Hsu and C.-J. Lin, A Comparison of Methods for Multi-class Support Vector Machines, *IEEE Transactions on Neural Networks* **13** (2002), no. 2, 415–425.

[15] T. Joachims, A Probabilistic Analysis of the Rocchio Algorithm with TFIDF for Text Categorization, *Proceedings of the ICML-97, 14th International Conference on Machine Learning* (San Francisco, CA, USA), Morgan Kaufmann Publishers Inc., 1997, pp. 143–151.

[16] Th. Joachims, Text categorization with support vector machines: learning with many relevant features, *Proceedings of the ECML-98, 10th European Conference on Machine Learning* (Heidelberg, DE), Springer Verlag, 1998, pp. 137–142.

[17] ______, Learning to Classify Text Using Support Vector Machines: Methods, Theory and Algorithms, Kluwer Academic Publishers, Norwell, MA, USA, 2002.

[18] C. Leacock and M. Chodorow, Combining local context and WordNet similarity for word sense identification, *WordNet: An Electronic Lexical Database* (1998), 265–283.

[19] D. Lin, An information-theoretic definition of similarity, *Proceedings of the 15th International Conference on Machine Learning (ICML)*, Morgan Kaufmann, San Francisco, CA, 1998, pp. 296–304.

[20] T. Pedersen, S. Pakhomov, S. Patwardhan, and C. Chute, Measures of semantic similarity and relatedness in the biomedical domain, *Journal of Biomedical Informatics* **40** (2007), no. 3, 288–299.

[21] J.P. Pestian, C. Brew, P. Matykiewicz, D.J. Hovermale, N. Johnson, K. Bretonnel Cohen, and W. Duch, A Shared Task Involving Multi-label Classification of Clinical Free Text, *Proceedings of the 2007 ACL BioNLP* (Prague) (ACL, ed.), Association of Computational Linguistics, June 2007.

[22] J. R. Quinlan, C4.5: programs for machine learning, Morgan Kaufmann Publishers Inc., San Francisco, CA, USA, 1993.

[23] R.Basili, M. Cammisa, and A. Moschitti, A Semantic Kernel to classify texts with very few training examples, *Informatica* **30** (2006), no. 2, 163–172.

[24] P. Resnik, Using Information Content to Evaluate Semantic Similarity in a Taxonomy, *Proceedings of the 14th International Joint Conference on Artificial Intelligence (IJCAI)*, 1995, pp. 448–453.

[25] R. Rifkin, G. Yeo, and T. Poggio, Regularized least squares classification, *Advances in Learning Theory: Methods, Model and Applications* **190** (2003), 131–153.

[26] G. Salton, A. Wong, and C. S. Yang, A Vector Space Model for automatic indexing, *Communications of the ACM* **18** (1975), no. 11, 613–620.

[27] F. Sebastiani, Machine learning in automated text categorization, *ACM Computing Surveys* **34** (2002), no. 1, 1–47.

[28] ———, Text categorization, Text Mining and its Applications to Intelligence, CRM and Knowledge Management (Alessandro Zanasi, ed.), WIT Press, Southampton, UK, 2005, pp. 109–129.

[29] J. Shawe-Taylor and N. Cristianini, Kernel Methods for Pattern Analysis, Cambridge University Press, 2004.

[30] G. Siolas and F. d'Alché Buc, Support Vector Machines Based on a Semantic Kernel for Text Categorization, *Proceeding of the IJCNN'00: International Joint Conference on Neural Networks*, IEEE Computer Society, 2000.

[31] H. Suominen, F. Ginter, S. Pyysalo, A. Airola, T. Pahikkala, S. Salanterä, and T. Salakoski, Machine Learning to Automate the Assignment of Diagnosis Codes to Free-text Radiology Reports: a Method Description, *Proceedings of the ICML/UAI workshop on Machine Learning in health care applications*, 2008.

[32] V. N. Vapnik, The nature of statistical learning theory, Springer-Verlag New York, Inc., 1995.

[33] Y. Yang, A Study on Thresholding Strategies for Text Categorization, *Proceedings of the SIGIR-01, 24th ACM International Conference on Research and Development in Information Retrieval*, ACM Press, New York, US, 2001, pp. 137–145.

In: Data Management in the Semantic Web
Editor: Hal Jin, pp. 81-104
ISBN: 978-1-61122-862-5

Chapter 4

ONTOLOGY REUSE – IS IT FEASIBLE?

Elena Simperl [*] ***and Tobias Bürger*** [†]
Semantic Technology Institute (STI), University of Innsbruck,
A-6020 Innsbruck, Austria

Keywords: Ontology engineering, ontology reuse, ontology economics.

1. Introduction

Paraphrasing the general understanding of reuse in related engineering disciplines (cf., for instance, [19]), *ontology reuse* can be defined as *the process in which existing ontological knowledge is used as input to generate new ontologies.* The ability to efficiently and effectively perform reuse is commonly acknowledged to play a crucial role in the large-scale dissemination of ontologies and ontology-driven technologies, thus being a prerequisite for the mainstream uptake of the Semantic Web. The sharing and reuse of ontologies increases the quality of the applications using them, as these applications become interoperable and are provided with a deeper, machine-processable and commonly agreed-upon understanding of the underlying domain of interest. Secondly, analogously to other engineering disciplines, reuse, if performed in an efficient way, reduces the costs related to ontology development. This is because it avoids the re-implementation of ontological components, which are already available on the Web, and can be directly – or after some additional customization – integrated into a target ontology. In addition, it potentially improves the quality of ontologies, as these are continuously revised and evaluated by various parties through reuse.

While it is generally accepted that building an ontology from scratch is a resource-intensive process, ontology engineering projects do not tap the full potential of existing domain knowledge sources. Often, when implementing an ontology-based application, the underlying ontology is built from scratch, does not resort to available ontological knowledge on the Web, and is implicitly tailored to specific application needs – which in turn means that it cannot be reused in other settings. Available ontology engineering methodologies address reusability issues only marginally. Though most of them mention the possibility

*E-mail addresses: elena.simperl@sti2.at
†E-mail addresses: tobias.buerger@sti2.at

of reusing existing knowledge sources as input for the conceptualization phase, they do not elaborate on how ontology discovery and the subsequent evaluation of candidate ontologies should be performed, and do not clarify the implications of reuse for the overall engineering process. For example, [75] describes in detail how to build ontologies from scratch, but gives a relatively sketchy recommendation for reusing existing ontologies. Some methodologies address reuse in the context of ontology customization or pruning i.e., extracting relevant fragments from very comprehensive, general-purpose ontologies [51, 71]. [52] gives a detailed description of the reuse process, but does not investigate its implications in the overall engineering process.

In current ontology engineering methodologies and guidelines, reuse is per default recommended as a key factor to develop cost-effective and high-quality ontologies (cf. the NEON methodology[1]). It is expected to reduce development costs, since it avoids rebuilding ontologies that might exist elsewhere. This process is, however, related to significant efforts, which may easily outweigh its benefits. First, as in other engineering disciplines, reusing an existing artifact is associated to costs to find, get familiar with, adapt, and update the relevant components in a new context. Second, building a new ontology means translating between different representation schemes, or performing matching, merging and integration, or both. The translation between representation formalisms is a realistic task only for similar modeling languages and even in this case current tools do face important limitations [15]. In addition, a large amount of knowledge, especially in the case of thesauri, classifications, and taxonomies is formalized in a proprietary language, making mainstream translation tools not applicable. Provided a common representation language, the source ontologies need to be compared and eventually merged or integrated. For this purpose, one needs a generic matching algorithm, which can deal with the heterogeneity of the incoming sources in terms of their structure, domain, representation language, or granularity. Matching algorithms, though containing valuable ideas and techniques, can not be currently applied in an efficient, operationalized manner to an arbitrary reuse scenario due to their limitations with respect to the issues mentioned above [38, 64]. On the other hand, the benefits of ontology reuse go beyond the obvious cost savings typically mentioned in the relevant engineering literature. Since ontologies are per definition understood as a means for a shared domain conceptualization, reusing them increases application interoperability both at the syntactic and at the semantic level. Humans or software using the same ontology are assumed to hold the same view upon the modeled domain, and thus define and use domain terms and concepts in the same way.

The decision whether to develop an ontology from scratch or by reuse, given a set of application requirements, is complex. It should be supported by means to estimate the costs and the benefits of the two engineering strategies in a comparable quantitative way. From an economic perspective, reuse can not be considered as a default option as it is more a matter of trade-offs between the costs implied by the reuse of the ontology and the benefits.

To understand the reuse process, we have analyzed the feasibility of ontology reuse based on which we discuss its economic aspects. In analogy to methods in the field of software engineering we relate costs of ontology development to the level of ontology reuse and to the costs of developing and maintaining reusable ontologies. Subsequently we propose

[1] `http://www.neon-project.org`

a cost model focusing on activities in ontology reuse whose goal is to support a trade-off analysis of reusable ontology development costs vs. the costs of the development from scratch. The research leading to this model aims to address the following questions:

1. *Which factors influence the costs for reusing ontologies?*
2. *How can the benefits of ontology reuse be shown in monetary terms?*
3. *Which general statement can be made about the financial feasibility of ontology reuse in specific settings?*

In order to answer these questions we elaborate on an extension of the ONTOCOM model for cost estimation of ontologies for reuse. Our aim is to isolate the costs of reuse of different artifacts on different levels of the ontology engineering process, that is, reuse on the requirements, the conceptual, or the implementation level. Secondly, following work by others on economic models for software reuse, we intend to show the monetary value of ontology reuse in different reuse scenarios on these levels (cf. [17, 20, 29, 76]).

The remainder of this chapter is organized as follows: Section 2. gives an overview of ontology reuse including the reuse process, the current state of practice, and existing methodologies for ontology reuse. Section 3. analyzes economic aspects of ontology development and reuse, presents an economic analysis, and a cost estimation model whose aim is to predict ontology reuse costs. Finally, Section 4. concludes the chapter.

2. Ontology Reuse

2.1. Process Overview

Ontology reuse is an integral part of ontology engineering. Resorting to the terminology in [25] the decision whether to build (fragments of) an application ontology by reusing (an adapted version of) existing ontological sources is one of the designated *support activities* performed in addition to the core *ontology development*. Consequently, ontology reuse can not be exercised in a stand-alone manner, but within an ontology engineering process. The latter pre-defines the characteristics of the ontology to be developed. Some of these form the basis for the requirements that should be satisfied by the potential ontology reuse candidates.

Once the analysis of the domain has been completed and this ontology development strategy has been positively evaluated by the engineering team, the ontology reuse process can start (cf. Figure 1). As input the participants are provided with an *ontology requirements specification document* that entails a compilation of the most important features of the planned ontology and of the application setting [70]. In particular, the sub-domains of the final ontology that are to be built by reuse are identified and described. The document also gives full particulars on the use cases, the scope, the purpose and the expected size of the outcomes. The reuse process is completed with the integration of the reused ontologies into the original application setting. Technically, this is equivalent to a new application ontology that incorporates the parts constructed by reuse and the parts resulting from other building activities—such as manual building, ontology learning, information extraction. This application ontology is then evaluated using the methods, and against the criteria that have been pre-defined in the overall ontology engineering methodology. If the ontology does not fulfill the expected requirements to a satisfactory extent, the engineering team may initiate a re-iteration of the ontology development process at various stages. This includes, under circumstances, a revision of the outcomes of the reuse process as well.[2]

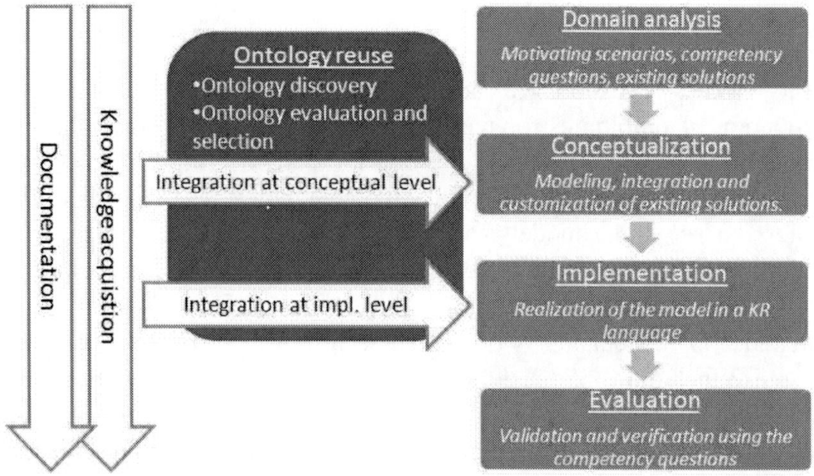

Figure 1. Ontology Reuse as Part of Ontology Engineering.

In the following we provide an overview of the main dimensions of our ontology reuse methodology.

Process steps The reuse process can be decomposed into three sequentially ordered steps (cf. Figure 2):

1. **Ontology discovery**: The first step of the reuse process is primarily technological. The engineering team resorts to conventional or Semantic Web-specific search engines and browses repositories of ontological resources in order to build a list of potential reuse candidates. At Web scale the search is usually performed automatically. The participants specify a minimal set of desired features in terms of machine-understandable queries and review the query results.

2. **Ontology evaluation and selection**: In the second step the reuse candidates are subject to an in-depth evaluation. While technological support is definitely helpful, this is targeted in principle at humans and is inconceivable without an adequate methodological background. The outcome is a set of reusable ontologies complemented by an inventory of actions to be taken for their customization in the next step.

[2]Note that Figure 1 does not commit to a particular ontology life cycle. The decision whether an ontology is built incrementally or as a result of a sequential workflow is out of the direct scope of ontology reuse, though it does have implications on the way this is eventually performed. See [25] for a discussion of ontology life cycles.

3. **Ontology integration**: The last step of the reuse process comprises the execution of the customization operations previously identified, followed by the integration of the reused ontologies into the application system. It requires both methodological and technological assistance. The choice upon a specific integration strategy is not trivial and should be therefore guided through dedicated methodologies. Feasible automatic tools and APIs are equally important. A manual processing is realistic, although involving significant effort, only for small inputs containing at most hundreds of ontological primitives (cf., for example, [2, 26]). The outcome is in the form of one or more ontologies represented in a particular representation language that can be utilized in the target application system.

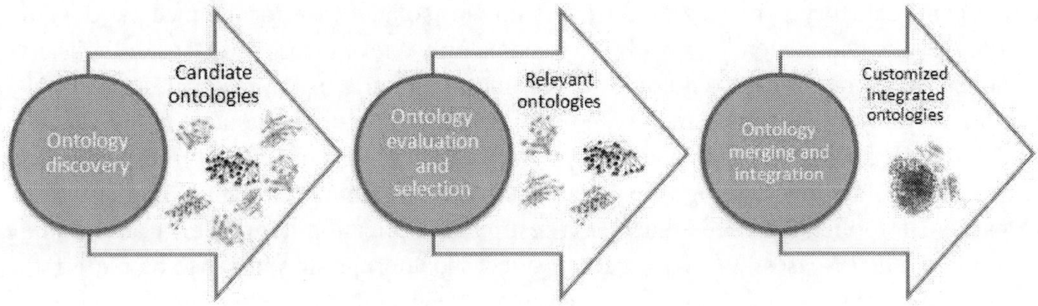

Figure 2. Ontology Reuse Process.

2.2. State of Practice

Ontologies are expected to play a significant role in various application domains on the emerging Semantic Web [18, 66]. Confirming these expectations, to date we have recorded an increasing number of industrial project initiatives choosing to formalize application knowledge using ontologies and Semantic Web representation languages RDFS,[3] OWL,[4] or WSML.[5] The emerging ontologies, however, seldom reflect a consensual, or at least application-independent, view of the modeled domain. Even when using Semantic Web representation languages, these ontologies are, in the sense of knowledge management, simple means of representing knowledge, without any claim of being *formal*, *application-independent* or the result of a *common agreement* within a community of practice. Paraphrasing the well-known definition of Gruber [27], they might indeed be *specifications of conceptualizations*, but they are rarely built to be *shared* or *reused*. The current state is confirmed by existing statistical studies on the size of the Semantic Web. For instance, according to the Semantic Web search engine Swoogle, the number of ontologies publicly available is estimated at approximately $10,000$.[6] Some of them, such as FOAF,[7] are

[3] `http://www.w3.org/TR/rdf-schema/`
[4] `http://www.w3.org/2004/OWL/`
[5] `http://www.wsmo.org/wsml/`
[6] `http://swoogle.umbc.edu/`
[7] `http://www.foaf-project.org/`

already used widely—a high percentage of the RDF data on the Web is FOAF data [9]. Others, particularly general ontologies such as DOLCE[8] or SUMO [50], have meanwhile found application in different settings as upper-level grounding of domain ontologies. The remaining, relatively large number of qualitatively heterogeneous ontologies, modeling the same or related domains of interests, are hardly being used beyond the boundaries of their originating context, though they are ubiquitously accessible. Their limited impact seriously impedes the uptake on semantic technologies in industrial settings.

The dimensions of this problem can be illustrated with the help of a simple example from the health care sector. This sector is a prime example for the adoption of semantic technologies and a high number of ontologies are already available. UMLS[9], which partially integrates over 100 independent medical libraries and contains over 1.5 million terms representing approximately three hundred thousand medical concepts, is representative for this category. The size of UMLS is not an isolated case for the medical domain: ontologies like OntoGalen,[10] or NCI [24] to name only a few, incorporate tens of thousands of concepts. Though these ontologies cover important parts of the medical domain, they can not be directly integrated into a medical information system, as stated for instance in [6, 22, 44, 45, 54, 62, 63]. The main reason for this situation is the lack of information and tools that would allow ontology designers and users to evaluate and adapt the ontologies to particular application needs (such as a restricted application domain e.g., an ontology describing lung diseases [45]). In order to select the appropriate sources to be reused, the engineering team currently has to "read through" over 100 extremely comprehensive ontologies and to gather additional information about them in an uncontrolled, ad-hoc manner. While information about the content and the usage of these ontologies might be available in text form on the Web, the search process is tedious in the absence of adequate instruments to present and organize the potentially large amount of informative material to the human user. Provided a list of useful ontologies, the reuse process goes on with the identification of relevant sub-ontologies and their extraction. Due to the huge size of common medical ontologies, a specific medical application would probably require certain fragments of the source ontologies, which are to be integrated into an application ontology. The identification of the fragments to be extracted is scarcely possible, since there is no available information about the structure or the domain covered by the studied ontologies. This leads to the adoption of domain- and ontology-specific heuristics, whose results can not be easily monitored or evaluated by the domain experts, hence decreasing the acceptance of ontology-based technology in the application setting [41, 44]. Furthermore, matching, merging, and integrating ontologies, besides serious performance and scalability problems, still necessitates considerable manual pre- and post-processing because of the lack of generality of the existing approaches in this area [43].

The limited reuse of existing ontologies is the result of a series of factors, some of which are specific to the Semantic Web context, others related to more general issues of knowledge representation and knowledge management. A common pre-condition for the reusability of an ontology is that it should be conceived and developed independently from

[8] `http://www.loa-cnr.it/DOLCE.html`

[9] The Unified Medical Language System (UMLS) Web site is available at `http://www.nlm.nih.gov/research/umls`.

[10] More information about the OpenGalen ontology is available at `http://www.opengalen.org`.

its usage context [28]. Consequently, reusable ontologies tend to be over-generalized, to model knowledge from a variety of domains of interest, and to omit relevant domain knowledge. They need considerable modifications before being reused, be that in terms of extensions and refinements, or of extraction of domain-relevant fragments. On the other hand, the more committed an ontology is to a specific domain or task, the less its terminological elements can be generalized and reused beyond this scope [1, 7]. A reusable ontology ideally achieves a balance between specificity and over-generalization, without compromising its cross-application usability. The difficulties associated with the realization of a shared ontological commitment are inherently related to the fact that the domain experts involved in the conceptualization process possess, even when belonging to the same community of practice, different, personal or organization-specific views upon the domain to be modeled, or are not necessarily willing to exchange and communicate their expertise within the engineering team [4]. A third factor contributing to the described state of practice is related to the still young nature of the Semantic Web field. Even if knowledge representation structures have been around in computer science for many decades, ontologies, and in particular Semantic Web ontologies, have only emerged so far in stand-alone systems—targeted at closed user communities—or as part of proof-of-concept applications. In addition to this, adequate methodological and technological support for ontology reuse processes is still under development.

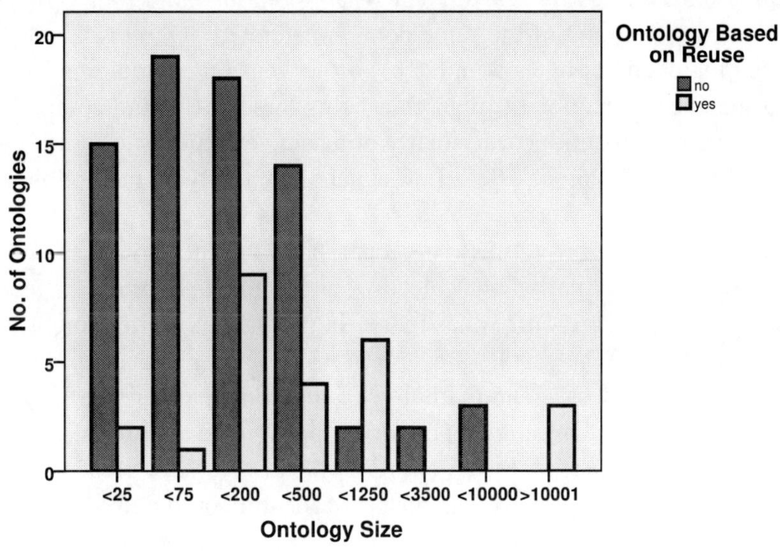

Figure 3. Size Distribution of Reused Ontologies.

To shed a light on the current practice of ontology engineering and reuse, we recently conducted a survey with participants in ontology engineering projects on which we report in [65]. The survey contains data from 98 ontology development projects. Approximately 50% of the data was collected during face-to-face or telephone interviews, the rest via a self-administered online questionnaire. 95% of the ontologies collected were built in Europe, whilst nearly 35% originated from industry parties. The size of the ontologies in the data set varied from only a few to 11 million entities. Most ontologies were implemented in OWL

DL (36.7%), followed by WSML DL and WSML Flight (around 15% each) and RDF(S) (13%). The duration of the projects varied from 0.1 to 52 person months.

Figure 3 shows the size distribution of the surveyed ontologies and indicates if the ontologies were built from scratch or reuse other ontologies. Approximately 60% of the ontologies were built from scratch. If other ontologies were reused they made up to 95% of the final ontology.

2.3. Methodologies, Methods and Tools

Though most of the available ontology engineering methodologies mention the possibility of reusing existing knowledge sources in building new ontologies, the reuse and re-engineering of ontologies has been rather poorly explored in this field. For example, Uschold and King describe in detail how to build an ontology from scratch, but on the matter of reusing existing ontologies they only give a general explanation of the approach [75]. Other methodologies address this issue only in the context of ontology customization. For instance [51, 71] propose methodologies for extracting relevant fragments of very comprehensive ontologies. A more extended account of the reuse process has been made by Pinto and Martins [52]. Differentiating between merging and integration, the authors give a general description of the steps and activities of the second one, defined as *''the process of building an ontology on one subject reusing one or more ontologies in different subjects"*. Reusing ontologies of the same domain is termed *"merging"*, which is studied from a methodological point of view in [22]. Further reuse methodologies often emerged in relation to specific application settings, thus being less general and comprehensive than the proposals previously mentioned. Evidence of reusing existing ontologies is attested in a number of case studies [2, 26, 60, 73, 74], in which the underlying methodology is usually left in the background of the work.

Several research initiatives address subjects related to ontology reuse, such as ontology discovery, ontology evaluation and selection, and ontology alignment. Technology for finding existing ontological resources has increasingly drawn the attention of the ontology engineering community. The results are on one side ontology repositories, such as the Protégé Library,[11] OntoSelect,[12] and Onthology,[13] and, on the other side, dedicated search engines such as Swoogle.[14] Ontology repositories appear to be a useful means of providing an access point for developers to locate ontologies. However, the present state of the art does not resolve a number of issues. The means of locating ontologies is quite haphazard, and relies on the same type of keyword matching that occurs in non-semantic search engines such as Google. Queries can not draw on the semantics of ontologies themselves in order to be able to find e.g., generalizations, specializations or equivalences of search terms or concepts. Finally, the repositories link to the complete ontologies from their descriptions, meaning that access is on an "all or nothing" basis, not taking into account the various needs of individual users. Approaches such as [49, 61] aim to alleviate this situation and propose designated algorithms for searching and ranking ontologies.

[11] `http://protege.stanford.edu/plugins/owl/owl-library/`.
[12] `http://views.dfki.de/ontologies/`.
[13] `http://www.onthology.org/`.
[14] `http://swoogle.umbc.edu/`.

Assessing the usability of an ontology in a target application context is addressed briefly in [52]. The authors identify a number of issues relevant on this matter, such as the compatible domain or representation language. Another exponent in area of research is OntoMetric [33], a framework for selecting among different ontologies. Provided a set of candidate ontologies, OntoMetric computes a quantitative measure of each of them using a framework of 160 features grouped in several dimensions. After specifying the objectives of the application the ontology engineers build a decision tree containing ontology characteristics required in the application setting. The suitability value of each candidate ontology is computed by comparing its features with the nodes of the decision tree. The usage of collaborative filtering techniques to evaluate reuse candidates has been proposed, for instance, in [5]. The tool WEBCORE [5] uses a series of similarity measures as a baseline to compare a pre-defined Golden Standard ontology with a set of available reusable ontologies, and retrieves the ones most similar to the domain based on user ratings. Gangemi et al. introduce in [21] a theoretical framework for various aspects of ontology evaluation and validation, including functionality and usability.

Ontology alignment is one of the most mature areas of research in the Semantic Web community [11, 13, 23, 34, 36, 37, 39, 55, 69]. Comprehensive studies, surveys, and classifications on this topic are given for example in [10, 23, 58]. Usually one distinguishes between individual matching algorithms (e.g., FCA-MERGE [69] or S-Match [23])—applying only a single method of matching items e.g., linguistic or taxonomical matchers—and combinations of the former ones that intend to overcome their limitations by proposing hybrid solutions. A hybrid approach (e.g., Cupid [34]) follows a black box paradigm, in which various individual matchers are molten together to a new algorithm, while the so-called composite matchers allow for increased user interaction (e.g., GLUE [13], COMA [11], or CMC [72]). Given the open nature of the Web environment, in which the emergence of a single ontology for a given application domain is considered both unrealistic and unnatural, application interoperability depends directly on consistent mappings between ontologies adopted by inter-communicating services. Approaches coping with this problem propose a (formal) specification of the semantic overlap between ontologies and integrate matching techniques to automatically discover mapping candidates [12, 14, 30, 35, 40]. Despite the relatively large number of promising approaches in the fields of matching, merging, and integration, their limitations with respect to certain ontology characteristics, such as format, size, and structure of the inputs, modeled domain, have been often emphasized in recent literature [23, 34, 37]. This diversity makes it difficult for an ontology developer to identify the algorithms that can be feasibly applied in a given reuse scenario, as these are *de facto* usable only for a certain class of ontologies.

Compared to classical knowledge bases, the importance of the ontology-maintenance problem has been recognized in a timely manner in the ontology-engineering community, resulting in a series of methodologies and (automatized) methods and tools supporting the systematic and consistent evolution of ontological contents, at both schema and data levels [32, 53, 68]. Last but not least, the advent of Web 2.0 can be seen as a first step towards the realization of widely accepted ontologies. Enhancing simple tagging structures with formal semantics provides an efficient means for exploiting the impressive amount of user-generated content for the realization of community-driven ontologies [8, 31, 59].

To summarize, within the last decade we have experienced impressive progress in various areas of research and development adjacent to ontology reuse. The reuse of knowledge in the Semantic Web context can benefit from the open, ubiquitous nature of the Web, from the emergence of standards for machine-processable knowledge representation, and from the methodological and technological ontology-engineering infrastructure, thus helping to alleviate some of the major obstacles so far impeding reuse in related engineering disciplines. Nevertheless, the costs of ontology reuse can not be underestimated.

3. An Economic Model for Ontology Reuse

3.1. An Economic Analysis of Ontology Reuse

As previously mentioned, software reuse is defined as the use of existing software to develop new software. Essentially, the principle of reuse allows saving money, time, and may lead to increased quality due to risen maturity of reused components. Current software projects tend to maximize the use of reusable components and by that minimize the total effort related to the realization of the overall project [29]. In the area of software engineering, it is well known that reuse of existing components can lead to reduced cost as well as promotes good practices: Typically software reuse happens on the design level (i.e., via design patterns), on the code level (i.e., by copy-and-pasting lines of code), on the class or component level via class libraries, on the application level via application frameworks, or on the system level by reusing a whole system. As explained in [76], two types of decisions are involved in software reuse: the first is whether or not to acquire the software to reuse and the second is whether or not to reuse the software in particular instances. From the point of view of a company, reuse is seen as an investment, which is accompanied with costs.

The goal of an economic model for software reuse is most notably to provide means to quantitatively measure reuse benefits or more precisely the relationship between cost and benefit of reuse. By that they are supposed to help CEOs to make decisions about investments.

There are plenty of economic models for software reuse available, which are summarized in [56] or [76]. These models typically try to estimate either net benefits of a potential reuse investment (a-priori) or try to estimate the net benefit due to reuse after reuse occurred (a-posteriori). Their output is typically a financial value denoting cost savings or a profitability ratio.

Two types of economic models of reuse can be distinguished [76]:

- **Cost Estimation** models which intend to quantify costs and benefits of a reuse investment. Popular models in this category include COCOMO whose aim is to predict costs of software development [3] or Poulin's business case or product line model which concentrates on the return-on-investment (ROI) for an individual project [57].

- **Investment Analysis** techniques try to provide a figure for the cash flow resulting from the reuse of a model (cf. [16]). These techniques are typically applied on an output of cost estimation models. Some well-known investment-analysis techniques include *Discounted Cash Flow (DCF)* which accounts for the time value of money, *Net Present Value (NPV)* which compares the net benefits of two investments, or

Profitability Index (PI) which compares total benefits with total costs to determine favorable investments.

Economic models for reuse either take a corporate viewpoint or a system viewpoint. The former aims to determine the costs and benefits that occur throughout the whole corporation while the latter only considers costs and benefits applied to one particular system.

Typically different types of costs and benefits are considered in these models. The following categorization covers the most frequently occurring costs/benefit types [76]:

- **Development Benefit (DB)** which refers to the savings that the consumer gains by reusing software rather than developing a new one from scratch. Costs to be considered should include all costs occurring in the software development life cycle including tool and management costs. An often applied metric in this category is *RCR (Relative Cost of Reuse)* which compares "cost with reuse" vs. "cost without reuse" [57].

- **Development Cost (DC)** refers to the costs of producing software to be reused. Reusable software is typically more expensive than normal software due to increased documentation or testing efforts. A distinction is made between creating reusable software from scratch and adding reusability features to existing software. The ratio "costs of producing reusable software" vs. "costs to produce equivalent non-reusable software" is often called *RCWR (Relative Cost of Reuse)* [57].

- **Maintenance Cost and Benefit (MC and MB)** take into account the effect which the reuse of software has on the maintenance phase. The assumption is that reused software has higher quality and might decrease the costs for maintenance.

- **Other Costs and Benefits** include startup costs such as costs for initial training or ongoing costs such as library maintenance or update costs. Furthermore costs which might occur to other systems are classified in this category. These type of costs are typically called *ORCA (Other's Reuse Cost Avoidance)*.

A simplified framework for combing the different cost and benefit factors has been proposed in [76]:

$$B = DB + MB + otherbenefits \tag{1}$$

$$C = DC + MC + othercosts \tag{2}$$

In each of the existing economic models for software reuse these terms are usually broken down. A set of simple models to determine costs and benefits are, for instance, provided by Jensen in [29]: In order to economically analyze software reuse, he presents a set of models which support the determination of the relation of relative development costs, to the amount of reused components and to the type of the reused artifact. His goal is to show when and if software reuse provides a positive incentive based on a comparison of acquisition costs of components to reuse and prospected development costs of components from scratch. In a simple black box model he concludes that the maximum cost reduction for a software system with 50 percent reused code is only about 37 percent. These figures are based on relative cost values for different software engineering stages determined by

Boehm and others [3].

In order to develop an economic model for ontology reuse, whose goal is to be able to make estimates and decisions about the prospected benefits of reusing ontologies in quantifiable terms, cost and benefit drivers have to be identified and an appropriate formula has to be selected which expresses the relation between costs and benefits in ontology reuse. Based on the principle economic benefits of software reuse, formulated in [20], benefits of ontology reuse can be:

- Lower development costs.
- Higher ontology quality due to multiple testing and error removal opportunities reused over a number of applications.
- Reduced development schedule due to a reduced amount of development work.
- Lower maintenance costs due to lower levels of error creation.
- Reduced life cycle costs due to reduced development and maintenance costs.

Economically speaking, ontologies lack typical characteristics to be reusable off-the-shelf in cases where they are supposed to be integrated in other ontologies. Thus a black box model, such as the one proposed by Jensen, can not be equally applied to the reuse of ontologies. A typical black box component behavior is characterized in terms of an input set, an output set, and a relationship between both sets. It is most often the case that ontologies have to be treated as a white box, whose modification is required to meet the requirements of an ontology project. This might include alignment, merging, transforming, or integration of ontological elements. If white-box-reuse has to be considered, we have to take into account customization costs and thus this simplification does not hold. In order to determine these customization costs, we intend to further extend an existing cost estimation model for ontologies.

3.2. Towards an Economic Model for Ontology Reuse

In this section we sketch our planned steps to develop an economic model for ontology reuse. After an analysis of existing economic models for software reuse we base our efforts on the economic model for reuse which is part of the COCOMO II framework [3]. This is due to the following reasons: (i) COCOMO II aims to predict the costs of adapting software which is similar to "reuse with modification". This reflects a considerable amount of cases in which ontologies are reused. (ii) Besides core development variables, COCOMO II takes into account variables for locating, testing, and evaluation and thus the model can be naturally mapped to the ontology reuse process. (iii) Furthermore COCOMO II takes into account effort which has been initially put into the development of a component in order to guarantee reuse which is an important aspect to consider in ontology engineering as our recent survey in the realm of ontology engineering indicated [65].

In the following we first present ONTOCOM, an adaptation of COCOMO for ontology cost estimation. Second, we sketch how to apply COCOMO's economic model of reuse to ontologies.

3.2.1. The ONTOCOM Model

ONTOCOM (Ontology Cost Model) is a model for predicting the costs related to ontology engineering processes. The model is generic with respect to the fact that it allows the generation of cost models suitable for any particular ontology development strategy which is shown in [46].

Cost estimation methods can be used to measure and predict costs related to ontology engineering activities. As many cost estimation methods exist (cf. [3, 67]), appropriate cost estimation methods have to be selected in accordance with the particularities of the current project regarding product, personnel and process related aspects. Different cost estimation methods that were seen as relevant for the application within ONTOCOM are explained in [42] and [48].

Based on the current state of the art in ontology engineering the following methods were selected for the development of cost estimation methods for ontology engineering: The top-down, parametric, and expert-based method. It is argued in [42] and [48] why these act as a viable basis for that purpose.

ONTOCOM is realized in three distinct phases:

1. First, a **top-down breakdown** is made in order to reduce the complexity of the overall estimation: The whole ontology engineering process is split into multiple subprocesses based on the ontology engineering methodology applied.

2. The associated costs are then elaborated using the **parametric method** which results in a statistical prediction model.

3. In order to calibrate the model based on previous project data, **expert evaluations** are used to evaluate and revise the predictions of the initial model (a-priori-model). Together with the combination of empirical data this results in an **a-posteriori-model**.

The Work Breakdown Structure According to the general structure of available ontology engineering methodologies, the overall process is split into multiple sub-processes (cf. Figure 1):

1. Requirements Analysis

2. Conceptualization

3. Implementation

4. Evaluation

Depending on the ontology life cycle of the underlying methodology, these process steps are seen in a sequential order or occur in parallel. In some ontology engineering methodologies the activities *documentation*, *evaluation* or *knowledge acquisition* are seen as so-called support actions that occur in parallel to the main activities. The work breakdown structure is further detailed in [47].

The Parametric Equation The parametric method now integrates the efforts associated with each component of the work breakdown structure into an overall equation. The necessary person months are calculated by the following equation:

$$PM = A * Size^{\alpha} * \prod CD_i \tag{3}$$

In this formula *PM* identifies the calculated person-months. *A* is a baseline multiplicative calibration constant in person-months. *Size* is the size of the ontology, and α is a parameter for handling a possible non-linear behavior of the estimated effort contingent on the ontology size. The cost drivers are represented by CD_i and have five rating levels from very low to very high, depending on their relevance in the ontology engineering process [48].

The Cost Drivers The ONTOCOM cost drivers were carefully selected based on a literature survey regarding the state of the art in ontology engineering and based on expert interviews [46].

During the course of the definition of the model, three groups of cost drivers that have direct impact on the predication of the estimation were identified [48]:

Product-related cost drivers account for the influence of product properties on the overall costs. These include cost drivers for ontology building such as *Complexity of the Domain Analysis (DCPLX)* or *Complexity of the Ontology Integration (OI)* and cost drivers for reuse and maintenance such as *Complexity of the Ontology Evaluation (OE)* or *Complexity of the Ontology Modifications (OM)*.

Personnel-related cost drivers that emphasize the role of team experience or ability in the process. These include cost drivers such as *Ontologist / Domain Expert Capability (OCAP/DECAP)* or *Language and Tool Experience (LEXP / TEXP)*.

Project-related cost drivers take into account the overall setting of the engineering process. Cost drivers in this category include *Tool Support (TOOL)* or *Multi-site Development (SITE)*.

A detailed overview of the cost drivers can be found on the ONTOCOM website.[15]

The first release of the ONTOCOM model was evaluated on a data set of 36 ontologies. Using regression and Bayes analysis as described in [48] the model was calibrated which resulted in an initial prediction quality of 75% of the data points within a range of ±75% of the estimates. For the corresponding ±30% range the model covered 32% of the real-world data. These results were further optimized in a calibration done on a larger data set of 148 ontology development projects. The calibration used a combination of statistical methods, ranging from preliminary data analysis to regression and Bayes analysis, and resulted in a significant improvement of the prediction quality of up to 50% as explained in [65].

3.2.2. Extensions of ONTOCOM for Reuse

According to the methodology presented in Section 2.1., the ontology reuse process can be split into three distinct phases:

[15] `http://ontocom.sti-innsbruck.at`

1. *Ontology discovery* in which relevant ontologies are retrieved from available sources.
2. *Ontology evaluation and selection* in which the selected ontologies are evaluated according to the requirements and finally chosen to be used in the project.
3. *Ontology integration* in which the ontologies are finally integrated in a target ontology which might include a translation of the ontology into the target knowledge representation language, the extraction of relevant parts, or the alignment of concepts from the reused ontology and the target ontology.

For the sake of simplicity we assume that relevant ontologies are available as the costs of finding relevant ontologies are hard to determine.

In the following we describe cost drivers which are relevant with respect to ontology reuse. Compared to earlier work described in [42] we explicitly added a cost driver to account for the alignment costs of the reused ontology with the target ontology. The extension of the costs drivers is due based on personal experiences in ontology projects in which frequent alignments had to be made.

- **Ontology evaluation and selection:**
  - **Ontology Understandability (OU)**: This cost driver takes into account that reusing an ontology significantly depends on the ability of the involved persons (domain experts or ontologists) to understand the ontology. OU is influenced by other factors including the complexity and clarity of the conceptual model. The complexity is dependent on the size and expressivity of the ontology and the number of imported ontologies. Clarity is strongly dependent on the documentation of the ontology and its readability. This cost driver is in turn influenced by the capability of the involved engineers and their (technical) know how.
  - **Ontologist/Domain Expert Unfamiliarity (UNFM)**: This accounts for the additional effort which occurs if the user is unfamiliar with an ontology.
  - **Ontology Evaluation (OE)**: This cost driver accounts for the effort needed to determine whether an ontology satisfies the requirements that were posed to it.
- **Ontology Integration:**
  - **Ontology Translation (OT)**: OT reflects the costs arising by translating between different representation languages. Depending on the compatibility of the source and target language as well as tool support in this process, different types of effort might occur
  - **Ontology Modification (OM)**: This cost driver reflects the complexity of the modifications required to reflect the full set of requirements initially posed to the reused ontology.
  - **Ontology Alignment (OA)**: This cost driver covers the costs needed to align the reused with the target ontology in case of overlapping concepts.

As it can easily be seen from the suggested cost drivers, ontology reuse can in most cases not be considered as reuse of "components of the shelf (cots)" as typically considerable adaptations occur. This is mainly due to the fact that many ontologies were not explicitly defined to be partially reused. This fact hinders reuse and increases its effort.

3.2.3. Calculating the Relative Costs of Ontology Reuse

As outlined above, our aim is show the benefits of ontology reuse in quantitative terms. Therefore we adapt an existing economic model for software reuse to assess the savings due to reuse and consequently to determine the relative costs of reuse (RCR) of ontologies. Compared to simpler models which are introduced in [56, 76], COCOMO's aim is to predict how the total software costs can be reduced by adapting existing software by taking into account so-called cost-drivers as introduced above.

Most notably, COCOMO's model takes into account the ease of understanding, the familiarity with the reused software, and variables for locating, testing, and evaluation of the integrated software. Further it takes into account a REUSE effort modifier which is in its intention similar to RCRW ("Relative Cost of Reuse") which accounts for additional reusability in the developed system.

Based on COCOMO's reuse model, a model to calculate development benefits (DB) and development costs (DC) for ontologies could look as follows:

$$B = DB \tag{4}$$

$$DB = RCR = DC_N - DC_R \tag{5}$$

$$DC_N = A * SIZE^{\alpha} * \prod CD_i * REUSE \tag{6}$$

$$DC_R = A * SIZE^{\alpha}_{Equiv} * \prod CD_i * REUSE \tag{7}$$

$$SIZE_{Equiv} = SIZE_{Scratch} + (Size_{Adapted} * (\frac{1 - OT}{100}) * AAM \tag{8}$$

$$AAM = \{ \begin{array}{ll} \frac{OE+AAF(1+(0.02*OU*UNFM))}{100} & if\ AAF \leq 50 \\ \frac{OE+AAF+(OU*UNFM)}{100} & if\ AAF > 50 \end{array} \tag{9}$$

$$AAF = \gamma_1(OM_{ConceptualModel}) + \gamma_2(OM_{Code}) + \gamma_3(OA) \tag{10}$$

where

B Overall benefit

DB Development benefit

DC Development costs; DC_N: Normal development costs; DC_R: Development costs with reuse

α, β, γ Empirically determined constants

RCR Relative cost of reuse (with modification)

AAM Amount of modification

AAF Adaptation adjustment factor

REUSE Required reuse; calibrated effort multiplier which is determined based on historical project data.

These formulas allow to calculate the benefits of reusing ontologies across a number of systems in quantitative terms. As outlined in [76], setting AAF to zero would mean that RCR becomes the cost of reuse "without modification". In order to operationalize the model, we have to calibrate it and get data to adjust the effort multipliers.

3.3. Application of the Model

In the subsequent section we outline an exemplary case study which demonstrates how to apply the model to calculate cost and benefit of reusing ontologies in a particular situation. The case study is fictive, however backed up with data gathered from real-world ontology development projects (cf. [65]).

The region of Tyrol intends to build an innovative information portal to inform visitors about the culture, relevant sights, and events and happenings taking place in the region. To represent this information, one or multiple ontologies shall be developed. The project manager, responsible for the portal, intends to discuss different development options: the development of the ontologies (1) from scratch or (2) by reusing already existing ontologies. He thus intends to compute the *development benefit* of both options.

Based on the requirements and an initial conceptual model, the size of the ontology to be developed is estimated at roughly 750 entities.[16] After an initial investigation of existing ontologies to represent, for instance, events or touristic information, the cost drivers relevant for the reuse model can be estimated as follows:[17]

- **Ontology Translation (OT)**: 100 percent of the existing ontologies have to be translated to the target knowledge representation language used.
- **Ontology Modification (OM)**: 10 percent of the existing ontologies have to be modified before reusing them, both at the conceptual and the implementation level.
- **Ontology Alignment (OA)**: 20 percent of the entities of the reused ontologies have to be aligned with other ontologies.
- **Ontology Evaluation (OE)**: The evaluation of the ontologies to be reused can be easily done because of their good documentation (Rating: *Very Low*).
- **Ontology Understanding (OU)**: Both the conceptual model as well as its implementation are not too hard to understand (Rating: *Nominal*).
- **Ontologist/Domain Expert Unfamiliarity (UNFM)**: Both domain experts and ontology engineers are not familiar with the ontologies to be integrated (Rating: *Very High*).
- **Required Reuse (REUSE)**: The ontology to be developed shall be usable as an application independent domain ontology (Rating: *Nominal*).

---

[16]including concepts, properties, and axioms

[17]The impact of some cost drivers is rated according to the guidelines from ONTOCOM on a five-point scale from *Very Low* to *Very High*; see `http://ontocom.sti-innsbruck.at/ontocom.htm`.

The factors used in the model can be calculated as follows:[18]

$$
\begin{aligned}
SIZE &= 750 \\
SIZE_{Scratch} &= 600 \\
Size_{Adapted} &= 150 \\
AAF &= 0.3 * 10 + 0.4 * 10 + 0.3 * 20 = 13 \\
AMM &= \frac{2 + 13(1 + (0.02 * 30 * 1))}{100} = 0.23 \\
SIZE_{Equiv} &= 600 + (150 * (\frac{1-1}{100}) * 0.23 = 634.5 \\
DC_N &= 4.00 \\
DC_R &= 3.90 \\
DB &= 4.00 - 3.90 = 0.10
\end{aligned}
$$

Based on the small development benefit of 0.1 PM, the project manager decides to reuse the existing ontologies. The reasons are the saved costs and other qualitative benefits such as increased compatibility with other applications using the same ontologies or increased maturity.

The development costs (DC) have been calculated using the calibrated ONTOCOM model. Further it has to be noted, that we used non-calibrated effort multipliers as proposed by the original COCOMO II – model to calculate the other factors of the reuse model. In order to operationalize the model, the effort multipliers used therein have to be estimated by experts and subsequently calibrated based on existing project data to reflect existing ontology engineering practices.

4. Conclusions and Outlook

It is widely acknowledged that the efficient and effective operation of the reuse process is a precondition for the large-scale take-up of semantic technologies. However, the challenges associated with achieving this objective – in the Semantic Web context or beyond – are also well-known, given the inherent limitations of realizing highly reusable, commonly agreed-upon knowledge conceptualizations. The current state of the art in the ontology-engineering field highlights the need for additional instruments to increase the reusability of existing ontological sources in new application settings, and to aid humans in carrying out this process.

We analyzed the technical feasibility of ontology reuse and surveyed recent ontology development projects which highlighted a considerable frequency of ontologies reused in practice. In contrast to that, methodological support for reuse is mostly lacking. In order to provide statements about the economic feasibility of ontology reuse we proposed an extension of the ONTOCOM model for the cost estimation of ontology engineering projects which is itself based on mature models from the area of software engineering. The model

[18] We use the scales for the factors as proposed in [3]: UNFM from 0-1 (steps of 0.2); OU from 50-10 (steps of 10); OE from 0-8 (steps 2). Further we use the pre-defined values for γ_1, γ_2, and γ_3: $\gamma_1 = 0.4$, $\gamma_2 = 0.3$, and $\gamma_3 = 0.3$.

is supposed to show the benefits of ontology reuse in monetary terms. Our next steps are to gather a considerable amount of data about ontology engineering projects in which ontologies have been reused in order to calibrate the model and instantiate it for practical use.

References

[1] A. Advani, S. Tu, and M. Musen, Domain Modeling with Integrated Ontologies: Principles for Reconciliation and Reuse, Tech. Report SMI-97-0681, Stanford Medical Informatics, 1998.

[2] J. Arpírez, A. Gómez-Pérez, A. Lozano-Tello, and H. Pinto, Reference Ontology and $(\mathrm{ONTO})^2$ Agent: The Ontology Yellow Pages, *Knowledge and Information Systems* **2** (2000), 387–412.

[3] B. Boehm, Software engineering economics, Prentice Hall PTR, Upper Saddle River, NJ, USA, 1981.

[4] M. Bonifacio, P. Bouquet, and P. Traverso, Enabling distributed knowledge management: Managerial and technological implications, *Informatik-Zeitschrift der schweizerischen Informatikorganisationen* **1** (2002), 23–29.

[5] I. Cantador, M. Fernandez, and P. Castells, *Proceedings of the 1st International Workshop on Social and Collaborative Construction of Structured Knowledge, collocated with WWW'07*, , , 2007.

[6] G. Carenini and J. Moore, *Proceedings of 17th Symposium on Computer Applications in Medical Care SCAMC1993*, , , 1993, pp. 725–729.

[7] B. Chandrasekaran and T.R. Johnson, *Second Generation Expert Systems*, , , 1993, pp. 232–272.

[8] C. Van Damme, M. Hepp, and K. Siorpaes, *Proceedings of the ESWC 2007 Workshop "Bridging the Gap between Semantic Web and Web 2.0"*, , , 2007.

[9] L. Ding and T. Finin, *Proceedings of the International Semantic Web Conference ISWC2006*, , , Springer, 2006, pp. 242–257.

[10] H. Do, S. Melnik, and E. Rahm, *Web, Web-Services, and Database Systems*, , , Springer, 2002, pp. 221–237.

[11] H. Do and E. Rahm, *Proceedings of the 28th Very Large Data Bases Conference VLDB2002*, , , 2002, pp. 610–621.

[12] A. Doan, J. Madhavan, and P. Domingos, *Proceedings of the 11th International World Wide Web Conference WWW2002*, , , 2002, pp. 662–673.

[13] A. Doan, J. Madhavan, P. Domingos, and A. Halevy, Ontology matching: A machine learning approach, *Handbook on Ontologies* (2004), 385–516.

[14] M. Ehrig and Y. Sure, *Proceedings of the 1st European Semantic Web Symposium ESWS2001*, , , 2004, pp. 76–91.

[15] J. Euzenat and P. Shvaiko, Ontology matching, Springer, 2007.

[16] J Favaro, *ICSR '96: Proceedings of the 4th International Conference on Software Reuse*, , (Washington, DC, USA), IEEE Computer Society, 1996, p. 136.

[17] J. Favaro, R. Kenneth, and F. Paul, Value based software reuse investment, *Ann. Softw. Eng.* **5** (1998), 5–52.

[18] D. Fensel, Ontologies: A silver bullet for knowledge management and electronic commerce, Springer, 2001.

[19] W. Frakes and C. Terry, Software Reuse: Metrics and Models, *ACM Computing Surveys* **28** (1996), 415–435.

[20] J. E. Gaffney, Jr. and R. D. Cruickshank, *ICSE '92: Proceedings of the 14th international conference on Software engineering*, , , 1992, pp. 327–337.

[21] A. Gangemi, C. Catenacci, M. Ciaramita, and J. Lehmann, *Proceedings of the European Semantic Web Conference (ESWC 2006)*, , , Springer, 2006, pp. 140–154.

[22] A. Gangemi, D. M. Pisanelli, and G. Steve, An overview of the ONIONS project: Applying ontologies to the integration of medical terminologies, *Data Knowledge Engineering* **31** (1999), no. 2, 183–220.

[23] F. Giunchiglia and P. Shvaiko, Semantic matching, *Knowledge Engineering Review* **18** (2004), no. 3, 265–280.

[24] J. Golbeck, G. Fragoso, F. Hartel, J. Hendler, B. Parsia, and J. Oberthaler, The National Cancer Institute's Thesaurus and Ontology, *Journal of Web Semantics* **1** (2003), no. 1.

[25] A. Gómez-Pérez, M. Fernández-Lopéz, and O. Corcho, Ontological engineering – with examples form the areas of knowledge management, e-commerce and the semantic web, Advanced Information and Knowledge Processing, Springer, 2004.

[26] A. Gómez-Pérez and D. Rojas-Amaya, *Proceedings of the 11th European Knowledge Acquisition Workshop EKAW1999*, , , 1999, pp. 139–157.

[27] T. R. Gruber, Toward principles for the design of ontologies used for knowledge sharing, *International Journal of Human-Computer Studies* **43** (1995), no. 5/6, 907–928.

[28] N. Guarino, *Proceedings of the 1st International Conference on Formal Ontologies in Information Systems FOIS1998*, , , IOS-Press, 1998, pp. 3–15.

[29] R. Jensen, An economic analysis of software reuse, *The Journal of Defense Software Engineering* **Dez** (2004).

[30] Y. Kalfoglou and M. Schorlemmer, *Proceedings of the Confederated International Conferences: On the Move to Meaningful Internet Systems (DOA, CoopIS and ODBASE 2002)*, , , 2002, pp. 1132–1151.

[31] R. Klamma, M. Spaniol, and D. Renzel, *Proceedings of I-Media'07, International Conference on New Media Technology and Semantic Systems, J.UCS (Journal of Universal Computer Science)*, , , 2007, pp. 163–171.

[32] M. Klein, A. Kiryakov, D. Ognyanov, and D. Fensel, *Proceedings of the 13th International Conference on Knowledge Engineering and Management EKAW2002*, , , 2002, pp. 197–212.

[33] A. Lozano-Tello and A. Gómez-Pérez, ONTOMETRIC: A Method to Choose the Appropriate Ontology, *Journal of Database Management* **15** (2004), no. 2, 1–18.

[34] J. Madhavan, P. A. Bernstein, and E. Rahm, *Proceedings of the 27th International Conference on Very Large Data Bases VLDB2001*, , , 2001, pp. 49–58.

[35] A. Maedche, B. Motik, N. Silva, and R. Volz, *Proceedings of the 13th European Conference on Knowledge Engineering and Knowledge Management EKAW2002*, , , 2002, pp. 235–250.

[36] D. L. McGuinness, R. Fikes, J. Rive, and S. Wilder, *Proceedings of the 17th International National Conference on Artificial Intelligence AAAI2000*, , , 2000, pp. 1123–1124.

[37] S. Melnik, H. Garcia-Molina, and E. Rahm, *Proceedings of the 18th International Conference on Data Engineering ICDE2002*, , , IEEE Computer Society, 2002, pp. 117–128.

[38] M. Mochol, The methodology for finding suitable ontology matching approaches, Ph.D. thesis, Free University of Berlin, 2009.

[39] N. F. Noy and M. A. Musen, *Proceedings of the 17th International National Conference on Artificial Intelligence AAAI2000*, , , 2000, pp. 450–455.

[40] B. Omelayenko, *Proceedings of the Workshop on Knowledge Transformation for the Semantic Web at the 15th European Conference on Artificial Intelligence IJCAI2002*, , , 2002, pp. 76–83.

[41] E. Paslaru-Bontas, *Proceedings of the 1st International ISWC Workshop on Semantic Web Case Studies and Best Practices for eBusiness SWCASE2005*, , , 2005.

[42] E. Paslaru Bontas and M. Mochol, A cost model for ontology engineering, Technical Report TR-B-05-03, Freie Universitt Berlin, Germany, 2005.

[43] E. Paslaru-Bontas, M. Mochol, and R. Tolksdorf, *Proceedings of the 5th International Conference on Knowledge Management IKNOW2005*, , , 2005, pp. 345–353.

[44] E. Paslaru-Bontas, D. Schlangen, and T. Schrader, *Proceedings of the 4th International Conference on Ontologies, Databases, and Applications of Semantics ODBASE2005*, , , 2005, pp. 1296–1313.

[45] E. Paslaru-Bontas, S. Tietz, R. Tolksdorf, and T. Schrader, *Proceedings of 3rd International Conference on Ontologies, Databases, and Applications of Semantics ODBASE2004*, , , 2004, pp. 637–653.

[46] E. Paslaru Bontas Simperl and C. Tempich, How much does it cost? applying ontocom to diligent, Tech. Report TRB-05-20, FU Berlin, 2005.

[47] E. Paslaru Bontas Simperl, C. Tempich, and M. Mochol, *Technologies for Business Information Systems*, , , Springer, 2006.

[48] E. Paslaru Bontas Simperl, C. Tempich, and Y. Sure, *Proceedings of the 5th International Semantic Web Conference ISWC2006*, , , 2006.

[49] C. Patel, K. Supekar, Y. Lee, and E. K. Park, *Proceedings of the 5th ACM international workshop on Web information and data management WIDM 2003*, , , 2003, pp. 58–61.

[50] A. Pease, I. Niles, and J. Li, *Working Notes of the AAAI-2002 Workshop on Ontologies and the Semantic Web*, , , 2002.

[51] B. J. Peterson, W. A. Andersen, and J. Engel, *Proceedings of the 5th International Workshop on Knowledge Represenation Meets Databases KRDB1998: Innovative Application Programming and Query Interfaces*, , , 1998, pp. 2.1–2.10.

[52] H. S. Pinto and J. P. Martins, *Proceedings of the International Conference on Knowledge Capture K-CAP2001*, , , ACM Press, 2001, pp. 131–138.

[53] H. S. Pinto, S. Staab, and C. Tempich, *Proceedings of the European Conference of Artificial Intelligence ECAI2004*, , , 2004, pp. 393–397.

[54] D.M. Pisanelli, A. Gangemi, and G. Steve, Ontological analysis of the UMLS metathesaurus, *JAMIA* **5** (1998), 810–814.

[55] J. Poole and J.A. Campbell, A novel algorithm for matching conceptual and related graphs, *Conceptual Structures: Applications, Implementation and Theory* (1995), 293–307.

[56] J. Poulin, Measuring software reuse: principles, practices, and economic models, Addison-Wesley Longman Publishing Co., Inc., Boston, MA, USA, 1996.

[57] J Poulin and J Caruso, *Software Reusability, 1993. Proceedings Advances in Software Reuse., Selected Papers from the Second International Workshop on*, , , 1993, pp. 152–166.

[58] E. Rahm and P. A. Bernstein, A survey of approaches to automatic schema matching, *Journal of Very Large Data Bases* **10** (2001), no. 4, 334–350.

[59] T. Rattenbury, N. Good, and M. Naaman, *Proceedings of the 30th Annual International ACM SIGIR Conference (SIGIR 07)*, , , 2007, pp. 103–110.

[60] T. Russ, A. Valente, R. MacGregor, and W. Swartout, *Proceedings of the 12th Workshop on Knowledge Acquisition, Modeling and Management KAW1999*, , , 1999.

[61] M. Sabou, V. Lopez, and E. Motta, *Proceedings of the 15th International Conference on Knowledge Engineering and Knowledge Management EKAW 2006*, , , Springer, 2006, pp. 96–111.

[62] S. Schulz and U. Hahn, Medical knowledge reegineering - converting major portions of the UMLS into a terminological knowledge base, *International Journal of Medical Informatics* **64** (2001), no. 2/3, 207–221.

[63] S. Schulze-Kremer, B. Smith, and A. Kumar, *Proceedings of the Medinfo2004*, , , 2004.

[64] P. Shvaiko and J. Euzenat, *Proceedings of The 7th International Conference on Ontologies, DataBases, and Applications of Semantics (ODBASE)*, , , 2008.

[65] E. Simperl, I. Popov, and T. Bürger, *Proceedings of the 6th European Semantic Web Conference (ESWC 2009), May 31 - June 04 2009 (forthcoming)*, , , 2009.

[66] S. Staab and R. Studer (eds.), Handbook on ontologies, International Handbooks on Information Systems, Springer Verlag, 2004.

[67] R. D. Stewart, R. M. Wyskida, and J. D. Johannes, Cost estimator's reference manual, Wiley, 1995.

[68] L. Stojanovic, A. Maedche, B. Motik, and N. Stojanovic, *Proceedings of the 13th European Conference on Knowledge Engineering and Management EKAW2002*, , , 2002, pp. 285–300.

[69] G. Stumme and A. Maedche, *Proceedings of the 17th International Joint Conference on Artificial Intelligence IJCAI2001*, , , 2001, pp. 225–230.

[70] Y. Sure, S. Staab, and R. Studer, Methodology for development and employment of ontology based knowledge management applications., *SIGMOD Record* **31** (2002), no. 4, 18–23.

[71] B. Swartout, R. Patil, K. Knight, and T. Russ, *Proceedings of the 10th Knowledge Acquisition for Knowledge-Based Systems Workshop*, , , 1996.

[72] K. Tu and Y. Yu, *Proceedings of the 10th International Conference on Database Systems for Advanced Applications DASFAA05*, , , 2005, pp. 888–893.

[73] M. Uschold, P. Clark, M. Healy, K. Williamson, and S. Woods, *Proceedings of the 11th Knowledge Acquisition Workshop KAW1998*, , , 1998.

[74] M. Uschold, M. Healy, K. Williamson, P. Clark, and S. Woods, *Proceedings of the 1st International Conference on Formal Ontology and Information Systems - FOIS'98*, , , 1998, pp. 179–192.

[75] M. Uschold and M. King, *Proceedings of the IJCAI1995, Workshop on Basic Ontological Issues in Knowledge Sharing*, , , 1995.

[76] E. Wiles, Economic models of software reuse: A survey, comparison and partial validation, Technical Report UWA-DCS-99-032, Department of Computer Science, University of Wales, 1999.

In: Data Management in the Semantic Web
Editor: Hal Jin, pp. 105-129
ISBN: 978-1-61122-862-5

Chapter 5

COMPUTATIONAL LOGIC AND KNOWLEDGE REPRESENTATION ISSUES IN DATA ANALYSIS FOR THE SEMANTIC WEB

***J. Antonio Alonso-Jiménez*[1], *Joaquín Borrego-Díaz*[2], *Antonia M. Chávez-González*[3] *and F. Jesús Martín-Mateos*[4]**
Department of Computer Science and Artificial Intelligence
E. T. S. Ingeniería Informática, Universidad de Sevilla, Sevilla, Spain

Abstract

The relationships between the logical and representational features on ontologies are analysed. Through several questions, this chapter restates the use of Computational logic in Ontology Engineering.

1. Introduction

The envisioned Semantic Web (SW) proposes the extension of the existing Web in order to process data as knowledge [11] . In order to achieve this aim, the project combines long standing traditions in Computer Science as Knowledge Engineering, Artificial Intelligence and Computational Logic, because the pair *data-ontology* will represent the knowledge bases (or *Knowledge DataBase*, KDB), aim of study in the SW. In spite of its benefits some realistic views claim several obstacles. Some of them come from the problematic use of ontologies in two ways: as formalized representations of consensual domain and as logical artefacts for automated reasoning. For example, an important problem is the need for creating and maintaining ontologies. On the one hand, such task is, from the point of view of

[1] E-mail address: jalonso@us.es
[2] E-mail address: jborrego@us.es
[3] E-mail address: tchavez@us.es
[4] E-mail address: fjesus@us.es

companies, dangerous and expensive, because every change in ontology would affect the overall knowledge of the organization. On the other hand, it is also hard to be automated, because some criteria for revision cannot be fully formalized, losing logical trust. Other example is the problem of providing metadata, a difficult task that the users tend to avoid: to save costs, the initial ontology may have been built by an ontology learning system, but then we have to debug it. An ontological analysis of the intended meaning of the elements of the ontology is even necessary (as [41]).

Despite its importance, the tools designed to transform do not analyze, in general, their effect on the (automated) reasoning. Thus, the realistic immediate future raises several challenges, some of them by dealing with foundational issues Semantic Web, the abstract (ontological) definition of data, and the work with incomplete or provisional ontologies through the evolution from current WWW to SW (as well as the evolution of the ontologies) [4].

In this chapter we discuss some issues (from the viewpoint of Computational Logic) that arise when ontologies are considered as logical theories with relevant features related to Knowledge Representation paradigm. We emphasize the problems found in an initial phase of data processing, namely *data analysis*. Some of the foundational challenges studied in [4] are restated according to new approaches or perspectives.

2. Automated Reasoning for Ontology Engineering

The role of Automated Reasoning (RA) in the Semantic Web project is concerned with the stack *proof* in SW cake (see fig. 1). Proof and Representation are two sides of the Knowledge Representation tradition in Artificial Intelligence field, according to Knowledge Representation Hypothesis (KRH) [74]. In spite of the splitting that KRH establishes, the reasoning with ontologies needs of some strong relations between these two aspects (especially when nonstandard reasoning services are considered). For example, SW can not be understood as a static environment, due to the dynamic nature of WWW. Also, there exists need for an explanation of the reasoning behind cleaning programs [34], because the ontologies represent consensual domains.

2.1. Logical Databases versus Knowledge Dynamism

Reasoning with KDB in a dynamic environment as SW is quite a hard task. On the one hand, as we said, KDB are continuously updated (because the user would add new facts in the future). Thus, even if we have a good KDB, the difficulties will begin again with the future introduction of data, and anomalies will therefore persist. On the other hand, usually the *intentional theory* of the KDB (i.e. the ontology) is not consistent with the classical axiomatization of database theory. Nevertheless, the self database represents a real model. In fact, reasoning with KDB works on “Open World Assumption" while classical database work on “Closed World Assumption".

Other reasons have to be found by means of a necessary revision of the verification and validation of Knowledge Based Systems problem [9]. It is also necessary to bear in mind, when we work with many information sources, that to focus query plans on selected sources we need to estimate the quality of the answer, which is a task that can become a critical issue[70].

In fact, an interesting option to integrate ARS in the SW framework consists of to consider ARS as a module of deliberative behaviour of SW agents. This idea enforces to keep the balance between real-time processing and complex reasoning [1, 2].

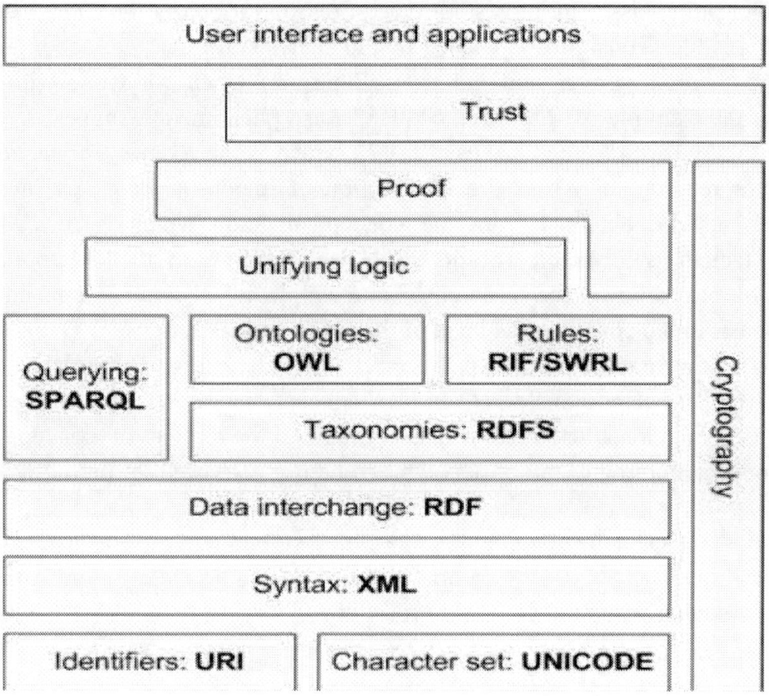

Figure 1. Semantic Web Cake.

3. Poor Representation and Deficient Ontologies

The relationship between poor representation and logical features of theories is an interesting research line in Model Theory. Since we assume that the content of SW is (explicitly or implicitly) in the form of logical formulas, that the use of ontologies in data management implies a logical reasoning deeper than the one that so far we believe is advisable. An ontology is not only a logical theory, but something with additional features like backward compatibility [42]. However, one must accept that logical trust provides a first security criterion, but representational issues must be considered.

In a logical setting, data are ground terms constrained by the ontology language, and, more important, whose behaviour is specified by the ontology. An ontology partially built constraints us to reason with a poor language or a deficient set of axioms.

There are several reasons for the persistence of unstable ontologies. Most of what the research does is related to the development of ontology representation paradigms and it has not a similar counterpart in other features associated with the evolution as persistence, transactions or scalability [57]. Experience has shown that the effort to build a *robust* ontology, including the large body of information of a company in the universe of metadata, is expensive. So the investment must be promoted in early stages, impeding significant changes later.

3.1. Skolem Noise and Poor Representation

In ATP-aided cleaning tasks, an interesting type of reason for *bottom-up change generation in ontologies* [57] is the *Skolem noise*, caused by the analysis of track interaction among KDB, the automated theorem prover and the user (Figure 2) when we work with provisional ontologies. In the example of Figure 2, Skolem noise phenomenon suggest that we should add to the ontology (even to the core used in [2], which is the *Region Connection Calculus*, RCC) the interpretation of $f1 as the intersection of regions (when they intersect). This interpretation must be obtained from the conceptualization which is formalized by the ontology. In fact, it is advisable to add weak specifications of this interpretation to the ontology in order to empower the reasoning. For example, in [2] some axioms on intersection are added in basis to the compactness level of the set of regions[1].

Returning to the representational perspective, a similar notion to Skolem noise in First Order Logic (FOL) can be considered: hidden concepts in data. Formal Context Analysis (FCA) [35] is a mathematical theory that formalizes the notion of concept and allows computing concept hierarchies out of data tables, and it is also used for ontology mining from folksonomies [48].

Lastly, note that specialized automated reasoning systems for SW (as Racer or Pellet) do not detect these kinds of logical symptoms because decidable Description Logics has been designed for reasoning with tableau-based procedures.

3.2. A Special Case: Semantic Mobile Web 2.0

An interesting challenge comes from a key convergence for the future of telecommunications. On the one hand, the great success of mobile networks implantation provide us with a global and ubiquitous net and, on the other hand, the exploding of social nets in Web 2.0 provides to users with tools for generating content of any kind. The convergence of the two global networks (see fig. 3, extracted from the book [47]) leads new kinds of personal communication and public sharing contents, example of mobile life streaming. Despite this convergence -seems to be the ultimate convergence- more work on knowledge interoperability among heterogeneous devices (mobile phones, Web 2.0 smash-ups, Semantic Web or Intranets) will be needed. This convergence is called *Metaweb*[2]. The special features of mobile devices make hard the convergence of Mobile Web 2.0 with the Semantic Web. These may lead a new digital divide between Mobile Nets and Semantic Web or Intranets. This problem should be (at least partially) solved before massive user content generation, and it seems advisable to work with lightweight ontologies (inspired in folksonomies, classifications systems, etc.).

1 The compactness level of a map $\pounds$ is the least $n > 0$ such that the intersection of a set of regions of $\pounds$ is equal to the intersection of n regions of the set.

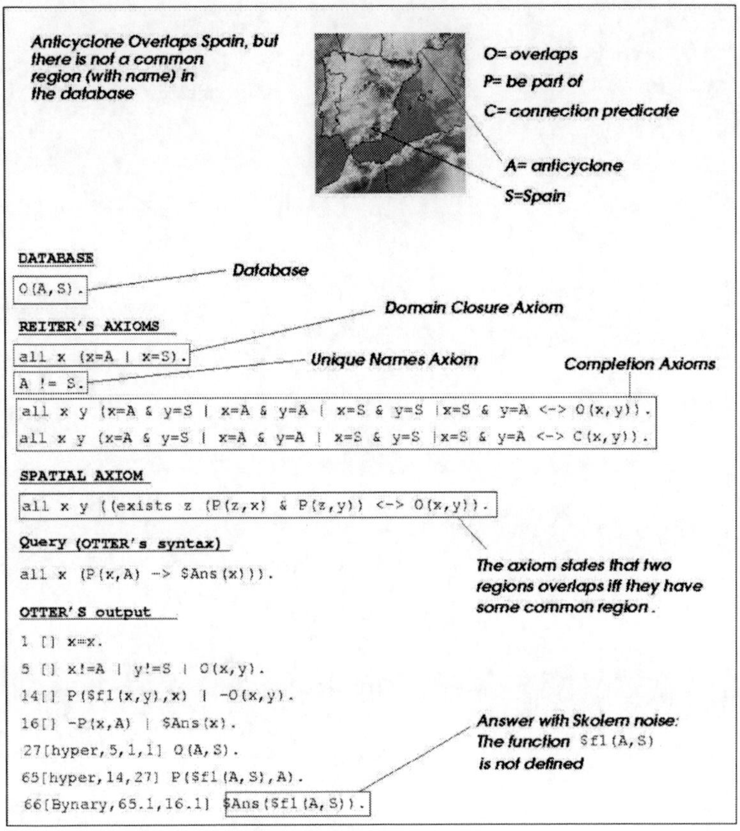

Figure 2. A naïf example of Skolem noise obtained by the system OTTER, reasoning with a poor ontology 2.0.

The convergence between Semantic Web and Mobile Web 2.0 depends on the specific management of ontologies. Ontologies and tags/folksonomies are two knowledge representation tools that must be reconciliated in Metaweb projects. In [7], a Metaweb platform which uses FCA as an ontological representation of tags is presented (Mowento). Roughly speaking, ontology class X, in Mowento ontology, is intended as the class of digital objects with tags X. In fact, Mowento ontology is extracted from several experiments with our mobile application and an arbitrary set of tags. Attribute exploration method is used to refine this ontology, as well as, to obtain a system for (post)suggesting tags. This decision was useful to solve the tedious task of tagging by means of mobile phones, because the ontology that is offered in a mobile application is a hierarchy of tags extracted from concept lattice, given by FCA. In this way, the interoperability among sets of tags from different users is (partially) solved. Nevertheless, it is necessary to augment and improve the set of tags, by means of suggestion tags method, related to original user's tags. Mowento use the stem basis [35], associated to the ontology of tasks, as knowledge basis for a production system of suggested tags. These will be implemented as a new agent's behaviour, associated to the document at the platform.

---

[2] See the text "New version of my "metaweb" graph { the future of the net in N. Spivack's blog *Minding the Planet* (2004), http://novaspivac.typepad.com/novaspivacks_ weblog/2004/04/new_version_of_html

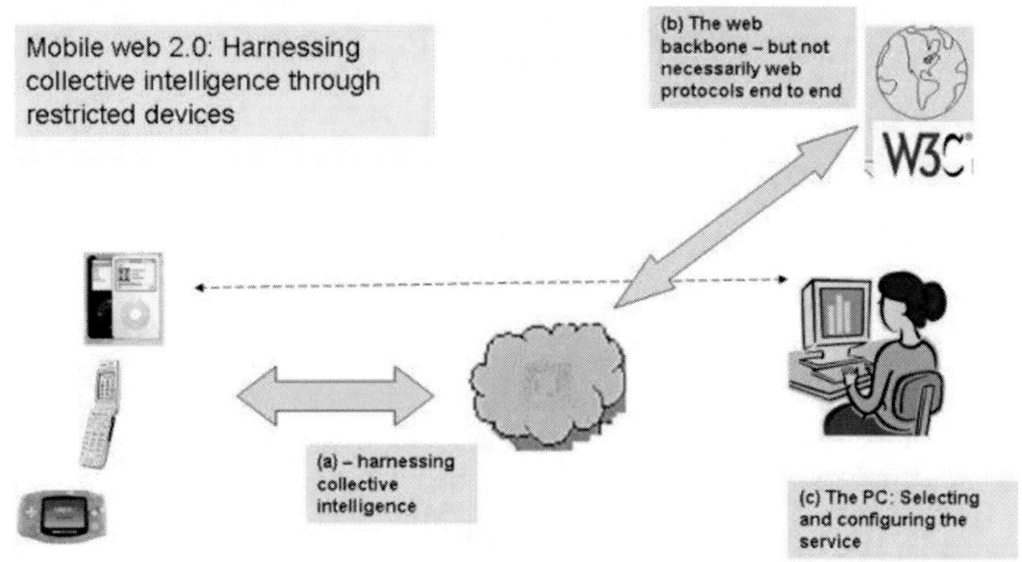

Figure 3. Mobile Web 2.0.

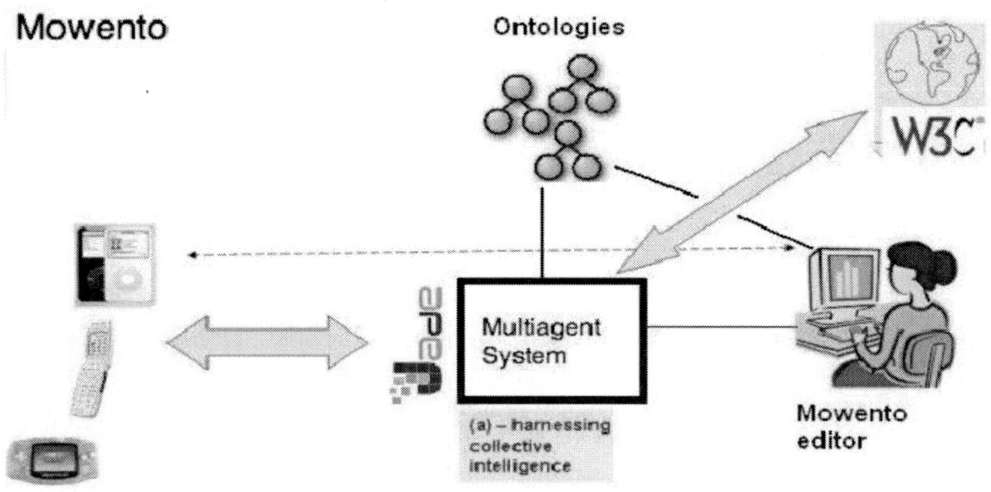

Figure 4. Mobile Semantic Web 2.0.

The semantic tasks are executed by a multiagent system, with a multi-role society where some different kind of agents can be found. Our aim is suggesting new knowledge (tags) to mobile-network users, which makes tagging process easier and improve the audiovisual contents organization. This task will be a post-tagging task by the WWW interface and it will be guided by the multiagent system, in order to improve the features of MW 2.0 explained above, like managing personal information, collecting and sharing digital objects.

4. When Is an Ontology Robust?

Above case study suggest several questions about ontology evolution. It seems unpredictable when tag-based ontology becomes stable. In general, the answer is no. Or at least until the meaning of stable, or better, *robust*, is clear.

4.1. Representational Perspective

The ontologies are presumably designed to protect us from incorrect management of information. But, can we be sure of the current ontology? Is it possible to predict that only minor changes will be applied? Ontologies need to be maintained just like other parts of a system (for example, by refinement [6] or versioning [50]). The definition of ontology robustness has several perspectives; all are necessary but none is sufficient.

From the SW perspective, the desiderata for a *robustness* notion come from some of the requirements to exploit SW ontologies, mainly in two of them [42]:

- *SW ontology should be able to extend other ontologies with new terms and definitions.*
- *The revision of an ontology should not change the well-foundness of resources that commit to an earlier version of the ontology.*

Nevertheless, even if it can be extended, it is evident that the *core* of the ontology should be stable. We understand *core* as a portion of the source of the ontology that we consider as the sound representation of a theory with well known properties, accepted as the best for the concepts contained in the ontology. It is advisable that the top of the ontology (general concepts) is included in the core, preferably by choosing a standard proposal for it, for example SUMO[3]. A formal and practical approach to this kind of extensions is the lattice-categorical ones [16] described in section 5.

4.2. Computational Logic Perspective

From a logical point of view, *robust ontology* should mean *complete logical theory*, and this definition might be applied in the context of OWL[4] full language, or in any case, it may be useful for some coherent parts of an ontology. However, this is not a local notion: minor changes compromise logical completeness in a dramatic way. Other logical notions, such as *categoricity*, clash with natural logical principles for reasoning in databases as Closed World Assumption or Unique Names Principles, or it is hard to achieve.

Therefore, robustness should be a combination of both perspectives, along with a notion of *clear* ontology, as opposed to messy ontology. In [4] we propose the following (informal) definition:

---

3 http://ontology.teknowledge.com/
4 http://www.w3.org/TR/owl-features/

An ontology is robust if its core is clear, stable (except for extensions), every model of its core exhibits similar properties with respect to the core language, and it is able to admit (minor) changes made outside of the core without compromising core consistency.

We understand *similar properties* as a set of metalogical properties, which brings us to the conclusion that all their models are, in essence, the same: they can not be distinguished by means of natural properties.

But the robustness can not be understood without considering some dynamic respects. Mainly, we regard robustness as a measure: ontology evolution extends the core to a big portion of the ontology almost only leaving out data. This evolution allows us to locate the possible inconsistencies in the data, thus approximating the problem to the integrity constraint checking.

5. Lattice Categorical Theories as Robust Ontologies

A weaker notion of robustness that combines representational and logic features is studied in a series of papers (see [16] for a compendium of main results, and [18]). Algorithms to solve several logical problems that ontological evolution raises are designed.

The lattice categoricity is based on categoricity of the structure of the concepts of the ontology. For the sake of clarity, it is supposed that the set of concepts has a lattice structure. Actually, this is not a constraint: there are methods to extract ontologies from data which produce such structure (such as the Formal Concepts Analysis [35]) and, in general, the ontology is easy to be extended by definition, verifying lattice structure. In [3] we have analysed the avaibility of FCA automated reasoning by means interactive theorem provers (in this case, PVS).

A theory T is called a lattice categorical (l.c.) theory if whatever pair of equational lattice descriptions of concept hierarchy of T are equivalent (modulo CWA and Unique Names principle). By using automated theorem provers and model finders we are able to decide if an ontology is lattice categorical.

On one hand, a *lattice categorical* theory is the one that proves the lattice structure of its basic relationships, specified by a set of equations called *skeleton*. This notion is weaker than categoricity or completeness. On the other hand, lattice categoricity is a reasonable requirement: the theory must certify the basic relationships among the primitive concepts. In [16] we argued that completeness can be replaced by *lattice categoricity* to facilitate the design of feasible methods for extending ontologies.

As we have already commented, the robustness of an ontology have to be related with the relationship between the ontology and its extensions. The knowledge preservation through extensions is both a logic problem and a KR problem.

5.1. Computational Viewpoint of Ontological Extensions

A theory T is a conservative extension of a theory T' (or T' is a *conservative retraction*) if every consequence of T in the language of T' is a consequence of T' too. Conservative extensions have been deeply investigated in Mathematical Logic, and they allow to formalize several notions concerning refinements and modularity in Computer Science (for example, in formal verification [55],[6],[62]). Therefore, it is a good choice for building extensions. One of the ways to build conservative extensions is to extend by definition. The extension by definition is the basis of definitional methodologies for building formal ontologies. It is based on the following principles[10]:

1. Ontologies should be based upon a small number of primitive concepts.
2. These primitives should be given definite model theoretic semantics.
3. Axioms should only be given for the primitive concepts.
4. Categorical axiom sets should be sought.
5. The remaining vocabulary of the ontology (which may be very large), should be introduced purely by means of definitions.

For extending lattice categorical theories, the first three principles are assumed. The fourth one will be replaced by lattice categoricity. Categoricity is a strong requirement that can be hard to achieve and preserve. Even when it is achieved, the resultant theory may be unmanageable (even undecidable) or unintuitive. This phenomenon might suggest that we restrict the analysis of completeness to coherent parts of the theory. However, it is not a local notion: since minor changes commit the categoricity and it is expensive to repeat the logical analysis. In [15] we show a formalization of *robust ontological extension*, based in the categorical extension of the ontology.

5.2. Representational Perspective: Knowledge Reconciliation and Ontological Extensions

The acceptation of ontology representation languages as OWL has facilitated the proliferation of ontologies. Thus, the necessity of relating ontologies arises in order to take advantage of the knowledge jointly contributed by different ontologies. Basically, there exist three kinds of reconciliation of the knowledge represented by ontologies:

- Ontology Merging, which builds a new ontology from initial ontologies
- Ontology Alignment, which establishes relationships between elements of different ontologies, and
- Ontology Integration does not join the ontologies into a new one, but it establishes mechanisms for joint reasoning instead.

Corresponding to the three kind of reconciliation, there exist methods to solve the tasks (see, for example, [51] and [66]), in the case of merging, as well as other methods that allow us to obtain knowledge about the consequences of ontology integration.

Any revision of an ontology may be considered, to some extent, from two points of view. On one hand, the task is similar to knowledge revision, thus the problem can be analysed by means of classic methods (see e.g. chapter 6 in [65]). On the other hand, ontology evolution should preserve some sort of backward compatibility, while possible. Therefore, the advantage of extension on revision is the feasibility of preserving ontological features of source theory (sect. 5.1).

Nevertheless, an ontological insertion is not interesting if it is not supported by a good theory about its relationship with the source theory, as well as a sound expansion of a representative class of models of the source theory to models of the new one (such class have to contain the *intended* models). For example, in the case of mereotopological reasoning, it can be necessary to show an intuitive topological interpretation of the new elements (and a re-interpretation of the older ones compatible with basic original principles), which should be formalized. This requirement is mandatory if one wishes to expand models of theory source to models of the new theory [25].

5.3. Merging Robust Ontologies

Therefore, one could consider ontology evolution as a sequence of extensions and revisions. As we have already commented, both methods are intimately tied. Likewise, above discussion is applicable for merging formal ontologies. Therefore, two ways for merging two ontologies *O*1 and *O*2 based on these ideas can be considered. A first one consists in repeatedly extending *O*1 by defining the terms of *O*2 (using the language of *O*1) producing this way a conservative extension of *O*1. Such definitions cannot exist in many cases, so it is necessary to consider a second method, based on the *ontological insertion* of the terms of *O*2 in *O*1 (possibly in parallel). For obtaining sound extensions, it is necessary to design axioms relating terms of both ontologies, for preserving basic features [15]. In [18] a proposal of ontology merging is presented (for lattice categorical theories). Also, a method for l.c. merging is presented.

5.4. Conservative Retractions

The inverse relation of conservative extension is the conservative retraction. This kind of retraction has not been deeply studied in Ontological Engineering due to high complexity. In [8] a tool to compute conservative retractions is presented, although it only serves for propositional description logic. Given a sublanguage *L'* of the language of *T*, a conservative retraction on *L'* has two basic properties: There always exists a conservative retraction of *T*, and whatever two conservative retractions of *T* to the same sublanguage are equivalent theories.

Denote by [*T;L'*] a conservative retraction of *T* to the sublanguage *L'*. The importance of the computing of conservative retractions, in any logic, is based on its potential applications. For example, *Location principle for Knowledge Based Systems (KBS) reasoning*: Suppose that *KB* is a knowledge base, and let *F* be a formula. Suppose also that the language of *F* is *L'*. The question

$$\neg KB \models F\star$$

can be solved in two steps:

- A conservative retraction [*KB;L'*] has to be computed
- We have to decide whether [*KB;L'*] |= *F*

Note that the second question usually has lower complexity than the original one, due to relatively small size of *L'*. This observation is extremely interesting when *KB* is a huge ontology.

It is usual to approach the retraction by means of syntactic analysis, in order to locate the reasoning on certain axioms ([76]). In these cases, the conservative retraction would be very useful. At higher levels of expressivity, one can observe that existing tools provide syntactic modularity, but no semantic modularity. The design of general methods for computing conservative retraction would solve interesting problems about ontological reasoning. One of these is the *Contextual reasoning*: a conservative retraction [*KB;L'*] ensures the maximality of context knowledge with respect to the ontology source.

A similar problem, in the complex case of ontological reasoning in OWL, is the use of partitioning methods by means *E*-connections ([27]). Indeed the partitioning to an *E*-Connection provides modularity benefits; it typically contains several "free-standing" components, that is, sub-KBs which do not "use" information from any other components (observation also made in [27]).

On one hand, to the best of our knowledge, there is no calculus specifically focused on the computing of conservative retractions for logics beyond propositional logic. On the one hand, the main reason for this is that the notion of *conservative extension* is more interesting (for example in incremental specification/verification of systems). For instance, the Isabelle and ACL2 theorem provers adopt this methodology by providing a language for conservative extensions by definition (even for the specification and verification of the logic itself, see e.g.[5]). On the other hand, although the conservative retraction of theories can be interesting itself, in expressive logics (as the first order logic) the retraction may not be finitely axiomatized (for example, in first order theories of arithmetic). It is even possible that it involves undecidable problems.

5.5. Conservative Retractions

The dynamics of ontology evolution lead us to adapt other ontologies to extend ours, or generally, to design systems for the management of multiple and distributed ontologies (as [58]). This question brings about another one: how to design sound ontology mappings for automated reasoning.

Ontology mapping will become a key tool in heterogeneous and competitive scenarios as e-commerce, the knowledge management in large organisations, and -in the SW- in the usual Extraction-Transformation-Loading process (see [71]) for data cleaning. However, the logical -and cognitive- effects of an ontology mapping on automated reasoning are not clear. Logical perspective once again gives a rigid concept, *interpretation among theories*, which is the most suitable for logical automated reasoning, but this approach has limited applications. In practice, a solution is the use of contexts (or micro theories), as in CyC[5] ontology. There are also proposals that may be useful in controlling the expansion of anomalies to the complete ontology, as the *contextual* such as OWL [20] (see also [59]).

There is a limit for ontology mapping. Intelligent KDB analysis aided by ATP will some time need a logical interpretation of basic data like integers (for example, when we accept that

5 http://www.cyc.com

number of parts is a positive integer). It is not easy to build an ontology on numeric data and their properties. Even if we have one, the ontology mapping can be understood as a logical interpretation of an arithmetic theory (remember that, in OWL, mappings are not part of the language). Since interpretation means, up to a point, incorporating a logical theory about such data to the target ontology, logical incompleteness is not only assumed, but unavoidable (also remember that, though OWL integrates data types, it includes nothing about integer arithmetic, for example). This phenomenon can be tamed by syntactical restriction of queries, but the solution will be hard in any case: extensions of OWL (regarding it as a logical theory) will add features for numerical data representation and reasoning. Moreover, undecidability will be intrinsic to any language for rules with powerful features and more complex tools. This is a definitive barrier to ontology language design. We have to find a way to escape form that in practice.

6. Anomalies in Ontologies

Roughly speaking, it can find four main types of errors or anomalies (presented as arguments):

- (A1): The contradictions of the base due to the bad implementation of data (for example, lack of data.
- (A2): The anomalies due to the inconsistency of the model: the theorem prover derives from the database the existence of elements which have not a name (possibly because they have not yet been introduced by the user). This anomaly can also be due to the *Skolem's noise*, produced when we work with the domain closure axioms but the domain knowledge is not clausal. Thus, it is also possible that the agent can not obtain any answer to the requirements of another agent.
- (A3): Disjunctive answers (a logical deficiency).
- (A4): Inconsistency in Knowledge Domain.

The anomalies come from several reasons, for example:

- The set of data is inconsistent with the Domain Knowledge due to formal inconsistencies produced by incorrect data.
- The database is never completed, that is, the user will keep on introducing data.
- Technically, the absence of certain facts about a predicate implies deduction with the Knowledge Domain, and -due to above reasons- non desired answers can be obtained.
- Another interesting aspect is that some languages for specifying ontologies as KIF[6] allow us to design theories of high expressivity, which can be hard to manage. Complex axioms in ontology description often come from a deficient or inconsistent set of concepts and relationships. A paradigmatic case is the following: in a company several programmers are concurrently developing the ontology and associated tools (inducing them from their own practical experience), and others concurrently introduce the data. The cooperative work may produce inconsistencies (due, for

6 http://logic.stanford.edu/kif/kif.html

example, to programmer's wrong interpretations of some concepts in the ontology) or complex axioms that make the ontology messy (a designer does not know any concepts which can simplify definitions). Another example is data warehouses. Finally, in some cases a lack of mechanisms exists to soundly evaluate the ontology engineering task. This is an obstacle for their use in companies [37].

6.1. Inconsistency: Debugging, Updating and Beyond

The larger the KDB, the less possibility it will have of being consistent. We may say that logical inconsistency, one of the main sources of distrust, is frequent whenever the KDB has big amount of hand-made information (and whenever it is a relatively interesting part of WWW). Big KDB escapes any model search (consistency checking) system. Thus, consistency analysis will only be partially solved by a semidecision procedure: if a refutation is found, KDB will be inconsistent. Thus inconsistency turns out to be the main anomaly. The main drawback of many of the methods for inconsistency handling is the computational complexity. Additionally, the relevant role of ontologies in KDB design for the SW requires a revision of both classical semantics for databases (which identify correct answer and logical consequence) and the definition itself of consistency (focused on integrity constraint checking).

Inconsistency is the main anomaly in logic terms. Some recent proposals for inconsistency handling are the following:

Paraconsistent logics:
Paraconsistent logics attempts to control the undesirable (logical) consequences obtained from an inconsistent database. See [45], for a general introduction, and [39].

Non repairing methods:
The idea behind these methods is to preserve the source of information and decide the trueness through an analysis of the retrieved knowledge. Some recent examples are:

- To establish Pre-orders on information sets (see e.g. [22], or [60], where the inference work on selected belief subbasis of the KDB, in the Paraconsistent pradigm).
- *Argumentative hierarchies*, that classify the arguments according to their robustness with respect to other subsets of the KDB [31] or their relationships with other arguments (for example, the argumentative framework based on the defeating relationship [30]). See [69] for an application to databases.
- A classic idea in Artificial Intelligence, *contextualization*, can be used (contextualizing ontologies [20] and data [59]).

Merging-oriented techniques:

- To design rules which allow the consistent fusion of joint inconsistent information (see [14]).
- Solutions provided by the theory of merging databases [26].

- Hierarchical merging [8].

Measuring anomalies

An option is to estimate the anomaly, for example:

- Evaluating by means of a Paraconsistent logic [46].
- Measuring inconsistent information by means of *measures for semantic information.* These measures estimate the information that the KDB gives on the model which it represents. Measures exist for working with inconsistencies [52].

Repairing techniques:

Mainly, there are two drawbacks to KDB repairing: the complexity of the revision of the full KDB and the possible discarding of inconsistent data which is potentially useful. So, it seems advisable to focus the repairing on relatively small datasets. The revision of ontologies is an essentially different, because these represent a key organization of the knowledge of the owner and minor changes may produce unexpected and dangerous anomalies. Some solutions are:

- The *Fellegi-Holt* method, was used in many government statistic bureaux, can be reviewed as a safe logical method [19]. It is based in the searching of *all deducible requirements* to decide which fields must be changed to correct an incorrect record.
- Once the notion of database repairing is defined in a logical form, the *entailment component* of the definition can be simulated by calculus; for example by tableaux method [12].
- Consistent querying to repair databases: The answer itself drives the repair. For example, by splitting the integrity constraints according to the character of the negation which involves each constraint we can produce consistent answers and repair the database [40].
- Consistent enforcement of the database. The aim is to systematically modify the database to satisfy concrete integrity constraints. A promising method uses greatest consistent specializations (adapting the general method which may be undecidable) [54].
- Ontology debugging. There exists tools that explain unsatisfiability of classes in Ontologies, that of improves debugging experience [49], [29].

Consistent answering without repairing:

- To transform the query to obtain consistent answers [24].
- Using paraconsistent inference (see e.g. [60]).

Preserving consistency:

The idea is to update the KDB preserving the consistency (in a wide sense, not only the satisfaction of integrity constraints). It is also necessary to prove the consistency of the method, and some type of completeness (see e.g. [63]).

6.2. Arguments, Logic and Trust

If we accept working with inconsistencies, the goal is to design logical formalisms that limit those that can be inferred from inconsistent KDB. An approach to the acquisition of trustworthy information consists in *argue* the information extracted from data. Argumenting is a successfully strategy in this scenario.

An argument is simply a pair <*L; fact* > where L is a subset of the KDB that proves *fact*. An argument with an unacceptable conclusion may be considered as a report about an anomaly, and the cleaner must find the reason for it. Any anomaly warns us about a mistake, but the expert decides which type of arguments has to be analysed. However, the ARS offers more arguments than human analysis can study. Though a referee layer for ARS's output could partially solve the overspill of arguments, we have to design very efficient criteria to discard the non interesting ones, but it is not easy an easy task. There is an interesting hierarchy of arguments that estimates -at least theoretically- their robustness [31]; hierarchy based on FOL notions as consistency and entailment, among others.

It would be extremately interesting to provide arguments and argumentative reasoning as a service to agents. Inference Web[7] aims to specify and to provide such service. Such service has components for interoperability (composing arguments from several resources), and a SW-based representation of explanations (based on Proof Mark-up language ontology[8]).

7. FOL as the Universal Provider for Formal Semantics

For the verification of KDB, FOL provides a formal framework where some anomalies in specifications can be defined. Ontology languages such as OWL[9] are actually verified and revised by translating specifications into FOL and then applying an ATP [32]. Reasoning services for this class of languages, based on their relationship with Description logics (a subset of FOL), are also investigated [44]. FOL is selected as a translation target because this way we have strong reasoning methods for several sublogics that expand the ontology language. In addition, we have an ideal framework where we can expand the expressivity of the language itself. Extensions of FOL (such as *F-logic* [77] that naturally solves problems like reification, a feature of RDF) language have been proposed.

Modal logics for beliefs lift the reasoning to mental attitudes. Mental attitudes do not seem adequate to be added to ontology reasoning, but other intentional operators exist, such as *Provable from Ontology O*, used in logic programming for meta-reasoning, which may be interesting to be considered. But how?

For the time being, we tend to think of the ontologies as *static theories*, that is, a set of axioms, separated from reasoning (or the set of rules). This option reduces the problem to investigate which rule language is the best for each purpose [43]. But it does not seem adequate for verification of KDB. It is advisable to solve this limitation for KDB cleaning tasks, and not only by means of *external* reasoners: an ontology should *ontologically define its reasoning framework*, or better, the ontology should be a potential reasoner itself. Later we will return to this question to briefly explore this solution.

7 http://inference-web.org/wiki/Main_Page
8 http://inference-web.org/2007/primer/
9 http://www.w3.org/TR/daml+oil-reference

7.1. Model Theory for Semantic Web

At the top of the SW cake proposed by Tim Berns-Lee, *Logic* and *Proof* appear as the bases of *Web of trust*. Logical trust, in a broad sense, is based on logical semantics, and this deals with models and the definition of truth. In the ontology design task, model theoretic analysis is often forgotten, because ontology designers have a particular model in mind (the real or *intended* model). A well known principle in Knowledge Representation states that no language or KB exists to faithfully represent the intended world where we want to work; that is, unintended models exist (see figure 5). In QSR, this principle turns into the *poverty conjecture*: there is no purely qualitative, general purpose kinematics. Therefore no categorical ontology exists for this field.

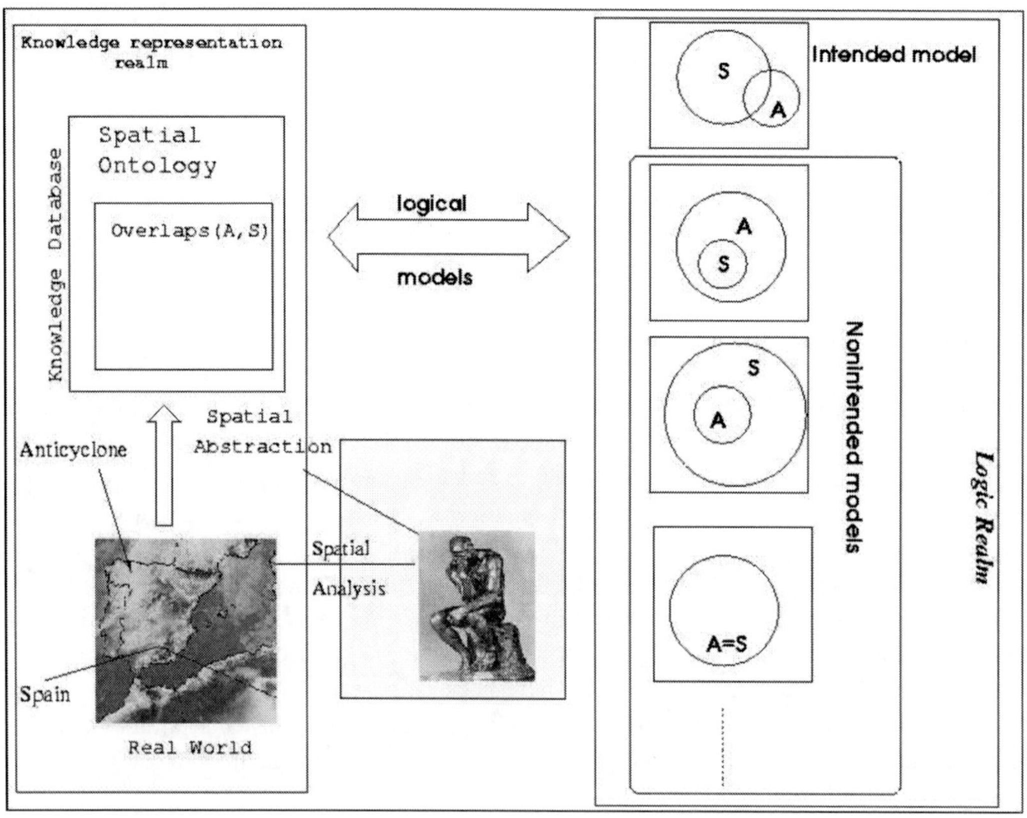

Figure 5. Unintended models for a poor KDB (with the natural notion of Overlaps role).

One of the goals of logical Model Theory is to study all the models of a theory, including non intended models. This is not only a semantic basis for good specification. It has impact on practical proving: the existence of unintended models is consequence of incompleteness and vice-versa. For example, in figure 5 the existence of a model where A = S implies that the theory RCC + {O(A; S)} does not entail that the region affected by the anticyclone and Spain are different.

Model Theory may be combined with other features, especially of linguistic nature. This way the designer may specify non-logical information. However the amount of linguistic and lexicographic problems that this option supposes warns us to carefully explore this combination. On the other hand, it is not strange to come up against inconsistent information in a KDB in the Web, and in this case Model Theory is useless: there are no models.

8. Untrustworthy Information versus Ontology and Knowledge

We have commented that the existence of an argument allows us to locate and repair an anomaly -if it is the witness of one- by means of expert analysis of its content. A deep analysis of the arguments reported by an ARS classifies them according to their trustworthiness. So, an argument hierarchy is a first step towards an ontology of trust. But we also need to clarify operational features of the ARS assistant. The autonomous behaviour that we expect of the automated argument searcher can be slanted. Much work about this topic could be accomplished using the background of automated reasoning field.

The task of recognizing fraudulent information represents a significantly different problem that will be more arduous. If the ontology represents a fraudulent world (an unintended model of the user's knowledge which is particularly dangerous for his/her purposes), the arguments reporting fraudulent information do not show anomalies. To make matters worse, fraudulent ontologies may use linguistic features to hide information. This takes the question beyond our interest: fraudulent, by definition, can not have logical legitimacy. A solution may be the combination of user's trustworthiness on other users (see [72]). One can also believe that the problem can be defeated with a precise analysis which deals with mental attitudes as *beliefs, desires or intentions* to specify the phenomenon for data-mining agents.

In [36] the applicability of social network analysis to the semantic web is studied, focusing on the specification of trust. In this paper, the authors propose a level of trust on a scale of 1-9 for each FOAF:Person (and with respect to each thematic area). The levels roughly correspond to the following: *Distrusts absolutely, Distrusts highly, Distrusts moderately, Distrusts slightly, Trusts neutrally, Trusts slightly, Trusts moderately, Trusts highly, Trusts absolutely*, and an ontology on trust is used.

8.1. Mental Attitudes and Ontology Reasoning

In a scenario with inconsistent information and/or several cleaning agents working, is it necessary to add an intentional level to the logical knowledge? We have already commented that it is not advisable to add mental attitudes to the ontology. But, in a multiagent system setting, the specification of knowledge extracted from inconsistent information is unavoidable. In fact, the specifications of agent communication languages as FIPA-ACL [10]use mental attitudes. A *multiagent data-mining* system should manage this kind of information.

A way to avoid the adoption of mental attitudes when one works with simple information items might be the design of fusion rules to solve agents' disappointments based on the nature of information (see the survey [14]). This option may need to preprocess data from heterogeneous databases. In another case, data needs to be extracted and translated (through ontology mapping) during cleaning runtime, making it difficult to achieve acceptable time responses, as occurs in classical data cleaning. But the preprocessing in KDB cleaning has another need: it is possible for the system to fire some rules to add new data, transforming the data source of the KDB into a consistent instance of the KDB target.

8.2. Emergent Ontologies

An interesting aspect of ontology evolution is the role that plays data and user, for example, when the change is induced by the user, who has detected the (cognitive) necessity of adding a *notion*. That is, a vague concept which comprises a set of elements with features roughly shaped by the existing concepts. In Ontological Engineering, careful consideration should be paid to the accurate classification of objects: the notion becomes a *concept* when its behaviour is constrained by new axioms that relate it to the initial concepts. This scenario emphasizes the current need for an explanation of the reasoning behind cleaning programs. That is, a *formalized explanation* of the decisions made by systems. Note that such explanations are necessary for the desirable design of logical algorithms to be used by general-purpose cleaning agents [4]. In [16] a type of entropy, called *cognitive entropy* is introduced to facilitate the extension of ontologies with these new concepts. This entropy combines classic information entropy with entailment. A conditional entropy based in the cognitive entropy allow to estimate the information change when ontologies are extended with vague concepts. Therefore, this entropy is similar to Kullback-Leibler distance or relative entropy (see [53]), but using the entailment to classify the elements.

There are other approaches that deal with probabilistic objects. J. Calmet and A. Daemi also use entropy in order to revise or compare ontologies [21], [29]. This is based on the self taxonomy defined by the concepts but provability from specification is not regarded. Note that reasoning services are necessary in order to build the extension with maximum entropy and they can be non-decidable for general first order theories, although it is feasible for ontologies expressed in several (decidable) Description Logics. M. Goldzmidt P. Morris and J. Pearl consider maximum entropy to default reasoning [38]. The method is also based on probability and, by means of this, non monotonic consequences are studied. J. Paris and A. Vencovska focus their work on the principles that characterize probabilistic inference process from a Knowledge Base (the *Maximum Entropy Inference Process*) [67]. See also [68]. We believe that those principles can be useful to discriminate a nice ontological reasoning and we will consider that idea.

M. Andreas and M. Egenhofer use semantic similarity to relate ontologies. They work with semantic distances, taking in account explicitness and formalizations [73]. They manage weights to drive the semantic similarity. Conditional entropy has already been considered in the similar task of Abductive Reasoning for learning qualitative relationships/concepts (usually in probabilistic terms, see e.g. [13]). The main difference between this approach and ours is that we work with probability mass distribution of *provable facts* from ontological specifications.

[10] http://www.fipa.org/specs/fipa00037/SC00037J.pdf

9. Understanding Ontologies: Mereotopology and Entailment-based Visualization

Ontologies are complex specifications that nonspecialist should be in a transparent way. A natural choice for representation and reasoning are the visual metaphor. Paraphrasing [64], visual cleaning of ontologies is important for future end-users of ontology debugging systems due mainly to three reasons:

1. It allows the user to summarize ontology contents.
2. User's information is often fuzzily defined. Visualization can be used to help the user to get a nice representation.
3. Finally, visualization can therefore help the user to interact with the information space.

There is not a generally accepted representation mechanism that translates every possible change in the visual representation into the specification of the ontology. In fact, this is an interesting problem in the design of visual reasoning tools. Current end-user tools are mostly based on facilitating the understanding of the ontology (see e.g. [33], [56]) facilitating very limited graphical changes to the user. In order to augment such features, we need formally sound mappings between (visual) representations and Knowledge Bases (KBs) (expressed, for example, in Description Logics). Note that such mappings have to translate logical notions for supporting the logical impact of arrangements on the spatial representation (for example, when new concepts are inserted), as it is possible in diagrammatic reasoning, for example [75]. These issues are critical and we need to solve them in order to integrate solutions in systems for visual representation of information [33]. This goal is far away of being achieved for classical Information Visualization (IV) tools. IV is the use of computer-supported, interactive and visual representations of abstract data to amplify cognition [23]. The goal of Visual Ontology Cleaning (VOC) should be to reason spatially for visually debugging and repairing of ontologies. Therefore, it should have additional features, different from classical user analysis, querying and navigation/browsing.

Therefore, it is interesting to investigate some KR issues behind the sound mereotopological representation of the conceptualization induced by small ontologies (namely the mentioned ontological arguments) [17]. The intended aim of such representation is the understanding and repairing of ontologies. Specifically, those considered as anomalous (although consistent) due to errors in the concept structure. In that paper the spatial representation and algorithmic repairing are described; we do not describe here the (future) implementation. The advantage of this approach is that visual reparation stage hides formal semantics that supports the change, facilitating in this way its use by non experts.

10. Meta-logical Trust

At this point, we have to reconsider if the formalization and the study of every element afore mentioned are enough to get the top of SW Cake: Trust. There exists a very interesting line of research to try to establish the supra-trust by formally verifying the automated theorem provers used to work with ontologies. Two possible approaches can be considered. The first one considers ontologies as potential reasoners and the second one aim to achieve a formal verification of logics and deduction algorithms involved in ontology reasoning.

10.1. Extend OWL to ROWL

A solution is the specification of the reasoning process in the ontology, for example, designing of a language that could be called ROWL (a Reasonable Ontology Web Language) [4], where ontologies are considered as potential reasoners.

The idea stems from the need to attach (specialised) certified logical inference to the ontology; that is, ontological information about how to reason with the information. To do this, we should add new features to OWL to specify what type of reasoning and which ARS are advisable to work with the OWL ontology (also keeping in mind that the ontology is optimized to reason with them). The idea is brought about the building of *Certified Generic Frameworks* (CGF), where the design of a certified *ad hoc* reasoner is simplified to provide some key features of the ATP that ontology must supply [61]. An ontology which accepts a reasoner that fits in this framework has to specify only simple elements: computation rules (to drive the deduction), representation rules (to normalize formulas), measure function on formulas (to deduce the halting of deduction methods) and model functions (to supply models in some basic cases). The CGF has been programmed in ACL2[11], which is both a programming language in which you can model computer systems and a tool to help you prove properties of those models. This way the ATP obtained is sound and complete, and formally verified by ACL2. A detailed presentation of the CGF will appear in [62], where its formal verification is described.

A generalization of this framework to others ARS will be an interesting task. Of course, prior to deciding what the key features of ROWL are, it is necessary to design an ontology about automated reasoning. There are some projects to build such an ontology, for example, within the *MathBroker*[12] and *MONET*[13] projects.

10.2. Verification of Description Logics

A second solution is the formal verification of satisfiability algorithms for description logics (DLs), as a previous stage to the formal verification of DLs reasoners. In [5] a formal proof of the well-known tableau algorithm for the ALC description logic in the PVS verification system is presented. The verification of reasoning systems for the SW poses a new challenge for the application of formal methods. In this case, a proof in PVS of correctness of the tableau algorithm for ALC described in theoretical papers is obtained. Since tableau algorithms for description logics are very specialized, the hardest part of this task is the termination proof, for which we have extended the multiset library of PVS in order to include well-foundness of the multiset order relation. This task needs of the specification in PVS of a prover for the ALC logic.

---

11 http://www.cs.utexas.edu/users/moore/acl2/

12 http://www.risc.uni-linz.ac.at/projects/basic/mathbroker/

13 http://monet.nag.co.uk/cocoon/monet/index.html

11. Final Remarks

This chapter is devoted to discuss relevant issues in Computational Logic and Knowledge Representation tightly related with the reasoning in the Semantic Web. These issues are related at once with usual problems in data cleaning, namely [71]: *data analysis, definition of mapping rules, verification, transformation and backflow of cleaning data.*

The emphasis is given on the complex relations among classic computational logic concepts and tools and representational issues (related at the same time with nonmonotonic reasoning and knowledge Engineering). The deep relation between the two perspectives of the concept of ontology in SW (considered as an Engineering tool for represent conceptualization that evolve, and considered as a logic theory with precise semantics) is scratched under the prism of several challenges and problems.

Acknowledgment

Partially supported by TIN2009-09492 project of Spanish Ministry of Science and Innovation, cofinanced with FEDER founds.

References

[1] J.A. Alonso-Jiménez, J. Borrego-Díaz, A. M. Chávez-González, M. A. Gutiérrez-Naranjo, J. D. Navarro-Marín, “A Methodology for the Computer Aided Cleaning of Complex Knowledge Databases", *Proc. of IEEE Int. Conf. on Industrial Electronics, Control and Instrumentation IECON 2002,* IEEE Press, 2003, pp. 1806-1812.

[2] J.A. Alonso-Jiménez, J. Borrego-Díaz, A. M. Chávez-González, M. A. Gutiérrez-Naranjo, J. D. Navarro-Marín, “Towards a Practical Argumentative Reasoning with Qualitative Spatial Databases". *Proc. of 16th Int. Conf. on Industrial and Engineering Applications of Artificial Intelligence and Expert Systems IEA/AIE 2003*, LNAI 2718, Springer-Verlag, 2003, pp. 789-798.

[3] J. Alonso-Jiménez, J. Borrego-Díaz, M.J. Hidalgo-Doblado, F.J. Martín-Mateos, J.L. Ruiz Reina: "Verification of the formal concept analysis". *RACSAM (Revista de la Real Academia de Ciencias), Serie A: Matemáticas*, Vol. 98, 2004, pp. 3-16.

[4] J.A. Alonso-Jiménez, J. Borrego-Díaz, A. M. Chávez-González, and F.J. Martín-Mateos: “Foundational Challenges in Automated Semantic Web Data and Ontology Cleaning", *IEEE Intelligent Systems* 21(1): 42-52 (2006).

[5] J. A. Alonso, J. Borrego-Díaz, M. J. Hidalgo, F. J. Martín-Mateos, J. L. Ruiz-Reina: “A Formally Verified Prover for the ALC Description Logic". 20th. Theorem Proving in Higher Order Logics TPHOLs 2007, *LNCS* 4732, 135-150 (2007).

[6] G. Antoniou, A. Kehagias. "On the Refinement of Ontologies". *Int. J. Intell. Syst.* vol. 15 2000, pp. 623-632.

[7] G.A. Aranda-Corral, J. Borrego-Díaz, F. Gómez-Marín, “Toward Semantic MobileWeb 2.0 through multiagent systems", to appear in *Lecture Notes in Artificial Intelligence* n. 5559 (2009).

[8] G.A. Aranda-Corral, J. Borrego-Díaz, M.M. Fernández-Lebrón: "Conservative retractions of propositional logic theories by means of boolean derivatives" to appear en Proceedings of Calculemus 2009, *Lecture Notes in Artificial Intelligence* (2009). Theoretical foundations.

[9] T. J. M. Bench-Capon, "The Role of Ontologies in the Verification and Validation of Knowledge-Based Systems" *Int. J. Intell. Syst.* 16(3): 377-390 (2001).

[10] B. Bennett, Relative Definability in Formal Ontologies, *Proc 3rd Int. Conf. Formal Ontology in Information Systems* (FOIS-04) pp. 107-118, IOS Press, (2004).

[11] T. Berners-Lee, J. Hendler, O. Lassila: The "Semantic Web", Scientific American Magazine May 2001 http://www.scientificamerican.com/article.cfm?id=the-semantic-web.

[12] L. E. Bertossi, C. Schwind, "Database Repairs and Analytic Tableaux", *Annals of Mathematics and Artificial Intelligence* 40(1-2): 5-35 (2004).

[13] R. Bhatnagar and L. N. Kanal Structural and Probabilistic Knowledge for Abductive Reasoning, *IEEE Trans. on Pattern Analysis and Machine Intelligence* 15(3):233-245 (1993).

[14] I. Bloch et al. "Fusion: General concepts and characteristics", *Int. J. Intell. Syst.* vol. 16, 2001, pp. 1107-1134.

[15] J. Borrego-Díaz, A.M. Chávez-González: "Extension of Ontologies Assisted by Automated Reasoning Systems". The 10th International Conference on Computer Aided Systems Theory. Lecture Notes in Computer Science, *EUROCAST 2005*, *LNCS* 3643, pp. 247-253, 2005.

[16] J. Borrego-Díaz, A. M. Chávez-González: "Using Cognitive Entropy to Manage Uncertain Concepts in Formal Ontologies". *Lecture Notes in Computer Science* Vol. 5327, 315-329 (2008).

[17] J. Borrego-Díaz, A. M. Chávez-González: "Visual Ontology Cleaning: Cognitive Principles and Applicability". *3rd. European Semantic Web Congress ESWC 2006*, *LNCS* 4011: 317-331 (2006).

[18] J. Borrego-Díaz, A. M. Chávez-González: "On the Use of Automated Reasoning Systems in Ontology Integration", *Ontology, Conceptualization and Epistemology for Information Systems*, *Software Engineering and Service Science* (ONTOSE 2009) to appear (2009).

[19] A. Boskovitz, R. Goré, M. Hegland, "A Logical Formalisation of the Fellegi-Holt Method of Data Cleaning", *Proc. of 5th Int. Symp. on Intelligent Data Analysis, IDA 2003, LNCS* vol. 2810, Springer-Verlag, 2003, pp. 554-565.

[20] P. Bouquet, F. Giunchiglia, F. van Harmelen, L. Serafini, and H. Stuckenschmidt, "C-OWL: "Contextualizing Ontologies," *Proc. of the 2nd Int. Semantic Web Conference ISWC 2003*, LNCS vol. 2870, Springer-Verlag, 2003, pp. 164-179.

[21] J. Calmet and A. Daemi, From entropy to ontology, *4th. Int. Symp. From Agent Theory to Agent Implementation AT2AI-4*, 2004.

[22] Cantwell, "Resolving Conflicting Information", Journ*al of Logic, Language and Information* vol. 7, 1998, pp. 191-220.

[23] S. Card, J. Mckinlay and B. Shneiderman (eds.) *Readings in Information Visualization: Using Vision to Think,* Morgan Kauffman, 1999.

[24] A. Celle, L. Bertossi, "Consistent Data Retrieval", *Information Systems* vol. 19, 1994, pp. 1193-1221.

[25] A. M. Chávez-González, *Automated Mereotopological Reasoning for Ontology Debugging*, Ph.D. Thesis, University of Seville, 2005.

[26] L. Cholvy, S. Moral, "Merging databases: Problems and examples", *Int. J. Intell. Syst.* vol. 16, 2001, pp. 1193-1221.

[27] B. Cuenca-Grau, B. Parsia, E. Sirin, and A. Kalyanpur, Automatic Partitioning of OWL Ontologies Using E-Connections, *Proc. 2005 Int. Workshop on Description Logics* (DL2005), http://sunsite.informatik.rwth-aachen.de/Publications/CEUR-WS/Vol-147/21-Grau.pdf

[28] A. Daemi and J. Calmet, From Ontologies to Trust through Entropy, *Proc. of the Int. Conf. on Advances in Intelligent Systems - Theory and Applications*, 2004.

[29] J. Du, Y.-D. Shen: "Computing minimum cost diagnoses to repair populated DL-based ontologies". WWW 2008: 565-574 (2008).

[30] P. M. Dung, "On the Acceptability of Arguments and its Fundamental Role in Nonmonotonic Reasoning, Logic Programming and n-Person Games", *Artificial Intelligence* vol. 77, 1995, pp. 321-358.

[31] M. Elvang-Goransson, A. Hunter, "Argumentative Logics: Reasoning with Classically Inconsistent Information", *Data and Knowledge Engineering* vol. 16, 1995, pp. 125-145.

[32] R. Fikes, D. L. McGuinness, R. Waldinger, "A First-Order Logic Semantics for Semantic Web Markup Languages", *Report n. KSL-02-01 of Knowledge Systems Laboratory*, Stanford University, 2002.

[33] C. Fluit, M. Sabou, F. Harmelen. Ontology-based Information Visualization, in V. Geroimenko, C. Chen (eds.), *Visualizing the Semantic Web*. Springer (2003).

[34] H. Galhardas, D. Florescu, D. Shasha, E. Simon, C. Saita, "Declarative Data Cleaning: Language, Model, and Algorithms" *Proc. of 27fh Very Large Databases Conference VLDB 2001,* Morgan-Kauffman, pp. 371-380.

[35] B. Ganter, R. Wille, "Formal Concept Analysis - Mathematical Foundations". Springer (1999).

[36] J. Golbeck, B. Parsia, J. A. Hendler: "Trust Networks on the Semantic Web" Cooperative Information Agents VII (CIA 2003) *Lecture Notes in Computer Science* vol. 2782, pp. 238-249 (2003).

[37] A. Gómez-Pérez, "Evaluation of Ontologies" *Int. Jounal. Intelligent Systems*. vol. 16, 2001, pp. 391-409.

[38] M. Goldzsmidt, P. Morris and J. Pearl, A Maximum Entropy Approach to Non-monotonic Reasoning. *IEEE Trans. on Pattern Analysis and Machine Intelligence* 15(3), pp. 220-232 (1993).

[39] J. Grant, V.S. Subrahmanian, "Applications of Paraconsistency in Data and Knowledge Bases", *Synthese* vol. 125, 2000, pp. 121-132.

[40] S. Greco, E. Zumpano, "Querying Inconsistent Databases", 7th International Conference on Logic for Programming and Automated Reasoning LPAR 2000, *LNCS* vol. 1955, Springer-Verlag, 2000, pp. 308-325.

[41] N. Guarino, C. A. Welty, "Evaluating ontological decisions with OntoClean", *Communications of ACM* vol. 45, 2002, pp. 61-65.

[42] J. He°in, "Towards the Semantic Web: Knowledge Representation in a Dynamic, Distributed Environment," Ph.D. Thesis, University of Maryland, College Park. 2001.

[43] I. Horrocks, J. Angele, S. Decker, M. Kifer, B. Grosof, G. Wagner, "Where are the rules?," *IEEE Intelligent Systems* vol. 18, no. 5, Sept./Oct. 2003, pp. 76-83.

[44] I. Horrocks and P.F. Patel-Schneider, "Reducing OWL Entailment to Description logics satisfiability," *Proc. of 2nd Int. Semantic Web Conf. (ISWC2003) LNCS* 2870, Springer-Verlag, 2003, pp. 17-29.

[45] A. Hunter, "Paraconsistent Logics", in D: Gabbay and Ph. Smets (eds.) Handbook of Defeasible Reasoning and Uncertain Information, Kluwer, 1998, 13-44.

[46] A. Hunter, "Evaluating the significance of inconsistencies", in *Proceedings of the International Joint Conference on AI (IJCAI'03),* Morgan Kaufmann, 2003, pp. 468-473.

[47] A. Jaokar and T. Fish: "MobileWeb 2.0: The Innovator's Guide to Developing and Marketing Next Generation Wireless/Mobile Applications". *Futuretext* (2006).

[48] R. JÄaschke, A. Hotho, C. Schmitz, B. Ganter, G. Stumme: "Discovering shared conceptualizations in folksonomies". *J. Web Sem.* 6(1): 38-53 (2008).

[49] A. Kalyanpur, B. Parsia, E. Sirin, J.A. Hendler: Debugging unsatisfiable classes in OWL ontologies. *J. Web Sem.* 3(4): 268-293 (2005).

[50] M. C. A. Klein, D. Fensel, "Ontology versioning on the Semantic Web", *Proceedings of the 1st Semantic Web Symposium SWWS 2001,* pp. 75-91.

[51] K. Kotis, G.A. Vouros: The Hcone approach to Ontology Merging, *Proc. European Semantic Web Symposium (ESWS 2004)*, *LNCS* vol. 3053, pp. 137-151, Springer (2004).

[52] K. M. Knight, "Two Information Measures for Inconsistent Sets", *Journal of Logic, Language and Information* vol. 12, 2003, pp. 227-248.

[53] S. Kotz and N.L. Johnson (eds). *Encyclopedia of Statistical Sciences* vol.4, pp. 421{425. John Wiley and Sons, 1981.

[54] S. Link, "Consistency Enforcement in Databases", *Proc. of 2nd Int. Workshop on Semantics in Databases 2001, LNCS* vo. 2582, Springer-Verlag, 2003, pp. 139-159.

[55] C. Lutz and F.Wolter, Conservative extensions in the lightweight description logic EL,*Proc. Conf. Automated Deduction* (CADE 2007), *Lecture Notes in Computer Science* 4603, 84-99 (2007).

[56] Y. Mao, Z. Wu, H. Chen, X. Zheng: An Interactive Visual Model for Web Ontologies. *Knowledge-Based Intelligent Information and Engineering Systems KES 2005, LNCS* 3682: 866-872 (2005).

[57] A. Maedche, B. Motik, L. Stojanovic, R. Studer and R. Volz, "Ontologies for Enterprise Knowledge Management," *IEEE Intelligent Systems* vol. 18, no. 2, March/April 2003, pp. 26-33.

[58] A. Maedche, B. Motik, L. Stojanovic, "Managing multiple and distributed ontologies on the Semantic Web", *The Very Large Database Journal* vol. 12, 2003, pp. 286-302.

[59] R. MacGregor, I.-Y. Ko, "Representing Contextualized Data using Semantic Web Tools", *Proceedings of the First InternationalWorkshop on Practical and Scalable Semantic Systems Services.*

[60] P. Marquis, N. Porquet, "Resource-Bounded Paraconsistent Inference", *Annals of Mathematics and Artificial Intelligence* vol. 39, 2003, pp. 349-384.

[61] F.J. Martín-Mateos, J.A. Alonso-Jiménez, M.J. Hidalgo-Doblado, J.L. Ruiz-Reina, "Verification in ACL2 of a Generic Framework to Synthesize SAT-Provers," *Proc. of*

12th Int. Workshop on Logic Based Program Development and Transformation LOPSTR '02, *LNCS* 2664, Springer-Verlag, 2003, pp. 182-198.

[62] F. J. Martín-Mateos, J. A. Alonso, M.J. Hidalgo, J.L. Ruiz-Reina: Formal Verification of a Generic Framework to Synthetize SAT-Provers. *J Aut. Reasoning* 32(4):287-313 (2004).

[63] E. Mayol, E. Teniente, "Consistency preserving updates in deductive databases", *Data and Knowledge Engineering* vol. 47, 2003, pp. 61-103.

[64] F. Murtagh, T. Taskaya, P. Contreras, J. Mothe and K. Englmeier: "Interactive Visual Interfaces: A Survey", *Artificial Intelligence Review* 19:263-283, 2003.

[65] B. Nebel, Reasoning and Revision in Hybrid Representation Systems, *LNAI* 422, Springer-Verlag, Berlin (1990).

[66] Noy, N.F., Musen, M.A.: The PROMPT suite: Interactive tools for ontology merging and mapping. *Int. J. of Human-Computer Studies*, 59(6):983-1024 (2003).

[67] J. B. Paris and A. Vencovská, A note on the inevitability of maximum entropy, *Int. Journal of Approximate Reasoning archive* 4(3): 183-223 (1990).

[68] G. S. Plesniewicz, Plausible Inference Based on Maximum Entropy, *IEEE Int. Conf. on Artificial Intelligence Systems (ICAIS'02)* pp.101-104 (2002).

[69] S. Pradhan, "Connecting Databases with Argumentation", *14th Int. Conf. On Applications of Prolog INAP 2001, LNCS* vol, 2543, Springer-Verlag, 2001, pp. 170-185.

[70] M. Peim, E. Franconi, N. W. Paton, "Estimating the Quality of Answers when Querying over Description Logic Ontologies", *Data and Knowledge Engineering* vol. 47, 2003, pp. 105-129.

[71] E. Rahm, H-H Do, "Data Cleaning: Problems and Current Approaches", *IEEE Data Engineering Bulleting* vol. 23, 2000, pp. 3-13.

[72] M. Richardson, R. Agrawal, P. Domingos, "Trust Management for the Semantic Web", Proc. of 2nd Int. Semantic Web Conference ISWC 2003, *LNCS* vol. 2870, Springer-Verlag, 2003, pp. 351-368.

[73] M. A. Rodríguez, M. J. Egenhofer, Determining Semantic Similarity among Entity Classes from Different Ontologies, *IEEE Trans. on Knowledge and Data Engineering* 15(2):442-456.

[74] D.E. Smith *Reflection and Semantics in a Procedural Language*, PhD Dissertation, Department of Electrical Engineering and Computer Science, *MIT*, 1982.

[75] G. Stapleton, J. Masthoff, J. Flower, A. Fish, J. Southern: "Automated Theorem Proving in Euler Diagram Systems". *J. Autom. Reasoning* 39(4):431-470 (2007).

[76] D. Tsarkov and I. Horrocks, Optimised Classification for Taxonomic Knowledge Bases, *Proc. 2005 Int. Workshop on Description Logics* (DL 2005), http://sunsite.informatik.rwth-aachen.de/Publications/CEUR-WS /Vol-147/39-TsarHorr.pdf

[77] G. Yang, M. Kifer, "Reasoning about Anonymous Resources and Meta Statements on the Semantic Web", *Journal of Data Semantics* vol. 1 (LNCS vol. 2800), 2003, pp. 69-97.

In: Data Management in the Semantic Web
Editor: Hal Jin, pp. 131-151
ISBN: 978-1-61122-862-5

Chapter 6

APPLYING SEMANTIC WEB TECHNOLOGIES TO BIOLOGICAL DATA INTEGRATION AND VISUALIZATION

Claude Pasquier*
Institute of Developmental Biology and Cancer (IBDC)
University of Nice Sophia-Antipolis, CNRS UMR6543
Parc Valrose, Nice, France

Abstract

Current research in biology heavily depends on the availability and efficient use of information. In order to build new knowledge, various sources of biological data must often be combined. Semantic Web technologies, which provide a common framework allowing data to be shared and reused between applications, can be applied to the management of disseminated biological data. However, due to some specificities of biological data, applying these technologies to life science is a real challenge. This chapter shows that current Semantic Web technologies start to become mature and can be used to develop large applications. However, in order to get the best from these technologies, improvements are needed both at the level of tool performance and knowledge modeling.

Keywords: Semantic Web, Data Integration, Bioinformatics

1. Introduction

Biology is now an information-intensive science and research in genomics, transcriptomics and proteomics heavily depend on the availability and the efficient use of information. When data were structured and organized as a collection of records in dedicated, self-sufficient databases, information was retrieved by performing queries on the database using a specialized query language; for example, SQL (Structured Query Language) for relational

*E-mail address: claude.pasquier@unice.fr

databases or OQL (Object Query Language) for object databases. In modern biology, exploiting the different kinds of available information about a given topic is challenging because data are spread over the World Wide Web (Web), hosted in a large number of independent, heterogeneous and highly focused resources. The Web is a system of interlinked documents distributed over the Internet. It allows access to a large number of valuable resources, mainly designed for human use and understanding. Now, hypertext links can be used to link anything to anything. By clicking a hyperlink on a Web page, one frequently gets another document that is related to the clicked element (this can be a text, an image, a sound, a clip, among others). The relationship between the source and the target of a link can have a multitude of meanings such as an explanation, a translation, a localization, a sell or buy order. Human readers are able to infer the role of links and are able to use the Web to carry out complex tasks. However, a computer cannot perform the same tasks without human supervision because Web pages are designed to be read by people, not by machines.

Hands-off data handling requires moving from a Web of documents, only understandable by humans, to a Web of data in which information is expressed not only in natural language, but also in a format that can be read and used by software agents, thus permitting them to find, share and integrate information more easily [1]. In parallel with the Web of data, which is mainly focused on data interoperability, considerable international efforts are ongoing to develop programmatic interoperability on the Web with the aim of enabling a Web of programs [2]. Here, semantic descriptions are applied to processes, for example represented as Web Services [3]. The extension of both the static and the dynamic part of the current Web is called the Semantic Web.

2. Semantic Web Technologies

The principal technologies of the Semantic Web fit into a set of layered specifications. The current components are the Resource Description Framework (RDF) Core Model, the RDF Schema language (RDF schema), the Web Ontology Language (OWL) and the SPARQL query language for RDF. In this chapter, these languages are designed with the acronym SWL for Semantic Web Languages. A brief description of these languages, which is needed to better understand this chapter, is given below.

The Resource Description Framework (RDF) model [2] is based upon the idea of making statements about resources. A RDF statement, also called a triple in RDF terminology is an association of the form (subject, predicate, object). The subject of a RDF statement is a resource identified by a Uniform Resource Identifier (URI) [3]. The predicate is a resource as well, denoting a specific property of the subject. The object, which can be a resource or a string literal, represents the value of this property. For example, one way to state in RDF that "the human gene BRCA1 is located on chromosome 17" is to build a statement composed of a subject denoting "the human gene BRCA1", a predicate representing the relationship "is located on", and an object denoting "chromosome 17". A collection of triples can be represented by a labeled directed graph (called RDF graph) where each vertex represents either a subject or an object and each edge represents a predicate.

RDF applications sometimes need to describe other RDF statements using RDF, for instance, to record information about when statements were made, who made them, or another similar information (this is sometimes referred to as "provenance" information). RDF provides a built-in vocabulary intended for describing RDF statements. A description of a statement using this vocabulary is called a reification of the statement. For example, a reification of the statement about the location of the human gene BRCA1 would be given by assigning the statement a URI (such as http://example.org/triple12345) and then, using this new URI as the subject of other statements, like in the triples (http://example.org/triple12345, information_coming_from, "Ensembl_database") and (http:/example.org/triple12345, specified_in, "human assembl_N").

RDF Schema (RDFS) [4] and the Web Ontology Language (OWL) [5] are used to represent explicitly the meanings of the resources described on the Web and how they are related. These specifications, called ontologies, describe the semantics of classes and properties used in Web documents. An ontology suitable for the example above might define the concept of Gene (including its relationships with other concepts) and the meaning of the predicate "is located on". As stated by John Dupré in 1993 [4], there is no unique ontology. There are multiple ontologies which each models a specific domain. In an ideal world, each ontology should be linked to a general (or top-level) ontology to enable knowledge sharing and reuse [5]. In the domain of the Semantic Web, several ontologies have been developed to describe Web Services.

SPARQL [6] is a query language for RDF. A SPARQL query is represented by a graph pattern to match against the RDF graph. Graph patterns contain triple patterns which are like RDF triples, but with the option of query variables in place of RDF terms in the subject, predicate or object positions. For example, the query composed of the triple pattern ("BRCA1", "is located on", ?chr) matches the triple described above and returns "chromosome 17" in the variable chr (variables are identified with the "?" prefix).

3. Semantic Web for the Life Sciences

In the life sciences community, the use of Semantic Web technologies should be of central importance in a near future. The Semantic Web Health Care and Life Sciences Interest Group (HCLSIG) was launched to explore the application of these technologies in various areas [7]. Currently, several projects have been undertaken. Some works concern the encoding of information using SWL. Examples of data encoded with SWL are MGED Ontology [8], which provides terms for annotating microarray experiments, BioPAX [9], which is an exchange format for biological pathway data, Gene Ontology (GO) [10], which describes biological processes, molecular functions and cellular components of gene products and UniProt [11], which is the world's most comprehensive catalog of information on proteins. Several studies focused on information integration and retrieval [12], [13], [14], [15], [16], [17] and [18] while others concerned the elaboration of a workflow environment based on Web Services [19], [20], [21], [22], [23] and [24].

Regarding the problem of data integration, the application of these technologies faces difficulties which are amplified because of some specificities of biological knowledge.

3.1. Biological Data Are Huge in Volume

This amount of data is already larger than what can be reasonably handled by existing tools. In a recent study, Guo and colleagues [25] benchmarked several systems on artificial datasets ranging from 8 megabytes (100,000 declared statements) to 540 megabytes (almost 7 millions statements). The best tested system, DLDB-OWL, loads the largest dataset in more that 12 hours and takes between few milliseconds to more than 5 minutes to respond to the queries. These results, while encouraging, appear to be quite insufficient to be applied to real biological datasets. RDF serialization of the UniProt database, for example, represents more than 25 gigabytes of data. Furthermore, this database is only one, among numerous other data sources that are used on a daily basis by researchers in biology.

3.2. Biological Data Sources Are Heterogeneous

Various sources of biological data must be combined to obtain a full picture and to build new knowledge, for example, data stored in an organism's specific database (such as FlyBase) with results of microarray experiments and information available on related species. However, a large majority of current databases does not use a uniform way to name biological entities. As a result, a same resource is frequently identified with different names. Currently, it is very difficult to connect each of these data seamlessly unless they are transformed into a common format with IDs connecting each of them. In the example presented above, the fact that the gene BRCA1 is identified by number "126611" in the GDB Human Genome Database [26] and by number "1100" in the HUGO Gene Nomenclature Committee (HGNC) [27] requires extra work to map the various identifiers. The Life Sciences Identifier (LSID) [28], a naming standard for biological resources designed to be used in Semantic Web applications should ease data interoperability. Unfortunately, at this time, LSID is still not widely adopted by biological data providers.

3.3. Bio-ontologies Do not Follow Standards for Ontology Design

To use ontologies at their full potential, concepts, relations and axioms must be shared when possible. Domain ontologies must also be anchored to an upper ontology to enable knowledge sharing and reuse. Unfortunately, each bio-ontology seems to be built as an independent piece of information in which every piece of knowledge is completely defined. This isolation of bio-ontologies does not enable the sharing and reuse of knowledge and complicates data integration [29].

3.4. Biological Knowledge Is Context Dependant

Biological knowledge is rapidly evolving; it may be uncertain, incomplete or variable. Knowledge modeling should represent this variation. The function of a gene product may vary depending on external conditions, the tissue where the gene is expressed, the experiment on which this assertion is based or the assumption of a researcher. Databases curators, who annotate gene products with GO terms, use evidence codes to indicate how an annotation to a particular term is supported. Another information that characterizes an annotation can also be relevant (type of experiment, reference to the biological object used to make the prediction, article in which the function is described). This information, which can be considered as a context, constitutes an important characteristic of the assertion which needs to be handled by Semantic Web applications.

3.5. Data Provenance Is of Crucial IMPORTANCE

In the life science, the same information may be stored in several databases. Sometimes, the contents of information are diverging. In addition to the information itself and the way this information has been generated (metadata encoded by the context), it is also essential, for researchers, to know its provenance [30] (for example, which laboratory or organism has diffused it). Handling information provenance is very important in e-science [31]. In bioinformatics, this information is available in several compendia; for example, in GeneCards [32] or GeneLynx [33]. A simplified view of the Semantic Web is a collection of RDF documents. The RDF recommendation explains the meaning of a document and how to merge a set of documents into one, but does not provide mechanisms for talking about relations between documents. Adding the notion of provenance to RDF is envisioned in the future. This topic is currently discussed in a working group called named graphs [34].

The two next sections describe a use case of biological data integration and visualization using Semantic Web technologies. The goal is to build a portal of gene-specific data allowing biologists to query and visualize, in a coherent presentation, various information automatically mined from public sources. The features of the portal, called "Thea online" are similar to other gene portals like GeneCards [32], geneLynx [33], Source [35] or SymAtlas [36].

4. Biological Data Integration with Semantic Web Technologies

Biological research, conducted in the post-genomic era, requires the analysis of large amounts of data. Such analyses often involve exploring and linking data from multiple different sources. However, with the unstoppable growth and the increasing number of biological databases, finding the relevant resources and making correct connections between their content becomes increasingly difficult.

Of course, today, biologists have access to bio-portals that provide a unified view on a variety of different data sources. However, the integration of each datasource in these aggregate databases is mostly designed, programmed and optimized in an ad hoc fashion by expert programmers.

The Semantic Web is about to revolutionize access to information. By enhancing the current Web with reasoning capabilities, the Semantic Web will enable automatic integration and combination of data drawn from diverse sources. From the user's point of view, the underlying technical solutions retained should be totally transparent. However, the adoption of Semantic Web technologies and languages will enable access to a virtually unlimited number of data sources.

4.1. Data Gathering

Various data about human genes or gene products were collected on the Web. This is an arbitrary choice intended to illustrate the variety of data available and the way these data are processed. Available data are either directly available in SWL, represented in a tabular format or stored in tables in relational databases.

Information expressed in SWL concerns protein centric data from UniProt [11], protein interactions data from IntAct [37] (data converted from flat file format into RDF by Eric Jain from Swiss Institute of Bioinformatics) and the structure of Gene Ontology from GO [10]. These data are described in two different ontologies. UniProt and IntAct data are described in an ontology called core.owl (available from the UniProt site). GO is a special case in the sense that it is not the definition of instances of an existing ontology, but it is an ontology by itself in which GO terms are represented by classes.

Data represented in tabular format concerns known and predicted protein-protein interactions from STRING [38], molecular interaction and reaction networks from KEGG [39], gene functional annotations from GeneRIFs [40], GO annotations from GOA [41], literature information and various mapping files from NCBI [42].

Information from relational databases is extracted by performing SQL queries. This kind of information concerns Ensembl data [43] which are queried on a MySQL server at address "ensembldb.ensembl.org".

A summary of collected data is presented in table 1 while Fig. 2 presents an overview of the different sources of data and the connections between these data. In the implementation described here, collected data about human genes are aggregated in a centralized data warehouse.

4.2. Data Conversion

In the future, when all sources will be encoded in SWL, downloaded data will be imported directly in the data warehouse. However, in the meantime, all the data that are not encoded in SWL needed to be converted. Tabular data were first converted in RDF with a simple procedure similar to the one used in YeastHub [44]. Each column which had to be converted in RDF was associated with a namespace that was used to construct the URIs identifying the values of the column (see the section "Principle of URIs encoding" below). The relationship between the content of two columns was expressed in RDF by a triple having the content of the first column as subject, the content of the second column as object and a specified property (Fig. 2). The conversions from tabular to RDF format were performed by dedicated Java or Python programs. The results obtained by SQL queries, which are composed of set of records, were processed the same way as data in a tabular format.

4.3. Ontology of Generated RDF Descriptions

The vocabulary used in generated RDF descriptions is defined in a new ontology called Biowl. Classes (i.e.: Gene, Transcript, Translation) and properties (i.e.: interacts_with, has_score, annotated_with) are defined in this ontology using the following namespace URI: "http://www.unice.fr/bioinfo/biowl#".

Table 1. List of collected data with the size of the corresponding RDF/OWL specification (in Kilobytes).

Source of information	**Size**
Gene Ontology *(at http://archive.geneontology.org/latest-termdb/)*	
go_daily-termdb.owl.gz	39,527
GOA *(at ftp://ftp.ebi.ac.uk/pub/databases/GO/goa/HUMAN/)*	
gene_association.goa_human.gz	25,254
Intact *(RDF description generated by Eric Jain from Uniprot)*	
Intact.rdf	28,776
Uniprot	
(at ftp://ftp.uniprot.org/pub/databases/uniprot/current_release/rdf/)	
citations.rdf.gz	351,204
components.rdf.gz	6
core.owl	128
enzyme.rdf.gz	2,753
go.rdf.gz	11,753
keywords.rdf.gz	550
taxonomy.rdf.gz	125,078
tissues.rdf.gz	392
uniprot.rdf.gz (human entries only)	897,742
String *(at http://string.embl.de/newstring_download/)*	
protein.links.v7.0.txt.gz (human related entries only)	388,732
KEGG *(at ftp://ftp.genome.jp/pub/kegg/)*	
ftp://ftp.genome.jp/pub/kegg/genes/organisms/hsa/hsa_xrefall.list	1,559
pathways/map_title.tab	1
NCBI GeneRIF *(at ftp://ftp.ncbi.nlm.nih.gov/gene/GeneRIF/)*	
generifs_basic.gz	40,831
interactions.gz	31,056
NCBI mapping files *(at ftp://ftp.ncbi.nlm.nih.gov/gene/DATA/)*	
gene2pubmed.gz	45,092
gene2unigene	4,036
Mim2gene	277
NCBI literature	
(at http://eutils.ncbi.nlm.nih.gov/entrez/eutils/efetch.fcgi)	
EFetch for Literature Databases	317,428
Ensembl *(at ensembldb.ensembl.org)*	
result of MySQL queries	50,768
TOTAL	**2,362,731**

4.4. Principe of URIs Encoding

In the RDF specifications generated from tabular files or from SQL queries, resources are identified with URIs. URIs were built by appending the identifier of a resource in

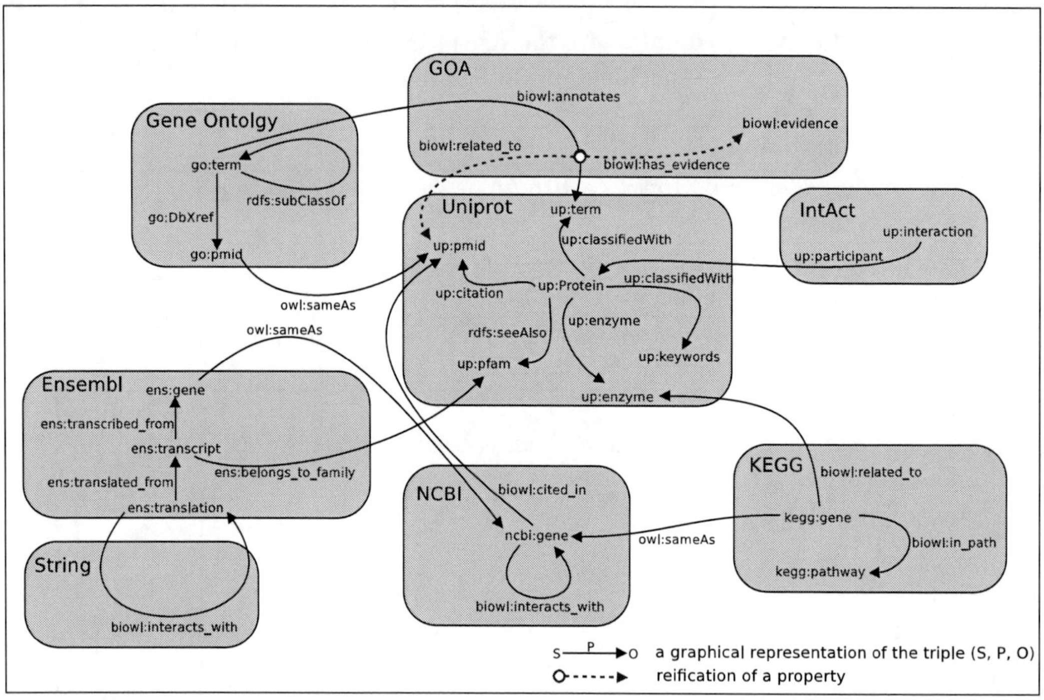

Figure 1. Graphical overview of the collected data. Each framed area represents a distinct source of data. Pieces of data are represented by vertices on the labelled graph. The relationships between pieces of data are represented by edges. Predicates that appear outside framed areas are defined during the unification of resources (see below).

a database to the database URL. For example, the peptide ENSP00000046967 from Ensembl database (accessible at the address http://www.ensembl.org) is assigned the URI "http://www.ensembl.org#ENSP00000046967" while the gene 672 from NCBI Entrez is assigned the URI "http://www.ncbi.nlm.nih.gov/entrez#672".

4.5. Unification of Resources

Several lists of mapping between identifiers used in different databases are available on the Web. The data from Ensembl, KEGG and the NCBI were used to generate OWL descriptions specifying the relationships that exists between resources. When two or more resources identify exactly the same object, they were unified with the OWL property "sameAs", otherwise, they were bound together with the most suitable property defined in the Biowl ontology (Fig. 3).

In the cases where the equivalences between resources are not specified in an existing mapping file, the identification of naming variants for a same resource was manually performed. By looking at the various URIs used to identify a same resource, one can highlight, for example, the fact that the biological process of "cell proliferation" is identified by the URI "http://purl.org/obo/owl/GO#GO_0008283" in Gene Ontology and by the URI "urn:lsid:uniprot.org:go:0008283" in UniProt. From this fact, a rule was built, stating that a resource identified with the URI "http://purl.org/obo/owl/GO#GO_$id" by GO is equiva-

a) Protein-protein interaction described in tabular format

```
9606.ENSP00000046967   9606.ENSP00000334051   600
```

b) Protein-protein interaction described in RDF

```
<Translation rdf:about="http://www.ensembl.org#ENSP00000046967">
  <interacts_with rdf:ID="SI3" rdf:resource="http://www.ensembl.org#ENSP00000334051"/>
</Translation>
<rdf:Description rdf:about="#SI3">
  <has_score>600</has_score>
</rdf:Description>
```

Figure 2. Principle of tabular to RDF conversion. a) a line from the STRING tabular file describing an interaction between a human proteins identified by "ENSP00000046967" in the Ensembl database and another protein identified by "ENSP00000334051" (in this file, downloaded from STRING, the relationship described in one line is directed, that means that the interaction between "ENSP00000334051" and "ENSP00000046967" is specified in another line). The reliability of the interaction is expressed by a score of 600 on a scale ranging from 0 to 1000. b) RDF encoding of the same information. The two proteins are represented with URIs and their interaction is represented with the property "interacts_with". The triple is materialized by a resource identified by "SI3". The score qualifying the reliability of the triple is encoded by the property "has_score" of the resource "SI3".

lent to a resource identified with the URI "urn:lsid:uniprot.org:go:$id" by Uniprot ($id is a variable that must match the same substring). The GO and Uniprot declarations were then processed with a program that uses the previously defined rule to generate a file of OWL statements expressing equivalences between resources (Fig. 4).

4.6. Ontologies Merging

As specified before, in addition to Biowl, two other existing ontologies defined by UniProt (core.owl) and GO (go_daily-termdb.owl) were used. These ontologies define different subsets of biological knowledge but are, nevertheless, overlapping. In order to be useful, the three ontologies have to be unified. There are multiple tools to merge or map ontologies [45] and [46] but they are quite difficult to use and require some user editing in order to obtain reliable results (see the evaluation in the frame of bioinformatics made by Lambrix and Edberg [47]). With the help of the ontology merging tool PROMPT [48] and the ontology editor Protégé [49], a unified ontology, describing the equivalences between the classes and properties defined in the three sources ontologies, was created. For example, the concept of protein is defined by the class "urn:lsid:uniprot.org:ontology:Protein" in Uniprot and the class "http://www.unice.fr/bioinfo/owl/biowl#Translation" in Biowl. The unification of these classes is declared in a separate ontology defining a new class dedicated to the representation of the unified concept of protein which is assigned the URI "http://www.unice.fr/bioinfo/owl/unification#Protein". Each representation of this concept in other ontologies is declared as being a subclass of the unified concept, as described in Fig. 5.

```
a)  <GeneProduct rdf:about=”http://www.genome.jp/kegg/gene#675”>
      <owl:sameAs rdf:resource=”http://www.ncbi.nlm.nih.gov/EntrezGene#675”/>
      <biowl:encodes rdf:resource=”http://www.ncbi.nlm.nih.gov/Protein#119395734”/>
      <biowl:in_pathway rdf:resource=”http://www.genome.jp/kegg/pathway#hsa05212”/>
    </GeneProduct>
b)  <Gene rdf:about=”http://www.ncbi.nlm.nih.gov/EntrezGene#675”>
      <biowl:cited_in rdf:resource=”urn:lsid:uniprot.org:pubmed:1072445”/>
    </Gene>
    <Gene rdf:about=”http://www.ncbi.nlm.nih.gov/EntrezGene#672”>
      <interacts_with rdf:ID=”NI8128” rdf:resource=”http://www.ncbi.nlm.nih.gov/EntrezGene#675”/>
    </Gene>
    <Gene rdf:about=”http://www.ncbi.nlm.nih.gov/EntrezGene#675”>
      <biowl:has_phenotype rdf:resource=”urn:lsid:uniprot.org:mim:114480”/>
    </Gene>
    <Gene rdf:about=”http://www.ncbi.nlm.nih.gov/EntrezGene#675”>
      <in_cluster rdf:resource=”http://www.ncbi.nlm.nih.gov/UniGene#Hs.34012”/>
    </Gene>
c)  <Gene rdf:about=”http://www.ensembl.org/gene#ENSG00000139618”>
      <owl:sameAs rdf:resource=”http://www.ncbi.nlm.nih.gov/EntrezGene#675”/>
    </Gene>
```

Figure 3. Description of some of the links between the gene BRCA2, identified with the id 675 at NCBI and other resources. a) descriptions derived from KEGG files. b) descriptions derived from NCBI files. c) descriptions built from the information extracted from Ensembl database.

The same principle is applied for properties by specifying that several equivalent properties are sub properties of a unified one. For example, the concept of name, defined by the property “http://www.unice.fr/bioinfo/owl/biowl#denomination” in Biowl and by the property “urn:lsid:uniprot.org:ontology:name” in UniProt is unified with the property “http://www.unice.fr/bioinfo/owl/unification#name”, as shown in Fig. 6.

One has to note that this is not the aim of this chapter to describe a method for unifying ontologies. The unification performed here concerns only obvious concepts like the classes “Protein” or “Translation” or the properties “cited_in” or “encoded_by” (for details, see supplementary materials at http://bioinfo.unice.fr/publications/DMSW_chapter/). The unification ontology allows multiples specifications, defined with different ontologies to be queried in a unified way by a system capable of performing type inference based on the ontology's classes and properties hierarchy.

4.7. Data Repository

Data collected from several sources which are associated with metadata and organized by an ontology represent a domain knowledge. This knowledge, represented by the set of collected and generated RDF/OWL specifications has to be stored in a Knowledge Base. In order to be able to fully exploit this knowledge, a Knowledge Bases System (KBS) [50] capable of storing and performing queries on a large set of RDF/OWL specifications (including the storing and querying of reified statements) is needed. It must include reasoning capabilities like type inference, transitivity and the handling of at least these two OWL

```
<rdf:Description rdf:about="http://purl.org/obo/owl/GO#GO_0008283">
  <owl:sameAs rdf:resource="urn:lsid:uniprot.org:go:0008283"/>
</rdf:Description>
```

Figure 4. Description of the equivalence of two resources using the owl property “sameAs”. The biological process of “cell proliferation” is identified by the URI “http://purl.org/obo/owl/GO#GO_0008283” in GO and by the URI “urn:lsid:uniprot.org:go:0008283” in UniProt. This description states that the two resources are the same.

```
<owl:Class rdf:ID="http://www.unice.fr/bioinfo/owl/unification#Protein"/>
<owl:Class rdf:about="http://www.unice.fr/bioinfo/owl/biowl#Translation">
  <rdfs:subClassOf rdf:resource="http://www.unice.fr/bioinfo/owl/unification#Protein"/>
</owl:Class>
<owl:Class rdf:about="urn:lsid:uniprot.org:ontology:Protein">
  <rdfs:subClassOf rdf:resource="http://www.unice.fr/bioinfo/owl/unification#Protein"/>
</owl:Class>
```

Figure 5. Unification of different definitions of the concept of protein (see the text for details).

constructs: “sameAs” and “inverseOf”. In addition, it should be capable of storing and querying the provenance of information.

For this application, a specifically designed KBS, called AllOnto, was used. However, other KBS, like Sesame (http://www.openrdf.org) might be used as well.

4.8. Information Retrieval with SPARQL

Triples stored in the KBS, information encoded using reification and the provenance of the assertions can be queried with SPARQL queries. An example of a query allowing retrieving every annotation of protein P38398 associated with its reliability and provenance is given in Fig. 7.

5. Data Visualization

The Web portal can be accessed at http://bioinfo.unice.fr:8080/thea-online/. Entering search terms in a simple text box returns a synthetic report of every available information relative to a gene or gene’s product.

Search in Thea-online has been designed to be as simple as possible. There is no need to format queries in any special way or to specify the name of the database a query identifier comes from. A variety of names, symbols, aliases or identifiers can be entered in the text area. For example, a search for the gene BRCA1 and its products can be specified using the following strings: the gene name “BRCA1”, the alias “RNF53”, the full sentence “Breast cancer type 1 susceptibility protein”, the NCBI gene ID “672”, the UniProt accession number “P38398”, the OMIM entry “113705”, the EMBL accession number “AY304547”, the RefSeq identifier “NM_007299” or the Affymetrix probe id “1993_s_at”.

```
<owl:DatatypeProperty rdf:ID="http://www.unice.fr/bioinfo/owl/unification#name"/>
<owl:DatatypeProperty rdf:about="urn:lsid:uniprot.org:ontology:name">
  <rdfs:subPropertyOf rdf:resource="http://www.unice.fr/bioinfo/owl/unification#name"/>
</owl:DatatypeProperty>
<owl:DatatypeProperty rdf:about="http://www.unice.fr/bioinfo/owl/biowl#denomination">
  <rdfs:subPropertyOf rdf:resource="http://www.unice.fr/bioinfo/owl/unification#name"/>
</owl:DatatypeProperty>
```

Figure 6. Unification of different definitions of the property "name" (see the text for details).

When Thea-online is queried, the query string is first searched in the KBS. If the string unambiguously identifies an object stored in the base, information about this object is displayed on a Web page. If this is not the case, a disambiguation page is displayed (Fig. 8).

Information displayed as a result of a search is divided in seven different sections: "Gene Description", "General Information", "Interactions", "Probes", "Pathways", "Annotations" and "Citations". To limit the amount of data, it is possible to select the type of information displayed by using an option's panel. This panel can be used to choose the categories of information to display on the result page, to select the sources of information to use and to specify the context of some kind of information (this concerns Gene Ontology evidences only at this time).

By performing SPARQL queries on the model, as described in Fig. 7, the application has access to information concerning the seven categories presented above and some metadata about it. In the current version, the metadata always includes the provenance of information, the articles in which an interaction is defined for protein interactions and the evidence code supporting the annotation for gene ontology association. The provenance of information is visualized with a small colored icon (see Fig. 9). Some exceptions concern information about "gene and gene products" and "genomic location" which comes from Ensembl and the extensive list of alternative identifiers which are mined from multiple mapping files.

Gene product annotations are displayed as in Fig. 10. By looking in details at the line describing the annotation with the molecular function "DNA Binding", one can see that this annotation is associated with no evidence code in UniProt, with the evidence code "TAS" (Traceable Author Statement) in GOA and UniProt and with the evidence code "IEA" (Inferred from Electronic Annotation) in GOA and Ensembl. The annotation of the gene product without an evidence code is deduced from the association of the protein with the SwissProt keyword "DNA-binding" which is defined as being equivalent to the GO term "DNA binding".

The unification of resources is used to avoid the repetition of the same information. In Fig. 10, the classification of the protein P38398 with the SwissProt keyword "DNA-binding" is considered as being the same information as the annotation with the GO term "DNA binding" as the two resources are defined as being equivalent. In Fig. 11, the unification is used in order to not duplicate an interaction which is expressed using a gene identifier in NCBI and a protein identifier in UniProt and IntAct.

```
PREFIX  up: <urn:lsid:uniprot.org:uniprot:>
PREFIX unif: <http://www.unice.fr/bioinfo/owl/unification#>
PREFIX  rdf: <http://www.w3.org/1999/02/22-rdf-syntax-ns#>
SELECT
  ?annotation ?reliability ?source
WHERE
  {
    GRAPH ?source
      { ?r rdf:subject up:P38398 .
        ?r rdf:predicate unif:annotated_by .
        ?r rdf:object ?annot .
        ?r unif:reliability ?reliability
      }
  }
```

Figure 7. SPARQL query used to retrieve annotations of protein P38398. This query displays the set of data representing an annotation, a reliability score and the information source for the protein identified by P38398 in UniProt. The KBS is searched for a triple "r" having the resource "urn:lsid:uniprot.org:uniprot:P38398" as subject, the resource "http://www.unice.fr/bioinfo/owl/unification#annotated_by" as predicate and the variable "annot" as object. The value of the property "http://www.unice.fr/bioinfo/owl/unification#reliability" of the matched triple is stored in the variable "reliability". The provenance of the information is obtained by retrieving the named graph which contains these specifications. The KBS performs "sameAs" inference to unify the UniProt protein P38398 with the same resource defined in other databases. It also uses the unified ontology to look for data expressed using sub properties of "annotated_by" and "reliability".

6. Discussion

Thea-online constitutes a use case of Semantic Web technologies applied to life science. It relies on the use of already available Semantic Web standards (URIs, RDF, OWL, SPARQL) to integrate, query and display information originating from several different sources.

To develop Thea-online, several pre-processing tasks were performed, like the conversion of data in RDF format, the elaboration of a new ontology and the identification of each resource with a unique URI. These operations will not be required in the future, when the data will be encoded in RDF. The process of resources mapping will be still needed until the resources are assigned with a unique identifier or that mappings expressed in SWL are available. The same applies to the task of ontology merging that will remain unless ontologies are linked to an upper ontology or until some descriptions of equivalences between ontologies are available.

From the user point of view, the use of Semantic Web technologies to build the portal is not visible. Similar results should have been obtained with classical solutions using, for example, a relational database. The main impact in the use of Semantic Web technologies concerns the ease of development and maintenance of such a tool. In the present version, our portal is limited to human genes, but it can be easily extended to other species. The addition of new kind of data if also facilitated because the KB doesn't rely on a static

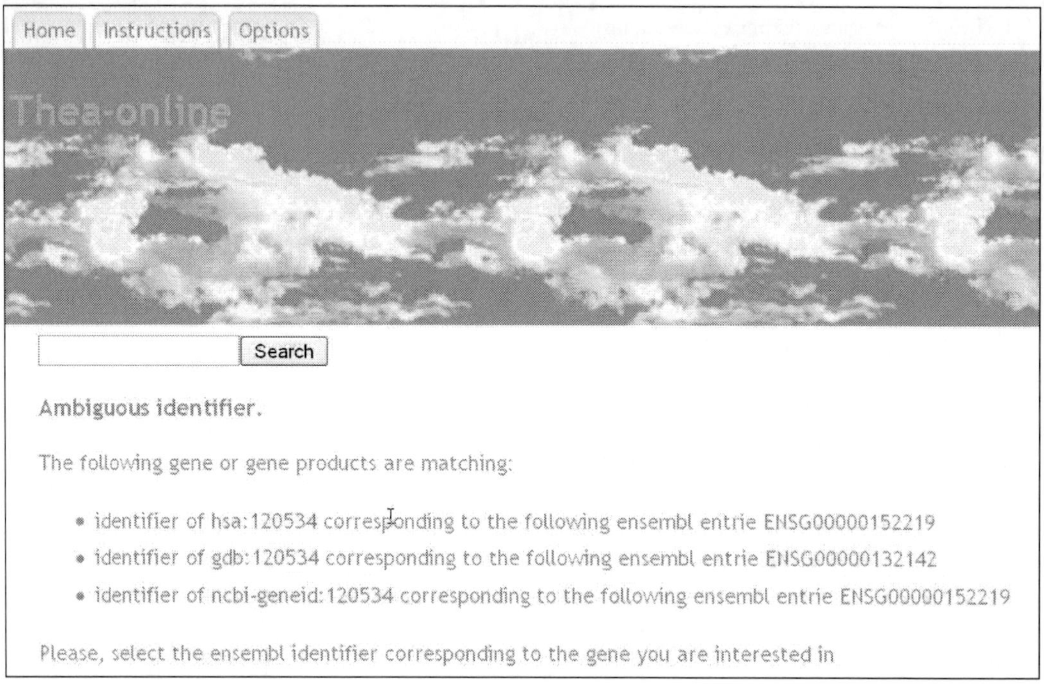

Figure 8. Disambiguation page displayed when querying for the string "120534". The message indicates that string "120534" matches a gene identifier from the Human Genome Database (GDB) corresponding to the Ensembl entry "ENSG00000132142" but also matches a gene identifier from KEGG and a gene identifier from NCBI which both correspond to the Ensembl entry "ENSG00000152219". A user can obtain a report on the gene he is interested in by selecting the proper Ensembl identifier.

modelization of the data like in a relational database. To access a new kind of data, one simply has to write or modify a SPARQL request.

Provided that information is properly encoded with SWL, generic tools can be used to infer some knowledge which, until now, must be generated programmatically. For example, when searching for a list of protein involved in the response to a temperature stimulus, an intelligent agent, using the structure of Gene Ontology, should return the list of proteins annotated with the term "response to temperature stimulus" but also the proteins annotated "response to cold" or "response to heat". By using the inference capabilities available in AllOnto, the retrieval of the information displayed in each section of a result page is performed with a unique SPARQL query.

Of course, the correctness of the inferred knowledge is very dependent on the quality of the information encoded in SWL. In the current Web, erroneous information can be easily discarded by the user. In the context of the Semantic Web, this filtering will be more difficult because it must be performed by a software agent. Let us take, for example, the mapping of SwissProt keywords to GO terms expressed in the plain text file spkw2go (http://www.geneontology.org/external2go/spkw2go). The information expressed in this file is directed: to one SwissProt keyword corresponds one or several GO terms but the reverse is not true. In the RDF encoding of Uniprot, this information is represented in

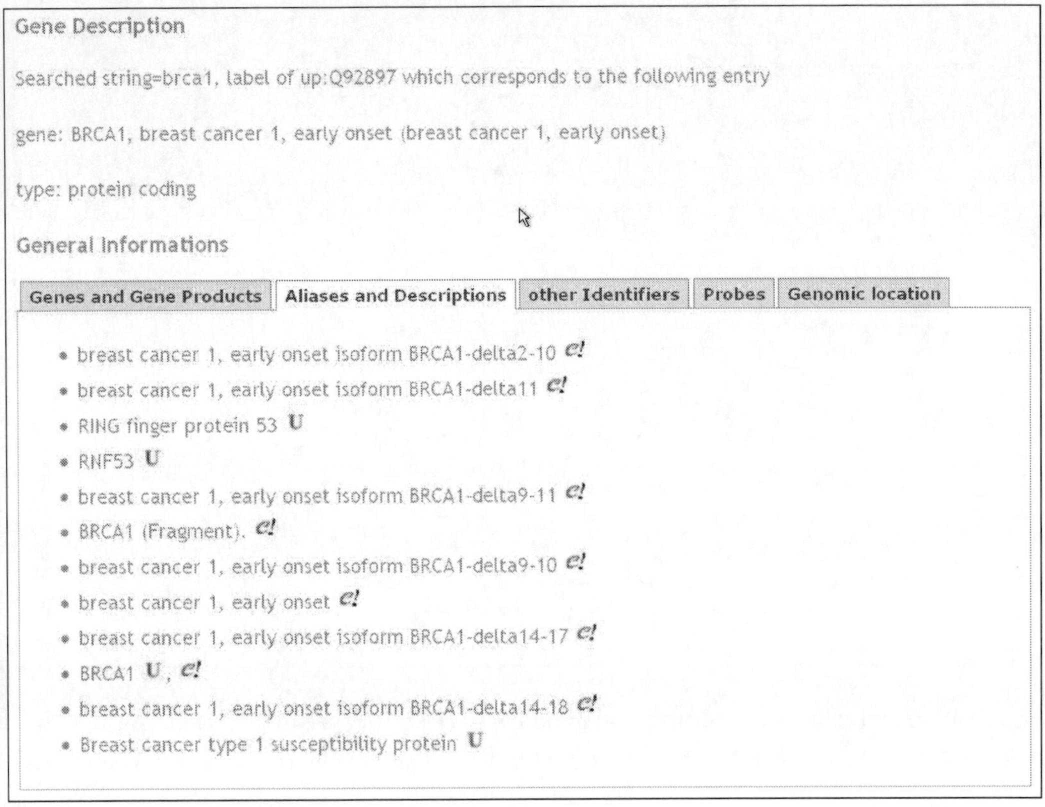

Figure 9. General information about the gene BRCA1 and its products. Selecting tab "Aliases and Descriptions" displays various names and descriptions concerning the gene BRCA1 and its products. Every displayed string is followed by a small icon specifying the provenance of the information: an uppercase red "U" for UniProt and a lowercase blue "e" followed by a red exclamation mark for Ensembl. Several labels are originating from a single database only (like the string "breast cancer 1, early onset isoform BRCA1-delta11" used in Ensembl or "RING finger protein 53" used in UniProt) while other labels are common to different databases (like BRCA1 used both in UniProt and Ensembl).

RDF/OWL format with the symmetric property "sameAs" (see the file keywords.rdf available from Uniprot RDF site). Thus, the information encoded in RDF/OWL is incorrect, but it will be extremely difficult for a program to discover it.

7. Conclusion

From this experiment, two main conclusions can be drawn: one which covers the technological issues, the other one which concerns more sociological aspects. Thea-online is built on a data warehouse architecture [51] which means that data coming from distant sources are stored locally. It is an acceptable solution when the data are not too large and one can tolerate that information is not completely up-to-date with the version stored in source databases. However, the verbosity of SWL results in amazing quantities of data which are

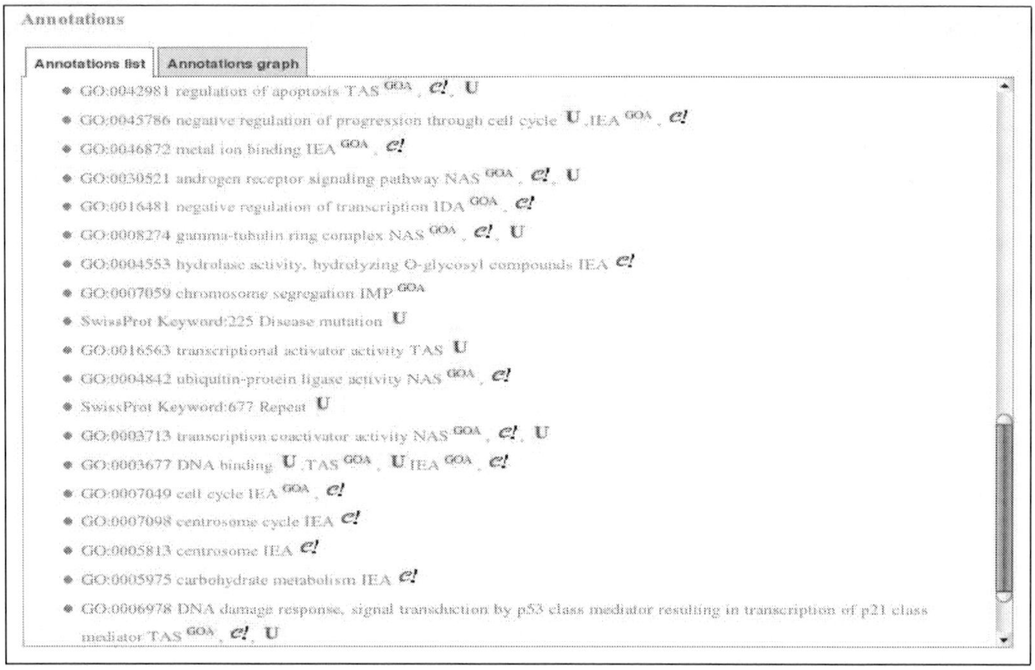

Figure 10. Annotations concerning the gene BRCA1 and its products. Selecting tab "Annotations list" displays the list of annotations concerning the gene BRCA1 and its products. Every displayed string is followed by a small icon specifying the provenance of the information. The first line, for example, represents an annotation of BRCA1 with the GO term "regulation of apoptosis" supported by the evidence code "TAS". This information is found in GOA, Ensembl and UniProt. The second line represents an annotation with the GO term "negative regulation of progression through cell cycle". This information is found in UniProt with no supporting evidence code and in GOA and Ensembl with the evidence code "IEA".

difficult to handle in a KBS. An import of the whole RDF serialization of UniProt (25 gigabytes of data) has been successfully performed but improvements are still required in order to deal with huge datasets. From the technological point of view, the obstacles that must be overcome to fully benefit from the potential of Semantic Web are still important.

However, as pointed out by Good and Wilkinson [52], the primary hindrances to the creation of the Semantic Web for life science may be social rather than technological. There may be some reticences from bioinformaticians to drop the creative aspects in the elaboration of a database or a user interface to conform to the standards [53]. That also constitutes a fundamental change in the way biological information is managed. This represents a move from a centralized architecture in which every actor controls its own information to an open world of inter-connected data, which can be enriched by third-parties. In addition, because of the complexity of the technology, placing data on the Semantic Web asks much more work than simply making it available on the traditional Web. Under these conditions, it is not astonishing to note that currently, the large majority of biomedical data and knowledge is not encoded with SWL. Even when efforts were carried out to make data available on the

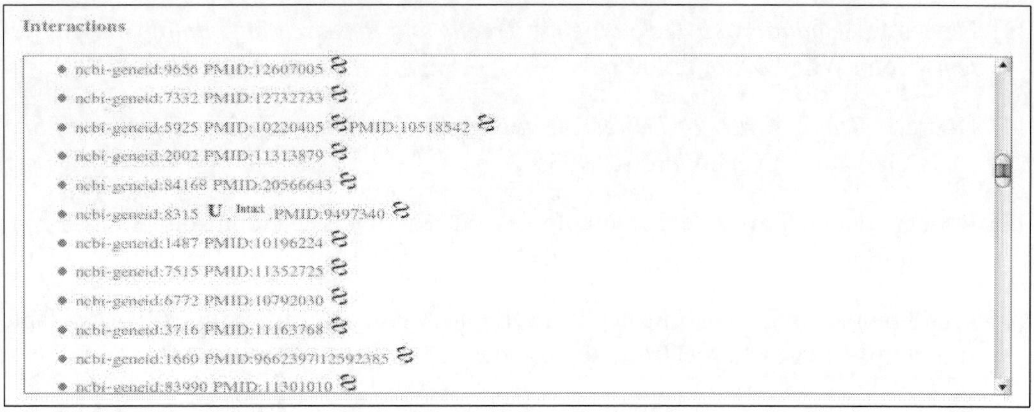

Figure 11. Interactions concerning the gene BRCA1 and its products. Most of the displayed information is coming from NCBI (the NCBI icon is displayed at the end of the lines). When information is available, the Pubmed identifier of the article describing the interaction is given. A line, in the middle of the list displays the same piece of information coming from UniProt, Intact and NCBI. This line is the result of a unification performed on data describing the information in different ways. In UniProt and Intact databases, the protein P38398 is declared as interacting with the protein Q7Z569. In the NCBI interactions file, an interaction is specified with the product of the gene identified by geneID "672" and the product of the gene identified by GeneID "8315". The KBS uses the fact that proteins P38398 and Q7Z569 are respectively products of the genes identified at NCBI by the IDs "672" and "8315" to display the information in a unified way.

Semantic Web, most data sources are not compliant with the standards [52], [29] and [14].

Even though our application works, a significant amount of pre-processing was necessary to simulate the fact that data were directly available on a suitable format. Other applications on the Semantic Web in life science performed in a similar fashion, using wrappers, converters or extraction programs [44], [15], [54], [55] and [56]. It is foreseeable that, in the future, more data will be available on the Semantic Web, easing the development of increasingly complex and useful new applications. This movement will be faster if information providers are aware of the interest to make their data compatible with Semantic Web standards. Applications, like the one presented in this chapter or in others, illustrating the potential of this technology, should gradually incite actors in the life science community to follow this direction.

References

[1] Berners-Lee T, Hendler J. Publishing on the semantic web. *Nature.* 2001;410(6832):1023–1024.

[2] Bratt SR. Toward a Web of Data and Programs. In: *IEEE Symposium on Global Data Interoperability - Challenges and Technologies;* 2005. p. 124–128.

[3] Davies J. *Semantic Web Technologies: Trends and Research in Ontology-based Systems.* John Wiley & Sons; 2006.

[4] Dupré J. *The Disorder of Things: Metaphysical Foundations of the Disunity of Science.* Harvard University Press; 1993.

[5] Bodenreider O, Stevens R. Bio-ontologies: current trends and future directions. *Briefings in Bioinformatics.* 2006;7(3):256–274.

[6] Prud'hommeaux E, Seaborne A. SPARQL Query Language for RDF; 2007. Available from http://www.w3.org/TR/rdf-sparql-query/.

[7] Ruttenberg A, Clark T, Bug W, Samwald M, Bodenreider O, Chen H, et al. Advancing translational research with the Semantic Web. B*MC Bioinformatics.* 2007;8(Suppl 3):S2.

[8] Whetzel PL, Parkinson H, Causton HC, Fan L, Fostel J, Fragoso G, et al. The MGED Ontology: a resource for semantics-based description of microarray experiments. *Bioinformatics.* 2006;22(7):866–873.

[9] BioPAX. BioPAX Biological Pathways Exchange Language Level 2; 2005. Available from http://www.biopax.org/.

[10] Ashburner M, Ball CA, Blake JA, Botstein D, Butler H, Cherry JM, et al. Gene Ontology: tool for the unification of biology. *Nature Genetics.* 2000;25(1):25–29.

[11] Consortium TU. The Universal Protein Resource (UniProt). *Nucleic Acids Research.* 2007;35(suppl_1):193–197.

[12] Smith A, Cheung K, Krauthammer M, Schultz M, Gerstein M. Leveraging the structure of the Semantic Web to enhance information retrieval for proteomics. *Bioinformatics.* 2007;23(22):3073–3079.

[13] Post LJG, Roos M, Marshall MS, van Driel R, Breit TM. A semantic web approach applied to integrative bioinformatics experimentation: a biological use case with genomics data. *Bioinformatics.* 2007;23(22):3080–3087.

[14] Quan D. Improving life sciences information retrieval using semantic web technology. *Briefings in Bioinformatics.* 2007;8(3):172–182.

[15] Smith A, Cheung KH, Yip K, Schultz M, Gerstein M. LinkHub: a Semantic Web system that facilitates cross-database queries and information retrieval in proteomics. *BMC Bioinformatics.* 2007;8(Suppl 3):S5.

[16] Jiang K, Nash C. Ontology-based aggregation of biological pathway datasets. In: Engineering in Medicine and Biology Society, *IEEE-EMBS.* vol. 7; 2005. p. 7742–5.

[17] Kunapareddy N, Mirhaji P, Richards D, Casscells SW. Information integration from heterogeneous data sources: a Semantic Web approach. *American Medical Informatics Association, Annual Symposium Proceedings.* 2006;p. 992.

[18] Lam HY, Marenco L, Shepherd GM, Miller PL, Cheung KH. Using web ontology language to integrate heterogeneous databases in the neurosciences. *American Medical Informatics Association, Annual Symposium Proceedings.* 2006;p. 464–8.

[19] Sabou M, Wroe C, Goble CA, Stuckenschmidt H. Learning domain ontologies for semantic Web service descriptions. *Journal of Web Semantics.* 2005;3(4):340–365.

[20] Wilkinson MD, Links M. BioMOBY: An open source biological web services proposal. *Briefings in Bioinformatics.* 2002;3(4):331–341.

[21] Kawas E, Senger M, Wilkinson M. BioMoby extensions to the Taverna workflow management and enactment software. *BMC Bioinformatics.* 2006;7(1):523.

[22] Pierre T, Zoe L, Herve M. Semantic Map of Services for Structural Bioinformatics. In: Scientific and Statistical Database Management, *18th International Conference.* vol. 0. Vienna; 2006. p. 217–224.

[23] Oinn T, Greenwood M, Addis M, Alpdemir N, Ferris J, Glover K, et al. Taverna: lessons in creating a workflow environment for the life sciences. *Concurrency and Computation: Practice and Experience.* 2006;18(10):1067–1100.

[24] Gomez JM, Rico M, García-Sánchez F, Liu Y, Mello MT. BIRD: Biomedical Information Integration and Discovery with Semantic Web Services. In: *IWINAC '07: Proceedings of the 2nd international work-conference on Nature Inspired Problem-Solving Methods in Knowledge Engineering.* Berlin, Heidelberg: Springer-Verlag; 2007. p. 561–570.

[25] Guo Y, Pan Z, Heflin J. An Evaluation of Knowledge Base Systems for Large OWL Datasets. In: *Third International Semantic Web Conference.* Hiroshima, Japan; 2004. p. 274–288.

[26] Letovsky SI, Cottingham RW, Porter CJ, Li PWD. GDB: the Human Genome Database. *Nucleic Acids Research.* 1998;26(1):94–99.

[27] Povey S, Lovering R, Bruford E, Wright M, Lush M, Wain H. The HUGO Gene Nomenclature Committee (HGNC). *Humam Genetics.* 2001;109(6):678–80.

[28] Clark T, Martin S, Liefeld T. Globally distributed object identification for biological knowledgebases. *Briefings in Bioinformatics.* 2004;5(1):59–70.

[29] Soldatova LN, King RD. Are the current ontologies in biology good ontologies? *Nature Biotechnology.* 2005;23(9):1095–1098.

[30] Cohen S, Cohen-Boulakia S, Davidson S. Towards a Model of Provenance and User Views in Scientific Workflows. In: DILS 2006, *Third International Workshop in Data Integration in the Life Sciences.* vol. 4075 of *Lecture Notes in Computer Science.* Springer; 2006. p. 264–279.

[31] Yogesh LS, Beth P, Dennis G. A survey of data provenance in e-science. *ACM SIGMOD Records.* 2005;34(3):31–36.

[32] Rebhan M, Califa-Caspi V, Prilusky J, Lancet D. GeneCards: a novel functional genomics compendium with automated data mining and query reformulation support. *Bioinformatics.* 1998;14(8):656–664.

[33] Lenhard B, Hayes WS, Wasserman WW. GeneLynx: A Gene-Centric Portal to the Human Genome. *Genome Research.* 2001;11(12):2151–2157.

[34] Jeremy JC, Christian B, Pat H, Patrick S. Named graphs, provenance and trust. In: *WWW '05: Proceedings of the 14th international conference on World Wide Web.* New York, NY, USA: ACM; 2005. p. 613–622.

[35] Diehn M, Sherlock G, Binkley G, Jin H, Matese JC, Hernandez-Boussard T, et al. SOURCE: a unified genomic resource of functional annotations, ontologies, and gene expression data. *Nucleic Acids Research.* 2003;31(1):219–223.

[36] Su AI, Cooke MP, Ching KA, Hakak Y, Walker JR, Wiltshire T, et al. Large-scale analysis of the human and mouse transcriptomes. *Proceedings of the National Academy of Sciences.* 2002;99(7):44654470.

[37] Kerrien S, Alam-Faruque Y, Aranda B, Bancarz I, Bridge A, Derow C, et al. IntAct–open source resource for molecular interaction data. *Nucleic Acids Research.* 2007;35(suppl_1):D561–565.

[38] von Mering C, Jensen LJ, Kuhn M, Chaffron S, Doerks T, Kruger B, et al. STRING 7–recent developments in the integration and prediction of protein interactions. *Nucleic Acids Research.* 2007;35(suppl_1):358–362.

[39] Kanehisa M, Goto S, Hattori M, Aoki-Kinoshita KF, Itoh M, Kawashima S, et al. From genomics to chemical genomics: new developments in KEGG. *Nucleic Acids Research.* 2006;34(suppl_1):D354–357.

[40] Mitchell JA, Aronson AR, Mork JG, Folk LC, Humphrey SM, Ward JM. Gene indexing: characterization and analysis of NLM's GeneRIFs. *American Medical Informatics Association, Annual Symposium Proceedings.* 2003;p. 460–4.

[41] Camon E, Magrane M, Barrell D, Lee V, Dimmer E, Maslen J, et al. The Gene Ontology Annotation (GOA) Database: sharing knowledge in Uniprot with Gene Ontology. *Nucleic Acids Research.* 2004;32(suppl_1):262–266.

[42] Maglott D, Ostell J, Pruitt KD, Tatusova T. Entrez Gene: gene-centered information at NCBI. *Nucleic Acids Research.* 2007;35(Database issue):26–31.

[43] Birney E, Andrews TD, Bevan P, Caccamo M, Chen Y, Clarke L, et al. An Overview of Ensembl. *Genome Research.* 2004;14(5):925–928.

[44] Cheung KH, Yip KY, Smith A, deKnikker R, Masiar A, Gerstein M. YeastHub: a semantic web use case for integrating data in the life sciences domain. *Bioinformatics.* 2005;21(suppl_1):i85–96.

[45] Kalfoglou Y, Schorlemmer M. Ontology mapping: the state of the art. *Knowledge Engineering Review.* 2003;18(1):1–31.

[46] Do HH, Rahm E. Matching large schemas: Approaches and evaluation. *Information Systems.* 2007;32(6):857–885.

[47] Lambrix P, Edberg A. Evaluation of ontology merging tools in bioinformatics. In: *proceeding of the Pacific Symposium on Biocomputing.* Lihue, Hawaii; 2003. p. 589–600.

[48] Natalya FN, Mark AM. The PROMPT suite: interactive tools for ontology merging and mapping. *International Journal of Human-Computer Studies.* 2003;59(6):983–1024.

[49] Rubin D, Noy N, Musen M. Protégé: A Tool for Managing and Using Terminology in Radiology Applications. *Journal of Digital Imaging.* 2007;20(0):34–46.

[50] John M, Vinay C, Dimitris P, Adel S, Thodoros T. Building knowledge base management systems. *The VLDB Journal.* 1996;5(4):238–263.

[51] Surajit C, Umeshwar D. An overview of data warehousing and OLAP technology. *ACM SIGMOD Record.* 1997;26(1):65–74.

[52] Good BM, Wilkinson MD. The Life Sciences Semantic Web is full of creeps! *Briefings in Bioinformatics.* 2006;7(3):275–86.

[53] Stein L. Creating a bioinformatics nation. *Nature.* 2002;417(6885):119–20.

[54] Schroeder M, Burger A, Kostkova P, Stevens R, Habermann B, Dieng-Kuntz R. Sealife: a semantic grid browser for the life sciences applied to the study of infectious diseases. *Studies in Health Technology and Informatics.* 2006;120:167–78.

[55] Neumann EK, Quan D. BioDash: a Semantic Web dashboard for drug development. In: *proceeding of the pacific Symposium on Biocomputing;* 2006. p. 176–87.

[56] Nardon FB, Moura LA. Knowledge sharing and information integration in healthcare using ontologies and deductive databases. *Medinfo.* 2004;11(Pt 1):62–6.

In: Data Management in the Semantic Web
Editor: Hal Jin, pp. 153-170
ISBN: 978-1-61122-862-5

Chapter 7

AN ONTOLOGY AND PEER-TO-PEER BASED DATA AND SERVICE UNIFIED DISCOVERY SYSTEM

***Ying Zhang*[1,*]*, Houkuan Huang*[2] *and Youli Qu*[2]**
1 School of Control and Computer Engineering, North China Electric Power University, Beijing, P.R. China
2 School of Electronics and Information Engineering, Beijing Jiaotong University, Beijing, P.R. China

Abstract

The next generation Internet has the potential ability to be a ubiquitous and pervasive medium communication carrier for all types of information. The World Wide Web is emerging with a broader variety of resources that include both data and services. Yet, a lot of research work focused on either service discovery or data discovery although they cannot be separated from each other. In addition, the current Network, due to its decentralized nature and weak support for semantic, is still chaotic and lacks of the ability to allow users to discover, extract and integrate information of interest from heterogeneous sources. In this paper, we present a scalable, high performance system for data and service unified discovery, and to increase the success rate, an ontology-based approach is used to describe data and services. As for service, we add quality of service (QoS) information to OWL-S files to get more accurate results for users. Moreover, we also bring JXTA, which is a suitable foundation to build future computer systems on, to our system.

1. Introduction

At present, many data or service discovery processes use keyword-matching technique to find published information. This method often discontents requesters with so many unrelated results that lead to certain amount of manual work to choose the proper service according to its semantics. In order to solve this problem, semantic web technique—OWL and OWL-S, which are innovative for data discovery and service discovery respectively, have been

[*] E-mail address: dearzppzpp@gmail.com; Phone: +8613261206198.

adopted. By using this semantic web technique, the information necessary for resource discovery could be specified as computer-interpretable [1-2].

We make use of four types of ontological data in this paper, namely, thesaurus ontology, resource domain ontology, service description ontology and QoS ontology. They will be specified in the next section.

There is a close relationship between data and service. However, much research work only concentrates on one part. Nowadays, users often search resources by keywords, and though they may want both data and related services, they can get only one kind of resource by a single query process. For one thing, user wants to choose a music file (mp3) for a special scene. In current Internet, he will type some words about the scene as his keywords and get much information of this scene, but no useful information about the music will he gain. The reason for this is that the current network is short of semantic information and correlation among multifarious resources. In this paper, we append semantic information and interrelationship to resource discovery process, and they meet with good results.

With regard to OWL-S, we apply it to describe services. It provides three essential types of knowledge about a service: a service profile (what the service does), a service model (how the service works), and a service grounding (how to use the service). The service profile describes what the service can do, for purposes of advertising, discovering, and matchmaking [3]. It describes the basic ability of service, so it is helpful for fulfilling the requirement of service discovery. In order to satisfy users' high-class requirements, we propose to add QoS descriptions to OWL-S to specify the service's QoS information.

Current proposals for data or service discovery focus on centralized approaches [4-5]. Resource descriptions are stored in a central repository which has to be queried in order to discover resource. Such centralized approach introduces single point failure and exposes vulnerability to malicious attacks and does not suit large number of resources. This disadvantage is fatal for evolving trend to ubiquitous and pervasive computing in which more and more devices and entities become services and the resource networks become extremely dynamic due to constantly arriving and departing resource providers [6-8].

In order to achieve high scalability, we focus on developing a decentralized discovery approach [9-12]. There are several P2P systems available, such as Gnutella and Napster. However, most of them are intended for one specific application like file sharing [3]. Therefore, our current research uses the P2P infrastructure JXTA. The JXTA Search discovery and access model exposes content unavailable through traditional indexing and catching search engines using a query routing protocol (QRP) for distributed information retrieval [13]. JXTA Search occupies a middle ground between the decentralized Gnutella and centralized Napster geometries, and is independent of platform, network transport and programming language.

The rest of this paper is as follows: In Section 2, we provide preliminary knowledge. In Section 3, we illustrate design of the unified discovery system. Next, we bring JXTA to our system design in Section 4. Resource registry and discovery are specified in Section 5. Then, experimental results and related work are presented in Sections 6 and 7 respectively. Last, in Section 8, we conclude and discuss our future work.

2. Preliminaries

2.1. Terms and Definitions

We give a definition of the service in this unified discovery system: service is a self-contained and modular application that can be described, published, located, and invoked over the network. Providing various qualities of services for different users is a significant feature of the next generation Internet. Quality depends on user's request and pay. Pay more can get more.

2.2. Ontological Data

As mentioned above, four types of ontological data are utilized in this paper; they are resource domain ontology, thesaurus ontology, service description ontology and QoS ontology. We will discuss them in detail in the context.

2.2.1. Resource Domain Ontology

The resource domain ontology is shown in Fig.1. In Fig.1, boxes represent classes in the resource domain ontology and ovals denote instances which are resources in the network.
Resources will be added as instances into ontology when providers register them. Data and services are denoted by ovals and dashed ovals respectively. To be on the simple side, this resource domain ontology comprises six domains: entertainment, engineering science, education, physical object, region and sport. Take education as an example, data mining and multi-agent system, which are data resources, belong to education domain; isbn book service, novel author service and country profession service are service resources and they belong to education domain as well.

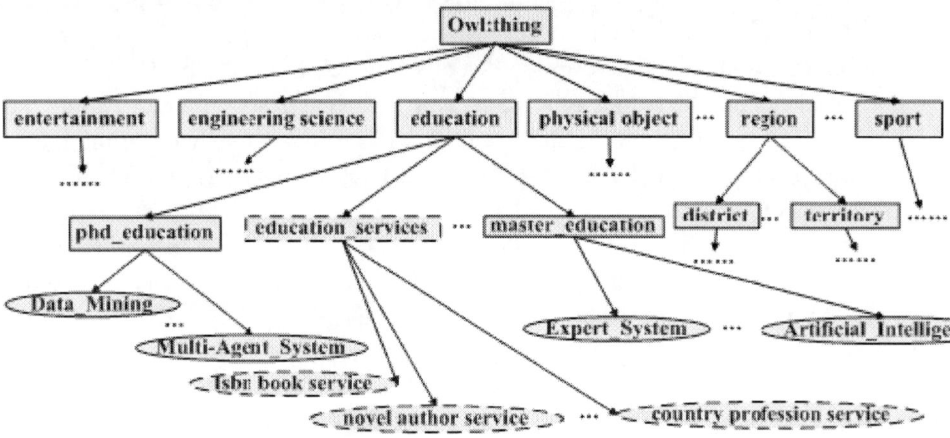

Figure 1. Resource domain ontology.

2.2.2. Thesaurus Ontology

Thesaurus maps synonymous and related words to each resource term in resource domain ontology. This can bring a higher degree of accuracy in finding correct node and information for registration and querying [5, 14]. Fig.2 gives an example of a partial graph which demonstrates synonyms and hyponymys of the terms within thesaurus ontology. Fillet boxes represent those terms that have appeared in the resource domain ontology and that means those resources exist in the network.

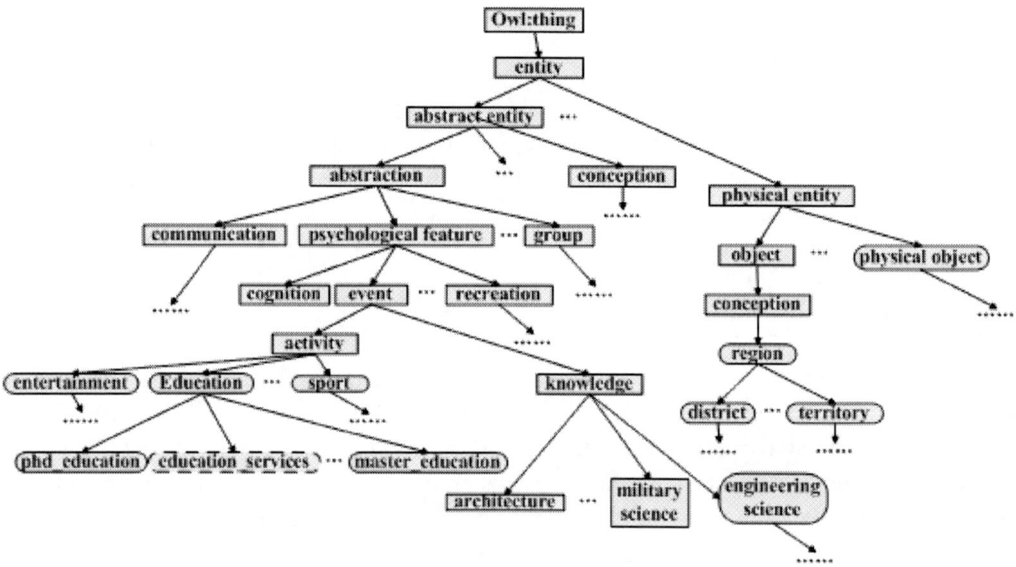

Figure 2. Thesaurus ontology.

Resource domain ontology is used for resource registry, while thesaurus ontology serves for discovery of resources. For same resource, it is impossible to require all providers and requesters to give a uniform definition, so key word based search is not a good choice. We propose a new inexact approach for resource discovery which is on the basis of thesaurus ontology. For instance, provided that requesters type knowledge as an index word, then engineering science, architecture and military science will be found for them by the unified discovery system. That's because there are some very close relationships among them according to thesaurus ontology.

We make use of Wordnet to create thesaurus ontology. Wordnet is an on-line lexical reference system whose design is inspired by current psycholinguistic theories of human lexical memory. Nouns, verbs and adjectives are organized into synonym sets and different relations link the synonym sets [15]. Wordnet is based on conceptual lookup and organizes concepts in a semantic network. It can be used as a thesaurus, because it organizes lexical information in terms of word meaning, rather than word form.

2.2.3. Service Description Ontology

As mentioned afore, data and service are parts of resources, so resource discovery involves data discovery and service discovery. However, most users can't recognize the distinctions between the above discoveries. That's why we plan to discovery both of them in a unified way. Descriptions of data and service are different from each other, because service has input, output, precondition, effect (IOPE) and so on.

For the sake of automatic service discovery, we adopt OWL-S markup for describing services and we call the services marked by OWL-S as semantic services. Service discovery with OWL-S description is addressed as semantic service discovery [16-17]. Semantic service discovery is a process for locating the semantic services that can provide a particular class of service capabilities and a specified QoS, while adhering to some client-specified constraints [2].

In order to satisfy user's high-level requirement, we append QoS measurement to service profile, the details have been discussed in our former work [18].

2.2.4. QoS Ontology

In QoS ontology, we provide QoS with several properties from network point of view: Latency, Reliability, Accuracy, Scalability, Availability, Capacity and Cost. Every property owns different grading.

Latency is the interval between the arrival time of a service request and the time that request is being served. It is classified into three grades.

1. Latency $\leqslant$5s (Applied to Interactive Service).
2. 5s < Latency$\leqslant$60s (Applied to Response-Service).
3. Latency > 60s (Applied to latency-Insensitive Service).

Reliability represents service's ability to perform its required functions under stated conditions for a specified period of time [19]. It can be measured by: mean time between failure (MTBF), mean time to failure (MTF), and mean time to transition (MTTT). In this paper, we classify reliability into three classes according to the threshold in the below:

1. Reliability $\ll \tau$.
2. Reliability is approximate to τ.
3. Reliability $\gg \tau$.

Every property owns different grading according to its character. In the following we give the definitions of the rest properties.

Accuracy – Defines the success rate produced by the service.

Scalability – The system's ability to process the number of operations or transactions in a given period. It is related to performance.

Availability – is the probability that a service can respond to consumer requesters [20].

Capacity – Limit number of concurrent requests for guaranteed performance.

Cost – captures the economic conditions of utilizing the service.

2.3. JXTA

The goals of JXTA [21] (short for "juxtapose") are platform independence, interoperability and ubiquity. Peers can interact with each other through the JXTA protocols. In JXTA, peers are often organized into peer groups. Any peer, which wishes to publish its resource on a JXTA network, needs to create an advertisement of the resource and publish it to one group. An advertisement is a piece of XML data that can describe resource information.

3. Design of Unified Discovery System

Unified discovery system has three layers: Physical Network Layer, Friend Group Layer and Location Network Layer. Physical Network Layer is the actual Internet topology; Friend Group consists of service providers who supply similar resources and all Friend Groups constitute Friend Group Layer; Every Friend Group votes a group leader [22] who has more capabilities and these group leaders form Location Network.

As Fig.3 shows, there are four kinds of elements in the system: Resource Requesters, Resource Providers, Friend Group Members and Friend Group Leaders.

Resource Requesters live in Physical Network Layer. They can also be resource providers.

Resource Providers register their resources to the unified discovery system, and then the system first leads providers to the related group according to resource domain ontology. Registry details will be specified later.

Friend Group Members are resource providers who provide similar resources.

Friend Group Leaders come from different friend groups, and they constitute Location Network Layer and have greater capabilities and higher bandwidth.

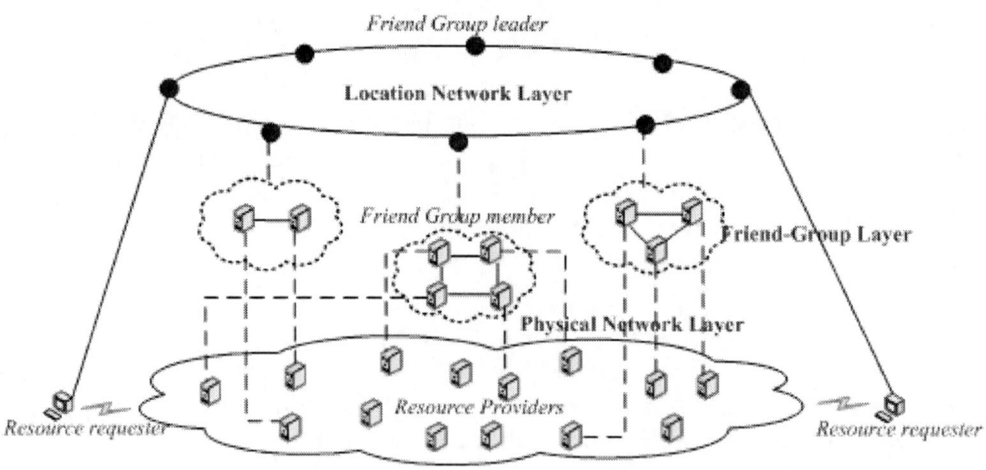

Figure 3. The architecture of the unified discovery system.

4. Combine with JXTA

In the fully decentralized Gnutella model, each request is propagated to every peer. In the Napster model, all queries are routed by a central server. In contrast, any peer in JXTA can act as the part of resource provider, resource consumer or hub.

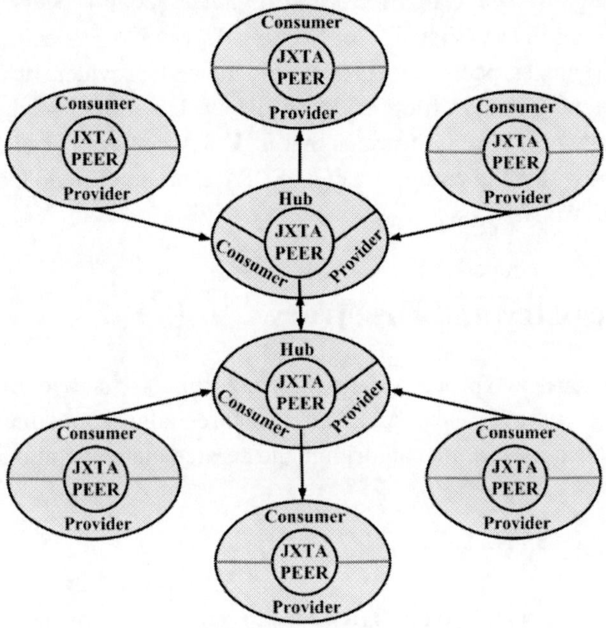

Figure 4. The architecture of JXTA search network.

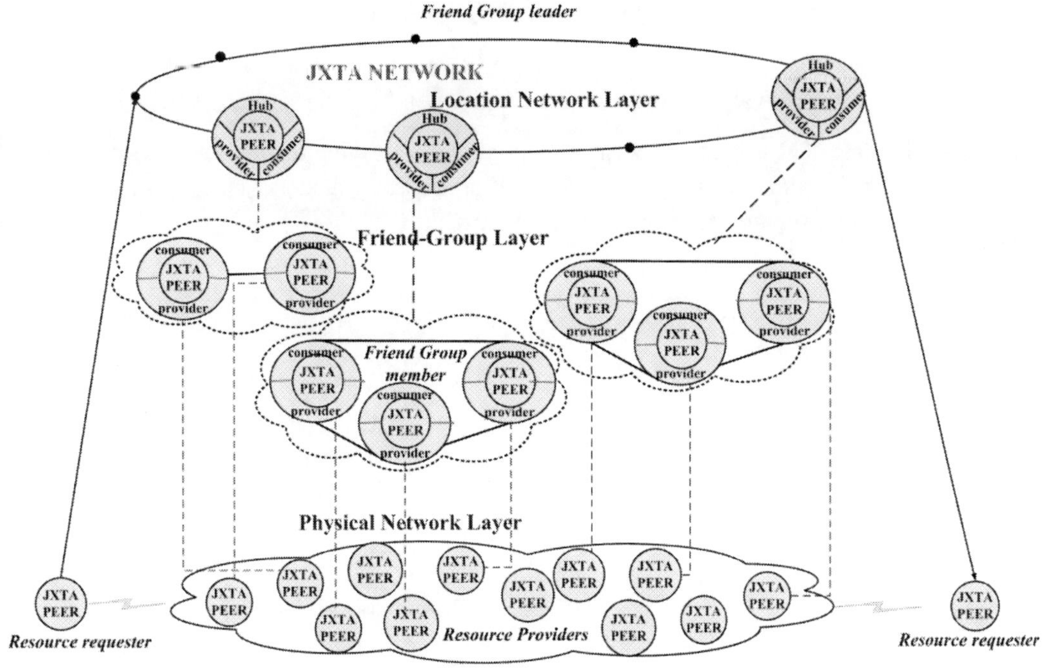

Figure 5. Combine the unified discovery system with JXTA.

JXTA Search can lay an efficient mechanism on distributing queries across a network of peers through hubs. Hubs can be organized by geography, peer content similarity [23] or application. Queries can be passed on from hub to hub [13]. A survey of peer relationships in JXTA search is given in Fig. 4. It illustrates every peer on the network interacts with a hub, and hub forwards requests to registered providers.

We take advantage of JXTA architecture to organize network peers, and implement our P2P-based resource discovery system. In Section 3, we have specified that the unified discovery system organizes peers into groups and related providers which publish similar resources form a Friend Group. Group leader in the system shows much resemblance to the hubs in the JXTA network. Fig. 5 illustrates that in JXTA network, Friend Group leader play a part of hub, both provider and requester act as JXTA peer; and Friend Group act as the same part of peer group in JXTA.

5. Resource Registry and Discovery

In this section, we discuss two processes and three algorithms. The two processes are resource registry process and discovery process, and the three algorithms include getting group location algorithm, locating resource algorithm and service matching algorithm.

5.1. Resource Registry Process

Resource providers need to go through three steps to publish their resources as Fig. 6 shows.

Step1: The unified discovery system makes use of getting group location algorithm to find friend groups (JXTA groups) which have close relationships with the resource.

Step2: A provider can publish his resource advertisement in the related JXTA groups found by step 1. For service, content of the advertisement include service name.

Step3: In the case that a provider wishes to publish his service to the network, it needs to upload its service profile to the related Friend Group leaders. This step prepares for the service discovery process in the next subsection.

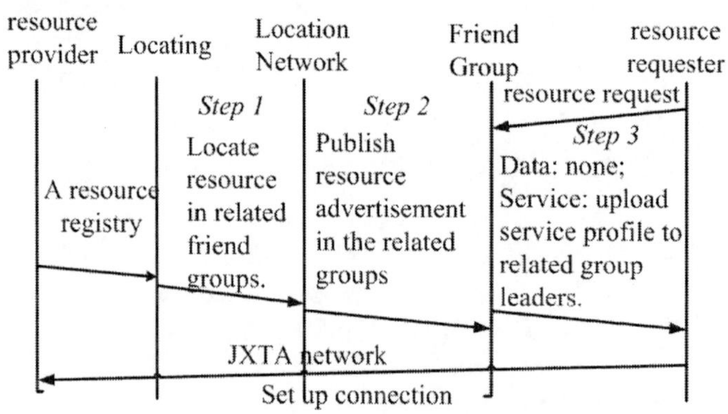

Figure 6. Resource registry process.

5.2. Resource Discovery Process

Requester plans to search some interested resource, however, he didn't know which kind of resources he wants. According to the requester's resource requirement advertisement, unified discovery system locates it in the related friend groups through getting group location algorithm firstly; then it utilizes locating resource algorithm to start searching resource in related groups; and finally, the discovery results containing both data and services, return to the requester. If a requester selects service as his interested resource, he needs to upload service query description file to discovery system. Users can put service input, output and QoS grading into that file. QoS grading is user's requirement for service quality. After receiving query description from user, discovery system begins to do service matching process with service matching algorithm. URLs of the matched services will be passed on to requester. With these URLs, requester gets access to the corresponding services as Fig. 7 shows.

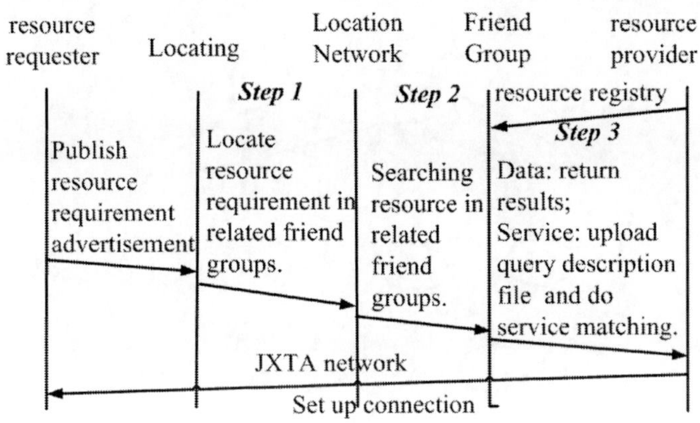

Figure 7. Resource discovery process.

5.3. Algorithms

5.3.1. Getting Group Location Algorithm

Input: Resource r 2R, Leader l 2L(Fgs), Threshold, thesaurus ontology Tho;

/*where R is a set of classes in thesaurus ontology; L(Fgs) is a set of Friend Group leaders; Threshold is the threshold value which is given by discovery system. */

Output: ListOfNum list;

/* One list of groups' numbers to which r belongs; */

step1:

BuildTree(Tho);

/* Build a tree structure for thesaurus ontology, and terms of the latter map to the nodes of the former; */

step2:

for (all l 2L(Fgs)) do

```
        if ( SimBetweenNodes (r, l) > Threshold)
            /* Compute degree of similarity between group leader l and resource r, and
            then select those degree values that are higher than Threshold. */
        then do
            numbern the group number of l;
            list.add(n);
            /*Add the selected Friend Group number to list. */
        end
    end
step 3:
    Return list;
```

The goal of this algorithm is to select related Friend Groups for resource r. It achieves its purpose via three steps. First of all, resource domain ontology is converted to a tree; secondly, we can get friend groups related with r by SimBetweenNodes (r, l); and finally, result list return back.

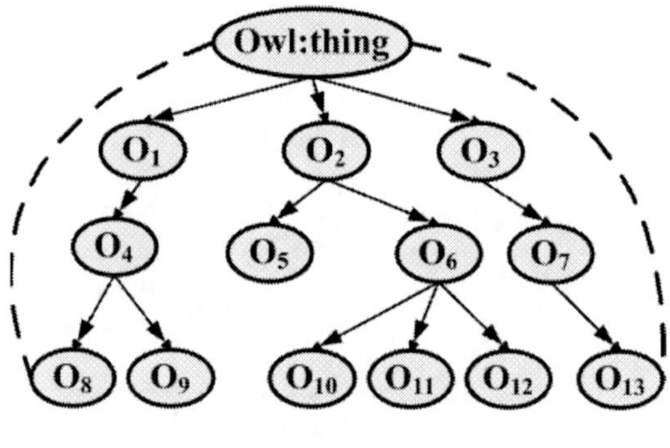

Figure 8. Tree structure.

Tree structure is shown in Fig. 8 and the formula below gives the definition of similarity degree between two nodes in the tree. Terms O_1 and O_2 live in layer l1 and layer l2 respectively. Dis(O_1, O_2) means the distance between O_1 and O_2. b is an adjustable parameter and it is a positive number. D represents depth of the tree.

$$SimBetweenNodes(O_1,O_2)=\begin{cases}\dfrac{\beta\times(l_1+l_2)\times\max(|l_1-l_2|,1)}{Dis(O_1,O_2)+\beta} & \big(Dis(O_1,O_2)=|l_1+l_2|\big)\quad(1)\\[2ex]\dfrac{\beta\times(l_1+l_2)\times D^2}{(Dis(O_1,O_2)+\beta)\times\max(|l_1-l_2|,1)} & \big(Dis(O_1,O_2)<|l_1+l_2|\big)\quad(2)\end{cases}$$

Along with the increase of two terms' distance, the similarity degree between them becomes smaller. For instance, Dis(O_8, O_{13})=6, l_8=3, and l_{13}=3, therefore, with formula (1) we can get SimBetweenNodes (O_8, O_{13})= $\frac{\beta\times 6}{6+\beta}$. In the same way, because Dis(O_8,

O_2)=4, l_8=3, and l_2=1, we can obtain SimBetweenNodes (O_8, O_2)= $\frac{\beta \times 8}{4+\beta}$. Since β is a positive number, SimBetweenNodes (O_8, O_2) is greater than SimBetweenNodes (O_8, O_{13}).

With the same distance, similarity degree of deep layer nodes is above and beyond that of low layer nodes [24] and in order to prove it, we give an example as follows. Terms O_1 and O_2 stay in the first layer, while O_8 and O_9 lay in the third layer. Dis(O_1 , O_2) is equal to Dis(O_8, O_9), however, similarity degree of the former is much lower than that of the latter, i.e. SimBetweenNodes(O_1,O_2)= $\frac{\beta \times 2}{2+\beta}$ < SimBetweenNodes (O_8, O_9)= $\frac{\beta \times 54}{2+\beta}$.

5.3.2. Locating Resource Algorithm

Input: Resource r 2R, Threshold, Resource domain ontology Ord;
Output: Instances Result_list;

```
        /* One list of instances which have close relationships with resource r; */
step1:
      ListOfNum list = getGrouplocation(r);
      /* Get a list of related groups for resource r */
step2:
      for (all groupNum 2list) do
          groupInstances = getGroupInstances(groupNum, Ord);
          /*Get all instances of the group in resource domain ontology*/
          for (all instance Ins in groupInstances) do
              if ( SimBetweenNodes (r, Ins) > Threshold )
                /* Calculate the degree of similarity between instance Ins and resource r,
                and then select those degree values that are higher than Threshold. */
              then do
                Result_list.add(Ins);
                //Add the selected instance to Result_list.
              end
          end
      end
step3:
      Return Result_list;
```

Given a resource to search, this algorithm restricts searching process within related groups firstly, and then extracts all instances from these groups of resource domain ontology to calculate their similarity degrees with search resource. Ultimately, those instances which have hyper-threshold similarity degree will be passed on to user.

5.3.3. Service Matching Algorithm

Service matching differs from data matching, because the former has some special essentials, such as IOPE. As set forth, if a user publishes an advertisement of a resource request, unified discovery system can return him with related resources which have been registered, and these resources involve both data and service. In the case that the user is interested in service, he needs to upload service description file (a service profile).

After receiving requester's profile, unified discovery system begins to match it with registered service profiles in the related JXTA groups. In this subsection, we present a flexible matching algorithm. The result of the match is not a hard true or false, however, it relies on the degree of similarity between the concepts in the match. Algorithm composes of two parts: basic ability matching and QoS matching. The main program is shown in the following.

main program:

```
match (request_profile, registered_profiles)
{
    ResultMatch = empty;
    for all profile in registered_profiles of a group
    do
        {
            if match(request_profile, profile)
            then ResultMatch.add(request_profile, profile);
        }
        return Sort(ResultMatch);
}
```

In the main program, request_profile is given by a user, and registered_profiles are registered service profiles in the related JXTA groups. The function of match(request_profile, profile) is to pick up related services with threshold. Sort(ResultMatch) is to rank related services for user and its sorting rules are specified in program 4.

program 1:

```
match(request_profile, profile)
{
    if (degreeMatch(OutR,OutA) > threshold_out & degreeMatch(InputA,InputR) >
        threshold_in & degreeMatch(QoSR,QoSA) > threshold_qos)
    then return true;
    else return false;
}
```

A match between a registered service profile and a request profile consists of the match of all the outputs of the request against the outputs of the registered service; all the inputs of the registered service against the inputs of the request; and all the QoS requirements of the request against QoS grading of the service. OutA, InputA and QoSA represent request's output, input and QoS grading respectively, while OutR, InputR and QoSR stand for registered service's output, input and QoS grading.

The algorithm for output matching is described as below. Success degree depends on the match degree. The matching algorithm of inputs is similar to that of outputs, but with the reversed order of the request and registered service, i.e. the latter inputs are matched against the former inputs [25]. Program 3 presents QoS matching.

program 2:

```
degreeMatch(OutR,OutA)
{
    if OutA = OutR then return Excellent
    if OutR is a subclassOf OutA then return Exact
    if OutA subsumes OutR then return PlugIn
    if OutR subsumes OutA then return Subsumes
    otherwise return error
}
```

program 3:

```
degreeMatch(QoSR,QoSA)
{
    if QoSR = QoSA then return Excellent
    if QoSR < QoSA then return Approximate
    if QoSR > QoSA then return Distinguishing
}
```

program 4:

```
SortingRule(Match1,Match2)
{
    if Match1.output > Match2.output
    then Match1 > Match2
    if Match1.output = Match2.output & Match1.QoS > Match2.QoS
    then Match1 > Match2
    if Match1.output = Match2.output & Match1.QoS = Match2.Oos & Match1.input >
      Match2.input
    then Match1 > Match2
    if Match1.output = Match2.output & Match1.QoS = Match2.Oos & Match1.input =
      Match2.input
    then Match1 = Match2
}
```

6. Implementation and Experimental Results

To measure the performance of ontology and P2P based data and service unified discovery system and to verify the means of service matching with QoS presented in this paper, we have developed a prototype of the system. In this prototype system, we make use of NetBeans 5.5.1, Protégé [26], Jena 2.5.1, JXTA and Apache Tomcat 6.0.14, for development.

Protégé is an open-source development environment for ontologies and knowledge-based systems. Protégé OWL Plugin has a user-friendly environment for editing and visualizing OWL classes and properties. It allows users to define logical class characteristics in OWL by a graphical user interface. It also makes users execute description logic reasoning by using Racer [14]. Protégé has an open-source Java API for developing arbitrary semantic services.

Jena is a Java framework for building Semantic Web applications. It provides a programmatic environment for RDF, RDFS, OWL and SPARQL and includes a rule-based inference engine. We adopt Jena in our system because it is a toolkit for developing applications within the semantic web. Jena allows users to create, query and parse OWL, and it also provides many interfaces to access RDF statement.

In this paper, we give four tests to measure performance of the unified discovery system. In the first one, we compare the performance of unified discovery with data discovery or service discovery separately. Fig. 9 illustrates that users prefer unified discovery system, in that they can get more related and heterogeneous resources at the same situation. Data or service discovery can only provide user with humdrum results. From user's point of view, it is not easy to make a distinction between data discovery and service discovery, so it is very useful to provide various search results for user to choose. We define satisfaction degree as $Sg=\frac{(1-\gamma)\times n+\gamma\times h}{|R|}$, $(0<\gamma<1)$. $|R|$ represents the number of results in searching result list; n is the amount of user's satisfied results; h means heuristic results which are related with satisfied results and can enlighten users.

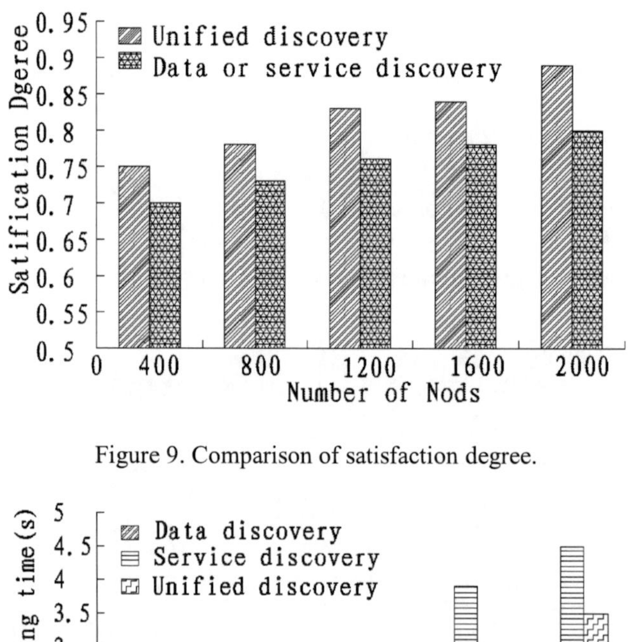

Figure 9. Comparison of satisfaction degree.

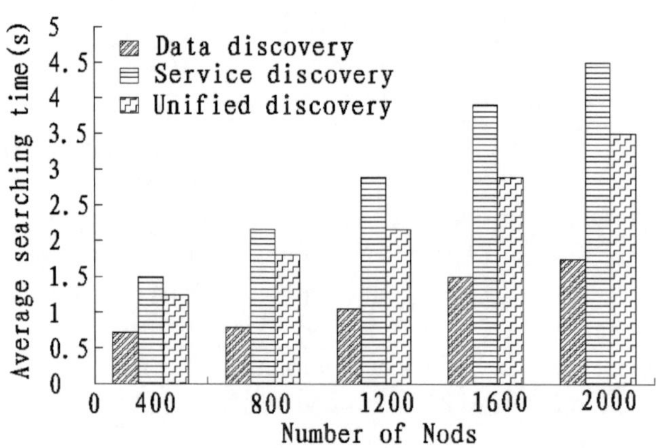

Figure 10. Comparison of efficiency.

Though unified discovery system is more complicated than data or service discovery, it does not cost more search time than them. Fig. 10 shows our second test result and it demonstrates that unified discovery costs less time than service discovery. The reason is that service discovery needs to match all service descriptions of the related domains with query description, however, unified discovery will be in need of match process only when user asks and uploads service query description.

In the third test, we compare service discovery with QoS and without QoS measurement in the unified discovery system. In Fig. 11, we can see that success rate of the former is higher than that of the latter. QoS measurement can filter out those services that have same function but low QoS grading, so it increases success rate.

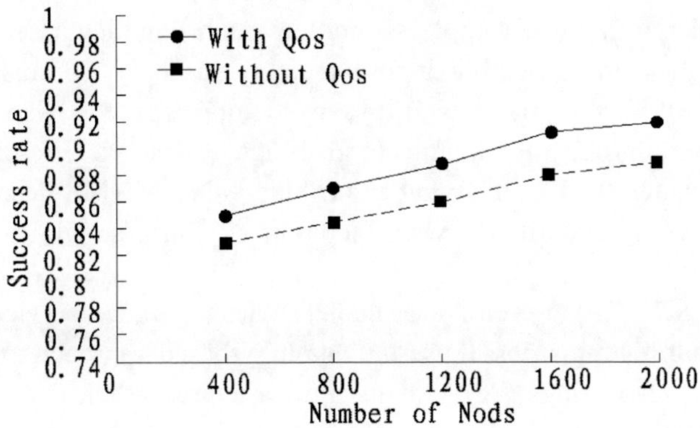

Figure 11. Comparison of success rate.

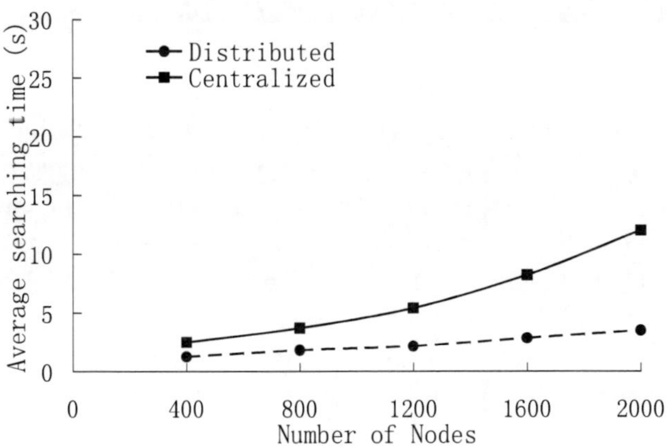

Figure 12. Distributed versus centralized.

Finally, we test the average cost time of distributed discovery system and centralized discovery system. Fig. 12 verifies that efficiency of the former is much higher than that of the latter. In our distributed system, we utilize resource domain ontology to divide resources into various groups and searching bound declines with these different groups, so it raises efficiency.

7. Related Work

In order to improve the performance of content searching in P2P system, Li and Vuong [27] propose a new decentralized P2P architecture—ontology-based community overlays. It is presented only for data discovery, but not for services.

Data in INS/Twine [28] are specified with hierarchies of attribute-value pairs by a convenient language (XML etc.) The approach of INS/Twine is to convert any such description into a canonical form: an attribute-value tree (AVTree). A resource matches a query when the AVTree formed by the query is the same as the AVTree of the service description. In order to allow more flexible queries, it separates string values into several attribute-value pairs. For instance, hmodeli One apple tree h/modeli could be divided into hmodlewiOneh/modlewi, hmodlewiapple < /modlew> and hmodlewitreeh/modlewi. Though this means making query more flexible, it costs memory space. By contrast, we use thesaurus ontology to implement inexact match, and it saves memory space. It also has greater logical capabilities in use of ontology for architectural design and service descriptions. The main difference between using OWL and any other attribute-value or XML description mechanism is that the former not only classifies services hierarchically but also allows logical restrictions on class relationships.

METEOR-S WSDI [29] presents a scalable environment for services publication and discovery among multiple registries. It uses an ontology-based approach to organize registries into domains, and it also brings JXTA to its infrastructure. When client peer sends query ontology to peer group, it will receive registries ontology and need to choose the most relevant domain specific ontology. This approach demands high performance of client peer. To bring down requirement of the client peer, we make peer group leader select relevant domain for the client. This method can also save time of transmitting ontology between client and peer group leader.

Oden (Ontology-based discovery enabled network) [3] is an ontology-based distributed service discovery system. It assumes a global namespace of services, which is very difficult to achieve in that different people may give different description when facing the same service. This problem is alleviated by using ‘‘*” in Oden at the expense of efficiency, so thesaurus ontology, not requiring a global namespace of resources, is adopted in our research.

GloServ [30-31] is a hybrid hierarchical and p2p ontology-based global service discovery system. It makes use of service classification ontology to locate service in the specific domain, however, it didn’t discuss such a situation that one query or registry may have very close relation with several domains. We solve this problem through calculating the similarity between query and different domains or between registry and different domains, and then choosing those whose similarity degree is above threshold value.

There is some research work focusing on service discovery with QoS, for instance, Ran [19] puts nonsemantic QoS information into UDDI. In contrast, we add QoS information to service description ontology and establish a special ontology for QoS.

8. Conclusion

At present, a lot of research work focuses on service discovery or data discovery as discussed in Section 7, but few of them concentrates on combining both of them though they have very close relation with each other. In this paper, we present a scalable, high performance system for data and service unified discovery. The unified discovery system has three layers and adopts four types of ontology to implement distributed and semantic resource discovery. Especially for the service, we add QoS measurement to OWL-S files so as to obtain more accurate results for users. Moreover, we combine unified discovery system with JXTA which is a suitable foundation to build future computer systems on. Finally, we give four tests to measure performance of our system.

References

[1] O. B. Kwon, S. C. Choi and G. R. Park, NAMA: A context-aware multi-agent based web service approach to proactive need identification for personalized reminder systems. *Expert Systems with Applications*, **29**(1), 17–32 (2005).

[2] D. Martin, OWL-S: *Semantic markup for web services*. http://www.daml.org/services/owl-s/OWL-S: SemanticMarkupforWebServices.htm (2003).

[3] D. Elenius and M. Ingmarsson, Ontology-based service discovery in P2P network. In *Proceedings of workshop on peer-to-peer knowledge management*, Boston (2004).

[4] M. Schlosser, M. Sintek, S. Decker and W. Nejdl, A scalable and ontology-based P2P infrastructure for semantic web services. In *Proceedings of the second international conference on peer-to-peer computing*. CA, USA: Stanford University, (2002).

[5] UDDI (2006). UDDI Technical white paper. <www.uddi.org>.

[6] C. Li and L. Li. Combine concept of agent and service to build distributed object oriented system. *Future Generation Computer Systems*, **19**(2), 161–171 (2003).

[7] C. Niu, J. Wang, R. Shen, L. Shen and H. Luo, Cooperativeness prediction in P2P networks. Expert Systems with Applications (in press, corrected proof, available online 15 August 2007) (2007).

[8] C. Sangpachatanaruk, and T. Znati, A P2P overlay architecture for personalized resource discovery, access, and sharing over the internet. In *Consumer communications and networking conference (CCNC'05)* (2005).

[9] R. Ahmed and R. Boutaba, Distributed pattern matching: A key to flexible and efficient P2P search. *IEEE Journal on Selected Areas in Communications*, **25**(1), 73–83 (2007).

[10] Y. Joung, L. Yang and C. Fang, Keyword search in DHT-based peer-to-peer networks. *IEEE Journal on Selected Areas in Communications*, **25**(1), 46–61 (2007).

[11] B. Yang, and H. Garcia-Molina, Comparing hybrid peer-to-peer systems. In P.Apers et al. (Eds.), *Proceedings of the very large data base* (pp. 561–570). Roma: Morgan Kaufmann, (2001).

[12] D. A. Menasce, Scalable P2P search. IEEE Internet Computing, 7(2), 83–87 (2003).

[13] S. Waterhouse, D. M. Doolin, G. Kan, and A. Faybishenko, Distributed search in P2P networks. *IEEE Internet Computing*, **6**(1), 68–72 (2002).

[14] V. Haarslev and R. Moller, Racer user's guide and reference manual version 1.7.19. Concordia University, Technical Universityh of Hamburg-Harburg, University Hamburg. (2004).

[15] G. Miller, R. Beckwith, C. Fellbaum, D. Gross and K. Miller, Introduction to WordNet: An on-line lexical database. *Journal of Lexicography*, **3**(4), 235–244. (1990).

[16] K. Sycara, M. Paolucci, J. Soudry and N. Srinivasan, Dynamic discovery and coordination of agent-based semantic web services. *IEEE Internet Computing*, **8**(3), 66–73 (2004).

[17] Y. Ganjisaffar, H. Abolhassani, M. Neshati and M. Jamali, A similarity measure for OWL-S annotated web services. In *IEEE/WIC/ACM international conference on web intelligence*, Hong Kong. (2006).

[18] Y. Zhang, K. Huang, Y. Qu and X. Zhao, Semantic service discovery with QoS measurement in universal network. In *Rough sets and emerging intelligent systems'07 international conference*. Poland: Warszawa. (2007).

[19] S. Ran, A model for web services discovery with QoS. *ACM SIGCOM Exchanges,* **14**(1), 1–10. (2003).

[20] E. M. Maximilien and M. P. Singh, A framework and ontology for dynamic web services selection. *IEEE Internet Computing*, **8**(5), 84–93 (2004).

[21] S. Oaks, B. Traversat and L. Gong, *JXTA in a nutshell.* Sebastopol, CA: O'Reilly. (2002).

[22] C. Mastroiannia, D. Taliab and O. Vertab, A super-peer model for resource discovery services in large-scale grids. *Future Generation Computer Systems*, **21**(8), 1235–1248 (2005).

[23] Y. Li, Z. A. Bandar and D. McLean, An approach for measuring semantic similarity between words using multiple information sources. *IEEE Transactions on Knowledge and Data Engineering*, **15**(4), 871–882 (2003).

[24] J. Wu, Z. Wu, Y. Li, and S. Deng, Web service discovery based on ontology and similarity of word. *Chinese Journal of Computers*, **28**(4), 595–602 (2005).

[25] M. Paolucci, T. Kawamura, T. R. Payne and K. Sycara, Semantic matching of web services capabilities. In Proceedings of the international semantic web conference (ISWC'02). *LNCS* (Vol. 2342, pp. 333–347). Springer Verlag. (2002).

[26] J. Gennari, M. A. Musen, R. W. Fergerson, W. E. Grosso, M. Crubzy, H. Eriksson, et al. Evolution of protg: *An environment for knowledge based systems development.* Technical report, Stanford University. (2002).

[27] J. Li, and S. Vuong, Ontology-based clustering and routing in peer-to-peer networks. In *Sixth international conference on parallel and distributed computing, applications and technologies.* (2005).

[28] M. Balazinska, H. Balakrishnan and D. Karger, INS/Twine: A scalable peer-to-peer architecture for intentional resource discovery. In Proceedings *of the first international conference on pervasive*. Switzerland: Zurich. (2002).

[29] K. Verma, K. Sivashanmugam, A. Sheth, A. Patil, S. Oundhakar and J. Miller, METEOR-S WSDI: A scalable P2P infrastructure of registries for semantic publication and discovery of web services. *Journal of Information Technology and Management, Special Issue on Universal Global Integration*, **6**(1), 17–39 (2005).

[30] K. Arabshian and H. Schulzrinne, An ontology-based hierarchical peer-to-peer global service discovery system. *Journal of Ubiquitous Computing and Intelligence (JUCI)* (2006).

[31] K. Arabshian and H. Schulzrinne, *Hybrid hierarchical and peer-to-peer ontology-based global service discovery system*, Columbia University Technical Report CUCS-016-05, New York, NY (2005).

In: Data Management in the Semantic Web
Editor: Hal Jin, pp. 171-194

ISBN: 978-1-61122-862-5

Chapter 8

The Design and Development of a Semantic Environment for Holistic eGovernment Services

***Luis Álvarez Sabucedo**, *Luis Anido Rifón*†
Rubén Míguez Pérez‡ *and Juan Santos Gago*§**
Telematics Engineering Department
Universidade de Vigo, Spain

Abstract

Most nations in the world are currently committed to provide advanced services for their citizens. The development of a software support capable of meeting the needs for this context requires to engage in a long term bet. The success for this kind of projects is deeply related to the provision of a solid back office support for services and the use of open technologies for the interconnection and interchange of information. In this chapter, it is presented a formal description of the business model involved in the provision of such solution using semantics as a tool to share this conceptualization. This characterization of the problem to be solved is derived from artifacts identified in the domain and described in relation with the interaction required to fulfill the citizen's needs. On the top of this description, an entire software platform is described. Also, some useful conclusions are presented for its consideration on further projects.

Keywords: eGovernment, semantics, interoperability.

1. Introduction

Applying Information and Communication Technologies (ICTs) to the labour of Public Administrations and Agencies (here after PAs) is not a recent phenomenon. Actually, during these last years, governments from all over the world have been devoting a large amount

*E-mail address: lsabucedo@det.uvigo.es
†E-mail address: lanido@det.uvigo.es
‡E-mail address: rmiguez@det.uvigo.es
§E-mail address: jsgago@det.uvigo.es

of resources to this new area of application for technology. The final goal is to evolve the mechanisms to fulfill the citizen's needs in order to update the service provision and match the current demands from its final users, the citizens.

Far from being concern just with upgrading the service interface to introduce web support for already available services, eGovernment solutions are striving to bring into scene new orientations for services, new interfaces for users and a larger support for operations.

Looking for formal definitions of eGovernment, several options can be identified. eGovernment is defined, according to the United Nations [40], as

> "the use of information and communication technology (ICT) and its application by the government for the provision of information and basic public services to the people"

According to the World Bank [44], eGovernment

> "refers to the use by government agencies of information technologies that have the ability to transform relations with citizens, businesses, and other arms of government".

From these definitions, it is clear that the real *ethos* in the domain is not merely to replace current fashion system with analogous systems that take advantage of the ICT support. On the contrary, this new paradigm of service is expected to reorient services and applications to put the citizen in the center of processes and redesign, if necessary, all workflows to make easier things for the citizens. In order to achieve this global goal there must be provided different kinds of projects, mainly:

- Legal updates. In order to provide a legal support for services, PAs involved must update the legal support for this sort of services. A clear example of these changes is, for example, the recognition of the legal value of digital signature.
- Aimed at providing final services for end-users. These projects are expected to develop solutions that tackle those services that are interesting for citizens. This would be the case for those services that offer functionalities such as paying taxes, requesting grants, or reporting a situation to the police using Internet.
- Supporting projects. These projects are oriented towards the provision of a basis to develop further solutions. The point is not to provide a service itself but to lay out the support to build on the top of them final services. This is the case of those projects concerned on the provision of digital identity cards or supporting broadband access to final citizens.

In the long term, it is clear that the development of platforms for eGovernment services has benefits for both government and citizens. Upon the review of already developed solutions, limitations were detected in deployed eGovernment web portals and some concrete problems to overcome were identified (see Section 2.). This set of problems and limitations have already been dealt with in previous works in the domain, at least, to a certain extension. A complete review of them can be found in Section 3.. Therefore, the next step is to propose a business model for the provision of services in the eGovernment domain that can deal with the unveiled drawbacks (see Section 4.).

Bearing these concepts in mind, a holistic software interface is designed. This platform is based on the use of LifeEvents (LEs hereafter). This artifact models services from the point of view of the citizen. LEs, as discussed in Section 5., can be seen as those situations where citizens are compelled to deal with a PA in order to fulfill an obligation (e.g., pay a fine) or to make use of a right (e.g., request a building license).

In order to increase the capabilities of the system regarding automatization and interoperability issues, semantic technologies are brought into scene. Nowadays, among the scientific community, this research area is usually considered the enabler technology to develop this sort of solutions. Within this approach, semantics is expected to play a role as a high-level support to make automatic discovery and orchestration of services possible. This technology offers us a new set of tools and mechanisms which have not been completely explored yet (see Section 6.1.). Its application to LEs introduces a fairly nice support to define the entire system in a formal way (see Section 6.2.).

The provision of a semantic characterization for LEs does not seem to be enough. We must provide a framework to capitalize the efforts already devoted to the system. Thus, a complete software architecture is developed by using LE as its foundation. In order to provide a complete software support (see Section 7.), we make use of Semantic SOA (Service Oriented Architecture) [30]. The general performance of the resulting platform is described in Section 8. where also some general details about the prototype implementation are presented. Finally, some conclusions are presented to the reader in Section 9..

2. Analysis of the Problem & Motivation

The vast majority of eGovernment solutions are presented to citizens by means of Web portals. The highest functioning Web portals show a complete system integration across agencies, whereas portals with the lowest level of functionality provide little more than access to forms and static pieces of information. High-functioning portals create a one-stop service for citizens. In particular, usability, customization, openness and transparency represent key aspects of portal functionalities. Regretfully, upon the review of web portals [33], the most common vehicle for solutions in the domain, some general drawbacks can be outlined:

Usability Locating services is not a simple task. When looking for a particular service in the web site of a PA, it is not a trivial task to find the proper place where the service is offered. This is due to the wide variety of classifications for services, mechanisms for its invocations, visual interfaces and even problems such as finding out beforehand if the administration is responsible for the wished service.

Traceability Very few administrations provide information about the evolution of services. Once the operation is requested, neither obtaining more information nor tracking its execution is possible. Therefore, in the case of services that take a lot of time to execute the requested action, citizens may not feel involved in the process.

Accessibility Web accessibility is not a highlight in most Web portals. Official web sites are often WAI-AA or WAI-AAA compliant [43] but this is not a general rule. Besides, the classification of the information itself and the interaction mechanisms are not always as simple and convenient as we would wish.

Lack of information Little information about the service, execution conditions or its evolution is provided. It is not common to find information about the level of security of invoked operations, the maximum life span for service allowed, laws that support and regulate that service and so on. Also, in some operations, there may be several administrations involved (e.g., moving to a new home), and that may drive citizens to confusion.

Authentication Different mechanisms for identification are required in different administrations for the same citizen. No single and horizontal mechanism to access services is available on most official web sites. Usually, a citizen must authenticate his/her identity by using different mechanisms in different administrations: a pair user/password, a digital certification, a smart card, etcetera.

Customization of services Usually, it is not possible to customize the access to services, e.g., lack of citizen profile managing. It is not possible for citizens, once they are logged in, to access the services they are most likely to invoke according to their profiles, their costumed interfaces. In most cases, no profiles are even stored.

The motivation of this work is to provide a software platform that overcomes the issues mentioned above. The proposal has the following two overall objectives:

- Provide a simple-to-use mechanism to discover which is the right service for a particular situation in the life of a citizen. For this, the concept of LifeEvent is modeled, and taken further through design and implementation stages.

  Service location may be an issue due to the variety of administrations that can be in charge (e.g., requesting a grant can depend on different administrations), to the difficulties in finding the services (e.g., the use of some searchers can be difficult if the user is not involved in administrative issues) or to the lack of information in the expected format.

- Simplify the interactions between the citizen and the administration, providing mechanisms to make the underlying needed operation, even involving different administrations, transparent to the end-user and offering tracking tools that allow those who requested a service check its actual state at any moment. In terms of one-stop services, this means a significant contribution given that administrations have not foreseen mechanisms to orchestrate services so far.

This platform introduces the artifacts LifeEvents and AdministrativeServices to define a holistic software architecture. By means of these concepts and further suggested models, it is possible to support real one-stop government services across different agencies facilitating the discovery and orchestration of complex services for the domain.

As we will prove in Section 8., the proposal presented along the rest of this paper contributes to improve in different sub-areas within the digital administration area, taken benefit from the implementation of several interoperability mechanisms based on standardized models and semantic technologies.

3. Related Work

The vast majority of countries have developed their own frames to host eGovernment solutions [24]. Mainly, most of them are oriented toward the provision of a framework for interoperability at some level or support in task related to eGovernment solutions. Regretfully, none of them provide a solid or holistic platform to actually carry out services. Briefly, we can outline some of those somehow related with our project:

- SAGA (Standards und Architekturen in eGovernment Anwendungen) [27] in Germany. It is a guideline for orientation to in the development of solutions in German administrations. This frame does not take care of semantic based solutions. It provides us, mainly, a with set of standards that must be used to deploy solutions in the domain.

- e-GIF (eGovernment Interoperability Framework) [39] in the United Kingdom. It covers issues related to specifications and policies for any cross-agency collaboration, eService access and content management. It also includes definitions of metadata to mark documents by using RDF [15]. This is one of the official projects making larger use of semantic based solutions. Regretfully, it only uses light-weighted semantic technologies such as RDF or taxonomies. Besides, it does not tackle issues rather relevant in the scope of this project such as semantic Web Services.

- CCI (Le Cadre Commun d'Intéroperabilité) from ADEA (l'Agence pour le dèveloppement de l'administration électronique) [20] in France. It establishes recommendations for systems related to public services and electronic delivery. Little attention is paid to details related to semantic definitions or services.

- EIF (European Interoperability Framework) [18] for European solutions. Mainly, it establishes a framework for discussion about interoperability, but it does not actually endorse any particular catalog or standard to build eGovernment solutions. Anyhow, it set the concern of European countries in the search for a interoperable frame for pan-European solutions.

- FEAF (Federal Enterprise Architecture Framework) [34] in USA. It focuses on the description of enterprise models to develop cross-border solutions. It does neither take care of particular architectures or technologies, nor does it actually deploy systems. It is quite useful as systematic way to design solutions where the point of all stakeholders is considered.

Most of these projects provide little semantic support as they just make use, at maximum, of very light-weighted semantic technologies. Further information about this particular topic can be found at [25].

Unfortunately, we can state that the support provided by these initiatives to develop actual platforms is limited. Additionally, as the use of the so-called heavy-weighted ontologies is, for the moment, a work to be done at this level, we can not take full advantage of any of the former in the frame of our proposal. These standards and proposals are useful in the frame of this contribution to depict the general panorama but they are of little use in our case.

Also, a number of projects from non-official institutions in the area have aims quite similar to ours. In this trend, it must be noted that the first time the concept of LE was used in eGovernment was within the eGov project [1]. In that context, Life Events were defined as "situations of human beings that trigger public services". This approach to the concept is mainly used to model the internal process in the own PA and as a guide to its implementation. Thus, it can be considered mainly a back-office contribution. Given that it was developed several years ago, no semantic support was used. On the contrary, the platform that we propose is oriented towards a front-office for the citizen on her/his daily tasks with public administrations. Taking advantage of current fashion technologies, we provide services not foreseen in the scope of this project such as orchestration, advanced discovery, etcetera.

In the literature, we can also find some interesting initiatives that make use, at different levels, of semantics applied to this concept in some manner:

- The Finnish Web site, Suomi.fi [6], implements a taxonomy that allows a more formal classification of LEs. Even though the approach is similar, the use of semantics is quite limited. The actual support provided is just interaction with human users. No orchestration procedures are provided or foreseen. On the contrary, our proposal goes a step further and uses LE and related artifacts to provide a holistic support for operations, not just support for searching.

- The SemanticGov project [4]. This ongoing project supported by the 6th Framework Program aims at developing a software infrastructure intended to provide support for PAs. Semantic technologies are expected to play a main role. The project is based on the use of WSMO to provide interoperability mechanisms. The definition of the preconditions and the postconditions turns out to be quite challenging within this project. It provides a two-level ontology that models in great detail an artifact also called life event. Contrary to our case, it is not provided how to actually compose calls to operations or track its evolutions.

- The Access-eGov project [3]. An initiative, also in the 6th Framework Program, based on a peer-to-peer and service-oriented architecture that also takes advantage of semantics to improve accessibility and connectivity. It focuses more on the reorientation of services to provide support and access to already provided services than on the provision of strategies for automatic composition services or semantic-based searching services. Also features related to the discovery and federation of services, those related to the BPS in our project, are not provided.

4. Business Model

In order to overcome the identified issues, this paper presents a semantic framework for the provision of services. The basis is a common software architecture to conduct operations in the eGovernment domain under the one-stop philosophy.

Based on the the analysis of the related work, the issues identified in the previous section, and the experience of the authors, a business model is characterized. This business model identifies the main actors and the general behavior of the system. This behavior is driven by the artifact of LifeEvents.

LifeEvents aim at tackling the definition of services from the point of view of citizens and at making possible their use within the framework in a holistic manner. A methodology to define and model LEs is presented which guides the process to express LEs in a replicable manner for any interested PA. The goal is to support interoperability mechanisms and advances in the composition of services in a feasible manner. LEs will make use of lower-level operations, namely Administrative Services (ASs hereafter) to actually conduct operations in the domain of PAs. Required ASs to complete a LE will be discovered at run-time and their composition will turn out into the accomplishment of a LE. The use of Documents (legal agreements between citizens and administrations) to execute and prove legal services from Public Administrations is a key aspect in order to achieve a high level of interoperability. Such Documents will be used, as shown below, to chain different ASs in order to accomplish a LE.

A global knowledge to define the entire system will be proposed by using the support of semantic technologies in order to make the above claims possible. This knowledge acts as the foundation for an entire software architecture which is derived by using SSOA (see Section 7.) as its architectural style.

In this scenario, the following agents are identified (see Fig. 1):

Client Agent This agent acts on behalf of citizens and it is the main agent in the system. It will invoke operations in the system , namely LEs, to satisfy their own needs.

Public Administrations (PA) These agents are responsible for the eventual execution of the expected services. In this approach, as we introduce ASs, we propose the provision of a fine-grained solution for services.

Digital Lawyer (DL) From the need to orchestrate ASs supported, in some cases, by different PAs, a broker-like agent arises. This agent will support LEs directly and will invoke different ASs to fulfill them. Its responsibility is to discover which ASs are required and to invoke them properly.

Blue Page Server (BPS) This agent supports searching operations to permit the discovery of suitable LEs for citizens and ASs for Digital Lawyers.

5. LifeEvents. The Knowledge Model

Taking into account the above mentioned considerations, LEs are proposed. The very first goal is to model services from the point of view of the citizen and no longer from the perspective of the PA and its internal procedures.

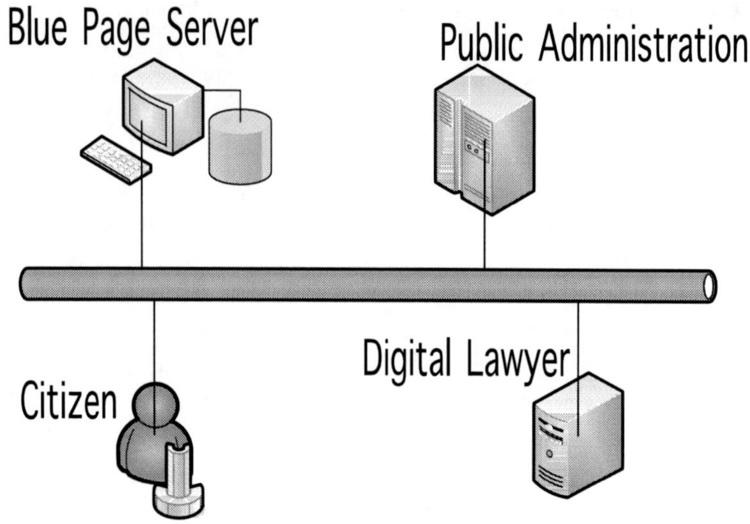

Figure 1. Business Model.

Therefore, LEs can be defined in the scope of this proposal as "any particular situation in the life of a citizen that must be dealt with and requires assistance, support or license from PAs". Those situations are considered from the point of view of the citizen and only include meaningful operations for the citizen.

We can consider as LEs, in the scope of this proposal, situations such as paying a fine, getting married, moving, losing one's wallet ...

Taking the analysis of the domain, already existing tools and the first evolution of the prototype as a basis, we are in a position to identify some relevant fields in the definition of LE:

- Task. Title for the considered operation.
- Description. High level description of the desired operation expressed in natural terms from the point of view of the citizen. This field will support human-driven selection procedure to finally choose the right LE.
- Input documents. All operations carried out by the administration require some input document. The citizen must provide, at least, a signed form in order to invoke the operation. This field states required documents to undertake the LE. We do not include simple forms or similar documents in this category since only meaningful documents for the citizen are taken into account at this point.
- Output documents. As a result of any performed operation, the PA in charge must provide an output expressed in terms of the ontology. This information will be put together into one or several documents. The content of the output will vary, ranging from the expected document (e.g., a certification, a license ...) to information about potential failures in getting the expected document. This field will state the legal

documents that will be issued to the citizen in response to his/her request. On the basis of these fields searches can be described.

- Scope. We must identify the scope in which we want an operation (local, national, international...) to be recognized. Therefore, we can choose the most suitable among different ASs.

- Security Conditions. The conditions for the security mechanism involved in the whole process, such as identification of both parties, cipher methods, etc. Using this field, the citizen can express the minimum conditions required to deal with his/her personal documents.

- Version. LEs can be modified and changed from one version to another. This information, which aims at tracking versions and providing coherent management of LEs, is not to be displayed to the citizen.

If we take the definition of LE as a basis, a single LE can –and normally does– involve different operations in different administrations. In order to model those interactions, another accessory artifact is introduced in the system: the Administrative Services. PAs can, and normally do, provide support to perform simple operations held directly by them. These operations may involve a more or less complex back-office mechanism but, in any case, they are invoked and fulfilled in a certain PA. Therefore, the fulfillment of a LE could involve several ASs in different PAs. ASs include the following data:

- Title. Brief name for the AS.

- Description. This information will be used in the description of ASs as components of LEs.

- Deadline. The maximum span of time for the response from the PA before the operation is considered approved/dismissed. This information is used to estimate how long an entire LE may last.

- Public Administration. Information about the PA; it is responsible for the execution of the PA and it is used to decide about the scope of the operation

- Law. Information about the supporting laws involved in the current AS. This could allow citizens to gather further information or support from government or lawyers in case of any eventuality.

- Input and Output documents. As in the case of LEs, these documents will provide the information about the required inputs to the system and the expected outputs. This information plays a main role in making decisions about the orchestration of ASs.

- Internal operations. Although an AS is easily executed in a PA, this process may have a number of steps that will be used to inform the citizen about the evolution of his/her request.

- Related ASs. This field informs about ASs that can usually fall together. These ASs will be the most likely to be coordinated.

6. Semantic Support

The semantic web has emerged as a new promising technology aimed at addressing information instead of data, i.e., it enables software agents to treat data in a meaningful manner. Making this possible would allow new mechanisms to operate on a higher level of abstraction. Also, by means of this technology, it is possible to express knowledge in a formal and interoperable way. These features will support the provision of the support claimed in this paper.

6.1. Semantics

The "semantic", as an IT researching field, was born in the early 2000's. In May 2001, Sir Tim Berners-Lee published the foundational article presenting the semantic web to the world [11].

> "The Semantic Web will bring structure to the meaningful content of Web pages, creating an environment where software agents roaming from page to page can readily carry out sophisticated tasks for users".

The *ethos* of this idea is to make machines capable of understanding the information within the web. This feature will allow them to make more complex interactions without the need of human support. To accomplish this ambitious goal, a long evolution on the technological side has taken place during these last years.

According to the previous article, the semantic web is:

> "an extension of the current web in which information is given well-defined meaning, better enabling computers and people to work in cooperation"

Therefore, semantics is compelled to provide information, not just data. In other words, semantics introduces meaning into the data in order to allow computers to deal with this information in a more interoperable manner. The objective of this discipline is the provision of information understandable by machines.

To achieve this ambitious goal, ontologies are a key element. In the literature, several definitions or approximations to the concept of ontology are provided. A rather suitable definition for ontology may be [23]:

> An ontology is a formal, explicit specification of a shared conceptualization of a domain of interest.

By means of this definition, we are addressing an ontology as a support to present abstract information about a certain domain in a concrete way by means of a machine-understandable data format.

To express an ontology in a formal manner, different languages [22] are at our disposal. OWL (Ontology Web Language) [41] is the W3C Recommendation intended to provide a fully functional way to express ontologies. To make different levels of complexity possible, OWL provides different sublanguages with increasing expressivity: OWL Lite, OWL DL and OWL Full. By using OWL, we are addressing a W3C recommendation that can be considered as solid and interoperable support for the provision of this solution. Besides, this option, OWL Full, allows us to include metadata expressed by means of RDF Schemas [14].

Ontologies are a way to express knowledge about entities in a broad sense. Nevertheless, they are, by themselves, of little use to describe services. In order to allow machines to discover and automatically invoke services, Web Services [45] in our case, the means for this task must be deployed. That is the reason why great effort has been devoted to the provision of semantic methods to describe Web Services. Semantic Web Services (SWS) are the result of describing Web Services by using outcomes of semantics.

Taking into account the current state of art, two different approaches are actually possible:

- It is possible to deal directly with services expressed under a semantic support. All the information to discover, compose or define services is provided by a single technology that involves all required data. This is the case of OWL-S (Ontology Web Language - Services) [32], WSMO (Web Service Modelling Object) [37] and SWSF (Semantic Web Services Framework) [10].
- Also, it is possible to define a global ontology to express and annotate web services by using it. We can outline two options by means of this approach:
  - WSDL-S (Web Service Description Language - Semantics) [16]. It provides a simple way to extend WSDL with semantic annotations.
  - SAWSDL [5]. This is the new Proposed Recommendation by the W3C. It is based on the semantical annotation of WSDL 2.0 [7]. So far, SAWSDL is just a proposed recommendation; however, it sounds a suitable option with a great potential.

6.2. Applying Semantics

Up to now, LEs and ASs, as tools to model services in the domain, have been presented with no binding to any technology in particular. For obvious reasons some technical support has to be chosen in order to advance in our proposal. In our case, we decided to make use of semantics to derive advantages in the system as shown below.

Semantics, in the present case, is presented by means of a modular system of ontologies that describes all entities involved in the process. Several acceptable options to develop an ontology that may fit our needs are available, such as Cyc [28], Kactus [36], Methontology [19], On-To-Knowledge [31], etc. The chosen option in our case was Methontology [19]. The main reasons for this election were good support with software tools (such as Protégé [38] or OntoEdit [8]), platform-independence; in addition, it is recommended by FIPA [21] and it has been tested in several large scale projects.

The resulting ontology includes the definition of all the meaningful data in the system. Therefore, this ontology must be known and shared by all agents. It is mainly made of some basic classes that characterize the ground.

citizens As the system final users, they are expected to be able to invoke all services available and interact with information in the system.

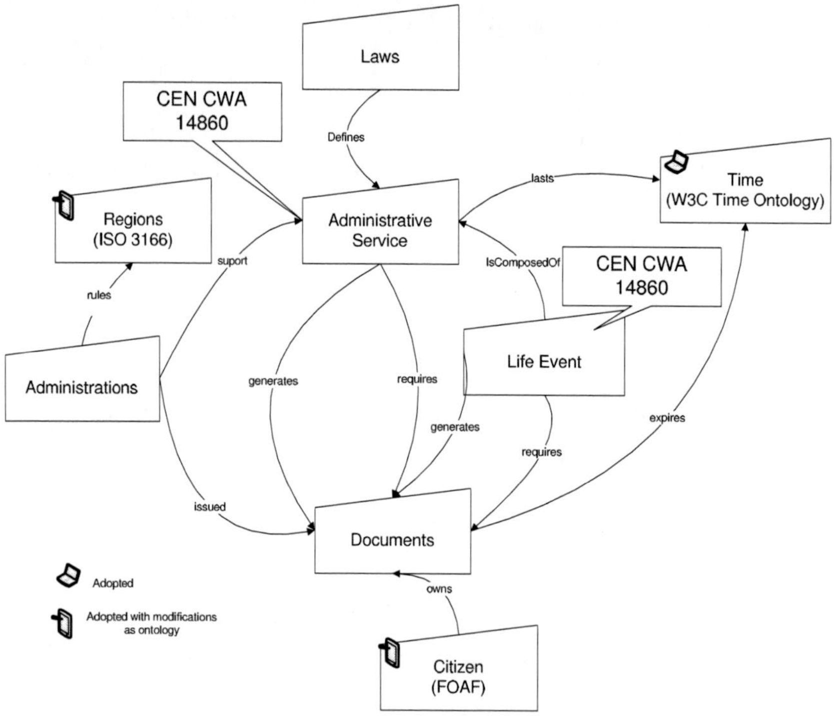

Figure 2. Ontologies included.

documents They provide the legal support for all operations in the system. Security concerns must be deployed in their management, since they compel agents to respect the contents of the documents.

LifeEvents These elements model the need of citizens and they are the drivers towards the service completion provided by the Digital Lawyers. Certainly, their definition includes already mentioned fields.

AdministrativeServices This class holds the properties to express all the knowledge about ASs as they are defined in previous sections.

In this ontology, we have reused previously proposed metadata. For example, in the task of defining the citizen, one of the main classes in the system, FOAF (Friend of a Friend) [2] has been reused. Also, metadata from European standardization bodies has been reused to mark documents in the system, in particular, CWA 14860 [12] from CEN [13]. Some of these metadata reused from this CWA included in our model are: *Status*, *Version*, *Title*, *Language*, and *Format*. Also, to express the maximun delay acceptable for the execution of an AS, the ontology from the W3C to express the time [46] was used. This is part of a general philosophy leading toward the maximum possible agreement and reusability both for the ontology and the software based on it (see Fig. 2).

Several properties have also been identified regarding the LEs (see Table 2). These permit the implementation of mechanisms to discover which LE can be invoked or how it can be composed. For example, by means of the property *generates*, it is possible to discover which document can be achieved as the result of the completion of a certain LE or AS.

Table 1. Some properties identified in the system

Property	Domain	Range	Explanation
issues	PA	Document	Refers to which Document is provided by who
requires	LE	Document	Refers to which Document is required for a LE
supports	PA	AS	Refers to which AS is supported by a PA
owns	Citizen	Document	Refers to which Document is owned by a Citizen
generates	LE	Document	Refers to which Document is the output of a certain LE

Some rules have been defined to ensure the consistency of current and future individuals in the ontology. These rules are defined by using the only support available in OWL. We can outline some of them, such as: every LE requires some input document, every AS is supported by some PA, or every LE generates some Document. The latter is displayed in the following lines both by means of logical notation and OWL code.

$R_1 = \{\forall LE \ \exists \ Doc, \ generates(LE) \ = \ Doc\}$

```
<owl:Class rdf:about="#LifeEvent">
    <rdfs:subClassOf>
     <owl:Restriction>
       <owl:onProperty>
         <owl:FunctionalProperty
                         rdf:ID="generates"/>
       </owl:onProperty>
       <owl:someValuesFrom>
         <owl:Class rdf:about="#Document"/>
       </owl:someValuesFrom>
     </owl:Restriction>
```

Further details about the conformance to local or national laws regarding documentation and legal procedures are not considered at this point and further implementations of the system should take care of them.

Some limitations regarding to the use of OWL have been noted. In particular, OWL does not support relations that link an individual to a class directly; relations can only involve individuals. This implies a number of shortcomings in the definition of some relations. In this case, for example, it is not possible to link, by using the property *requires* (see Table 1), a certain LE (an individual from class "LE") with a sub-class of Document; the LE can only be bound to another individual. To overcome this issue, we chose to define meaningless individuals, with no content in them, to make links to.

7. Supporting Architecture

Several architectural styles were considered to deploy this solution. Nevertheless, the use of a semantic version of SOA (Service Oriented Architecture) was chosen as the most appropriate as justified below.

The actual use of SOA as the architectural style provides to developers with an entire software model to be use in a quite straightforward manner. Anyhow, we have to admit that the definition of what a SOA architecture is may not be quite clear, as each software provider defines it in a slight different manner. Nevertheless, the OASIS [29] definition seems suitable [30] to us:

> "A paradigm for organizing and utilizing distributed capabilities that may be under the control of different ownership domains. It provides a uniform means to offer, discover, interact with and use capabilities to produce desired effects consistent with measurable preconditions and expectations."

We can consider Service Oriented Architecture, SOA hereafter, as an architectural style, according to the Bass terminology [9]. The gist of this proposal lays on the definition and modeling of Services themselves. This philosophy leads us to pay no attention to other details such as the network or the format for the messages. From this point of view, a service is a software resource accessible and defined by means of some key concepts: advertisement, service, contract, data model and policy. All of them together define and model the service in a holistic manner. This approach will provide interesting features such as loosely coupled, platform independent and protocol independent. Nowadays, the most common support for systems modeled under this style are Web Services.

In our case, we are prone to apply semantics to these considerations and to suggest the use of Semantic Service Oriented Architecture, hereafter SSOA. Hence, SSOA is considered, in our proposal an architectural style that takes SOA as its basis but in which the advantages of semantics are also applied. Thus, a semantic description of services and properties is provided by means of ontologies defined within the proposal. In this context, a semantic version of the usual agents of the SOA architecture is provided. A costumed version of the schema is adapted to our solution as shown in Figure 3.

These agents will perform similar operations to those present in the SOA environments. However, as services and data are marked with knowledge by means of semantics, it is possible to provide new mechanisms which are not available in "non-semantic" environments to discover and orchestrate services on execution-time.

Upon the adoption of SSOA as the architectural style, the matching of the agents identified (see Section 4.) with the aim of the proposal went smooth:

- Service provider. It is responsible for actually providing the service. As mentioned previously, the reader should note that now this agent is considered as a smart actor. Therefore, it can undertake complex task as publish its services using semantic support and support invocations described under this technology. In our case, two different agents are linked to this role. Even their tasks are quite close, they are concerned with different levels of service:

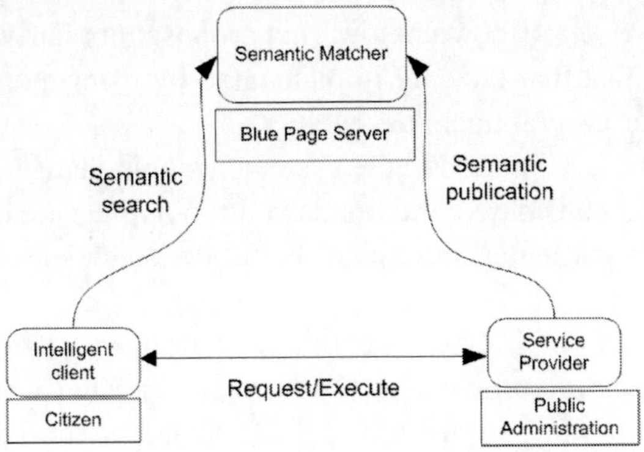

Figure 3. SSOA Services.

- PAs. They will be responsible for the execution of ASs. As they are responsible for their fulfillment, they will provide support for them.
- Digital Lawyers. As previously stated, LEs will involve the execution of several ASs. Thus, no particular PA will be responsible for their execution. Therefore, we introduce a new agent in the system, the Digital Lawyer, which will be responsible for supporting the execution of the LE in a holistic way. In the real world, this role may be performed by a number of *real* entities: lawyers, other PAs, interregional official entities ... Anyhow, its operations will be signed and a single identifiable agent will be in charge for the operation.

• The Semantic Matcher. This agent has a twofold mission: to support the publication of services (LEs and ASs) and to support the client in locating the wished service. Within our proposal, it is called Blue Page Server and it will accept the publication of semantically tagged services that will be at the citizen's disposal. As a result of the semantic support for operations, this agent is enabled to perform advanced operations due to the extra information obtained from the semantic annotations.

• Client, the intelligent agent. It is the one that will make use of the provided services. In this case, the citizen will discover services in the Blue Page Servers and will invoke them on PAs and Digital Lawyers. This is the agent that benefits from the use of semantics the most. With the provided technology, it is enabled to make the discovery of complex services to fulfill its needs.

As previously stated (see Section 6.1.), currently there are two different approaches for describing Web Services. In our case, we decided to take advantage of both philosophies. On the one hand, a semantic annotation of WS is provided, mainly for choreography support by means of SAWSDL. On the other hand, the definition of LE stored in the Blue Page Server using OWL ontologies to support the discovery and the orchestration is also provided.

As previously mentioned, SAWSDL was chosen to support the semantic annotation of services on the server side. The motivation is its simplicity and its power to express all the required information. Also, as shown below, this proposal fits fairly well in our definition of LEs/ASs due to the fact that they are implemented by using a single Web Service that provides an interface for programmers/developers.

Therefore, for each LE supported in the system, a single Semantic Web Service is provided. In each operation considered, the inputs and the outputs are defined in terms of the ontology developed. In particular, input and output documents are the ones identified as documents in the ontology.

The formal description of LEs, as previously mentioned, is stored in the Blue Page Server. These descriptions are provided as OWL instances. They are used to decide which ASs should be invoked in the composition of a LE or in a direct request from the citizen. It is quite simple, in general, to orchestrate LEs by using a semantic reasoner as it will only have to link outputs and inputs expressed in terms of the same ontology and related properties identified.

Under this approach, they can be considered an alternative to WSMO or OWL-S since they play a similar role, although very specialized for our solution. The interaction with this pool of LEs made solely of OWL instances is supported by means of SPARQL [42] queries where the wished conditions are introduced.

From the already introduced concepts, a particular software architecture is derived. The review of requirements from the citizen and the administration leads us to the identification of use cases.

This review involves a large number of use cases that cooperatively solve the entire problem. For the sake of clarity, we include the most important high-level use cases on Figs 4 and 5. Briefly, these use cases are responsible for:

InvokeLE This use case supports the invocation by the citizen of an LE in a Digital Lawyer to fulfill his/her final need.

InvokeAS The invocation of an AS in a PA by a Digital Lawyer is supported by this use case.

GetStatus To check the status of an AS or a LE, the citizen can invoke this use case.

RequestNotification Once the operation is completed, the citizen, using this use case, gets the final output of the LE (or AS in the case of a Digital Lawyer), i.e., the output document.

ManageLE The Digital Lawyer needs to manage (create, update or remove) the LE it is offering. This is done by this use case.

ManageAS Conversely, the PA needs to perform the very same operation. This is the suitable use case.

SearchLE The citizen needs to locate the proper LE before its invocation. This use case fulfills this need: upon the receipt of the semantic parameters for the search, the BPS responds with the proper LEs.

SearchAS In the same way, the Digital Lawyer needs to find out the proper AS it is going to invoke in order to perform the LE supported.

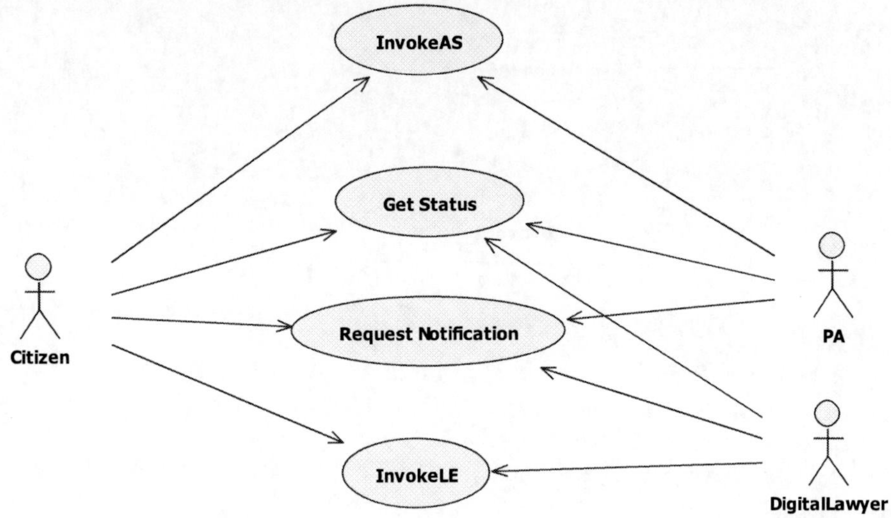

Figure 4. Use cases related to the citizen.

Regardless of the refinements of the previous ones, additional use cases are considered within this solution such as: RequestApplicationForm, CheckPossibleASs, ExploreTotal-LifeSpan, etcetera. These use cases provide support for non-critical task that are considered to be useful for the citizen.

8. LEs in Motion

The system will evolve and provide support to operations according to the schema shown on Fig. 6. The final aim of the citizen is to fulfill the desired LE, thus achieving the legal documents to prove the status or the completion of an operation.

LEs are available to the intelligent agents by means of the Blue Page Server, which stores LEs in a pool managed by a semantic engine. Upon the request from the citizen, the Blue Page Server submits the LE that best fits the conditions expressed by the client by means of a SPARQL [42] query (phase 1). This suitability is defined according to the profile of the citizen, the documents he/she is providing, the service that is being described and so on. The result is provided by the semantic engine in the XML format defined by SPARQL and sent to the client.

The LE within the response from the Blue Page Server includes a property containing the URL for the SAWSDL file with all the required data to actually invoke the LE in the suitable Digital Lawyer (phase 2). In response, the client receives a confirmation of the request, but not the result of the operation itself. At this point, we would like to make clear that Digital Lawyers are software agents that are responsible for the execution of LEs. Therefore, according to legal constraints, this role may be performed by other PA of a higher range, international offices, NGOs, etc.

Once the LE is requested, the Digital Lawyer will look for the AS required to accomplish the current LE (phases 3 and 4). The Digital Lawyer must search for a path of feasible ASs that leads toward the fulfillment of the LE. New searches are launched to the Blue

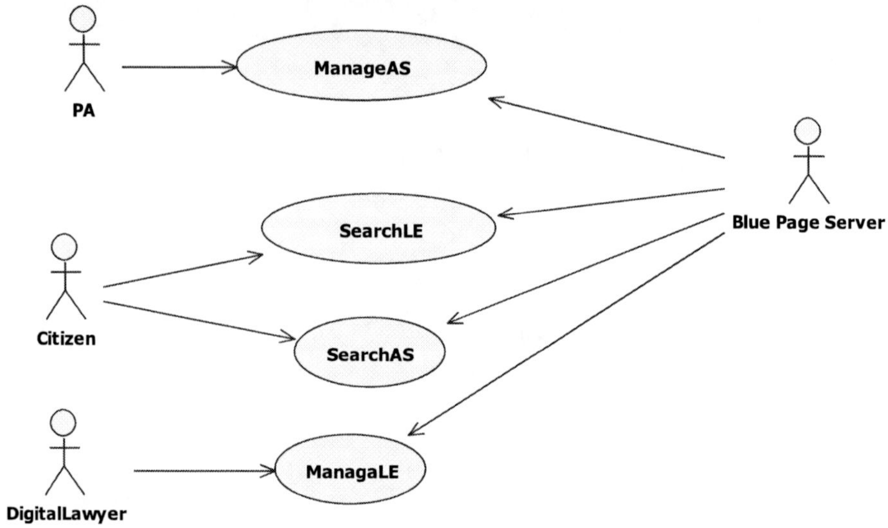

Figure 5. Use Cases related to the blue page server.

Page Server in order to accomplish this search and compositions of ASs. These searches are composed by taking advantage of the input/output documents and by using only the suitable Administration according to the scope of the LE. At this point, the Digital Lawyer must perform the tasks related to choreography. Once the analysis of the SAWSDL file stored on the PAs is performed, data fields for the request are adapted to make the invocation possible.

Once the required ASs are discovered, the Digital Lawyer will invoke those services (phases 5 and 6). In the process, the citizen can check the status of the operation (phase 7). In this case, the citizen will get a piece of data providing all available information regarding his/her operation. This information is provided under the form of a RSS file [35] with a new *item* for each step overtaken. The aim of this feature is to keep the citizen properly informed and engaged in the operation. The Digital Lawyer can also check the status of ASs requested to the PAs (phases 8 and 9). This operation works exactly the same way in both cases. After this step, and once the ASs have been already completed, the Digital Lawyer can request the final result of the operation (phases 10 and 11). If the citizen asks again about the completion of the LE (phase 12), he/she will discover that the operation is accomplished. So, he/she can get the final result (phase 13).

To carry out the implementation of these agents, authors decided to make use of a Java platform. Main reasons for this are due to its long background in large scale solutions, its capacity to run on nearly any hardware support and the existence of software libraries suitable to our interests. Also, for the implementation of agents, the use of Web Services was a key technology. And under this platform there are available plenty of libraries especially designed for this task. As a result, users of the system, both citizens and Public Administrations, are provided with an user friendly local application (see Figure 7).

In order to implement the most relevant semantic features required in this solution, the Jena library [26] was selected among other libraries. This library was the chosen option due to the large community of programmers currently working on its development and the support for required semantic operations such as executing queries or merging new

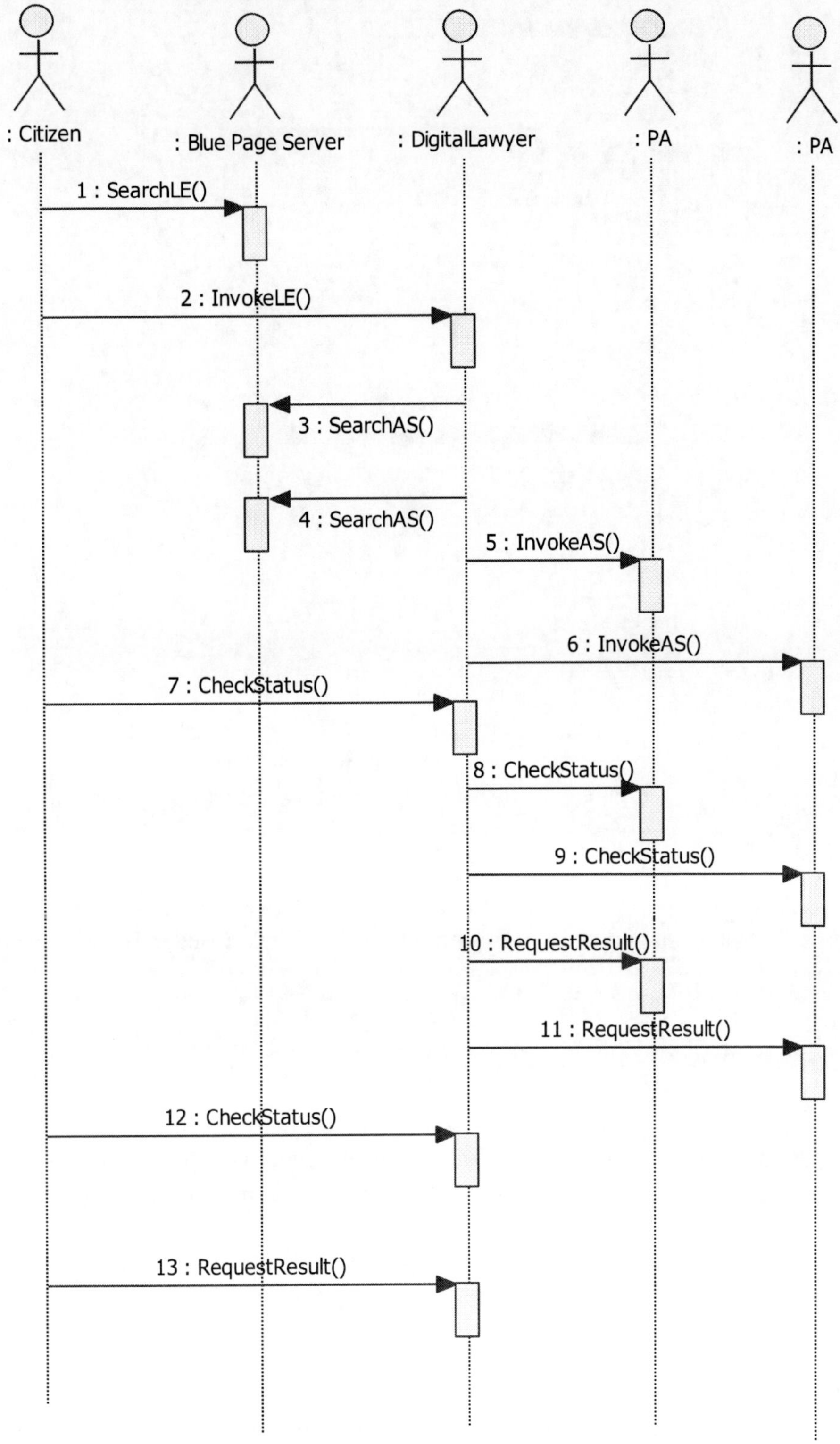

Figure 6. Example of use.

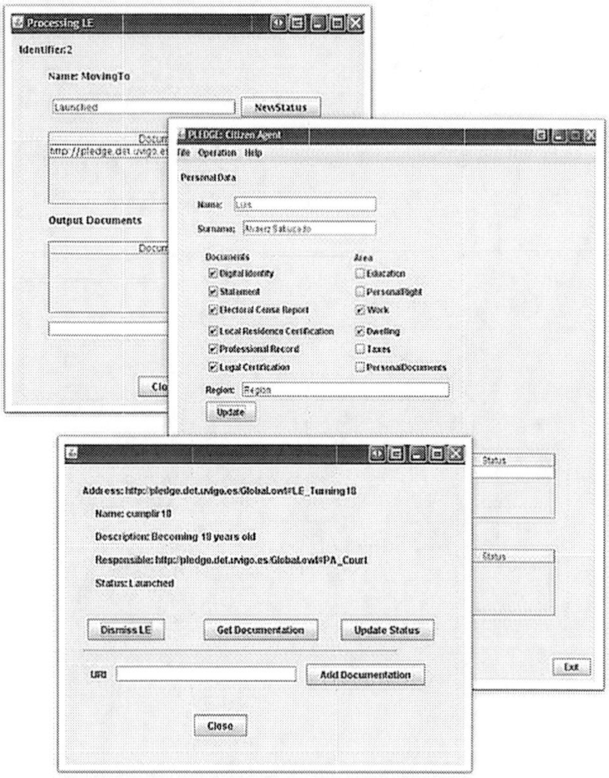

Figure 7. Screenshots from the prototype.

instances. Also, we would like to mention the use of the SAWSDL4J [47] as the tool that makes possible the managing of the description of services expressed in terms of SAWSDL definitoin.

9. Conclusion

eGovernment is getting more mature as more resources are devoted to the domain and more experienced become developers. These new and more complex projects require the provision of an integral support for services understood as an end-to-end support in the needs of citizens.

This chapter describes all the aspects required to duplicate this effort and it is intended to be used by any interested party. By means of this platform, Public Administrations or Agencies will get a simplified mechanism to provide their services. In addition, citizens will get access to services from a number of PAs in a quite simplified manner.

From a technological point of view, the use of semantics turned out to be a quite useful support. It provides us with a highly interoperable manner to define knowledge in the system that is actually shared among different entities with quite little binding. Also, it enables the provision of a way to recover information from different sources, to make discoveries about the current status of the citizen and to add new knowledge to the system.

Its actual adoption in a Public Administration should involve a review of the local/national legislation in order to make sure its compliance with their own regulation. Also we must mention that the level of interaction of the PA with the proposed schema is not very deep as the PA will still have to take care of the service on their own. This approach is acceptable in the current phase of maturity for eGovernment as more advanced mechanism could turn out in situations where PAs will not be willing to take part in the platform due to the extra effort required on its side. And in current state of eGovernment, it is a matter of utter importance to get involved as many PAs as possible in order to achieve an acceptable critic mass.

Acknowledgment

This work has been funded by the Ministerio de Educación y Ciencia through the project "Servicios adaptativos para e-learning basados en estándares" (TIN2007-68125-C02-02) and by the Xunta de Galicia, Consellería de Innovación e Industria "SEGREL: Semántica para un eGov Reutilizable en Entornos Locais" (08SIN006322PR).

References

[1] eGov: Online one-stop government. Web available, 2008. http://www.egov-project.org/.

[2] the foaf project. Web available, 2008. http://www.foaf-project.org/.

[3] Access-eGov. Web available, 2008. http://www.accessegov.org/.

[4] The SemanticGov Project. Web available, 2008. http://www.semantic-gov.org.

[5] Semantic Annotations for WSDL and XML Schema. Web available, 2008. http://www.w3.org/TR/sawsdl/.

[6] SW-Suomi.fi - Semanttinen informaatioportaali. Web available, 2008. http://www.museosuomi.fi/suomifi.

[7] Web Services Description Language (WSDL) Version 2.0. Web available, 2008. http://www.w3.org/TR/2007/REC-wsdl20-primer-20070626/.

[8] AIFB, University of Karlsruhe. Ontoedit. Web available, 2007. http://www.ontoknowledge.org/tools/ontoedit.shtml.

[9] L. Bass, P. Clements, and RickKazman. *Software Architecture in Practice*. Addison Wesley, 2003.

[10] S. Battle et al. Semantic Web Services Framework (SWSF) Overview. Web available, 2008. http://www.w3.org/Submission/SWSF/.

[11] T. Berners-Lee, J. Hendler, and O. Lassila. A new form of web content that is meaningful to computers will unleash a revolution of new possibilities. *Scientific American*, May-2001.

[12] CEN. Dublin Core eGovernment Application Profiles. Web available, 2008. http://www.cenorm.be/cenorm/businessdomains/businessdomains/isss/cwa/cwa14860/.asp.

[13] CEN. CEN home page. Web available, 2008. http://www.cenorm.be/cenorm/index.htm.

[14] W. W. W. Consortium. Rdf. Web available, 2008. http://www.w3.org/TR/rdf-schema/.

[15] W. W. W. Consortium. Rdf. Web available, 2008. http://www.w3c.org/RDF/.

[16] W. W. W. Consortium. Web service semantics - wsdl-s. Web available, 2008. http://www.w3.org/Submission/WSDL-S/.

[17] Council of Europe. Democratic institutions. Web available, 2008. http://www.coe.int/t/e/integrated_projects/democracy/.

[18] D. Enterprise and I. I. Unit. European interoperability framework for pan-european egovernment services. Web available, 2008. http://europa.eu.int/idabc/en/document/2319/5644.

[19] Fernández-López, M., Gómez-Pérez, A, and Juristo, N. Methontology: From ontological art towards ontological engineering. *Symposium on Ontological Art Towards Ontological Engineering of AAAI.*, pages 33–40, 1997.

[20] French Government. Adea. Web available, 2008. http://www.adae.gouv.fr/adele/.

[21] Fundation for Intelligent Physical Agents. Fipa. Web available, 2005. http://www.fipa.org/.

[22] A. Gómez-Pérez, M. Fernández-López, and O. Corcho. *Ontological Engineering*. Springer, 2003.

[23] T. Gruber. A translation approach to portable ontology specifications. *Knowledge Acquisition*, pages 199–220, 1993.

[24] L. Guijarro. Interoperability frameworks and enterprise architectures in e-government initiatives in europe and the united states. *Government Information Quarterly*, pages 89–101, 2007.

[25] L. Guijarro. Semantic interoperability in eGovernment initiatives. *Comput. Stand. Interfaces*, doi:10.1016/j.csi.2007.11.011, 2008.

[26] Hewlett-Packard. Jena. 2008. http://www.hpl.hp.com/semweb/.

[27] KBSt. Saga. Web available, 2008. http://www.kbst.bund.de/-,182/SAGA.htm.

[28] Lenat, DB and Guha, RV. *Building Large Knowledge-based Systems: Representattion and Inference in the Cyc Project*. 1990.

[29] OASIS. Oasis. Web available, 2008. http://www.oasis-open.org/.

[30] OASIS. Reference Model for Service Oriented Architecture 1.0. Web available, 2008. http://www.oasis-open.org/committees/download.php/19679/soa-rm-cs.pdf.

[31] Ontoknowledge project. Oil. Web available, 2008. http://www.ontoknowledge.org/.

[32] OWL-S Coalition. OWL-S: Semantic Markup for Web Services. Web available, 2008. http://www.daml.org/services/owl-s/1.1/.

[33] X. Papadomichelaki, B. Magoutas, C. Halaris, D. Apostolou, and G. Mentzas. A review of quality dimensions in e-government services, 2007.

[34] POPKIN Software. FEAF. Web available, 2007. http://government.popkin.com/frameworks/feaf.htm.

[35] RSS Advisory Board. RSS 2.0 Specification. Web available, 2008. http://www.rssboard.org/rss-specification.

[36] Schreiber, ATh et al. The KACTUS View on the 'O' World. *IJCAI95. Workshop on Basic Ontological Issues in Knowledge Sharing.*, pages 28–37, 1995.

[37] SDK WSMO working group. Wsmo. Web available, 2008. http://www.wsmo.org/TR/d2/v1.1/.

[38] Stanford Medical Informatics. Protege. Web available, 2008. http://protege.stanford.edu/.

[39] UK GovTalk. e-GIF. Web available, 2008. http://www.govtalk.gov.uk/.

[40] United Nations. Benchmarking e-government: A global perspective. Web available, 2008. http://unpan1.un.org/intradoc/groups/public/documents/un/unpan019207.pdf.

[41] W3C. Web ontology language. Web available, 2008. http://www.w3.org/2004/OWL/.

[42] W3C. SPARQL Query Language for RDF. Web available, 2008. http://www.w3.org/TR/rdf-sparql-query/.

[43] W3C. Web Accessibility Initiative. Web available, 2008. http://www.w3.org/WAI/.

[44] World Bank. About e-government. Web available, 2008. http://www.worldbank.org/egov.

[45] W3C. Web Services Activity. Web available, 2008. http://www.w3c.org/2002/ws/.

[46] W3C. Web Accessibility Initiative. Web available, 2008. http://www.w3.org/TR/2006/WD-owl-time-20060927/.

[47] K. G. Douglas Brewer Zixin Wu Ajith Ranabahu. SAWSDL4J Home. Web available, 2008. http://knoesis.wright.edu/opensource/sawsdl4j/.

In: Data Management in the Semantic Web
Editor: Hal Jin, pp. 195-214
ISBN: 978-1-61122-862-5

Chapter 9

SEMANTIC TOPIC MODELING AND ITS APPLICATION IN BIOINFORMATICS

***B. Zheng*[1] *and X. Lu*[2*]**

[1] Center for Neurologic Diseases, Harvard Medical School and Brigham and Women's Hospital, Cambridge, MA, U. S.

[2] Department of Biostatistics, Bioinformatics and Epidemiology, Medical University of South Carolina, Charleston, SC, U. S.

Abstract

In this chapter, we discuss utility of semantic topic modeling with the latent Dirichlet allocation model (LDA) and its application in bioinformatics domain. Through capturing the statistical structure of word usage patterns, LDA is capable of identifying semantic topics from a collection of text documents in an unsupervised manner. We show that semantic topic modeling with LDA can be used to automatically identify biological concepts from corpora of biomedical literature, thus providing more concise representation of the biomedical knowledge. We further demonstrate that representing text documents in semantic topic space facilitates classification of text documents. Finally, we show that connecting proteins in the semantic topic space enables efficient evaluation of the functional coherence of a group of proteins.

1. Introduction

Biomedical research has generated a wealth of knowledge, and the majority of this body of knowledge is stored in the form of free text, e.g., journal articles and in bibliographic databases such as PubMed. Recent two decades have witnessed significant progress in the text mining and natural language processing in the bioinformatics domain [1-4]. In particular, while it remains a challenge to fully analyze and represent the semantic meaning of natural language using computational technologies, significant progresses have been made to analyze

* E-mail address: lux@musc.edu.

the semantic context of free text [5-8], and these techniques have applied in the biomedical informatics domain [9-14].

In its most general form, semantic modeling is based on the premises that the semantic context of free text can be reflected by the word co-occurrence patterns—the topics; different semantic modeling methods employ different approaches to capture these patterns. In early 1990s, the latent semantic analysis (LSA) [6], also referred to as latent semantic indexing (LSI), was first introduced to capture the characteristics of word usage in text documents. In an LSA model, a collection of text documents is represented as a word by document matrix with dimension of $V \times D$, where V denotes the size of vocabulary and D represents the number of documents and an element represents how frequently a word is used in a document. The singular value decomposition (SVD) method is used to decompose the document matrix into two matrices: a $V \times K$ matrix $\mathbf{L}$ and a $K \times D$ matrix $\mathbf{C}$. The matrix $\mathbf{L}$ contains a total of K orthogonal vectors, with $K << D$, to provide low rank representation of the original document matrix. While capable of representing the intrinsic word co-occurrence structure, an individual vector from $\mathbf{L}$ does not convey any comprehensible semantic meaning, and therefore semantics in this analysis remains latent. The non-negative matrix factorization (NMF) [15] was later used to capture the intrinsic structure of the word-document matrix by relaxing the requirement of orthogonality of the recovered vectors but introducing a constraint that all elements of the vectors are non-negative. A vector recovered from NMF clearly reflects the co-occurrence of words that are comprehensible to human, which can be thought as topics. LSA and NMF are deterministic models, and as such the models cannot represent the uncertainty regarding the semantic context of documents. Furthermore, LSA and NMF are only capable of identifying topic context at document level but incapable of inferring to which topic each word (token) in a document belongs. To address this issue, a family of probabilistic topic models has been introduced, including the probabilistic latent semantic indexing (PLSI) [8], multinomial PCA [16] and latent Dirichlet allocation (LDA) [5, 7]. In these models, a topic reflecting the word co-occurrence pattern is represented as a multinomial distribution over the space of vocabulary. The models are capable of learning the topics from a corpus of text in an unsupervised manner, and more interestingly, the presence of topics in text document can be represented by latent variables indicating to which topic a word in a document belongs. The probabilistic topic models have the following characteristics: 1) identified topics are clearly comprehensible for human interpretation, 2) information encoded by latent topic variables can be used to segment the text into different topic regions to enhance information extraction, 3) probabilistic approach entertains uncertainty of topic content, and 4) Bayesian learning approach can incorporate information from new training documents in online learning manner, without re-running the whole learning process.

The chapter is organized as follows. Section 2 introduces the LDA model; Section 3 discusses the application of LDA model in bioinformatics domain, including identifying biological topics from the Gene Ontology (GO) [17] annotation corpus, enhancing text categorization with semantic representation, and evaluate protein functional coherence; and finally Section 4 provides general discussion of the utility of semantic modeling in the above domains.

2. Latent Dirichlet Allocation (LDA) Model

2.1. Model Specification

The LDA model is a probabilistic topic model [5, 7, 8], which simulates the process of generating a text. Let the corpus $C = \{d_1, d_2, ..., d_D\}$ be a set of documents, where D denotes the number of documents in the corpus; a document $d = (w_1, w_2,..., w_{Nd})$ consists of a sequence of words; and w be a word that takes a value from the vocabulary $\{v_1, v_2, ..., v_V\}$. Let T be the number of topics of an LDA model and V be the size of the vocabulary of the corpus. The LDA model simulates the generation of a document with following stochastic processes:

For each document, sample a topic proportion vector $\theta = (\theta_1,\theta_2,...,\theta_T)'$ from a Dirichlet distribution with a parameter vector $\boldsymbol{\alpha}$: $\theta \sim \mathrm{Dir}(\theta \mid \boldsymbol{\alpha})$. This is equivalent to an author deciding what topics to include in the paper and how the contents of the document are distributed among the topics.

For each word w_i in the document, sample a topic z_i according to multinomial distribution governed by θ: $z_i \sim \mathrm{Multi}(z| \theta)$. This can be thought as assigning the word to a topic.

Conditioning on the topic for the word, z_i, sample the word w_i according multinomial distribution with parameter $\boldsymbol{\phi}_z$: $w_i \sim \mathrm{Multi}(w \mid \boldsymbol{\phi}_z, z_i)$. This corresponds to picking words to represent the concept.

The parameter $\phi_{t,}$ with $t = 1,2,\ldots,T$, is a V-dimension vector that defines the multinomial word distribution of a topic, which in turn is distributed as Dirichlet with a parameter β: $\boldsymbol{\phi}_t \sim \mathrm{Dir}(\varphi_t \mid \beta)$.

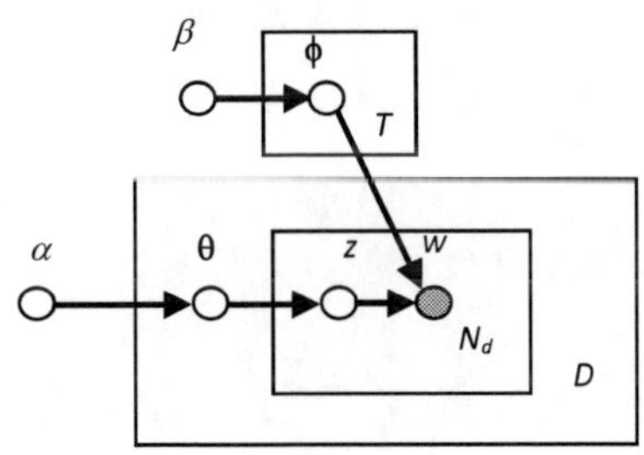

Figure 1. A directed acyclic graphical representation of the LDA model in plate notation.

The probabilistic directed acyclic graphical representation of the LDA model is shown in **Figure 1**. In a probabilistic graph, nodes represent random variables and edges represent the probabilistic relationship, i.e., the conditional probability, between the variables. The shaded and un-shaded nodes represent the observed and unobserved variables, respectively. Each rectangular plate represents a replica of the data structure; the number at the bottom right of each plate indicates the number of the replicates. In this graph, each document is associated with a topic composition variable θ and total of N_d replicates of topic variable z and word w. The graph also shows that there are T topic word distributions.

2.2. Statistical Learning

Given the observed documents, the learning task is to infer the topic-composition θ_d for each document d; the topic variable, z_i, for each word, w_i, within the document; and the word distribution $\boldsymbol{\phi}_t$ for each topic t. The exact inference of these unobserved variables is intractable; approximation algorithms such as variational methods and Markov chain Monte Carlo (MCMC) have been employed. We adopted the MCMC inference algorithm developed by Griffiths and Steyvers [7] to perform approximate inference. Let **z** denote a vector of the instances of all latent topic variables and **w** denote a vector of all the observed words of the corpus. The algorithm concentrates on calculating the joint probability $p(\mathbf{w}, \mathbf{z})$ by applying Gibbs sampling to instantiate the latent topic variables for all words in the corpus, **z**. Gibbs sampling is a technique to generate samples from a complex posterior distribution $p(\mathbf{z} \mid \mathbf{w})$ by iteratively sampling and updating each component variable z_i according to the conditional distribution $p(z_i \mid \mathbf{z}_{-i}, \mathbf{w})$, where $\mathbf{z}_{-i}$ denotes the current instantiation of all the latent topic variables except z_i, and **w** denotes the vector of all observed words of the corpus. The Gibbs sampling procedure follows these steps: (1) randomly initialize the latent variables **z**; (2) each element z_i of **z** is iteratively sampled and updated; (3) repeat step (2) until the Markov chain converges to the target posterior distribution $p(\mathbf{z} \mid \mathbf{w})$—a process commonly referred to as "burning in"; and (4) samples of **z** from the Markov chain can be used to denote the topics of the words, to calculate the joint and marginal probability of the corpus, to estimate the parameters θ and $\boldsymbol{\phi}$. The conditional distribution $p(z_i \mid \mathbf{z}_{-i}, \mathbf{w})$ is defined as follows:

$$p(z_i = j \mid \mathbf{z}_{-i}, \mathbf{w}) \propto \frac{n_{-ij}^{(W)_i} + \beta}{n_{-ij}^{(\cdot)} + V\beta} \times \frac{n_{-ij}^{(d_i)} + \alpha}{n_{-i}^{(\cdot)} + T\alpha} \tag{1}$$

In equation (1), $n_{-ij}^{(w_i)}$ denotes the count of the words in the corpus that are indexed by w_i and assigned to the topic j, excluding the word w_i; $n_{-ij}^{(\cdot)}$ is the count of all words assigned to the topic j, excluding the word w_i; $n_{-ij}^{(d_i)}$ is the count of words assigned to the topic j in document d_i that contains topic variable z_i, excluding w_i; $n_{-i}^{(d_i)}$ stands for the count of all the words in that document excluding w_i; and α, β, V and T were defined previously. During training of the LDA model, the values for the corpus level parameters were set as follows: $\alpha = 1$, $\beta = 0.01$. Once the vector of the latent topics **z** is instantiated by sampling, the parameters governing the posterior distribution of θ and ϕ can be estimated analytically as follows:

$$\hat{\theta}_j^{(d)} = \frac{n_j^{(d)} + \alpha}{n_{\cdot}^{(d)} + T\alpha} \tag{2}$$

$$\hat{\phi}_j^{(v)} = \frac{n_j^{v} + \beta}{n_j^{(\cdot)} + V\beta} \tag{3}$$

where n_j^d is the number of words assigned the topic j in the document d; $n_\cdot^{(d)}$ is the total number of words in the document d; $n_j^{(v)}$ stands for number of times a word indexed by v belongs to the topic j; and $n_j^{(\cdot)}$ denotes total number of words assigned to the topic j.

Since an LDA model can use different number of topics to represent a corpus, determining the optimal number of topics can be treated as a Bayesian model selection task, in which the optimal model, $\hat{M}$, is the model with the highest posterior probability defined as follows:

$$\begin{aligned}\hat{M} &= \underset{M}{\operatorname{argmax}}\, p(M \mid \mathbf{w}) \\ &\propto p(\mathbf{w} \mid M)p(M)\end{aligned} \tag{4}$$

Assuming the prior for each model is equal, the posterior probability of a model is determined by its marginal likelihood, written as:

$$p(\mathbf{w} \mid M) = \int_\phi \int_\theta \sum_z p(\mathbf{w}, \mathbf{z}, \phi, \theta \mid M) d\theta d\phi \tag{5}$$

However, the summation and integration in the equation (5) was intractable. Instead, the results from Gibbs sampling can be used to calculate the conditional probability based on a sample of instantiated **z**:

$$\begin{aligned}p(\mathbf{w} \mid \mathbf{z}, M) &= \int_\phi \int_\theta p(\mathbf{w}, \mathbf{z}, \phi, \theta \mid M) d\theta d\phi \\ &= \left(\frac{\Gamma(V\beta)}{\Gamma(\beta)^V}\right)^T \prod_{j=1}^{T} \frac{\prod_{i=1}^{V} \Gamma\left(n_j^{(i)} + \beta\right)}{\Gamma\left(n_j^{(\cdot)} + V\beta\right)}\end{aligned} \tag{6}$$

Then the marginal likelihood can be approximated by repeatedly sampling the latent variables **z**, calculating the conditional probabilities and averaging the conditional probabilities.

3. Applications of LDA in Biomedical Research

3.1. Identifying Biological Related Topics

When writing a scientific article, a scientist usually refers to multiple real world objects and/or concepts, thus a paper usually consists of multiple topics/subjects, e.g., a paper may discuss a protein that is located in *mitochondrion* and involved in a cellular process of *apoptosis*. When discussing an object or concept, an author tends to choose certain words to convey the semantic meaning. For instance, when discussing the topic *mitochondria*, words like 'electron,' 'cytochrome,' and 'ATP' are commonly used, while words like 'apoptosis,' 'programmed,' 'death' and 'caspase' are commonly used to discuss the concept of *apoptosis*. The LDA model represents such a notion by explicitly encoding multi-topicality of a document with a topic-composition variable and then simulating the "generation" of words by accordingly mixing words from topics, which are represented as multinomial distributions over a vocabulary, i.e., a word usage pattern. **Figure 2** shows how a topic can be represented as word-usage pattern in a probabilistic topic model.

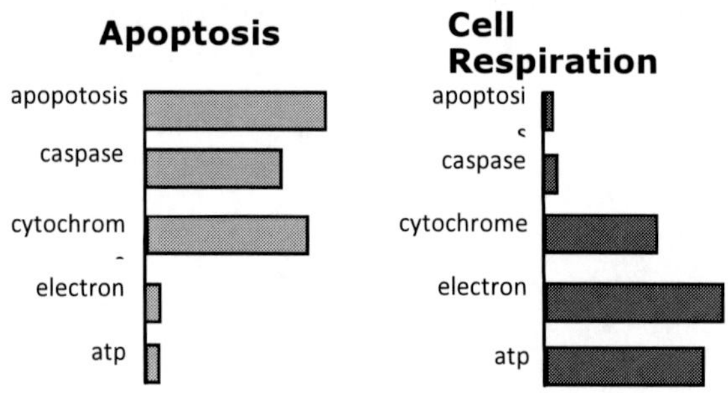

Figure 2. Representing concepts with word distributions. Two hypothetical topics are depicted. The bar lengths indicate the word-usage preference or the conditional probability of observing a word for a given topic.

We applied the LDA model to extract the semantic topics from a corpus of MEDLINE titles and abstracts, which were downloaded from the GOA annotation data (version 28.0) from the European Bioinformatics Institute. In this dataset, proteins from the Uniprot database are annotated with GO terms. Many of these GO annotations are associated with a PubMed identification number (PMID), indicating sources of information for the annotations. This dataset bridges proteins and their associated literature. We extracted 26,084 PMIDs from the dataset and retrieved the corresponding MEDLINE titles and abstracts through the batch service provided by the National Center for Biotechnology Information (NCBI). There are 39,336 proteins associated with this document set. The documents were pre-processed by removing 'stop words' and stemming [12]. The total number of unique words in this corpus is 52,350. In order to determine whether a word was relevant to biology, we calculated the mutual information (MI) of a word with respect to the GO terms associated with the corpus. The MI is determined as follows:

$$MI(w,g) = \sum_{w,g \in \{0,1\}} p(w,g) \log \frac{p(w,g)}{p(w)p(g)} \tag{7}$$

where $p(w,g)$ is estimated by counting the documents in which a word w and a GO term g are present or absent (1or 0, respectively). The biological relevance of a word is determined as its maximal MI with respect to any GO term. When the words were sorted in descending order according to their MI, we found that words with low MI tended to be either very common or very rare words. The final vocabulary list contained 18,725 unique terms.

Training of an LDA model requires specification of the number of topics for the models, an issue of interest from both semantic analysis and statistical learning viewpoints. From a semantic analysis point of view, this is equivalent to determine the granularity of abstraction of the concepts that can be used to summarize the semantic contents of the corpus. From the statistical learning point of view, this is equivalent to select among the models with different complexity. A Bayesian model selection framework was employed to determine the "optimal" number of topics based on the posterior probability of a model, $p(M \mid \mathbf{w})$. To perform the Bayesian model selection, samples of the latent semantic topics, $\mathbf{z}$, were collected for a model with a given number of topics, T, and the approximate the posterior probabilities were calculated according to equation (6). **Figure 3** shows that the model with 300 topics had the highest approximate marginal likelihood, and the results from this model were used for further analyses.

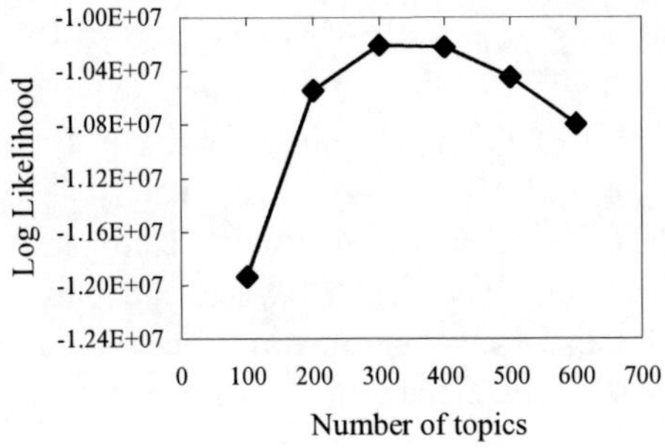

Figure 3. Bayesian model selection. The means of approximated evidence for different models are plotted; standard error bars ware within the symbols.

Table 1. The ten most common topics from a trained LDA model

Topic #	Topic words
51	receptor coupl ligand agonist subtype pharmacolog antagonist orphan adrenerg desensit
156	Kinas phosphoryl serin threonin pkc autophosphoryl casein akt catalyt ste20
136	cerevisia saccharomyc strain yeast plasmid multicopi lacz floccul auxotroph gal1
67	Famili member belong multigen subfamily mrg Dalton cabp28k heterogen transmembran
154	patient syndrom diseas disord autosom inherit recess ref caus clinic
124	Cdna librari clone probe screen isol lambda obtain oligonucleotid gt11
37	neuron axon migrat motor glial spinal cord neurit dendrite outgrowth
229	mutant defect doubl phenotyp fail rescu restor impair pleiotrop unable
112	Exon intron genom kb flank region span upstream bp start
172	nuclear nucleu export cytoplasm nuclei pore ran hnrnp envelop import

A trained LDA model returns estimated distributions of the following parameters and latent variables: (1) the word-usage distribution, $\boldsymbol{\phi}_{t,}$ for each topic; (2) the latent topic labeling z_i for each word w_i; and (3) the topic-composition distribution $\boldsymbol{\theta}_d$ for each document. The parameter vector $\boldsymbol{\phi}_t$ is a distribution representing a word-usage pattern for the topic t. High probability words of each $\boldsymbol{\phi}_t$ can be thought as the words frequently used to discuss the topics. **Table 1** contains the 10 most commonly observed topics and their high probability words of the trained LDA model. The topics were sorted in descending order according to the number of words assigned to them in the corpus. High probability words of these topics constitute clusters of words that coherently convey biological concepts. For example, topic # 51 reflects the concept of *ligand-activated receptors,* and the topic # 156 is related to *serine/threonin kinase activity*. Because an LDA model attempts to capture the major topics that can be used to "generate" the data, the concepts extracted by this model should reflect the recurring themes of the corpus. Indeed, when multiple models with 300 topics were trained with different random-number seeds, similar major topics were extracted although the index of the topics differed among the models. Thus, the topics listed in **Table 1** do reflect common biological themes in the corpus.

Mitochondria[73] play a key part[160] in the regulation[113] of apoptosis[147] (cell[200] death[147]). Their intermembrane[73] space[73] contains[131] several proteins[265] that are liberated[224] through the outer[73] membrane[219] in order[294] to participate[87] in the degradation[299] phase[209] of apoptosis[147]. Here we report[33] the identification[208] and cloning of an apoptosis[147]-inducing[147] factor[19], AIF[147], which is sufficient[3] to induce[147] apoptosis[147] of isolated[76] nuclei[191]. AIF[147] is a flavoprotein[73] of relative[122] molecular[177] mass[185] 57,000 which shares[168] homology[212] with the bacterial[213] oxidoreductases[73]; it is normally[122] confined[123] to mitochondria[73] but translocates[166] to the nucleus[191] when apoptosis[147] is induced[147]. Recombinant[279] aif[147] causes[141] chromatin[51] condensation[279] in isolated[76] nuclei[191] and large-scale[41] fragmentation[174] of dna[126]. It induces[147] purified[213] mitochondria[73] to release[5] the apoptogenic[147] proteins[265] cytochrome[73] c and caspase9[147]. Microinjection[217] of aif[147] into the cytoplasm[81] of intact[257] cells[200] induces[147] condensation[279] of chromatin[51], dissipation[292] of the mitochondrial[73] transmembrane[206] potential[64], and exposure[280] of phosphatidylserine[68] in the plasma[219] membrane[219]. None of these effects[257] is prevented[147] by the wide-ranging[132] caspase[147] inhibitor[170] known[140] as zvad.fmk[172]. Overexpression[150] of bcl2[147], which controls[113] the opening[101] of mitochondrial[73] permeability transition[209] pores[191], prevents[147] the release[5] of aif[147] from the mitochondrion[73] but does not affect[257] its apoptogenic[147] activity[23]. These results[150] indicate[144] that aif[147] is a mitochondrial[73] effector[147] of apoptotic[147] cell[200] death[147].

Figure 4. Semantic analysis for a MEDLINE abstract (PMID 9989411). The topics associated with the words were inferred by the LDA model and are shown as the superscript number next to the words. The words from the topics # 73 and # 147 are highlighted with blue and red colors, respectively.

The instantiated latent variables of a document, $\mathbf{z}_d$, can be used to reflect the semantic contents of the document. For the text in the training data set, the topic contents for each document were returned as the estimated latent variables $\mathbf{z}_d$ of the trained model. For a newly observed text, the topic contents can be inferred by invoking the sampling algorithm with the estimated parameters as described in the Methods section. **Figure 4** shows an example of a MEDLINE abstract, in which topic assignment for the words were inferred using a trained LDA model. This abstract discusses a protein referred to as apoptosis inducing factor (AIF), a mitochondrial protein that induces apoptosis. In the figure, the inferred semantic topic for each word (excluding "stop" words) is shown as the superscript numbers next to it. The abstract is associated with the following GO terms: (1) GO:0008630, DNA damage response, signal transduction resulting in induction of apoptosis; (2) GO:0009055, electron carrier activity; (3) GO:0005739, mitochondrion; and (4) GO:0006309, DNA fragmentation during apoptosis. In **Figure 4**, two major topics, # 73 and # 147, are the dominant topics of the abstract. Topic # 73 is related to the *mitochondrion* and topic # 147 reflects the concept of *apoptosis*. Interestingly, several words, which may belong to multiple topics depending on context, were found in the abstract, e.g., "space" and "outer." The LDA model has captured their common occurrence in the context of *mitochondrion* and correctly assigned these common words to this topic based on the context. With the inferred topics, this abstract can be readily indexed with these two major topics, which agree well with the human GO annotations of this abstract. Furthermore, a document can also be indexed as a vector containing the counts of the words in each topic or with the normalized estimated $\hat{\theta}$, which be treated as a vector in the space spanned by the topics. Such representation effectively projects the document from the high dimensional vocabulary space onto the reduced-dimensionality of topic space. Such information could be used to automatically index the text.

The LDA model simulates the "generation" of a corpus. By its generative nature, it will incorporate topics needed to capture the common characteristics in the corpus. However, some common features may not be necessarily relevant to biology but merely reflect the linguistic feature of the corpus. To determine the biological relevance of topics, we further inspected the high probability words and assigned a biological relevance score, ranging from 0 (indicating no biological relevance) to 5 (representing strong biological relevance) to each topic. **A histogram of the assigned biological relevance scores (Panel A of** Figure 5) **indicates that most topics/concepts extracted from this corpus were biologically relevant, with only a fraction with biological relevance scores equal to zero, indicating no biological relevance.**

Each MEDLINE abstract from the GOA corpus was associated with one or more GO terms, providing an opportunity to study the relationship between the semantic topics extracted by the LDA model and the GO annotations. The correlation between a semantic topic and the GO annotation was quantified by mutual information (MI) between the latent topic and the annotated GO terms. MI is a symmetric, non-negative quantity that measures the relevance (amount of information) of one variable with respect to another variable, which equals zero if and only if the variables are independent. Topics highly relevant to biological objects/concepts should have high MI with some GO terms, while the topics irrelevant to biology should have low MI values for topic-GO association. Indeed, as shown in **Figure 5**, topics rated low relevance have very low MI with any GO terms, while topics with high relevance have the highest topic-GO MI (Panel B). However, there were some topics that were assigned high relevance scores but had low MI with GO terms. This disparity was likely due to the way the MI for a topic-GO association was calculated in this study, which specifies that, if a document was annotated with a GO term *g*, every word in the document was considered as annotated with that GO term. This method was adopted due to the lack of supervised training data specifying which words in a document were responsible for the GO annotations. MI calculated under this assumption is skewed for the relatively uncommon topics in the corpus. Nonetheless, the MI of topic-GO association serves as a criterion of evaluating the biological relevance of a topic. When a topic had a high MI value for a topic-GO association, it usually reflected a coherent biological concept. Interestingly, a topic with low biological relevance did not mean that it was not a coherent semantic concept. For example, topics # 224 and # 227 (**Table 2** in ref. 12) consisted of common English words that therefore had the lowest MI with any GO term. However, the topics did contain the words that constitute coherent semantic concepts, e.g., topic # 224 contains words related to the concept of *being unique*.

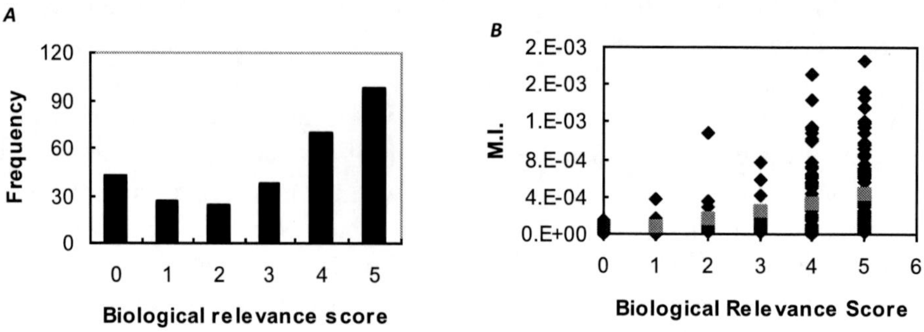

Figure 5. Determining the biological relevance of the topics. Panel A. Histogram of human assigned biological relevance scores. A score of 0 indicates no biological relevance, while scores of 1 through 5 indicate increasingly relevant and coherent biological relevance. Panel B. Relationship between the human assigned biological relevance score and the topic-GO MI.

3.2. Enhancing Text Categorization with Semantic-Enriched Representation and Training Data Augmentation

Information retrieval, in general, can be divided into two types: ad hoc retrieval and text categorization or filtering. Text categorization or filtering refers to meeting the long-term information needs of users, where users' preferences are predefined and new text is divided into groups according to such preferences. Since examples of documents labeled with preference categories are often available, the task is usually cast as a supervised classification problem. Support vector machine (SVM) [18, 19] is considered as one of the best text categorization algorithms. However, when trained with a small number of high dimensional training cases, SVM, like other classification methods, does not perform well because a combination of high-dimensionality of the text data and scarcity of training cases makes it difficult to classifiers that generalize well. To address these problems, we investigated the utility of using semantic-preserving dimension reduction in text categorization task, by representing text with semantic-enriched features.

As a baseline experiment, we used the data from the TREC 2005 text categorization task, which consisted of full articles published during the years of 2002~2003 from three journals: the Journal of Cell Biology, the Proceedings of the National Academy of Sciences, and the Journal of Biological Chemistry. There were four text categorization subtasks: (1) the allele subtask (A) is to retrieve documents related to allele mutation; (2) the expression subtask (E) is to retrieve documents related to gene expression during embryonic development; (3) the gene ontology subtask (G) is to retrieve documents that contain the contents which warrant GO annotations; and (4) the tumor subtask (T) is to retrieve documents related to tumors. The training data consist of 5,837 full article documents, and the numbers of positive training cases for the subtasks A, E, G, and T are 338, 81, 462, and 36, respectively.

The documents were preprocessed by removing stop words, stemming, and discarding terms that appeared less than ten times in the corpus. As a result, the size of the vocabulary (V) was trimmed to 23,484, and a document was represented by the V-dimensional vector, $d = (w_1, w_2, \ldots, w_V)^T$, in which an element, w_i, represents the number of times the ith word of the vocabulary occurs in the document. The elements of the vector were further weighted using a modified term frequency and inverse document frequency (*tf-idf*) scheme, which calculates the weight $w_d(t)$ for the term t in the document d:

$$w_d(t) = (1 + \log n(t,d)) \times \log(D / n(t)) \quad (8)$$

where n(t, d) is the number of times the term t occurs in the document d, D is the total number of documents in the corpus and n(t) is the number of the documents that contain t. To remove the influence of the documents that contain the weights, the document vectors were further normalized to have Euclidean norm of 1.0:

$$w_d^{'}(t) = \frac{w_d(t)}{\sqrt{\sigma_u w_d(u) \times w_d(u)}} \quad (9)$$

where $w'_d(t)$ is the normalized weight, $\sigma_u(.)$; u=1,2,..., V is summation over all elements of the vector.

The SVM^{light} program [20] was used to train the data set with each document represented as a vector in the original vocabulary vector space, which we referred to as *VocRep*. To deal with the situations of unbalanced positive and negative training cases, the SVM^{light} implementation allows users to specify a cost-factor parameter to indicate how training errors on positive cases outweigh those of the negative cases. The cost-factor is specified through the option parameter "-j" of the program. When training the SVM^{light} classifier on the TREC 2005 VocRep corpus, we tested different cost weights, with option "–j" set to 1, 1.5, 2, 3, 4, 6, 8, and 10. The classification performance was evaluated by the built-in leave-one-out (LOO) test of the SVM^{light} implementation.

Figure 6 shows that increasing cost-factor for the positive training cases enhances the classification performance of SVM. However, the performance of the SVM^{light} reached plateaus when "*-j*" parameter was set higher than 3. Overall, the classification performance of SVM on this data set is not very satisfactory, especially on the categories E, G, and T task. These results are not surprising as they agree with the observations from the benchmark studies by Lewis *et al* [18], in which the F values for the low frequency categories in the Reuter's corpus are equivalent to our results. These results indicate that, although the SVM^{light} implementation is capable of alleviating the problem of skewed training data with an adjustable cost-factor parameter, the insufficient training data remain an obstacle to effective text classification. Such a problem manifests itself further when the training cases are represented as sparse vectors in a high dimensional space. In such a scenario, the data points represented by these vectors tend to share few common elements and thus are far apart in the high-dimensional space. The decision surface learned under such a condition tends to over-fit the data. To determine if the SVM algorithm was over-fitting on our training data, we further evaluated the training error of the program by invoking the trained classifiers on the training data. The training errors for all these classifiers were zeros, while the LOO estimation of testing errors were around 20 ~ 80%. Thus, these experiments indicate that, although utilizing maximal margin to protect itself from over-fitting on the high dimensional data, the SVM algorithm suffered from over-fitting in this scenario.

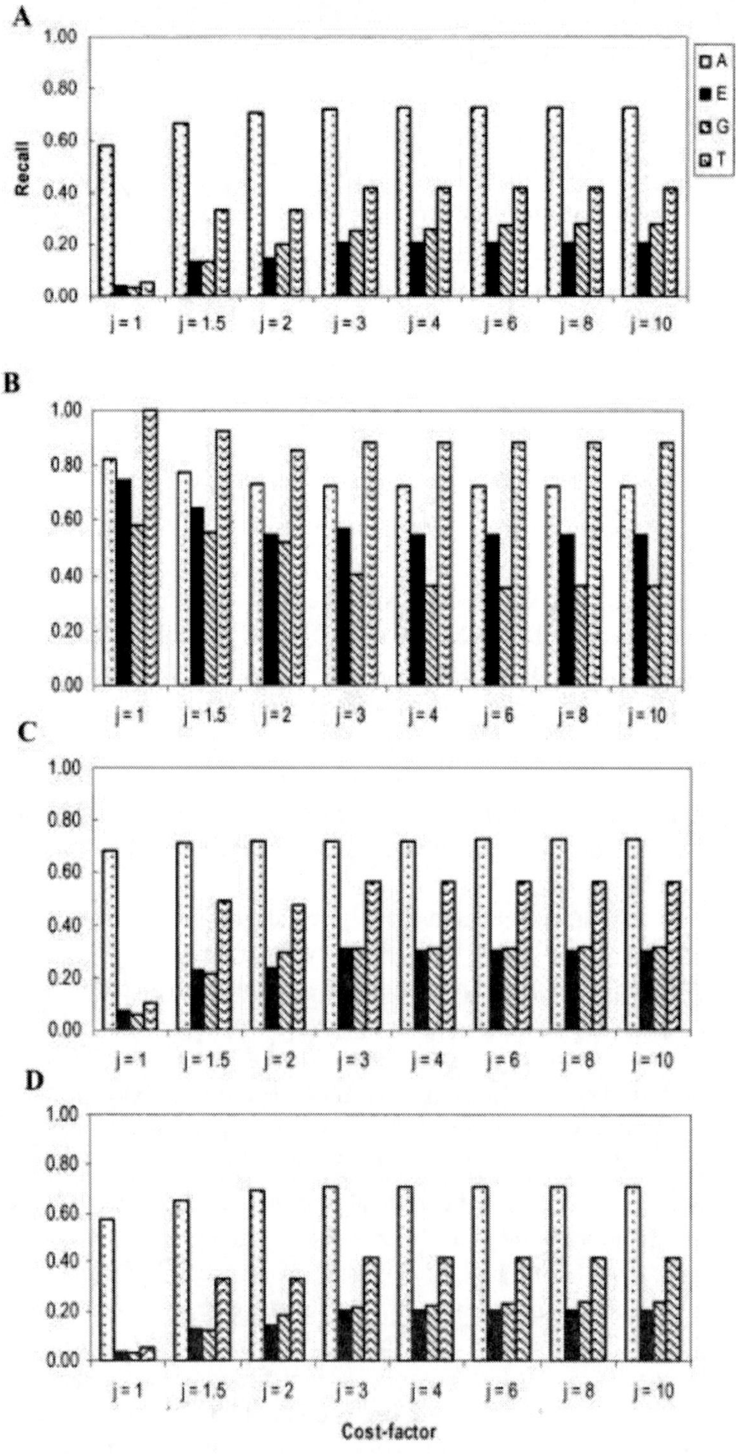

Figure 6. Baseline performance of SVM. Different with different cost-factor setting were used for training SVM. Panel A: Recall; Panel B: Precision; Panel C: F scores; and Panel D: normalized utility.

The possible reasons for the relative poor baseline classification performance are the sparseness in both the non-zero elements of the vector representation and the number of data points within a high dimensional space. The first problem potentially can be addressed by reducing the dimensionality of the data while maintaining the semantic structure of the original vector space. The LDA model is a full probabilistic generative model that can capture human understandable semantic topics, which are represented by a relatively small number of distributions over the vocabulary. By representing a document in the topic space instead of in the vocabulary space, the LDA model effectively reduces dimension of the texts while maintains the semantic content of the document.

We trained an LDA model with 400 topics using the TREC 2005 data. Inspecting the topics extracted from the corpus, we found that most of topics were coherent biological topics while some were not specifically related to biology. Associating every word with a topic enables us to represent a document within a lower-dimensional vector space spanned by semantic topics, in our case the dimension of topic space $T = 400$, instead of the original high-dimensional vocabulary space. In this semantic space, each document is represented by a T-dimensional vector, whose elements indicate the number of words belonging to each topic in the document thus projecting the document from the vocabulary space to the topic space. The projection addresses the problem of sparseness of the elements of original vocabulary vector space. We refer to the documents represented with the semantic-enriched features as *SemRep* and examined the effect of such transformation on the text categorization performance of the SVM^{light}.

The text documents of TREC 2005 represented in SemRep form were used to train the SVM^{light} program, and the performance was evaluated with the LOO estimation of the test errors as in the baseline experiments. To avoid differences in the performance introduced by the different parameter settings, we fixed the cost-factor parameter "-j" to 10, a value that gave rise to the saturated performance on the baseline experiments. **Figure 7** shows the comparison of the classification performance of SVM^{light} for these experiments.

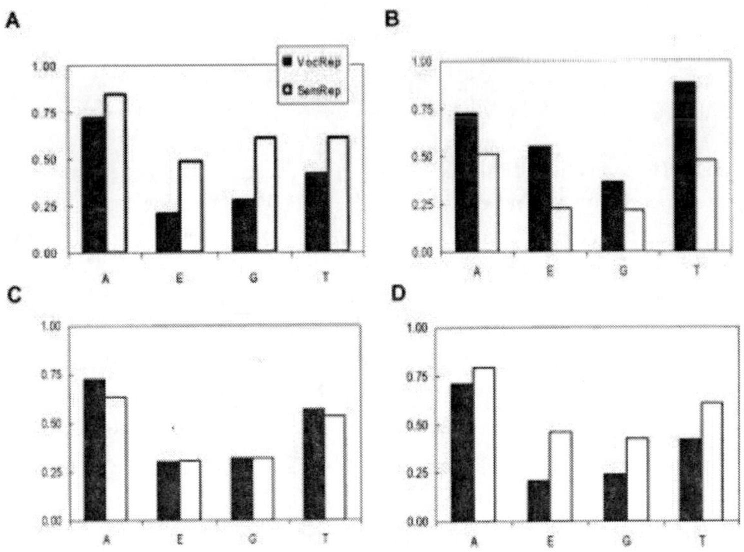

Figure 7. Semantic representation and classification. Text documents are represented in vocabulary (VocRep) and semantic space (SemRep). Panels A, B, C, D correspond to the recall, precision, F value and utility score comparisions of VocRep and SemRep.

The results indicate that representing the text in the form of SemRep significantly enhances the recall and utility of the SVM^{light} on the SemRep data set compared to the results on the VocRep data. The increase in recall is most noticeable (more than one fold) for categories E and G, while it is also clear for categories A and T. Due to the well-known trade off between recall and precision, the precision for all categories declined to different degrees. However, the metrics that measure the overall performance of the classifier, the utility score and *F* values, increased for both E and G categories, indicating that SemRep produced balanced improvement for these subtasks. On the other hand, the utility scores for the subtasks A and T are significantly increased while the *F* values declined slightly. An F value is a balanced metrics considering both recall (sensitivity) and precision (positive predictive value). Since the total numbers of positive cases for these classification tasks are small, precisions are sensitive to a relative small change of false positive number which may dominant the true positive number, which in turn influence the *F* values.

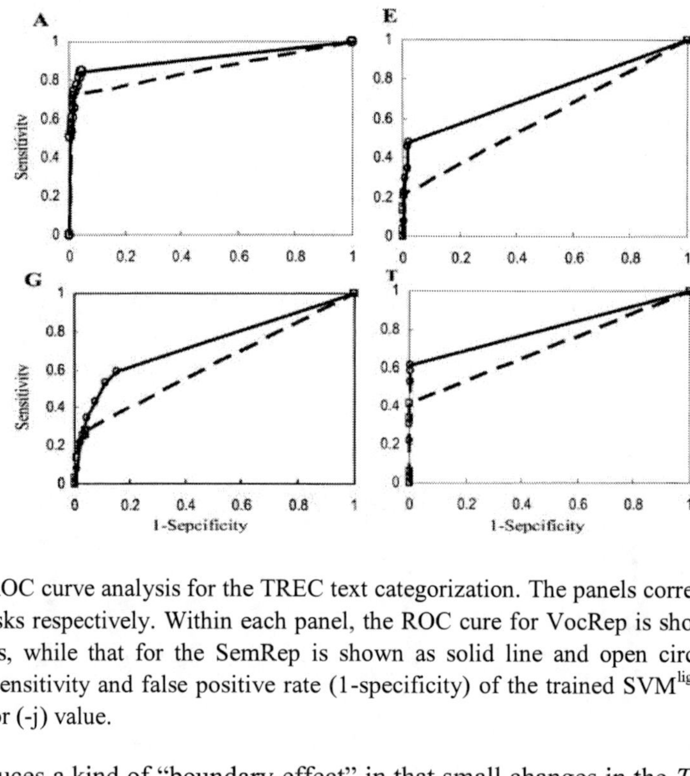

Figure 8. The ROC curve analysis for the TREC text categorization. The panels correspond to the A, E, G, and T subtasks respectively. Within each panel, the ROC cure for VocRep is shown as dashed line and open boxes, while that for the SemRep is shown as solid line and open circles. Each symbol represents the sensitivity and false positive rate (1-specificity) of the trained SVM^{light} classifier with a given cost-factor (-j) value.

This produces a kind of "boundary-effect" in that small changes in the *TP* and *FP* counts significantly change the values of precision and *F* values. To address this issue, an ROC curve, another balanced metric considering both recall and false positive rate, was used to evaluate the performance of SVM^{light} based on VocRep and SemRep for all four subtasks (**Figure 8**). The results show that, for every subtask, representing the documents in SemRep clearly increases the AUCs, i.e., the discriminative power of SVM^{light}, in comparison to those for VocRep. In summary, representing the text document in the form of SemRep can significantly increase recall (sensitivity), utility scores and the AUC of the SVM^{light}, thus the SemRep enhances the discriminative power of the SVM^{light} program.

3.3. Evaluating the Functional Coherence of Protein Groups

In the era of high throughput biology, analysis of results of these technologies commonly results in a list of genes of potential interest, e.g., genes that differentially expressed before and after a treatment. An ensuing problem is to determine if the genes within a list perform coherently related functions. Currently, determining the functional coherence of protein groups requires either manual inspection of the associated biomedical literature or utilization of currently available protein annotations. Manually studying of literature is a labor intensive task and does not scale well with high throughput methodology. Recently, some researchers directly tap into the knowledge in the form of biomedical literatures and perform semantic analysis on the literatures associated with the proteins to study their functional relationship [21]. Raychaudhuri and Altman developed a sophisticated scheme and a metric, referred to as neighbor divergence per gene (NDPG), to evaluate the functional coherence of a group of proteins. However, their method requires many heuristic setting of parameters and threshold, whose "optimal" values may be hard to be determined. Furthermore, their metric is essentially the Kullback-Leibler divergence of two distributions whose value is not normalized, thus the values and their interpretations are training-data-dependent.

We developed a novel metric to measure the functional coherence of a group of proteins. The idea is that biomedical literature describing a group of proteins that have similar functions or participate in common pathways should share common biologic concepts. This allows us to extract biological concepts from literature and to connect proteins through their shared biologic concepts in a bipartite graph, referred to as protein-semantic network (ProSemNet). In the graph, proteins are connected to each other only through the shared biological concepts, extracted through semantic analysis, such that proteins participating in a related function tend to be closely located in the graph. The functional coherence of a group of proteins is measured by their "closeness" or "strength of connectivity" on the graph. Furthermore, methods for evaluating statistical significance of functional coherence metrics are also developed.

Using the results from the experiments described in Section 3.1, the semantic content of each of MDELINE document is represented as the presence of topics in the document, and relative strengths of the topics can be estimated through counting the words belonging to each topic. With such information available, we were able to connect proteins with the semantic topics based on the MEDLINE documents associated with them. Furthermore, the strength of association of a protein with a topic can be represented as the number of words assigned to the topic among all the documents associated with the protein. Combining the associations between proteins and topics, we constructed a protein-topic associated matrix, which can be thought of as an adjacency matrix of a weighted, undirected bipartite graph consisting of proteins and topics—protein semantic network. In this network, proteins are connected to each other only through shared biologic concepts, and therefore proteins with shared functions tend to be closely located or strongly connected.

The assumption underlying our approach of evaluating the functional coherence of a group of proteins is that the biomedical literature describing proteins with similar functions should share similar biologic topics, and therefore these proteins should be closely connected in the ProtSemNet. Therefore, the 'closeness' of the proteins on the ProtSemNet graph can be used as a metric for evaluating the functional coherence of the group of protein. Given a ProtSemNet, one can extract a subgraph connecting any arbitrary number of proteins, provided that they are represented in the graph, such that the total semantic distance of the subgraph is shortest. A subgraph satisfying such requirement is referred to as the Steiner tree problem, which is a NP-hard problem. We adopted a proximate algorithm developed by Kou *et al* [22] to extract Steiner trees from ProtSemNet. furthermore, we designed two metrics, the group functional coherence score (GFCS): the total number of edges of the Steiner tree, GFCSe; and the total semantic distance of the Steiner tree, GFCSd.

Examples of Steiner trees for a randomly grouped proteins and a functionally coherent KEGG pathway (ribosome) are shown in **Figure** 9, a Steiner tree from randomly selected proteins tends to spread over (left) while a Steiner tree from a functional coherent group forms tight clusters (right).

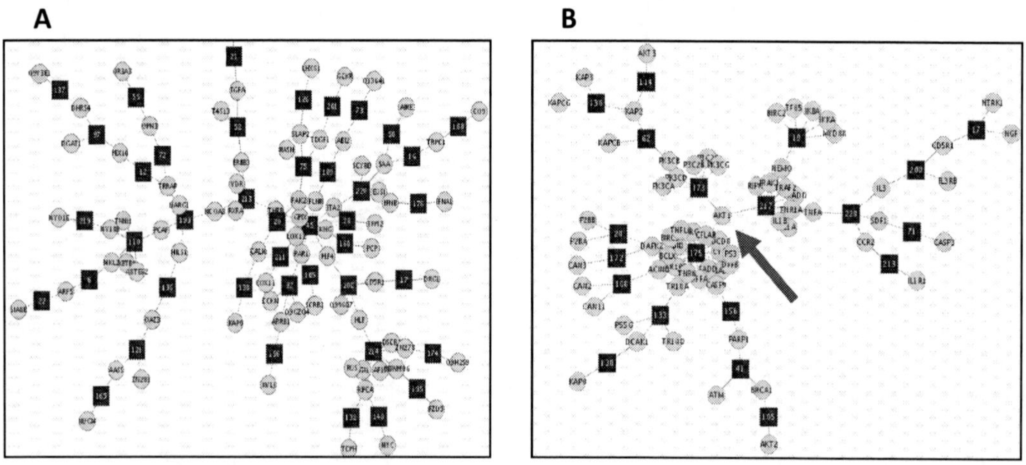

Figure 9. Steiner trees for random and KEGG protein groups. The biologic topic are represented by square vertices, whereas proteins are represented by circle vertices. (a) A Steiner tree of a random protein group. (b) The Steiner tree of human apoptosis pathway proteins. KEGG, Kyoto Encyclopedia of Genes and Genomes.

When given a set of proteins, the most common question is: what is the probability that the group consist of random proteins. This can be achieved by comparing the ProtSemNet statistics (GFCSe and GFCSd) to those derived from a population of randomly grouped gene sets—null distributions of the statistics. We applied a sampling approach to generate the populations of randomly grouped gene sets by randomly selecting sets of proteins from a given genome, e.g., yeast, mouse and human. For each random protein set, we extracted its Steiner tree and collected network statistics from the tree. Since the size of the Steiner tree for a protein set is proportional to the number of proteins in the set, we further applied linear regression to estimate the relationship between the protein set size and the network statistics. The probability of an observed GFCSe and GFCSd was determined according to a Gaussian distribution with estimated mean and variance.

To test whether GFCSs can correctly discriminate the functionally coherent protein groups from randomly picked groups, we selected 30 pathways of human, mouse, and yeast from the KEGG database as the functionally coherent protein clusters and evaluated whether their GFCSs are significantly different from the distributions for the random protein groups. We used the sensitivity, specificity, and receiver operating characteristic (ROC) analysis to evaluate the discriminative power of the GFCSs obtained from the species specific ProtSemNet. For this experiment we randomly drew 30 protein groups, with sizes similar to those from KEGG pathways, from the human, mouse, and yeast ProtSemNet, respectively. At the significance level of $P = 0.05$, the sensitivity and specificity for GFCSe are 0.97 and 1.0, respectively, and the sensitivity and specificity for GFCSd are 0.73 and 1.0, respectively. Using random groups as negative cases and the KEGG pathway groups as positive cases, we progressively set the significance threshold at 1E-4, 1E-3, 5E-3, 1E-2, 5E-2 to perform ROC analysis. **Figure 10** shows the ROC curves for both GFCSee and GFCSd. The results indicate that the metrics have excellent discriminative power, with the area under the ROC curve being 0.98 and 0.86 for GFCSe and GFCSd, respectively.

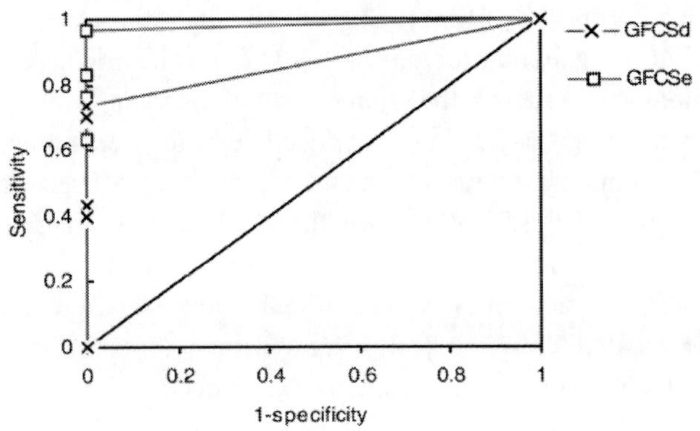

Figure 10. ROC curves for GFCSe and GFCSd. GFCS, group functional coherence score; ROC, receiver operation characteristic.

4. Discussion

Most biomedical knowledge is stored as free text in biomedical literature, and the size of biomedical literature is increasing rapidly. There is an urgent need for automatically acquiring and representing this body of knowledge in a computable form to facilitate the discovery of new knowledge, which requires the development of computational methods to extract knowledge form text. The current state of the art of text mining approaches have applied to biomedical literature and reported in several recent challenge evaluations, such as the KDD, the BioCreative, and the TREC. However, most of these approaches are within the conventional NLP, IE, and IR framework, and the application of probabilistic or non-probabilistic semantic modeling of biomedical literature remains relative sparse.

In this chapter, we show several examples of applying LDA to solve problems in biomedical research. In sections 3.1, we reported that using LDA to extract a set of semantic topics from a corpus of protein-related MEDLINE titles and abstracts. The key advantages of applying an LDA model to perform statistical semantic analysis include: 1. it can extract major recurring themes from a corpus of text in a unsupervised manner; 2. the assumption that a document is a mixture of topics naturally simulated real world text and allows modeling of text at finer granularity; and 3. an LDA model effectively resolves the uncertainties and ambiguities caused by polysemes and synonyms, which is a common problem associates with natural language. One limitation of an LDA model is that it requires a specified number of topics in order to model the data, which may not be valid in the real world. To address this issue, recent development in the nonparametric approaches, such as Dirichlet process based methods may be more reasonable to model the data without a specified number of topics [23].

In Section 3.2, we showed using LDA to enhance text categorization, therefore to improve the performance of SVM in the sparse training data scenario. Contemporary supervised learning algorithms, e.g., SVM, usually perform well when sufficient training data are available. However, in real world, it is not uncommon for a classifier to face a scenario of data scarcity and high-dimensionality, as in our case. In such cases, even a state of the art classifier like SVM may perform poorly as demonstrated in our baseline experiments and other benchmark studies [18]. A combination of high dimensionality and sparse training data almost inevitably leads to over-fitting. Such difficulty does not only occur in text categorization tasks but is a general problem for many classification tasks. We addressed both aspects of the problem by reducing the dimension of the data with the LDA model and augmenting the training cases with semi-supervised learning techniques and demonstrated such low-dimensional semantic representation resulted in significant improvements in the classification performance of the SVM^{light} over the original high-dimensional representation [18]. The enhancements were demonstrated as cross-board increases in both recall and utility, together with increased precision and F values in many subtasks. We believe that the benefit of SemRep may be attributed to the following reasons: (1) the semantic representation strengthens the signal contained in the original text, therefore increases the discriminative power of the representation; and (2) the decision rules learned within the low dimension space generalize better than those learned from in the high dimension space. We believe that the former is likely to play a major role in improving the performance because SVM aims at finding a decision surface with maximal margins and is relatively insensitive to the dimensionality of the data in comparison to other classifiers. In fact, SVM can perform well by implicitly projecting the data into higher dimensional space using the kernel tricks.

In Section 3.3, we used LDA to extract biological concepts from the literature associated with proteins and constructed protein networks, a bipartite graph, by effectively connects proteins through their shared functions. The bipartite trees not only group proteins according to function description, but it also establishes connections between biological concepts via proteins. Connecting proteins via biologically meaningful semantic topics in the literature has the following advantages. First, it allows us to evaluate the ‘functional closeness’ of a set of proteins without requiring them to interact physically, which is sensible in that proteins involved in a pathway do not necessarily bind to each other physically. Second, it does not require proteins to be co-mentioned within the same biomedical article in order to establish connections. Thus, it overcomes a difficulty encountered by other natural language processing or information retrieval approaches that require proteins to be co-mentioned in order to establish associations. Third, the multiple topic nature of the LDA model captures the multifaceted character of proteins; for example, a protein can be part of an electron-carrier chain in mitochondria and be involved in the cellular process of apoptosis. Thus, such proteins provide connections between biological concepts.

The method does not require manual annotation like GO does, which can be a bottleneck to accumulation of knowledge. Also, it overcomes the limitation of GO that concepts from one domain of GO (for example, molecular function) cannot be connected to concepts of other domains (such as cellular component). As demonstrated in the example of the human apoptosis pathway (**Figure 10**), the proteins are closely connected by their functional descriptions, such as apoptosis, phosphoinositide 3-kinase, chromatin structure, and tumor necrosis factor pathway.

In summary, semantic modeling with LDA model, potentially with other probabilistic topic models, provides useful means to automatically extract semantic topics from a corpus of text. The inferred semantic topics can be further used to enhance information retrieval, information extraction, and provide semantic connections among entities associated with the topics.

Acknowledgments

This work is partially supported by a grant, R01 LM009153, from the National Library of Medicine, the National Institutes of Health of the United States. The content is solely the responsibility of the authors and does not necessarily represent the official views of the National Library Of Medicine or the National Institutes of Health.

References

[1] Cohen, K.B. and L. Hunter, Getting started in text mining. *PLoS Comput Biol,* 2008. 4(1): p. e20.

[2] Krallinger, M., A. Valencia, and L. Hirschman, Linking genes to literature: text mining, information extraction, and retrieval applications for biology. *Genome Biol,* 2008. 9 Suppl 2: p. S8.

[3] Winnenburg, R., et al., Facts from text: can text mining help to scale-up high-quality manual curation of gene products with ontologies? *Brief Bioinform*, 2008. 9(6): p. 466-78.

[4] Zweigenbaum, P., et al., Frontiers of biomedical text mining: current progress. *Brief Bioinform*, 2007. 8(5): p. 358-75.

[5] Blei, D., A. Ng, and M. Jordan, Latent Dirichlet allocation. *Journal of Machine Learning Research*, 203. 3: p. 993-1022.

[6] Deerwester, S., et al., Indexing by latent semantic analysis. *J Am Soc Inf Sci* 1990. 41: p. 391.

[7] Griffiths, T.L. and M. Steyvers, Finding scientific topics. *Proc Natl Acad Sci U S A,* 2004. 101 Suppl 1: p. 5228-35.

[8] Hofmann, T. *Probabilistic latent semantic analysis*. in *The Fifteenth Conference on Uncertainty in Artificial Intelligenece*. 1999.

[9] Chute, C.G. and Y. Yang, An evaluation of concept based latent semantic indexing for clinical information retrieval. *Proc Annu Symp Comput Appl Med Care,* 1992: p. 639-43.

[10] Homayouni, R., et al., Gene clustering by latent semantic indexing of MEDLINE abstracts. *Bioinformatics*, 2005. 21(1): p. 104-15.

[11] Zheng, B. and X. Lu, Novel metrics for evaluating the functional coherence of protein groups via protein semantic network. *Genome Biol,* 2007. 8(7): p. R153.

[12] Zheng, B., D.C. McLean, Jr., and X. Lu, Identifying biological concepts from a protein-related corpus with a probabilistic topic model. *BMC Bioinformatics*, 2006. 7: p. 58.

[13] Lu, X., et al., Enhancing text categorization with semantic-enriched representation and training data augmentation. *J Am Med Inform Assoc,* 2006. 13(5): p. 526-35.

[14] Khatri, P., et al., A semantic analysis of the annotations of the human genome. *Bioinformatics*, 2005. 21(16): p. 3416-21.

[15] Lee, D.D. and H.S. Seung, Learning the parts of objects by non-negative matrix factorization. *Nature*, 1999. 401(6755): p. 788-91.

[16] Buntine, W., *Variational extensions to EM and multinomial PCA*, in *European Conference on Machine Learning (ECML-02)*. 2002.

[17] Ashburner, M., et al., Gene ontology: tool for the unification of biology. The Gene Ontology Consortium. *Nat Genet,* 2000. 25(1): p. 25-9.

[18] Lewis, D., et al., *RCV1:* A new benchmark collection for text categorization research. *Journal of Machine Learning Research,* 2004. 5: p. 361-397.

[19] Yang, Y., An evaluation of statistical approaches to text categorization. . *Information Retrieval*, 1999. 1: p. 67-88.

[20] Joachims, T. Text Categorization with Support Vector Machines: Learning with Many Relevant Features. in *The European Conference on Machine Learning*. 1998: Springer.

[21] Raychaudhuri, S. and R.B. Altman, A literature-based method for assessing the functional coherence of a gene group. *Bioinformatics*, 2003. 19(3): p. 396-401.

[22] Kou, L., G. Markowsky, and L. Berman, A fast algorithm for Steiner trees. *Acta Inform.*, 1981. 15(2): p. 141-145.

[23] Teh, Y., et al., Hierarchical Dirichlet processes. *J Am Stat Assoc,* 2006. 101: p. 1566.

In: Data Management in the Semantic Web
Editor: Hal Jin, pp. 215-251
ISBN: 978-1-61122-862-5

Chapter 10

SUPPORTING A USER IN HIS ANNOTATION AND BROWSING ACTIVITIES IN FOLKSONOMIES

***G. Barillà*[1], *P. De Meo*[2], *G. Quattrone*[3] *and D. Ursino*[4]**
DIMET, Università Mediterranea di Reggio Calabria, Via Graziella,
Località Feo di Vito, 89122 Reggio Calabria, Italy

Abstract

In this chapter we present a new approach to supporting users to annotate and browse resources referred by a folksonomy. Our approach proposes two hierarchical structures and two related algorithms to arrange groups of semantically related tags in a hierarchy; this allows users to visualize tags of their interests according to desired semantic granularities and, then, helps them to find those tags best expressing their information needs. In this chapter we first illustrate the technical characteristics of our approach; then we describe the prototype implementing it; after this, we illustrate various experiments allowing its performance to be tested; finally, we compare it with other related approaches already proposed in the literature.

1. Introduction

The term *collaborative tagging* (also known as *social tagging* or *social annotation*) refers to the practice of collaboratively annotating resources of various types (e.g., URLs, photos, videos, scientific papers, and so on) by means of plain keywords, also known as *tags* [6, 20, 31]. The result of the collaborative tagging process is also called *folksonomy*; this term derives by the fusion of the term *folk* (i.e., people) and the Greek term *nomos* (i.e., management). A folksonomy can be, thus, depicted as a set of resources and a set of users who collaborate to classify these resources by means of tags.

The number of Web sites capable of supporting collaborative tagging is rapidly increasing since 2004. In the meantime, also the number of resources stored in each

[1] E-mail address: barilla.giuseppe@gmail.com.
[2] E-mail address: demeo@unirc.it
[3] E-mail address: quattrone@unirc.it
[4] E-mail address: ursino@unirc.it

folksonomy, as well as the number of users who exploit folksonomies, are rapidly growing [6]. Popular examples of folksonomies are Flickr [3] (which allows users to annotate their photos), del.icio.us [2] (which allows users to store and share their Web bookmarks), and Bibsonomy [1] (which allows users to share bibliographic data on scientific papers).

The explosive rise of folksonomies on the Web underscores a more general trend [30]; in fact, in the early phase of the Web, there was a small elite of people capable of authoring and publishing their contents through it; today, powerful, simple and cheap authoring and publishing tools are allowing masses of new users to produce and disseminate their contents through the Web. Folksonomies are a significant example of the transformation of the Web to a participatory and interactive platform; as a matter of fact, in a folksonomy, users intensively cooperate to classify available resources.

Actually, folksonomies are gaining a wider and wider popularity not only on the Web but also in large organizations and businesses. For instance, IBM has recently proposed DOGEAR [33], a system allowing employees to create and share their personal collections of Web bookmarks. Analogously, Oracle has implemented some modules capable of building and handling collaborative tagging systems, and has included these modules in its Enterprise Content Management suite, a software package conceived to capture, store and delivery contents and documents related to business organizational processes [15].

Many authors conjecture that the usage of folksonomies (in particular, those regarding Web bookmarks) can enhance the performance of traditional Web search engines [6,25]. Finally, folksonomies are useful to highlight hidden social ties among users.

However, as neatly pointed out in [20,40], despite these advantages, folksonomies suffer from some, quite crippling, disadvantages that can be summarized in: *(i)* ambiguity, *(ii)* lack of synonymies, and *(iii)* discrepancy on granularity.

Ambiguity refers to the fact that some terms may have multiple meanings. The basic example of ambiguity are homonymies; we say that two terms are homonymous if they have the same name but different meanings; for instance, the term "bark" is a root of homonymies because it may represent both the sound made by a dog and the outermost layer of trees. Lexical ambiguities are a key problem for a user who wants to retrieve resources from a folksonomy. In fact, assume that he is sifting through a folksonomy for resources labelled with the tag "bank"; in this case he could receive resources regarding both river banks and financial institutions. As a consequence, homonymies can dilute the result of a user search because they mix both relevant and irrelevant resources.

The lack of synonymies in a folksonomy implies that there could be a lack of consistency in the choice of tags; consequently, different users could exploit different tags to label the same type of resource. Therefore, some resources could be relevant to a user query even though they are not labelled with the tags specified in the query itself. As a consequence, a user could receive a complete set of answers to his query only if his vocabulary is rich enough to allow him to encompass an arbitrary tag with the whole set of its variants. This hypothesis is clearly unrealistic because user vocabularies are often quite limited.

Discrepancy on granularity of tags could arise because a certain resource can be reasonably described by various tags, ranging from terms having a broad meaning to terms characterized by a narrow meaning. Therefore, some users, according to their level of expertise and cultural background, may prefer to exploit generic tags, whereas other ones are driven to exploit specific tags. This can weaken the ability of a user to find relevant resources. As an example, assume that a resource about Web programming is labelled with the tag "javascript". An expert programmer may consider this term too generic and, then, he may decide to not use it in his search, since he is inclined to use more specific tags; as a consequence, he is not able to retrieve the list of resources labelled only with the tag "javascript", even though some of them may be potentially relevant to him. On the other side, a novice may not use the tag "javascript" in his search because it is too specific and, then, it does not belong to his vocabulary yet; as in the previous case, he is not able to retrieve potentially meaningful resources.

In order to better face the three problems mentioned above, it would be extremely useful a tool capable of parsing the set of tags a user is inserting (for either cataloguing a resource in a folksonomy or defining a query over it) in such a way as to interactively suggest new related tags. As a matter of fact, these new tags could help him to more properly label the resource he is inserting or to more precisely specify the query he is submitting.

In the literature various approaches to helping a user in querying a folksonomy or cataloguing folksonomy resources have been proposed. These approaches have been designed to find pairs of semantically related tags (in such a way as to deal with the ambiguity and the lack of synonymies problems) and to arrange tags in a hierarchical structure (in such a way as to solve the discrepancy of granularity problem).

In particular, a first category of approaches relies on the usage of external data sources, like thesauri (e.g., WordNet) [28] or ontologies [4,40,41]. The main advantage of these approaches is that they are fast and unsupervised (i.e., they do not need any training phase) [28]. In addition, as for approaches based on ontologies, there is a strong correspondence between ontology concepts and folksonomy tags [40]. As a consequence, the knowledge encoded in an ontology can be fruitfully used to check if two tags are semantically related or to determine if the meaning of a tag is more general than that of another tag. Conversely, data stored in a folksonomy can be used to automatically populate and update the corresponding ontology.

However, these approaches suffer from some disadvantages. For instance, approaches based on thesauri use only syntactical criteria (e.g., the distance function implemented in WordNet) to check if two tags are related, and these criteria may produce unsatisfactory results in some cases. In addition, many thesauri are general-purpose and, then, may miss many relevant terms present in the folksonomy. As for approaches based on ontologies, experimental studies prove that they are able to achieve accurate results; however, a strong human effort to build and update ontologies is required [4].

A second category of approaches uses Data Mining techniques, such as the EM algorithm [42], other clustering approaches [7,10,31], classification algorithms [8], approaches detecting association rules [37] and probabilistic modeling techniques [38]. These approaches analyze the set of resources labeled by two tags to determine if these tags are related. As a consequence, they create a link between the semantics of a tag and the behavior of the users adopting it.

These approaches are able to produce both rigid (e.g., trees) [7] and loose classification schemes [31]. Their main disadvantage is that they often require an initial training phase. In addition, they are generally time expensive and this makes it difficult to design interactive applications running on a folksonomy (e.g., an application that receives a set S of tags specified by the user and generates on-the-fly a list of tags semantically related to S).

A third category of approaches model folksonomies as graphs (and often as hypergraphs). These approaches apply techniques typical of Social Network Analysis to discover pairs/groups of related tags [32,43] or to organize tags into hierarchical structures [24]. For instance, the approach of [32] computes a closeness coefficient to find pairs of related tags, the approach of [43] applies the Girwan-Newman algorithm to find clusters of semantically similar tags, and, finally, the approach of [24] uses the centrality coefficient to organize tags into a tree.

These approaches are quite fascinating because they put into evidence the associative and participatory nature of the tagging process. However, they are computationally expensive and require to examine the whole folksonomy. On the contrary, in many cases, a user would prefer to focus only on a small folksonomy fragment strictly related to his needs.

This chapter provides a contribution in this setting; in fact, it proposes an approach to supporting social annotations and browsing activities in folksonomies.

Our approach operates as follows. Assume that a user wants to query a folksonomy or to label a resource he is inserting in it. Initially he starts by specifying a set $TSet_{Input}$ of tags; this set could be incomplete and/or imprecise. Our approach first derives a set $NeighTSet_{Input}$ of tags semantically related to those of $TSet_{Input}$ and capable of making the query or the set of labels more complete and precise. After this, it visualizes this supplementary set of tags as a hierarchy and allows the user to interactively "drill down" or "roll up" it in such a way as to easily find the desired level of granularity and, then, the most adequate tags.

In order to construct $NeighTSet_{Input}$, our approach defines and uses a suitable semantic distance function which receives two tags and returns a value in the real interval [0,1]; the lower this value is the more related the two tags will be. This function relies on the assumption, widely accepted in the literature [7, 31], that two tags are semantically related if they often label the same type of resource.

In order to organize the tags of $NeighTSet_{Input}$ into a hierarchy, our approach proposes two different algorithms.

The first algorithm is called *MST-based*; it initially constructs a suitable weighted and directed graph (called *generalization graph*) whose nodes represent the tags of $NeighTSet_{Input}$ and whose arcs denote the generalization relationships among tags. After this, it derives the hierarchy by computing the maximum spanning tree associated with the constructed generalization graph.

The second algorithm is called *Concentric*; it associates each tag of $NeighTSet_{Input}$ with a coefficient stating its semantic granularity; the higher (resp., the lower) this parameter is, the more general (resp., more specific) the corresponding tag will be. Tag semantic granularities can be used to build a suitable data structure; this can be graphically depicted as a set of concentric circles such that the innermost ones are associated with the most specific tags, whereas the outermost ones are associated with the most general tags.

Observe that the information contents implied by the two hierarchies constructed by the *MST-based* and the *Concentric* algorithms are different. In fact, the hierarchy constructed by the *MST-based* algorithm is a tree and, therefore, it emphasizes the generalization relationships among tags. By contrast, the hierarchy returned by the *Concentric* algorithm puts in each circle tags having very close semantic granularities. As a consequence, given a tag t_i, the first hierarchy allows the detection of other tags having the same semantics as t_i but being more general or more specific than it; the second hierarchy, instead, allows the detection of other tags having the same semantic granularity as t_i but a semantics possibly related to (but not the same as) that of t_i. The previous observation points out that the two algorithms are orthogonal; as a consequence, in the prototype implementing our approach, a user can choose to exploit the former, the latter, or both of them.

The general features of our approach and its capability of suggesting tags make it capable of successfully facing the problems of ambiguity, lack of synonymies and discrepancy on granularity introduced above. Specifically:

- The first step of our approach analyzes all tags of $TSet_{Input}$ and explores the whole space of available tags to construct the neighborhood $NeighTSet_{Input}$ of $TSet_{Input}$, i.e., the set of tags semantically close to those of $TSet_{Input}$. $NeighTSet_{Input}$ is computed by simultaneously considering all tags of $TSet_{Input}$, rather than each tag separately from the other ones. This simple form of "context" definition allows our approach to disambiguate the sense of terms specified by the user and, then, to avoid possible homonymies. As a consequence, our approach is capable of solving the "ambiguity" problem mentioned above.
  As an example, consider the set of tags $TSet_{Input}$ = {apple, grapefruit} and assume that it is necessary to compute $NeighTSet_{Input}$. If, in this computation, each tag of $TSet_{Input}$ would be considered separately from the other ones, then tags like "computer" and "iPod" would be included in $NeighTSet_{Input}$, even though they are likely to be not relevant to the user; by contrast, if all tags are jointly examined, "noisy" tags can be found and discarded.
- Given a set $TSet_{Input}$ of tags, the exploitation of the semantic distance function allows all tags having a low semantic distance from tags of $TSet_{Input}$ to be considered in the construction of $NeighTSet_{Input}$. As previously pointed out, a low semantic distance between two tags implies that they are semantically close. Therefore, $NeighTSet_{Input}$ presumably contains, among all its elements, also those tags synonymous with tags of $TSet_{Input}$. This makes our approach capable of facing also the "lack of synonymies" problem introduced above.
- During the second step, our approach organizes the tags of $NeighTSet_{Input}$ into a hierarchy; each level of this hierarchy stores concepts at a certain granularity level. As a consequence, when a user must specify his tags, he can choose the hierarchy level that he considers the most adequate to his knowledge background, needs and desires. In this way, our approach is capable of facing the "discrepancy on granularity" problem described above.

In addition to the three problems mentioned above, our approach aims to face two further problems, arising when folksonomies to handle are very large and rapidly variable over time (think, for instance, of Flickr or del.icio.us). These problems, and the corresponding solutions proposed by our approach, are as follows:

- *The number of resources populating a folksonomy is often huge and rapidly varies over time.* As will be clear in the following, this problem could negatively influence the computation of tag semantic distances and, ultimately, the construction of both $NeighTSet_{Input}$ and the associated hierarchy. In order to solve this problem we have defined a refined heuristics for the semantic distance computation. This heuristics has been derived from a corresponding one proposed in [13]. It allows a quick and accurate computation of semantic distance; moreover, its accuracy can be suitably tuned.

- *The number of tags present in a folksonomy can be very large and can rapidly vary over time.* As will be clear in the following, the construction of $NeighTSet_{Input}$ requires the computation of the semantic distances associated with all possible pairs of tags; clearly, this task is very time consuming. In order to face this problem, our approach associates a suitable data structure, called *neighborhood list* with each tag. The neighborhood list of a tag stores the set of those tags semantically closest to it. The presence of this data structure allows our approach to inspect, for each tag, only those tags belonging to its neighborhood list, instead of all available tags; this allows a considerable reduction of its execution time.

It is worth pointing out that the material presented in this chapter represents a consolidation of the ideas illustrated in a previous paper [16]. In particular, in the Introduction of this chapter we have provided a summary of the existing approaches and of the remaining problems that the proposed algorithm tries to solve; this allows our work to be placed in the right research context and allows the reader to better and easily understand the research problems it aims at solving and the novelties it introduces. Moreover, we have added a section, namely Section 5, in which we provide all details about the design and the implementation of our system. In particular, we have used the UML formalism to describe all the software components of our system as well as their interactions.

The plan of this chapter is as follows: in Section 2 we provide some preliminary concepts largely used throughout this chapter. In Section 3 we describe the first phase of our approach, i.e., the construction of $NeighTSet_{Input}$. Section 4 illustrates the second phase, i.e., the construction of hierarchies. The description of the prototype we have constructed to implement the proposed approach is presented in Section 5. Some experiments carried out to evaluate the performance of our approach are reported in Section 6. A comparison between our approach and other related ones previously proposed in the literature can be found in Section 7. Finally, in Section 8, we draw our conclusions.

2. Preliminaries

2.1. Basic Definitions

In this section we illustrate some preliminary concepts that will be extensively exploited in the next sections of this chapter. The first concept is that of folksonomy[26].

Definition 2.1. Let $USet = \{u_1, ..., u_p\}$ be a set of users, let $RSet = \{r_1, ..., r_m\}$ be a set of resource URIs and let $TSet = \{t_1, ..., t_n\}$ be a set of tags. A *folksonomy* F is a tuple $F = <USet, RSet, TSet, ASet>$, where $ASet \subseteq USet \times RSet \times TSet$ is a ternary relationship called *tag assignment set.* □

In this definition we do not make any hypothesis about the nature of involved resources; they could be URLs, photos, videos, music files, text documents, and so on.

An element $a = <u, r, t>$, belonging to *ASet*, indicates that the user u has labelled the resource r with the tag t. A user can tag many resources and a resource can be labelled with multiple tags by a user.

Table 1. Distribution of resources and tags in our reference folksonomy

Tag/resource	r1	r2	r3	r4	r5	r6	r7	r8	r9	r10	r11	r12	r13	r14	r15
t1 = "AJAX"						X	X	X							
t2 = "Computer Science"	X														
t3 = "CSS"								X							
t4 = "Database"		X	X	X	X										
t5 = "Design"														X	
t6 = "Entity/ Relationship"					X										
t7 = "Javascript"						X	X	X	X						
t8 = "Join"				X						X	X				
t9 = "MySQL"												X			
t10 = "Oracle"										X	X	X	X	X	
t11 = "Outer Join"											X				
t12 = "PHP"														X	
t13 = "PL/SQL"											X	X	X		
t14 = "Programming"									X						
t15 = "Projection"				X											
t16 = "RDBMS"										X	X	X	X		
t17 = "Relational Algebra"		X	X	X											
t18 = "Selection"				X											
t19 = "SQL"	X	X	X												X
t20 = "XML"						X		X						X	X
t21 = "XQuery"														X	X

Example 2.1. As an example consider the scenario shown in Table 1. It refers to a folksonomy covering topics about Databases and Information Systems and will be exploited as the reference scenario in the examples throughout the chapter. In Table 1 rows are associated with tags and columns with resources; the symbol "X" at the intersection of the row associated with the tag t_i and the column associated with the resource r_j indicates that t_i is one of the tags labelling r_j. For instance, Table 1 shows that r_1 has been labelled with the tags "Computer Science" and "SQL" whereas r_2 has been labelled with the tags "Database", "Relational Algebra" and "SQL". □

Definition 2.2. Let *RSet* be a set of resources, let *TSet* be a set of tags and let t_i be a tag of *TSet*. The *projection* of *RSet* onto t_i, indicated by $ProjRSet_i$, is the set of resources of *RSet* labelled with t_i. □

Example 2.2. Consider the tags t_1 = "AJAX" and t_{10} = "Oracle" in our reference folksonomy reported in Table 1. We have that $ProjRSet_1 = \{r_6, r_7, r_8\}$ because t_1 labels resources r_6, r_7 and r_8. For the same reasons $ProjRSet_{10} = \{r_{10}, r_{11}, r_{12}, r_{13}, r_{14}\}$. □

Authors of [7,31] performed an analysis about the semantics of a tag. They concluded that: *(i)* the semantics of a tag directly depends on the resources labelled by it, and *(ii)* tags semantically similar annotate similar resources and, vice versa, similar resources are annotated by semantically similar tags. We agree with this analysis and assume that, *given a pre-defined set of resources* (like those related to a folksonomy), the larger the set of resources labelled by two tags is the higher the tags' similarity degree will be. As a consequence of this reasoning, given two tags t_i and t_j belonging to *TSet*, we considered the set of resources $ProjRSet_i$ and $ProjRSet_j$ labelled by them to determine if they are semantically related; more specifically, the larger the overlap of $ProjRSet_i$ and $ProjRSet_j$ is, the larger the semantic similarity of t_i and t_j will be. This reasoning leads us to define a function $sim(t_i, t_j)$, called *semantic similarity*, which specifies to what extent t_i and t_j are semantically similar.

Definition 2.3. Let *RSet* be a set of resources, let *TSet* be a set of tags and let t_i and t_j be two tags of *TSet*; let $ProjRSet_i$ and $ProjRSet_j$ be the projections of *RSet* onto t_i and t_j, respectively. The *semantic similarity* $sim(t_i, t_j)$ between t_i and t_j is defined as:

$$sim(t_i, t_j) = \frac{|ProjRSet_i \cap ProjRSet_j|}{|ProjRSet_i \cup ProjRSet_j|}$$

□

In other words, $sim(t_i,t_j)$ is determined by computing the *Jaccard Coefficient* [23] of $ProjRSet_i$ and $ProjRSet_j$. Observe that $sim(t_i, t_j)$ ranges in the real interval [0,1]; the higher it is, the more similar t_i and t_j will be.

Example 2.3. Consider the tags t_1="AJAX" and t_7="Javascript" in our reference folksonomy reported in Table 1. From this table it is easy to check that $ProjRSet_1 \cap ProjRSet_7 = \{r_6, r_7, r_8\}$ and $ProjRSet_1 \cup ProjRSet_7 = \{r_6, r_7, r_8, r_9\}$ and, consequently,

$$sim(\text{“AJAX”,“Javacript”}) = \frac{|ProjRSet_1 \cap ProjRSet_7|}{|ProjRSet_1 \cup ProjRSet_7|} = \frac{3}{4} = 0.75$$

In an analogous fashion, it is possible to compute that *sim("Oracle","RDBMS")* = 4/5 = 0.8 and that *sim("Javascript", "Join")* = 0/7 = 0. □

Actually, we are more interested in defining a function that expresses the semantic distance, rather than the semantic similarity, of two tags. As a consequence, we consider a function $dist(t_i, t_j)$, called *semantic distance*, by complementing $sim(t_i, t_j)$ to 1.

Definition 2.4. Let *TSet* be a set of tags and let t_i and t_j be two tags of *TSet*. The *semantic distance* $dist(t_i, t_j)$ between t_i and t_j is defined as: $dist(t_i, t_j) = 1 - sim(t_i, t_j)$. □

Observe that, due to the properties of the Jaccard coefficient [23], the function *dist* is a *metric distance*.

In our approach, in some cases, it is also necessary to verify how much the meaning of a tag t_i is "subsumed" by the meaning of a tag t_j and, vice versa, how much the meaning of t_i "subsumes" the meaning of t_j. According to the ideas presented in [31], it is possible to assume that the "subsumption" of t_i in t_j depends on the fraction of resources of t_i that are tagged also by t_j, and vice versa. In fact, if this fraction is large, it is possible to conclude that most of the resources tagged by t_i are also tagged by t_j. By contrast, if this fraction is small, then most of the resources tagged by t_i are not tagged by t_j; this could imply either that t_i and t_j have different meanings or that t_j is more specific than t_i. This reasoning is formalized by the following definitions.

Definition 2.5. Let *RSet* be a set of resources, let *TSet* be a set of tags and let t_i and t_j be two tags of *TSet*. The *inclusion degree* of t_i in t_j is defined as:

$$inc(t_i, t_j) = \frac{|ProjRSet_i \cap ProjRSet_j|}{|ProjRSet_i|}$$

□

Observe that the *inc* function is *asymmetric*; in other words, given a pair of tags $<t_i, t_j>$, we have that, generally, $inc(t_i, t_j) \neq inc(t_j, t_i)$; as a consequence, the order of input arguments of the function *inc* influences the output values returned by it.

Definition 2.6. Let *TSet* be a set of tags and let t_i and t_j be two tags of *TSet*. The *generalization degree* of t_i vs. t_j is defined as:

$$gen(t_i, t_j) = \frac{|ProjRSet_i \cap ProjRSet_j|}{|ProjRSet_j|} = inc(t_j, t_i)$$

□

Observe that, due to its definition, also the function *gen* is asymmetric.

Example 2.4. Consider the tags t_{17} = "Relational Algebra" and t_{18} = "Selection" in our reference folksonomy reported in Table 1. We have that $ProjRSet_{17} = \{r_2, r_3, r_4\}$ and $ProjRSet_{18} = \{r_4\}$, and this implies that *inc("Selection", "Relational Algebra")* = $(|ProjRSet_{18} \cap ProjRSet_{17}|)/(|ProjRSet_{18}|) = 1/1 = 1$ and that *gen("Selection", "Relational Algebra")* = *1/3 = 0.33*. □

In an analogous fashion we have that *inc("Outer Join", Join") = 1* and *gen("Outer Join", "Join")= 1/3*. □

It is worth pointing out that the worst case computational complexity of $dist(t_i, t_j)$ and $gen(t_i, t_j)$ would be $O(min(|ProjRSet\_j| \cdot log|ProjRSet\_i|, |ProjRSet\_i| \cdot log|ProjRSet\_j|))$. Now, since folksonomies are generally very large, the involved *ProjRSets* are generally very large too; as a consequence, $|ProjRSet_i|$ and $|ProjRSet_j|$ and, ultimately, the computational complexity of $dist(t_i, t_j)$ and $gen(t_i, t_j)$ would be quite high.

However, since both $dist(t_i, t_j)$ and $gen(t_i, t_j)$ are based on the computation of the Jaccard Coefficient between $ProjRSet_i$ and $ProjRSet_j$, for their computation it is possible to apply the Monte Carlo technique introduced in [13], which allows the corresponding computational complexity to be reduced to $O(l)$, where l is a fixed integer number usually ranging from 70 to 120 (see [13] for all details).

3. Phase 1: Neighborhood Computation

In this section we illustrate Phase 1 of our approach, i.e., that phase which receives a set $TSet_{Input}$ of tags specified by a user and returns a set $NeighTSet_{Input}$ of semantically related tags.

The problem of deriving tags semantically related to other ones has been studied in the past and proposed solutions are generally based on data clustering techniques (see, for instance, [7, 10, 31]). The computational cost associated with a graph clustering algorithm is $O(n^3)$, where n is the number of involved tags. As observed in [31], this cost is prohibitively high in real scenarios in which a user is involved in real-time browsing activities. For this reason, authors of [31] propose to use a fast, but approximate, clustering algorithm.

Actually, techniques for detecting semantically similar tags based on clustering algorithms are not adequate to fulfill the requirements of our approach. In fact, in our approach, $NeighTSet_{Input}$ must be computed at *query time* (i.e., when the user specifies $TSet_{Input}$). In addition, our approach must be able to promptly react to any change both in the set *TSet* of available tags and in the set *RSet* of available resources. Now, the reasons that make techniques for detecting semantically similar tags based on clustering algorithms unsuitable to fulfill the requirements of our approach are the following:

1. A clustering algorithm operates on the whole *TSet* which is, generally, extremely large. Such an effort is presumably unjustified and unnecessary for the goals of our approach. In fact, in our reference context, it is necessary an approach that, at query time, constructs $NeighTSet_{Input}$ starting from the tags of $TSet_{Input}$ and expanding its search to only those tags semantically close to them.
2. If the computation of $NeighTSet_{Input}$ is based on a preliminary clustering of *TSet*, the risk arises that it is not capable of capturing all the features of $TSet_{Input}$, since it is strongly guided by the already defined tag partitioning generated by clustering.
3. Many off-the-shelf clustering algorithms return disjoint portions of *TSet*; however, in the reality, as observed in [39], the tag definition process is ambiguous and loose and, then, a tag might belong to multiple clusters.

Due to the reasons specified above, our technique for computing $NeighTSet_{Input}$ is not based on clustering algorithms and operates in a very different way. In fact, for each tag t_i of $TSet_{Input}$, it generates a set of candidate tags semantically close to t_i. After this, it examines all sets of candidate tags and determines which of them are eligible to belong to $NeighTSet_{Input}$.

More formally, our technique consists of the following steps:

1. It sets $NeighTSet_{Input}$ equal to the empty set.
2. For each $t_i \in TSet_{Input}$, it generates a set $CandTSet_i$ of candidate tags comprising all tags of $TSet$ - $TSet_{Input}$ whose distance from t_i (computed by applying the approach described in Section 2.3) is less than a certain threshold θ_{cand}. The value of θ_{cand} can be suitably set in such a way as to tune the dimension of $CandTSet_i$ according to user desires and needs.
3. It applies a function *compute-neighborhood* aiming to determine what tags of $CandSet_1$, ..., $CandSet_{|TSetInput|}$ are eligible to belong to $NeighTSet_{Input}$. We have

considered three strategies implementing *compute-neighborhood*; they will be discussed in the following.

4. It returns $NeighTSet_{Input}$.

In the following subsections we illustrate in detail the core of our technique, i.e., Steps 2 and 3.

3.1. Step 2: Construction of the Sets of Candidate Tags Starting from$\mathbf{TSet_{Input}}$

A key issue to be considered in our technique for the computation of $NeighTSet_{Input}$ starting from $TSet_{Input}$ regards the number $|TSet|$ of tags present in a folksonomy. In fact, as long as $|TSet|$ increases, the search space to be explored for constructing the candidate sets associated with the tags of $TSet_{Input}$ increases too. In the worst case, the execution of this task requires the computation of $O(|TSet| \cdot |TSet_{Input})$ tag distances. In real application contexts $_{\mathrm{TSet}}$ can be very large; for instance, an experimental study described in [11] estimated that the number of distinct tags in del.icio.us in November 2006 was about $2.5 \cdot 10^6$. As a consequence, even if a query consists of only one tag (i.e., $TSet_{Input}=1$), the number of tag distances that should be computed forexecuting it would be about $2.5 \cdot 10^6$.

In order to reduce this computational cost our approach associates a support data structure with each tag $t_i \in TSet$. This structure is called *neighborhood list* of t_i and is denoted as $NeighTList_i$; it consists of a list of pairs $<t_j, dist(t_i, t_j)>$, where t_j is a tag of $TSet$ and $dist(t_i, t_j)$ is the distance between t_i and t_j. A pair $<t_j, dist(t_i, t_j)>$ is inserted in $NeighTList_i$ if $dist(t_i, t_j)$ is less than a threshold θ_{nlist}; $NeighTList_i$ is sorted, in an ascending order, on the basis of the values of tag distances. As a consequence, when our technique must extract the set of tags whose distance from a tag t_i is less than a threshold θ_{cand}, $0 \leq \theta_{cand} \leq \theta_{nlist}$, it simply needs to scan $NeighTList_i$, instead of scanning the whole $TSet$.

Interestingly enough, the construction and/or the update of the neighborhood lists (which is much more expensive than their scan) can be performed off-line and asynchronously. According to the terminology adopted in the context of Web search technology, we say that our technique builds each neighborhood list at *index construction time*, whereas, at *query execution time*, it simply scans one or more neighborhood lists.

The presence of the neighborhood lists allows an easy computation of the set of candidate tags. In fact, for each tag $t_i \in TSet_{Input}$, $CandTSet_i$ can be obtained by scanning $NeighTList_i$ and putting the corresponding pairs in $CandTSet_i$ until a pair $<t_k, dist(t_i, t_k)>$, such that $dist(t_i, t_k) > \theta_{cand}$, has been reached. Interestingly enough, in this way, the construction of all sets of candidate tags can be performed in parallel.

A particular attention must be paid to the value of θ_{nlist}; in fact, since $CandTSet_i$ is constructed by selecting all pairs $<t_i, t_j>$ of $NeighTList_i$ such that $dist(t_i, t_j) < \theta_{cand}$, θ_{nlist} must be greater than or equal to θ_{cand}; in fact, if this condition is not satisfied, $CandTSet_i$ cannot be computed starting from $NeighTList_i$. However, the higher θ_{nlist} is the higher the amount of space required to store $NeighTList_i$ will be. As a natural consequence of these two reasonings, it is possible to conclude that the best tradeoff between the two exigencies presented above is obtained when $\theta_{nlist} = \theta_{cand}$.

3.2. Step 3: Construction of $NeighTSet_{Input}$ Starting from the Sets of Candidate Tags

The core of our technique for the construction of $NeighTSet_{Input}$ is the function *compute_neighborhood*; as previously pointed out, we propose three different strategies to implement this function. These strategies are:

- *OR-like strategy*. In this case we have that:

$$NeighTSet_{Input} = \bigcup_{i=1}^{|TSet_{Input}|} CandTSet_i$$

  This strategy generates quite a large $NeighTSet_{Input}$ whose tags could be loosely related each other; in fact, with this strategy, a tag is eligible to belong to $NeighTSet_{Input}$ if it is close to *at least* one tag of $TSet_{Input}$, even if it is far from all the other tags. As a consequence, this strategy is adequate each time a user has a vague and imprecise knowledge of a domain and prefers to handle a broad range of options to label or to search for his resources.

- *AND-like strategy*. In this case we have that:

$$NeighTSet_{Input} = \bigcap_{i=1}^{|TSet_{Input}|} CandTSet_i$$

  This strategy constructs quite a narrow $NeighTSet_{Input}$ whose tags are closely related each other; in fact, in this case, a tag is added to $NeighTSet_{Input}$ only if it is close to *all* tags of $TSet_{Input}$. As a consequence, this strategy is well suited each time a user has a precise and detailed picture of a domain and prefers to manage few and highly related tags to label or to search for his resources.

- *Hybrid strategy*. In this case we have that:

$$NeighTSet_{Input} = \{t_j \mid t_j \text{ belongs to at least } k \text{ candidate sets OR } dist(t_i, t_j) \leq \theta_{strong}, t_i \in TSet_{Input}\}$$

  In other words, a tag is added to $NeighTSet_{Input}$ if it is sufficiently close to at least k tags of $TSet_{Input}$ or, even if this does not happen, its closeness with at least one of them is very strong, i.e., they are almost identical. k and θ_{strong} are suitable thresholds that can be tuned in such a way as to increase or decrease both the dimension and the cohesiveness of $NeighTSet_{Input}$ according to user needs and desires.

Observe that this strategy is extremely general and flexible; as a matter of fact, it we set $k=1$ and $\theta_{strong}=0$, we obtain the *OR-like* strategy, whereas if we set $k = |TSet_{Input}|$ and $\theta_{strong}=0$ we obtain the *AND-like* strategy.

4. Phase 2: Hierarchy Construction

In this section we illustrate Phase 2 of our approach; it receives the set $NeighTSet_{Input}$ of tags returned at the end of Phase 1 and organizes them in a hierarchical fashion.

In order to carry out all tasks of this phase we have defined two orthogonal algorithms, called *Maximum Spanning Tree based* (hereafter, *MST-based*) and *Concentric*, each characterized by some specific features.

4.1. The *MST-based* Algorithm

MST-based starts by associating a rooted, directed and weighted graph, called *generalization graph* and denoted by *GGen*, with $NeighTSet_{Input}$. *GGen* consists of a set *NGen* of nodes and a set *AGen* of arcs. Each node n_i of *NGen* is associated with exactly one tag t_i of $NeighTSet_{Input}$; in addition, there exists a fictitious node n_0 in *NGen* representing the root of *GGen*. An arc from n_i to n_j indicates that: *(i)* t_i labels more resources than t_j, and *(ii)* the generalization degree of t_i vs t_j (i.e., $gen(t_i, t_j)$) is greater than a certain threshold θ_{gen}; the weight of this arc is equal to $gen(t_i, t_j)$. A node n_i is directly linked to the root n_0 if the generalization degree of all tags labelling more resources than t_i vs t_i is lower than θ_{gen}; in this case the weight of the arc linking n_0 to n_i is θ_{gen}.

Intuitively, *GGen* stores all tags of $NeighTSet_{Input}$ along with the set of all potential relationships of the form "father-child" existing among them. Observe that, in *GGen*, a "father" node may link to multiple "child" nodes and each "child" node may have several "father" nodes; moreover, each node in *GGen* is connected (either directly or indirectly) to the root. Therefore, there exists at least one tree spanning *GGen* whose root coincides with the root of *GGen*.

GGen is the key element to construct the final hierarchy; in fact, *MST-based* computes the maximum spanning tree *MSTGen* associated with *GGen* and returns it as the final output. We recall that the maximum spanning tree associated with a weighted graph is the spanning tree such that the sum of the weights of its arcs is maximum [14]. This problem, with some trivial modifications, can be reduced to the problem of computing the minimum spanning tree of a directed and weighted graph.

As for the computational cost of *MST-based*, it is possible to state the following theorem.

Theorem 4.1. Let $NeighTSet_{Input}$ be a set of tags. The worst case computational complexity of *MST-based*, when applied on $NeighTSet_{Input}$, is $O(|NeighTSet_{Input}|^2)$. □

A first important feature of *MST-based* can be inferred by observing that the generalization graph *GGen* = <*NGen, AGen*> constructed by this algorithm and the corresponding hierarchy derived by it store only "strong" generalization relationships among tags. In fact, consider a tag t_j and assume that $gen(t_i, t_j) < \theta_{gen}$ for all tags $t_i \in NeighTSet_{Input}$; in this case, the node n_j corresponding to t_j is directly linked to the root of G_{Gen}. This implies that "very uncertain" generalization relationships among tags are cut off by this algorithm.

A second important feature of *MST-based* is that the maximum spanning tree *MSTGen* returned by it satisfies the so called *cut property* [14]. This property implies that, among all arcs connecting a node of $V = \{n_1, ..., n_k\}$ with n_j, *MSTGen* contains that having the highest weight. This is equivalent to state that *MST-based* selects, among all possible generalization relationships involving a tag t_j, that having the highest value of the generalization degree.

A third important feature regards the structure of *MSTGen*. In fact, it is a data structure having an intuitive and effective graphical representation. Thanks to this, a user can, *at a glance*, locate the tag (or the tags) potentially relevant to him and move toward upper and lower levels of the tree in order to identify those tags best fitting his needs and desires. This graphical representation is particularly valuable if the number of involved tags becomes very large.

As a final important feature, we observe that the "shape" of *MSTGen* is influenced by user information needs. In fact, if a user is willing to accept only strong (resp., also weak) generalization relationships, he will choose high (resp., low) values of θ_{gen}; in this case, in the corresponding generalization graph, a large (resp., low) number of nodes will be directly attached to the root and *MSTGen* will be flat (resp., lengthened).

4.2. The *Concentric* Algorithm

In this section we describe our second algorithm to build a hierarchy of tags; it is called *Concentric*.

The aim of this algorithm is quite different from that of *MST-based*; in fact, it does not produce a tree-based representation of tags but associates each tag with a coefficient stating its *semantic granularity*; the higher (resp., the lower) this parameter is, the more general (resp., more specific) a tag will be.

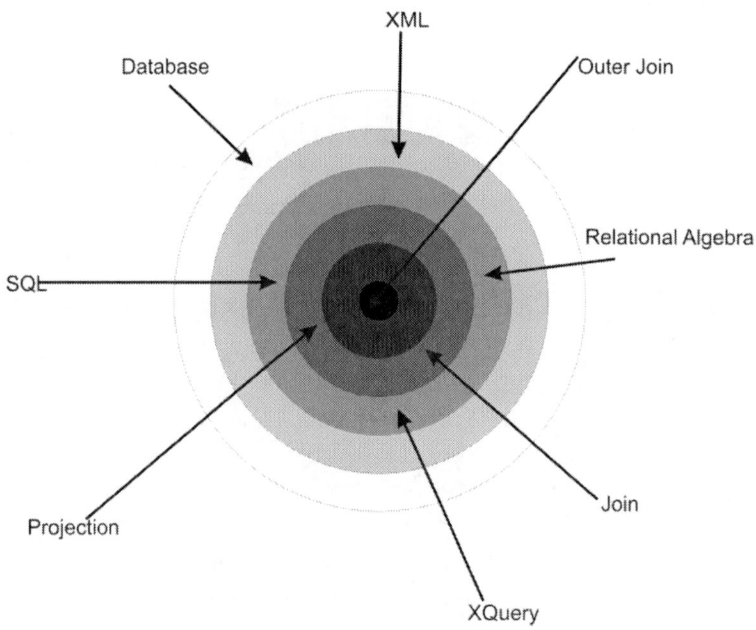

Figure 1. An example of hierarchy built by *Concentric*.

Semantic granularities of tags can be used to build a suitable data structure; this consists of a set of concentric circles such that the inner (resp., outer) ones are associated with the most specific (resp., general) tags. For instance, consider our reference folksonomy reported in Table 1; the external circles would host tags like "Database" or "XML", whereas the internal ones would contain tags like "Projection" or "Outer Join" (see Figure 1).

Concentric exploits a semantic granularity function, called *sem_gran(·)*, which receives a tag $t_i \in NeighTSet_{Input}$ and returns a value belonging to the real interval [0,1]. Its behaviour relies on the following intuitions:

1. The larger the number of resources labelled by a tag t_i is, the higher the semantic granularity of t_i will be. Due to this reasoning $sem\_gran(t_i)$ must be proportional to $|ProjRSet_i|$; in order to normalize this value to 1, $sem\_gran(t_i)$ is set proportional to the ratio:

$$\tau_i = \frac{|ProjRSet_i|}{|\bigcup_{t_j \in NeighTSet_{Input}} ProjRSet_j|}$$

2. A tag t_i has a high value of semantic granularity if there exist some tags $t_1, \ldots, t_k$ such that: *(i)* $t_1, \ldots, t_k$ have a high value of semantic granularity, and *(ii)* t_i is "more general" than $t_1, \ldots, t_k$. Due to this reasoning, $sem\_gran(t_i)$ must be proportional to the ratio:

$$\kappa_i = \frac{\sum_{t_j \in NeighTSet_{Input}, t_j \neq t_i} gen(t_i, t_j) \cdot sem\_gran(t_j)}{|NeighTSet_{Input}| - 1}$$

Here, the term $|NeighTSet_{Input}|-1$ has been used to normalize κ_i to 1.

We can combine the previous intuitions and we can express the semantic granularity of a tag as a *weighted mean* of two terms such that the former reflects the contribution provided by τ_i and the latter that provided by κ_i. This ultimately leads to the following set of equations:

$$sem\_gran(t_i) = \alpha\tau_i + (1 - \alpha)\kappa_i \qquad \forall t_i \in NeighTSet_{Input}$$

whose solution provides the semantic granularity of each tag of $NeighTSet_{Input}$.

Observe that if α is close to 0 the contribution of τ_i can be disregarded and the semantic granularity of t_i depends only on the generalization relationships of t_i against the other tags of $NeighTSet_{Input}$. On the contrary, if α is close to 1 the contribution of κ_i can be disregarded and, then, the number of resources labelled by t_i is the only factor contributing to the computation of its semantic granularity.

From our experience, setting α to either excessively high or excessively low values leads to negative effects. This can be easily seen also by considering some examples taken from our reference folksonomy reported in Table 1. For instance, consider the tags t_4="Database" and t_{17}="Relational Algebra". Assume that $NeighTSet_{Input} = \{t_4, t_{17}\}$ and that $\alpha = 1$. Since t_4 labels 4 resources and t_{17} labels 3 resources we have that the semantic granularity of "Database" is 4/7 whereas the semantic granularity of "Relational Algebra" is 3/7.

Therefore, these two tags would have an almost equal semantic granularity. Such a result clashes with the general knowledge that the semantic granularity of "Database" is higher than that of "Relational Algebra". As a further example, consider the tags t_4="Database" and t_{21}="XQuery". Assume that $NeighTSet_{Input} = \{t_4, t_{21}\}$. If $\alpha = 0$ we would obtain that the semantic granularities of "Database" and "XQuery" are equal. This result, again, clashes with the general knowledge that the semantic granularity of "Database" is much higher than that of "XQuery".

In order to confirm our experience and to concretize it by providing a numeric value for α we have performed many experiments. At the end of these experiments we have found that the best value for α is 0.6. This is also the value we have used in our system.

With some simple algebraic manipulations the previous system of equations can be rewritten in matrix form, i.e., in the form **Ax** = **b**. Observe that **A** is a square matrix having $|NeighTSet_{Input}|$ rows and $|NeighTSet_{Input}|$ columns. This system can be efficiently solved by a heuristics based on the Singular Value Decomposition (hereafter, *SVD*) technique [18].

We are now able to illustrate the behaviour of *Concentric*. It receives a set $NeighTSet_{Input}$ of tags and an integer N_{Circ} stating the number of circles of the hierarchy. It consists of the following steps:

1. Computation of the semantic granularity of all tags of $NeighTSet_{Input}$.
2. Computation of the lowest and the highest semantic granularities gr_{min} and gr_{max} associated with the tags of $NeighTSet_{Input}$.
3. Computation of the ratio $\rho = (gr_{max} - gr_{min})/N_{Circ}$. This allows the interval of possible semantic granularity values $[gr_{min}, gr_{max}]$ to be partitioned into N_{Circ} intervals of size ρ. Specifically, the first (resp., the second, the kth, the last) interval stores tags whose semantic granularity belongs to the real interval $[gr_{min}, gr_{min}+ \rho)$ (resp., $[gr_{min}+ \rho, gr_{min}+ 2\rho)$, $[gr_{min}+ (k-1)\rho, gr_{min}+ k\rho)$, $[gr_{min}+ (N_{Circ}-1)\rho, gr_{max}]$). We call *circle* each of these intervals and denote the kth circle as $Circ_k$.
4. Computation, for each $t_i \in NeighTSet_{Input}$, of the circle which it belongs to.

As for the computational cost of *Concentric*, we can state the following theorem:

Theorem 4.2. Let $NeighTSet_{Input}$ be a set of tags. The worst case computational complexity of *Concentric*, when applied on $NeighTSet_{Input}$, is $O(|NeighTSet_{Input}|^3)$. □

With regard to this theorem, it is worth pointing out that there exist heuristic algorithms capable of quickly and accurately performing the computation of the *SVD* of **A**. As an example, in [18] the authors propose a technique, based on the exploitation of both sampling and the Lanczos method, which computes the *SVD* of **A** in $O(|NeighTSet_{Input}|^2)$. Therefore, if this heuristics is chosen, the computational complexity of *Concentric* is $O(|NeighTSet_{Input}|^2)$.

As a first important feature, *Concentric* favours *serendipity*, i.e., the faculty of finding valuable and unexpected things without explicitly looking for them. This property is due to the fact that a user can first select an initial tag and, then, can freely browse the hierarchy from the outermost (resp., innermost) circles to the innermost (resp., outermost) ones, or, alternatively, he can move within the circle which the initial tag belongs to. During his exploratory search he could run into relevant tags and could progressively create a collection of interlinked tags which could represent a valuable and rich source of unexpected information.

As a second important feature, *Concentric* is very friendly and intuitive. In fact, it requires a user to specify only the number of circles *NCirc* forming the hierarchy; the meaning of this parameter is clear also to inexpert users.

The final relevant feature of *Concentric* is that it can be easily tuned in such a way as to take both user needs and user expertise level into account. In fact, if a user is a novice, he presumably chooses low values for N_{Circ}; the resulting hierarchy consists of few circles and, therefore, privileges simplicity to refinement. On the contrary, an expert user generally tends to choose high values of N_{Circ}; the resulting hierarchy consists of many levels and, therefore, is quite complex and articulated. This makes hierarchy exploration more difficult, on one side, but, on the other side, it allows a user to discover a higher number of properties.

5. Prototype Description

In order to evaluate our approach we built a prototype in Java and MySQL. In this section we describe this prototype by means of the UML formalism. More specifically, we first illustrate its class diagram; then, we describe the use case diagram and, finally, for each use case, we present the corresponding sequence diagram.

5.1. Class Diagram

Figure 2 shows the class diagrams of our system.

From the analysis of this diagram we can observe that the basic classes of our system are:

- *Tag*: it models a tag. It is very important because, besides representing the key element of our system, it has the methods *dis(Tag)* and *gen(Tag)* that allow the computation of the distance and the generalization coefficients. These coefficients play a key role in the construction of both $NeighTSet_{Input}$ and the tag hierarchy associated with *MST-based*. This class is connected through an association link to the class *DBConnection.*
- *Resource*: it models a resource. It has two very important methods, i.e., *addTag(Tag)* and *removeTag(Tag)*. The former labels a resource with a specified tag and stores this association on the support database; the latter, instead, removes the associations between a resource and a tag from the database. The class is connected through an association link to the classes *Tag* and *DBConnection*.
- *DBConnection*: it models a connection between the system and the database in which the tags and the resources of a generic folksonomy are stored. It executes suitable queries whose results are exploited by the system to perform its tasks.
- *Folksonomy*: it models a folksonomy. It is the most important class of our system. In fact, it provides all methods necessary to our system to perform its tasks. This class is connected through an association link to the classes *Tag*, *DBConnection*, *Matrix* and *Tree*.
- *Matrix*: it models a support matrix exploited by the classes *Folksonomy* and *Tree*. It provides a very important method, called *solution(boolean)*, used by *Concentric* to construct its hierarchy.
- *Tree*: it models a support tree for the class *Folksonomy*. Specifically, its method addNodes(Tag, Tag)} allows the construction of the tree structure, whereas its method *visualizes()* allows the visualization of the hierarchy constructed by *MST-Based*. This class is connected through an association link to the classes *Tag* and *Matrix*.

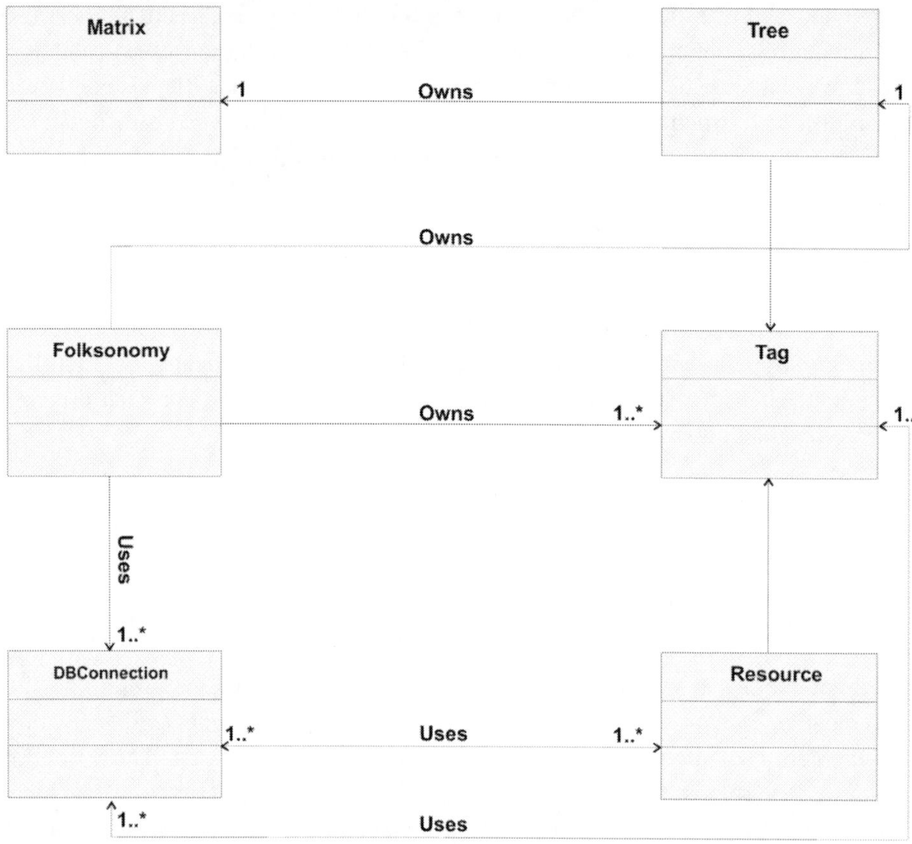

Figure 2. Class diagrams of our system.

In order to represent a set of tags (for istance, $TSet_{Input}$, $NeighTSet_{Input}$ or *CandTSet*) we have used a generic class *Vector<E>*, where *E* is a tag. *Vector* allows the representation of a sequence of objects with different lengths. The methods of this class that we have used most frequently are:

- *add(Tag)*: it allows the addition of a specific tag to the structure;
- *remove(Tag)*: it allows the removal of a specific tag from the structure;
- *elementAt(int)*: it returns the object contained in a specified position;
- *size()*: it returns the vector dimension;
- *contains(Tag)*: it returns *true* if the specific tag is present in the vector, *false* otherwise.

It is worth pointing out that all the basic classes, except *DBConnection* and *Matrix*, have the methods *get* and *set*: the former return the value of a specific property, the latter assign a value to a given property.

5.2. Use Case and Sequence Diagrams

The use case diagram associated with our system is shown in Figure 3. This diagram shows that there is only one actor for the system, i.e., the generic user; the possible use case are, instead, four, i.e. "Insertion of Input Tags", "Hierarchy Construction", "NeighTSetInput Computation" and "Resource Labelling".

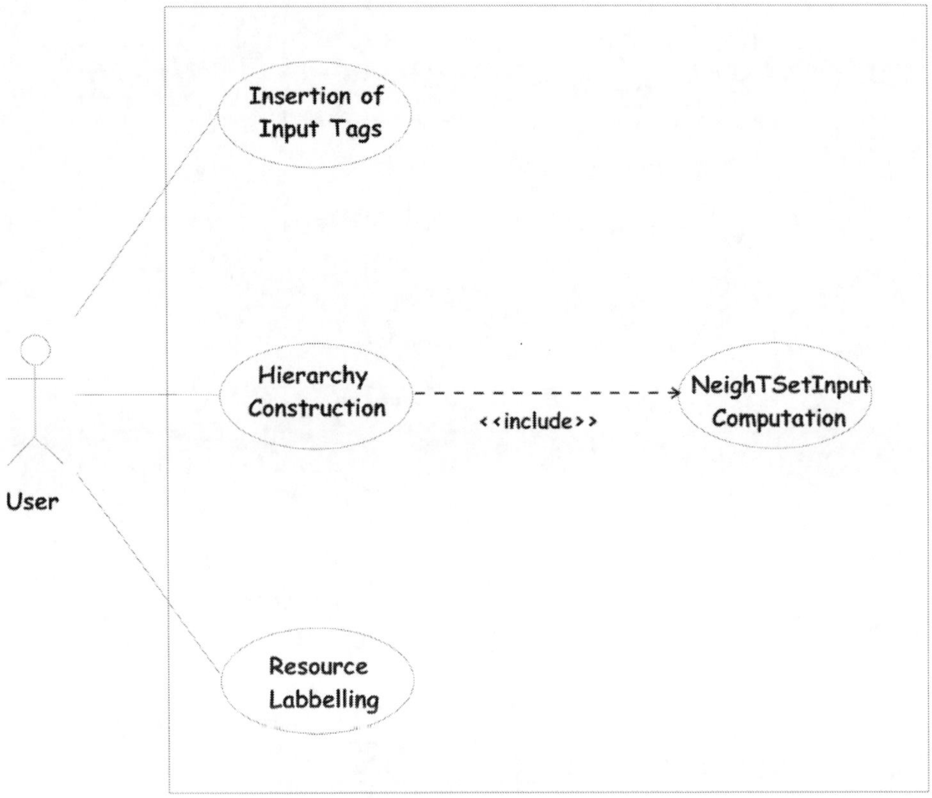

Figure 3. Use case diagram of our system.

In the following we analyze the design of each use case by illustrating the corresponding sequence diagram.

The sequence diagram associated with the use case "Insertion of Input Tags" is shown in Figure 4. This diagram starts when the user, through the User Interface, accesses the system and inserts $TSet_{Input}$ by means of a suitable form. $TSet_{Input}$ is, then, forwarded to *Folksonomy* that performs the following steps: *(i)* it requires *DBConnection* to verify that all tags belonging to $TSet_{Input}$ are stored in *TSet*; *(ii)* it requires *TSet* to *DBConnection*; *(iii)* for each pair of tags belonging to *TSet*, it requires *Tag* to get the corresponding distance value; *(iv)* it inserts the returned distance value in the Similarity Matrix; *(v)* it stores the obtained Similarity Matrix in a text file.

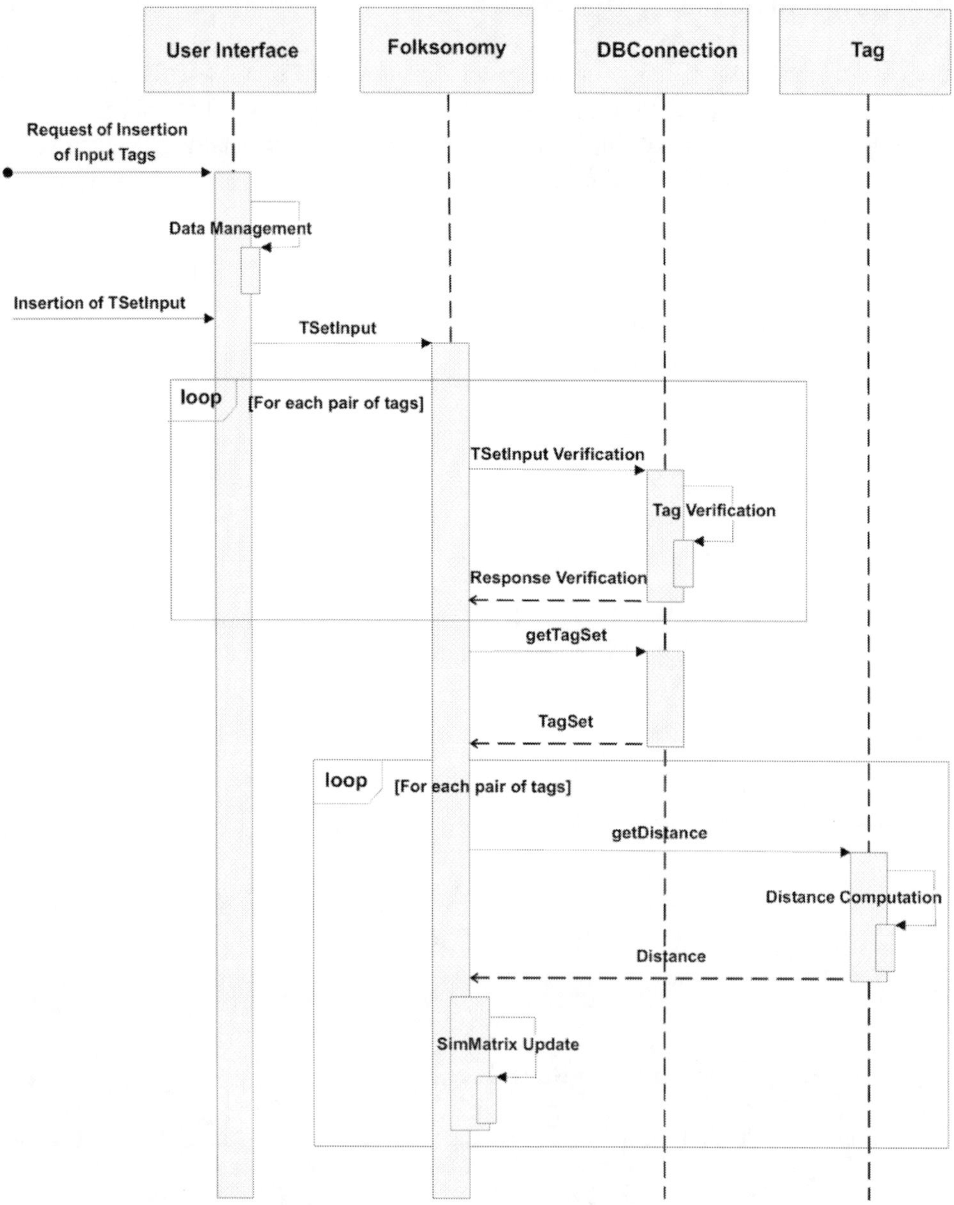

Figure 4. Sequence diagram of the use case "Insertion of Input Tags".

Figure 5 shows the sequence diagram of the use case "NeighTSetInput Computation".

Initially, the user specifies, through a suitable form, the strategy to be adopted for the computation of $NeighTSet_{Input}$. This choice is forwarded to *Folksonomy* that performs the following steps: *(i)* If the choice is "OR", it receives from the user, through the User Interface, the value θ_{cand}; for each element of $TSet_{Input}$, it computes *CandTSet* by applying the *getCandidate* method. After this, it derives $NeighTSet_{Input}$ by applying the *union* method. *(ii)* If the choice is "AND", for each element of the $TSet_{Input}$, it computes *CandTSet* by applying the *getCandidate* method. After this, it derives $NeighTSet_{Input}$ by applying the *intersection* method. *(iii)* If the choice is "Hybrid", it receives from the user, through the User Interface, the value of θ_{cand} and k. After this, it computes two sets of tags by applying the methods *NeighTSetInputOR* and *NeighTSetInputK*. Finally, it obtains $NeighTSet_{Input}$ by applying the method *union* which computes the union of these two sets.

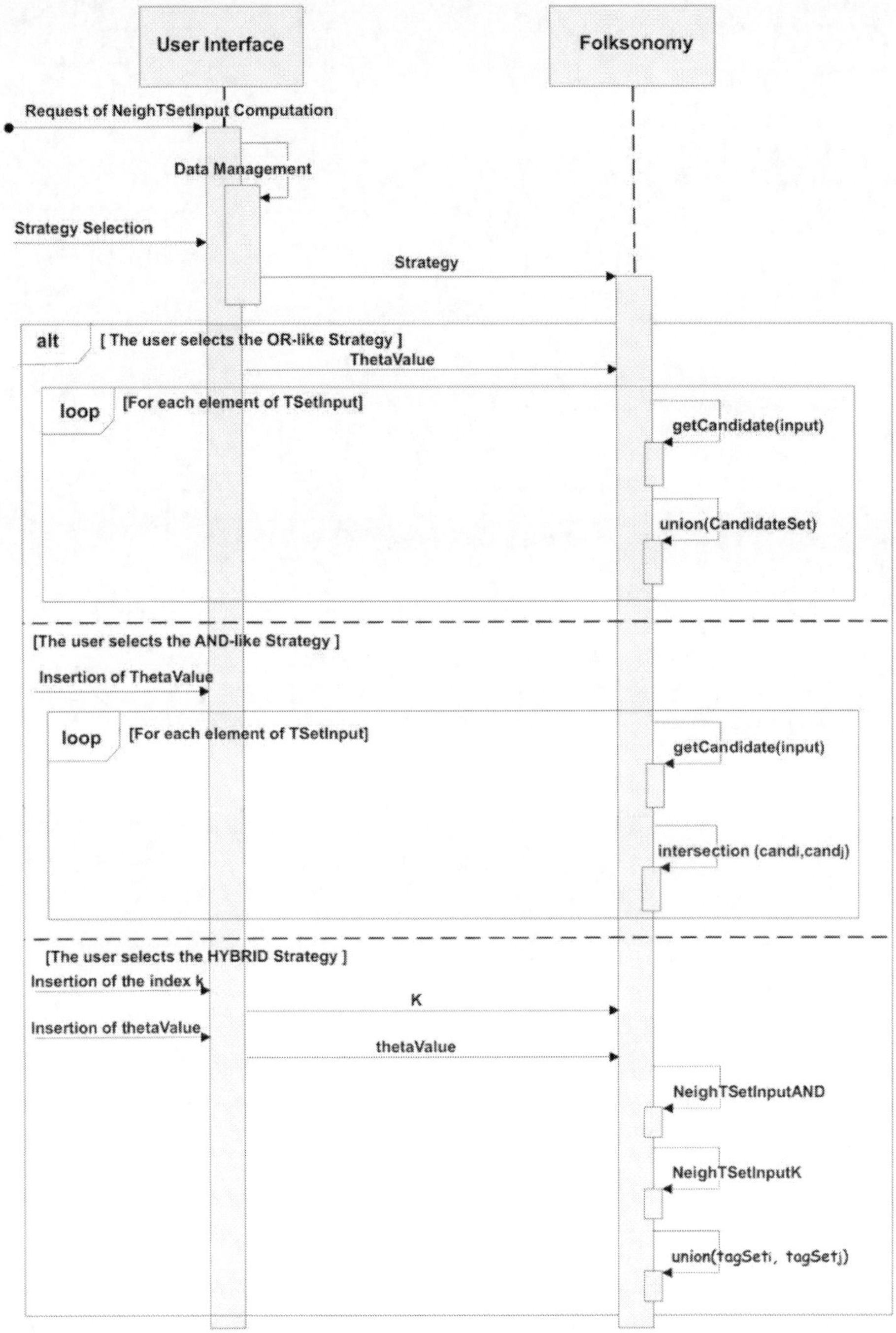

Figure 5. Sequence diagram of the use case "NeighTSetInput Computation".

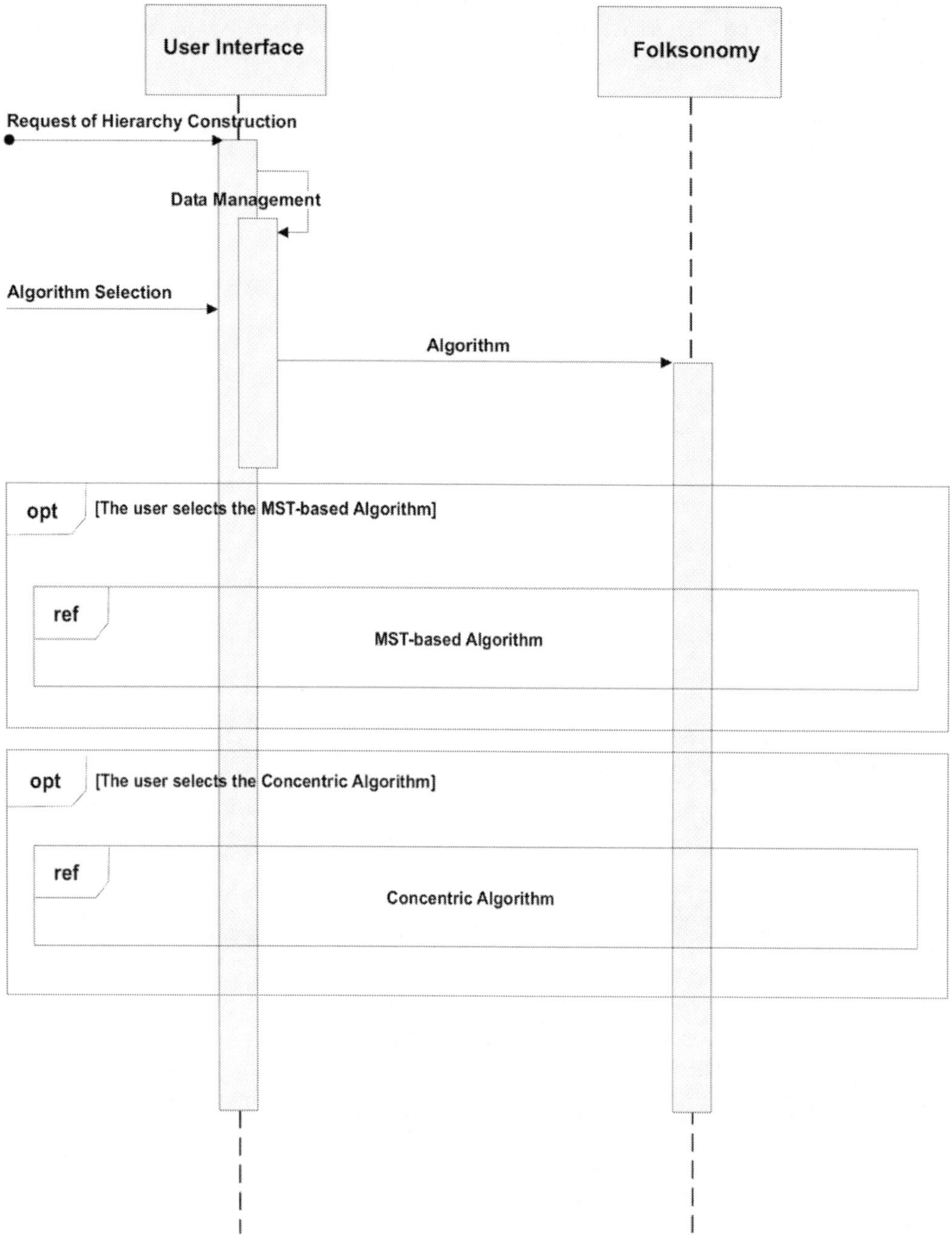

Figure 6. Sequence diagram of the use case "Hierarchy Construction".

Figure 6 shows the sequence diagram of the use case "Hierarchy Construction". This use case can start only after that *Folksonomy* has computed $NeighTSet_{Input}$. Initially, the user specifies, through a suitable form of the User Interface, the algorithm to be applied for the construction of the tag hierarchies. If the user chooses the *MST-Based* algorithm, *Folksonomy* performs the steps shown in Figure 7. On the contrary, if the user chooses the *Concentric* algorithm, *Folksonomy* performs the steps shown in Figure 8.

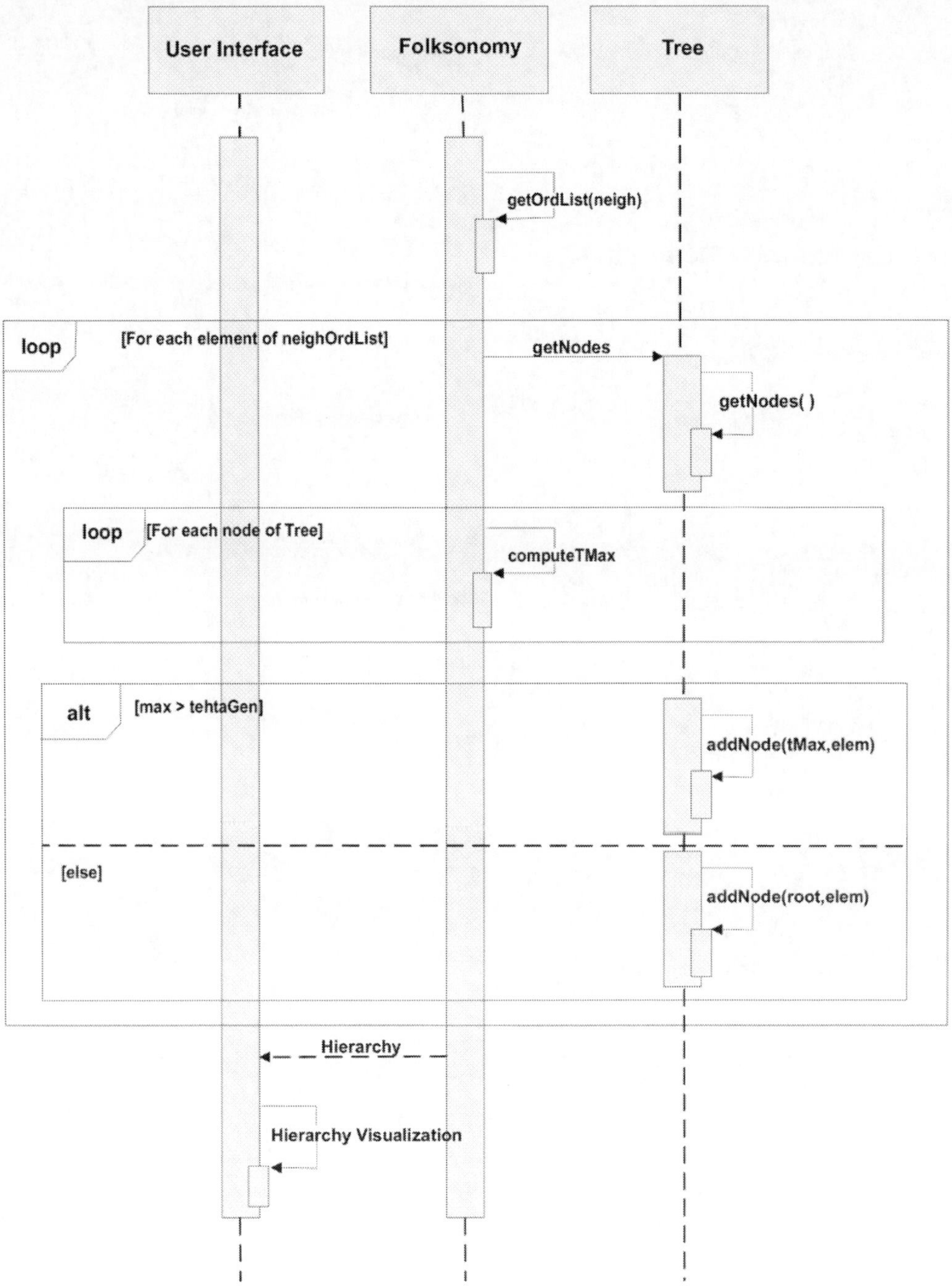

Figure 7. Sequence diagram of the use case "MST-Based Algorithm".

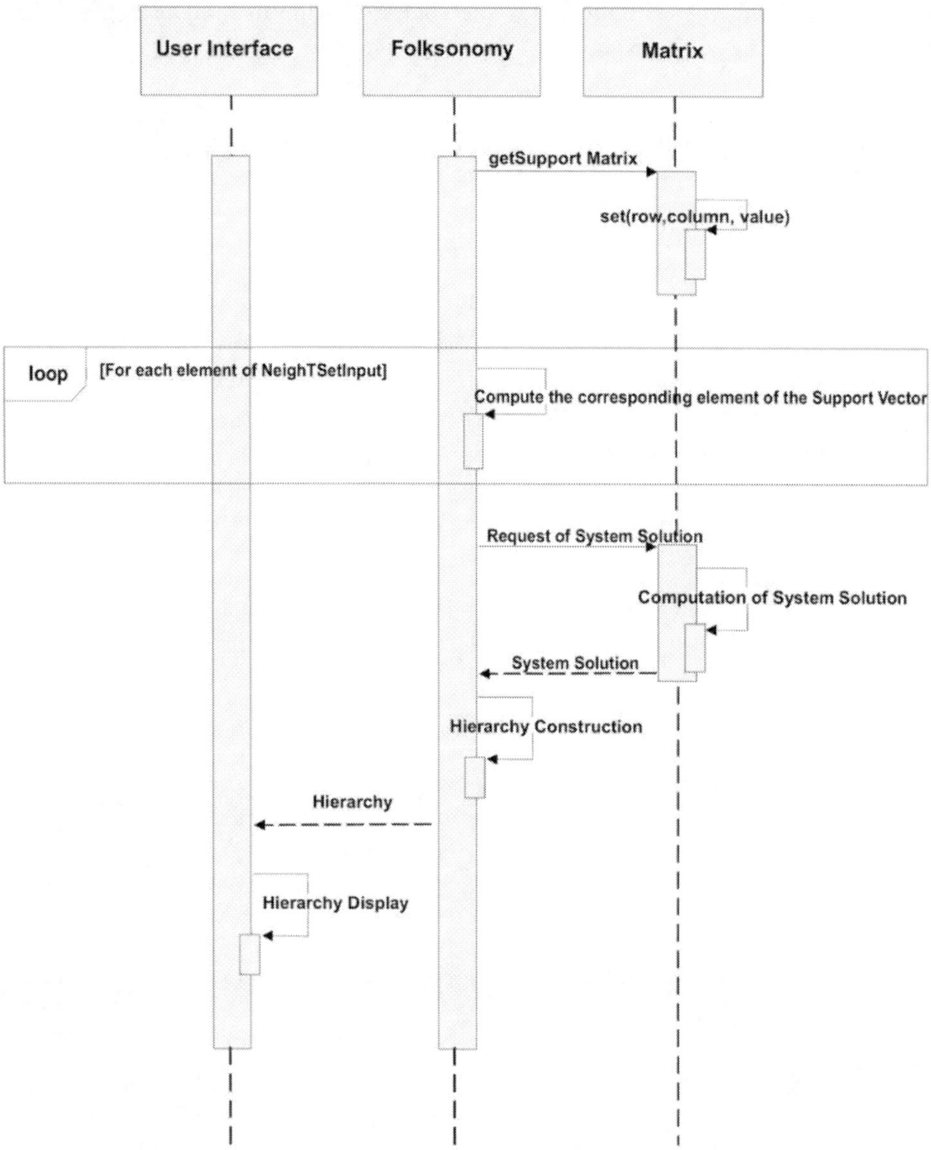

Figure 8. Sequence diagram of the use case "Concentric Algorithm".

Finally, Figure 9 shows the sequence diagram of the use case "Resource Labelling". From the analysis of this diagram we can see that the user initially requires the activation of the resource labelling task. After this, he specifies, by means of a suitable form of the User Interface, the resource to label and the associated tags. When these parameters have been specified, *DBConnection* performs the following steps: *(i)* it verifies if the input resource has already been labelled with the specified tag; *(ii)* in the negative case, it verifies if the input resource is present in *RSet*; *(iii)* if it is not present, it applies the method *insertRisSet* to put the resource in *RSet*; *(iv)* it verifies if the input tag is present in *TSet*; *(v)* in the negative case, it applies the method *insertTagSet* to insert the input tag in *TSet*; *(vi)* it labels the input resource with the specified tag; *(vii)* it sends an acknowledgement to the user through the User Interface.

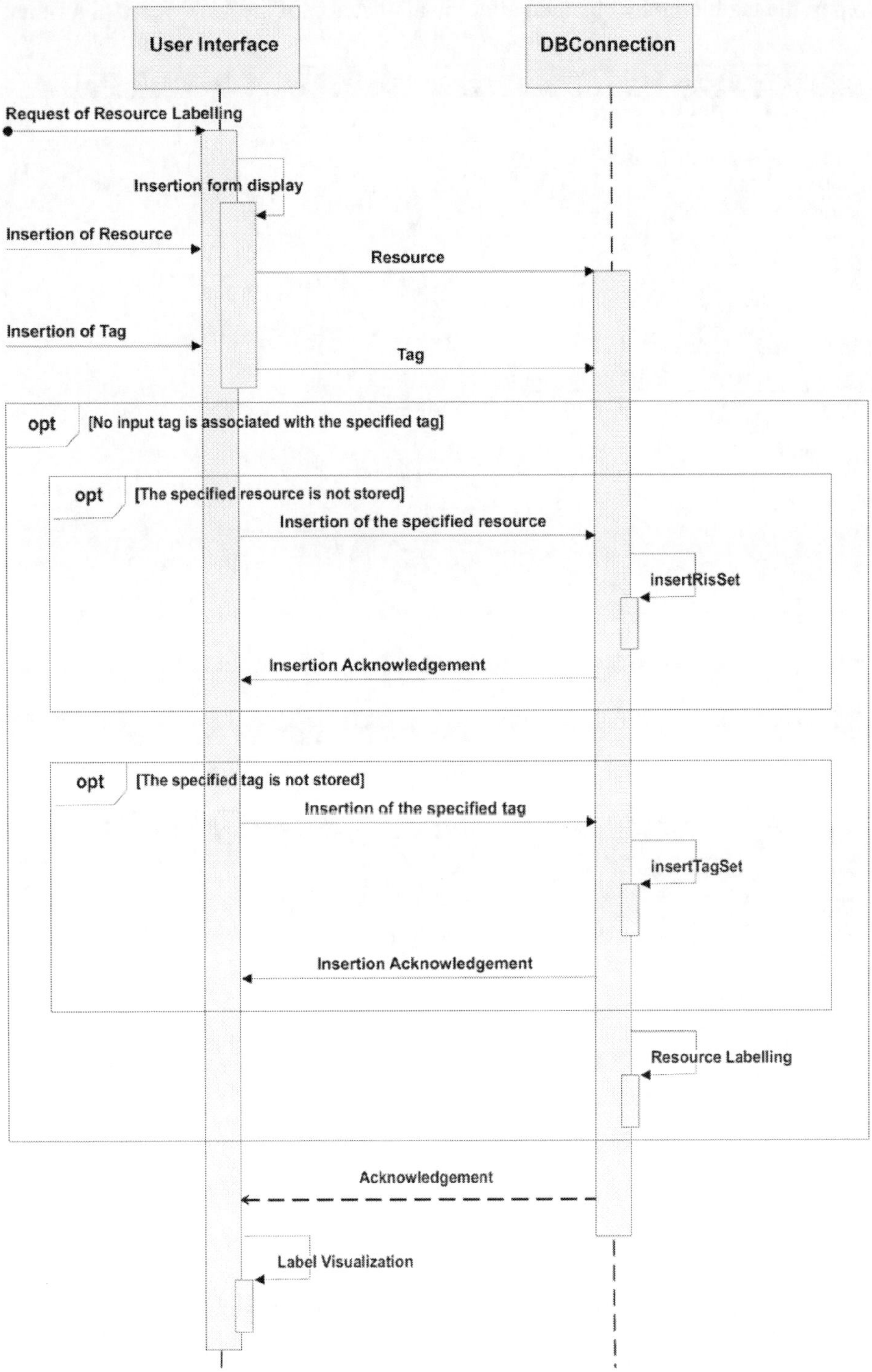

Figure 9. Sequence diagram of the use case "Resource Labelling".

In Figures 10 and 11 we report some screenshots of our prototype. Specifically, Figure 10 shows the original set of tags specified by the user ($TSet_{Input}$) along with the "expanded" set of tags ($NeighTSet_{Input}$) returned by our system when the *AND-like* strategy is applied. In Figure 11 we report the tag hierarchy obtained after the application of the *MST-based* algorithm.

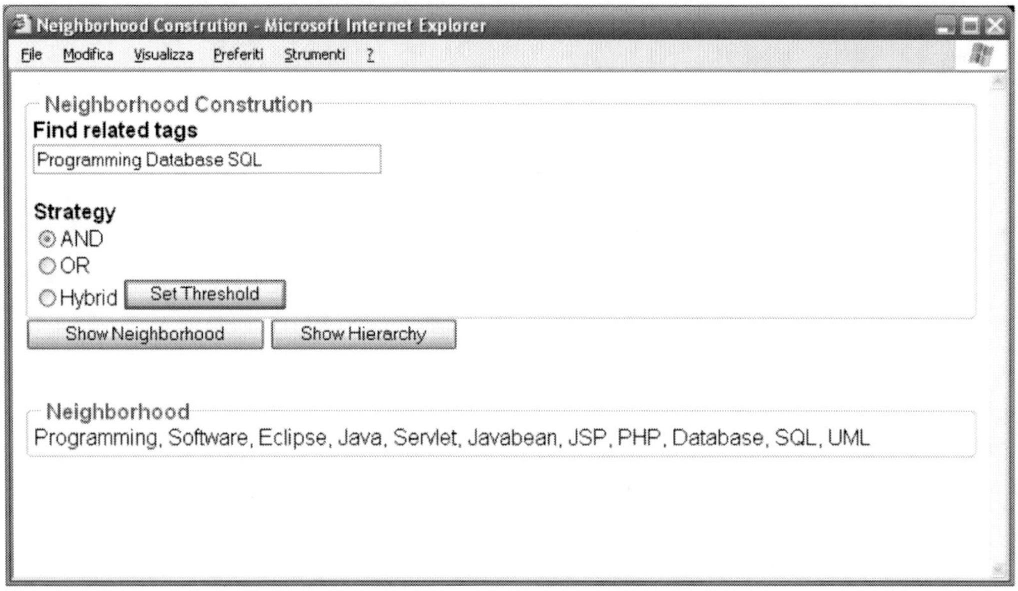

Figure 10. The Graphical Interface showing *TSetInput*, the strategies and *NeighTSetInput*.

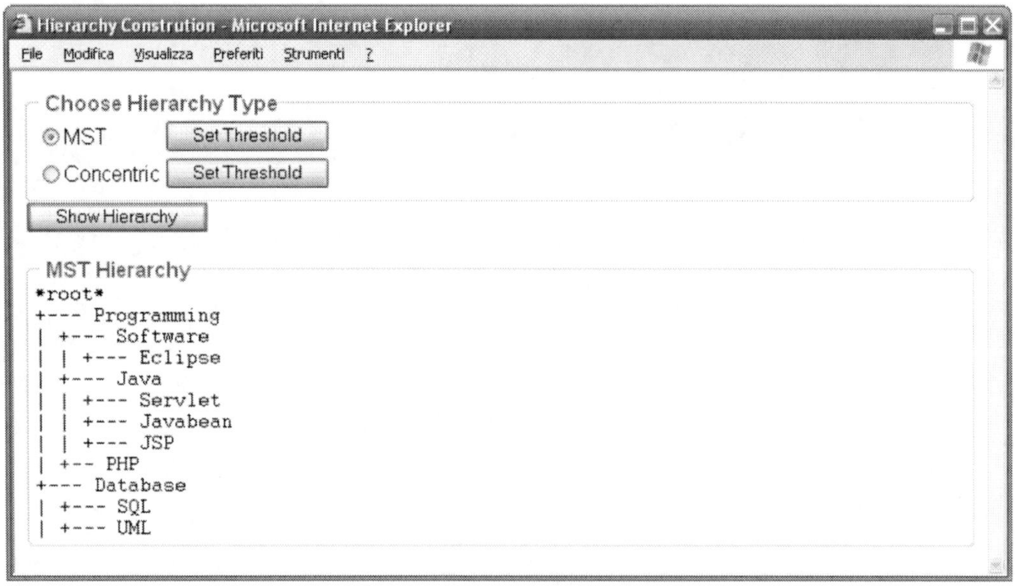

Figure 11. The Graphical Interface showing the hierarchy obtained by applying the *MST-Based* algorithm.

6. Experiments

We carried out all experiments on a Personal Computer equipped with a 3.4 GHz CPU and 1 GB of RAM.

The dataset used in our tests was extracted from del.icio.us [2]. Del.icio.us is a Web-based social bookmarking tool; it allows a user to manage a personal collection of links (*bookmarks*) to Web sites and to annotate these links with one or more tags. Users of del.icio.us are young and technologically aware [32]. Each time a user introduces and annotates new bookmarks he receives an instant gratification in the form of bookmarks to other Web pages. These factors contribute to making del.icio.us as one of the most popular examples of folksonomies. In this scenario, problems due to ambiguity, usage of synonymous tags and discrepancy on granularity of tags may frequently occur [32]; this makes del.icio.us an ideal benchmark for the evaluation of our approach.

We collected data from del.icio.us according to the methodology described in [26]. Specifically, we used an open source Web crawler called *wget*. Initially, we applied it to del.icio.us starting from its top page and we obtained 496 folksonomy users, 146,326 tags and 710,495 resources. After this, we applied *wget* in a recursive fashion on del.icio.us users, to obtain new resources, and on resources, to obtain new del.icio.us users. At the end of this process we obtained a dataset whose features are summarized in Table 2. Retrieved tags and resources refer to the Database and Information Systems domains; in Table 3 we report the topics they refer to along with their distribution over these topics.

Table 2. Features of the dataset adopted in our experiments

Total number of del.icio.us users	8,267
Maximum number of tags per del.icio.us user	17,057
Minimum number of tags per del.icio.us user	2
Mean number of tags per del.icio.us user	295
Maximum number of resources per del.icio.us user	31,465
Minimum number of resources per del.icio.us user	1
Mean number of resources per del.icio.us user	614

Table 3. Distribution of retrieved tags and resources over the corresponding topics

Topic	Percentage of Tags	Percentage of Resources
Database Design	19.68 %	19.53 %
Querying	21.19 %	24.57 %
Storage and Indexing	2.18 %	2.38 %
DataWarehouse	12.99 %	11.11 %
SQL Server/PL SQL	18.12 %	15.34 %
Other	25.85 %	27.07 %

Finally, we selected a pool of 20 users (different from those present in del.icio.us) and we asked them to take part to our experiments. Selected users showed the following features:

- Five users were undergraduate students who had to take an introductory course in Databases and Information Systems. They had no knowledge about Databases but they had some knowledge about programming and algorithm design.
- Five users were graduate students who had already taken a course in Databases and Information Systems. They were familiar with conceptual data modelling, relational model and SQL.
- Five users were students enrolled in a PhD programme on Databases and Information Systems.
- Five users were engineers with 3-5 years of experience in the development/administration of Databases.

In order to analyze our approach's capability of properly identifying groups of related tags we adopted two popular parameters defined in Information Retrieval, namely *Precision* and *Recall* [5]. The computation of these parameters in our reference scenario was performed as follows. First, a user was asked to specify a set $TSet_{Input}$ of tags; then, an expert was required to specify a set $ExpTSet_{Input}$ of tags that he considered related to those of $TSet_{Input}$; after this, our system was applied to compute $NeighTSet_{Input}$. Since there exist three possible strategies to carry out this last activity (see Section 3.2), in the following we denote as $NeighTSet_{Input}^{str}$ the set $NeighTSet_{Input}$ obtained by applying the strategy *str* (here *str* ∈ {*OR-like*, *AND-like*, *Hybrid*}). The Precision Pre^{str} and the Recall Rec^{str} obtained by applying the strategy *str* are defined as follows:

$$Pre^{str} = \frac{|NeighTSet_{Input}^{str} \cap ExpTSet_{Input}|}{|NeighTSet_{Input}^{str}|} \qquad Rec^{str} = \frac{|NeighTSet_{Input}^{str} \cap ExpTSet_{Input}|}{|ExpTSet_{Input}|}$$

Both these two measures range in the real interval [0,1]; the higher they are, the better our system works.

This experiment was performed as follows. We asked the 20 users described above to specify 8 different queries; the ith query specified by each user was composed by i tags (i.e., the corresponding $|TSet_{Input}|$ was equal to i). As a consequence, we obtained 8 sets, each consisting of 20 queries. The set $QSet_i$, $1 \leq i \leq 8$, contained all queries submitted by users and consisting of i tags.

For each set $QSet_i$ we computed Pre_i^{str} and Rec_i^{str} for all its queries and we averaged the corresponding values across the 20 users.

Figures 12 and 13 show the values of Pre_i^{str} and Rec_i^{str} obtained by applying the three strategies specified above on each set of queries (i.e., when i ranges from 1 to 8). As for the *AND-like* and the *OR-like* strategies, we report only the results obtained when the threshold θ_{cand} (see Section 3) is equal to 0.5. A lower (resp., higher) value of this threshold would produce smaller (resp., larger) neighborhoods and, ultimately, an increase of Precision (resp., Recall) and a decrease of Recall (resp., Precision). As for the *Hybrid* strategy, we considered different values of the thresholds k and θ_{strong} (see Section 3.2).

Specifically, we assumed that $k \in \{\lceil 1/3\ |TSet_{Input}| \rceil, \lceil 1/2\ |TSet_{Input}| \rceil, \lceil 2/3\ |TSet_{Input}| \rceil\}$ and $\theta_{strong} \in \{0.00, 0.15, 0.30\}$ and considered all possible combinations of these parameters.

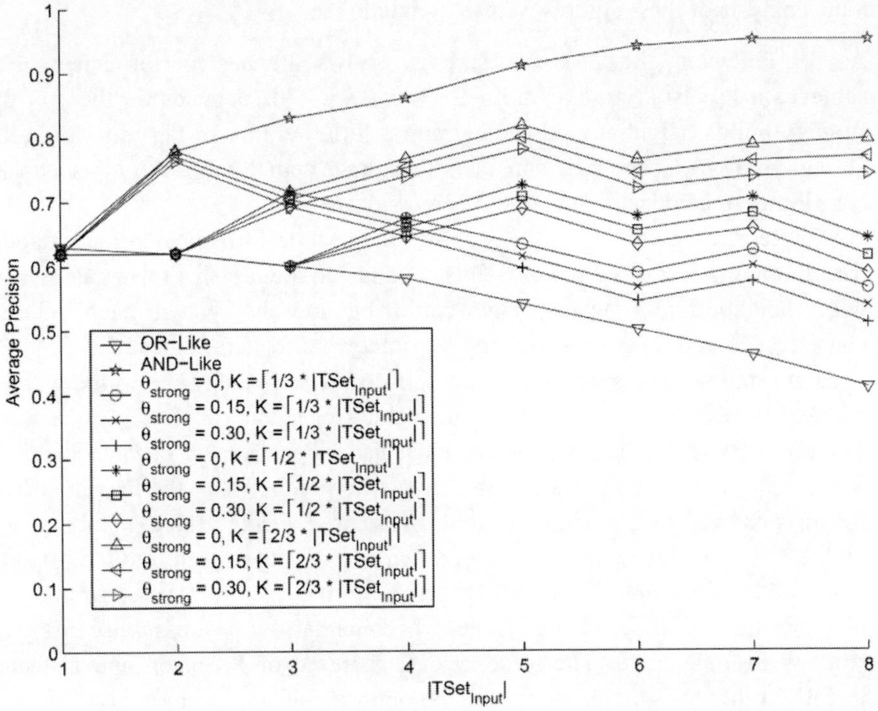

Figure 12. Average Precision obtained by applying the *OR-like*, the *AND-like* and the *Hybrid* strategies.

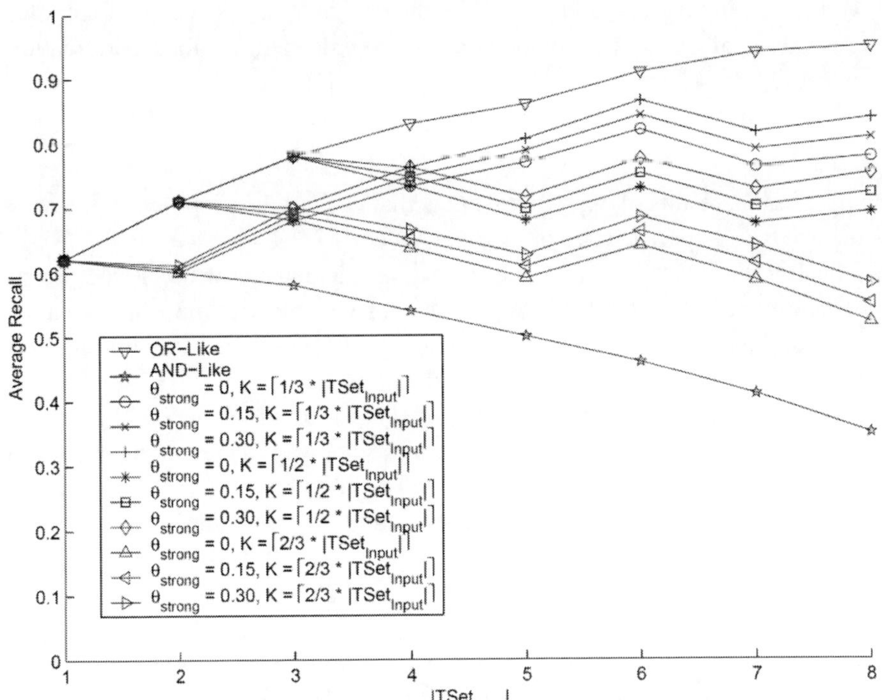

Figure 13. Average Recall obtained by applying the *OR-like*, the *AND-like* and the *Hybrid* strategies.

From the analysis of these figures we can conclude that:

1. As for Precision, the *AND-like* strategy shows the best performance; in fact, it achieves a Precision ranging from 0.63 to 0.95. This depends on the fact that this strategy builds neighborhoods containing a little number of tags strongly related to all tags of $TSet_{Input}$; the user considers these tags actually close to his needs and this contributes to achieve high values of Precision.
2. As for Recall, the *OR-like* strategy shows the best performance; in fact, it achieves a Recall ranging from 0.62 to 0.94. This depends on the fact that this strategy generates wide neighborhoods whose tags could be loosely related each other; as a consequence, it does not rule out any tag somewhat related to those of $TSet_{Input}$.
3. For the same reasons specified above, the *AND-like* strategy shows the worst Recall whereas the *OR-like* strategy shows the worst Precision.
4. The size of $TSet_{Input}$, i.e., the parameter i, has a deep impact on both Precision and Recall. In fact, when i ranges from 1 to 8, the gap between the Precision (resp. the Recall) achieved by the *AND-like* strategy (resp., *OR-like* strategy) and that achieved by the *OR-like* strategy (resp., *AND-like* strategy) ranges from 0 to 0.54 (resp., from 0 to 0.60). This behaviour is explained by the fact that when i increases the neighborhoods of the *AND-like* strategy become narrow whereas those of the *OR-like* strategy become large. This produces an increase of Precision and a decrease of Recall for the *AND-like* strategy, and the opposite behaviour for the *OR-like* strategy.
5. The results returned by the *Hybrid* strategy are intermediate between those returned by the *OR-like* and the *AND-like* strategies. The oscillatory behaviour of Precision and Recall in this case is explained by the choice to use the ceiling function to define the values of k; these oscillations are to be intended as slight perturbations to the intrinsic trend characterizing Precision or Recall. However, it is worth observing that, when i increases, the oscillations of Precision and Recall become smaller and smaller.

One of the main results of our experiment is that each of the proposed strategies is able to address the needs of a specific class of users.

Specifically, the *AND-like* strategy is particularly adequate for users who are starting to study a certain matter; in fact, it tends to provide tags very close to those specified by users in $TSet_{Input}$ even at the expense of filtering out some tags that could be partially suitable to satisfy user desires.

By contrast, the *OR-like* strategy is very suitable for users who know a given matter and want to enlarge their knowledge by studying topics someway related to this matter; in fact, it tends to provide tags also partially close to those specified by users in $TSet_{Input}$; this produces a decrease of Precision that, however, is less important than Recall in this scenario and, therefore, can be partially "sacrificed".

Finally, *Hybrid* strategy is useful for all "intermediate" categories of users. These have a partial knowledge of a matter and are interested both in deepening their search and enlarging their knowledge. They can apply the *Hybrid* strategy to obtain an initial set of results; after this, by means of a "guess-and-check" approach, according to their personal needs, they can tune k and θ_{strong} in such a way as to obtain an increase of Precision (resp., Recall) at the expense of Recall (resp., Precision). In the experiments described in the next sections we applied the *Hybrid* strategy with $\theta_{cand} = 0.50$, $k = \lceil 1/2\ |TSet\mathit{Input}| \rceil$ and $\theta_{strong} = 0.15$; this choice of parameter values is explained by the fact that this configuration achieves the best tradeoff between Precision and Recall.

7. Related Work

Some authors have suggested to exploit external data sources in the detection of groups of semantically related tags and in the construction of a hierarchy [4, 28, 40, 41]. Exploited data sources range from simple thesauri (e.g., WordNet [34]) to complex ontologies.

Approaches relying on external data sources provide many advantages. In fact, there is a strong correspondence between folksonomies and ontologies, in particular between folksonomy tags and ontology concepts. As a consequence, if a relationship between a folksonomy and an ontology is established, any enrichment or improvement performed in the folksonomy can be fruitfully extended to the ontology, and vice versa. In addition, many of these approaches are *unsupervised*, i.e., they do not require a preliminary training phase.

Some of the approaches cited above introduce the concept of *paradigmatic association* [40] which largely resembles the ideas we introduced to compute the neighborhood of a tag. Paradigmatic association implies that a tag is assigned to a group of related tags if it is similar to multiple tags of this group; this perspective strongly differs from traditional approaches based on clustering algorithms which assign a tag to a cluster according to its similarity with the corresponding centroid. In our approach paradigmatic associations are captured by *AND-like* and *Hybrid* strategies for neighborhood computation. In fact, if *AND-like* (resp., *Hybrid*) strategy is adopted, a tag is included in a neighborhood if it is similar to all tags (resp., to at least *k* tags) of the neighborhood itself.

As a final interesting feature characterizing approaches of this category, we observe that those of them which use only thesauri as external data sources are often very fast; for instance, the algorithm proposed in [28] runs in a linear time against the number of input tags.

However, approaches based on external data sources suffer also from some drawbacks. Specifically:

- As far as approaches using thesauri are concerned, we observe that the inference of the relationships existing among concepts is carried out by applying only syntactical criteria (think, for instance, of the metrics used in WordNet to assess the semantic relatedness of two words). By contrast, in our approach, the similarity of two tags directly depends on the number of resources jointly labelled by them and, ultimately, on the joint behaviour of users involved in labelling activity. As a consequence, high (resp., low) values of the semantic similarity of two tags indicate that a broad (resp., narrow) consensus on their meaning emerged in user community.
  A further drawback concerning thesauri-based approaches is that many thesauri are *general-purpose* and, then, might not store many specialistic entries which could have a great relevance in some domains.
- As far as approaches using ontologies are concerned, we observe that they generally depend on the suitability of the exploited ontologies to the context which they are operating on. Indeed, if adopted ontologies are adequate, these systems can achieve a high accuracy; by contrast, if exploited ontologies are lacking or incomplete, they achieve a bad performance.

Some authors (e.g., those of [4,40]) suggest to use Semantic Web search engines, such as Swoogle [17], to find proper ontologies; however, many of these search engines offer quite limited query facilities; for instance, they do not provide tools capable of distinguishing concepts, instances and properties. As a consequence, in many cases, a human user is required to manually download, parse and modify the selected ontology [4]. In these aspects our approach is considerably different in that it requires quite a limited human intervention which can be carried out also by inexpert users.

Data Mining and statistical techniques have been widely applied to find groups of related tags as well as to build hierarchies in folksonomies [7, 8, 10, 31, 37, 38, 42].

We can recognize some similarities between our approach and those relying on Data Mining and statistical techniques. Specifically, given a pair of tags, these approaches generally consider the set of resources jointly labelled by them to determine to what extent they share the same meaning or one of them has a broader meaning than the other [42].

A remarkable exception to this idea is represented by the approach of [10] where the authors propose and exploit a *syntactic* parameter relying on the frequency of a word in blog articles; this metrics is adequate in this context because blog articles have a typical narrative structure with few hyperlinks to other Web pages.

Our approach is similar to those based on Data Mining and statistical techniques in that it considers the resources jointly labelled by two tags in the computation of tag semantic similarity or generalization degrees. In this context it introduces a relevant novelty in that it uses a probabilistic framework to quickly and accurately estimate these coefficients.

Some of the approaches described previously build rigid classification schemas [7], i.e., they define precise tag categories and specific subsumption relationships among tags. Other approaches, instead propose looser classification models not characterized by rigid relationships among tags or categories [31]. Our approach shares some features with both these philosophies; in fact, if *MST-based* is applied, the constructed hierarchy is a tree and, therefore, specifies precise subsumption relationships among tags; by contrast, if *Concentric* is adopted, the constructed hierarchy is much more loose and does not specify relationships among tags.

As for differences between these approaches and ours we observe that, generally, approaches based on Data Mining and statistical techniques are computationally costly. For instance, some of them apply clustering techniques whose computational cost is excessively high for interactive browsing activities (see [31] for some considerations about this topic). In other cases, they operate by performing loops in which the cost of each iteration is proportional to the size of tag space. Some approaches (e.g., [31]) remedy high computational costs by applying approximate algorithms for clustering tags [31]. Like these approaches, our own defines a methodology to reduce its computational costs. However, differently from them, it obtains this cost reduction by using a suitable data structure that avoids the whole space of tags to be explored when tag similarities must be determined.

Moreover approaches relying on Data Mining and statistical techniques generally try to determine semantic relationships among *all* available tags. As a consequence, they are able to extract hidden relationships also among tags traditionally regarded as independent by users; this enhances user capability of retrieving relevant resources. However, they do not consider if semantic relationships they are extracting are potentially relevant to their users; as a consequence, they could waste many computational resources to derive complex tag relationships that are next judged uninteresting by users. By contrast, our approach is always guided in its search by user interests since it derives neighborhoods and constructs hierarchies starting from the set of input tags specified by user and, therefore, surely interesting to him. As a consequence, it focuses all efforts only on a small portion of the folksonomy presumably capable of satisfying user needs and desires.

Social Networks theory offers many relevant methods to analyze folksonomies and derive semantic relationships among tags [24, 32, 43].

Approaches based on Social Networks are quite fascinating because they put into evidence the associative and participatory nature of tagging process. In fact, they depict users as autonomous entities who organize knowledge according to their own rules and negotiate the meaning of tags when they want to cooperate. In this scenario the meaning of a tag emerges through a collective usage of it as well as through a broad consensus about its meaning reached among users.

Some authors (e.g., the author of [30]) suggest that the rich interlacement of social relationships can complement and enhance traditional information processing techniques; specifically, a user, rather than searching resources by keywords or subscribing to special interest groups, can browse through the resources posted by other users that he considers similar to him.

Approaches based on Social Networks are also useful to explain the emergence of serendipity in folksonomies. With regard to this, the authors of [11] carried out an experimental analysis about the properties of the tripartite graph representing a folksonomy. The corresponding datasets were extracted from del.icio.us [2] and Bibsonomy [1]. Experiments revealed that this graph was highly connected and enjoyed *small world* property. This implies that the average length of the shortest path between two random nodes of the graph is small even if the number of its nodes is high; as a consequence, few hops are necessary to move from one node to another in the graph; this favors serendipitous search over folksonomies.

Approaches based on Social Networks usually compute parameters assessing the centrality of a node within a graph; these parameters determine the importance of a node by considering its relative relevance w.r.t. the other nodes of the graph. This idea resembles our definition of semantic granularity; in fact, in our approach, the semantic granularity of a tag depends on the semantic granularity of the other tags. These mutual reinforcement relationships lead to a system of linear equations whose solution returns the semantic granularity of each tag.

It is worth observing that the computation of centrality measures in social networks is quite expensive; for instance, the betweenness centrality can be computed in $O(n^3)$ time, where n is the number of the nodes of the corresponding graph and, therefore, the number of available tags; this effort becomes very heavy as long as the number of available tags becomes large. Some authors (e.g., those of [24]) observe that the small world hypothesis allows an efficient computation of centrality parameters. However, to the best of our knowledge, there are only few experimental studies about network properties of folksonomies and, then, it is still unclear if the small world property holds for all existing folksonomies. Generally speaking, the problem of efficiently approximating centrality measures is an open research problem and many research papers have been recently devoted to study this topic [19, 36].

Our approach follows a different philosophy; in fact, it builds its hierarchies starting from the tags of $NeighTSet_{Input}$, i.e., from the tags similar to those provided in input by the user. Both the derivation of $NeighTSet_{Input}$ and the construction of hierarchies require a limited amount of computational resources. In fact, at the implementation level, the derivation of $NeighTSet_{Input}$ is performed with the support of the neighborhood lists whereas the construction of hierarchies is performed on $NeighTSet_{Input}$, i.e., on a generally small sample of the whole tag space.

8. Conclusions

In this chapter we have presented a new approach to supporting users to perform social annotations and browsing activities in folksonomies. Our approach receives a set $TSet_{Input}$ of tags specified by a user. It first constructs a set $NeighTSet_{Input}$ of tags semantically related to those specified in $TSet_{Input}$. After this, it organizes tags of $NeightTSet_{Input}$ in a hierarchy in such a way as to allow a user to visualize the tags of his interest according to the desired semantic granularity as well as to find those tags best expressing his information needs. Our approach proposes two suitable data structures and two related algorithms to organize $NeighTSet_{Input}$ in a hierarchy.

In this chapter we have provided all technical details about our approach; then, we have described the corresponding prototype and we have illustrated various experiments devoted to measure its performance; finally, we have compared it with other related ones previously presented in the literature.

In our opinion the ideas proposed in this chapter present various interesting developments. Specifically, since the annotations of a user can be regarded as a reliable indicator of his preferences, we plan to design a recommender system capable of learning the profile of a user from his annotations. In particular, we plan to design both a content-based recommender system (relying on the analysis of tags specified by a user in the past) and a collaborative-filtering one (based on the analysis of tags jointly adopted by multiple users presumably sharing some common interests).

A further research direction consists of defining complex hierarchies capable of capturing different types of semantic relationship among tags and displaying it in an intuitive fashion. Specifically, we think of exploiting graph visualization techniques to represent tags as charged particles whose interaction is regulated by attractive or repulsive forces. These techniques graphically display tags in a bi-dimensional layout by finding a (locally) minimum energy state for the associated physical system. The result is that two tags appear close in this space if they are semantically similar, and distant otherwise.

References

[1] Bibsonomy. `http://bibsonomy.org/, 2008.`
[2] Delicious. `http://del.icio.us/, 2008.`
[3] Flickr. `http://www.flickr.com/, 2008.`

[4] R. Abbasi, S. Staab, and P. Cimiano. Organizing Resources on Tagging Systems using T-ORG. In *Proc.of the International Workshop on Bridging the Gap between Semantic Web and Web 2.0*, pages 97–110, Innsbruck, Austria, 2007.

[5] R. Baeza-Yates and B. Ribeiro-Neto. *Modern Information Retrieval*. Addison Wesley Longman, 1999.

[6] S. Bao, G. Xue, X. Wu, Y. Yu, B. Fei, and Z. Su. Optimizing Web search using social annotations. In *Proc. of the International Conference on World Wide Web (WWW '07)*, pages 501–510, Banff, Alberta, Canada, 2007. ACM.

[7] G. Begelman, P. Keller, and F. Smadja. Automated tag clustering: improving search and exploration in the tag space. In *Proc. of the Collaborative Web Tagging Workshop*, Edinburgh, Scotland, UK, 2006.

[8] D. Benz, K.H.L. Tso, and L. Schmidt-Thieme. Supporting collaborative hierarchical classification: Bookmarks as an example. *Computer Networks*, **51**(16):4574–4585, 2007.

[9] A. Broder. On the resemblance and containment of documents. In *Proc. of the International Conference on the Compression and Complexity of Sequences (SEQUENCES '97)*, pages 21–29, Positano, Italy, 1997. IEEE Computer Society.

[10] C.H. Brooks and N. Montanez. Improved annotation of the blogosphere via autotagging and hierarchical clustering. In *Proc. of the International Conference on World Wide Web (WWW '06)*, pages 625–632, Edinburgh, Scotland, UK, 2006. ACM.

[11] C. Cattuto, C. Schmitz, A. Baldassarri, V.D.P. Servedio, V. Loreto, A. Hotho, M. Grahl, and G. Stumme. Network properties of folksonomies. *Artificial Intelligence Communications*, **20**(4):245–262, 2007.

[12] Z. Chen, F. Korn, N. Koudas, and S.Muthukrishnan. Generalized substring selectivity estimation. *Journal of Computer and System Sciences*, **66**(1):98–132, 2003.

[13] E. Cohen. Size-estimation framework with applications to transitive closure and reachability. *Journal of Computer and System Sciences*, **55**(3):441–453, 1997.

[14] T.H. Cormen, C.E. Leiserson, R.L. Rivest, and C. Stein. *Introduction to Algorithms*. The MIT Press, 2001.

[15] B. Cripe. Folksonomy, keywords, & tags: Social & democratic user interaction in enterprise content management. Technical report, An Oracle Business & Technology White Paper `http://www.oracle.com/technology/products/content-management/pdf/OracleSocialTaggingWhitePaper.pdf`, 2007.

[16] P. De Meo, G. Quattrone, D. Ursino. Exploitation of semantic relationships and hierarchical data structures to support a user in his annotation and browsing activities in folksonomies. *Information System*, **34**:511-535, 2009.

[17] L. Ding, T. Finin, A. Joshi, R. Pan, R.S. Cost, Y. Peng, P. Reddivari, V. Doshi, and J. Sachs. Swoogle: a search and metadata engine for the Semantic Web. In *Proc. of the ACM International Conference on Information and Knowledge Management (CIKM '04)*, pages 652–659, Washington, Washington D.C., USA, 2004. ACM.

[18] P. Drineas, A.M. Frieze, R. Kannan, S. Vempala, and V. Vinay. Clustering in large graphs and matrices. In *Proc. of the ACM-SIAM Symposium on Discrete Algorithms (SODA 1999)*, pages 291–299, Baltimore, Maryland, USA, 1999. ACM-SIAM.

[19] D. Eppstein and J. Wang. Fast approximation of centrality. In *Proc. of the ACM-SIAM Symposium on Discrete Algorithms (SODA '01)*, pages 228–229. Society for Industrial and Applied Mathematics, 2001.

[20] S.A. Golder and B.A. Huberman. Usage patterns of collaborative tagging systems. *Journal of Information Science*, **32**(2):198–208, 2006.

[21] S. Gollapudi, M. Najork, and R. Panigrahy. Using Bloom Filters to Speed Up HITS-Like Ranking Algorithms.

[22] In Proc. of the International Workshop on Algorithms and Models for the Web-Graph (WAW 2007), *Lecture Notes in Computer Science,* pages 195–201, San Diego, CA, USA, 2007. Springer. Community Systems Group. Community systems research at Yahoo! *SIGMOD Record*, **36**(3):47–54, 2007.

[23] J. Han and M. Kamber. Data Mining: Concepts and Techniques - Second Edition. Morgan Kaufmann Publishers, 2006.

[24] P. Heymann and H. Garcia-Molina. Collaborative creation of communal hierarchical taxonomies in social tagging systems. *Technical Report InfoLab 2006-10*, Computer Science Department, Stanford University, 2006.

[25] P. Heymann, G. Koutrika, and H. Garcia-Molina. Can Social Bookmarks Improve Web Search? In Proc. *of International Conference on Web Search and Data Mining (WSDM 2008)*, pages 195–206, Stanford, California, USA, 2008. ACM Press.

[26] A. Hotho, R. Jaschke, C. Schmitz, and G. Stumme. Information Retrieval in Folksonomies: Search and Ranking. In *Proc. of the European Semantic Web Conference (ESWC'06),* pages 411–426, Budva, Montenegro, 2006. Lecture Notes in Computer Science, Springer.

[27] J.M. Kleinberg. Authoritative sources in a hyperlinked environment. *Journal of the ACM*, **46**(5):604–632, 1999.

[28] D. Laniado, D. Eynard, and M. Colombetti. Using WordNet to turn a folksonomy into a hierarchy of concepts. In *Proc. of the Italian Semantic Web Workshop - Semantic Web Application and Perspectives (SWAP 2007),* pages 192–201, Bari, Italy, 2007.

[29] R. Lempel and S. Moran. SALSA: the stochastic approach for link-structure analysis. *ACM Transactions on Information Systems,* **19**(2):131–160, 2001.

[30] K. Lerman. Social information processing in news aggregation. *IEEE Internet Computing,* **11**(6):16–28, 2007.

[31] R. Li, S. Bao, Y. Yu, B. Fei, and Z. Su. Towards effective browsing of large scale social annotations. In Proc. *of the International Conference on World Wide Web (WWW '07),* pages 943–952, Banff, Alberta, Canada, 2007. ACM Press.

[32] P. Mika. Ontologies are us: A unified model of social networks and semantics. Web Semantics: Science, *Services and Agents on the World Wide Web,* **5**(1):5–15, 2007.

[33] D.R. Millen, J. Feinberg, and B. Kerr. Dogear: Social bookmarking in the enterprise. In *Proc. of the International Conference on Human Factors in computing systems* (CHI '06), pages 111–120, Montreal, Quebec, Canada, 2006. ACM Press.

[34] A.G.Miller. WordNet: *A lexical database for English. Communications of the ACM*, **38**(11):39–41, 1995.

[35] S. Raghavan and H. Garcia-Molina. Representing Web Graphs. In *Proc. of International Conference on Data Engineering (ICDE 2003),* pages 405–416, Bangalore, India, 2003. IEEE Computer Society.

[36] M.J. Rattigan, M. Maier, and D. Jensen. Using structure indices for efficient approximation of network properties. In *Proc. of the ACM SIGKDD International Conference on Knowledge Discovery and Data Mining (KDD '06),* pages 357–366, Philadelphia, PA, USA, 2006. ACM.

[37] C. Schmitz, A. Hotho, R. Jaschke, and G. Stumme. Mining Association Rules in Folksonomies. In *Proc. of the International Conference on Data Science and Classification (IFCS 2006),* pages 261–270, Ljubljana, Slovenia. Springer.

[38] P. Schmitz. Inducing ontology from Flickr tags. In *Proc. of the Collaborative Web Tagging Workshop,* Edinburgh, Scotland, UK, 2006.

[39] N. Shadbolt, T. Berners-Lee, and W. Hall. The Semantic Web Revisited. IEEE Intelligent Systems, 21(3):96–101, 2006.

[40] L. Specia and E. Motta. Integrating Folksonomies with the Semantic Web. In *Proc. of the European Semantic Web Conference (ESWC 2007)*, pages 624–639, Innsbruck, Austria, 2007. Springer, Lecture Notes in Computer Science.

[41] C. van Damme, M. Hepp, and K. Siorpaes. FolksOntology: An Integrated Approach for Turning Folksonomies into Ontologies. In *Proc. of the International Workshop on Bridging the Gap between Semantic Web and Web 2.0,* pages 57–70, Innsbruck, Austria, 2007.

[42] X. Wu, L. Zhang, and Y. Yu. Exploring social annotations for the Semantic Web. In *Proc. of the International Conference on World Wide Web (WWW '06),* pages 417–426, Edinburgh, Scotland, UK, 2006. ACM.

[43] C.A. Yeung, N. Gibbins, and N. Shadbolt. Tag meaning disambiguation through analysis of tripartite structure of folksonomies. In *Proc. of the International Conference on Web Intelligence and International Conference on Intelligent Agent Technology - Workshops (WI-IAT 2007 Workshops),* pages 3–6, Silicon Valley, California, USA, 2007. IEEE Press.

In: Data Management in the Semantic Web
Editor: Hal Jin, pp. 253-275
ISBN: 978-1-61122-862-5

Chapter 11

DATA MANAGEMENT IN SENSOR NETWORKS USING SEMANTIC WEB TECHNOLOGIES

Anastasios Zafeiropoulos*[1], *Dimitrios-Emmanuel Spanos*, *Stamatios Arkoulis*, *Nikolaos Konstantinou and Nikolas Mitrou
National Technical University of Athens, Zografou, Athens, Greece

Abstract

The increasing availability of small-size sensor devices during the last few years and the large amount of data that they generate has led to the necessity for more efficient methods regarding data management. In this chapter, we review the techniques that are being used for data gathering and information management in sensor networks and the advantages that are provided through the proliferation of Semantic Web technologies. We present the current trends in the field of data management in sensor networks and propose a three-layer flexible architecture which intends to help developers as well as end users to take advantage of the full potential that modern sensor networks can offer. This architecture deals with issues regarding data aggregation, data enrichment and finally, data management and querying using Semantic Web technologies. Semantics are used in order to extract meaningful information from the sensor's raw data and thus facilitate smart applications development over large-scale sensor networks.

1. Introduction

Sensor networks have attracted a lot of attention lately and have been increasingly adopted in a wide range of applications and diverse environments, from healthcare and traffic management to weather forecasting and satellite imaging. A vast amount of small, inexpensive, energy-efficient, and reliable sensors with wireless networking capabilities is available worldwide increasing the number of sensor network deployments [6]. Advanced networking capabilities enable transmission of sensory data through their connection to the Internet or to specific gateways and provide remote access for management and configuration

[1] E-mail address: tzafeir@cn.ntua.gr, Phone: +302107722425

issues. The adoption of IPv6 also provides a huge address space for networking purposes in order to address the large sensor networks on a global scale while concurrently leads to the rapid development of many useful applications. Thus, it is not unreasonable to expect that in the near future, many segments of the networking world will be covered with sensor networks accessible via the Internet. Archived and real time sensor data will be available worldwide, accessible using standard protocols and application programming interfaces (APIs).

Nevertheless, as stated in [1], too much attention has been placed on the networking of distributed sensing while too little on tools to manage, analyze, and understand the collected data. In order to be able to exploit the data collected from the sensor network deployments, to map it to a suitable representation scheme, to extract meaningful information (e.g. events) from it and to increase interoperability and efficient cooperation among sensor nodes, we have to devise and apply appropriate techniques of data management. Towards this direction, data aggregation and processing have to be done in a way that renders it valuable to applications that receive stored or real time input and undertake specific actions. It is important to note that, special characteristics of sensor nodes, such as their resource constraints (low battery power, limited signal processing, limited computation and communication capabilities as well as small amount of memory) have to be considered while designing data management schemes.

Sensory data has to be collected and stored before being aggregated. Various techniques for data aggregation have been proposed in accordance with the type of the network and the imposed requirements [2] [3] [4]. However, aggregated data is raw data that has little meaning by itself. Hence, it is crucial to interpret it according to information that is relevant to the deployed applications. This will increase interoperability among different types of sensors as well as provide contextual information essential for situational knowledge in the sensor network. Moreover, appropriate methods of data processing can be proven helpful, especially in cases where data from many heterogeneous sources need to be compared and/or combined and different events have to be correlated. Towards this direction, the Open Geospatial Consortium (OGC) recently established the Sensor Web Enablement (SWE) initiative to address this aim by developing a suite of sensor related specifications, data models and Web services that will enable accessibility to and controllability of such data and services via the Web. The Sensor Web is a special type of Web-centric information infrastructure for collecting, modeling, storing, retrieving, sharing, manipulating, analyzing, and visualizing information about sensors and sensor observations of phenomena.

A promising technology that is able to address the technical challenges of extracting meaningful events and enabling interoperability among data from different sources, is the Semantic Web. The contribution of the Semantic Web is the semantic-level content annotation. Content existing either on the Web or in restricted access repositories should be annotated in order to become retrievable. This purpose is served by a number of prevalent Semantic Web technologies like content description languages, query languages and annotation frameworks. Semantic annotation in the form of metadata can be added to any form of context, in order to add well-defined semantics that will ease its use and the use of domain specific ontologies could enhance the use of knowledge extracted from the available information as well as add relationships between context data and application defined rules. In other words, Semantic Web can connect the sensory data to the features of their environment.

Taking into account the aforementioned considerations, in this chapter we present the basic characteristics of sensor networks and analyze in detail the problem of gathering, processing and intelligently exploiting real-time or stored streams of data produced by mostly heterogeneous sources of sensor nodes. Special emphasis has been given on the aspects of sensory data description, data transformation into meaningful information as well Semantic Web aided data processing that enables high level information extraction and sharing among different applications. Furthermore, we introduce a layered architecture that unifies the majority of the proposed approaches in the sensor data management research area and suggests a more straightforward recommendation for a complete solution for efficient data management in sensor networks.

2. Sensor Networks

2.1. Sensor Nodes: Functionality and Characteristics

A sensor node, also known as "mote", was an idea introduced by the Smart Dust project [46] in early 00's (2001). Smart Dust was a promising research project that first studied and supported the design of autonomous sensing and communication micro-computing devices of size as small as a cubic millimeter (or the size of a "dust particle"). In other words, this project acted as the cornerstone for the development of today's wireless sensor networks.

The key functionality of a modern sensor node, in addition to sensory data gathering, is the partial processing and transmission of the collected data to the neighbouring nodes or to some central facility. A modern node could be considered as a microscopic computer embedding all the units required for sensing, processing, communicating and storing sensory information, as well as power supply units able to support such operations. The most important units that are present in a sensor node are the following [48]:

- *the Processing Unit*, that is responsible not only for processing the collected data, but also for orchestrating the cooperation and synchronization of all other mote's units towards realizing the promised functionality. Its operation is most often supported by on-chip memory modules.
- *the Communication Unit*, also known as transceiver, that enables motes to communicate with each other for disseminating the gathered sensory data and aggregating them in the sink nodes (nodes with usually higher hardware specifications than simple sensor nodes). The two most popular technologies considered here are either the Radio Frequency (RF) one, where the unlicensed industrial, scientific and medical (ISM) spectrum band is worldwide and freely usable by anyone, or the Optical or Infrared (IR) one, where line-of-sight between communicating nodes is highly required – making communication extremely sensitive to the atmospheric conditions.
- *the Power Supply Unit*, that provides power for the operation of such tiny devices. A typical power source does not exceed the 0.5Ah under a voltage of 1.2V and is most commonly a battery or a capacitor. While operations like data sensing and processing consume some power, the communication between neighbouring nodes is proved to

be the most energy-consuming task (by a factor of 1000, as compared to the power consumed for taking a sample or performing a trivial aggregation operation [3]).

- *the Sensor Unit*, that is responsible for sensing the environment and measuring physical data. Sensors are sensitive electronic circuits turning the analog sensed signals into digital ones by using Analog-to-Digital converters. There is a large variety of sensors available today with the most popular of them being able to sense sounds, light, speed, acceleration, distance, position, angle, pressure, temperature, proximity, electric or magnetic fields, chemicals, and even weather-related signals. Such units must be able to provide the accuracy the supported application demands, while consuming the lowest possible energy.

Modern sensor nodes are required to be inexpensive, multifunctional, cooperative, microscopic, as well as able to cope efficiently with low power supplies and computational capacity. Consequently, contradictory issues are introduced regarding both motes' design and operation, with the most important of all being their limited lifetime, tightly related to their limited power resources, given that power supplies' replenishment, storing and harvesting is not a trivial issue until now. This is due to the fact that sometimes it is either extremely difficult, expensive, or even impossible to replenish motes' power supplies. This phenomenon is mainly due to the common practice followed today – in the case of terrestrial deployments – where sensor nodes are thrown randomly in mass, instead of being placed one by one in the sensor field according to special planning or engineering. Despite the fact that such an approach results in both pushing down the installation costs and increasing the overall deployment's flexibility, it leads most of the times to situations where the deployed sensors are hardly reachable, or even unreachable. As a result, redeploying a new sensor in a given area is rather preferable – in terms of cost, feasibility and provided effort – to getting in proximity with already deployed sensor nodes in order to replenish or fix them. Last but not least, a similar statement holds for the sensor nodes deployed either underwater or underground. The solution here would be to enable sensor nodes storing as much power as possible. However, their limited size does not allow for the use of large and heavy battery cells, while the use of cutting edge technology would violate their low manufacturing cost requirement. Alternatives such as harvesting power resources by exploiting solar energy, fuel cells or vibration are very popular today, but not so widely used yet in current deployments.

2.2. Sensor Networks Topologies

When a number of sensor nodes is clustered together, a special type of autonomic and power efficient network is formed, a so-called Wireless Sensor Network (WSN). WSNs are mainly consisting of the Sensor Nodes, the Sink Nodes that aggregate the measured data from a number of Sensor Nodes and the Gateway Nodes that interconnect the Sink Nodes with the network infrastructure (e.g. Internet) and route the traffic to proper destinations. There are cases where the Sink Nodes have embedded network interfaces for data forwarding and thus coincide with the Gateway Nodes. Regarding the topology of the sensor network, it may form either a single-hop network where each Sensor Node sends directly the data to the Sink Node through a star topology, or a multi-hop network where each Sensor Node relies on its neighbours to forward its sensory data to the respective Sink Node. Multi-hop networks may form a mesh, a serial or a tree topology, as it is shown in Figure 1. It is important to note that in most cases, the sensor nodes do not present mobility functionality.

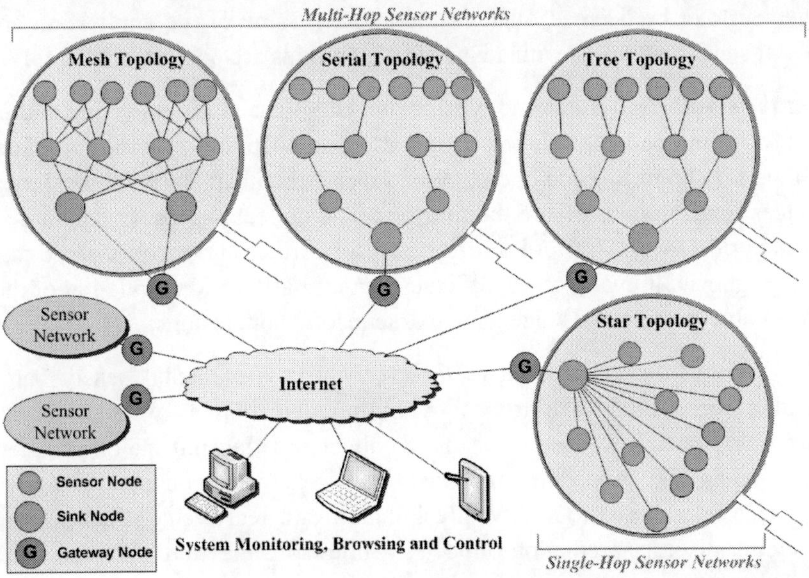

Figure 1. Sensor Network Topology.

Sensor networks carry several characteristics that make them unique. First of all, a sensor network's main objective is diametrically opposed to those of the traditional communication networks. The main concern and goal of sensor networks is their lifetime maximization instead of the provision of Quality of Service (QoS), a goal directly translatable into the need their overall power consumption minimization during operation. However, this is not always the case, since there are also sensor networks consisting of multimedia sensor nodes – able to cope with multimedia content (video, audio, and imaging) – where terms like QoS provisioning, high bandwidth demand, and small delay are more crucial than the power efficiency itself [47]. Furthermore, sensor networks must be fault tolerant, a term closely related to the required autonomicity of every single sensor node, since their underlying topologies are highly volatile and dynamic, as nodes continuously join or leave the network. New nodes may either be redeployed at a specific area to support the operation of an existing sensor network or have just overcome a critical problem that was obstructing their normal operation (e.g., environmental interference). As already mentioned before, a node's lifetime is proportional to its power supplies. When the latter drain out, the node becomes automatically inactive. Since such failures are very common in sensor networks, their overall operation should not be affected by them in any case. Thus, autonomic functionalities (self-healing, self-configuration, self-optimization, self-protection) should be developed in a sensor node. Fortunately, such techniques are fully supported by modern sensor networks, where millions of sensor nodes are deployed in extremely dense topologies; these techniques provide nodes with enough alternatives regarding their potential neighbors, cooperators, and routing paths. In such dense deployments, shorter communication distances have to be covered during the exchange of sensory data between Nodes/Gateways, thus leading to larger power savings during such an energy-consuming operation.

2.3. Application Areas

Sensor networks have been adopted in a wide set of scenarios and applications where proper data management can be deemed of high importance. Some of the application areas where deployments of sensor networks with advanced capabilities are popular are the following:

- *Health Monitoring*: Biometric sensors are usually used for collecting and monitoring data regarding patients, administrating issues in hospitals, provision of patient care as well as for supporting the operation of special chemical and biological measurement devices (e.g. blood pressure monitoring). The collected sensory data are also stored for historical reasons in order to be used for further survey on disease management and prognosis. In many cases, efficient representation and correlation of the acquired data enable doctors and students to extract useful conclusions.
- *Meteorology and Environment Observation*: Environmental sensors are used for weather forecasting, wildfire and pollution detection as well as for agricultural purposes. Special observation stations collect and transmit major parameters which are used in the procedure of decision making. For example, in agriculture, air temperature, relative humidity, precipitation and leaf wetness data are needed for applying disease prediction models, while soil moisture is crucial for proper irrigation decisions towards understanding the progress of water into the soil and the roots.
- *Industrial applications*: Different kind of sensors are deployed for serving industries including aerospace, construction, food processing, environmental & automotive. Applications are being developed for tracking of products and vehicles in transportation companies, satellite imaging, traffic management, monitoring the health of large structures such as office buildings and several other industry-specific fields.
- *Smart Homes*: Home automation applications are being developed in order to support intelligent artifacts and make the users' life more comfortable. Special sensors are attached to home appliances while the created sensor network can be managed or monitored by remote servers accessible via the Internet (e.g. user's office, police office and hospital etc). Sensor networks also play a significant role on facilitating assisted living for the elderly or persons in need of special care.
- *Defense (Military, Homeland Security)*: Sensors are also used for military purposes in order to detect and gain as much information as possible about enemy movements, explosions, and other phenomena of interest. Battlefield surveillance, reconnaissance (or scouting) of opposing forces, battle damage assessment and targeting are some of the fields where large sensor networks have been already deployed.

2.4. Sensor Web: Data and Services in a Sensor Network

The term Sensor Web is used by the Open Geospatial Consortium (OGC) for the description of a system that is comprised of diverse, location aware sensing devices that report data through the Web. In a Sensor Web, entire networks can be seen as single interconnected nodes that communicate via the Internet and can be controlled and accessed through a web interface. Sensor Web focuses on the sharing of information among nodes, their proper interpretation and their cooperation as a whole, in order to sense and respond to changes of their environment and extract knowledge. Hence, one could say that the process of managing the available data is not just a secondary process simply enhancing the functionality of a Sensor Web, but rather the reason of existence of the latter. According to [3], data management can be defined as the task of collecting data from sensors (sink or gateway nodes), storing data in the network, and efficiently delivering data to the end users.

One of the most appealing and popular approaches in sensor data management is to regard the sensor network as a distributed database system. Data management on distributed database environments is a far more mature research field than the rapidly evolving sensor networking field, thus it sounds tempting to use the experience gained in the former in order to deal with open issues in the latter. However, this parallelism that regards sensor nodes as databases, is obviously, not entirely realistic, since a sensor node does not have the computational capabilities or the energy sufficiency that a database management system (DBMS) has. In other words, the technological constraints, mentioned in the previous section, should be taken into account towards devising efficient data management methods. Frequent failures of sensor nodes, unreliable radio communication and tradeoff between low energy consumption and network efficiency have to be considered when designing redundant and robust data management approaches, ensuring the proper functionality of a sensor network. Furthermore, the usually large number of sensor nodes in a Sensor Web system creates the demand for scalable solutions of data management and thus promotes local, asynchronous approaches that use short-range transmissions among the interconnected nodes. Thus, although data management in sensor networks borrows heavily from research on distributed databases, extra constraints are imposed due to innate characteristics of sensor nodes.

Primarily, the acquired data have to be stored taking into account methods for low energy consumption. Data storage can be either external (all data are collected on a central infrastructure), local (every node stores its data locally) or data-centric (a certain category of data is stored to a predefined node). External storage is not considered as a viable solution, because of the high energy cost of data transmission from each sensor node to the central infrastructure. Local storage overcomes this drawback, since every node stores only self-generated data. The option of local storage is also referred to as Data-Centric Routing (DCR), where a routing algorithm is needed in order to answer a query or to perform an aggregation, focusing on minimizing the cost of communication between sensor nodes. In early examples of DCR [19, 20], queries are flooded throughout the entire network and on the same time, a routing tree is built. Then, data from the individual sensor nodes or aggregated data are returned, following the query tree path to the node that initiated the query or the request. This procedure is repeated for every different query and therefore, is efficient only for queries that are executed on a continuous basis, e.g. query tracking or repeated computation of aggregates for some sensors. The third option of following a data storage policy is the most recent one, known in the literature as Data-Centric Storage (DCS). In this approach, data and events with common properties or the same attribute (e.g. temperature readings) are stored to specific nodes, regardless of where the data has been generated. Example methods include DIM [21] and GHT [22], which, by using distributed data structures (an index and a hash table respectively) avoid query flooding, and instead, direct the query to the node that is delegated to store the relevant data. It is obvious that the choice of data storage strategy affects the way that queries are answered, the data flow among sensor nodes and the ability of the Sensor Web to answer questions regarding both historical and present data.

Another aspect of data management is data aggregation, a common operation in sensor networks regardless of the deployment scenario. Data aggregation can be defined as the collection of data originating from a number of distributed sensor nodes to a sink node, offering the advantage of less data being transferred across the network. Sometimes, in a sensor network, there are two or more proximate sensors that measure the same phenomenon; in this case, an aggregated view (e.g. the mean value) of these sensors' observations is equally or even more desirable than the individual readings, due to the possible redundancy of the measurements. Thus, it becomes clear that there are at least two issues to be taken into account: a) the selection of the sink nodes, based on their computational capabilities (unless the final processing takes place in a centralized server in the network) and b) the selection of the most power-efficient strategy to be followed for the aggregation procedure. Of course, these two issues are correlated and the selection of the so-called "leader" node should not ignore the goal of minimum energy consumption. There are several criteria that could be used for the election of the leader node; for example, the leader node could be the node with the greatest remaining energy supply or the node that will minimize the exchange of messages across the network based on its topology. Furthermore, more sophisticated election algorithms could be devised [24].

Computational procedures usually need to be performed on the aggregated data. Two alternative strategies have been widely used for computational issues. In the more simplistic centralized approach, all the nodes send their data to the central node, while in the distributed approach, every node performs a part of the total processing and passes on to the neighbouring nodes the result of this partial computation along the path of a routing tree built for this purpose. In the distributed approach, each sensor node must have computational capabilities in order to be able to process the available data. Synchronization issues arise as well, since nodes have to know if they are expecting any data from their children in the routing tree in order to pass on the partial result to their parent. In most cases, the sensor node is not aware if there is a big communication delay with another node or if an existing link is broken. Hence, the problem here is how long the parent node has to wait: either a fixed time interval [23] or until it receives a notification from all of its children that have not sent any data yet [24]. Data aggregation methods are being evaluated on the basis of accuracy (the difference between the aggregated value that reaches the sink and the actual value), completeness (the percentage of readings included in the aggregation computation), latency and the message overhead that they introduce.

Data management includes also delivery of data generated by sensor nodes to the users that request it. Query answering is tightly connected to data storage and aggregation, which we have already analyzed. In fact, data aggregation can be considered as a special case of query answering, since aggregation queries are simply one case of possible queries that a user may submit to the sensor network. Other kinds of queries are one-shot queries, asking for a value of a specific sensor at a specific time, event-based queries, triggered by an event defined in the query and lifetime-based queries, specified to run for a larger time period. Of course, the goal here is the same: execute queries with as little energy consumption as possible. Depending on the type of query issued and the type of sensor, sampling rate can be adjusted accordingly in order to save energy. For example, in the case of PIR (Passive

InfraRed) motion detectors, sensor data become quickly outdated, and therefore, in a monitoring scenario, the query retrieving these sensors' values has to be executed frequently. On the contrary, temperature or other environmental variables exhibit small variance and approximate results are satisfactory, allowing for caching previous results and lowering the query update rate. Efforts have been made to reduce energy consumption in all stages of query answering: query optimization, dissemination and execution [23]. However, there is a tradeoff between energy-efficient and complete query answering schemes; in other words, the more energy-saving a query answering approach is, the less correct and accurate the answer will be. Typically, the process of query answering is based on the formulation of a routing tree, along which the query is first disseminated and then data is returned, following the opposite direction. From this point on, approaches vary: some simply choose the most energy-efficient query plan, based on the form of the query and the topology of the network [25], some apply extensively in-network aggregation constructing appropriate routing trees [26], while others modify accordingly the sampling rate of the sensors [23].

Another feature of sensor networks that poses further challenges to query answering is the fact that, unlike database management systems that follow a pull-based model for data dissemination, sensor networks usually follow a push-based model, where new data is constantly generated and may trigger event-based queries. This differs radically from the usual scenario of a user (or a node) submitting a query and having the answer returned to him. In this case, when streams of data (readings) are being pushed in the Sensor Web, continuous queries must react to this data and then, answers are submitted to the interested user. Several architectures have been proposed in order to deal with push-based data stream processing, such as Aurora [27], TelegraphCQ [28] and Borealis [29].

So far, we have assumed that nodes in a Sensor Web are stationary and the main challenge is to keep the energy consumption as low as possible. But, there are cases where sensor nodes are mobile and thus pose further challenges to data management. For instance, the external data storage is not an option for mobile sensor networks, since mobile nodes may not always be able to access the sink node, making in-network storage the only choice. Similarly, approaches for data aggregation and query answering must be adaptive because of the constantly changing topology.

All of the previously mentioned issues have emerged due to the inherent restrictions of sensor networks. However, with the introduction of the Sensor Web notion, challenges and demands increase. Further interoperability and flexibility play central roles in the Sensor Web vision, since different kinds of sensors must be linked and communicate with each other, while at the same time it should be easy for new sensors to be added in an existing Sensor Web. For this purpose, the Open Geospatial Consortium (OGC) has developed and maintains, in the context of its Sensor Web Enablement (SWE) initiative [7], a series of standards. These standards include, on one hand, markup languages defining a vocabulary for the common understanding and encoding of observations, measurements, sensor processes and properties, such as Observations & Measurements Schema (O&M), Sensor Model Language (SensorML) and Transducer Markup Language (TransducerML) and on the other hand, web service interfaces for the request and retrieval of sensor measurements, acquisition of measurements planning and subscription to event alerts, such as Sensor Observations Service (SOS), Sensor Planning Service (SPS), Sensor Alert Service (SAS) and Web Notification Services (WNS). Obviously, to achieve cooperation among different sensor networks, agreement on some common representation scheme must be made; it is believed that OGC standards will play the role of the bond that glues together all of the Sensor Web components.

3. Knowledge Management in Sensor Networks

As stated earlier, the rapid development and deployment of sensor technology involves many different types of sensors, both remote and in-situ, with diverse capabilities. However, the lack of integration and communication between the deployed sensor networks often isolates important data streams and intensifies the existing problem of too much data and not enough knowledge. The absence of ontological infrastructures for high-level rules and queries restricts the potential of end users to exploit the acquired information, to match events from different sources and to deploy smart applications which will be capable of following semantic-oriented rules.

Current efforts at the OGC Sensor Web Enablement (SWE) aim at providing interoperability at the service interface and message encoding levels. Sensor Web Enablement presents many opportunities for adding a real-time sensor dimension to the Internet and the Web. It is focused on developing standards to enable the discovery, exchange, and processing of sensor observations. The functionality that OGC aims to supply a Sensor Web with, includes discovery of sensor systems, determination of a sensor's capabilities and quality of measurements, access to sensor parameters that automatically allow software to process and geo-locate observations, retrieval of real-time or time-series observations, tasking of sensors to acquire observations of interest and subscription to and publishing of alerts to be issued by sensors or sensor services based upon certain criteria [7].

However, these Sensor Web Enablement functionalities are not enough, when it comes to real-life applications, where requirements are extended beyond simple "readings-retrieval" queries. In such cases, the need for well-defined semantics that will enhance the sensors by providing situation awareness is evident. Technologies and standards issued by the World Wide Web Consortium (W3C) will be used in this context to implement the Semantic Sensor Web (SSW) vision [8], an extension of the Sensor Web, where sensor nodes will be able to discover their respective capabilities and exchange and process data automatically without human intervention. Components playing a key role in Semantic Sensor Web are ontologies, semantic annotation, query languages and rule languages.

Ontologies are formal representations of a domain that can serve as dictionaries containing the definitions of all concepts (phenomena, temporal and spatial concepts) used throughout the Sensor Web. Semantic annotation languages, such as Resource Description Framework - in - attributes (RDFa), do just what their name suggests: they enrich existing content with semantic information. Since Sensor Web Enablement standards are XML-based, RDFa can be used for annotating sensors' measurements and observations. Then, standard reasoning services can be applied to produce inferences on existing facts and spawn new knowledge. Rules can be defined using SWRL (Semantic Web Rule Language) and additional knowledge can be extracted by applying rule-based reasoning. Moreover, complex queries written in SPARQL Query Language for RDF - a W3C recommendation (or equivalently, a standard for the Web) - can be submitted to the Sensor Web for meaningful knowledge extraction and not just for simple retrieval of sensor readings. The previously mentioned Semantic Web technologies are the most prominent ones, but there are several others as well that could be proven useful in the context of Semantic Sensor Web. The application of these technologies will transform the Sensor Web Enablement service standards to Semantic Web Service interfaces, enabling sensor nodes to act as autonomous agents being able to discover neighbouring nodes and communicate with each other.

3.1. Current Approaches

In this section we present the state of the art in the field of knowledge management in sensor networks. Many approaches are available today for managing sensor networks, regarding especially the aggregation and processing of data, and several architectures have been proposed that provide services to the end user through the exploitation of the collected data. Existing approaches combine data from sensors in order to carry out high-level tasks and offer to the end user a unified view of the underlying sensor network. They usually provide a software infrastructure that permits users to query globally distributed collections of high bitrate sensors' data powerfully and efficiently. Following this approach, the SWAP framework [11] proposes a three tier architecture comprising a sensor, a knowledge and a decision layer, each one of them consisting of a number of agents. Special care is taken for the semantic description of the services available to the end user, allowing the composition of new applications. In the same direction, IrisNet [10] envisions a worldwide sensor web, in which users can query, as a single unit, vast quantities of data from thousands or even millions of widely distributed, heterogeneous sources. This is achieved through a network of agents, responsible for the collection and storage organization of sensor measurements. Data are stored in XML format and XPath is used as the mean to answer user queries.

Recently proposed approaches go one step further and apply Semantic Web technologies on top of a sensor network in order to support the services provided in the existing and the newly deployed sensor networks. These technologies allow the sensor data to be understood and processed in a meaningful way by a variety of applications with different purposes. Ontologies are used for the definition and the description of the semantics of the sensor data. Such an approach is the ES3N architecture [9] that develops an ontology-based storage mechanism for sensor observations that let the end user of the system to post semantic queries. This is accomplished through the use of an RDF repository containing daily records of all sensor measurements. Then, rudimentary SPARQL queries are posed in order to extract a specific observation. Another proposed architecture that exploits Semantic Web technologies is the SWASN architecture [17] where mechanisms for context aware processing of sensor data in pervasive communications scenarios are defined and the Jena API is used for sensor data processing to query sensor data and extract meaningful information through inference. Finally, Priamos [12] is a middleware architecture for automated, real-time, unsupervised annotation of low-level context features and their mapping to high-level semantics. It enables the composition of simple rules through specific interfaces, which may launch a context aware system that will annotate content without the need for user technical expertise.

Going one step further, Semantic Sensor Web (SSW) is proposed as a framework for providing enhanced meaning for sensor observations so as to enable situation awareness [8]. This is accomplished through the addition of semantic annotations to existing standard sensor languages of the Sensor Web Enablement. These annotations provide more meaningful descriptions and enhanced access to sensor data in comparison with the Sensor Web Enablement alone, and they act as a linking mechanism to bridge the gap between the primarily syntactic XML-based metadata standards of the Sensor Web Enablement and the RDF/OWL-based vocabularies driving the Semantic Web.

As we have described earlier, the semantic representation of sensory data is significant because ontologies specify the important concepts in a domain of interest and their relationships, thus formalizing knowledge about the specific domain. In association with semantic annotation, ontologies and rules play an important role in the Semantic Sensor Web vision for interoperability, analysis, and reasoning over heterogeneous multimodal sensor data. Several ontologies for describing entities and relationships in sensor networks have already been designed. A universal ontology is designed for describing concepts and relationships of the sensor network units and data [13]. The source for collecting commonly used terms in sensor domain and the taxonomic class diagram that forms the foundation of the ontology was the IEEE 1451.4 smart transducers template description language [18]. In a more practical approach, the development of comprehensive sensor ontologies is based upon deep knowledge models rather than capturing only superficial sensor attributes [14]. Thus, the OntoSensor ontology has been proposed, providing formal definitions of the concepts and relations in sensor networks, being influenced from SensorML and extending concepts from the IEEE SUMO ontology [13]. It presents a practical approach to building a sensor knowledge repository aiming to serve as a component in comprehensive applications that include advanced inference mechanisms, which can be used for synergistic fusion of heterogeneous data. Furthermore, there are some service-oriented approaches that describe sensor ontologies which enable service-oriented services in future ubiquitous computing [15]. The main sources for collecting commonly used terms in the service domain are the Geography Markup Language (GML), SensorML, SUMO and OntoSensor.

Finally, it is important to note that environmental sensor data captured by an ontology can be combined with a rule-based system that can reason over the ontology instances creating alarm-type of objects if certain conditions are met [16]. The rules are fired based on data obtained from sensors in real-time and classified as instances of fundamental ontologies. The rule-based system is used as an advisor in the complex process of decision making, applying corrective measures when needed. The decision combines the real-time data with a-priori sensor data stored in various warehouses. The platform controls also the whole environment in order to make the user aware of any glitches in the functionality of the whole system.

3.2. A Unifying Generic Architecture for Sensor Data Management

However varied and divergent some of the above approaches might seem, they share enough common traits allowing us to propose, in this section, a generic scheme for efficient sensor data management, combining as many desirable features and interesting aspects as possible. This generic scheme is applicable to a wide range of different categories of sensor networks and deployed applications. After completing a review of the already deployed systems, we can infer that the downside of the majority of the proposed approaches are the limitations regarding the size of the sensor network, the amount of data transferred, the support of distributive sensor deployments and the lack of semantic data representation. It is questionable whether these approaches will scale with the mass increase in the deployment of heterogeneous sensor networks and the abilities for remote communication and management of the sensor resources. The limited presence of semantic context annotation and ontological descriptions for high-level rules and queries restricts the potential of end users to exploit the acquired information.

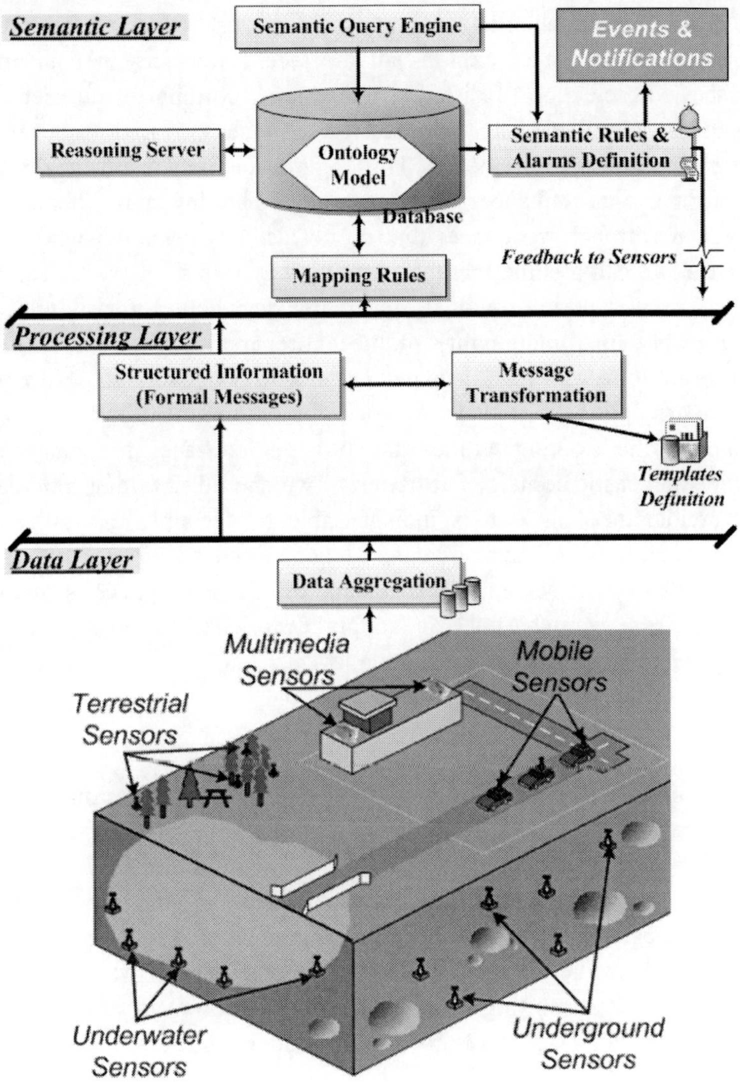

Figure 2. Abstract Overall Architecture.

The architecture we describe tries to tackle with these issues and provide a flexible and modular scheme for easily deploying and managing large scale sensor networks, consisting of heterogeneous data sources. It consists of three layers (see Figure 2): the Data Layer for data discovery, collection and aggregation, the Processing Layer for integration and processing of the aggregated data and the Semantic Layer for the addition of context annotation and ontological descriptions. The advantage of such a scheme is the fact that each layer can be considered independent from the others and consequently, layer-specific decisions about the implementation and strategies followed in one layer do not affect other layers. This allows for harvesting and reusing previous work on traditional data management in sensor networks, where the emphasis has been given on dealing with the limited energy restriction.

In more detail, in the Data Layer, this architecture does not reject past data management techniques, but builds on the most successful ones. Different topologies and data aggregation techniques are supported, providing flexibility to administrators to select the most suitable topology and aggregation scheme for optimizing energy consumption and bandwidth utilization. The Processing Layer exploits all the recent advances in data processing and provides interfaces for selection of different templates according to the user needs and the transformation to new templates when required (e.g. new sensors are introduced in the sensor network that provide extra measurements). Thus, aggregated data is always represented in the most suitable format that enhances their meaning. The layered scheme we introduce incorporates even traditional approaches that do not use any semantics and are not context aware; in this case, we can assume that the Semantic Layer is simply omitted. The existence of the Semantic Layer is purely optional, depending on whether the addition of semantics improves considerably the functionality of the entire application or not. But, the use of Semantic Web technologies for data management in sensor networks gives to developers the opportunity to create applications that can sense the environment and deploy, identify the relationships among the existing entities and provide interfaces for enhanced query and reasoning within the sensor domain. Furthermore, we should note that modularity is a key aspect of this architecture, since it is indispensable to decouple the collection from the processing and semantic enrichment of data. Hence, when trying to build a sensor-based application that will exploit semantic web technologies, an engineer is not compelled to design everything from scratch, but can simply deal with the construction of efficient algorithms and implementation details in the top layers.

3.2.1. Data Layer

This layer handles raw sensor data discovery, collection and aggregation in a central entity. Efficient data aggregation is crucial for reducing communication cost, thereby extending the lifetime of sensor networks. As we have described in Section 2.2 different kinds of topology may be present in a sensor network. Based on the topology of the network, the location of sources and the aggregation function, an optimal aggregation structure can be constructed. Optimal aggregation can be defined in terms of total energy consumption, bandwidth utilization and delay for transporting the collected information from simple nodes to the sink nodes. Data gathering can be realized following structured or structure-free approaches [2]:

- Structured approaches are suited for data gathering applications where the sensor nodes are following a specific strategy for forwarding the data to the sink nodes. Due to the unchanging traffic pattern, structured aggregation techniques incur low maintenance overhead and are therefore suited for such applications. But, in case of dynamic environments, the overhead of construction and maintenance of the structure may outweigh the benefits of data aggregation. Furthermore, structured approaches are sensitive to the delay imposed from the intermediate nodes, the frequency of the data transmission and the size of the sensor network. The central entity is responsible for the discovery of new nodes and the specification of the data acquisition policy. The data acquisition can be event-based where data are sent from the source and a method is called to collect them (serial ports, wireless cameras) or polling based where the central node periodically queries the data from the managed sensors.

- In structure-free approaches, there is no predefined structure and routing decisions for the efficient aggregation of packets need to be made on-the-fly. As nodes do not explicitly know their upstream nodes, they cannot wait on data from any particular node before forwarding their own data. These approaches can be applied in dynamic environments and in ad-hoc sensor networks where nodes continuously join and leave the network and thus a predefined static routing and aggregation scheme will possibly be unsuitable.

In addition to raw data aggregation, security awareness is an important aspect that is considered due to the reason that sensor networks often store, process and interact with sensitive data in hostile and unattended environments. Security in sensor networks has attracted the interest of many researchers and, thus, the requirements (data confidentiality / integrity / freshness, availability, self-organization, time synchronization, secure localization, authentication) and the obstacles (inherent resource and computing constraints, unreliable communication, unattended operation) for security have been defined. The current attacks have been carefully classified and the corresponding defensive measures have already been listed in detail [42]. In cases where the location of important sensor-observed aspects must be hidden, anonymity mechanisms [43] have to be implemented in order to ensure the confidentiality of this information. Especially in location sensors, due to the location sensitive nature of the transmitted data, the information should, under no circumstances, be accessed by unauthorized persons.

We must make clear that depending on the type of sensors used and the deployment scenario, the exact routing and aggregation scheme and the trade-off between safety and efficiency have to be taken into account for the optimal solution to be selected.

3.2.2. Processing Layer

Due to the raw nature of sensory data and the fact that it cannot provide us with high-level information extraction, several XML-based models are being used in order to interpret it. This will leverage its usability, allow further processing and finally make it meaningful for the end user. Proper processing is necessary, especially in cases of aggregation of data from many heterogeneous sources and the need for discovery of possible correlations among the aggregated data. Furthermore, the processed data can be distributed to other network devices (e.g. PDAs) without the need for sensor-specific software. Different XML templates can interpret in a different way the sensory data according to the application related view. The aggregated data has to be processed and integrated in a manner that shortens the data exchanging transactions. Integrating the data and transforming it into an XML (possibly a SensorML) format makes it meaningful for the end user.

Initially, the Processing Layer integrates the bulk of the incoming data. It is not necessary neither optimal, in certain cases, to maintain the total amount of data. Consider for instance a sensor network consisting of some dozens of sensors measuring the temperature over a field. While keeping track of the temperature levels is useful, processing every single datum originating from every single sensor is not needed. Such practice would overload the network, augment its maintenance needs and consequently decrease its autonomicity. Moreover, the volume of the archived information would soon require a substantial storage capacity. Aggregated reports (such as the maximum or an average of the values reported) may be sufficient to describe the conditions that are present in the area of interest.

Subsequently, the integrated information collected by the sensors has to be forwarded to the upper Semantic Layer. In order for this to be achieved, the information needs to be encapsulated in messages suitable for further machine processing. For instance, XML-based languages such as OGC's SensorML, Geography Markup Language (GML), Observations and Measurement (O&M) can stand up to the challenge. It is important to note that SensorML is currently encoded in XML Schema, but the models and encoding patterns for SensorML follow Semantic Web concepts of Object-Association-Object. Therefore, SensorML models could easily be transformed to a more "semantic" representation form. Furthermore, SensorML makes extensive use of soft-typing and linking to online dictionaries for definition of parameters and terms.

The process of creating a message with information originating from the observations of the sensor network constitutes a substantial computational burden for conventional sensor nodes, which means that this processing should take place at a central infrastructure, i.e. a server that administers the sensor network. The message templates and their transformation constitute a common agreement on the messages interchanged in the network. The template definition and its corresponding transformation can be thought of as an XML Schema Definition (XSD) and an Extensible Stylesheet Language Transformation (XSLT) in order to produce an XML message. It is needed that the user will have the ability to specify his preferred message templates in order to ensure adaptability to the system's requirements, according to the data that has greater significance for his application. Thus, after the creation of the XML messages, data has to be forwarded to the Semantic Layer.

3.2.3. Semantic Layer

The Semantic Layer abstracts the processed outputs from the heterogeneous, low-level data sources such as sensors and feature extraction algorithms, combined with metadata, thus enabling context capturing in varying conditions. Context annotation is configured through application-specific ontologies and it can be automatically initiated without any further human intervention. It must be noted that the Semantic Layer is not an indispensable part of a sensor network architecture, in the same way that semantics do not need necessarily to be part of systems. However, the benefits provided by a Semantic Layer justify its existence, regardless to the additional computational burden. As we analyze in this section, Semantic Web technologies allow for complex context descriptions, reusable rule definitions, concept satisfiability and consistency, and finally, integration with third-party systems and services. A Semantic Layer can be viewed as consisting of the following modules, as depicted in Figure 2.

Rules: First, the incoming messages must be mapped to ontology concepts. The use of rules is essential in depicting the desired behaviour of context-aware systems. Since the model-theoretic background of the OWL language is based on Description Logics systems that are a subset of the First Order Logic, the designed model has fully defined semantics and, also, Horn clauses can be formed upon it. These clauses can be seen as rules that predefine the desired intelligence in the system's behavior.

In general, two distinct sets of rules can be applied: one containing rules that specify how sensor measurements represented in an XML-based format will be mapped to a selected ontology and another set of rules deriving new facts, actions or alerts based on existing facts and the underlying knowledge represented by the ontology. The first set can be referred to as Mapping Rules and the second one as Semantic Rules. The rules are formed according to the following event-condition-action (ECA [31]) pattern:

on *event* if *condition* then *action*

where the event in a sensor network is a message arrival indicating a new available measurement. Mapping Rules can fetch data from the XML-like message and store it into the ontology model in the form of class individuals. They can be perceived as the necessary step bridging the gap between semi-structured data presented in an XML form and ontological models. Semantic Rules, on the other hand, can perform modifications, when needed, solely on the ontology model. This set of rules depend on the semantics of the specific domain or deployment scenario and involves high-level concepts that are meaningful to humans e.g. "when a certain area under observation is "too hot", open the ventilating system". Of course, the "too hot" conclusion will probably be inferred from a set of current observations coupled with the knowledge stored in the ontology.

Ontology model: Contemporary Semantic Web practices dictate that the ontological model is stored in a relational database in triples (statements of the form Subject, Property, Object) and form the underlying graph of the model. The model can be stored as an RDF graph using one of the various so called triple-store implementations available (3Store [32], Corese [33], Sesame [34], Openlink's Virtuoso [44] to name a few).

In order to guarantee system's scalability, sampling techniques or caching for future processing can be used. For instance, an ontology model that handles the incoming messages, i.e. a temporary ontology model, can be kept in a different database from the persistent ontology model. The tradeoff for this approach is that the reasoning that takes place for every new message is aware of the facts that are stored in the temporary ontology model. Additionally, scheduled maintenance can be responsible for migrating the facts from the temporary ontology to the persistent storage. This scheduled task can take place either synchronously or asynchronously. The former case indicates that the migration can be triggered by an incoming message while the latter that the migration schedule can be running as a background process according to specified time intervals.

We also must note that the use of several Semantic Web vocabularies is desirable and should be encouraged in order to allow unambiguous definitions of the concepts involved in any application. Vocabularies, such as the Dublin Core Metadata Initiative for digital content, DBPedia [45] for reference to Wikipedia's entries, the Friend Of A Friend network or the Creative Commons for licensing purposes, provide the means for effective semantic interoperability between applications.

As far as the ontology content is concerned, we should keep in mind that the ontology should describe the system's context. According to [35], context means situational information and involves any information that can be used to characterize the situation of an entity. An entity can be a person, a place, or an object that is considered relevant to the interaction between a user and a system, including the user and the system themselves. Therefore, specific ontology authoring can be inspired by approaches to describe context, such as the approach presented in [30] where the authors provide a rough categorization of context into four classes: location, time, activity and identity. The choice of an authoring environment is up to the user. According to [37] the most used ontology authoring environments are Protégé, SWOOP and OntoEdit.

Reasoning Server: As stated in [36], a Knowledge Base is the combination of an ontology and a software engine, also known as reasoner, capable of inferring facts from the facts explicitly defined in the ontology (sometimes referred to as axioms). The presence of a reasoner is indispensable, since it is the module that spawns new knowledge. Furthermore, a reasoner inspects an ontology model and can check its consistency, satisfiability and classification of its concepts [38], leading to the existence of a "healthy" and robust context model that does not contain any disaccords among its term definitions.

Reasoning is an important and active field of research, investigating the tradeoff between the expressiveness of ontology definition languages and the computational complexity of the reasoning procedure, as well as the discovery of efficient reasoning algorithms applicable to practical situations. There is a variety of available reasoners, commercial ones like RacerPro or OntoBroker, free of charge like KAON2 [39] and open-source like Pellet [40] and FaCT++ [41], which have different features and performance characteristics according to the application specific needs, e.g. in case of voluminous knowledge bases, a reasoner that scales well to millions of facts should be used. All of these reasoning servers can function stand-alone and communicate via HTTP with the deployed system, leaving the reasoner choice up to the user.

Semantic Queries: The Semantic Layer should also provide the user with a way to ask and derive information from the underlying Knowledge Base, similarly to relational database queries. Hence, an important component of this layer is a semantic query interface that will allow for the creation and execution of intelligent queries, based on the semantics of the stored knowledge, in contrast to the conventional keyword-based queries such as in SQL for relational databases or XQuery for XML. SPARQL, a W3C recommendation since 2007 as a query language for the Semantic Web, is the practical choice for querying RDF graphs and a SPARQL endpoint can essentially serve as the gateway to access the stored knowledge from remote systems.

3.2.4. Use Case Scenario

This section illustrates a scenario where all the previously described features come into play. Arrays of sensors can be placed inside art exhibitions or museums for monitoring purposes. In the current example, we consider a museum where temperature, humidity, light and passive infrared sensors are placed in proximity to each exhibit: paintings, sculptures and other, possibly sensitive in environmental changes, artifacts. These sensors have a fixed known location, forming a static sensor network. Location sensors (such as Bluetooth Tags [49]) are also located in each room and are used for positioning purposes. Such a deployment may exist either in open air or, for the purpose of our example, in an indoor environment.

The collected data is aggregated on several sink nodes connected to specific gateways which forward the measured data to a central repository either on the museum or in a remote site. Then, the aggregated data is processed and mapped to an Observations and Measurement (O&M) template, which optimally encodes sensor observations. Safety intervals are denoted explicitly for every exhibit – in the form of rules – and stored in an ontology that contains additional information about the artifacts and their creators and describes adequately the important entities of the current scenario as well as the relationships among them.

Each exhibit has different properties and different temperature, light and humidity levels are required for its optimal preservation. Specific rules can be defined for triggering the desired alarms, allowing application developers to provide location-aware services in the museum. Museum's personnel can move around the museum with a mobile device, recognize the current position through proper localization and check whether the existing artifacts in this room are under optimal conditions or not. Of course, when sensors deployed near an exhibit report a temperature or humidity value that is outside the respective safety interval, an alarm fires off automatically and an action selected by the system administrator is performed: either a direct notification to the museum personnel or the appropriate notification to the museum's Heating, Ventilating, and Air Conditioning (HVAC) system for automatic temperature, light or humidity adjustment. The reasoning server is responsible to reason over the acquired data towards providing the required information to the administrators.

The combination of sensor readings and the ontology information can be used for precautionary reasons as well. A SPARQL endpoint provides access to the system's ontology and can answer complex questions, such as:

"Return the positions and the names of all the 18th century landscape paintings in this room, created by a Dutch artist, whose temperature, or light or humidity readings are higher than 80% of the maximum allowed values" or

"Return the most suitable room for installation of a new artifact according to its category and its prerequisite conditions"

Furthermore, the passive infrared sensors detect possible motion of the exhibits and thus, can be used for security reasons to inform when someone touches or tries to remove an artifact or enter a banned region near an artifact, and in this case, an appropriate notification is also being sent to the museum personnel. Of course, more scenarios of usage can be thought of, depending on the defined rules and actions residing in the semantic layer of the system. Finally, the already stored data can be used for offline analysis and useful statistics extraction for each area.

4. Conclusions – Open Issues

In this chapter we have presented the available techniques that are being used for data management in sensor networks. Sensor network characteristics, possible topologies, data aggregation and data querying schemes are described in detail. The use of Semantic Web technologies for extracting meaningful events from the aggregated data is investigated. A generic modular architecture for knowledge management in sensor networks that consists of the Data, the Processing and the Semantic Layer is presented. We envision that such an architecture will add flexibility to the sensor world to form associations over the raw data, extract information and valuable results, and create specific management and notification rules, in accordance with the nature of each application. It will also facilitate developers to create new services for the end users and to provide them with context-aware information.

Open issues include a) the energy efficiency trade-off under several routing schemes and data aggregation architectures: selection of the suitable gathering strategy under different topologies can optimize use of resources in the sensing field, b) the proper dissemination of the available information among the sensor nodes: collaborative data processing can minimize the amount of data transferred and information exchange can help sensor nodes improve their self-functionalities (e.g. self-configuration), c) the analysis of mechanisms for the establishment of accurate synchronization: participating nodes will be synchronized either by exchanging messages with other nodes or by communicating with a central entity in order to acquire a common notion of time, d) the implementation of different scenarios combining several aggregation, security and processing methods and the evaluation of the discrete components of the proposed architecture. Special attention also has to be given to the performance of each layer entity depending on the amount and the rate of the received data.

References

[1] M. Balazinska, A. Deshpande, M. J. Franklin, P. B. Gibbons, J. Gray, M. Hansen, M. Liebhold, S. Nath, A. Szalay, V. Tao, Data Management in the Worldwide Sensor Web, *IEEE Pervasive Computing*, **6(2)**, p. 30-40 (2007).

[2] K.W. Fan, S. Liu, P. Sinha, Structure-Free Data Aggregation in Sensor Networks, *IEEE Transactions on Mobile Computing*, **6(8)**, p.929-942 (2007).

[3] V. Cantoni, L. Lombardi, P. Lombardi, Challenges for Data Mining in Distributed Sensor Networks, *18th International Conference on Pattern Recognition (ICPR'06)*, p. 1000-1007 (2006).

[4] P. Sridhar, A.M. Madni, M. Jamshidi, Hierarchical Data Aggregation in Spatially Correlated Distributed Sensor Networks, *World Automation Congress (WAC '06)*, p.1-6 (2006).

[5] K. Romer, F. Mattern, The Design Space of Wireless Sensor Networks, *IEEE Wireless Communications*, **11(6)**, p. 54-61 (2004).

[6] S. Rajeev, A. Ananda, C. M. Choon, O. W. Tsang. Mobile, Wireless, and Sensor Networks - Technology, Applications, and Future Directions, John Wiley and Sons, 2006.

[7] C. Reed, M. Botts, J. Davidson, G. Percivall, OGC® Sensor Web Enablement: Overview and High Level Architecture, *IEEE Autotestcon, 2007*, p.372-380 (2007).

[8] A. Sheth, C. Henson, S. Sahoo, Semantic Sensor Web, *IEEE Internet Computing*, **12(4)**, p.78-83 (2008).

[9] M. Lewis, D. Cameron, S. Xie, B. Arpinar, ES3N: A Semantic Approach to Data Management in Sensor Networks, *Semantic Sensor Networks Workshop (SSN06)* (2006).

[10] P. B. Gibbons, B. Karp, Y. Ke, S. Nath, S. Seshan, Iris-Net: An Architecture for a Worldwide Sensor Web, *IEEE Pervasive Computing*, **2(4)**, p. 22–33 (2003).

[11] D. Moodley, I. Simonis, A New Architecture for the Sensor Web: The SWAP Framework, *Semantic Sensor Networks Workshop (SSN06)* (2006).

[12] N. Konstantinou, E. Solidakis, S. Zoi, A. Zafeiropoulos, P. Stathopoulos, N. Mitrou, Priamos: A Middleware Architecture for Real-Time Semantic Annotation of Context Features, *3rd IET International Conference on Intelligent Environments (IE'07)* (2007).

[13] M. Eid, R. Liscano, A. El Saddik, A Universal Ontology for Sensor Networks Data, *IEEE International Conference on Computational Intelligence for Measurement Systems and Applications (CIMSA 2007)*, p. 59–62 (2007).

[14] D. Russomanno, C. Kothari, O. Thomas, Sensor Ontologies: from Shallow to Deep Models, *IEEE Computer Society*, p. 107–112 (2005).

[15] J. H. Kim, H. Kwon, D. H. Kim, H. Y. Kwak, S. J. Lee, Building a Service-Oriented Ontology for Wireless Sensor Networks, *Proceedings of the Seventh IEEE/ACIS International Conference on Computer and Information Science (ICIS 2008)*, p.649-654 (2008)

[16] M. Trifan, B. Ionescu, D. Ionescu, O. Prostean, G. Prostean, An Ontology based Approach to Intelligent Data Mining for Environmental Virtual Warehouses of Sensor Data, *IEEE Conference On Virtual Environments, Human-Computer Interfaces and Measurement Systems (VECIMS 2008)*, p.125-129 (2008).

[17] V. Huang, M. K. Javed, Semantic Sensor Information Description and Processing, *Second International Conference on Sensor Technologies and Applications, 2008 (SENSORCOMM '08)*, p.456-461 (2008).

[18] C. H. Jones, IEEE 1451.4 smart transducers template description language, http://standards.ieee.org/regauth/1451/IEEE_1451d4_TDL_Introduction_090104.pdf, accessed September 15, 2009.

[19] C. Intanagonwiwat, R. Govindan, D. Estrin, J. Heidemann, F. Silva, Directed Diffusion for Wireless Sensor Networking, *IEEE/ACM Transactions on Networking*, **11**, p. 2-16 (2003).

[20] S. Madden, M. Franklin, J. Hellerstein, W. Hong, TAG: A Tiny Aggregation Service for Ad-Hoc Sensor Networks, *Proceedings of the USENIX Symposium on Operating Systems Design and Implementation* (2002).

[21] X. Li, Y.J. Kim, R. Govindan, W. Hong, Multi-dimensional Range Queries in Sensor Networks, *Proceedings of the 1st international conference on Embedded Networked Sensor Systems*, p. 63-75 (2003).

[22] S. Ratnasamy, B. Karp, S. Shenker, D. Estrin, R. Govindan, L. Yin, F. Yu, Data-centric Storage in Sensornets with GHT, a Geographic Hash Table, *Mobile Networks and Applications*, **8(4)**, p. 427-442 (2003).

[23] S. Madden, M. Franklin, J. Hellerstein, W. Hong, TinyDB: An Acquisitional Query Processing System for Sensor Networks, *ACM Transactions on Database Systems (TODS)*, **30(1)**, p. 122-173 (2005).

[24] Y. Yao, J. Gehrke, The Cougar Approach to In-Network Query Processing in Sensor Networks, *SIGMOD Record*, **31(3)**, p. 9-18 (2002).

[25] Y. Yao, J. Gehrke, Query Processing for Sensor Networks, *First Biennial Conference on Innovative Data Systems Research (CIDR)* (2003).

[26] M. Sharaf, J. Beaver, A. Labrinidis, P. Chrysanthis, Balancing Energy Efficiency and Quality of Aggregate Data in Sensor Networks, *The VLDB Journal*, **13(4)**, p. 384-403 (2004).

[27] M. Cherniack, H. Balakrishnan, M. Balazinska, D. Carney, U. Çetintemel, Y. Xing, S. Zdonik, Scalable Distributed Stream Processing, *First Biennial Conference on Innovative Data Systems Research (CIDR)* (2003).

[28] S. Chandrasekaran, O. Cooper, A. Deshpande, M. Franklin, J. Hellerstein, W. Hong, S. Krishnamurthy, S. Madden, V. Raman, F. Reiss, M. Shah, TelegraphCQ: Continuous Dataflow Processing for an Uncertain World, *First Biennial Conference on Innovative Data Systems Research (CIDR)* (2003).

[29] D. Abadi, Y. Ahmad, M. Balazinska, U. Çetintemel, M. Cherniack, J.-H. Hwang, W. Lindner, A. Maskey, A. Rasin, E. Ryvkina, N. Tatbul, Y. Xing, S. Zdonik, The Design of the Borealis Stream Processing Engine, *Second Biennial Conference on Innovative Data Systems Research (CIDR)* (2005).

[30] G. D. Abowd, A. K. Dey, P. J. Brown, N. Davies, M. Smith, P. Steggles, Towards a Better Understanding of Context and Context-Awareness, *Proceedings of the 1st international Symposium on Handheld and Ubiquitous Computing, LNCS*, **1707**, p. 304-307 (1999).

[31] G. Papamarkos, A. Poulovassilis, P. T. Wood, Event-Condition-Action Rule Languages for the Semantic Web, *Workshop on Semantic Web and Databases (SWDB 03)*, p. 309–327 (2003).

[32] S. Harris, N. Gibbins. 3store: Efficient Bulk RDF Storage, *Proceedings of the 1st International Workshop on Practical and Scalable Semantic Systems (PSSS'03)*, p. 1–15 (2003).

[33] O. Corby, R. Dieng-Kuntz, C. Faron-Zucker, Querying the Semantic Web with the Corese Search Engine, *Proceedings of the 15th European Conference on Artificial Intelligence (ECAI 2004)*, p. 705–709, (2004).

[34] J. Broekstra, A. Kampman, F. van Harmelen, Sesame: An Architecture for Storing and Querying RDF Data and Schema Information, *Towards the Semantic Web*, p. 71–89, John Wiley & Sons, Ltd, DOI: 10.1002/0470858060.ch5, (2003).

[35] A. Dey, Understanding and Using Context, *Journal of Ubiquitous Computing*, **5(1)**, p. 4-7 (2001).

[36] F. Baader, W. Nutt, Basic Description Logics, in the Description Logic Handbook, p. 47–100, Cambridge University Press (2002).

[37] J. Cardoso, The Semantic Web Vision: Where are We?, *IEEE Intelligent Systems*, **22(5)**, p. 84–88 (2007)

[38] F. Donini, M. Lenzerini, D. Nardi, A. Schaerf, Reasoning in Description Logics, in Gerhard Brewka, ed., Principles of Knowledge Representation, p. 191–236. CSLI Publications, 1996.

[39] B. Motik, U. Sattler, A Comparison of Reasoning Techniques for Querying Large Description Logic ABoxes, *Proceedings of the 13th International Conference on Logic for Programming Artificial Intelligence and Reasoning (LPAR'06)*, LNCS, **4246**, p. 227–241 (2006)

[40] E. Sirin, B. Parsia, B. Grau, A. Kalyanpur, Y. Katz, Pellet: A Practical OWL-DL Reasoner, *Journal of Web Semantics*, **5(2)**, p. 51–53 (2007)

[41] D. Tsarkov, I. Horrocks, FaCT++ Description Logic Reasoner: System Description, *Proceedings of the International Joint Conference on Automated Reasoning (IJCAR 2006)*, LNAI, **4130**, p. 292-297 (2006).

[42] J. P . Walters, Z. Liang, W. Shi, V. Chaudhary, Wireless Sensor Network Security: A Survey, in Security in Distributed, Grid, and Pervasive Computing, Auerbach Publications, CRC Press, 2006.

[43] L. Kazatzopoulos, C. Delakouridis, G. F. Marias, and P. Georgiadis, iHIDE: Hiding Sources of Information in WSNs, *Second International Workshop on Security, Privacy and Trust in Pervasive and Ubiquitous Computing (SecPerU 2006)*, p. 41–48 (2006).

[44] O. Erling, I. Mikhailov, RDF Support in the Virtuoso DBMS, *Proceedings of the 1st Conference on Social Semantic Web (CSSW 2007)*, LNI, **113**, p. 59-68 (2007).

[45] S. Auer, C. Bizer, G. Kobilarov, J. Lehmann, R. Cyganiak, Z. Ives, DBpedia: A Nucleus for a Web of Open Data, *6th International Semantic Web Conference (ISWC 2007)*, p. 11-15 (2007).

[46] B. Warneke, M. Last, B. Liebowitz, K. S. J. Pister, Smart Dust: Communicating with a Cubic-Millimeter Computer, *Computer*, **34(1)**, p. 44-51 (2001).

[47] J. Yick, B. Mukherjee, D. Ghosal, Wireless Sensor Network Survey, *Computer Networks*, **52(12)**, p. 2292-2330 (2008).

[48] I. F. Akyildiz, W. Su, Y. Sankarasubramaniam, E. Cayirci, Wireless Sensor Networks: a Survey, *Computer Networks*, **38(4)**, p. 393-422 (2002).

[49] A. Zafeiropoulos, E. Solidakis, S. Zoi, N. Konstantinou, P. Papageorgiou, P. Stathopoulos and N. Mitrou: A lightweight approach for providing Location Based Content Retrieval, *In 18th IEEE International Symposium on Personal, Indoor and Mobile Radio Communications (PIMRC'07)*, Athens, Greece (2007)

In: Data Management in the Semantic Web
Editor: Hal Jin, pp. 277-293
ISBN: 978-1-61122-862-5

Chapter 12

CHINESE SEMANTIC DEPENDENCY ANALYSIS

***Jiajun Yan*[1] *and David B. Bracewell*[2]**
[1] LN3GS Language Consulting,
Niskayuna, NY, U. S.
[2] General Electric Global Research,
Niskayuna, NY, U. S.

Abstract

The first and overwhelmingly major challenge of the Semantic Web is annotating semantic information in text. Semantic analysis is often used to combat this problem by automatically creating the semantic metadata that is needed. However, semantic analysis has been proven difficult to get ideal results, because of two controversial problems; semantic scheme and classification. This chapter presents an answer to these two problems. For semantic scheme, semantic dependency is chosen and for classification a number of machine learning approaches are examined and compared. Semantic dependency is chosen as it gives a deeper structure and better describes the richness of semantics in natural language. The classification approaches encompass standard machine learning algorithms, such as Naive Bayes, Decision Tree and Maximum Entropy, as well as multiple classification and rule-based correction approaches. The best results receive a state-of-the-art accuracy of 85.1%. In addition, an integrated system called SEEN (Semantic dEpendency parsEr for chiNese) is introduced, which combines research presented in this chapter as well as segmentation, part-of-speech, and syntactic parsing modules that are freely available from other researchers.

1. Introduction

The semantic web has the potential to create numerous new possibilities in how we search and interact with web data. However, as Benjamins et. al. point out there are some major challenges [1]. One of these challenges, which is arguably the biggest, is the availability of semantically annotated content. The reason that content availability is a challenge is because extending normal data with semantic metadata is not an easy process and until recently has mostly been done manually. In order to lessen the metadata creation burden, researchers have used semantic analysis to automate the process, most notably Dill et. al. [2]. However, semantic analysis is a difficult problem that has not been solved and has vastly varying performance and maturity across languages.

When doing semantic analysis there are two questions that have to be asked before attempting to solve the problem.

1. Which semantic annotation task to perform?
2. How to classify semantic relations?

This chapter presents one such way of doing semantic analysis for Chinese. Semantic dependency analysis is the undertaken task. A variety of machine learning approaches are experimented with to attempt to solve the second problem of classification.

Semantic Dependency Analysis (SDA) has been gaining interest among theoretical linguists and natural language processing experts alike. SDA has many direct applications, such as knowledge representation, Question & Answering [3], cross-language information retrieval, and machine translation [4]. The amount of research on SDA has been steadily growing for European languages. In particular, English has seen a large amount of research in semantic parsing using statistical and machine learning methods [5]. Additionally, annotated corpora such as FrameNet [6] and the proposition Bank [7] are widely available.

However, much less research has been undertaken for Chinese. This is largely due to the lack of publicly available semantically annotated corpora. While some corpora, such as the work done by Gan and Wong [8] on the Sinica Treebank [9] and the 1 million word scale corpora created by Li et al. [10] are available, these corpora are either not publicly available or have problems that may make them less optimal for some researchers. In later sections, more background in semantic analysis and the reasons behind choosing SDA will be fully explained.

The most straightforward way of classifying the semantic relations is to use machine learning. In this chapter, Naïve Bayesian, Naïve Possibilistic, Decision Tree and Maximum Entropy classifiers are examined. They are looked at individually and combined in a multi-classifier with a couple of winning classification selection methods.

After being classified using one of the above approaches, the results are corrected using a set of rules mined using transformation-based learning. The results of each classifier, a winner-takes-all selection based multi-classifier and the rule-based correction will be given in a later section.

This chapter will continue as a follows. In section 0, greater detail on the two major semantic annotation tasks and why SDA was chosen will be given. Next, in section 0 details on the corpus and its annotation will be discussed. Then, in section 0, an overview of the different classifiers and selection mechanisms used in classifying semantic dependency relations will be given. Section 0 presents the experimental results. Next a prototype system is introduced in section 0. Finally, concluding remarks are given in section 0.

2. Semantic Annotation

There are mainly two different semantic annotation tasks: Semantic Role Labeling (SRL) and Semantic Dependency Analysis. The goal of the Semantic Role Labeling task is to determine the semantic arguments of the main verb of a sentence and assign semantic roles to them. In contrast, the Semantic Dependency Analysis task assigns semantic relations between any two words that have a link between them as determined by the underlying dependency grammar.

Semantic Role Labeling

SRL assigns the main verb of the sentence as the headword and the rest of the text as arguments of the verb. An example of SRL is shown in figure 1. The main verb is “wrote” and the modifier and complement are “Liuxiang” and “strong-minded women biography” with “agent” and “result” assigned as the semantic roles.

A great deal of research has been done on Chinese semantic role labeling. Xue and Palmer [10] used a Maximum Entropy classifier with a tunable Gaussian to do semantic role labeling for Chinese verbs using a pre-release version of the Chinese Proposition Bank [11]. You and Chen [12] presented a system for semantic role labeling of structured trees from the Sinica corpus. Their system adopts dependency decision-making and example based approaches.

```
(IP (ADVP (AD 同时)) (PU ，) (NP-PN-SBJ (NR 刘向)) (VP (VV 写)(NP-TTL-OBJ
    (PU 《) (NN 列女) (NN 传) (PU 》))))
English: At the same time, Liuxiang wrote <<The Biography of Strong-minded Women>>

                         A) Original sentence

                           ARG0: 刘向 (agent)
                           ARG1: 列女传 (result)
                           REL:  写 (verb)

                           B) Semantic Role Labeling
```

Figure 1. Semantic Role Labeling Example.

Semantic Dependency Analysis

SDA builds a dependency tree with semantic relationships labeled between parent (headword) and child (dependent) nodes, between which there is a dependency link according to underlying dependency grammar. The headword is chosen as the word that best represent the meaning of the headword-dependent pair. Like SRL, the main verb of the sentence is chosen as the headword of the sentence. In a compound constituent the headword inherits the headword of the head sub-headword-dependent pair and headwords of other sub-headword-dependent pairs are dependent on that headword. SDA labels the semantic relations between all headword-dependent pairs. This gives SDA a deeper structure and allows a richer understanding of the sentence. Moreover, it has advantages over traditional representations, as the dependency links are closer to semantic relationships [13].

An example of SDA, using the same sentence as in figure 1, is shown in figure 2. It can be seen that SDA is not limited to verb-modifier pairs. Extra semantic relationships such as "time" and "restrictive" are assigned between dependents and non-verbal headwords. The utilization of these extra relationships could prove to be useful in different NLP tasks.

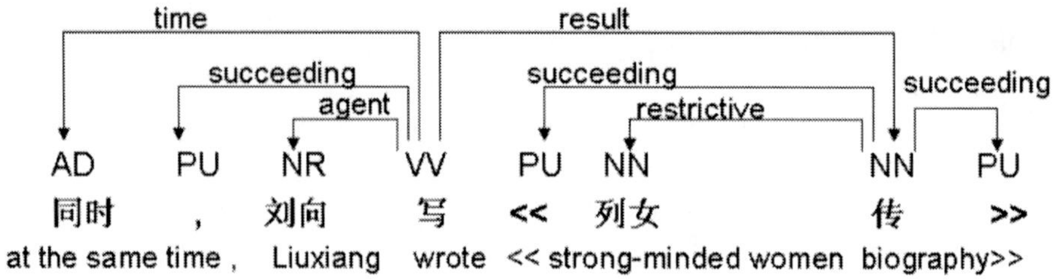

Figure 2. Semantic Dependency Analysis Example.

The differences between SDA and SRL can be thought of as being similar to those between chunking and parsing. SRL, like chunking, is not exhaustive and gives a much flatter tree. In contrast, SDA is more like parsing in that it exhaustively determines all semantic relations in the sentence and creates a deeper structure. Two of the major advantages of SDA over SRL are as follows…

1. ***Allsidedness and Uniqueness:*** The goal of semantic dependency relations is to obtain a set of semantic relations that can be applied to all the words in a sentence. Except for the main headword of the sentence, every dependent has one and only one headword. For every two words between which there is a dependency link, one and only one semantic relation is assigned.
2. ***Distinctness:*** The assigned semantic relation distinguishes a word from the others in a sentence. In this case, each word is assigned a different semantic relation from other dependent words of the same headword. Because semantic relations are assigned in a parse tree, the boundary between any two semantic relations is distinct. The differences between semantic relations are shown clearly with the respective dependency link

Because of the above-mentioned reasons, semantic dependency grammar was chosen as the representation scheme for Chinese sentences. It is believed to be the best and most natural way of representing and visualizing semantics in natural language.

Little research has been done on automatic methods of determining semantic dependency relations for a complete sentence. The most notable research is by Li et al. [14] who built a large corpus annotated with semantic knowledge using dependency grammar structure. The selections of semantic relations were taken from HowNet, which is a Chinese lexical database. In addition, a computer-aided tagging tool was developed to assist annotators in tagging semantic dependency relations. Manual checking and semiautomatic checking were carried out. Auto-tagging this type of semantic information still has not been completed and is the goal of the current research.

3. Chinese Semantic Dependency Corpus and Tag Set

Semantically labeled corpora for Chinese are still scarce, due to the fact that the corpora that have been created are rarely made publicly available. To our knowledge, the Sinica Treebank [15] is currently the only publicly available semantically annotated corpora for Chinese. However, it presents a number of problems. The first is that the sentences in the corpus were segmented on punctuation making a majority of the annotated trees just phrases or even single words. In Chinese punctuation plays a critical role and should not be ignored. The second problem is that it is made up of mostly Mandarin as used in Taiwan, which has enough differences with its mainland counterpart that the corpus may not be as useful for researchers in mainland China.

Because of this, we chose to manually annotate part of the Penn Chinese Treebank 5.0 [16]. In total 4,000 sentences containing 32,000 words were manually annotated with headwords and semantic relations according to Dependency Grammar, which means that only the words between which there is a unique dependency link were assigned a relation. Headword annotation started at the bottom most chunks in the parse tree and for each chunk the word that best represented the meaning of the chunk was assigned as its headword. The headword was then passed up the tree to represent the chunk. This process continued until the root was reached. The sentence headword, or root word, was the word that best describes the meaning of the sentence.

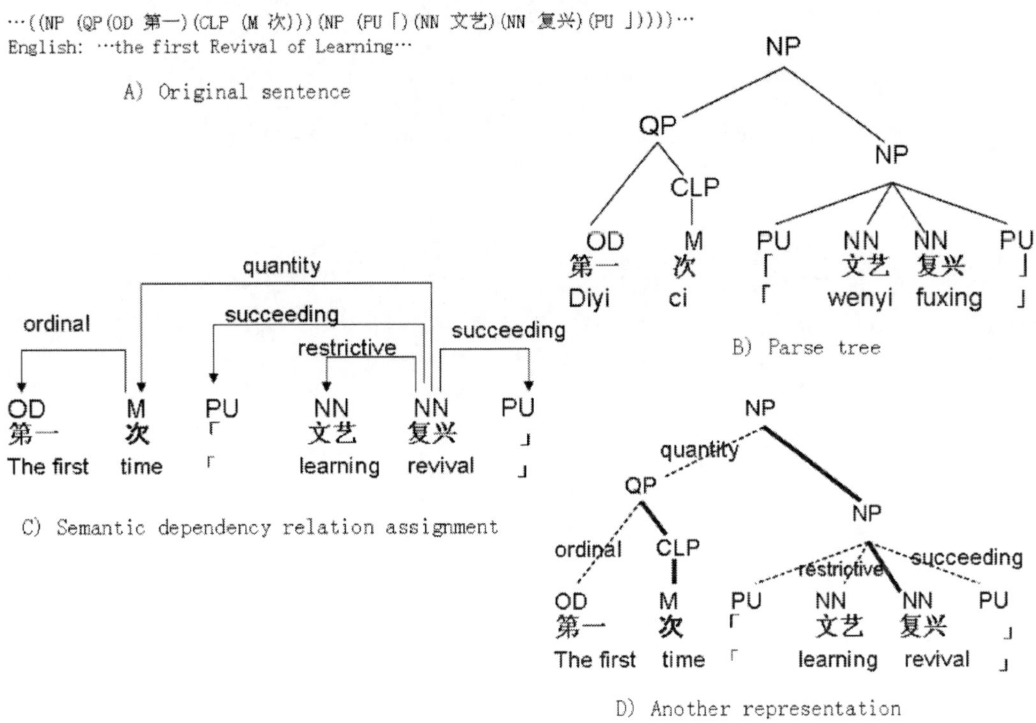

Figure 3. Manually Annotating the Corpus with Headword and Semantic Dependency Relations.

Figure 3 gives a simple example of a portion of an annotated sentence. 3-c shows the results of semantic dependency relation labeling. The start point of the arrow denotes headword, the end point of the arrow denotes dependent. The labeled arrows with "ordinal", "quantity", "restrictive" and so forth represent the implicit meaning from dependents to headwords. The relations for punctuations "PU" and other words are tagged with "succeeding." 3-d shows another representation of the semantic dependency analysis result (headwords marked with bold lines), in which the parse tree of 3-b was preserved.

The semantic dependency relation tag set was taken from HowNet, which is a Chinese lexical dictionary that describes the inter-conceptual relations and inter-attribute relations among words and concepts as a network [17]. HowNet is growing in popularity amongst Chinese NLP researchers, which makes adopting its tag set more beneficial. In addition, a Chinese-English semantic hierarchy was assigned to HowNet by [18].

The tag set, shown in figure 4, is made up of 70 tags, which includes 55 semantic relations and 14 syntactic relations and one special tag, which describes the relation between punctuations and other words. Semantic relations are the main content of the annotations that describe the underlying meaning from dependents to headwords. Syntactic relations are used to annotate the special dependency links that do not have an exact sense in terms of semantics. In Chinese, punctuation plays an important role, which acts as a connecting link for the context in the sentence, and in the Penn Treebank the punctuation is annotated. The relations between punctuations and other words are annotated mainly as "succeeding."

Semantic Relations (55)			
accompaniment	descriptive	locationIni	relevant
AccordingTo	determiner	locationThru	restrictive
agent	direction	logicSubject	result
appositive	emphasis	manner	scope
beneficiary	event	material	speed
cardinal	existent	modifier	state
cause	experiencer	ordinal	stateFin
comment	extent	partner	stateIni
condition	focus	patient	target
content	frequency	possession	time
contentCompare	instrument	possessor	timeIni
contrast	isa	purpose	timerange
cost	location	quantity	topic
degree	locationFin	question	
Syntactic Relations (14)			
addition	connection	modality	trend
besides	coordinate	negative	voice
but	de-dependency	parenthesis	
concession	except	tense	
Special Relations (1)			
succeeding			

Figure 4. Semantic Dependency Tag Set.

4. Semantic Dependency Relation Classification

The semantic dependency analysis task requires that a semantic dependency relation be assigned between a headword-dependent pair. The straightforward way of dealing with this problem is to use machine learning based classifiers. Here we give information on the individual classifiers that we experimented with as well as information about multi-classifier based and rule-based correction approaches. The individual classifiers were Naïve Bayesian, Decision Tree, Naive Possibilistic and Maximum Entropy.

The Naive Bayesian classifier (NBC) is widely used in machine learning due to its efficiency and its ability to combine evidence from a large number of features. It is a probabilistic model that assigns the most probable class to a feature vector. Even though it relies on an assumption that the features are independent and this is not normally true, it has been shown to generally do well in classification [19].

The NBC is based on Bayes theorem. The idea of Bayes theorem is that the probability of a class (***C***) given observed data for a set of features (***X***) can be determined by equation 1. The naive part of the Naive Bayesian classifier comes in its assumption that the features are independent of one another. After simplification of equation 1 and making the independence assumption a classifier can be built using equation 2.

$$P(C \mid X_1 ... X_N) = \frac{P(X_1 ... X_N \mid C) x P(C)}{P(X_1 ... X_N)} \tag{1}$$

$$\hat{C} = \arg\max_{C} P(C) \prod_{i=1}^{N} P(X_i \mid C) \tag{2}$$

Decision Trees (DT) use a tree structure where at each node a decision is made until a leaf node is reached where the class is given. The most widely used variant is the ID3 decision tree introduced by [20]. The ID3 decision tree uses information gain, see equation 3, which is based on entropy to induce the tree structure. One of the main reasons of using a decision tree is that they are very easy to understand and to visualize, while also giving good results.

$$IGain(i) = -\sum_{j=1}^{N} f(i,j) \log_2 f(i,j) \tag{3}$$

The Naive Possibilistic Classifier (NPC) is based on possibilistic networks. They are able to handle imprecise data better than Naive Bayesian Classifiers. Borgelt and Gebhardt showed that for certain data sets the Naive Possibilistic Classifier can perform as well and sometimes better than Naive Bayesian Classifiers and Decision Tree Classifiers [21].

Maximum Entropy modeling creates a model based on facts from the underlying data while trying to stay as uniform as possible [22]. As a classifier it uses the principal of maximum entropy to estimate the probability distribution of a model based on observed events. It achieves state-of-the-art results and often performs as well or better than Support Vector Machines. It is also extremely useful for NLP, as [23] shows, and has been widely adopted in the NLP field. For a more in depth explanation we refer the reader to [23].

Mutli-Classifier Classification

Multi-classifier approaches have been used for everything from handwriting recognition [24] to segmentation of biomedical images [25]. They combine many different classifiers to create better results than individual classifiers could do alone. Recently, these techniques have found their way into NLP applications. Zelai et al. [26] used a multi-classifier technique with singular value decomposition for document classification. Giuglea and Moschitti used multi-classifiers for semantic parsing using FrameNet [27].

When using multiple classifiers, the important part is in choosing the selection method. The selection method decides how to combine results of the individual classifiers and choose the final classification.

We chose to use a majority wins approach in a Naïve Bayesian, Decision Tree and Maximum Entropy combined multi-classifier. The majority wins selection method works as follows. If two of the classifiers agree on a relation then that relation is chosen. If no two classifiers agree then the Maximum Entropy classifier's relation is chosen, as it has a higher overall accuracy in our experiments. In the following subsections an introduction to the features used in classification will be given.

Classification Features

Currently, five features are used for classification. Since the headword and its dependents are the most important indicators of semantic dependency relation assignment, they are the basis for the chosen characteristics. These features can be easily and directly obtained from parsed data and, we believe, they are the most important. The five chosen features are described below.

- Headword-Dependent parts-of-speech (POS): The headword and dependent parts-of-speech feature is the parts-of-speech for the headword-dependent pair.
- Headword-Dependent words (WORDS): The headword and dependent feature is the words that makeup the headword and the currently looked at dependent.
- Context (CON): The context feature is the set of dependent parts-of-speech that fall between the headword and the currently looked at dependent.
- Phrase Type (PT): The phrase type feature uses the phrase head, i.e. NP, PP, VP, etc.
- Phrase Length (PL): The phrase length is the number of dependents that makes up the phrase plus one for the headword

Rule-Based Correction

To correct classification errors, transformation based learning (TBL) was used for rule-based correction system. Brill originally pioneered TBL for use in part-of-speech tagging [28]. Since then it has been used in many areas of NLP including chunking, parsing, etc. We used the fnTBL [29] implementation to generate and evaluate rules for correcting errors from classification. fnTBL introduced some improvements to the learning process that allow for a faster training time while still achieving the same precision in classification.

Here we will briefly describe the learning process for TBL. TBL is an iterative process where at each step new rules are created and scored based on how well they change the underlying corpus. The rule with the highest score is chosen, added to the rule list and the corpus is modified using the rule. This process is repeated until the score of the best rule falls below some given threshold. The characteristics of this approach can be summarized as following.

1. All five features were used
2. Rules were generated from a set of templates covering all possible combinations of the features.
3. All rules with a score over a given threshold were used.

5. Experimental Results

For the classifiers, a 10-fold-cross-validated test was adopted. Each classifier was trained and tested on a varying combination of features. Table 1 shows the results of the tests. Each combination of classifier and features shows the average accuracy and standard deviation.

It can be seen that the most important feature is POS, headword-dependent parts-of-speech. Using it alone results in an average accuracy of over 70% for all four classifiers. The CON (context) feature is the next important feature. All the accuracies of using only CON are over 61%. The WORDS feature resulted in a lower average accuracy, possible due to a large amount of ambiguities and not enough data to make an accurate statistical model. Also it can be seen that, PT gives more information than PL does. Even though the average accuracy is very low, maybe it will help improve the disambiguation.

When the POS and WORDS features were combined they produced a synergistic effect resulting in the DT, ME and NBC classifiers accuracy being increased by about 10%, 8% and 7% respectively. The POS and CON features combination also show strong increase of the average accuracy.

After the performance of single features and combination of double features, the next important combination is triple. The POS, WORDS and CON combination was able to increase about 10% in NBC, DT and ME classifiers. The DT and ME classifiers were able to achieve their highest accuracies of 83.4% and 84.0% respectively. The ME had a higher average accuracy with a lower standard deviation.

As one would expect the ME classifier gave the best results. However, they were not much better than those of the NBC and DT classifiers. When the feature space was small the NPC classifier performed nearly as well or better than the NBC and ME classifiers.

After combining PT or PL with the most three important features, it did not show much improvement in the results. The NPC classifier was not able to handle these attributes. All in all, the classification-based approach proved to work well and produced highly accurate results. Both the DT and ME classifiers seem to be suitable for the job at hand. These tests were the basis for choosing the Maximum Entropy classifier as the fall back classifier.

Table 1. Individual Classifier Results

Features	NBC	NPC
POS	70.4% (±1.7%)	70.2% (±1.5%)
WORDS	65.6% (±4.6%)	49.4% (±4.0%)
CON	62.2% (±2.6%)	61.1% (±2.7%)
PT	39.4% (±2.2%)	39.4% (±2.2%)
PL	16.6% (±2.4%)	0.0% (±0.0%)
POS + WORDS	77.9% (±2.2%)	64.4% (±2.2%)
POS + CON	73.9% (±2.0%)	74.0% (±2.8%)
POS + WORDS + PT	77.6% (±2.5%)	64.7% (±2.1%)
POS + WORDS + CON	80.3% (±2.6%)	67.6% (±2.5%)
POS + CON + PT	73.9% (±2.2%)	74.1% (±2.6%)
POS + WORDS + CON + PT	80.3% (±2.6%)	67.7% (±2.5%)
POS + WORDS + CON + PL	80.3% (±2.6%)	0.0% (±0.0%)
POS + WORDS + CON + PT + PL	80.3% (±2.6%)	0.0% (±0.0%)
Features	**DT**	**ME**
POS	70.9% (±1.6%)	70.0% (±1.8%)
WORDS	61.0% (±3.2%)	61.1% (±5.0%)
CON	62.1% (±2.5%)	62.2% (±2.8%)
PT	39.4% (±2.2%)	39.4% (±2.2%)
PL	26.5% (±1.9%)	26.7% (±1.5%)
POS + WORDS	81.0% (±2.8%)	78.3% (±2.7%)
POS + CON	74.6% (±2.4%)	74.3% (±2.8%)
POS + WORDS + PT	81.3% (±2.6%)	78.4% (±2.6%)
POS + WORDS + CON	83.4% (±3.6%)	84.0% (±2.2%)
POS + CON + PT	74.7% (±2.5%)	74.5% (±2.4%)
POS + WORDS + CON + PT	83.4% (±3.7%)	83.9% (±2.3%)
POS + WORDS + CON + PL	83.4% (±3.6%)	84.1% (±2.1%)
POS + WORDS + CON + PT + PL	83.4% (±3.7%)	84.0% (±2.2%)

For testing the multi-classifier, a 10-fold-cross-validated experiment was also used. Table 2 shows the average accuracy and the standard deviation with the same features combination as the single classifiers. It can be seen that almost all the results got a little increase for all the features. The best result 84.9% using POS, WORDS, and CON features is 0.9%.

For testing the rule-based correction method, all 10-folds of the NBC, DT ME and multi-classifier with all features were combined and used. The first 8 folds of classifier testing data were taken as training data and the other 2 folds as testing data. Ten thresholds (1-10) were used in testing.

The results before applying the rules for NBC, DT, ME and the multi-classifier were 80.6%, 83.7%, 83.7% and 84.8% respectively. Table 3 shows the post rule accuracy for the ten different thresholds. The best post rule accuracy was 84.6% for NBC, 83.9% for DT, 84.1% for ME and 85% for the multi-classifier.

Table 2. Multi-Classifier Results

Features	Avg. Accuracy
POS	70.7% (±1.7%)
WORDS	65.4% (±3.9%)
CON	62.1% (±2.5%)
PT	39.4% (±2.2%)
PL	26.5% (±1.9%)
POS + WORDS	80.7% (±2.8%)
POS + CON	74.7% (±2.4%)
POS + WORDS + PT	80.7% (±2.9%)
POS + WORDS + CON	84.9% (±2.1%)
POS + CON + PT	74.7% (±2.4%)
POS + WORDS + CON + PT	84.8% (±2.2%)
POS + WORDS + CON + PL	84.9% (±2.1%)
POS + WORDS + CON + PT + PL	84.9% (±2.1%)

Table 3. Rule-Based Correction Results

	Threshold									
	1	**2**	**3**	**4**	**5**	**6**	**7**	**8**	**9**	**10**
NBC	81.9%	83.8%	84.3%	**84.6%**	**84.6%**	**84.6%**	84.4%	84.4%	84.4%	84.4%
DT	80.1%	82.6%	83.4%	83.7%	83.8%	83.8%	**83.9%**	83.7%	83.7%	83.6%
ME	81.6%	83.4%	83.9%	83.8%	83.8%	84.0%	**84.1%**	**84.1%**	**84.1%**	**84.0%**
Multi-Classifier	81.2%	83.8%	84.6%	84.8%	84.8%	85.0%	**85.1%**	**85.0%**	**85.0%**	**85.0%**

6. The SEEN System

The SEEN (Semantic dEpendency parsEr for chiNese) system is a culmination of the research presented in this chapter. It combines the work we have done on headword assignment and semantic dependency analysis with other research on word segmentation, POS tagging and parsing to create a full system.

SEEN is one of only a few systems to integrate the steps needed to perform semantic dependency analysis on Chinese text. The Stanford Parser allows Chinese text to be entered and will out syntactic dependency [32]. Other systems focus mainly on semantic role labeling.

The SEEN system is broken into 3 main modules, as seen in Figure 5. The first module is syntactic analysis. This module takes care of morphological analysis and parsing. The second module is headword assignment. This module assigns headwords to sentences and phrases. The final module is semantic dependency relation assignment. Each of the modules will be described in more detail in the following subsections.

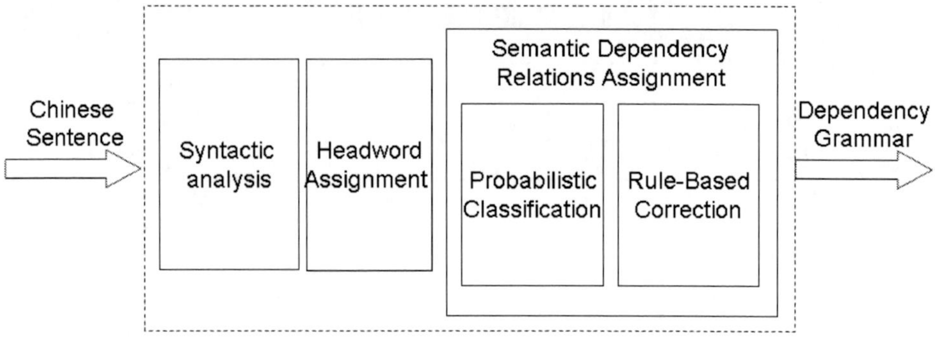

Figure 5. Architectural Overview of the SEEN System.

Syntatic Analysis Module

The syntactic analysis module is made up of morphological analysis and parsing. While not as far along as English, Chinese programs do exist and are rapidly improving. In the following subsections Chinese morphological analysis and parsing will be briefly discussed.

Morphological analysis consists of word segmentation and part-of-speech tagging. It is a widely researched topic and many languages have these tools available including Chinese. ICTCLAS 2.0 [30], based on Hidden Markov Models, is a free morphological analyzer that has a precision of 97.58% for segmentation and 87.32% for part-of-speech tagging. In SEEN, this morphological analyzer will be used.

There has been a lot of research done in Chinese Parsing. Some of the notable research is [31], which reported that their statistics-based Chinese parser had 86% precision and 86% recall. Levy and Manning [32] developed a factored-model statistical parser and used on the Penn Chinese Treebank. Because the parser was used on the Penn Chinese Treebank, and it is freely available, it was chosen as the parser for the SEEN system.

Headword Assignment Module

The headword assignment module takes the output of the parser and converts it into a dependency structure by assigning headwords. Headwords are assigned using a set of handcrafted rules. The rules were created from linguistic observations made from the Penn Chinese Treebank and were designed to look at the syntactic head of a phrase and the other constituents. It was found that the different syntactic heads followed certain patterns that could easily be defined in rules. For example, normally, in the right direction, the last noun is always taken as the headword of the noun phrase in Chinese. Such research can also be seen in [33].

From the observation of 560 sentences with 2,396 phrases, 118 original phrase types were extracted. Neglecting the functional tags or dash tags, such as CP-ADV, IP-CND, LCP-PRD, etc. (All the functional tags are shown in Table 4), 21 unique phrase types were extracted and had handcrafted rules created for the most general case. Table 5 shows the created rules.

Table 4. Functional Tags

ADV adverbial	IMP imperative	Q question
APP appositive	IO indirect object	SBJ subject
BNF beneficiary	LGS logic subject	SHORT short form
CND condition	LOC locative	TMP temporal
DIR direction	MNR manner	TPC topic
EXT extent	OBJ direct object	TTL title
FOC focus	PN proper names	WH wh-phrase
HLN headline	PRD predicate	VOC vocative
IJ interjective	PRP purpose or reason	

Table 5. Headword Assignment Rules

ADJP	the last ADJP or JJ
ADVP	the last AD or ADVP
CLP	the last CLP
CP	the last CP or IP
DNP	the first tag
DP	the last tag
DVP	the first tag
IP	the last IP or VP
LCP	the last LC
NP	the last NN or NP
PP	the last P or PP
PRN	the last NN or NP
QP	the last QP or CLP
UCP	the last tag
VCD	the last tag
VCP	the last tag
VNV	the last tag
VP	the last tag that begins with V
VPT	the first tag
VRD	the first tag
VSB	the last tag that begins with V

Semantic Dependency Assignment Module

The semantic dependency assignment module uses the NBC, DT and ME based multi-classifier with rule-based correction. It assigns relations between each headword-dependent pair in a sentence, which was previously shown to have an accuracy of 85%.

7. Conclusion

As far as we know, this is the first research that tried to automatically determine semantic dependency relations for Chinese sentences. By comparing semantic dependency relation labeling and semantic role labeling, it was shown that semantic dependency grammar is a perfect scheme to describe the implicit meaning of a full sentence. It will be extremely helpful not only for most of the tasks in Chinese natural language processing, but also for cross-linguistic tasks. Using the semantic dependency grammar, it is not only a turning point to spread Chinese but also a bridge to connect Chinese with other languages.

This research played an important role in introducing the HowNet knowledge dictionary for disambiguation of semantic relations in Chinese. After the relationships between syntactic tags and other constituents were initially defined and given examples, the semantic dependency tag set for a full sentence was improved.

A subset of the Penn Chinese Treebank 5.0 was manually assigned with headwords and semantic dependency relations. This manually constructed corpus is the first data in which the Penn Chinese Treebank 5.0 was assigned with semantic information more than semantic roles.

A hybrid system that combined probabilistic classification and a rule based correction system was proposed for semantic dependency analysis. In the probabilistic classification part, after examining the flexibility of some simple classifiers, a multi-classifier was implemented. The multi-classifier integrated four different classifiers, Naive Bayesian classifier, Naive Probabilistic classifier, Decision Tree and Maximum Entropy. After the output from each classifier, majority wins method was used for selecting the best results. It was shown that the multi-classifier based method is capable of assigning semantic dependency relations between headword-dependent pairs. Also the fusion of information brought together when dealing with multiple classifiers helps to overcome weaknesses in any of the individual classifiers. This allowed for a higher accuracy 84% to be obtained with simple features performance. Rule-based correction was then done, by applying transformation-based learning. The system achieved a state-of-the-art result with an accuracy of 85%.

Although we have not completely reviewed the essentials of the Chinese grammar and the SDA treatment of various fundamental phenomena, the current research grasped the important aspects of describing implicit meaning of Chinese sentences based on semantic dependency theory. Semantic dependency grammar was shown to be very effective in representing and analyzing Chinese sentences in computational aspect of Chinese. Even though every semantic dependency relation was defined and examples shown, because the corpus came from news articles, a lot of linguistic phenomena still did not show up, such as the semantic relations between interrogative, interjection, mimetic word and other constituents. For the defined dependency relationships, it is necessary to investigate a wider area of linguistic phenomena to testify the semantic dependency theorem.

The corpus needs to be enlarged. This includes two kinds of data enlargement. In this thesis, only a subset of Penn Chinese Treebank 5.0 was used. The first way for us to do is to tag the whole Penn Chinese Treebank 5.0 by using the proposed classification, and then do manually checking. Second, not only corpora based on articles but also corpora based on other topics need to be tested to get closer to the real essence of Chinese sentences.

Although we automatically annotated the sentences with semantic dependency structure successfully, much further work is still needed. The test set we used was made manually and thus was very small. We will aim at enlarging the size of the annotated corpus by using the algorithms in this paper to first assign a relation and then manually correcting the errors. After a larger annotated corpus is created we can use other machine learning algorithms. In particular we would like to examine the use of Support Vector Machines.

References

[1] V.R. Benjamins, J. Contreras, O. Corcho, A. Gomez-Perez, Six challenges for the Semantic Web, *Proceedings of the Semantic Web workshop held at KR-2002*, (2002)

[2] S. Dill, N. Eiron, D. Gibson, D. Gruhl, R. Guha, A. Jhingran, T. Kanungo, S. Rajagopalan, A. Tomkins, J. Tomlin, J. Zien, SemTag and Seeker: Bootstrapping the Semantic Web via automated semantic annotation, *Proceedings of the 12th international conference on World Wide Web*, pp. 178-186, (2003)

[3] Molla, D. and B. Hutchinson, Dependency-based semantic interpretation for answer extraction, in: 5th AUSTRALASIAN NATURAL LANGUAGE PROCESSING WORKSHOP (ANLP2002), 2002.

[4] Fox, H. J., Dependency-based statistical machine translation, in: *Proceedings of the 2005 ACL Student Workshop*, Ann Arbor, America, 2005.

[5] Gildea, D. and D. Jurafsky, Automatic labeling of semantic roles, *Computational Linguistic* **28** (2002), pp. 496–530.

[6] Johnson, C. R. and C. J. Fillmore, The framenet tagset for frame-semantic and syntactic coding of predicate-argument structure, in: *Proceedings of the 1st Meeting of the North American Chapter of the Association for Computational Linguistics (ANLP-NAACL 2000)*, Seattle, WA, 2000, pp. 56–62.

[7] Palmer, M., D. Gildea and P. Kingsbury, The proposition bank: An annotated corpus of semantic roles, *Computational Linguistics Journal* **31** (2005), pp. 71–106.

[8] Gan, K. W. and P. W. Wong, Annotating information structures in chinese texts using hownet, in: *Proceedings of Second Chinese Language Processing Workshop, HongKong, 2000.*

[9] Chen, F.-Y., P.-F. Tsai, K.-J. Chen and C.-R. Hunag, The construction of sinica treebank, *Computational Linguistics and Chinese Language Processing* **4** (1999), pp. 87–104.

[10] Xue, N. and M. Palmer, Automatic semantic role labeling for chinese verbs, in: *Proceedings of the 19th International Joint Conference on Artificial Intelligence*, Edinburgh, Scotland, 2005.

[11] Xue, N. and M. Palmer, Annotating the propositions in the penn chinese treebank, in: *Proceedings of the Second Sighan Workshop*, Sapporo, Japan, 2003, pp. 47–54.

[12] You, J. and K. Chen, Automatic semantic role assignment for a tree structure, in: *Proceedings of the third SIGHAN Workshop*, *Barcelona, Spain, 2004*, pp. 109–115.

[13] Covington, M. A. (2001). A fundamental algorithm for dependency parsing. In *Proceedings of the 39th Annual ACM Southeast Conference*, pages 95–102.

[14] Li, M., J. Li, Z. Dong, Z. Wang and D. Lu, Building a large chinese corpus annotated with semantic dependency, in: *Proceedings of the Second SIGHAN Workshop*, Sapporo, Japan, 2003.

[15] Huang, C., K. Chen, F. Chen, Z. Gao and K. Chen, Sinica treebank: Design criteria, annotation guidelines, and on-line interface, in: *Proceedings of 2nd Chinese Language Processing Workshop, Hong Kong, China*, 2000, pp. 29–37.

[16] Xia, F., M. Palmer, N. Xue, M. E. Okurowski, J. Kovarik, F.-D. Chiou, S. Huang, T. Kroch and M. Marcus, Developing guidelines and ensuring consistency for chinese text annotation, in: *Proceedings of the 2nd International Conference on Language Resources and Evaluation (LREC-2000)*, Athens, Greece, 2000.

[17] Z. Dong and Q. Dong. *Introduction to hownet.* In HowNet, http://www.keenage.com, 2000

[18] Levow, G.-A., B. J. Dorr and M. Katsova, Construction of chinese-english semantic hierarchy for cross-language retrieval, in: *Proceedingd of the workshop on English-Chinese Cross Language Information Retrieval, International Conference on Chinese Language Computing*, Chicago, IL, 2000.

[19] Rish, I., An empirical study of the naive bayes classifier, in: *Proceedings of IJCAI-01 workshop on Empirical Methods in Artificial Intelligence*, 2001, pp. 41–46.

[20] Quinlan, J., Induction of decision trees, *Machine Learning* **1** (1986), pp. 81–106.

[21] C. Borgelt and J. Gebhardt. A naive bayes style possibilistic classifier. In *Proc. 7th European Congress on Intelligent Techniques and Soft Computing,* Aachen, Germany, 1999.

[22] Berger, A., S. D. Pietra and V. D. Pietra, A maximum entropy approach to natural language processing, *Computational Linguistics* **22** (1996), pp. 39–77.

[23] Ratnaparkhi, A., *A simple introduction to maximum entropy models for natural language processing*, Technical report, Institute for Research in Cognitive Science, University of Pennsylvania (1997). URL citeseer.ist.psu.edu/128751.html

[24] Xu, L., A. Krzyzak and C. Suen, Methods of combining multiple classifiers and their applications to handwriting recognition, *IEEE Transaction on systems Man and Cybernetics* **22** (1992), pp. 418–435.

[25] Rohlfing, T., D. Russakoff, R. Brandt, R. Menzel and C. Maurer, Performance-based multi-classifier decision fusion for atlas-based segmentation of biomedical images, in: *Proceedings of the IEEE International Symposium on Biomedical Imaging: Macro to Nano,* 2004.

[26] Zelai, A., I. Alegria, O. Arregi and B. Sierra, A multiclassifier based document categorization system: profiting from the singular value decomposition dimensionality reduction technique, in: *Proceedings of the workshop on Learning Structured Information in Natural Language Applications*, 2006.

[27] Giuglea, A.-M. and A. Moschitti, Towards free-text semantic parsing: A unified framework based on framenet, verbnet and propbank, in: Proceedings of the workshop on Learning Structured Information in Natural Language Applications, 2006.

[28] Brill, E. (1992). A simple rule-based part-of-speech tagger. In *Proceedings of 3rd Applied Natural Language Processing*, pages 152–155.

[29] Ngai, G. and Florian, R. (2001). Transformation-based learning in the fast lane. In *NAACL-2001*

[30] Zhang, H., Yu, H., Xiong, D., and Liu, Q. (2003b). Hmm-based chinese lexical analyzer ictclas. In *2nd SIGHAN Workshop*.

[31] Zhou, Q. (1997). A statistics-based chinese parser. In the *Fifth Workshop on Very Large Corpora,* pages 4–15.

[32] Levy, R. and Manning, C. (2003). Is it harder to parse chinese, or the chinese treebank? In *Proceedings of the Association of Computational Linguistics 2003*.

[33] Sun, H. and Jurafsky, D. (2004). Shallow semantic parsing of chinese. In *Proceedings of NAACL-HLT 2004*.

In: Data Management in the Semantic Web
Editor: Hal Jin, pp. 295-322
ISBN: 978-1-61122-862-5

Chapter 13

Creating Personal Content Management Systems using Semantic Web Technologies

Chris Poppe[1], Gaëtan Martens, Erik Mannens and Rik Van de Walle
Department of Electronics and Information Systems - Multimedia Lab
Ghent University – IBBT
Gaston Crommenlaan 8 Bus 201, B-9050 Ledeberg-Ghent, Belgium

Abstract

The amount of multimedia resources that is created and needs to be managed is increasing considerably. Additionally, a significant increase of metadata, either structured (metadata fields of standardized metadata formats) or unstructured (free tagging or annotations) is noticed. This increasing amount of data and metadata, combined with the substantial diversity in terms of used metadata fields and constructs, results in severe problems to manage and retrieve these multimedia resources. Standardized metadata schemes can be used but the plethora of these schemes results in interoperability issues. In this chapter, we propose a metadata model suited for personal content management systems. We create a layered metadata service that implements the presented model as an upper layer and combines different metadata schemes in the lower layers. Semantic web technologies are used to define and link formal representations of these schemes. Specifically, we create an ontology for the DIG35 metadata standard and elaborate on how it is used within this metadata service. To illustrate the service, we present a representative use case scenario consisting of the upload, annotation, and retrieval of multimedia content within a personal content management system.

1. Introduction

These days, the amount of multimedia content is increasing considerably. Several concurrent trends made this happen. Current software made creating, sharing, and editing of multimedia resources a common and easy task. Digital camera sales overtook film-based cameras in 2003

[1] E-mail address: Chris.poppe@ugent.be, Phone: +32 9 33 14959, Fax: +32 9 33 14896

and the numbers keep on increasing [1]. Online communities that allow sharing of pictures or videos are blooming and users can easily and rapidly annotate their own or others content. This increasing amount and diversity of content, metadata, and users, makes it a hard task to manage, retrieve and share the multimedia content. In this sense, Content Management Systems (CMS) have been used for several years. However, nowadays the user is becoming a producer of content, and there is a need to manage this personal content as well, hence the introduction of a Personal Content Management System (PCMS). In this case, the user creates, annotates, organizes and shares his personal content. In this context, the metadata have never had such an important impact on the capability of PCMSs to manage, retrieve, and describe content [2]. Nevertheless, creating a PCMS that can work with different sorts of metadata is a difficult task. Numerous metadata formats exist and generally their structure is defined in a metadata scheme (e.g., using XML Schema), while the actual meaning of the metadata fields is given in plain text [3, 4, 5]. This leads to several interoperability issues since there is no formal representation of the underlying semantics. For example, different MPEG-7 metadata constructs can be used to denote the same semantic concept [6]. Even in more recent standards, like MPEG-21, we can see problems by not formally defining the semantics as discussed in our previous work [7]. This interoperability problem was the main topic of the W3C Multimedia Semantics Incubator Group (MMSem) in which the authors have actively participated within the photo use case [9]. We adopt the vision of this group and use semantic web technologies to solve these interoperability issues within the context of a PCMS.

This chapter is an extended version of our previous work [8], in which we introduce a semantic approach to build a PCMS. This work is part of the PeCMan (PErsonal Content MANagement) project (http://www.ibbt.be/en/project/pecman), in which a PCMS is created that is completely metadata-driven. We propose a metadata model, representing system-, security-, and user-related metadata in the context of a PCMS. The model is used as an upper ontology (expressed by an OWL schema) that is linked to a set of lower-level metadata ontologies (e.g., formal representations of MPEG-7, Dublin Core, and DIG35). To show the extensibility of our system we create an ontology conform the DIG35 specification and incorporate it within the proposed model.

The next section gives related work within the context of using semantic technologies to align different XML sources. In Section 3., we elaborate on the created PCMS metadata model. Subsequently, in Section 4. we discuss the interoperability issues that we faced when trying to incorporate existing metadata schemes with our metadata model. Accordingly, a layered approach is presented that builds upon and combines formal representations of existing metadata schemes. In Section 4.3. we elaborate on the DIG35 ontology that we created and Section 4.4. shows the mappings between the different ontologies. Section 5. presents the metadata service that is built around our model and discusses the used technologies. A use case scenario is shown in Section 6. to illustrate our system and, finally, conclusions are drawn in Section 7.

2. Related Work

Semantic technology is a vivid area of research and a number of different approaches exist in creating semantic multimedia management systems. Two broad categories can be found in the related work, consisting of approaches that focus on integration of metadata standards and approaches that propose semantic multimedia systems.

The first category tries to integrate the various multimedia metadata formats by creating formal representations and/or frameworks to integrate them. The following paragraphs describe related work that represents this category.

Hunter et al. describe a semantic web architecture in which RDF schema [10] and XML schema are combined [11]. The RDF schema defines the domain-specific semantic knowledge by specifying type hierarchies and definitions, while the XML schema specifies recommended encodings of metadata elements by defining structures, occurrence constraints, and data types. A global RDF schema (called MetaNet) is used to merge domain-specific knowledge and it is combined with XSLT to accomplish semantic, structural, and syntactic mapping. MetaNet is a general thesaurus of common metadata terms that contains semantic relations (e.g., broader and narrower terms) and is used as a sort of super ontology. However, to reach its full potential, the super ontology should provide more and diverse semantic relations between the commonly used metadata terms. Consequently, using MetaNet allows for some semantic relations but it is not suited to act as a super ontology. The actual mapping between different ontologies happens through XSLT transformations. Since XSLT only relies on template matching, it can be used to transform one XML construct in another, but it is not suited to represent actual semantic relations between different concepts. Consequently, Hunter reports on the difficulties that arise due to lexical mismatching of metadata terms. Moreover, the stylesheets do not make the actual semantic relations publically available for other ontologies.

The structure of the ontologies in our system is mostly related to the work of Cruz et al. [12]. They introduce an ontology-based framework for XML semantic integration in which, for each XML source that they integrate, a local RDF ontology is created and merged in a global RDF-based ontology. During this mapping, a table is created that is used to translate queries over the RDF data of the global ontology to queries over the XML sources. The major difference with their approach is that we make explicit use of OWL to create and link the ontologies whereas they define a proprietary mapping table and introduce an extension to RDF. Moreover, they assume that every concept in the local ontologies is mapped to a concept in the global ontology. In our case, we have defined the global ontology by analyzing the specific needs of a PCMS. Consequently, not all the concepts present in every included metadata standard need to be mapped to our upper ontology.

Hunter and Little defined a framework enabling semantic indexing and retrieval of multimedia content based on the ABC ontology [13]. As in our approach, ontologies are manually created based on the XML schemas that are used. The ontologies are manually linked by using the ABC ontology as a core ontology [14]. This core ontology offers concepts and relations that allow to describe knowledge (events, actions, entities, etc.) at a high level. As such, domain-specific ontologies can use the ABC ontology to map specific concepts on each other, creating rich semantic representations across domains. However, the ABC ontology is not suitable to relate different multimedia metadata formats (which describe multimedia and not that much existing concepts or events) to each other. Indeed, only one multimedia metadata format (MPEG-7) is used in combination with two domain-specific ontologies, which are linked through the ABC ontology. XML schemas are linked to the ontologies through a proprietary system that extends the given schemas with specific attributes. Using XPath queries that process these schemes, XML instances are accordingly mapped upon instances of the corresponding ontologies. Rules are used to deduce additional relations between instances.

Vallet et al. used ontological knowledge to create a personalized content retrieval system [15]. They presented ways to learn and predict the interest of a user for a specific multimedia document to personalize the retrieval process. More specifically, the system adds a weight to concepts of the available domain ontologies and these are adjusted with every query a user does. However, the way that these concepts are related to the actual multimedia documents is similar to free-tagging systems. Each multimedia document is associated with a vector of weighted domain concepts. For example, if a picture is annotated with the concept *Paris* it is not possible to decide whether the image depicts the city of Paris or if the picture is taken in Paris.

Arndt et al. created a well-founded multimedia ontology, called the Core Ontology for Multimedia (COMM) [6]. The ontology is based on the MPEG-7 standard and uses the Descriptive Ontology for Linguistic and Cognitive Engineering (DOLCE) as modeling basis [16]. In this sense they formally describe MPEG-7 annotations, however mapping other existing metadata formats onto this model is a cumbersome task.

The second category presents general solutions to make a semantic multimedia management system. These include metadata representations and an architecture that allows to reason upon, adapt, and query this information.

Dönderler et al. presented an overview of the design and implementation of a video database management system [17]. The system allows to create semantic annotations of multimedia (video) by annotation or extraction. For this purpose a video-annotation tool and a feature extractor were proposed. The resulting annotations are subsequently used by a query processor to allow advanced querying. However, the semantic knowledge is hard-coded as a database, which makes it hard to change the system.

Shallauer et al. presented a description infrastructure for audiovisual media processing systems [18]. The system consists of an internal metadata model and access tools to use it. The model used to describe the audiovisual media is a self-defined profile of the MPEG-7 standard (called the Detailed Audiovisual Profile). By defining this profile they tried to discard the generality and complexity of the entire MPEG-7 standard.

Petridis et al. created a knowledge infrastructure and experimental platform for semantic annotation of multimedia content [19]. They use DOLCE as core ontology to link domain-specific ontologies (e.g., describing sport events like tennis) to multimedia ontologies. The latter consist of the Visual Descriptor Ontology (VDO) [20], an ontology based on MPEG-7's Visual Part [21] and a Multimedia Structure Ontology (MSO) using the MPEG-7 Multimedia Description Scheme [22]. However, their infrastructure is solely made to semi-automatically combine low-level visual features into semantic descriptions of the multimedia resource. Unfortunately, they do not consider other relevant metadata (e.g., creation location and human annotations) that is usually available and can be used to infer semantic information. Moreover, they do not allow other multimedia metadata schemes in their system.

Asirelli et al. presented an infrastructure for MultiMedia Metadata Management (4M) [23]. The infrastructure enables the collection, analysis, and integration of media for semantic annotation, search, and retrieval. It consists of an MPEG-7 feature extraction module, an XML database for storage of MPEG-7 features as XML files, an algorithm ontology, an MPEG-7 ontology, and an integration unit that merges the different modules together. As such, they succeed in reasoning about MPEG-7 features and linking different algorithms to extract MPEG-7 features. However, the restriction of using MPEG-7 XML files prevents the use of other existing metadata formats.

Garcia and Celma proposed a system architecture to achieve semantic multimedia metadata integration and retrieval by building upon an automatically generated MPEG-7 ontology [24]. They presented an automatic XML Schema to OWL mapping and apply it to the MPEG-7 standard to create an OWL Full MPEG-7 ontology. However, this mapping is fully automatic and can only extract semantics out of the structure of the XML schema. Hence, semantics not defined within the schema are not present in the resulting ontology. A system architecture to achieve semantic multimedia metadata integration and retrieval is proposed. This system uses the MPEG-7 ontology as upper ontology to which other ontologies are mapped. An RDF storage system is used for management and the data are queried using RDQL (RDF Data Query Language). However, by using the automatically generated MPEG-7 ontology, the semantic knowledge that can be represented is restricted. Additionally, MPEG-7 has gained only moderate popularity due to its complexity, and numerous metadata standards exist that work on the same conceptual level [25]. Therefore, building the upper ontology solely out of MPEG-7 concepts is too restrictive.

As the related work shows, no current architecture allows to incorporate and combine several different existing metadata formats for use within a PCMS. The possibility to include and work with different metadata formats is a prerequisite for the creation of a practically useful PCMS. Different metadata standards exist and instances of these metadata schemes are everywhere. Therefore, to work with these formats, we need to address the interoperability between the different standards and cannot rely on one metadata standard alone (like MPEG-7). Consequently, we present a semantic layered metadata model and describe a metadata service tailored for a PCMS.

3. PCMS Metadata Model

When talking about a PCMS, we imagine a metadata-driven distributed management system where the multimedia content can be placed on several devices (e.g., desktop PC or cell-phone) connected over different networks. The actual content is indexed in a separate module, called indexer that makes intelligent decisions on the technical details of the content storage. As such, the storage capacities and network traffic can be optimized [26]. The metadata related to the content is managed by a metadata service. The indexer makes use of this metadata service to decide upon the location of the content. For this purpose, system related metadata is created and linked to the content. As such, an end-user only adds metadata to content, while the system interprets this to move the content to its best location. Accordingly, a security service maintains policy rules, based on specific security related metadata fields of the content. Lastly, to allow personalized management of the content and to enforce the community aspect of the content management system, user-centric metadata is used.

To structure the metadata within the PCMS, we present a metadata model, which is depicted in Fig. 1. These metadata fields were defined according to a number of use cases inherent to a PCMS. These are:

- Registration of a resource.
- Retrieval of a resource.

- Annotation of the resource (to enhance the retrieval of content).
    - Manual annotation of the resource. This involves tagging or adding metadata according to a specific metadata scheme.
    - Automatic annotation of the resource. This includes feature extraction (e.g., face recognition tools) and importing existing metadata (e.g., reading EXIF header of a picture file).
- Metadata-driven security. This means the possibility to include access rules based on the metadata of the content.

Fig. 1 shows the metadata classes that can be regarded as independent of the actual type of the multimedia document (e.g., image, video, or audio) and are discussed in the next section. Metadata that is specific for a certain type is collected within subclasses of the *ManualAnnotation* class and is the topic of Section 3.2.

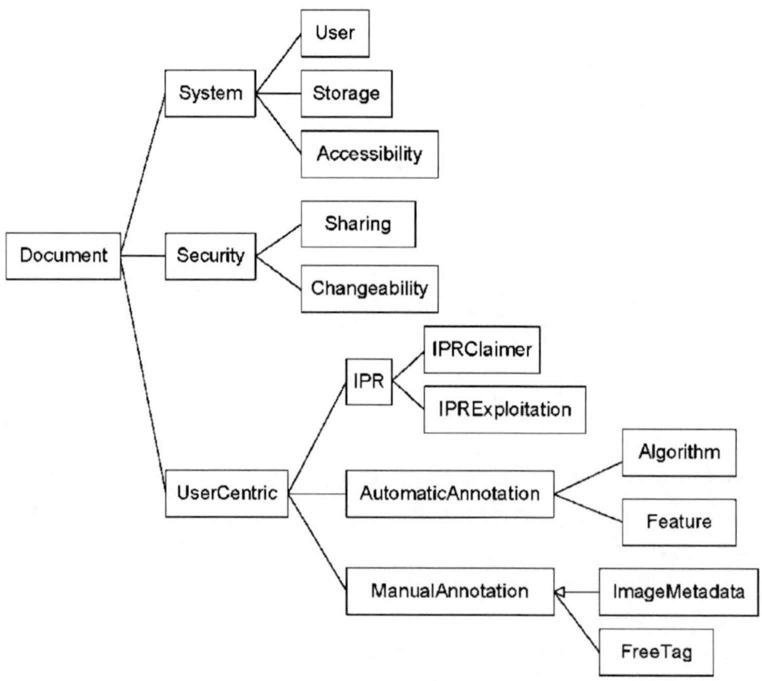

Figure 1. PCMS Class Hierarchy.

3.1. Content-Independent Metadata

A resource (e.g., a picture, video, audio file, or textual document) is called a *Document* and forms the base of our metadata model. The metadata itself reflects the modular architecture of a PCMS and is split up into system-, security-, and user-related metadata fields.

3.1.1. System Metadata

The system metadata holds the owner, storage info, and accessibility rules. The owner is a registered user within the PCMS. The user has an ID, login name, and some additional settings. The storage info holds information about the current location of the document. This location is influenced by the accessibility rules. If the accessibility is set to “online”, the document is placed on an accessible server. A value of “offline”' signifies that the document is never accessible from other devices connected to the PCMS. The last option is to set the accessibility to “always online” which infers that the document is stored both online and on a detachable device.

3.1.2. Security Metadata

The security-related metadata describes the rights that govern the access of other users concerning a specific document. This access is twofold; it includes access to the multimedia resource and to the available metadata. We refer to sharing settings for the former and changeability settings for the latter. The sharing settings hold a share level which states whether the document is shared with some users, or is private. If the document is shared, specific permission settings can be used that contain the rights of a user or user group upon the document (e.g., view or modify). If the document is not shared, the permissions are ignored. To manage the access to the metadata, the permissions of a user or user group concerning the metadata are stored within the changeability settings. Fragment 1 shows an XML serialization of the security-related metadata. This fragment shows that the actual content is private, but the metadata is visible. This allows our system to deal with copyright issues so that the content is inaccessible but the metadata can still be browsed.

```
<Security>
  <SharingSettings>
    <ShareLevel>private</ShareLevel>
  </SharingSettings>
  <ChangeabilitySettings>
    <Permissions>tag</Permissions>
    <Permissions>see</Permissions>
    <User>urn:pecman:user001</User>
  </ChangeabilitySettings>
</Security>
```

Fragment 1. Example of PCMS metadata fragment expressing copyrighted content, serialized in XML.

3.1.3. User Metadata

The user-centric metadata contains metadata for describing IPR (Intellectual Property Rights), a reference to a thumbnail which is interpreted as a summarization of the actual content, and automatic and manual annotations. We split IPR-related metadata on the security and user level. The security-related metadata as discussed above is typically only accessible through and within the PCMS. The subjects of the permissions are consequently the PCMS-users. On the other hand, the IPR-related metadata on the user level is regarded as a global protection scheme. The owner of the document defines the exploitation rights of a certain IPRClaimer. The latter is a person (which could be a PCMS-user) or organization. The actual exploitation can hold metadata to identify a specific IPR mechanism (e.g., watermark or registration), metadata to impose restrictions upon the use of the document, and metadata to specify obligations resulting from the use of the document (e.g., a fee for watching a movie). This IPR mechanism is in line with the IPR systems described in MPEG-21 Rights Expression Language (REL) and Rights Data Dictionary (RDD) [27]. These define standardized language constructs that can be used to create a licensing system that allows a user to define the rights that other persons have upon his content [28].

Automatic annotation concerns the algorithmic extraction of relevant features from the multimedia resource. The need for this kind of metadata increases with the number of multimedia resources that are stored within the PCMS. If many documents need to be annotated, manual annotation is not an option. Accordingly, automatic annotations are used that describe the content as accurate as possible. Numerous approaches and algorithms exist that try to bridge the semantic gap [29].

A generic approach is used to allow a plethora of algorithms. In this approach, the algorithm itself is described on a high level (e.g., name and reference) and the result of the algorithm can be stored as features, consisting of a header and actual data.

The last category of user-centric metadata consists of the manual annotations. A manual annotation differs from an automatic annotation in the sense that the former is metadata generated by a human expert, whereas the latter is created by an algorithm that works on the actual multimedia resource.

One general form of manual annotation is free tagging of multimedia content. As can be seen from the numerous web applications that allow tagging content (e.g., Flickr or Facebook), the popularity and, consequently, necessity of tagging is enormous. However, due to its nature, it is difficult to assign a semantic meaning to free tagging. Different users assign different keywords or tags to the same content. Moreover, several different tags can be used to identify the same conceptual entity (e.g., house, home, building, or auntie's place). Finally, different spellings, languages, or dialects cause even more problems. To reduce the semantic gap, we introduce a *Context* field that tries to represent, on a high level, the semantic meaning of the actual tag. This structuring of free tags was inspired by MPEG-7 [3]. The field can take the values “who”', “what”', “where”', “when”, or “misc”' to refer to a person(s), a subject, a place, the time, or something else, respectively. The major advantage of tagging is the degree of freedom that the user has and the ease of tagging a multimedia resource. Therefore, we restrict the context fields to those mentioned above.

In addition to the free tagging scenario, we can have other metadata that describes the multimedia resource. However, these are mostly dependent on the actual type of the resource. In this chapter, we restrict our discussion of the PCMS metadata model to images (the class *ImageMetadata* is a subclass of the *ManualAnnotation* class), but the metadata structure of other document types (e.g., audio, video, and textual documents) is similar and some constructs are reused.

3.2. Image-related Metadata

We have actively participated in the creation of an overview on the state-of-the-art of multimedia metadata formats within MMSem [30]. This overview was matched with the general requirements of the PeCMan project to yield the structure of the image metadata incorporated in our metadata model. In this sense common metadata concepts in different existing metadata formats were analyzed to see whether they aid in solving the use cases. This image metadata is split up in basic, creation, and content metadata as shown in Fig. 2.

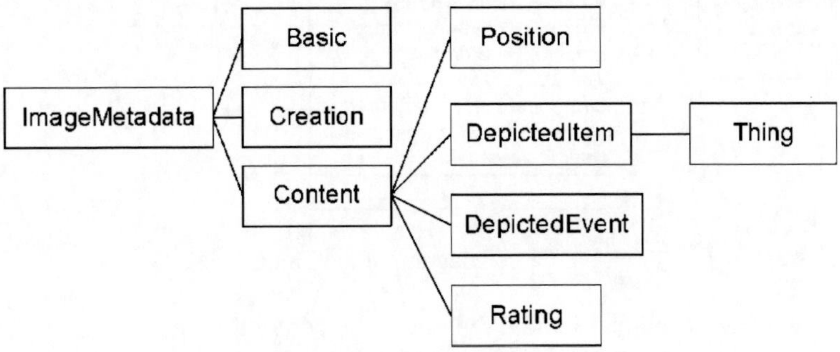

Figure 2. Model of image-related metadata.

The basic image parameters define general information about the content (e.g., file name, width and height, and the coding format).

The creational metadata encompasses both general as detailed creation information. The general creation information has fields for the creation time, the image creator, and the image source. This image source field can take the values “digital camera” or “computer graphics” to denote that the image was taken by a digital camera or was created using software, respectively.

With the detailed image creation information, one can specify which software or what camera was used in the creation process.

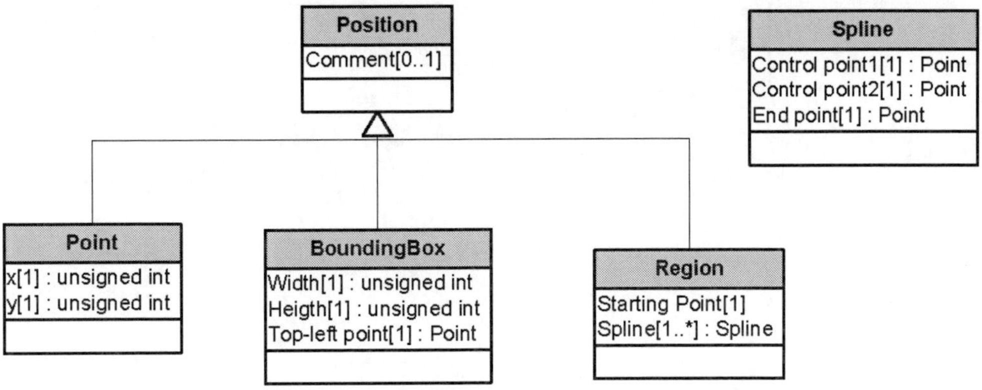

Figure 3. Class Diagram of the Position class.

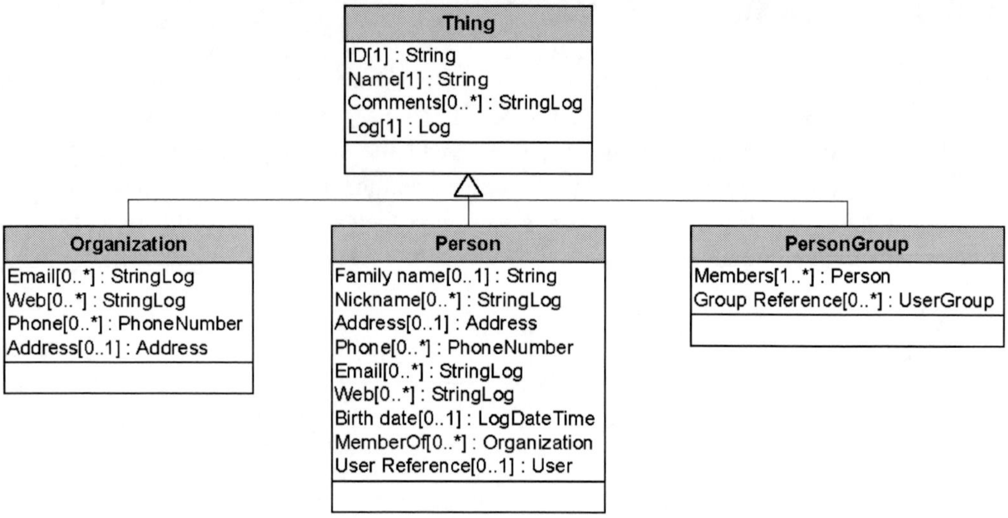

Figure 4. Class Diagram of the Thing class.

The third category of image metadata, namely the content descriptive metadata, describes the content of an image or a specific region of the image as described by the *Position*. By explicitly including this field we can make an annotation about an actual region within an image. This region can be described as a comment (*Comment*), as a point (*Point*), a bounding box (*BoundingBox*), or as a region (*Region*). The latter is defined in terms of *Splines*, as shown in Fig. 3.

The actual annotation that describes the defined region can be a textual comment, depicted item, depicted event, and rating. The *DepictedItem* field describes a tangible *Thing* (see Fig. 4) that is depicted; this can be an object or living thing but also a person (*Person*), a group of people (*PersonGroup*) or an organization (*Organization*).

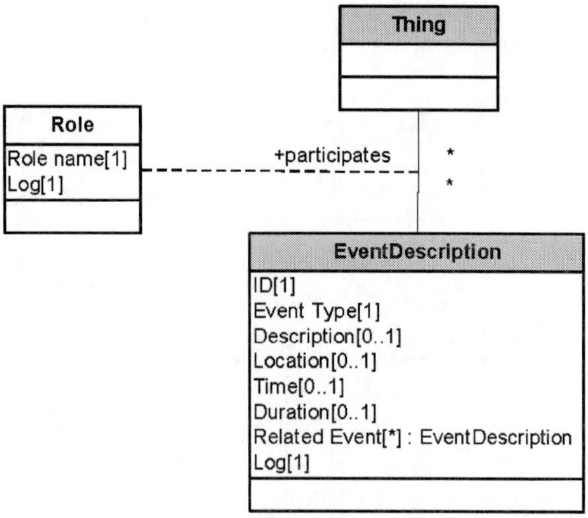

Figure 5. Class Diagram of the EventDescription class, showing the connection with the Thing class.

An event is described by an *EventDescription* and relates to participating things, as shown in Fig. 5. The field *Event Type* specifies the type of event (e.g., "soccer game" or "wedding party") and events can be related with each other through the *Related Event* field.

The rating is defined by a value or score that is given to the content and a minimum and maximum value to denote the range of the score (e.g., the rating is 3 on a scale from 0 to 5). The possibility to rate each others content is especially interesting in a community context where people can tag other users' content (e.g., Flickr).

As shown in this section, we have created a compact metadata model specifically tailored for personal content management systems. The model offers a general overview of the metadata fields of interest and has a large descriptive potential, due to the allowance of automatic annotations, free tagging, and content descriptive metadata. In the next section, we elaborate on the practical implementation of this model and show how existing metadata standards are combined with the model to allow the description of the content in various formats.

4. Semantic PCMS

4.1. Interoperability Issues

The metadata model, introduced in the previous section, is specifically tailored to be compact and easy to reuse. Therefore, it is not intended to replace existing multimedia metadata standards. Based on the metadata model, we created an XML Schema that allows specifying the structure of the metadata used in our system. To allow the actual end-user to freely annotate content, other existing standardized metadata schemas need to be included. However, when trying to match the XML Schemas of different standards we face interoperability problems. These problems were already signaled by the W3C Multimedia Semantics Incubator Group [9].

Although each of the standardized formats present interoperability amongst applications which use that standardized metadata scheme, issues occur when using different metadata schemes together. Fragment 2 and Fragment 3 show two annotations of the same picture but according to different metadata schemes. Both annotations describe a unique identifier, the person who created the picture and the software that was used, the location and time of the creation, and give an identifier used for IPR purposes.

These examples illustrate the issues of interoperability created when using multiple metadata standards. The same concepts are described but in a totally different format. Note that even when using one single standard (e.g., MPEG-7) to describe a resource, issues in interoperability can exist due to a lack of precise semantics [31].

As these examples show, using XML Schema is not sufficient. Consequently we use semantic web technologies to deal with these issues by creating a semantic metadata model, discussed in the next section.

```xml
<METADATA>
 <BASIC_IMAGE_PARAM>
  <BASIC_IMAGE_INFO>
   <IMAGE_ID>
    <UID>098f2470-bae0-11cd-b579-08002b30bfeb</UID>
    <ID_TYPE>http://www.digitalimaging.org/dig35/UUID</ID_TYPE>
   </IMAGE_ID>
  </BASIC_IMAGE_INFO>
 <BASIC_IMAGE_PARAM>
 <IMAGE_CREATION>
  <IMAGE_CREATOR>
   <PERSON_NAME>
    <NAME_COMP TYPE="Given">Yoshiaki<NAME_COMP>
    <NAME_COMP TYPE="Family">Shibata<NAME_COMP>
   </PERSON_NAME>
  </IMAGE_CREATOR>
  <SOFTWARE_CREATION>
   <SOFWARE_INFO>
    <MODEL>Wizzo Extracto</MODEL>
    <VERSION>2</VERSION
    </SOFTWARE_INFO>
  </SOFTWARE_CREATION>
 </IMAGE_CREATION>
 <CONTENT_DESCRIPTION>
  <LOCATION>
   <ADDRESS>
    <ADDR_COMP TYPE="City">Tokyo</ADDR_COMP>
    <COUNTRY>jp</COUNTRY>
   </ADDRESS>
   <CAPTURE_TIME>
    <EXACT>2000-10-10T19:45:00+09:00<EXACT>
   </CAPTURE_TIME>
  </LOCATION>
 </CONTENT_DESCRIPTION>
 <IPR>
  <IPR_IDENTIFICATION>
   <IPR_IDENTIFIER><IPR_ID>RID#</IPR_ID></IPR_IDENTIFIER>
  </IPR_IDENTIFICATION>
 </IPR>
</METADATA>
```


Fragment 2. Example of XML metadata expressed in DIG35-format.

```
<Mpeg7>
  <DescriptionMetadata>
    <Confidence>1.0</Confidence>
    <Version>1.1</Version>
    <LastUpdate>2001-09-20T03:20:25+09:00</LastUpdate>
    <PublicIdentifier type="UUID">
                                098f2470-bae0-11cd-b579-08002b30bfeb
    </PublicIdentifier>
    <PrivateIdentifier>completeDescriptionExample</PrivateIdentifier>
    <Creator>
      <Role href="creatorCS"><Name>Creator</Name></Role>
        <Agent xsi:type="PersonType">
          <Name>
            <GivenName>Yoshiaki</GivenName>
            <FamilyName>Shibata</FamilyName>
          </Name>
        </Agent>
    </Creator>
    <CreationLocation>
       <Region>jp</Region>
       <AdministrativeUnit>Tokyo</AdministrativeUnit>
    </CreationLocation>
    <CreationTime>2000-10-10T19:45:00+09:00</CreationTime>
    <Instrument>
      <Tool><Name>Wizzo Extracto ver. 2</Name></Tool>
      <Setting name="sensitivity" value="0.5"/>
    </Instrument>
    <Rights><RightsID>RID#</RightsID></Rights>
  </DescriptionMetadata>
  <Description xsi:type="ContentEntityType">
    <MultimediaContent xsi:type="ImageType">
      <Image>
         <!-- more elements here -->
      </Image>
    </MultimediaContent>
  </Description>
<Mpeg7>
```

Fragment 3. Example of XML metadata expressed in MPEG-7 format.

4.2. Semantic Metadata Model

Semantic web technologies allow alleviating the interoperability issues within one metadata standard. For example, efforts have been undertaken to translate MPEG-7 into ontology and through appropriate frameworks to enable its integration with other ontologies, thus enhancing interoperability [11, 24, 31, 6].

To solve interoperability issues inherent to the use of several different metadata schemes, the ideal scenario would be to create a commonly accepted multimedia (metadata) ontology that encompasses all the concepts needed for annotation of multimedia resources. However, this is not feasible as can be seen by the many different existing metadata standards. Therefore, we chose to create a specific upper-ontology, based on our metadata model, called the PeCMan ontology using OWL [32]. Different multimedia metadata ontologies are subsequently linked to this upper-ontology. As such, we create a hierarchical system of two layers. The upper layer contains concepts on the system, security, and user level suited for content management systems. The lower layer exists of several multimedia ontologies which can be used to describe multimedia resources in various application scenarios.

The plethora of multimedia metadata standards has shown that there is not one commonly accepted standard that provides everything. Different standards are used, whether they are small and simple (PhotoRDF [33]) or broad and complex (MPEG-7). Conceptually, the multimedia metadata formats are on the same level, i.e. they all describe content. Consequently, we regard each metadata format as equally important and will handle the ontologies representing them as such.

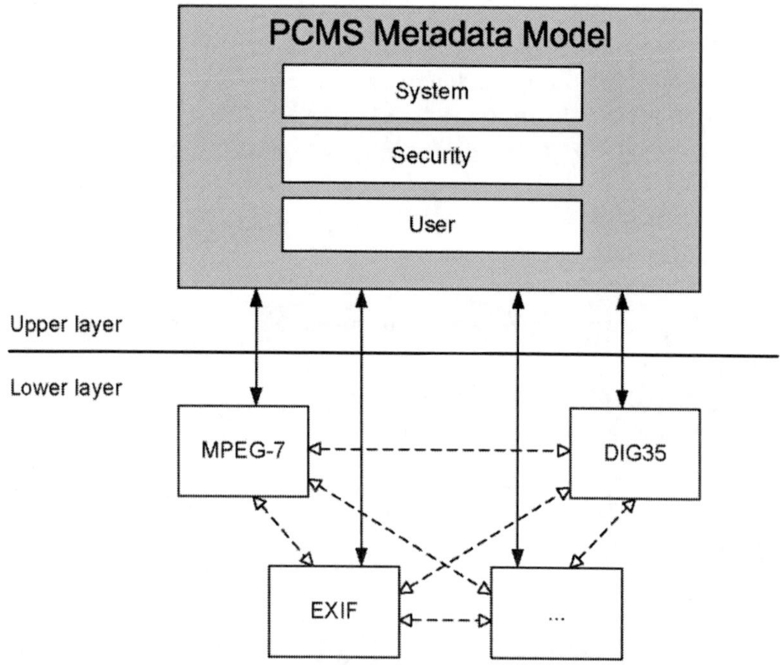

Figure 6. Layered metadata model; the dashed arrows denote mappings between ontologies in the lower layer, the full arrows denote cross-layer mappings.

Fig. 6 shows the layered metadata model consisting of the created PCMS model and the underlying metadata standards. Between the different ontologies there are so called mappings which consists of mapping ontologies and inference rules. These define the relations between classes, properties, and instances of involved ontologies and are discussed in Section 4.4.

The way we organize the different metadata schemes allows intelligent reasoning on different levels. The combination of the formal representation of different metadata standards in the lower layer allows broadening the search space when looking for content based on certain fields of a specific metadata scheme. The personal content management model that works as an upper ontology allows the application of the semantic knowledge to make intelligent decisions on system level (e.g., make content accessible for the depicted user and if the size of an image is large, move it to another storage device).

4.3. Lower Layer

The layered approach allows including new and existing ontologies. To show the extensibility of the system, we add a new metadata ontology based on the DIG35 metadata format. Since for this standard no formal representation exists today, we have built a DIG35 ontology.

DIG35 was developed by the DIG35 Initiative Group which is part of I3A (not-for-profit International Imaging Industry Association), the largest imaging industry group worldwide. The DIG35 specification includes a standard set of metadata for digital images, which promotes interoperability and extensibility, as well as a uniform underlying construct to support interoperability of metadata between various digital imaging devices. The DIG35 Initiative Group chose for XML as the recommended reference implementation structure for their metadata scheme (see Fragment 2 for an example of DIG35 XML instance data). Although this allows to define the structure of the actual metadata, it cannot sufficiently describe the underlying semantics. When semantic reasoning is the goal, a formal representation of this metadata schema is needed. Therefore, within the context of MMSem, we created the DIG35 ontology using OWL (The ontologies can be found at http://multimedialab.elis.ugent.be/users/gmartens/ontologies/DIG35/).

For the development of the formal representation we have chosen not to use an automatic conversion like Garcia et al. [24], since, like within the MPEG-7 standard, DIG35 defines the underlying semantics of the different metadata fields within a textual specification. Consequently, we manually created classes and properties based on the DIG35 specification, which allows us to define semantic relationships that are not derivable from the provided XML Schema. The final ontology is an OWL DL ontology, consisting of approximately 150 classes.

According to the different parts that are covered by the metadata specification, different ontologies were created. These consist of an image creation, basic image parameters, content description, image history, and IPR ontologies. Note that the image related metadata in the PeCMan ontology is similar. Additionally, a number of fundamental ontologies were created which actually are domain-independent and could be reused for different purposes. These ontologies represent fundamental concepts like addresses, persons, dates and times, events, locations, and other concepts which are also used in the DIG35 specification. These concepts can easily be matched with other existing ontologies (like FOAF or Dublin Core) through a separate mapping ontology.

4.4. Mapping and Rules

A mapping ontology typically consists of basic OWL or RDFS constructs (e.g., owl:equivalentClass and rdfs:subPropertyOf) between concepts of different ontologies. Fragment 4 shows an excerpt of a mapping ontology between the DIG35 ontology and the PeCMan ontology. The figure shows for example how the standard constructs are used to map a DIG35 *Person* class on the conceptually equivalent PeCMan *Person* class.

```
<owl:ObjectProperty rdf:about="../DIG35/PersonDescription.owl#person">
        <rdfs:subPropertyOf rdf:resource="../Pecman/Content.owl#depictedItem"/>
</owl:ObjectProperty>

<owl:Class rdf:about="../DIG35/Person.owl#Person">
        <owl:equivalentClass rdf:resource="../Pecman/Person.owl#Person"/>
</owl:Class>

<owl:Class rdf:about="../DIG35/Content.owl#Content">
 <owl:equivalentClass rdf:resource="../Pecman/Content.owl#ImageContentDescription"/>
</owl:Class>
```

Fragment 4. Example of mapping using OWL-constructs within the DIG35 to PeCMan mapping (the namespaces were abbreviated for layout purposes).

Note that, for practical implementations, a mapping ontology as presented above is not sufficient. Rules are needed to create advanced conditional relationships, for example to declare instance equivalence when certain properties match. Within the PCMS, we want to offer content retrieval based on metadata. As such, the actual instances of these data are sometimes not known beforehand. Hence, we cannot define relations on them in the pre-determined mapping ontologies. However, by defining rules we can automatically link new instances to those that are stored within the system. Fragment 5 shows such a rule (we adopt the informal notation declared in the SWRL (Semantic Web Rule Language) submission to give a human readable form of the rules [34]). The rule relates individuals of the class *Person* within the DIG35 ontology to individuals of the class *Person* within the PeCMan ontology. If instances of these classes have the same values for their corresponding name and family name properties, they are considered to be equal. This rule makes it possible to match an instance of a PeCMan *Person* to an instance of a DIG35 *Person* based on their properties.

```
dig35:Person(?x1) □ pecman:Person(?x2)
□ dig35:givenName(?x1,?y1) □ pecman:name(?x2,?y2)
□ dig35:familyName(?x1,?y3)□ pecman:familyName(?x2,?y4)
□ (?y1=?y2) □ (?y3=?y4)
    => owl:sameAs(?x1,?x2)
```

Fragment 5. Rule for mapping PeCMan Person instances to DIG35 Person instances.

Furthermore, rules are needed to relate certain constructs in different ontologies. For example the rule shown in Fragment 6 states that if an instance of the DIG35 *Content* class *x1* is related to an instance *x3* through the *contentPersonDescription* and *person* object properties, it can be inferred that *x1* is the subject and *x3* is the object of the property *depictedItem* from the PeCMan ontology (in this example the actual classes of instances *x2* and *x3*, being *PersonDescription* and *Person* respectively, can be omitted). As such we can find depicted persons within the PeCMan ontology, based on descriptions in the DIG35 ontology.

```
dig35:Content(?x1) □ dig35:contentPersonDescription(?x1,?x2)
                   □ dig35:person(?x2,?x3)
=> pecman:depictedItem(?x1,?x3)
```

Fragment 6. Rule to relate the *depictedItem* property to a specific construct in DIG35.

The next section discusses the practical aspects of the creation of a semantic PCMS. More specifically, we elaborate on how it is used within the PeCMan project.

5. Metadata Service

The underlying framework for the metadata service is a distributed architecture based on Web services, from the BRICKS project, which is discussed in the next section [35]. This framework incorporates the metadata schema as we defined above and allows to reason on RDF triples based on the present ontologies.

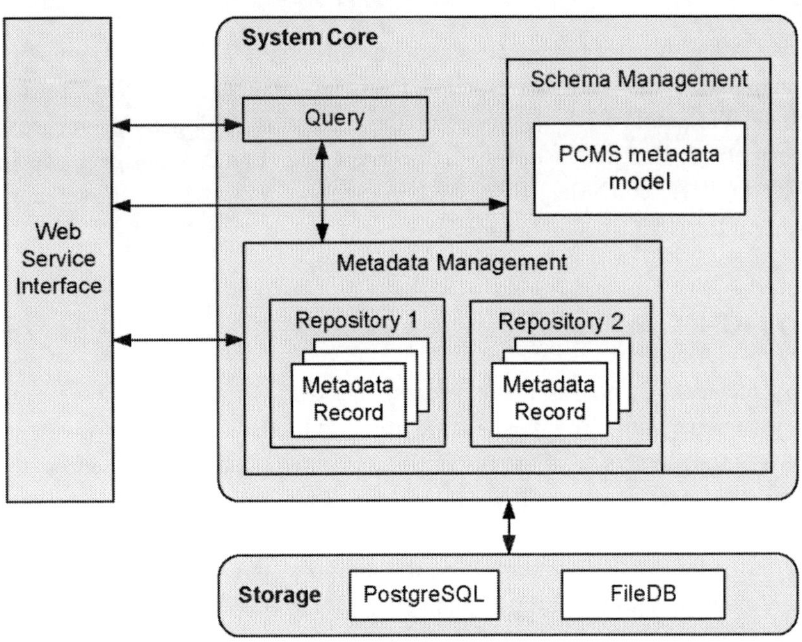

Figure 7. Metadata architecture of Bricks environment showing the interface, system core and storage capacities.

5.1. Metadata Management

BRICKS (Building Resources for Integrated Cultural Knowledge Services) is a European project, funded by the IST priority in FP6. It aims to establish the organizational and technological foundations of a digital library, which refers to a networked system of services over globally available collections of digital multimedia documents, providing several layers of knowledge to a variety of users and access methods.

The actual infrastructure consists of integrated, but independent, software units, which are deployed on the nodes of the architecture. These nodes, called *Bnodes*, can connect to each other through a peer-to-peer mechanism and use available resources for content and metadata management. Each node is characterized by a web-based interface giving access to administration, cataloguing, consultation, annotation, and personalization of content. Our metadata service is implemented within such a *Bnode*. Fig. 7 shows the internal structure of the metadata service. The *Schema Management* module stores arbitrary metadata schemas, both standard and proprietary, which are described in OWL DL. These schemas describe the actual metadata, denoted as *Metadata Records*. The query module uses Lucene for simple text-search querying. Moreover, advanced ontology queries are expressed in SPARQL (SPARQL Protocol And RDF Query Language [36]) and executed by an underlying Jena RDF query processor.

An external content manager is used to store and manage object identifiers that refer to the actual multimedia content. Within PeCMan, the management of this content is done through a global index that keeps track of the location of the resources. Consequently, within the metadata service, the metadata is linked to these object identifiers. The metadata service holds a Web service giving acces to setters and getters of specific metadata fields. Internally these are translated to the appropriate operations on the RDF triple store, according to the OWL schemas.

Within PeCMan, the metadata access happens through a Web service, invoking methods upon specific metadata fields. However, since many metadata exists in XML format, we need a way to obtain the actual RDF instances of the different ontologies, as such avoiding the usage of the methods for the insertion of the metadata. For this purpose, we introduce a generic XML to RDF converter, discussed in Section 5.2., which allows the automatic transformation of the XML metadata to RDF.

5.2. XML to RDF Conversion

Today, many metadata standards are expressed in XML Schema and there are numerous multimedia documents with XML-based annotations. Moreover, several software agents have specific XML-based parsers to interpret multimedia metadata. Consequently, to make the system practically usable, we allow communications expressed in XML format. To implement this within the PCMS, a conversion tool is needed to automatically generate the RDF triples out of the XML fragments. For this purpose, two major approaches exist: fixed XML to RDF mapping and ontology-dependent XML to RDF mappings. The former uses a mapping based on the XML Schema and disregards the actual ontology [24, 37, 38]. The ontology-dependent mappings specify a XML to RDF mapping document that is specifically tailored for the actual ontology [39, 40, 12, 41]. They mostly differ in the way the mapping document is created. We have chosen the generic XML to RDF convertor presented by Van Deursen et al. [41]. This uses an XML document as mapping document that defines specific mapping rules between an XML instance document and the resulting RDF document. A generic *XMLtoRDF* tool takes this mapping document and the used ontology as input and then automatically transforms corresponding XML documents to RDF instances, as shown in Fig. 8.

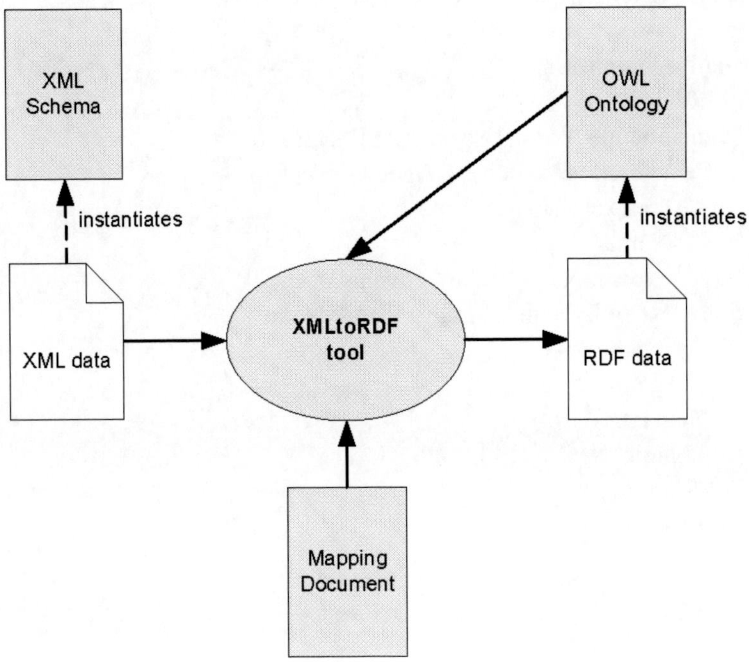

Figure 8. Working of the XMLtoRDF tool.

The XML-based mapping document is built from specific elements which form a mapping language and can be interpreted by the *XMLtoRDF* tool. This language allows to create a simple mapping of XML nodes to corresponding OWL classes or properties. Conditional mappings are avialable in case a mapping not always holds. In that case, a condition can be made of XPATH (XML Path Language) or SPARQL ASK expressions. Finally, value processing is included which specifies different ways to infer the value of a resulting OWL property. These specific language constructs ease the development of such XML to RDF mappings.

6. Use Case Scenario

6.1. Solving the Use Case Scenario with the Proposed System

When a PeCMan user uploads a multimedia document, the related XML-based metadata is imported. This metadata could be stored in the multimedia file itself (e.g., JPEG), in which case an extractor retrieves the metadata from the file, or the XML fragments could be uploaded separately. Consider that a user has employed a face recognition tool on a picture to create an MPEG-7 annotation as output. The annotation, shown in XML format in Fragment 7, states that a specific person (John Smith) is depicted.

```
<Mpeg7>
  <Description xsi:type="ContentEntityType">
    <MultimediaContent xsi:type="ImageType">
      <Image>
        <SpatialDecomposition>
          <StillRegion>
            <Semantic id="FormalAbstractionDescription">
              <SemanticBase xsi:type="AgentObjectType">
                <Agent xsi:="PersonType">
                  <Name>
                    <GivenName>John</GivenName>
                    <FamilyName>Smith</FamilyName>
                  </Name>
                </Agent>
              </SemanticBase>
            </Semantic>
          </StillRegion>
        </SpatialDecomposition>
      </Image>
    </MultimediaContent>
  </Description>
<Mpeg7>
```

Fragment 7. Example of XML metadata expressed in MPEG-7 format.

When this picture and its MPEG-7 annotation are uploaded to the system, the *XMLtoRDF* tool is used to create corresponding RDF triples. Fragment 8 shows the RDF/N3 notation of an instance of the *PersonType* class within the MPEG-7 ontology of Garcia et al. [24].

```
@prefix mpeg7: <http://rhizomik.upf.edu/ontologies/2005/03/MPEG7-2001.owl#>.

<#mpeg7_0> a mpeg7:PersonType;
               mpeg7:Name [mpeg7:GivenName "John", mpeg7:FamilyName "Smith"] .
```

Fragment 8. RDF/N3 notation of the MPEG-7 description of a person.

Now consider that a different user utilizes a DIG35 application to annotate a newly created picture in which he is depicted. The application provides the end-user with means to select a region in an image and to add an annotation. When the user selects a region, possible DIG35 metadata fields are presented and an XML annotation is created (e.g., the XML annotation shown in Fragment 9). Afterwards, the user uploads the content and metadata to the PCMS, in which the metadata is added to the metadata service.

```
<METADATA>
  <CONTENT_DESCRIPTION>
    <PERSON_NAME>
      <NAME_COMP type="Given">John</NAME_COMP>
      <NAME_COMP type="Family">Smith</NAME_COMP>
    </PERSON_NAME>
  </CONTENT_DESCRIPTION>
</METADATA>
```

Fragment 9. Example of DIG35 metadata in XML format. It expresses that the person John Smith is depicted on the image.

Within the metadata service, this XML annotation is converted to RDF triples, by the *XMLtoRDF* tool, and stored for future retrieval (the RDF/N3 annotation is given in Fragment 10).

```
@prefix dig35: <../DIG35/V0.2/DIG35.owl#>.

<#person_0> a dig35:Person;
        dig35:givenName "John";
        dig35:familyName "Smith".
<#personDescription_0> a dig35:PersonDescription;
        dig35:person <#person_0> .
<#content_0> a dig35:Content;
        dig35:contentPersonDescription <#personDescription_0> .
<#metadata_0> a dig35:Metadata;
        dig35:imageContent <#content_0> .
```

Fragment 10. Example of DIG35 metadata expressed in RDF/XML-format.

Finally, the PCMS system offers the user the possibility to search for depicted persons through a Web interface. When invoked, the user fills in a name and family name. The Web service interprets this and constructs a SPARQL query solely based on PeCMan metadata as shown in Fragment 11. This is indeed a normal query that retrieves instances of the *ImageContentDescription* class that describe a depicted person with name "John" and family name "Smith". The actual pictures can be retrieved and shown to the user since the metadata service internally stores a digital object identifier that relates the annotations to corresponding multimedia resources.

Since the semantic representations of our PeCMan metadata model and the underlying MPEG-7 and DIG35 standards are linked together, through the ontology mapping and rules as explained in Section 4.4., the system retrieves both pictures. For example, following the mapping and rules, the information from the DIG35 annotation of the second picture is linked to PeCMan triples within the RDF triple-store. The *Content* class of DIG35 is matched with the *ImageContentDescription* class of the PeCMan ontology and the *depictedItem* property is deduced from the DIG35 constructs following the rule shown in Fragment 6. As a result, the software agent retrieves the two pictures depicting the requested person.

```
PREFIX rdf: <http://www.w3.org/1999/02/22-rdf-syntax-ns#>
PREFIX pecman: <../PecMan/V1.0/PDocument.owl#>

SELECT ?content
WHERE { ?content rdf:type pecman:ImageContentDescription.
        ?content pecman:depictedItem ?person .
        ?person rdf:type pecman:Person.
        ?person pecman:name "John" .
        ?person pecman:familyName "Smith"
        }
```

Fragment 11. Example of SPARQL query to retrieve.

```
PREFIX rdf: <http://www.w3.org/1999/02/22-rdf-syntax-ns#>
PREFIX pecman: <../PecMan/V1.0/PDocument.owl#>

SELECT ?doc
WHERE { ?doc rdf:type pecman:PecmanDocument.
        ?doc pecman:securityCentric ?security.
        ?security pecman:share ?shareLevel.
        ?shareLevel pecman:shareLevel "Shared".
        ?security pecman:permission ?policy.
        ?policy pecman:user "urn:pecman:someUserID".
        ?policy pecman:permission "View".

         ?doc pecman:userCentric ?userMetadata.
         ?userMetadata pecman:manualAnnotation ?imageMetadata
         ?imageMetadata pecman:imageContent ?content.
         ?content pecman:depictedItem ?person.
         ?person rdf:type pecman:Person.
         ?person pecman:name "John" .
         ?person pecman:familyName "Smith"
         }
```

Fragment 12. Example of SPARQL query to retrieve shared content.

The use case presented here can be extended to deliver only those resources for which a user is granted access, or that are currently stored in some location, etc. The related work focuses on the (semantic) annotation of multimedia content and does not include metadata on the security or system level; hence it cannot enforce such restrictions. However, in the proposed system, all this metadata is part of the same search space, so metadata relevant for the working of a PCMS can be combined with the actual multimedia metadata. For example, to show only those resources that are shared with a user (with id *urn:pecman:someUserID*), the query of Fragment 11 is extended to check the sharing settings (see Fragment 12). The query finds all resources that are shared and for which the specific user has been given permission to view the resource.

6.2. Solving the Use Case Scenario with the Related Work

This section discusses whether the related work could be used to implement the use case scenario presented above (without the security restrictions). Note that the use case scenario consists of 2 steps. First resources with metadata, according to two different formats (MPEG-7 and DIG35), are inserted into the system. Secondly, by querying the high-level metadata model that is used within the PCMS, the according resources are retrieved.

Hunter used XSLT transformations to map concepts of different metadata standards on each other [11]. This means that XML fragments according to different metadata schemas need to be mapped upon each other using these transformations for each request. In the proposed system, these mappings are available as an OWL schema by itself. Hence, the relations between the different metadata schemas are part of the search space, so only one query is needed to retrieve the right results.

Cruz et al. use a proprietary mapping table that links an upper ontology to local RDF ontologies [12]. A query upon this upper ontology is therefore first translated, using the mapping table, to different queries on the local RDF ontologies. Moreover, according to their architecture, these queries are translated to XML queries that are executed upon the XML sources. This introduces overhead compared to the proposed system where only one query is executed on the RDF data to retrieve the same results.

Hunter and Little use the ABC ontology as core ontology [13]. However, the ABC ontology is not suitable to relate different multimedia metadata formats (which describe multimedia and not that much existing concepts or events) to each other. In contrast, our system allows to relate those formats to each other by using the general user centric metadata within the top layer. In fact, the lower layer of our system could include the ABC ontology to link different domain-specific ontologies. These links can be regarded as a mapping ontology, which was described in Section 4.4.

If the system of Hunter and Little is applied to find the resources that depict a person with given name, the following steps are needed. First a reasoner is used to find concepts within the participating ontologies that represent a person, or the name of a person. Next, these concepts need to be mapped upon the XML instances. To accomplish this an XPath query is needed to find the according XML element defined in the XML schema. Finally, an additional XPath expression is needed to find the actual value of that element within the XML instance, so that it can be used for retrieval.

Dønderler et al. presented a semantic video database management system [17]. A video annotation tool could be incorporated in their system that takes MPEG-7 or DIG35 metadata and stores this in the database according to the semantic model for future querying. A proprietary textual query language, called BilVideo, has been developed, which allows for example to retrieve video (fragments) that depict a certain person. Such a query is formulated in Fragment 13. The query is very simple since it is internally translated on semantic relations, which need to be explicitly defined in the database. Moreover, only relations between instances are possible. As a result, a query that is looking for all persons cannot be used to retrieve specific individuals.

```
select video from all
    where appear(somePerson);
```

Fragment 13. Example of BilVideo query to retrieve a video that depicts a specific person.

Additionally, since the database has a fixed semantic model to describe multimedia, including domain-specific ontologies would infer a new database structure, which makes the system not practical.

Asirelli et al. presented an infrastructure that they are planning to implement, so details are missing about the actual system [23]. Their system totally relies on MPEG-7 descriptors, stored in an XML database, no ways for translating other metadata formats to MPEG-7 descriptors are presented, which is necessary for retrieval across metadata formats.

In this sense, their work resembles that of Petridis et al. [19], meaning they regard MPEG-7 descriptions as low-level features from which high-level semantic concepts are learned. Accordingly, the latter cannot work with other metadata formats.

Garcia et al. use XSD2OWL to automatically create an ontology based on an existing XML schema [24]. However, this tool is made to allow the automatic conversion from MPEG-7 XML schema to an OWL ontology (and only results for MPEG-7 conversions were presented). We noticed that this tool is not usable for the conversion of the DIG35 XML schema. For example, an XSD2OWL translation is used that translates an XML sequence to an intersection of classes (denoted by the *OWL:intersectionOf* construct). Within the DIG35 schema the element *Content Description* is defined as a sequence of different elements (*Caption*, *Location*, *Person*, *Thing*, *Comment*, etc.). Some of these would be translated to *owl:Class* constructs, others to *owl:DatatypePropery* constructs, which would invalidate the intersection.

Moreover, Garcia et al. did not define ways to map different ontologies on each other. By using the XSD2OWL conversions, making a mapping would only be possible if the different metadata schemes use the same names for the same concepts, which is obviously not the case as can be seen from Fragment 2 and Fragment 3.

Note that the use case scenario presented here is a very generic case study, which consists of importing metadata according to different specific multimedia metadata formats and using queries upon the proposed metadata model to retrieve the content. The actual implementation of this use case can vary; we have presented a use case of retrieving pictures that depict a certain person. Comparable studies can be made to retrieve content based on other metadata fields (finding pictures taken in a specific location, retrieve all pictures created by a specific person, retrieve pictures that correspond to a given set of tags, etc.). However, within the related work the same problems will reoccur, regardless the actual implementation of this use case.

7. Conclusion

This chapter introduced a semantic metadata service, tailored for personal content management systems. A novel layered metadata model has been created that is both compact and efficient to allow intelligent semantic reasoning. An upper layer consists of an OWL representation of a PCMS metadata model and allows for system, security, and user level management. This ontology is linked to a lower layer containing a pool of multimedia metadata ontologies that represent commonly accepted metadata formats. To show the usability of our system, we created the first semantic representation of the DIG35 metadata standard. Subsequently, we showed how mapping ontologies and inference rules were defined to integrate this ontology in the layered metadata model. As such, we succeeded in reducing the interoperability issues inherent to the use of different standards. Additionally, the architecture and practical implementation of the semantic metadata service was outlined. Finally, a general use case scenario of retrieving multimedia content based on annotations in different metadata formats was presented. This evaluation showed that the proposed architecture is better suited to deal with the case study than the related work, and that it allows reducing the interoperability issues inherent to the use of different metadata standards.

Acknowledgments

The research activities that have been described in this chapter were funded by Ghent University, the Interdisciplinary Institute for Broadband Technology (IBBT), the Institute for the Promotion of Innovation by Science and Technology in Flanders (IWT-Flanders), the Fund for Scientific Research-Flanders (FWO-Flanders), and the European Union.

References

[1] D. Gussow, *New lens on war*, St. Petersburgh Times online (2004). http://www.sptimes.com/

[2] *Photo Metadata*, White Paper, International Press Telecommunications Council (IPTC) (2007).

[3] *MPEG-7 Overview*, International Organization for Standardisation, Klagenfurt ISO/IEC JTC1/SC29/WG11, (2002). http://mpeg.telecomitalialab.com/standards/mpeg-7

[4] I. Burnett, F. Pereira, R. Van de Walle, R. Koenen, *The MPEG-21 Book*, Whiley, New Yersey, (2006).

[5] I3A DIG35 Initiative Group, http://www.i3a.org/i dig35.html

[6] R. Arndt, R. Troncy, S. Staab, L. Hardman, M. Vacura, *COMM: Designing a Well-Founded Multimedia Ontology for the Web*, in: *Lecture Notes of Computer Science*, p. 30-43 (2007).

[7] C. Poppe, F. De Keukelaere, S. De Zutter, S. De Bruyne, W. De Neve, R. Van de Walle, Predictable Processing of Multimedia Content, Using MPEG-21 Digital Item Processing, in: *Proc. Pacific Rim-Conference on Multimedia (PCM),* p. 549-558, (2007)

[8] C. Poppe, G. Martens, E. Mannens, R. Van de Walle, Personal Content Management System: A Semantic Approach, in: *Journal of Visual Communication and Image Representation*, Vol. 20, p. 131-144, (2009).

[9] *W3C Multimedia Semantics Incubator Group*, http://www.w3.org/2005/Incubator/mmsem/

[10] F. Manola, E. Miller, RDF Primer. *W3C Recommendation*, W3C, (2004).

[11] J. Hunter, Adding Multimedia to the Semantic Web - Building an 7 Ontology, in*: Proc. the First Semantic Web Working Symposium (SWWS),* p. 261-281, (2001).

[12] I.F. Cruz, H. Xiao, F. Hsu, *An Ontology-Based Framework for XML Semantic Integration*, in: *Proc. International Database Engineering and Applications Symposium*, p. 217-226 (2004).

[13] J. Hunter, S. Little, A Framework to enable the Semantic Inferencing and Querying of Multimedia Content, in: *International Journal of Web Engineering and Technology*, Vol. 2, p. 264-286, (2005).

[14] C. Lagoze, J. Hunter, The ABC Ontology and Model, in: *Journal of Digital Information*, Vol. 2(2) (2001).

[15] D. Vallet, P. Castells, M. Fernandez, P. Mylonas, Y. Avrithis, *Personalized Content Retrieval in Context Using Ontological Knowledge*, in: IEEE Transactions on Circuits and Systems for Video Technology, Vol. 17, p. 336-346, (2007).

[16] C. Masolo, L. Vieu, E. Bottazzi, C. Catenacci, C. Ferrario, R. Gangemi, N. Oltramari, A. Schneider, The WonderWeb Library of Foundational Ontologies (WFOL*)*, Technical report, *WonderWeb Deliverable* **17**, (2002).

[17] M. E. Dönderler, E. Saykol, U. Arslan, Ö. Ulusoy, U. üdükbay, BilVideo: Design and Implementation of a Video Database Management System, in: *Multimedia Tools and Applications*, Vol. 27, p. 79-104, (2005).

[18] P. Schallauer, W. Bailer, G. Thallinger, A Description Infrastructure for Audiovisual Media Processing Systems Based on MPEG-7, in: *Journal of Universal Knowledge Management*, Vol. 1, pp. 26-35, (2006).

[19] K. Petridis, S. Bloehdorn, C. Saathoff, N. Simou, S. Dasiopoulou, V. Tzouvaras, V.Tzouvaras, S. Handschuh, Y. Avrithis, Y. Kompatsiaris, S. Staab, Knowledge Representation and Semantic Annotation of Multimedia Content, in: *IEE Proceedings Vision, Image and Signal Processing,* Vol. 153, 3, p. 255-262, (2006).

[20] N. Simou, V. Tzouvaras, Y. Avrithis, G. Stamou, S. Kollias, A Visual Descriptor Ontology of Multimedia Reasoning, in: *Proc. Workshop on Image Analysis for Multimedia Interactive Services*, (2005).

[21] ISO/IEC 15938-3 *FCD Information Technology - Multimedia Content Description Interface - Part 3:Visual*, Singapore, (2001).

[22] P. Salembier, J.R. Smith, MPEG-7 Multimedia Description Schemes, in *IEEE Trans. Circuits and Systems for Video Technology*, vol. 11, p. 748-759, (2001).

[23] P. Asirelli, S. Little, M. Marinelli, O. Salvetti, MultiMedia Metadata Management: a Proposal for an Infrastructure, in: *Proc. Semantic Web Applications and Perspectives (SWAP),* p. 255-261, (2006)

[24] R. Garcia, O. Celma, Semantic Integration and Retrieval of Multimedia Metadata, in: *Proc. 5th Knowledge Markup and Semantic Annotation Workshop*, p. 69-80, (2006).

[25] V. Tzouvaras, R. Troncy, J. Z. Pan, Multimedia Annotation Interoperability Framework, *W3C Incubator Group Report* (2007),

http://www.w3.org/2005/Incubator/mmsem/

[26] N. Sluijs, K. Vlaeminck, T. Wauters, B. Dhoedt, F. De Turck, P. Demeester, Caching strategies for Personal Content Storage Grids, in: *Proc. the International Conference on Parallel and Distributed Processing Techniques and Applications*, p. 396-404, (2007).

[27] X.Wang, T. DeMartini, B. Wragg, M. Paramasivam, C. Barlas, The MPEG-21 Rights Expression Language and Rights Date Dictionary, in: *IEEE Transactions on Multimedia, International Conference on Parallel and Distributed Processing Techniques and Applications*", Vol. 7, No. 3, p. 408-417, (2005).

[28] C. Poppe, I. Wolf, S. Wischnowsky, S. De Zutter, R. Van de Walle, *Licensing System in an online MPEG-21 Environment*, in: *Proc. the International Conference WWW/Internet*, p. 315-319, (2006)

[29] J. S. Hare, P. A.S. Sinclair, P. H. Lewis , K. Martinez, P. G.B. Enser, C. J. Sandom , *Bridging the Semantic Gap in Multimedia Information Retrieval*, in: *Proc. the third European Semantic Web Conference Workshop on Mastering the Gap: From Information Extraction to Semantic Representation, (2006),* http://ceur-ws.org/Vol-187/19.pdf

[30] M. Hausenblas, S. Boll, T. Burger, O. Celma, C. Halaschek-Wiener, E. Mannens, R. Troncy, Multimedia Vocabularies on the Semantic Web, *W3C Incubator Group Report* (2007), http://www.w3.org/2005/Incubator/mmsem/XGR-vocabularies/

[31] R. Troncy, W. Bailer, M. Hausenblas, P. Hofmair, R. Schlatte, Enabling Multimedia Metadata Interoperability by Defining Formal Semantics of MPEG-7 Profil*es*, *Lecture Notes in Computer Science* 4306, p. 41-55, (2006)

[32] P. Patel-Schneider, P. Hayes, I. Horrocks, OWL Web Ontology Language Semantics and Abstract Syntax, *W3C Recommendation*, (2004) http://www.w3.org/TR/2004/REC-owl-semantics-20040210/

[33] *Describing and retrieving photos using RDF and HTTP*, W3C Note, (2002), http://www.w3.org/TR/photo-rdf/

[34] I. Horrocks, P. Patel-Schneider, H. Boley, S. Tabet, B. Grosof, M. Dean, SWRL: A Semantic Web Rule Language - Combining OWL and RuleML, W3C Member Submission, (2004), http://www.w3.org/Submission/SWRL/

[35] BRICKS - *Building Resources for Integrated Cultural Knowledge Services,* (2007), http://www.brickscommunity.org/prj

[36] SPARQL Query Language for RDF, *W3C Recommendation* (2008), http://www.w3.org/TR/rdf-sparql-query/

[37] S. Battle, Gloze, XML to RDF and back again, in: *Proc. First Jena User Conference,* (2006).

[38] M. Ferdinand, C. Zirpins, D. Trastour, Lifting XML Schema to OWL, in: *Proc. Web Engineering - 4th International Conference*, p. 354-358 (2004).

[39] M. Klein, Interpreting XML Documents via an RDF Schema Ontology, in: *Proc. DEXA Workshop*, p. 889-894, (2002)

[40] B. Amann, C. Beeri, I. Funulaki, M. Scholl, Ontology-Based Integration of XML Web Resources, in: *Proc. the First International Semantic Web Conference on The Semantic Web,* p. 117-131, (2002).

[41] D. Van Deursen, C. Poppe, G. Martens, E. Mannens, R. Van de Walle, XML to RDF Conversion: a Generic Approach, in: *Proc. the 4th International Conference on Automated Solutions for Cross Media Content and Multi-Channel Distribution*, (2008).

[42] R. Wilkinson, M. Wu, Evaluation Experiments and Experience from the Perspective of Interactive Information Retrieval, in: *Proc. 3rd Workshop Empirical Evaluation Adaptive Systems*, p. 221-230 (2004).

In: Data Management in the Semantic Web
Editor: Hal Jin, pp. 323-344
ISBN: 978-1-61122-862-5

Chapter 14

A HYBRID DATA LAYER TO UTILIZE OPEN CONTENT FOR HIGHER-LAYERED APPLICATIONS

M. Steinberg* and J. Brehm
Institute of Systems Engineering, System- and Computer Architecture,
Leibniz Universität Hannover, Germany

Abstract

Increasing heterogeneous Open Content is an ongoing trend in the current Social Semantic Web (S2W) [1]. Generic concepts and how-tos for higher-layered reuse of the arbitrary information overload for interactive knowledge transfer and learning - mentioning the Internet of Services (IoS) [2] - are not covered very well yet. For further directed use of distributed services and sources, inquiry, interlinking, analysis, machine- and human-interpretable representation is as essential as lightweight user-oriented interoperation and competence in handling. In the following, we introduce the qKAI application framework (qualifying Knowledge Acquisition and Inquiry) [3] - a service-oriented, generic and hybrid approach combining knowledge related offers for convenient reuse. qKAI aims at closing some residual gaps between the "*sophisticated*" Semantic Web and "*hands-on*" Web 2.0 enabling loose-coupled knowledge and information services focused on knowledge life cycles, learning aspects and handy user interaction. Accomplishing user interoperation and standardized web techniques is a promising mixture to build a next generation of web applications. The focus of this chapter lies on the qKAI data layer as part of the application framework and basic prerequisite to build user interaction scenarios on top of it. The qKAI data layer utilizes available, distributed semantic data sets in a practically manner using an affordable Quadcore hardware platform and preselected data dumps. Overall, we boost Open Content as an inherent part of higher-layered, lightweight applications in knowledge and information transfer via standard tasks of knowledge engineering and augmented user interaction. Beyond giving an overview of research background and periphery assumption, this chapter introduces the hybrid data concept - a minimalistic data model with maximized depth - implementation results and lessoned learned. We discuss the Semantic Web query language SPARQL[1] and the Resource Description Format[2] (RDF) critically to enlighten their limitations in current web application practice. qKAI implements search space restriction

* E-mail address: steinberg@sra.uni-hannover.de, Phone: +49 0511 762 19726, Fax: +49 0511 762 19733
[1] http://www.w3.org/TR/rdf-SPARQL-query, visited: 09.05.09
[2] http://www.w3.org/RDF/, visited: 09.05.09

(Points of Interests) by smart enabled RDF representation and restriction to SQL as internally used query language. Acquiring resources and discovering the Web of Data is a massively multithreading part of the qKAI application framework that serves as basis for further knowledge based tasks.

1. Introduction

Currently, the borders between Semantic Web and Web 2.0 wipe out more and more and let us create new synergies in the Web 3.0 or also called the Social Semantic Web [1]. The combination of social user involvement, employing desktop-alike rich interfaces (RIA [4]), and the Semantic Web with technologically oriented operability for data representation and processing is a promising conceptual basis to solve two pending problems. On the one side, there is still a lack of lightweight user participation in Semantic Web contexts because of handling hurdles and missing fancy interoperation ability. On the other side, there are claims for less trivial and more unitary content in Web 2.0 contexts. Currently, DBpedia[3] and Freebase[4] start bringing these efforts together by offering collaborative content collection, creation, refinement, or semantic interlinking to increase Open Data that is well interpretable by humans and machines. Twine[5] is another semantic knowledge-enhancing platform, but it does not offer its content with open access yet.

Metadata is an important factor for analyzing and categorizing content. In case of missing metadata automated and manual annotation are approved workarounds to get information about the information for processing useful knowledge out of it. Conclusions about information quality (e.g. provenance, reputation, timeliness, correctness) are important for further deployment in knowledge transfer scenarios. These conclusions can be deduced out of metadata analyses and further interactive assessment.

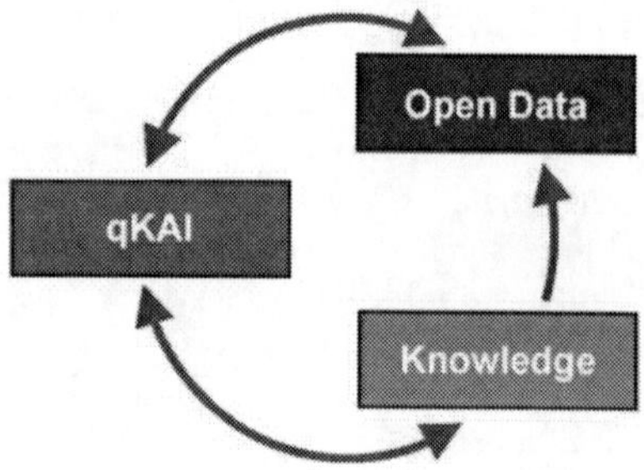

Figure 1. qKAI concept scheme to derive knowledge out of Open Data.

We have to develop enjoyable interoperation scenarios that permit interactive knowledge transfer and learning. We see facilitating access to Open Data by intuitive learning interaction concepts as a promising combination to increase Open Knowledge and to prepare it for further learning purposes. In contrast to learning, knowledge transfer is a non-linear process. Learners are able to move free in the created environment and may

[3] http://dbpedia.org/About, visited: 13.05.09
[4] http://www.freebase.com/, visited: 13.05.09
[5] http://www.twine.com, visited: 13.05.09

decide on their own which learning order to take. Furthermore, users are embedded and actively involved to influence learning sequences. Proved learning concepts have to be active, self-controlled, constructive, situative and social following successful didactic concerns [5]. Gradually, we realize linear and non-linear learning scenarios on top of the qKAI application framework to allow different interaction forms like exploring, questioning, answering or annotating. Also fundamental are incentive and motivation of the users to interoperation and collaboration. Next to common methods for annotating and exploring data, using questionnaires and data browsers, we see especially learning games as a motivating way to implicitly inquire, analyze and annotate content while knowledge is interceded. Well-designed gaming flows can impart handling of suspenseful information in an easy understandable manner to the user. Open Knowledge that is well comprehensible for its users and machine-readable, increases this way. Newly developed learning interaction services and enriched content are combined with conventional Learning Management Systems (LMS) and learning standards (e.g. SCORM[6] or IMS/QTI[7]).

Obviously, there are many different tasks to perform utilizing arbitrary available Open Data for higher-level, extensible and standardized applications with rich interoperation for knowledge transfer and learning. Our research showed that there are several knowledge bases, services and software components available that are required for sub tasks of qKAI. The challenge is to merge and expand existing APIs, frameworks, autonomous services and distributed sources to perform our jobs here. According to C. Schroth and T. Janner [2] we see the relation of our needs to service-oriented software design (SOA): "*The first major analogy between product design in the fields of Web 2.0 and SOA is the notion of reusing and composing existing resources. Both concepts let users reuse, remix, and enrich existing resources and components to new and potentially higher-level applications. The second commonness is the affinity to collaboration and coupling of remote resources or services. Both Web 2.0 and SOA applications enable the loose coupling of distant and possibly heterogeneous resources. A third apparent resemblance between Web 2.0 and SOA is the shared principle of agility and the support of permanent structural change.*" [2]

Long-term objective is to embed different types of services (atomic, simple and composite services) and resources in qKAI for systematically utilizing Open Data and enhancing Open Knowledge. Design concepts from service -oriented and mediator -wrapper-based [6] information systems are applied in the system specification of the qKAI framework. We identified three main service categories and packaged them in three service bundles as interaction, representation and discovery manager in a mediation layer (s. Fig.2). To keep the system structure comprehensive and easy extensible we take a 4-tier-layer concept paired with Rich Client MVC2 paradigms to structure and model desired service managers and types.

Resources and Open Content

Open Content is interpreted in qKAI following the Open Knowledge specification "*Defining the Open in Open Data, Open Content and Open Information*" by the Open Knowledge

[6] http://en.wikipedia.org/wiki/Scorm, visited: 18.05.09
[7] http://en.wikipedia.org/wiki/IMS_Global, visited: 18.05.09

Foundation[8]: "*A piece of knowledge is open if you are free to use, reuse, and redistribute it.*" qKAI adds processing differentiation between Open Data, as raw input information and Open Knowledge, which represents qualified information – checked or enriched yet. The semantic Web of Data (RDF stores and ontologies) and User Generated Content (Wikis, communities, Blogs) stand by and grow up in structured, unstructured and semi-structured manner. DBpedia offers an extensive knowledge base in RDF format (generated out of Wikipedia content), allows semantic browsing and detailed thematic inquiring by applying SPARQL queries for refinishing and further assignment.

The aim of RDF is the unique description of entities, their relations and properties on the internet [7] according to a standardized scheme. These are the resources or "*things*" if we talk about the renewed "*Internet of Things*". The access to resources is realized by using representations. One resource can have several representations like HTML, RDF, XML or JSON.

Open, shared databases like Freebase offer a free API to reuse its content by its own Metaweb query language (MQL)[9]. Relational databases can be easily converted into the Web of Data embedding existing components like the D 2R server [8]. Additionally, there are many unstructured sources like HTML sites or PDF files that do not apply to machine-interpretable web concepts yet. Serializing this data to standardized formats with open access is a first step towards enhanced machine and user interpretability. Aperture[10] and Virtuoso Spongers[11], for example, enable comprehensive solutions for these tasks. In case more text engineering is needed, there are comprehensive solutions for standard Natural Language Processing (NLP) tasks (e.g. by OpenNLP[12]) to perform sentence detection, NER (Named Entity Recognition), POS (Part-Of-Speech) tagging or even semantic chunking.

Web 3.0 Alias Social Semantic Web behind the Scenes

Resource Description Framework (RDF): The Semantic Web, increasingly transcribed as "*Linked Data*"[13], is supposed to bring new quality to the internet: What was formerly known in form of internet pages only to human beings, shall now be applied to automatic processing. In order to achieve this, the formerly in continuous text existent data will be classified, its properties transformed into defined forms and, as their aggregation, connected through labeled links. The scheme of the "*Resource Description Framework*" (RDF) - developed for this purpose - follows a natural speaking sentence structure. It consists out of the following information carrier: The "*subject*", "*resource*" or "*node*" is represented as an URI (Unified Resource Identifier) just like the "*predicate*" and the "*object*". All of them might contain properties following their description. Properties are typed and if we imagine RDF as a tree, they represent the leaves. Their type is normally declared like for example the number 34 is of type "*integer*", but functionally dependent from its predicate. RDF models the relation of the information carriers implicitly, always directed and qualified through the predicate.

[8] http://opendefinition.org/, visited: 15.05.09
[9] http://www.freebase.com/view/freebase/api, visited: 13.05.09
[10] http://aperture.sourceforge.net/, visited: 13.05.09
[11] http://virtuoso.openlinksw.com/dataspace/dav/wiki/Main/VirtSponger, visited: 13.05.09
[12] http://opennlp.sourceforge.net/, visited: 13.05.09
[13] http://linkeddata.org/, visited: 10.05.09

Instead of speaking about "*subject*", „*predicate*" and „*object*" (the object might be a subject as well), it is more efficient to name them "*properties*" that are assigned to resources. RDF connects resources over relations in three ways: As source, target and identifier.

SPARQL: With SPARQL (SPARQL Protocol and RDF Query Language), the W3C designed a search and query language for RDF repositories. SPARQL is a W3C specification since the beginning of 2008. SPARQL's syntax is similar to SQL while columns can be defined to answer requests. Filtering expressions are possible in SPARQL that are placed in the WHERE clause in SQL for example. Up to now, there is no efficient functionality to implement full text search yet. Next to ASK there are no aggregate functions available in the SPARQL specification at this time. ASK allows only a true/false statement about whether a request delivers a result or not. To abandon the special case of an identity, regular expressions should be used for full text search. Such expressions do not fit properly to a large amount of data, because there are no database indices available to speed up them upon text. That is why every expression has to be evaluated for any RDF property and all of the properties have to be fully loaded too. To get more aggregate functionality next to ASK, many providers implement additional, proprietary extensions[14]. These not standardized extensions use the strength of the traditional, relational query language SQL and a combination of SPARQL and SQL[15]. For this reasons also qKAI does not use SPARQL only. Temporary query results have to be stored anyway, to allow acceptable performance while requesting and combining distributed RDF resources. These results are stored in a relational database and we utilize SQL for effective, internal data processing (see section 5).

REST: Representational State Transfer (REST) is an architectural style - not tied to any particular technology - although it is used as a guide for designing architectures following four key constraints: identification of resources handled by URIs, manipulation of resources through representations using the HTTP's uniform protocol (GET, PUT, POST, DELETE), self-descriptive messages and hypermedia as the engine of application state. Roy Fielding defined REST [9] in his dissertation as an architectural style he used for foundational Web specifications - in particular HTTP and URIs. REST offers important architectural properties to improve reliability, scalability or simplicity. These properties are mainly named as superior to SOAP[16] web services. Therefore, we can speak about REST as a "*thin*" style SOA alternative. Especially in Web 2.0 applications, REST web services are very popular these days.

Rich Clients: Regarding today's browser-based user interfaces, Rich Clients using especially asynchronous JavaScript and XML (AJAX) are a wide spread trend. The aim of Rich Internet Applications (RIA) is to bring desktop-alike and easy to use interoperation to the Web. Next to AJAX and Adobe Flash/Flex[17], Java based User Interfaces (UI) are technical alternatives. The best technique to choose depends on the main requirements that have to be fulfilled [4]. FLASH/Flex3 for example offers the advantage of less scripting work and easier event handling to reach highly interactive functionality, if the focus lies on multimedia and design

[14] http://www.w3.org/2009/sparql/wiki/Extensions_Proposed_By_OpenLink, visited: 03.04.09
[15] http://docs.openlinksw.com/virtuoso/rdfsparqlaggregate.html, visited: 03.04.09
[16] http://www.oasis-open.org/specs/, visited: 03.06.08.
[17] http://en.wikipedia.org/wiki/Adobe_Flex, visited: 04.04.09

issues. All these Rich Clients can be seen as an extended and enhanced view in the traditionally Model-View-Controller (MVC2) concept. Advantages Rich Clients offer are e.g. faster reaction to user requests with partially reloads of site parts without refreshing the whole site, less network traffic and server load as well as offline usage possibility. A so-called Rich UI Engine delivers the General User Interface and the presentation logic is separated from visualization components. RIAs as standalone Web clients that interact with the server side through web services are a promising combination. One of the most important advantages of the Client-Server model is the idea that we develop the User Interface independently of the business logic and data persistence technology. Nevertheless, to be honest, in today's Web programming practice before RIA, the UI is in fact tightly coupled with the server-side technology of choice. If we like to change our backend functionality for example from Java to PHP we also have to rework all the scripts generating the HTML UI from *.jsp to *.php. To avoid this problem we can now choose a Rich Client communicating over standardized interfaces like web services only and put the most of the UI logic to client side to get a real separated solution.

2. How to Utilize Open Content for Higher-layered Applications?

In this section, we outline what we see as requisite to turn Open Content into an organized, useful knowledge base for higher-level applications. Powerful but easy to handle by the user mechanisms for acquisition and inquiring relevant data out of heterogeneous sources have to be established. We have to serialize formats for unitary, comprehensive analysis and mediation of distributed, inconsistent content. In this context, mediation means to utilize input data for higher layered applications by offering personalized query plans, transformation, annotation and interoperation. Open access to knowledge and data in e.g. RDF representation brings advantages in interlinking and easily accessing distributed data on the Web as Linked Open Data. Data processing concepts allowing machine- and human-interpretable staging without storing redundant data permanently become possible by semantic interlinking.

Information chunking for easy to digest knowledge bits without losing context information is a prerequisite for better understanding and human-capable representation during interaction. In qKAI (semi-)automatic extracted information units represent a piece of information that can be qualified by annotation and interaction to a knowledge unit – always aware of its context not to lose information and to allow effective change management (actuality).

Knowledge life cycle concerns have to be matched with content cycles of the Read-Write-Web. Acquiring (inquire, discover, categorize, index) maintaining and mediating (manage, analyze, enrich, transform) and particularly reusing (interoperation for information, learning, knowledge transfer) services have to be established.

The more we know about a source, the better we can reuse it. Therefore, metadata and its annotation are essential for accurate thematic, semantic analysis and quality determination. Determining the quality of content allows rearrangement according to source criterions like provenance, timeliness or correctness. Emerging qualitative valence of information units and sources raises information to valid knowledge. To get the emerging qKAI knowledge base applicable, we see the need for interaction services to learn, rate, rank, inquire, explore and annotate. Motivation and user involvement are important aspects and learning games are proficient for easily accessible, intuitive forms of interactivity. Synergy effects between learning, gaming and annotating content arise. We see content enrichment by the user as an implicit, positive side effect in qKAI application services.

Learning scenarios in qKAI enable self-controlled and directed concepts embedded as interaction services. We are starting with the scenarios shortly outlined in section 0, but kept extension simple by architectural division of presentation, its logic and managing interaction services. Learning targets are to increase competency in handling information and to learn in an enjoyable manner with the Internet of Services. Visual building of SPARQL queries (compare SPARQLizer section 7) out of own questions using template and rule services lets the user implicitly learn about search strategies, query structures and plans on the Web. RESTful SOA paradigms harmonize with Web 2.0 concerns and support Semantic Web technologies as a scalable, reusable and unified software concept, while retaining application autonomy.

3. State of the Art and Related Work

Currently, there arise some novel Social Semantic Web applications (e.g. Twine, Freebase, Knol)[18] that regroup existing knowledge, allow manual annotation and creation. There is still a lack in all-embracing, standardized frameworks, integration practice and reusing interoperation scenarios so far. There are a few examples for game-based interaction with Open Data like Quizzer[19] embedding User Generated Content (UGC) or annotating the Web of Data. Interaction and learning applications that combine arbitrary sources in an extensible SOA way are not available yet, as far as we know. DBpedia mobile [10] is an ideal example for browser accessible Linked Data combined out of different sources on mobile devices, but interactive learning scenarios and change management still have to be applied. SOA concepts find more and more their way into university and campus management systems. New qKAI interactive learning services can be loosely coupled and integrated. Frameworks helpful for the GUI side use Asynchronous JavaScript und XML (AJAX: Prototype, Dojo, YUI)[20] or Flash/Flex (e.g. FlowUI Open Source RIA Enterprise Mashup Framework). The Jena RDF framework[21] brings comprehensive Java functionality for semantic data discovery, querying (Jena ARQ) and transformation. The Semantic Web Application Framework[22] enables further semantic tasks.

Semantic search engines[23] like Swoogle, Sindice or Watson deal with searching, exploitation and large scale access to the Semantic Web of Data and are useful as gateways to find further relevant input resources for the qKAI data store. However, beyond getting to know where to find these resources, qKAI wants to transform and embed the resources'

[18] http://www.twine.com, http://www.freebase.com, http://knol.google.com/k, visited: 17.05.09
[19] http://www.d-elina.de/2008/index.php?option=com_content&task=view&id=97&Itemid=64, visited: 3.2.09
[20] http://www.prototypejs.org/, http://dojotoolkit.org/, http://developer.yahoo.com/yui, visited: 18.06.08
[21] http://jena.sourceforge.net, visited 05.03.08
[22] http://doi.ieeecomputersociety.org/10.1109/MS.2007.126, visited: 15.09.08
[23] http://swoogle.umbc.edu/, http://www.sindice.com, http://watson.kmi.open.ac.uk/WatsonWUI/, visited: 15.05.09

content after mediation in own application scenarios. Therefore, we have to add its own open and transparent data processing, storage concept, representation and change management that is outlined in section 5. To crawl the Web of Data we can use available solutions, but for effective storage, recombination and real time access of the resources' content during user interaction we developed the hybrid qKAI data layer. Additionally, existing crawlers are pluggable into the qKAI data layer.

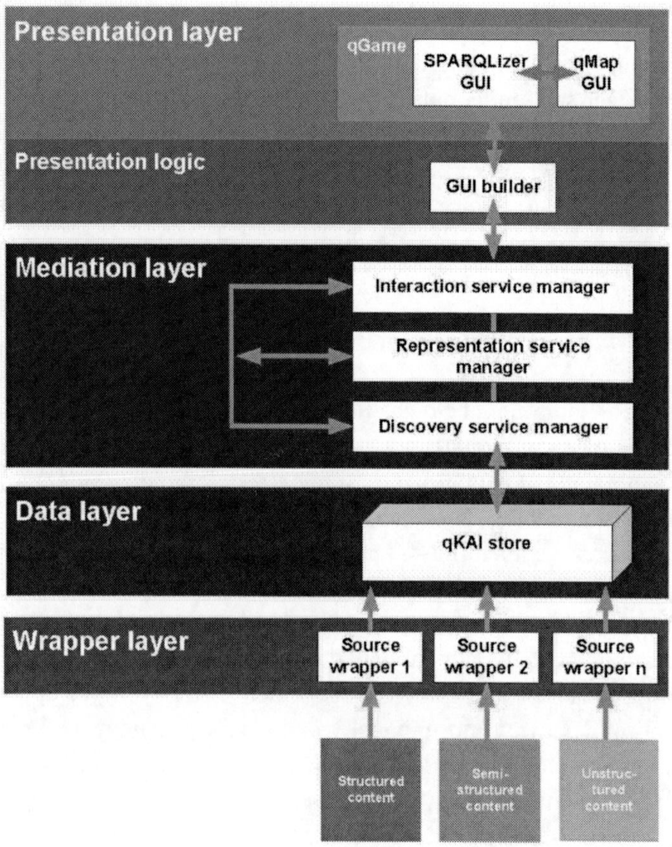

Figure 2. Conceptual system design of the qKAI application framework as a combination of Mediator-Wrapper, Rich Client MVC2 und RESTful SOA paradigms.

4. qKAI Application Framework

We organized the system design of the qKAI application framework in four main layers as a combination of mediator-wrapper-concepts, service oriented approaches (Internet of Services) and conventional web application N-tier design. In this chapter, we explain the components and tasks of applied layers as shown in figure 2.

qKAI System Layer

The presentation layer implements the General User Interfaces and its necessary logic. To fulfill extended MVC2 separation, the mediation layer presents the business logic and controller functionality. Regarded in a SOAP style, service-oriented way we would place the Enterprise Service Bus (ESB) and the service broker here - belonging to the discovery manager. The mediation layer acts as middleware that connects available services (service mediation) and other technical components. The definition of "*mediation*" in qKAI is also interpreted according to Wiederhold [11]: „*A mediator is a software module that exploits encoded knowledge about certain sets or subsets of data to create information for a higher layer of applications.*"

The data layer meets the model level in the Model View Controller pattern and extends it with wrapper services at the wrapper layer to embed various distributed sources. The data layer has to manage hybrid data processing enabling RDF and XML related data as well as relational database content. It retains existing data sources temporarily for mediation purpose. qKAI processes provide new generated data as open RDF or serialized JSON representation after mediation.

Data Storage and Change Management

The qKAI knowledge representation consists for example of RDF graphs and superior metadata about them. Existing graphs outside of qKAI are first stored as link to the origin source in the qKAI service and source repository e.g. using the URI of a SPARQL endpoint like http://dbpedia.org/sparql. New generated information is stored separately and sustainable at the qKAI data layer. The data processing concept contains a persistent, relational database component (e.g. MySQL), flexible representation (RDF, N3, JSON) and temporary fetching of working data during discovery and enrichment. To allow persistent storage and to handle relational data with only a small set of classes in an effective way we deployed the Java persistence JPA with the EclipseLink implementation[24].

Linked Data concepts[25] enable persistent, resource-related storage, change management and non-redundant, context-aware data processing by interlinking identifiable distributed resources. New knowledge about available sources that qKAI services generated is stored in MySQL additionally. qKAI represents it as Linked Data on demand. Following the Linked Data keynote [12] and overall desire of next generation web applications, to combine different, distributed RDF stores on demand in real time without buffering, our first trials to embed content while querying exemplary the DBpedia endpoint failed. Without fetching a copy of relevant data, results showed unacceptable response times forcing us to develop a more practically solution. Main reason for the bad response times is the SPARQL endpoints performance itself as outlined in the following (section "Fetching and indexing"). Now the qKAI data layer buffers relevant resources in a traditional, relational database structure to allow adequate performance to users' requests and ability to further processing and annotation of the acquired content. Furthermore, affordable hardware can be used to reach good performance results without the need to investigate in high-end enterprise server technology.

[24] http://www.eclipse.org/proposals/eclipselink/, visited: 13.05.09

[25] http://esw.w3.org/topic/SweoIG/TaskForces/CommunityProjects/LinkingOpenData, visited: 10.04.09

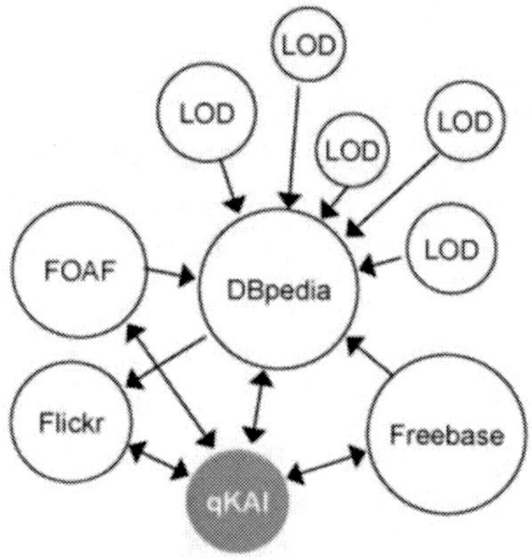

Figure 3. The qKAI data layer embeds Linked Open Data resources and represents its data store as another node in the Linked Open Data cloud.

This section gives an introduction into the qKAI data management based on the concept that every RDF resource is portable into a relational database structure and vice versa[26]. DBpedia serves as an exemplary knowledge base accessed via its SPARQL endpoint to demonstrate first results while building the hybrid qKAI data store out of distributed web resources. Main criteria for the qKAI data store are easy, affordable, scalable reusability, possibility to mediation and representation of acquired resources of different kinds and varying provenance. We deploy Points of Interest (POI) to give a starting point into the knowledge base by users or further applications and to update the qKAI store partially on demand in an effective way.

Discovering Linked Data by Setting Points of Interest

Because of the wide web discovery space (open world assumption) and conceivable performance problems while answering and updating comprehensive queries in real-time, among others we are integrating POI (Point of Interest) setting functionality in qKAI. The users and further applications need an interface to define points of interest and to limit inquiry space and knowledge base according to own interests. Setting and storing several POIs according to different domains and topics becomes possible. Once set, POIs are stored for reuse and link to each other. The POIs enable defined entry points to the large RDF knowledge base. Browsing Linked Data stores requires semantic browsing functionality for different devices like web browsers or mobile devices. Representational Web services fulfill device specific representation requests of the qKAI knowledge base.

A single geographically and/or thematically oriented Point of Interest (POI) is now using the qKAI implementation completely reproducible by the qKAI data layer through a single and effective SQL query. In the current implementation, we assume that the topic the user is interested in is a part of the knowledge base yet – now DBpedia for testing purposes. DBpedia contains all thematically categories out of Wikipedia – so we know approximately,

[26] http://www.w3.org/2006/Talks/0518-SPASQL/#(1), visited: 19.05.09

what we got up to now. Under this condition a thematically search space limitation is representable through the following SQL statement:

```
-- POI for persons
SELECT DISTINCT r.resource, r.resourceURI
FROM resources r
JOIN relations l ON (r.resource=l.resource)
WHERE l.predicate
= ANY (SELECT resource FROM resources WHERE
resourceURI="…/22-rdf-syntax-ns#type")
AND l.target = ANY (SELECT resource FROM resources
WHERE resourceURI="http://dbpedia.org/ontology/Person");
```

POIs offer combination without limitation. In SQL, this means an implementation as follows („NATURAL JOIN" is a substitute for „INTERSECT" which is not supported by MySQL):

```
SELECT resource FROM
(/* SELECT from POIa */)
NATURAL JOIN
(/* SELECT from POIb */)
NATURAL JOIN … -- for further POI
```

The derivation of this high-performance, multithreading solution to embed distributed Linked Open Data in higher-layered web applications is exemplary enlightened in the following. We applied a *minimalistic data model* with *maximized depth*, because the implementation is suitable for several semantic data purposes on a Quadcore hardware platform that is available for about 500 € (May 2009). Because every table is transferable to RDF and vice versa, there is no need for further extension. Further on, relational data storage brings the advantage of flexible, independent representation and delivery on demand e.g. in JSON next to RDF or N3 Turtle.

SQL Replaces SPARQL

Considering the current infirmity of SPARQL shown in the introduction and regarding the fact that popular SPARQL implementations are still a facade for relational databases, it seems to be consequent at this time to abstain from the broad adoption of SPARQL. Significantly, even DBpedia uses Virtuoso[27] for a SPARQL endpoint with proprietary extensions, but MySQL handles query processing in the background. Thus, we decided to choose MySQL directly for the qKAI data layer and reduced the data processing bulk to SQL that most developers are more familiar with. On the one side, we can resort to a broad pool of proofed SQL solutions – enabling hierarchical queries for example – on the other side following developers save incorporation time to get started with the qKAI data layer.

[27] http://www.openlinksw.com/virtuoso/, visited: 14.05.09

SPARQL only acquires DBpedia content or other RDF stores using hybrid indexing. Our first approach, sending complex SPARQL requests without SQL background support to the endpoint, failed. Even for a tree out of more than two nodes, results often are not returnable and the endpoint timed out. Under these conditions, we discarded this approach. Present practice showed that too many dependencies on distributed resources constrain further work that relies on the qKAI data layer, because the reliability of reaching SPARQL endpoints is not well calculable this times.

Hybrid Knowledge Index

An initial qKAI knowledge base e.g. out of DBpedia can be easily imported using the qKAI dump reader. Proper connected resources complement this initial knowledge base on demand via SPARQL. The dump reader accepts requests and queries the buffered qKAI data layer instead of the distant resource. A hybrid knowledge index arises this way by and by.

Change Management

The qKAI knowledge base buffered in MySQL will become obsolete earlier or later. Thereby, the qKAI data store might be soon as large that synchronizing all entries with their provenance resource is not possible anymore all at once. The hybrid knowledge index allows updating the buffered data store partially at runtime. If a user or an application indicates that more elements out of e.g. DBpedia are needed while setting Points of Interest, they can be additionally loaded and their content can be updated on demand. If the update amount and interval are set properly, "*fluent*" actualization of the whole qKAI knowledge base is possible. We fetch only small and relevant amounts of data out of the provenance source. Parallel processing is possible in the qKAI data layer. Data provision is reliable at any time this way. Setting POIs enables huge databases to update temporarily redundant stored data to be efficient synchronized with their provenance source on demand when requested. Interesting parts of domains and knowledge bases will be updated more often than irrelevant ones and weighting is set implicitly for further statistically tasks. We implemented a thin, asynchronous updatable and practicable data layer this way.

Reusability and Extensibility

All database connectivity of the qKAI data layer is autonomic and persistent without relying on other qKAI components. To embed further SPARQL endpoints we only have to deploy the new endpoint's address. The implementation of generic classes allows using even different protocols – what we showed exemplary with the qKAI dump reader. Integrating new sets of POIS is as easy. At this time, we offer POI setter for thematically, geographically and full text POIs. Full text POIs search like traditional search engines for matching phrases.

Multithreading

Without to beware of it, most developers of web applications work with multithreading on multicores. In case of Java, the Container manager treats every request as a separate thread. Most of the time, there are no negative side effects, if the result is not especially tweaked for this purpose. The qKAI data layer needs parallel processing to reach practicable performance. In addition, multithreading avoids blockades while querying resources with slow answering times.

Fetching and Indexing

A first, not yet thread optimized version of the qKAI data layer claimed **over 30 seconds** to fetch a test data item and all of its properties. The one thread of the application waiting for DBpedia answers wasted most of the time. To understand the underlying processes and their problems to infer a more reactive solution, we analyzed the tasks to do while fetching our test data from a SPARQL endpoint:

1. For a given word, the URI has to be found.
2. All properties and relations of the constant URI and their neighborhood are fetched. This happens gradually because SPARQL does not allow binding constants to variables.
3. Step 2 has to be repeated for every fund

DBpedia Search Example with the Term „*Nietzsche*"

Now we take the famous search term „*Nietzsche*" to get the following results with numbers and processes shown below:

Table 1. Steps, document count and necessary requests searching for the example term "*Nietzsche*" in DBpedia using SPARQL only

Step	Document count	Requests
1	444 hits for search term „Nietzsche"	1
2	8458 properties 41804 outgoing links 2068 mutual properties among	444

In general, all hits have to be loaded, because SPARQL does not know any word quantifier ordering and the wanted term might be at the end of the result list. We get a serial waiting time for 445 query results with 50.000 new created documents or even markers. This result can be constructed much shorter enabling qKAI buffering DBpedia and then applying the following SQL queries to the qKAI data layer:

```
SELECT resource
FROM properties_fulltext
WHERE q="Nietzsche"
```

Repeated for table „*properties*":

```
SELECT COUNT(*)
FROM (
SELECT resource FROM properties_fulltext
WHERE q="Nietzsche"
) sub JOIN relations p ON (sub.resource=p.resource);
```

Also for "*relations*":

```
SELECT p.property, COUNT(*) amount
FROM (
SELECT resource
FROM properties_fulltext
WHERE q="Nietzsche"
) sub JOIN properties p ON (sub.resource=p.resource)
GROUP BY p.property HAVING amount > 1;
```

A trivial DBpedia answer takes 2 seconds at its best. Thus, without synchronous loading we have to wait 14 minutes at least. To solve this problem, we divided the process in a pipeline of five steps to identify especially working and waiting intensive tasks. Finally, we matched these tasks to a suitable number of threads and processor cores. In our implementation, the Java classes do not communicate directly. Instead, they use the „*FetchingMediator*" as broker. For every step represented through a class, a predefined amount of „*ThreadPoolExecutors*"[28] is started. Class instances are lined up in a queue. Every started thread will work constantly and multiple threads accomplish tasks parallelized. With four concurrent „*RelatedResourceProducers*" the waiting time of the above mentioned example theoretically increases to a quarter. Practically, DBpedia answers slower with increasing concurrent numbers of requests. Next to qKAI, there are several other applications querying DBpedia what makes the answering times unforeseeable. Waiting times of several minutes are not avoidable. The parallelized approach prevents the bottleneck in qKAI: Successive requests get their answers faster allowing queued search terms to be processed further on despite of small blockades.

Evaluation

Initial search space creation without preselected data dumps

If data is fetched only by requesting a SPARQL endpoint like DBpedia without buffering, the used time until the whole search space is available, depends on its connection: qKAI itself uses only very simple SPARQL expressions and - if implemented in the endpoint - the

[28] http://java.sun.com/javase/6/docs/api/, visited: 16.03.09

Virtuoso extension "*bif:contains*" [13] to allow faster full text search. According to our samples, it takes about 20 seconds until 10 results are available: To be presentable, we have to find a result and must load it completely as well. Resulting out of this unacceptable response times while only using SPARQL requests on distant resources, qKAI uses a prepared data store as copy of the provenance resource to utilize distributed data for further application scenarios in real time. Therefore, we currently dissuade from deploying "*SPARQL only*" installations in productive environments – even if this approach is desirable regarding the long term, it is not realizable in an affordable way. Instead, a minimal data store - with at best domain or application customized data - should be prepared like explained in the following using the example of the qKAI data layer.

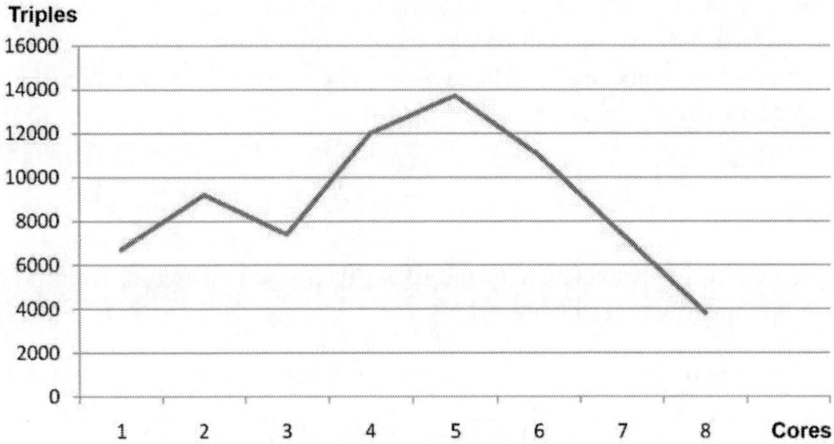

Figure 4. Reading in the Dbpedia dumps on test system 2 (see table 3): Count of read triples per second and amount of processors per second, measured over 80h. The peak lies at five by qKAI used processors because there is an optimal balance reached between 5 cores for qKAI resources and 3 cores for MySQL.

Initial search space creation with preselected data dumps

A "*dump*" is a view of a database written down in a file. In case of DBpedia, we speak of 40 compressed files that reach decompressed 25 GB. The decompressing time took about half an hour on test system 2 (see table 3). qKAI optimizes this data in N-Triples[29] format for further queries. N-Triples are a rather redundant data structure because e.g. a RDF subject is repeated for each of its properties. Direct transfer of N-Triples into the qKAI data store is a quite ineffective task. It would mean to get tables with over 200 million lines and expensive JOINs with more than one property concurrently. The fastest known SPARQL implementation Virtuoso [13] uses just like qKAI OpenRDF Sesame[30] to transform data into a more effective representation. After that, the representation is transformable into the qKAI data model. We turned off the database indices in MySQL because it is a rather time intensive tasks too.

[29] http://www.w3.org/2001/sw/RDFCore/ntriples/, visited: 14.05.09

[30] http://www.openrdf.org/, visited: 14.05.09

Result concerning the qKAI hybrid data layer

If a distant RDF store like DBpedia is portable to the qKAI data layer as relational structure, efficient search space limitation and processing of the content is realizable with good performance using internal SQL selection. Requesting and combining distributed RDF resources using SPARQL only currently turned out to be not practicable. Therefore, we implemented the transformation into an own, efficient relational data structure. At this time, the qKAI data store consists out of DBpedia and we will enhance it through further resources by and by. The qKAI data layer is usable to embed available semantic search services to build a hybrid knowledge index for the Semantic Web - and in future work for further Open Content resources. Embedding e.g. the Sindice and Watson crawling functionality is under development. Sindice offers a large RDF data index; qKAI is able to mediate with to acquire further resources next to DBpedia. The algorithm for change management introduced in section 5 can be used for periodic and on demand synchronization with provenance sources. Relying on a modular architecture, qKAI can be easily extended by further Points of Interest e.g. for multimedia content.

Test Systems

We tested the current implementation of the qKAI data layer on two different systems to determine the ideal distribution strategy:

Table 2. Benchmark data for test system 1, the qKAI data layer was deployed on

Processor	AMD Phenom 9550, Quadcore, 4x 2,2 GHz
RAM	8 GB DDR2 667MHz RAM
Internet connection	14 MBit
Storage	Four Western Digital WD6400AAKS SATA 2 hard disks, Adaptec 3805 RAID Controller in RAID 5
Throughput storage	380 MB/s read, 300 MB/s write

Table 3. Benchmark data for test system 2 (Amazon Elastic Computing Cloud 2), the qKAI data layer was deployed on

Processor	2x Intel XEON, Quadcore, 8x 2,33 MHz
RAM	7 GB, unknown
Internet connection	1 GBit
Storage	Amazon EBS Storage, Western Digital WD6400AAHS
Throughput storage	60 MB/s read, 50 MB/s write

6. Services and Components in qKAI

We are dividing qKAI functionality into two main developer levels:

1. RESTful backend web services acquire, select and represent textual and multimedia data. qKAI performs read and write access to resources over the HTTP protocol by

the GET and POST method. Working at this level means extensive use of the Java Jersey API (JAX-RS specification) to build atomic web services for several subtasks. qKAI's backend web services and the hybrid data layer altogether build the qKAI application framework.

2. Rich User Interface components build on top of the qKAI application framework let the user interact with different kinds of activities. We built frontend components according to their type of interactivity with AJAX and/or Flash/Flex.

To perform backend and frontend tasks, there are some available and proofed libraries merged up and extended.

Further Techniques and Libraries

We are developing qKAI as a Java web application with Servlets and Java Server Pages deployed in a Tomcat Servlet Container[31]. Prototype, Dojo and YUI libraries support the AJAX frontend interaction. The frontend is next to AJAX designed using Adobe Flex and Flash components for highly interactive tasks with extended design issues (e.g. learning game sequences). Most of the qKAI service and component offer is reusable in nearly any information and knowledge transfer scenario. Additionally, some gaming services and components allow specialized functionality for social educational gaming.

To keep the qKAI application structure flexible, extensible and autonomic, we decided to encapsulate functional subtasks in small web services. Web service interaction will follow RESTful Web 2.0 paradigms. Self-descriptive messaging is the most important constraint of REST. It means that every message needs to include all the information necessary in order to understand the message itself. We do not see a web service description language like WSDL as mandatory for REST – also it is possible to describe RESTful web services using WSDL 2. The fundamental advance of REST over the styles of e.g. SOAP or CORBA is that all service interfaces are the same - there is no need for explicit description. After registering all available services and resources in the qKAI data store according to a broker, we are looking towards embedding structured databases by converting them to RDF. The last challenge is to enhance unstructured content for qKAI integration developing more complex wrapper services.

Project Management and Build Automation

qKAI is using the build and management tool Apache Maven [14] with support of Subversion to automate working tasks. qKAI offers fast start up and good documentation facility of all working processes to reuse them as much as possible this way. We can use interface classes without knowing about the classes' Weaving[32] this way. In addition, we adopted the standard for (JUnit) tests deploying Maven. The programmers get hints and suggestions for code snippets to allow better handling of the framework and its language. Maven dissolves all

[31] http://tomcat.apache.org/, visited: 25.05.09

[32] Enriching Java's byte code for EclipseLinks persistence implementation to allow efficient handling with the database

dependencies among packages and downloads them automatically in the correct version. Developers can use their IDE of choice. To adjust qKAI to e.g. Netbeans or Eclipse we only need one Maven command. qKAI's currently deployed server and database are exchangeable that easy, too.

7. Further qKAI Use Cases and Application Scenarios

The qKAI application framework with its hybrid data layer builds a well-suited foundation for various use cases of user interaction. qKAI services enable embedding, querying and enriching distributed web sources for any kind of higher-level applications that like to integrate a broad, structured knowledge base with interoperation ability based on a suitable tools and services collection. We are focusing on process plans suitable for learning - realized by composite services. In the following, we give a few precise examples for use cases that are currently under development using a first prototype of the qKAI framework. qKAI will offer services published in a service broker way for reuse in other web applications like Learning or Content Management Systems. Embedding enriched qKAI content by RDF representation service will be available soon for testing and evaluation. A qKAI user for instance places a question like "*Which authors are influenced by Stanislav Lem?*" using the SPARQLizer, gets five automatically generated Multiple-Choice answers presented with relational author images from Flickr[33] and he has to choose the right ones out of it.

Learning Game Services

Currently, we are developing question-answer-game-types generated out of well suitable Open Data in RDF format. We see two main modes as most interesting for creating first learning game scenarios out of Open Data: Players assign questions to (semi) automatically extracted information units. Players create questions and get (semi)automated answers, which are transformable into playable answers (IMS/QTI).

SPARQLizer: With the SPARQLizer, a visual query interface is under design that allows intuitive question to query plan transformation on distributed RDF stores deploying SPARQL endpoints and dynamic graph interlinking. SPARQL queries constructed by the user will be stored as graphs enlarging the qKAI knowledge base and are ready to query against in further query plans.

qMAP: With qMAP a map-based geocoding frontend is under development. We place questions, answers and their combination (knowledge units) at the qMAP and enrich them with geocodes. qMAP acts as a kind of gaming board for placing, exploring and editing stored question-answer-pairs. The qMAP will interact with SPARQLizer and represents submitted questions and related answers. Beyond embedding RDF sources by SPARQL queries, we plan to integrate Metawebs MQL to place queries against Freebase. Furthermore,

[33] http://www.flickr.com, visited: 10.04.09

mapping between MQL and the W3C standardized SPARQL is an interesting task for further transformation services in the mediation and wrapper layer.

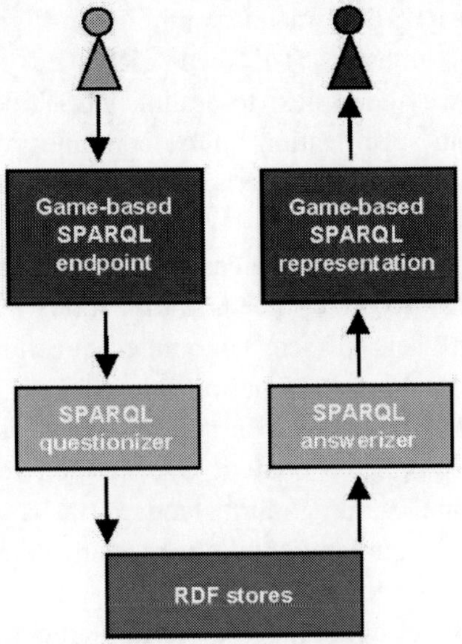

Figure 3. Concept scheme of the query and answer transformation in the SPARQLizer.

Annotating and Qualifying Services

Joker option services for annotating, rating and qualifying are currently under design. They belong to the interaction manager of the mediation layer. qKAI jokers allow game-based functionality to add additional sources and to qualify metainformation by rating and ranking input to the qKAI knowledge base. Playing the "*Know-it-all-Joker*" bounds the player to add a source (or information) that proves contrary statements. The "*Nonsense-Joker*" marks an information unit as semantically wrong or inconsistent and defers it to review mode by other qKAI users. The "*Hint-Joker*" allows looking up related sources or other users' answers as solution suggestion. The "*Explorer-Joker*" allows exploring the right answer on the web outside of qKAI during a predefined time. The "*History-Joker*" enables lookups in played answers, ratings of other users by logged interaction and transaction protocols. Statistical protocol analysis is suitable to infer further metainformation.

Global Point and Level System

qKAI provides global point and level system services to document learning progress, personal interests and to implement incentive and reputation ability. Every kind of interaction is rewarded with qPOINTS according to its grade of interoperation.

8. Conclusion

We introduced the qKAI application framework for utilizing arbitrary Open Data sources and services in a standardized, RESTful manner aiming at highly interactive scenarios in information and knowledge transfer. To keep qKAI easy extensible with reusable, autonomous service design, we added next to a slim, RESTful SOA a 4-layered mediator-wrapper-schema to the system specification. qKAI combines Web 2.0, Semantic Web and SOA paradigms to apply and enable the Internet of Services for higher level, user-oriented applications with open access.

Current focus lies on implementing use cases like the SPARQLizer and qMAP based on the qKAI data layer. SPARQLizer needs a dynamic, adaptive GUI, template and ontology structure to support users in (semi)automated question and answering generation out of SPARQL requests. Chunking information into capable knowledge units is work in progress. The specification of qKAI information units is finished and exemplary implemented based on live Wikipedia content. We derived requirements to utilize Open Content for social educational gaming and standard tasks in knowledge engineering. Atomic services and frontend components allow rearrangement and are suitable for any other purpose in information and knowledge transfer – not only for game-based learning. Services are adaptable to several domains. We are implementing first educational gaming prototypes and we are gaining at further features to utilize current web trends like social interaction for learning purpose and sustainable, knowledge-related interoperation on Open Content.

Reusing and composing is a precept at all levels in qKAI, the challenge is to merge and to expand: Resources, ontologies, web services or available frameworks. We are aiming at standardized, machine- and human readable staging of Open Content with lightweight interoperation to develop incentive, web-based knowledge transfer and learning scenarios. Therefore, we deploy Linked Data, Rich Clients and REST. The qKAI application framework serves as conceptual basis and system specification for further work exemplary highlighted in this chapter. We want to offer learning scenarios based on user-oriented web services with lightweight interaction grounded on Open Content. Therefore, we have to implement standard tasks of knowledge engineering for extended interaction as a generic application framework. qKAI combines and respectively extends available Java APIs for subtasks to a scalable, reusable and unifying software concept.

Overall, our research focus lies on three main aspects:

1. Provide standard tasks of knowledge engineering (acquisition, formalization, representation, visualization).
2. Determine and enhance the quality of content (analyzes and enrichment of metainformation. The user's opinion and knowledge annotate, rate and rank the content additionally).
3. Tackle extended interaction and incentive for user's attendance while interoperating with Open Content.

We implemented an aware compact and hybrid data layer that serves as basis for further knowledge-processing applications and as interface to semantic search engines. The missing possibilities of the therefore designed query language SPARQL are substituted by the transformation into a relational database scheme. Resulting models are flexible and reusable, because any relational data structure can be mapped onto. The chosen approach of parallel data fetching and processing was not that easy to implement concerning thread safe programming, but it is very profitable regarding sustainable deployment - independent of external, at this time still unsecure circumstances:

- Time intensive requests will not block successive queries in qKAI.
- Only this way data can be loaded additionally with adequate response times, if a request is not answerable through the pre-buffered data store.

Further Development of SPARQL and the Semantic Web

Our research showed that the power of SPARQL is not yet applicable to the efforts of the qKAI data layer. Even if suggested extensions like OpenLink are integrated into the final specification, it is not obvious whether SPARQL alone will be properly suited for large, distributed data requests soon. Currently we noticed an ongoing trend to deploy relational database concepts because of their majority and performance – like nearly all SPARQL endpoint and RDF repository implementations do [15]. Future work in qKAI will implement available algorithms and APIs to crawl distributed resources and to amplify the mapping optimization between SPARQL and SQL (SPARQLtoSQL[34]). We implemented some MySQL optimizations like the Sphinx full text indexer [16] yet to allow faster search. For geographically search spaces, a GIS extension is ready to use for periphery searches.

In summary, the interface to Open Data resources over SPARQL endpoints offers new ways to combine, enrich and explore the data web as an open, semantically connected graph. Data sources are presented in a standardized, machine interpretable and extensible manner deploying RDF repositories. They offer many advantages like Linked Open Data ability and annotation compared to traditional relational databases under closed world assumption. Further SPARQL functionality is under development and will be part of its specification. We decided to mix up proven and new concepts to get a nowadays realistic data layer implementation while buffering preselected data dumps in a relational database and acquiring Open Content out of RDF repositories using SPARQL. Additionally, we developed with POI setting for applications and users a practically solution to update pre buffered resources partially on demand when they are requested.

[34] http://semanticweb.org/wiki/SPARQL-to-SQL_Query_Translation_for_Optional_Graph_Patterns, visited 15.05.09.

Acknowledgments

The BMBF (Bundesministerium für Bildung und Forschung) co-funded this work under the HELCA (Hannover E-Learning Campus) project. We thank especially M. Kubacki and J. Hein for their support in implementing and advancing the qKAI application framework.

References

[1] T. Berners-Lee, "Web 2.0 and Semantic Web", http://www.w3.org/2006/Talks/1108-swui-tbl/#(1), W3C, last update: 2006.

[2] Schroth, C.; Janner, T., "Web 2.0 and SOA: Converging Concepts Enabling the Internet of Services", *IT Professional,* Volume 9, Issue 3, 2007, pp 36 – 41.

[3] M. Steinberg, J. Brehm, "Towards utilizing Open Data for interactive knowledge transfer". *DigitalWorld 2009, International Conference on Mobile, Hybrid, and On-line Learning (eL&mL),* Mexico, 2009.

[4] M. Domenig, "Rich Internet Applications und AJAX, Entwickler-Magazin, http://www.canoo.com/news/entwickler.pdf", 2006.

[5] H. Mandl, G. Reinmann-Rothmeier, "Unterrichten und Lernumgebungen gestalten", *Forschungsbericht* Nr. 60, Instituts für Pädagogische Psychologie und Empirische Pädagogik, München, Ludwig-Maximilians-Universität, 1995.

[6] F. Naumann, "Mediator/Wrapper-Architektur & Peer-Data-Management", Lecture in information integration, http://www2.informatik.hu-berlin.de/mac/lehre/WS04/InfoInt_15_MediatorWrapperPDMS.pdf, Berlin, Humboldt Universität, last update: 2004.

[7] J. H. Dieter Fensel, H. Lieberman, W. Wahlster, "Spinning the Semantic Web: Bringing the World Wide Web to Its Full Potential", The Mit Press, Massachusetts, 2005.

[8] C. Bizer, R. Cyganiak, D2R server: Publishing Relational Databases on the Semantic Web, http://www4.wiwiss.fu-berlin.de/bizer/d2r-server/, last update: 2008.

[9] Fielding, R.: *Architectural Styles and the Design of Network-based Software Architectures*. Dissertation, Irvine, 2000.

[10] Becker, C; Bizer, C.: "DBpedia Mobile: A Location Enabled Linked Data Browser", *17th International World Wide Web Conference WWW2008*, China, 2008.

[11] G. Wiederhold, "Mediators in the Architecture of Future Information Systems, *IEEE Computer, Journal*, 25(3), 38-49, 1992.

[12] Bizer, C.; Heath, T; Berners-Lee, T.: Linked Data: Principles and State of the Art, *17th International World Wide Web Conference, WWW2008*, China, 2008.

[13] C. Weiske, *Implementierung eines effizienten datenbankbasierten SPARQL-Prozessors und Erweiterungen zu SPARQL,* Institut für Informatik, Abteilung Betriebliche Informationssysteme, Universität Leipzig, Leipzig, 2007.

[14] M. Loukides, „Maven - The Definitive Guide", O'Reilly Media, Inc., Sebastopol, 2008.

[15] M. Völkel, SparQL Implementations, ESW Wiki, 2008, http://esw.w3.org/topic/SparqlImplementations.

[16] J. Kumar, "Benchmarking results of mysql, lucene and sphinx", 2006, http://jayant7k.blogspot.com/2006/06/benchmarking-results-of-mysql-lucene.html.

In: Data Management in the Semantic Web
Editor: Hal Jin, pp. 345-381
ISBN: 978-1-61122-862-5

Chapter 15

USING SEMANTICS EQUIVALENCES FOR MRL QUERIES REWRITING IN MULTI-DATA SOURCE FUSION SYSTEMS

Gilles Nachouki[1,*] and Mohamed Quafafou[2]
[1] LINA-UMR CNRS 6241, Faculté des Sciences et des Techniques, F-4432 Nantes Cedex 03, France
[2] LSIS-UMR CNRS 6168, Domaine Universitaire de St-Jerome, F-13397 Marseille Cedex 20, France

Abstract

Classical approaches of data integration, based on schemas mediation, are not suitable for the World Wide Web (WWW) environment where data is frequently modified or deleted. This chapter describes a new approach of heterogeneous data source fusion called Multi-data source Fusion Approach (MFA). Data sources are either static or active: static data sources can be structured or semi-structured, whereas active sources are services. The aim of MFA is to facilitate data sources fusion in dynamic contexts such as the Web. We introduce an XML-based Multi-data source Fusion Language (MFL). MFL provides two sub-languages: the Multi-data source Definition Language (MDL) - used to define the multi-data source - and the Multi-data source Retrieval Language (MRL) - that aims to retrieve conflicting data from multiple data sources.

In this chapter, we also study how to reconciliate semantically data sources. This study is based on OWL/RDF technologies. Our main objective is to combine data sources with a minimal effort required from the user. This objective is crucial because, in our context, we suppose that the user is not an expert in the domain of data fusion, but he/she understands the meaning of data being integrated. The results of semantic reconciliation between data sources are used to improve the problem of rewriting MRL semantic queries into a set of equivalent sub-queries over the data sources. We show the design of the Multi-Data Source Management System called MDSManager. Finally, we give an evaluation of our MRL language. The results show that our language improves significantly the XQuery language especially considering its expressiveness power and its performances.

* E-mail address: Gilles.Nachouki@univ-nantes.fr, Phone: +33240306049, Fax: +33240306001

1. Introduction

Interoperability is the problem of interconnecting and accessing heterogeneous data sources. As organizations have evolved, this problem has become an important field of research in both academic and industry. In the past, intensive researches related to data integration were focused on databases. A federated database (FDB) [38] is a collection of cooperative and autonomous database systems (DBs). A federated database management system (FDBMS) provides a controlled and coordinated manipulation of DBMS component. FDBMSs are characterized by the following three dimensions: distribution, autonomy and heterogeneity. Distribution concerns data which may be distributed among multiple databases that are stored on one or several computers. Autonomy refers to different DBs, which have independent control. Heterogeneity means technical and semantic differences in database management systems (DBMSs) – technical differences include several data models and languages; semantic differences represent several meaning, interpretation or use of the same related data. FDBMSs are divided into two main categories: tightly coupled and loosely coupled [38]. Tightly coupled FDBMS requires the DB component to be created, maintained and access-controlled by its administrator(s). It is always static because the creation of a federated schema is similar to databases schema integration process. In a loosely coupled FDBMSs, the user controls the creation and maintenance of DB component. Furthermore, loosely coupled FDBMS and its administrator(s) do not enforce access control to the DB. It is considered as dynamic because the federated schema may be managed on the fly: it can be easily created, changed and dropped. Each user is the administrator of his/her own federation: he/she has to understand the semantics of the federated schema data sources and to solve all ambiguous problems raised.

With the advent of the Web, data management has moved away from the traditional framework to match the variety of information available on the Web [37]. Nowadays, web documents are largely used for storing data especially over the web, whilst XQuery language [42] has become the standard data retrieval in such documents. The main architecture of data integration systems on the Web is based on the mediator approach [40] which consists on defining an interface between an agent (user or application program) and a set of data sources. The role of the agent is to submit queries over the mediation schema. This process is transparent to the user: it seems as he/she manipulates a single homogeneous and centralized data source. Two interesting characteristics of the Web are to be noted: the growing number of data sources and their frequent updates and volatility. Major data sources are freely accessible on the Web and users often need to integrate them quickly without any help. Classical approaches based on mediator's reasoning do not facilitate the user's task since it is hard to unify data sources in a dynamic way. Rather, they assume a global mediated schema to model data sources. As such, these approaches often require an administrator to control the mediated schema.

Our main objective is to provide a flexible integration of data sources on dynamic environments which is the web case. In our system, we are using a loosely coupled approach where there is no integration of data sources schema into a global one. We assume that the user, who is the administrator of his/her own integrated schema, is able to understand, build, manage these schemas and formulate separate queries over them. We have chosen this type of model because the construction of a global schema is a very difficult task, particularly on the web, where data sources are frequently updated or deleted.

In this chapter, we address two major aspects related to multi-data source fusion. The first one concerns conflicts that take place between different data sources. Our approach of reconciliation between data sources uses the concept of ontologies. Our main objective is to integrate automatically, just after web data extraction, several data sources with minimal effort required from the user. We suppose that the user understands the meaning of the extracted data of data sources he/she want to integrate in the multi-data source. The second aspect concerns the rewriting of semantic queries submitted by the user on the multi-data source schema. In order to satisfy the objective mentioned above, we propose a Multi-data source Fusion Language (MFL) that allows defining and retrieving data from conflicting data sources or multi-data source. A multi-data source schema is defined in a specific structure. MFL is a simple and powerful language that allows users to formulate their need in a single query. It facilitates query's expansion over conflicting data sources and controls the semantics expressed in users' queries: For each query submitted, MFL will search for conflicts in the query's body. If no conflict is detected, the query will be accepted and executed. Otherwise, three cases may arise: (1) Conflicts are solved through query processing; in this case, the query will be accepted and executed. (2) Conflicts cannot be solved; in this case, the query will be rejected (e.g. case of homonyms conflicts). (3) Some conflicts are solved where others not; in this case, a part of the query related to the solved conflicts will be executed and results will be returned to the user with a warning message informing him/her of the detected conflict nature (e.g. case of scale conflicts).

The chapter is organized as follows: section 2 describes related work concerning data integration. Section 3 introduces MFL language. Section 4 shows our approach based on ontologies in order to reconciliate different data sources. Section 5 illustrates our proposal concerning the rewriting of MRL semantic queries. Section 6 shows an implementation of our approach with MDSManager system. Section 7 discusses and evaluates the Rewriting Semantic Queries (RSQ) algorithm. Section 8 concludes and summarizes some future research directions.

2. Related Work

MSQL [22] and MDSL [23], are two multi-database languages developed in the late 70th for data integration in a loosely coupled approach. Both languages were designed to access structured data only (e.g. relational databases). Many researches in data integration's domain based on mediators use the mapping method between mediated schema and integrated data sources schemas. Two main approaches are proposed: Global As View (*GaV*) and Local As View (*LaV*) [15] [20] [21]. The *GaV* approach comes from the federated databases' process presented above. It involves the definition of a mediated schema as global view over local schemas. This view is created by assembling together different local views (called also local schemas). The *LaV* approach is a dual one. It involves the definition of local schemas as views over a given mediated schema.

Many researches have been developed in order to integrate data sources in Peer-To-Peer (P2P) context where the definition of a unique mediated schema is unrealistic because of the autonomy and volatility of peers. Most of P2P systems avoid the maintenance of a single global schema and their approaches can be classified in tow categories: mediation between a small group of peers and mediation between super-peers.

Many projects and systems were developed according to a centralized or P2P approaches. Among these systems, (the list is not exhaustive), we quote TSIMMIS [12], DISCO [39], GARLIC [7], MIX [3], MOMIS [4], AGORA [25], [26], INFORMATION MANIFOLD [19], C-WEB [1] and XYLEME [11]. Other systems like AXML [6], PIAZZA [9] and SENPEER [8] were developed in a P2P context. In order to show the diversity of these systems, we present some of them by giving the data model used, the language and the type of mapping (*GaV, LaV*). TSIMMIS follows a *GaV* approach. It integrates structured and unstructured data sources. The common model is an Object-based information Exchange Model (OEM). The objective of GARLIC (following the *GaV* approach) is the integration of multimedia data sources (image, video, text etc.). The common model is object oriented and the query language is an extension of SQL called GQL (Garlic Query Language).

Given the popularity of XML as a data description format, more and more DBMS vendors have added to their systems the capability to export relational or object schema to an XML format. In this direction, AGORA uses XML as user interface format, while all data inside the query processor consist of relational tuples. AGORA follows *LaV* approach. Queries are expressed using an XML query language and the results are formatted as XML documents, making the underlying relational engine transparent to user. C-Web proposes an ontology based integration approach of XML web resources. C-WEB, like AGORA starts from a global virtual schema (data lies in some external sources) expressed with a given model. The virtual schema allows users to formulate queries without being aware of the source's specific structure. Xyleme project, provides a semantic integration model for heterogeneous XML schemas. This model uses views that connect (through path-to-path mappings) a virtual tree-like schema (called abstract DTD) to the heterogeneous schemas (called concrete DTDs). A query on the view (abstract query) is translated into several concrete queries and the results are returned according to the view schema.

In P2P context, AXML (Active XML) is an XML document that may include some special elements such as the tag <sc> (for service web call). This tag contains calls to web services (SOAP, WSDL) for data integration. Some of the data are given explicitly in the AXML documents whereas the other ones are returned in these documents by web services calls. The use of calls to web services, embedded in XML documents, allows integrating or updating data included in these documents in a dynamic way. PIAZZA integrates sources that are semi-structured data based on XML data model and XQuery language. The peers, interested by exchanging data, establish semantic links between them. PIAZZA combines the two approaches of mediation *LaV/GaV*. SENPEER is a P2P system where data sources are expressed using various data models (e.g. Relational, XML etc.). SENPEER assumes an unstructured P2P where peers are connected to super-peers according to their semantic domains expressed with an ontology. Super-peers exchange messages to discover semantic links between them. A query formulated with the language of a peer is expressed with the query exchange format SQUEL and sent to its process owner for execution. Most of these systems use an architecture with single global schema (or ontology). This approach is interesting if all sources have similar attributes or concepts; otherwise, a source cannot be changed without reconsidering the global schema and the other sources, to make sure that there are no conflicts. For the other systems, which are based on multiple schemas (or ontology), it is hard to make a comparison between them since no common vocabulary were defined. Moreover, mapping between several couples of ontology needs to be defined. Unlike these systems, our approach uses a multi-data source language, based on XQuery, to data fusion: we can smoothly add or delete data sources since no global schema is required. Our approach is based on the use of ontologies in order to reconciliate between data sources. We suppose that the user is not an expert in data fusion tasks but he/she understand the meaning of data that should be integrated. Compared to existing languages and approaches, our work demonstrates good system achievements when the user frequently formulates queries.

In the following section, we describe our Multi-data source Fusion Language (MFL) for data sources fusion.

3. Multi-data Source Fusion Language

MFL provides two sub-languages [32]: the Multi-data source Definition Language (MDL) - used to define the multi-data source - and the Multi-data source Retrieval Language (MRL) - used to retrieve data from multi-data source. One characteristic of MDL resides on the simplicity of the multi-data source's definition: users can give a collective name called multi-data source name to some data sources. A collective name simplifies the expression of queries; users declare inter-sources conflicts between elements composing the multi-data source. It is useful to declare these conflicts for some types of queries described below. MRL extends XQuery language in order to access multiple conflicting data sources. Furthermore, in conflicting data sources, user's need is expressed through a single query. With MRL, it is easy to smooth out all semantic data differences which often exist in autonomous data sources.

3.1. Multi-data Source Definition Language

The purpose of MDL is to define the multi-data source schema starting from a set of data sources schemas.

3.1.1. Multi-data Source Description

Definition 3.1.1. (Multi-data source) *A multi-data source schema is a collection of data sources' schemas or multi-data sources according to the syntax of a Document Type Definition (DTD) of XML:*

<!ELEMENT multisources (source | multisources)+)>
<!ATTLIST multisources name CDATA #REQUIRED>
<!ELEMENT source (feature)+>
<!ATTLIST source name CDATA #REQUIRED>
<!ATTLIST source url CDATA #REQUIRED>
<!ELEMENT feature (#PCDATA)>
<!ATTLIST feature name CDATA #REQUIRED>

In this schema, <multisources> and <source> refer to a specific multi-data source or a data source. <name> designates the name of a multi-data source or simply a property in a data source. <url> describes the path to reach this data source. <feature> contains the properties of a data source. The following example shows how to integrate many data sources in a multi-data source.

Example 1 (Multi-data source creation): Consider the multi-data source given in Figure 1 describing an *AirLine* domain. In this example, the three (static) data sources *IndiAir, BritishAirway* and *FineAir* represent a multi-data source called *Company2*. Similarly, *Company2* with company *AirFrance* form a multi-data source called *Company1* and *Company* is the root of the multi-data source. Conflicts between these data sources are given in a specific data source called *Conflicts*. *Services* represent a multi-data source which describes two (active) data sources called *Dollar2Euro* and *Euro2Dollar*. The first service converts currencies from Dollar to Euro whereas the second one converts currencies from Euro to Dollar. In Figure 1, the name of a static or active data source (e.g. *AirFrance*) represents the root of a document (e.g. *AirFrance.dtd*) that describes the schema of this source. In this example, the schema of data sources *AirFrance*, *IndiAir* and *FineAir* are expressed in French and the data source *BritishAirway* in English. The structure of multi-data source Conflicts is expressed in the section below.

3.1.2. Conflicts Description

Data sources present heterogeneity that consists of differences in names, data structures, types, scale etc. Several perceptions of the same real world lead to different data sources. To integrate all these data sources together, we need first to solve their conflicts. Conflicts are classified as follows [18][38]: data models conflicts, data conflicts, structural conflicts, descriptive conflicts, abstraction conflicts and semantic conflicts. Conflicts between data models appear when data sources are designed using distinct data models (relational, XML etc.). Data conflicts refer to differences among definitions, such as attribute types, formats, or precision. Structural conflicts consist on describing the same idea in different ways and in different data sources. For example, a concept is defined as an attribute in a relational schema Sch1 and as a relation in another schema Sch2 etc. Descriptive conflicts concern different names given to a same entity (e.g. homonymous, synonymous), identity conflicts (e.g. a person is identified by a number in Sch1 and social-security number in Sch2), scale conflicts (e.g. salaries are given in Dollar and Euro respectively in Sch1 and Sch2) etc. Abstract conflicts concern generalization (e.g. the concept of employee in Sch1 generalizes the concept of teacher in Sch2) and aggregation (e.g. date of birth in Sch1 is a string while in Sch2 it is composed of three fields month, day and year). Semantic conflicts refer to differences and similarities in the meaning of elements in the data sources. Many works have studied semantic conflicts in the literature, we quote: [10] and [36].

```
<?xml version="1.0" encoding="ISO-8859-1"?>
<!DOCTYPE ms SYSTEM "my_mds.dtd">
<multisources name="Company">
    <multisources name="Company1">
        <source name="AirFrance"url="AirFrance.xml">
            <feature name="agence">
            <feature name="nom"/>
            <feature name="client">
            <feature name="nom"/>
            </feature>
            </feature>
        </source>
    <multisources name="Company2">
      <source name="BritishAirway" url=" BritishAirway.xml">
                <feature name="branch">
                <feature name="name"/>
                <feature name="employee">
                <feature name="name"/>
                <feature name="salaire"/>
                </feature>
                </feature>
      </source>
     <source name="AirIndia"url="AirIndia.xml">
                <feature name="agence">
                ...
                </feature>
                ...
     </source>
   </multisources>
    ...
</multisources>
```

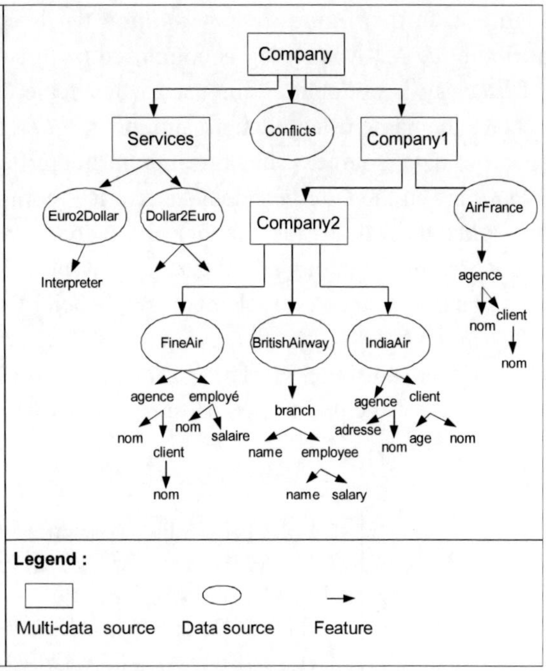

Figure 1. Multi-data source schema *AirLine.*

In [10], authors propose an algorithm called H-MATCH which takes two schemas as input and returns the mappings that identify corresponding concepts in the two schemas, namely the concepts with the same or the closest meaning. In [36], authors provide a survey of different approaches to automatic schema matching. In this chapter, we consider the most important conflicts detailed above, such as data models conflicts, descriptive conflicts and semantic conflicts. In order to solve conflicts between data models, we express data sources schemas with DTD formalism which represents in our case a common data model of all integrated data sources. Another model like XML schema can be chosen. Semantic conflicts between elements are detected using contexts of elements. A context of an element E is the set of elements connected directly to E and on which it depends semantically. In other words, if a node E2 is a child of a node E1, the term E2 has to be interpreted in the scope of E1's meaning. Thus, the different occurrences of a same term do not have the same meaning (e.g. Name can appear different times, and may represent the name of different entities). We suppose the following descriptive conflicts between elements of two data sources: synonymous, equivalence, homonymous, disjoint and scale conflicts. Two elements are considered semantically synonymous if their names are synonymous and have the same context (i.e. synonymous conflicts). Two elements are considered semantically equivalent if their names are the same and have the same context (i.e. equivalence conflicts). Such elements are connected between them by a similarity link in the Conflicts data source (given below). Two elements are linked by a dissimilarity (or difference) link if their names are the same or synonymous and have two distinct contexts (i.e. homonymous conflicts). Finally, two elements are linked by a dissimilarity link if their names are distinct and not synonymous (i.e. disjoint conflicts). A scale link describes two elements which are similar and each one uses a specific scale unit (i.e. scale conflicts). The structure of the data source Conflicts is given in

Figure 2. In this figure each *<Similar>* tag is composed of several *<Node>* tags and of an attribute *id*. A *<Node>* tag is composed of three elements *<Elt>*, *<Path>* and *<Unit>*. The *<Unit>* tag is optional and is used when scale conflicts are raised. The *<Elt>* tag allows to declare the name of an element and the *<Path>* tag shows the path to reach this element in a specific data source. The attribute *id* identifies the element *<Elt>* among all the tags *<Similar>* in the *Conflicts* data source. It is composed of two symbols: the first one is a letter that takes the value *s* (as similar); the second symbol is a number that gives the value of the tag *<Similar>* (among all the tags of type *<Similar>*) in the *Conflicts* data source that contains this element. An element *<Elt>* belongs to at most one tag of type *<Similar>. Each <Dissimilar> tag in the data source Conflicts combines an < Elt >* tag, at least two *<Path>* tags and an attribute id. The *<Elt>* tag allows to declare the element's name. The tags *<Path>* show the paths to reach the elements which are dissimilar in specific data sources.

```
<!ELEMENT Conflicts (Dissimilar*,Similar*,Scale*,Services*)>
<!ELEMENT Dissimilar (Elt,Path,Path+)>
<!ELEMENT Similar (Node*)>
<!ATTLIST Similar id CDATA #REQUIRED>
<!ATTLIST Dissimilar id CDATA #REQUIRED>
<!ELEMENT Node (Path,Elt,Unit?)>
<!ELEMENT Scale (Node*)>
<:ATTLIST Scale Type CDATA #REQUIRED>
<!ELEMENT Services (Service*)>
<!ATTLIST Services Type CDATA #REQUIRED>
<!ELEMENT Service (Name, Path, Convert)>
<!ELEMENT Name (#PCDATA)>
<!ELEMENT Convert (Unit1, Unit2)>
<!ELEMENT Unit1 (#PCDATA)>
<!ELEMENT Unit2 (#PCDATA)>
<!ELEMENT Elt (#PCDATA)>
<!ELEMENT Path (#PCDATA)>
<!ELEMENT Unit (#PCDATA)>
```

Figure 2. Structure of Conflicts data source.

The attribute *id* identifies the element *<Elt>* among all the tags *<Dissimilar>* in the *Conflicts* data source. It is composed of two symbols: the first one is a letter that takes the value *d* (as dissimilar); the second symbol is a number that gives the number of the tag *<Dissimilar>* (among all the tags of type *<Dissimilar>*) in the *Conflicts* data source to which this element is affected. An element *<Elt>* may belong to one or several tag(s) of type *<Dissimilar>*. A *<Scale>* tag describes the scale unit of an element. It has an attribute type, which describes the domain in which this scale is applied (e.g. Currency). The structure of the scale conflict consists on the *<Node>* tag mentioned above. The *<Services>* tag describes the services that can be used to solve the scale conflicts between two elements (e.g. to convert the value of an element from a scale unit to another one). This tag is made up of several tags called *<Service>*. Each *<Service>* tag specifies a service of conversion from an origin unit denoted by <*Unit*$_1$> to a destination unit denoted <*Unit*$_2$>. The two tags <*Name*> and <*Path*> respectively indicate the name of the service and its location in the multi-data source schema.

```
<?xml version="1.0" encoding="UTF-8"?>
<!DOCTYPE CONFLICTS SYSTEM "conflicts.dtd">
<CONFLITS>
<DISSIMILAR id= 'd1'>
     <ELT>nom</ELT>
  <PATH>Comp/Comp1/Comp2/IndiAir/agence</PATH>
  <PATH>Comp/Comp1/Comp2/IndiAir/client</PATH>
  <PATH>Comp/Comp1/Comp2/FineAir/employé</PATH>
</DISSIMILAR>

<DISSIMILAR id= 'd2'>
     <ELT>nom</ELT>
  <PATH>Comp/Comp1/AirFrance/agence</PATH>
  <PATH>Comp/Comp1/Comp2/IndiAir/client</PATH>
  <PATH>Comp/Comp1/Comp2/FineAir/employé</PATH>
</DISSIMILAR>
<DISSIMILAR id= 'd3'>
     <ELT>nom</ELT>
  <PATH>Comp/Comp1/AirFrance/agence</PATH>
  <PATH>Comp/Comp1/AirFrance/client</PATH>
  <PATH>Comp/Comp1/Comp2/FineAir/employé</PATH>
</DISSIMILAR>
  ...
```

```
 <SIMILAR id='s2'>
 <Node>
  <PATH>Comp/Comp1/Comp2/FineAir/employé</PATH>
  <ELT>nom</ELT>
 </Node>
 <Node>
  <PATH>Comp/Comp1/Comp2/BritishAirway/
      branch/employee</PATH>
  <ELT>name</ELT>
 </Node>
</SIMILAR>
SIMILAR id='s3'>
 <Node>
  <PATH>Comp/Comp1/Comp2/FineAir/employé</PATH>
  <ELT>salaire</ELT>
 </Node>
 <Node>
  <PATH>Comp/Comp1/Comp2/BritishAirway/
      branch/employee</PATH>
  <ELT>salary</ELT>
 </Node>
</SIMILAR>
...
</CONFLICTS>
```

Figure 3. Fraction of conflicts of the integrated data sources.

Example 2 (Conflicts between AirLine *sources):* Consider the multi-data source of *AirLine* field given in Figure 1. A fraction of the conflicts between data sources composing this multi-data source is described in Figure 3. In this figure, the first tag <*Dissimilar*> (id='d1') designates dissimilarity between the following features : the *'nom'* of an *'agence'*, the *'nom'* of a *'client'* and the *'nom'* of an *'employé'* (given in French language) in the two data sources *IndiAir* and *FineAir*. The second tag <*Similar*> (id='s2') indicates a similarity between the two features: the *name* of an employee in *BritishAirway* and the *'nom'* of *'employé'* (given in French language) in *FineAir*. Each tag <*Similar*> or <*Dissimilar*> is identified with a unique identifier *id*.

In the following section, we introduce the Multi-data source Retrieval Language MRL in order to retrieve data. This language is based on the structure of multi-data source.

3.2. Multi-data Source Retrieval Language

Query form: MRL query is defined as follows:

Use (multi-)datasource$_1$ *name*$_1$ *[,(multi-)datasource*$_j$ *name*$_j$]*
Allow $ < semantic-variables >
(E)XQuery query
Close name$_1$ *[,name*$_j$]*

The clauses *Use*, *XQuery query* and *Close* are mandatory in MRL queries, whereas the clause *Allow* is optional. The clause *Use* determines the scope of the query and connects to data sources for processing whilst *Close* disconnects from data sources. The *name* is a given alias for either a data source or multi-data source and the clause *Allow* permits the declaration of semantic variables. Through these variables, the user declares his/her intention to access data, in a given query, semantically similar and differently named. The (E)XQuery query can be formulated like a query w.r.t. to XQuery language [42] or as an EXQuery query given in [29] that allows an active data source to be called. In MRL, we distinguish two categories of queries: elementary query and semantic query illustrated in Figure 4.

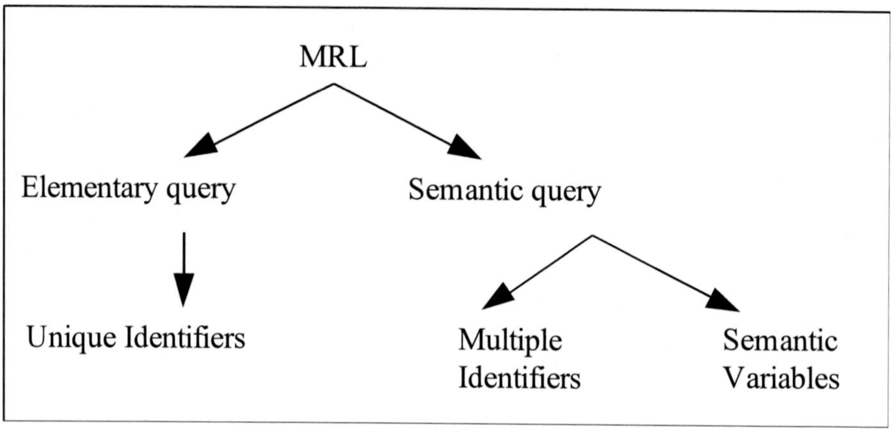

Figure 4. Classification of MRL queries.

3.2.1. Kinds of Data

Typically, a data source is built with one data model. However, such focus on one data model makes hard to deal with more complex applications which need different data models and query languages. Data sources are often expressed with relational or XML data models. We refer to Kinds of data all objects expressed, one or many times, in one or multiple data sources schema, within the same data model or distinct data models. For example, an object named *Car* can be modeled, many times, within XML or relational data model, in several data sources schemas. We say that the name *Car* refers to several kinds of data. But if the name *Car* appears only one time in a single data source schema, we say that it refers to only one kind of data.

3.2.2. Elementary Query

Elementary queries are used when various data sources represent distinct domains, used conjointly in queries, like in the example of the Leisure given in Figure 5.

Definition 3.2.1 (Unique identifiers) *A unique identifier is a designator (i.e. name) that refers to only one kind of data.*

An MRL query is an elementary query, if all its designators are unique identifiers in its scope. We distinguish two types of elementary queries: mono-data source and multi-data source. An elementary mono-data source query involves only one data source (static or active). An elementary multi-data source query involves several data sources. In the next example we show the situation in which we formulate an elementary mono-data or multi-data source query.

Example 3 (unique identifiers): In this example, we consider the multi-data source given in Figure 5(c). It is composed of one multi-data source called *Leisure* (the root). *Leisure* is also composed of two data sources: the bank and the underground station (XML and Sql), which respectively model the following two contexts: *Bank* (Figure 5(a)) and *Underground* (Figure 5(b)).

```
<!ELEMENT bank (banks+)>
<!ELEMENT banks(name,ban-street)>
<!ELEMENT name (#PCDATA)>
<!ELEMENT ban-street (#PCDATA)>
```

(a)

```
<!ELEMENT underground (lines+)>
<!ELEMENT lines(und-street,station)>
<!ELEMENT und-street (#PCDATA)>
<!ELEMENT station (#PCDATA)>
```

(b)

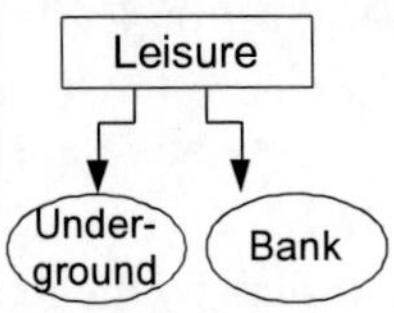

(c)

Figure 5. (a) Bank (b) Underground (c) Multi-data source Leisure.

If a user wants to retrieve the names of the banks in Saint-Michel street, the corresponding MRL query, in this case, is an elementary mono-data source query because it concerns one data source and unique identifiers (e.g. Ban-street and name):

Q_1: use bank c
for $a in document("my_mds")/leisure
where $a/*/ban-street/text()="Saint-Michel"
return *<result >*$a/*/name/text()*</result>*
close c

If the user wants to retrieve the names of the banks and the underground stations that are in the same street, we formulate the following query:

Q_2: use leisure l
for $a in document("my_mds")/l
where $a/*/ban-street/text() = $a/*/und-street/text()
return*<results><bank >*$a/*/name/text()*</bank>*,
<underground >$a/*/station/text()*</underground ></results >*
close l

The scope of Q_2 is the multi-data source *Leisure*. This query is an elementary multi-data source query since it joins two unique identifiers in both data sources *Bank* and *Underground.*

3.2.3. Semantic Query

Semantic queries are used when various data sources represent the same universe like the companies example given above (Figure 1). Semantic queries are also called broadcast queries [24] because a user may have to broadcast the same retrieval query to several conflicting data sources. XQuery language, in its current form, does not easily allow to express such situations. With XQuery, the user needs to formulate as many queries as there are data sources. In contrast, semantic queries allow to broadcast the user's intention in a single query. This is a considerable simplification, especially for a larger scope. Syntactically, semantic queries are basically formulated as elementary queries. In MRL, semantic queries are formulated according to the following concepts: multiple identifiers and semantic variables.

Definition 3.2.2 (Multiple identifiers) *A semantic query with multiple identifiers contains at least one designator that represents more than one kind of data in its scope.*

A semantic query q with multiple identifiers represents the set of all elementary queries $Sq_1, Sq_2, \ldots Sq_n$, also called subqueries, which are the result of substituting all multiple identifiers by their corresponding unique ones. Each designator becomes a unique identifier in a subquery Sq_i, i=1..n. This choice of unique identifiers may lead to a subquery that cannot be executed. We say that an executable subquery is a pertinent subquery. The result of such query q is the set of results returned by all its pertinent subqueries. We consider the example that describes the AirLine multi-data source given in Figure 1. We show an example of a semantic query with multiple identifiers.

Example 4 (multiple identifier and conflict): Select the names of all the branches of the companies *AirFrance*, *IndiAir* and *FineAir*.

If a user chooses to use XQuery language to answer this question, he/she would have to formulate three distinct subqueries (Sq_1, Sq_2 and Sq_3). Each subquery is executed over the corresponding data source. The union of the three subqueries' results constitutes the last result.

Sq_1: for $a in document("AirFrance")/AirFrance, $b in $a/agence/nom
return <*result*>$b/text()</*result*>
Sq_2: for $a in document("IndiAir")/AirIndia, $b in $a/agence/nom
return <*result*>$b/text()</*result*>
Sq_3: for $a in document("FineAir")/FineAir, $b in $a/agence/nom
return <*result*>$b/text()</*result*>

If this user chooses to use the Multi-data source Retrieval Language MRL to answer this question he/she would have to formulate only one query (Q_1) as follows:

Q_1: use AirFrance b, IndiAir c, FineAir s
for $a in document("my_mds")/company/company1, $b in $a/*/nom
return <*result*>$b/text()</*result*>
close b,c,s

This example highlights the simplicity of our language MRL. This query is a semantic query. Its scope is *AirFrance*, *IndiAir* and *FineAir*. Starting from the following path: */company/company1* in the multi-data source my_mds (For $a in document("my_mds")/

company/company1) and for each data source (*AirFrance*, *AirIndia* and *FineAir*) reached from this path, we return the names of the branches ($b/text()). In this query, the attribute *'nom'* is a multiple identifier since it designates the three attributes *'nom'* in *AirFrance*, *IndiAir* and *FineAir*. The designator *'nom'* in the scope of this query does not present any conflict of dissimilarity in the Conflicts data source (Figure 3). Let us consider another example, instead of selecting in (Q_1) the names of all the branches of the companies *AirFrance*, *AirIndia* and *FineAir* we want to select the names of the company in *BritishAirway*. The following MRL query (Q_2) is formulated:

***Q*₂:** use BritishAirway c
for $a in document("my_mds")/company/company1/company2, $b in $a/*/name
return *<result>*$b/text()*</result>*
close c

In this query, the designator name is a multiple identifier since it designates the branch name and the employee name in the data source *BritishAirway*. Dissimilarity (homonymous conflict) is detected in the scope of this query. In this case, a warning message informs the user of this conflict. In addition, the branches name in *FineAir* and *BritishAirway* are written in two distinct languages: French (*'nom'*) and English (*name*). We cannot use a multiple identifier to refer the branches names in these two data sources. In such a case, we use a semantic variable whose domain is *'nom'* and *name* as follows:

Definition 3.2.3 (Semantic variables) *A semantic variable is a variable whose domain are the names of data types which are semantically similar. A query can invoke one or several semantic variables. The aim of these variables is to enable the user to broadcast his/her intention over differently named data types which are semantically linked between them by similar links in the Conflicts data source (e.g.* name *and* 'nom'*).*

A semantic query, with semantic variables, consists of a set of pertinent elementary subqueries resulting from all possible substitutions of semantic variables and multiple identifiers by unique identifiers. The syntax of the clause *Allow* is given as follows:

Allow $< *semantic-variable* > = < *designator* >[,< *designator* >]+
< *semantic-variable* > ::= < *simple-variable* > | < *composed¡variable* >
< *composed-variable* > ::=< *simple-variable* >[.< *simple-variable* >]+
< *simple-variable* > ::= < *string* >
< *designator* > ::= < *string* >[.< *string* >]+

Consider the following example where the clause *Allow* appears: Allow $\$x_1.x_2...x_k = n_{1,1}.n_{2,1}...n_{k,1},...,n_{1,m}.n_{2,m}...n_{k,m}$. Each x is a semantic variable. Each n is a designator. The domain of the semantic variable x_i is $n_{i,j}$, for j=1..m. To preserve semantics in the query, we assume that the data type names $n_{i,j}$, for j=1..m are semantically similar. The ith subquery corresponds to the simultaneous substitutions of $n_{j,i}$ to x_j, for j=1..k. For example, the semantic variables $\$x_1.x_2...x_k$, for the first subquery, are replaced by the unique or multiple identifiers $n_{1,1}.n_{2,1}..n_{k,1}$.

The following query is a semantic query with one semantic variable (x) and multiple identifiers (*name*). This query contains conflicts in its scope, including similarity (i.e. synonymous) and dissimilarity (i.e. homonymous) conflicts.

Example 5 (One semantic variable) : Select the name of the branches in the two data sources *FineAir* and *BritishAirway*.

```
Q1: use FineAir b,BritishAirway c
allow $x=nom,name
for $a in document("my_mds")/company/company1/company2, $b in $a/*/$x
return <result>$b/text()</result>
close b,c
```

The clause *Allow* declares one semantic variable x. The domain of this variable is the pair of values (*'nom'*, *name*). For each value of x, a subquery is generated. Moreover, the designator name is a multiple identifier since it designates the name of a branch and the name of an employee in the data source *BritishAirway*. In the same way, the designator *'nom'* is a multiple identifier since it designates the *'nom'* of an *'agence'*, the *'nom'* of a 'client' and the *'nom'* of an *'employé'* in the data source *FineAir*. Similarity and dissimilarity conflicts are detected through query processing. An example of conflicts resolution is shown here: the meaning of *'nom'* of an *'agence'* in *FineAir* is found to be dissimilar from the name of an employee but it is similar to the name of a branch in *BritishAirway*. In this case, we keep the possibility, for the variable x, to take the two features: *'nom'* of an *'agence'* in *FineAir* and *name* of a *branch* in *BritishAirway*. Another possibility for the variable x is to take the two features : *'nom'* of an *'employé'* and *name* of a *employee*. We discard the possibility for the variable x to take the following features : *1. 'nom'* of a *'client'* and *name* of an *employee* or *2. 'nom'* of a *'client'* and *name* of a *branch* because dissimilarity between these elements are detected in the Conflicts data source. This query seeks in its scope some elements which are coherent semantically (e.g. *'nom'* of an *'agence'*, name of a branch) and some other elements which are heterogeneous semantically (e.g. *'nom'* of an *'employé'*, name of a branch). The responses to this query are given in two distinct sets S^i, i=1,2. S^1 returns the names of branches whilst S^2 returns the names of employees in the data sources *FineAir* and *BritishAirway*. Each set contains two pertinent Xquery subqueries (Sq^i_1 and Sq^i_2), resulting from the substitution of the semantic variable (x) by its corresponding unique identifiers:

```
Sq11: for $a in document("BritishAirway")/BritishAirway,
$b in $a/*/branch/name
return <result> $b/text()</result>
Sq12:for $a in document("FineAir")/FineAir,
$b in $a/*/agence/nom
return <result>$b/text()</result>
Sq21: for $a in document("BritishAirway")/BritishAirway,
$b in $a/*/employee/name
return <result>$b/text()</result>
Sq22: for $a in document("FineAir")/FineAir,
$b in $a/*/employé/nom
```

```
return <result> $b/text()</result>
```

The first subquery $\boldsymbol{Sq^1_1}$ (of the first set S^1) corresponds to the substitution of *name* (name of a branch) in *BritishAirway* to the semantic variable x. The second subquery $\boldsymbol{Sq^1_2}$ corresponds to the substitution of *'nom'* (*'nom'* of a *'agence'*) in *FineAir* to the semantic variable x. The first subquery $\boldsymbol{Sq^2_1}$ (of the second set S^2) corresponds to the substitution of *name* (name of an employee) in *BritishAirway* to the semantic variable x. The second subquery $\boldsymbol{Sq^2_2}$ corresponds to the substitution of *'nom'* (*'nom'* of an *employé'*) in *FineAir* to the semantic variable x. The user is alerted, in this case, of the presence of several semantics in its query. This is due to the large scope of the query. The user can either refine the query or accept the subqueries.

The following query shows a semantic query with two semantic variables. Each semantic variable in this query designates two different names. Each name may be a unique or a multiple identifier in the query's scope. This query contains two conflicts in its scope: similarity and dissimilarity conflicts. This query leads to two subqueries formulated differently, one per data source in the scope.

Example 6 (Several semantic variables): Select the branches names in the two data sources *BritishAirway* and *AirFrance*.

```
Q1: use BritishAirway c,AirFrance s
allow $x.y=branch.name, agence.nom
for $a in document("my_mds")/company/company1,
$b in $a/*/$x/$y
 return <result>$b/text()</result>
close c,s
```

Here, the clause *Allow* declares a couple of semantic variables (x,y), where x designates the pair of values (*branch*, *'agence'*) and y the pair of values (*name*, *'nom'*). These two features *'nom'* and name are two multiples identifiers in the scope of the query. To resolve the conflicts detected in this query, as in example 5, the feature name is substituted by the corresponding unique one (the branch name) and the feature 'nom' is substituted by the corresponding unique one (the *'nom'* of an *'agence'*). After that, we search for similar pair of values in the data sources conflicts (Figure 3). This query is equivalent to two XQuery subqueries (Sq_1 and Sq_2) coherent semantically:

```
Sq1: for $a in document("BritishAirway")/BritishAirway,
$b in $a/*/branch/name
return < result >$b/text()< =result >
Sq2: for $a in document("AirFrance")/AirFrance,
$b in $a/*/agence/nom
return < result >$b/text()< =result >
```

The first subquery corresponds to the substitution of *branch* and *name* respectively by the two semantic variables x and y. In the same perspective, *'agence'* and *'nom'* are related respectively to x and y, in the second subquery.

The following example, like the previous one, presents a semantic query with scale conflicts in its scope. This query uses the clause *Allow* with one semantic variable.

Example 7 (Scale conflict): Select the salaries of employees of *FineAir* and *BritishAirway*.

```
Q1: use FineAir b ,BritishAirway c
allow $x=salaire,salary
for $a in document("my_mds")/company/company1/company2, $d in $a/*/$x
return <result>$d/text()</result>
close b,c
```

In the scope of this query, a scale conflict is detected between the two elements *'salaire'* and *salary*. After execution, this query returns to the user a result with a warning message that points out the unit scale of each value selected. In this case, the user has the possibility to accept the result, to convert all the salaries into the same unit of scale (e.g. Dollar or Euro) or to choose a part of the salaries (e.g. only salaries expressed with Euro). To achieve this goal, we use the clause *Service* that calls an active data source.

Definition 3.2.4 (EXQuery) *EXQuery (Extended XQuery) (E)XQUERY is an extension of XQuery language in which we have integrated the clause* Service *[29]. The syntax of this clause is given below:*

```
< service >::=service "("< interpreter >","< name >","< argument >
","< locate >","< display >")"
< interpreter >::=< string >|(empty)
< name >::=< string >
< argument >::=< arg >[,< arg >]+
< arg >::=< string >|< number >
< locate >::=< ch >(< / >< ch >)*
< ch >::=< string >
< display >::=0|1
```

The first argument is optional and is specified only if an interpreter software is used to run the service required. The second argument is the service name. The third argument provides a list of parameters required to execute the service. The next argument specifies the location of the service in order to reach it. Display is optional; if this option is used, the result is displayed on the user's standard output. Otherwise, it is included into the query result.

For each active data source an XML document [43] is defined according to the document's structure given as follows:

```
<!ELEMENT service(interpreter; name; parameter; locate) >
<!ELEMENT interpreter(#PCDATA) >
<!ELEMENT name(#PCDATA) >
<!ELEMENT parameter(para¤) >
<!ELEMENT para(#PCDATA) >
<!ELEMENT locate(#PCDATA) >
```

This document provides information about a service such as its name, interpreter, parameters and location. The following query uses the clause *Service* that calls an active data source.

Example 8 (Service): Convert the salaries of employees of company BritishAirway into Euro.

```
Q1: use BritishAirway c, dollar2euro d
for $a in document("my_mds")/company/company1/comany2, $b in $a/*/salary
let $c := document("my_mds")/services
return < result >service($c/*/interpreter/text(),$c/*/name/text(),$b/text(),
$c/*/locate/text(),display)</result>
close c,d
```

Query Q_1, is an elementary multi-data source query that uses the clause *Service* in order to convert the salaries of BritishAirway' employees in Euros currency using the service *Dollar2Euro*. In this query, $b designates the salaries of BritishAirway' employees, and $c designates the multi-data source *Services*. The salaries selected from *BritishAirway* are passed as arguments to the clause *Service* (e.g. $b/text()).

In conclusion, MFL gives the possibility to integrate, dynamically, heterogeneous data sources, in particular, data sources coming from the Web. Data sources are integrated without the administrators' involvement. The proposed MFL language takes into account semantic and scale conflicts between data sources. The following section, describes our approach of semantic reconciliation between data sources. This approach is chosen for its simplicity. Its advantage is to allow the user to reconciliate between data sources with minimal difficulties.

4. Semantic Reconciliation Based on Ontology

In this section we present our approach for conflicts detection in the multi-data source. We start by introducing briefly the benefit of using ontologies in the domain of data sources fusion. For this purpose, we build a conceptual representation of the AirLine's domain with a terminolgical model. This representation is translated using the OWL/RDF language and stored as XML document. This document represents the basis of our study to reconciliate semantically different data sources.

4.1. Ontology Overview

An ontology is an explicit specification of a conceptualization [13]. It provides a set of constructors which are used to model a specific domain of knowledge. Constructors are classes, properties and relationships between them. An ontology allows also to model knowledge about individuals (i.e. instances), and the relationships between them. Ontologies are independent from lower level data models (logical or physical). They are useful especially in the fields of Web Semantic [5] and also for integrating heterogeneous data sources [17],[41]. In the early stage of the Web, information was shared as HTML pages. These pages were designated to be read only by a human user. The first language designed by the consortium W3C [35] in the domain of Web Semantic is the RDF (Resource Description framework) language. RDF is an XML language used to describe metadata and to facilitate their treatment by specific applications programs. After that, RDFS (RDF Schema) [35] language was developed in order to give RDF more expressive power. However, many limitations restrict the ability to express knowledge. Indeed, it is not possible to carry out an automated reasoning on knowledge modeled using RDFS. To overcome this lack, a new language for Web called OWL was developed (Ontology Web Language) [27]. OWL is based on logic description [2]. Using OWL, we can describe the knowledge about a domain in terms of a set of classes and a set of properties. Classes represent entities of interest in a specific domain and a property represents a feature (i.e. data type property) of an entity or a relationship between entities (i.e. object properties). OWL, like RDF, is based on XML language. OWL provides tools for comparing and reasoning on classes, their features and the relations between them. It gives a great ability to interpret the web content because it contains a wide range of vocabulary and a full semantic formal. The W3C provides three types of languages to better express OWL: Lite, DL (Description Logic) and Full.

4.2. Integrating Ontologies in Our Approach

Ontologies are used in integration tasks to describe the semantics of data sources. In [41], three different approaches are discussed to use ontologies in the process of integration of data sources: single ontology, multiple ontologies and hybrid ontologies. In the single ontology approach, all data sources are related to one global ontology. In the second approach, each data source has its own ontology. In this case, mapping between ontologies is necessary for integrating data sources. The hybrid approach is a combination of the two previous ones. In [17], the authors describe the role of ontologies in data integration in two settings: central and P2P. The single approach is appropriate for *GaV* systems. Hybrid approach is more appropriate for *LaV* systems; hybrid peer-to-peer system, where a global ontology exists in a super-peer, can also use hybrid ontology approach. The multiple ontology approach can be better used to create pure peer-to-peer data integration systems, where there are no super-peers. Figure 6 shows, with a terminological model, a sample of AirLine's domain knowledge. This domain is expressed using the four following components:

- A concept is a collection of individuals that constitute the entities of the modeled domain. The concepts can be compared to notion of class (i.e. object model) or type of entity in the conceptual models (i.e. Entity/ Relationship).
- A role is a binary relationship between concepts. Roles are used to specify properties of instances and are compared to notion of attributes in the conceptual models. A role is viewed as a function linking a concept (called domain) to another concept (known as co-domain).
- An inheritance relationship. A class *C1* subsumes a Class *C2* if and only if every instance of *C2* is also an instance of *C1*. i.e. *C1* is a superclass of *C2*. This inheritance relationship is applied if the constraint attributes of class *C1* involve logically the constraint attributes of class *C2*.
- ANYTHING represents a topmost concept and NOTHING represents a bottom concept.

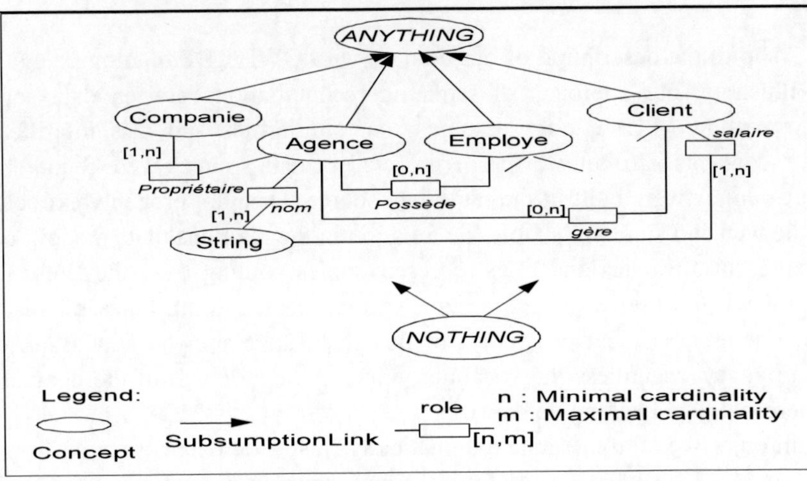

Figure 6. Description of AirLine's domain (in French).

```
<rdf:RDF ...
 xml:base="http://www.owl-ontologies.com/Ontology1228248595.owl">
 <owl:Class rdf:ID="Employe">
 </owl:Class>
 <owl:Class rdf:ID="Client">
 </owl:Class>
 <owl:Class rdf:ID="Agence">
  </owl:Class>
 <owl:Class rdf:ID="Companie"/>
 <owl:ObjectProperty rdf:ID="proprietaire">
   <rdfs:range rdf:resource="#Agence"/>
   <rdfs:domain rdf:resource="#Companie"/>
 </owl:ObjectProperty>
<owl:DatatypeProperty rdf:ID="chemin_Agence">
   <rdfs:domain rdf:resource="#Agence"/>
   <rdfs:range rdf:resource="http://www.w3.org/2001/XMLSchema#string"/>
 </owl:DatatypeProperty>
 <owl:DatatypeProperty rdf:ID="age_client">
   <rdfs:domain rdf:resource="#Client"/>
   <rdfs:range rdf:resource="http://www.w3.org/2001/XMLSchema#string"/>
 </owl:DatatypeProperty>
 <owl:DatatypeProperty rdf:ID="nom_agence">
   <rdfs:domain rdf:resource="#Agence"/>
   <rdfs:range rdf:resource="http://www.w3.org/2001/XMLSchema#string"/>
 </owl:DatatypeProperty>
 <owl:DatatypeProperty rdf:ID="adresse_agence">
   <rdfs:domain rdf:resource="#Agence"/>
   <rdfs:range rdf:resource="http://www.w3.org/2001/XMLSchema#string"/>
 </owl:DatatypeProperty>
 <owl:DatatypeProperty rdf:ID="salaire_client">
   <rdfs:range rdf:resource="http://www.w3.org/2001/XMLSchema#string"/>
   <rdfs:domain rdf:resource="#Client"/>
 </owl:DatatypeProperty>
 <owl:DatatypeProperty rdf:ID="salaire_employe">
   <rdfs:domain rdf:resource="#Employe"/>
   <rdfs:range rdf:resource="http://www.w3.org/2001/XMLSchema#string"/>
 </owl:DatatypeProperty>
 <owl:DatatypeProperty rdf:ID="nom_client">
   <rdfs:range rdf:resource="http://www.w3.org/2001/XMLSchema#string"/>
   <rdfs:domain rdf:resource="#Client"/>
 </owl:DatatypeProperty>
...
</rdf:RDF>
```

Figure 7. Airline's domain expressed with OWL/RDF (AirLine.owl).

Figure 7 shows the description of our domain with OWL/RDF ontology language which is used to illustrate, our approach of semantic reconciliation between data sources. The process of rewriting MRL queries assumes that similarities and dissimilarities between elements (i.e. concepts, attributes or properties etc.) of data sources were found and that the data source *Conflicts* were built in the multidata source. Data are probably extracted (by the user) from the web and stored in a table (i.e. relation in the relational data model): columns of this table represent attributes and rows represent tuples coming from the Web. During the extraction process, the user is free to assign, various names to attributes of this table. For example, a user assigns the word 'emp' to designate an employee in a Bank or 'ag' to designate an agency, regardless the vocabulary and/or the structure of the domain to which he/she is interested (e.g. banking domain).

Our main objective is to integrate automatically (just after data extraction from the web) several data sources (specially coming from the web) with a minimal effort required from the user. But, we suppose again that the user understands the semantic of the extracted data he/she wants to integrate in the multi-data source. Figure 8 summarizes our approach in order to generate the *Conflicts* data sources. The data source *Conflicts.xml*, which constitutes the primary component for rewriting queries, is presented in the section 5.

4.3. Methodology for Semantic Reconciliation

The methodology applied for semantic reconciliation between data sources is based on the use of ontology that defines properties, concepts and relationships between these concepts. Using such ontology allows the user to specify clearly the domain of his/her interest. In our context, using ontology improves the user's knowledge about data source by clarifying the meaning of all its elements. For example, a user, interested by an Airline's domain, must specify an ontology conformed to this domain. Therefore, the user can assign to each element of the data source the equivalent semantic element in the specified ontology. This step involves a semantic enrichment of the integrated data source schema stored as an XML document, which is conformed to the following DTD called *SemEnr.dtd*.

<!*ELEMENT source* (*ontology*+) >
<!*ATTLIST source name CDATA #REQUIRED* >
<!*ATTLIST source url CDATA #REQUIRED* >
<!*ELEMENT ontology* (*feature*) >
<!*ATTLIST ontology name CDATA #REQUIRED* >
<!*ELEMENT feature* (*ontology*?) >
<!*ATTLIST feature name CDATA #REQUIRED* >

Figure 9(a) shows a part of the data source BritishAirway. This data source describes two main elements which are : Branch and Employee, with their respective names and salaries (for employee). Figure 9(b) shows the extracted DTD of this data source. Figure 9(c) associates, to each element in this DTD, an element of the chosen ontology (in AirLine.owl) with respect to the given DTD *SemEnr.dtd*. The next step is to generate instances in the AirLine's ontology using the wrapper component (Figure 8).

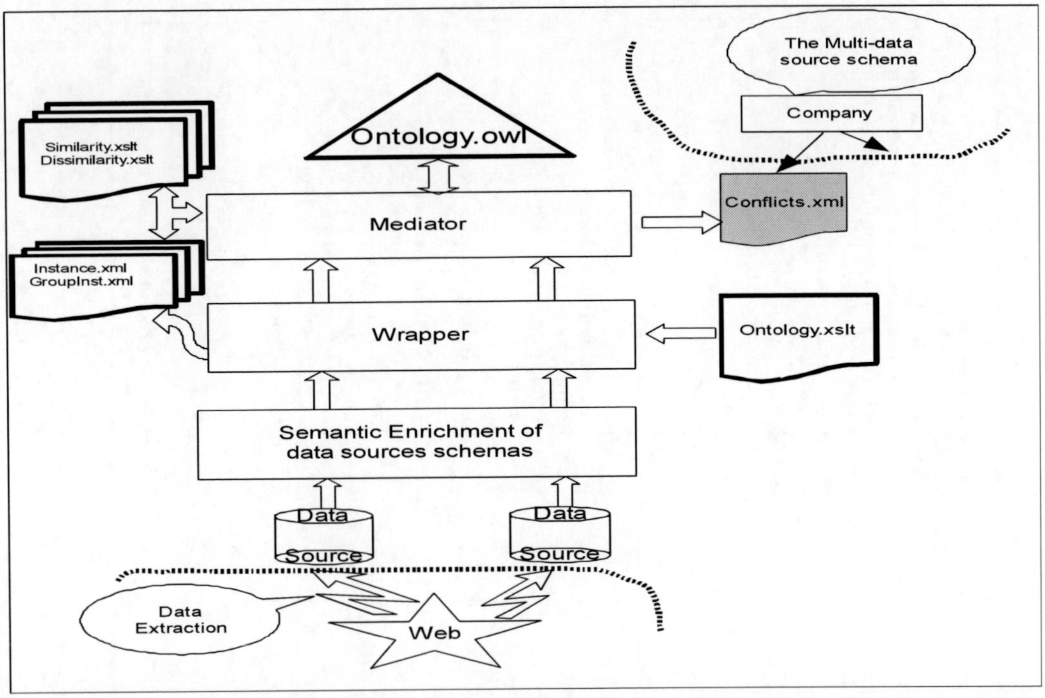

Figure 8. Approach for semantic reconciliation between data sources.

```
<!DOCTYPE BritishAirway SYSTEM
"BritishAirway.dtd">
<BritishAirway>
    <branch>
        <name>Londre</name>
      <employee>
        <name>Dupond</name>
        <salary>1500</salary>
      </employee>
    </branch>
    ...
</BritishAirway>
```

(a) A part of the data source BritishAirway (XML document)

```
<!ELEMENT BritishAirway (branch,employee)>
<!ELEMENT branch (name)>
<!ELEMENT name (#PCDATA)>
<!ELEMENT employee (salary)>
<!ELEMENT salary (#PCDATA)>
```

(b) DTD corresponding to data source BritishAirway

```
<!DOCTYPE source SYSTEM "SemEnr.dtd">
<source name="BritishAirway"
url="AirLines/BritishAirway.xml">
  <ontology name="agence">
    <feature name="branch">
      <ontology name="nom">
        <feature name="name"/>
      </ontology>
      <ontology name="employe">
        <feature name="employee">
          <ontology name="nom">
            <feature name="name"/>
          </ontology>
        <ontology name="salaire">
            <feature name="salary"/>
        </ontology>
        </feature>
      </ontology>
    </feature>
  </ontology>
</source>
```

(c) Semantic enrichment of the BritishAirway schema

Figure 9. Semantic enrichment of the BritishAirway schema.

```xml
<xsl:stylesheet ... />
  <xsl:template match="/">
    <Instance>
      <AirLine>
        <xsl:attribute name="rdf:ID">
          <xsl:value-of
           select="concat('AirLine_',//source/@name)"></xsl:value-of>
        </xsl:attribute>
      </AirLine>
     <Client>
        <xsl:attribute name="rdf:ID">
        <xsl:value-of select="concat('Client_',//source/@name)"></xsl:value-of>
        </xsl:attribute>
        <chemin_Client rdf:datatype="...#string">
          <xsl:variable name="nomAirLine" select="//source/@name"></xsl:variable>
          <xsl:variable name="courant" select="concat('/',//ontology[@name='client']/
                               feature/@name)"></xsl:variable>
          ...
        </chemin_Client>
        <nom_client rdf:datatype="...#string">
          <xsl:value-of select="//ontology[@name='client']/*/ontology[@name='nom']/
                                feature/@name"></xsl:value-of>
        </nom_client>
        <age_client rdf:datatype="...#string">
          <xsl:value-of select="//ontology[@name='client']/*/ontology[@name='age']/
                               feature/@name"></xsl:value-of>
        </age_client>
        <salaire_client rdf:datatype="...#string">
          <xsl:value-of select="//ontology[@name='client']/*/ontology[@name='salaire']/
                               feature/@name"></xsl:value-of>
        </salaire_client>
      </Client>
...
    </Instance>
  </xsl:template>
</xsl:stylesheet>
```

(a) XSLT Template (Generation of instances)

```xml
<Instance xmlns:rdf="http...">
<AirLine rdf:ID="AirLine_BritishAirway"/>
    <Employe rdf:ID="Employe_BritishAirway">
        <chemin_Employe rdf:datatype="http...">
            BritishAirway/employee
        </chemin_Employe>
        <salaire_employe rdf:datatype="http...">
            salary
        </salaire_employe>
        <nom_employe rdf:datatype="http...">
            name
        </nom_employe>
        <age_employe rdf:datatype="http..."/>
    </Employe>
    <Agence rdf:ID="Agence_BritishAirway">
        <chemin_Agence rdf:datatype="http...">
            BritishAirway/branch
        </chemin_Agence>
        <nom_agence rdf:datatype="http...">
            name
        </nom_agence>
        <adresse_agence rdf:datatype="http..."/>
    </Agence>
    <Client rdf:ID="Client_BritishAirway">
        <chemin_Client rdf:datatype="http...">
            BritishAirway/
        </chemin_Client>
        <nom_client rdf:datatype="http..."/>
        <age_client rdf:datatype="http..."/>
        <salaire_client rdf:datatype="http..."/>
    </Client>
</Instance>
```

(b) Instance of BritishAirway with OWL/RDF

Figure 10. Part of the template AirLine.xslt and an instance of BritishAirway.

```
declare namespace owl="http://www.w3.org/2002/07/owl#";
declare namespace rdf="http://www.w3.org/1999/02/22-rdf-syntax-ns#";
declare namespace rdfs="http://www.w3.org/2000/01/rdf-schema#";
for $dtp in doc("airlines.owl")//owl:DatatypeProperty
let $domain := substring($dtp/rdfs:domain/@rdf:resource/string(),2)
let $nom_dtp := $dtp/@rdf:ID/string()
 return <dtp><domain>{$domain}</domain><nom>{$nom_dtp}</nom>
  <valeurs>{
for $inst in doc("instances.xml")//*[name() = $domain]
let $valeur := $inst/*[name() = $nom_dtp]/text()
return
  <valeur inst="{$inst/@rdf:ID/string()}">{$valeur}</valeur>
}</valeurs>
</dtp>
```

Figure 11. Querying the ontology AirLine.

The improved data source schema, obtained in the previous step, is now expressed as instances using the ontology's language (i.e. OWL/RDF). This conversion is based on a defined template (AirLine.xslt) given in Figure 10(a). The result of this step is an XML document called *Instance.xml*, describing an instance in the ontology of the data source being integrated. Figure 10(b) shows an instance obtained by applying this template on the enrichment schema of BritishAirway data source (given in Figure 9(c)). The final step consists in generating Conflicts data source (Conflicts.xml) by the mediator, which has three main tasks: *a.* Create each instance in the document *instance.xml*, returned by the wrapper, in the ontology; *b.* Regroup together, for each Data Type Property (DTP) (of a class) all its instances in the ontology: let us consider, the DTP *'nom'* of *'Agence'* in the AirLine's ontology. The instances of this DTP are the names of *'Agence'* (or Branches) in each company in the multi-data source schema. This step may be accomplished by querying directly the ontology with one of the ontologies' languages (i.e. DLQuery etc.) or with an XQuery query as given in Figure 11. In this query *AirLine.owl* represents our ontology and *Instances.xml* contains all the instances created in the AirLine's ontology. This result is stored in an XML document named *GroupInst.xml*. A part of this document is given in Figure 12; *c.* Generate similarities (dissimilarities) by transforming the document *GroupInst.xml*, using the template *Similarity.xslt* (*Dissimilarity.xslt*) (not shown in this chapter). The result of this step is stored in the Conflicts.xml (a part of this result is given in Figure 3). In Conflicts.xml file, a node with a tag Similar represents a semantic link between two elements of equivalence (e) or synonym (s) types. A node with a tag dissimilar represents a semantic link between two elements of homonym (h) or disjoint (d) types. For each node, with a tag similar or dissimilar, we associate an identifier. The nodes with similar (dissimilar) tags are identified with the following identifier: $s_i(d_i)$. The index i represents the ith node similar or dissimilar among all nodes with the same tag. The following section describes the algorithm of rewriting semantic queries.

```
<result>
<dtp>
  <domain>Client</domain>
  <nom>age_client</nom>
  <valeurs>
    <valeur inst="Client_IndiAir">age</valeur>
    <valeur inst="Client_BritishAirWay"/>
    <valeur inst="Client_FineAir"/>
    <valeur inst="Client_AirFrance"/>
  </valeurs>
</dtp>
<dtp>
  <domain>Agence</domain>
  <nom>nom_agence</nom>
  <valeurs>
    <valeur inst="Agence_IndiAir">nom</valeur>
    <valeur inst="Agence_BritishAirWay">name</valeur>
    <valeur inst="Agence_FineAir">nom</valeur>
    <valeur inst="Agence_AirFrance">nom</valeur>
  </valeurs>
</dtp>
...
<dtp>
  <domain>Client</domain>
  <nom>salaire_client</nom>
  <valeurs>
    <valeur inst="Client_IndiAir"/>
    <valeur inst="Client_BritishAirWay"/>
    <valeur inst="Client_FineAir"/>
    <valeur inst="Client_AirFrance"/>
  </valeurs>
</dtp>
<dtp>
  <domain>Employe</domain>
  <nom>salaire_employe</nom>
  <valeurs>
    <valeur inst="Employe_IndiAir"/>
    <valeur inst="Employe_BritishAirWay">salary</valeur>
    <valeur inst="Employe_FineAir">salaire</valeur>
    <valeur inst="Employe_AirFrance"/>
  </valeurs>
</dtp>
</result>
```

Figure 12. Regrouping instances of the ontology AirLine.

5. Rewriting Semantic Queries (RSQ) Algorithm

In this section, we study, using an example, the steps of our (RSQ) algorithm. Let us consider the following query:

Use AirFrance af, FineAir fa, BritishAirway ba, IndiAir ia
Allow $x.y.z=branch.employee.name, agence.employé.nom
For $a in document("my_mds.xml")/Company/Company1,
$b in $a/*/$x/*/$z, $c in $a/*/$y, $d in $c/$z, $e in $a/*/$x/adresse
Return
<results>
<result1>$b/text()</result1><result2>$d/text()</result2>,
<result3>$e/text()</result3>
</results>
Close af,fa,ba,ia

The above code corresponds to an MRL semantic query over the multi-data schema AirLine given in Figure 1. The scope of this query contains four data sources: *AirFrance*, *FineAir*, *BritishAirway* and *IndiAir*. This query is composed of three semantic variables x,y and z. Each of these variables is related to two identifiers: (*branch*, *'agence'*), (employee,'employé') and (*name,'nom'*). Some of these identifiers are multiples (e.g. 'nom' etc.). This query contains a set of five variables called context variables: {$a,$b,$c,$d,$e}. It returns values for the variables $b, $d and $e.

To obtain the required results, the following steps must be executed:

***Step 1:** Analyze the clauses Use, Allow, For (or Let) and Return of the query*
Input : MRL query which is syntactically correct
Output : MsoVarTab is a table containing the data sources or multi-data source with their respective alias; *SemVarTab* is a table containing the various semantic variables (*$x.y.z*) specified in Allow and their respective values; *ConVarTab* is a table containing the different context variables (*$a, $b*, etc..) specified in For (or Let) and their respective values (*/root/*/$x/...; $a/*/$y/..., etc.*). *ResVarTab* is a table containing the (sub-)set of context variables specified in the clause Return. In this table, a context variable takes the value *true* if it is specified in the clause Return. Otherwise it takes the value *false*. Figure 13 shows the results of this step.

***Step 2 :** Create the tree context*
Input : MsoVarTab, SemVarTab, ConVarTab, ResVarTab
Output : ConTree

The information obtained from step 1 is used to build the tree of the query called *ConTree*. This tree is obtained after substituting each variable in the tables given in input, based on the multi-data source schema (given in Figure 1). *ConTree* describes the context for each element of the query. Recall that the context of an element E is the path that connects the root to E in the multi-data source schema. Figure 14 represents the tree of the given query. In this figure, each child node of the Root node (here four nodes) represents a valid path toward a data source (e.g. document("my_mds.xml")/company/company1/AirFrance is a valid path reached by $a). Moreover, the children of these nodes are again valid paths in the scope of the context variable $b. For example, the two childrens '/agence/nom' and '/agence/client/nom', of the node *AirFrance*, are two valid paths in the scope of the variable $b. In this example, the element *'nom'* is a multiple identifier in the data source *AirFrance*, which designates respectively the name of an *'agence'* and the name of a *'client'* of this *'agence'*. The context variables $c, $d and $e are empty elements because it is not possible to reach *'nom'* of *'employé'* and *'adresse'* in the data source *AirFrance* (i.e. *'employé'* and *'adresse'* are two missing elements in this data source).

AirFrance	af	FineAir	fa	BritishAirway	ba	IndiAir	ia

MsoVarTab

Semantic variables	Values
x	{agence, branch}
y	{employé, employee}
z	{name,nom}

SemVarTab

Context variables	Values
$a	document("my_mds")/Compny/Company1
$b	$a/*/$x/*/$z
$c	$a/*/$y
$d	$c/$z
$e	$a/*/$x/adresse

ConVarTab

$a	false	$b	true	$c	false	$d	true	$e	true

ResVarTab

Figure 13. Analysis of the query's clauses.

Step 3: *Control conflicts between elements*
Input: ConTree
Output : ConTab

This step controls, using the data source Conflicts.xml, all the semantics equivalences between the tree's elements *ConTree*. For the sake of presentation, we construct a table called *ConTab* (starting from the *ConTree*), where the intersection between each involved data source in the query (given in column) and each variable specified in the clause Return of the query (given in row) is an element with a Null value or one or several contexts (i.e. unique or multiple identifier(s)). For each element within a context in *ConTab*, we search for all the identifiers (i.e. s_i, d_j etc.) in the Conflicts data source which are associated to that context. In Figure 15, each column of the table *ConTab* represents a data source. Each row represents a context variable in *ResVarTab* initialized to true. The intersection between a row and a column contains an element within a single or several context(s). For example, in this table, in the intersection of \$b and *AirFrance*, we found the element *'nom'* within two distinct contexts (*'agence'* and *'client'*). For each context (e.g. *\$a/agence/nom*) we search for all its identifiers (e.g. $\{s_1,d_2,d_3\}$) in the file *Conflict.xml*. If we analyze the variable \$b in this table, we observe that: *1.* the four data sources have similar identifier (s_1) in their respective sets of identifiers (i.e. *'\$a/agence/nom'* in AirFrance, *'\$a/agence/nom'* in FineAir, *'\$a/branch/name'* in BritishAirway and *'\$a/agence/nom'* in IndiAir are semantically similar); *2.* the two elements *'\$a/agence/client/nom'* and *'\$a/agence/nom'* in AirFrance (for example) are dissimilar. In such a case, we can not be sure that the user is interested by the branches' names (*'agence'*) or their customers' names (*'client'*). At this stage, we conclude that *ConTab* is ambiguous and it cannot be used to generate subqueries.

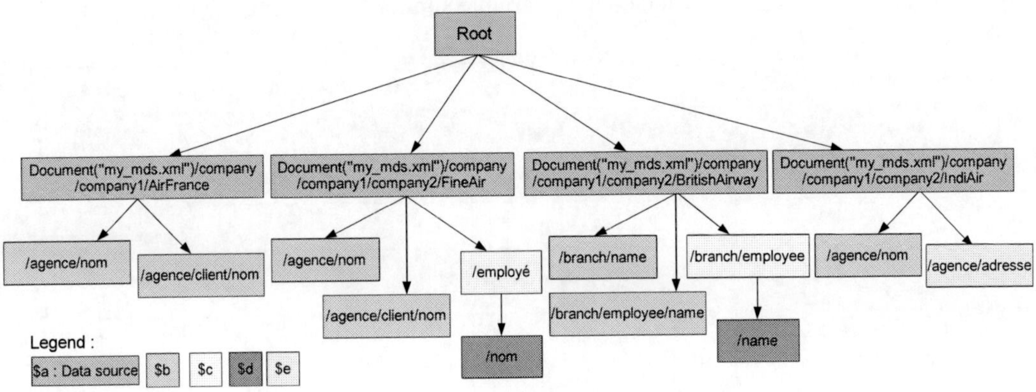

Figure 14. Creation of the ConTree.

Step 4: *Generate Semantic Tables*
Input : ConTab
Output : SemTab

This step is called only if *ConTab* is considered ambiguous in the previous step, otherwise we skip it and we pass to step 5. Recall that, *ConTab* contains all semantics information about the user's query. This table allows controlling all semantic equivalences and therefore the query's conflicts. *SemTab* is a semantic table having the same structure as *ConTab* with, in addition, the following restriction: for each variable and for each data source in *SemTab*, there is an element defined within only one context (or missing element). *SemTab* is considered as coherent semantically and it contains all useful elements to convert the MRL query into a set of pertinent subqueries.

When *ConTab* is considered ambiguous in the previous step, at least two sets of identifiers are associated to an element. In this case at least two semantic tables *SemTab* are built. Each *SemTab* permits to generate a set of pertinent subqueries, which are semantically coherent. The user has three choices: 1) to refine more his/her query semantically; 2) to obtain the response which requires the maximal number of data sources (and/or a minimum number of missing elements in the subqueries), or by default 3) to consult all the possible responses. This last choice is not realistic since exploring all the responses needs considerable time.

	AirFrance	FineAir	BritishAirway	IndiAir
$b	$a/agence/nom {s1,d2,d3] $a/agence/client/nom {s4,d3,d4}	$a/agence/client/nom {s4,d5,d6} $a/agence/nom {s1,d6}	$a/branch/name {s1,d5} $a/branch/employee/name {s2,d5,d6 }	$a/agence/nom {s1,d1,d4}
$d		$a/employé/nom {s2,h1,d2,d3,d4}	$a/branch/employee/name {s2,d5,d6}	
$e				$a/agence/adresse {s5}

Figure 15. Construction of the ConTab.

From the resulting table *ConTab* in Figure 15, we generate three tables *SemTab* (Figure 16). Each *SemTab* contains for each context variable similar (or missing) elements.

	AirFrance	FineAir	BritishAirway	IndiAir
$b	$a/agence/nom {s1,d2,d3}	$a/agence/nom {s1,d6}	$a/branch/name {s1,d5}	$a/agence/nom {s1,d1,d4}
$d		$a/employé/nom {s2,h1,d2,d3,d4}	$a/branch/employee/name {s2,d5,d6}	
$e				$a/agence/adresse {s5}

SemTab 1

	AirFrance	FineAir	BritishAirway	IndiAir
$b	$a/agence/client/nom {s4,d3,d4}	$a/agence/client/nom {s4,d5,d6}		
$d		$a/employé/nom {s2,d1,d2,d3,d4}	$a/branch/employee/name {s2,d5,d6}	
$e				$a/agence/adresse {s5}

SemTab 2

	AirFrance	FineAir	BritishAirway	IndiAir
$b			$a/branch/employee/name {s2,d5,d6 }	
$d		$a/employé/nom {s2,d1,d2,d3,d4}	$a/branch/employee/name {s2,d5,d6}	
$e				$a/agence/adresse {s5}

SemTab 3

Figure 16. Generation of the semantic tables.

***Step 5:** Generate pertinent sub-queries*
Entry : SemTab
Output : Sub-queries

For each SemTab, we generate a set of pertinent subqueries, which are semantically coherent with each others. Each generated subquery is an XQuery query (or an MRL elementary query) with only unique identifiers defined in its body.

Subquery 1 :

```
for $a in document("AirFrance.xml")/AirFrance,
$b in $a/agence/nom
return
<result1>$b/text()</result1>
```

Subquery 2 :

```
for $a in document("FinAir.xml")/FinAir,
$b in $a/agence/name
$d in $a/employe/nom
return
<result1>$b/text()</result1>
<result2>$d/text()</result2>
```

Subquery 3 :

```
for $a in document("BritishAirway.xml")/BritishAirway,
$b in $a/branch/name
$d in $a/branch/employee/name
return
<result1>$b/text()</result1>,
<result2>$d/text()</result2>
```

Subquery 4 :

```
for $a in document("AirIndia.xml")/AirIndia,
$b in $a/agence/nom
$e in $a/agence/adresse
return
<result1>$b/text()</result1>
<result3>$e/text()</result3>
```

Figure 17. Generation of the subqueries associated to SemTab1.

Figure 17 shows four XQuery subqueries generated from table *SemTab1*. A subquery corresponds to one data source. It is generated by returning the values of variables $b, $d and $e asked by the user initially in his/her query. For example, the first subquery returns the names of agency in *AirFrance*. The second one returns the name of agency in FineAir and their employees. The third subquery returns the name of agency in *BritisAirway* and their employees. The last one returns the name of agency *IndiAir* and their addresses.

The following section describes an implementation of our proposed data source fusion approach.

6. MDSManager Architecture

This section describes the design of MDSManager (Multi-Data Source Manager) system developed according to our approach [28],[30]. The design of this system is given in Figure 18. MDSManager has five principal components: Wrapper, Mediator, Extractor, Petri-Nets Engine (PN-Engine) and Interfaces. The Wrapper component offers two main modules which include Data Source Server and T-Engine. The Data Source Server (DSS) manages several data sources (static or active). A DSS represents a data source for the outer world. It represents the interface of this source. There is no way to reach data sources directly in this model. All communications toward data sources have to be done through the DSS. This design provides the possibility to reach all data sources of any type and to communicate with them using the same interface. The DSS hides the implementation differences between data source types and provides a common prototype for data retrieval and query. In contrast, T-Engine provides specific classes (e.g. java classes) which describe how to communicate with data sources. For static data sources, we have developed T-Wrapper which corresponds to the most important sources of information existing over the web (e.g. SQL databases and XML documents). The role of the T-Wrapper is to extract DTDs from data sources and to register them beside the mediator. The T-Wrapper executes also the XQuery queries on the data sources and returns the results to the mediator.

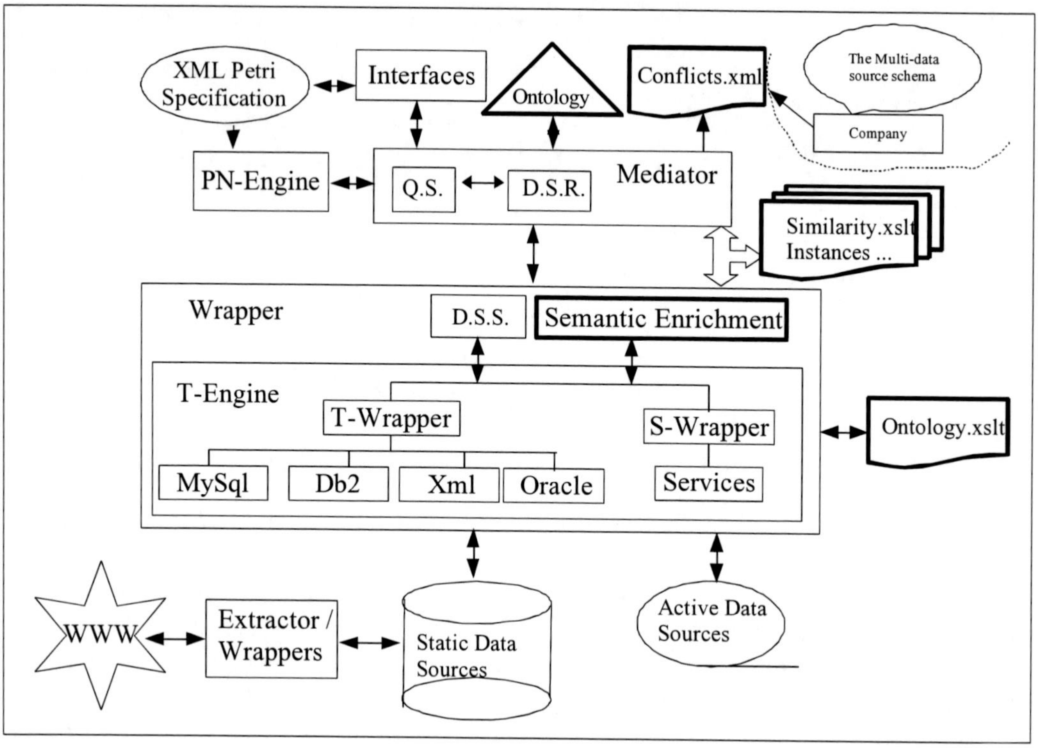

Figure 18. Design of MDSManager system.

For the active data sources, we have developed S-Wrapper with main objective to extract the DTD from a given XML document that describes an active data source. The S-Wrapper accepts EXQuery queries, which integrate the clause Service in their bodies. The S-Wrapper runs the active data source specified in Service and returns results to the mediator. The mediator component offers users' views of multi-data sources expressed with their DTDs. A mediator receives MRL or XQuery queries from user interfaces; it processes queries and returns the results to the user as XML documents. The mediator has the right information to forward a specific query to the relevant DSS server. The main two modules of this component are Data Source Repository and Query Server.

The goal of the Data Source Repository (DSR) is to collect information about data sources (references, addresses, names, descriptions and the DTD of the associated data source, which is the most important information). All the DSS have to register themselves at start-up at the central DSR, providing all the needed information about the requested data source. Therefore, a repository contains information about the connected data sources. It has the possibility also to share this information with the clients in a centralized way.

The Query Server (QS) receives MRL or XQuery queries and processes them. Processing an MRL query (or rewriting MRL queries) consists of analyzing this query, eventually substituting semantic variables and multiple identifiers with unique ones, and generating (E)XQuery pertinent subqueries. Processing an MRL query was presented in section 5. The QS communicates with both DSR and Wrapper in order to obtain more information about data sources and to execute subqueries respectively.

The Extractor module extracts information from web pages. We only require the user to give a set of example instances of the relation that he/she wants to extract. Our method generates a wrapper (a set of patterns) corresponding to a web page. This wrapper allows the user to daily update the extracted data without running the extractor module completely. A wrapper returns an XML document containing information, from web pages. More details about the extractor algorithm are given in [31]. In this paper, we do not consider how to extract efficient information from the Web. Many works have studied this problem and several solutions have been proposed. These works are described in different approaches, which are found in reference [14].

The main objective of the Petri-Nets Engine (PN-Engine) is to build a fully automated process of data extraction from the web and to query multi-data sources. To achieve this goal, there is a need to specify a set of basic operators and to coordinate these operators. For example, an extractor operator takes as input a web page and returns the list of results extracted from the page. A parsing operator takes as input an XML or HTML document, parses it and returns a DOM (Document Object Model) object. A filter operator takes as input a predicate in order to refine the results returned by a resource and so on.

In order to build automatically a complete information extraction and fusion, it is important to coordinate the basic operators. In our work the component PN-Engine supports the composition and the interpretation of scenarios (i.e. advanced operators) which are expressed with Petri-Nets model [34]. In our approach and language, these scenarios are built starting from basic operators and constructs. Constructors can be Sequence, Alternative, Iterative, Parallel etc. These constructors are given in more details in [16]. PN-Engine, takes as input a scenario which is expressed with XML, interprets it and returns the result to the user. This component communicates with the mediator in order to retrieve data from multi-data sources.

The interface modules provide an administrator interface and a user interface. The administrator interface defines mainly the structure of the future multi-data source and describes conflicts existing between them. For each data source involved in the multi-data source, T-Engine extracts and stores, using the DSR module, all information about the data source (in particular its DTD, references etc.). The administrator interface extracts data from Web pages, stores data in XML documents and generates corresponding wrappers. User interface allows expert users to submit their queries directly. In other hand, it allows users, who are not familiar with MRL or XQuery languages, to generate their queries and then to submit them to the mediator. After analysis of these queries, the Query Server (QS) module generates a set of (E)XQuery subqueries and asks each Data Source Server (DSS) responsible of a data source to execute the corresponding subquery. Each DSS, in its turn, sends the subquery to the Wrapper able to run it. The Wrapper module executes the subquery on the data source and the final result is returned to the user.

The rectangles in bold in figure 18 represent the components used in order to reconciliate semantically between data sources. This was presented in detail in section 4. Finally, the user interface allows to formulate several queries and to specify an order to execute them using the Petri-Nets specification. To interpret this specification, PN-Engine generates an XML document and uses QS module to run, for example, a sequence of queries.

7. Evaluation of RSQ Algorithm

In this section, we study the performances of RSQ algorithm. First, we focus on step 2 of the algorithm. This step deals with the generation of the query's tree (i.e. tree context). We recall that, this step substitutes each context variable (e.g. $a) in the tables given in input, by their corresponding values, and validates the correctness of their paths on the multi-data source schema. The processing of this step is compared with a baseline version that uses a Cartesian Product *(Cart. Prod.)* between the set of values taken by the semantic variables in order to find the valid paths on the multi-data source schema.

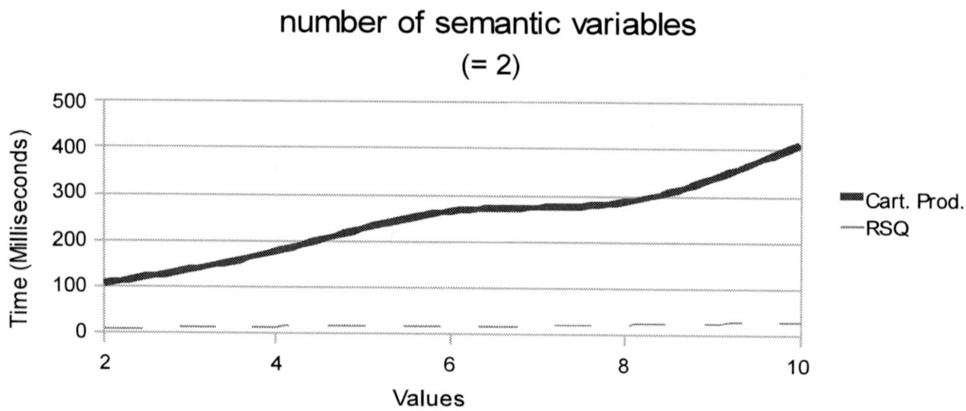

Figure 19. Two semantic variables; each variable takes values varying from 2 to 10.

The number of data sources considered in each experiment is equal to 20. In each experiment, the values taken by each semantic variable vary from 2 to 10. We observe that the response time is more sensitive to variations concerning the number of semantic variables in a query and the number of values taken by these variables. Figure 19 shows the case of a query that uses in its body two semantic variables. In this experiment, the response time increases faster in the baseline method, based on *'Cartesian Product'*, with the increase of the number of values taken by the semantic variables. Figure 20 shows the case of a query that uses in its body five semantic variables. In this experiment, the response time in the baseline method increases dramatically -compared to RSQ algorithm- with the increase of the number of values taken by the semantic variables.

Next, we compare the performance of MRL with XQuery (our baseline language). We consider a multi-data source composed of 100 data sources. Each data source is an XML document that contains at least 8 elements linked together with similar links. We consider two settings: (1) the first one is our baseline. It is used when a user chooses to formulate his/her queries manually with XQuery language. In this setting, in order to select the values of the first element, the user must formulate and submit 100 XQuery queries on the respective data sources (the user does not have any information about the conflicts given in the multi-data source). Similarly, if he/she selects the values of two elements from the multi-data source he/she must formulate 200 XQuery queries and so on until he/she selects 8 elements (800 XQuery queries).

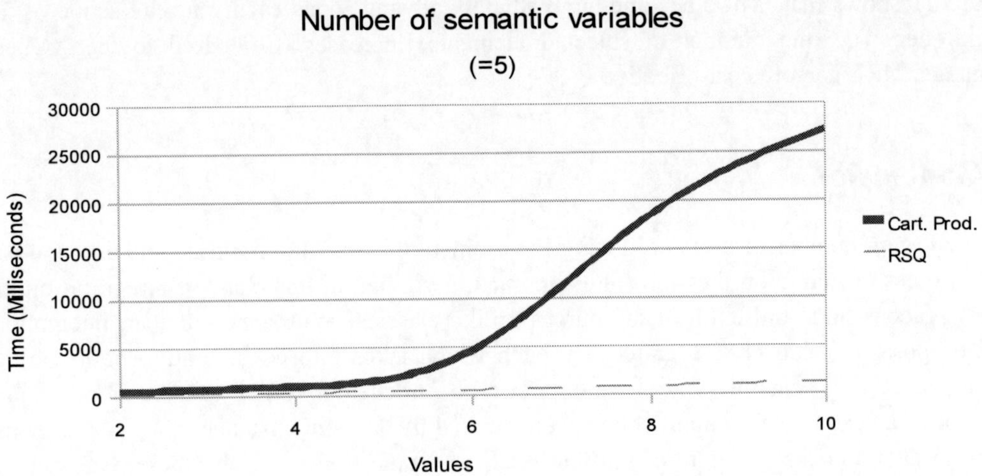

Figure 20. Five semantic variables; each variable takes values varying from 2 to 10.

In this setting, the total response time is the time to run queries in the corresponding data sources; (2) in the second setting, the user chooses to use MRL language. In this case, he/she submits only one MRL query whatever the number of elements to select. Each MRL query contains a semantic variable S. The domain of this variable varies at each time. For example, for the first query, S takes only one value and for the last query (8 queries in total) the domain of S is the set of values (8 elements). In addition, each element is a multiple identifier in the MRL query's scope. Based on conflict management and semantic rules mentioned above, the first MRL query generates only 10 pertinent XQuery queries (instead of 100 XQuery queries in setting 1), the second MRL query generates 20 XQuery queries and the last one generates 80 queries. The total response time is the sum of: (a) the time to generate pertinent XQuery queries (e.g. the research of eventual conflicts between the elements and the generation of queries) and (b) the time to run these queries in the corresponding data sources.

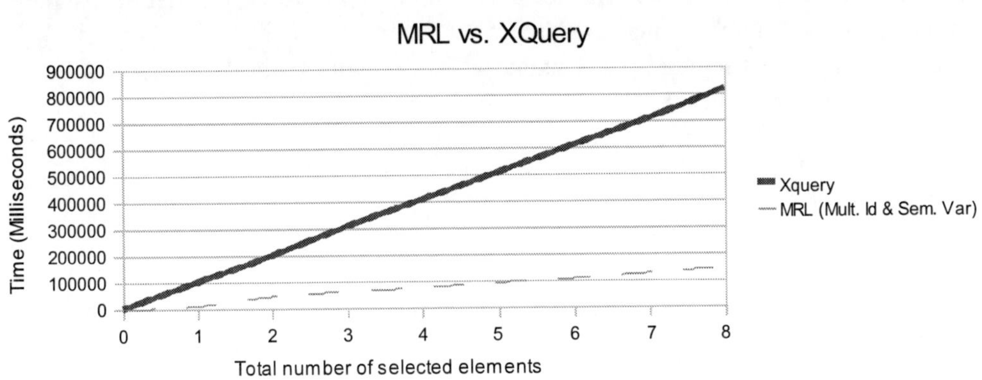

Figure 21. Data sources contains up to 100 various prices by product.

Figure 21 shows the time needed to obtain answers to queries using Xquery and MRL. The abscise represents the total number of elements to select from the multi-data source and the range represents the total response time (in Milliseconds) to return the answers to the user.

Figure 21 shows that, MRL becomes immediately advantageous each time the scope of the MRL query (i.e. the number of selected elements) increases. Compared to the XQuery language, MRL is more cost-effective.

8. Conclusion

An increasing number of users are facing the problem of accessing multiple and autonomous data sources available on the web. The approach, described in this chapter, integrates online heterogeneous and conflicting data sources unlike classical approaches of data integration. Our proposal is a loosely integrated approach which takes into consideration both conflict management and semantic rules, which must be enriched in order to take into account additional data source. Our approach is characterized by the non existence of a global schema because data sources integration is a hard task, especially on the web where data sources schema are frequently updated. In this chapter, we showed how to reconciliate between heterogeneous data sources and how to rewrite MRL semantic queries using semantics equivalences. This approach is validated by a prototype called MDSManager. Two other main approaches have been discussed in the related work section: *GaV* and *LaV*. In the *GaV* approach, the global schema is defined in terms of sources and the mapping provides direct information about which data satisfy the elements of the global schema. Consequently, the global schema needs to be rebuilt each time a source is added or deleted, but query rewriting is straightforward: a simple rule unfolding process is needed to rewrite the query in terms of the source relations. In the *LaV* approach, data sources are described in terms of the global schema. In this case, the mapping does not provide direct information about which data satisfies the global schema. Consequently, there is no need to modify the global schema when sources disappear, but it is harder to rewrite queries in terms of data sources views: the system has to control the sources interaction and their data combination in order to answer the query (the Bucket algorithm) [20]. The MRL contribution is beyond *GaV/LaV* approaches. In fact, our approach looks like P2P as we have no global schema. Our rules for conflicting management and semantic may be considered as a subset of assertions that define mapping in P2P context. In the future, we plan to study MRL queries including joined operations and algorithms in order to discover, in a dynamic way, similarities and dissimilarities between elements in the context of Peer-to-Peer [33].

References

[1] B. Amann, C. Beeri, I. Fundulaki, M. Scholl, Ontology-Based Integration of XMLWeb Resources, in: P*roceedings of the International SemanticWeb Conference (ISWC),* 2002, pp. 117-131

[2] F. Baader, D. Calvanese, D.L. McGuinness, D. Nardi, P.F. Patel-Schneider (eds.), TheDescription Logic, in(Handbook): *Theory, Implementation and Applications*. Cambridge University Press, Cambridge, 2003

[3] C. Baru, A. Gupta, B. Ludaesscher, R. Marciano, Y. Papakonstantinou, P. Velikhov, V. Chu, XML-based information mediation with MIX, in: *Proceedings of the international conference on Management of data*, 1999, pp. 597-599

[4] D. Beneventano, S. Bergamaschi, The MOMIS methodology for integrating heterogeneous data sources, in: *IFIP Congress Topical Sessions*, 2004, pp. 19-24
[5] T. Berners-Lee, J. Hendler, O. Lassila, *The Semantic Web*, in: Scientific American, 284(5), 2001, pp. 34-43
[6] O. Benjelloun, *Active XML: A Data-Centric Perspective on Web Services*, Phd Thesis of Paris XI University, Orsay, France, 2004
[7] M.J. Carey, L.M. Haas, P.M. Schwarz, M. Arya, W.F. Cody, R. Fagin, M. Flickner, A.W. Luniewski, W. Niblack, D. Petkovic, J.Thomas, J.H. Williams, E.L. Wimmers, Towards heterogeneous multimedia information systems: the Garlic approach, in: *Proceedings of the 5th International Workshop on Research Issues in Data Engineering-Distributed Object Management (RIDE-DOM'95),* 1995, pp. 161-173
[8] D.C. Faye, G. Nachouki, P. Valduriez, SenPeer : un système pair-à-pair de médiation de données, in: *Int. journal ARIMA*, Volume 4, 2006, pp. 24-48
[9] A.Y. Halvey, Z.G. Ives, P. Mork, I. Tartarinov, Piazza: Data Management Infrastructure for Semantic Web Applications, in: *Proceedings of the twelfth international conference on World Wide Web,* 2003 , pp. 556- 567
[10] S. Castano, A. Ferrara, S. Montanelli, C. Quix, H-MATCH: an Algorithm for Dynamically Matching Ontologies in Peer-based Systems, in: *Proceedings of the VLDB International Workshop on Semantic Web and Databases (SWDB),* 2003, pp. 231-250
[11] C. Delobel, C. Reynaud, M.C. Rousset, J.P. Sirot, D. Vodislav, Semantic Integration in Xyleme: a Uniform Tree-based Approach, in: *Journal of Data and Knowledge Engineering,* 44(3), 2003, pp. 267-298
[12] H. Garcia-Molina, J. Hammer, K. Ireland, Y. Papakonstantinou, J. Ullman, J. Widom, Integrating and Accessing Heterogeneous Information Sources in TSIMMIS, in: *Proceedings of the AAAI symposium on information gathering*, 1995, pp. 61-64
[13] H. Garcia-Molina, J. Hammer, K. Ireland, Y. Papakonstantinou, J. Ullman, J. Widom, Integrating and Accessing Heterogeneous Information Sources in TSIMMIS, in: *Proceedings of the AAAI symposium on information gathering*, 1995, pp. 61-64
[14] B. Habegger, M. Quafafou, Building Web Information Extraction Tasks, in: Proceedings of the *IEEE/WIC/ACM International Conference on Web Intelligence (WI),* 2004, pp. 349-355
[15] A.Y. Halevy, Answering queries using views: A survey, in: *Journal of the VLDB*, 10(4), 2001, pp. 270-294
[16] R. Hamadi, B. Benatallah, A Petri Net-based Model for Web Service Composition, in: *Proceedings of the Australasian Database Conference (ADC),* Volume 17, 2003, pp. 191-200
[17] I.F. Cruz, X. Huiyong, The Role of Ontologies in Data Integration, in: *Journal of Engineering Intelligent Systems,* Volume 13, 2005, pp. 245-252
[18] V. Kashyap, A. Sheth, Semantic and Schematic Similarities between Database objects: A Context-based Approach, in: *Journal of the VLDB,* 5(4), 1996, pp. 276-304
[19] T. Kirk, A.Y. Levy, Y. Sagiv, D. Srivastava, The Information Manifold, in: *The American Association for Artificial Intelligence (AAAI) Press*, 1995, pp. 85-
[20] A.Y. Levy, Logic-based techniques in data integration. In: Jack Minker, editor, *Logic-Based Artificial Intelligence*. Kluwer Academic Publisher, 2000, pp. 1-27
[21] M. Lenzerini, Data Integration: A Theoretical Perspective, In: *Proceedings of the ACM symposium on Principles Of Database Systems (PODS),* 2002, pp. 233-246

[22] W. Litwin, A. Abdellatif, A. Zeroual, B. Nicolas, Ph. Vigier, MSQL: a multidatabase language, in: *Journal on Information Sciences* Volume 49(1-3), 1989, pp. 59-101

[23] W. Litwin, A. Abdellatif, An overview of the multidatabase manipulation language MDSL (Invited paper), in: *Proceedings of the IEEE* 75(5), 1987, pp. 621-632

[24] P. Lyngbaek, D. McLeod, An Approach to Object Sharing in Distributed Database Systems, in: *Proceedings of the international conference on Very Large Databases (VLDB),* 1983, pp. 364-375

[25] I. Manolescu, D. Florescu, D. Kossmann, D. Olteanu, F. Xhumari, Agora: Living with XML and Relational, in: *Proceedings of the international conference on Very Large Databases (VLDB),* 2000, pp. 623-626

[26] I. Manolescu, D. Florescu, D. Kossmann, Answering XML Queries over Heterogeneous Data Sources, in: *Proceedings of the international conference on Very Large Databases (VLDB),* 2001, pp. 241-250

[27] D.L. McGuinness, F. Van Harmelen, *OWL Web Ontology Language Overview*, in: W3C Recommendation, W3C, 2004

[28] G. Nachouki, M.P. Chastang, On-Line Analysis of a Web Data Warehouse, in: *Proceedings of the International Workshop of Databases in Networked Information Systems (DNIS),* 2003, pp. 112-121

[29] G. Nachouki, Integration of Static and Active Data Sources, in: *Proceedings of the Eighteenth International Symposium on Computer and Information Sciences (ISCIS),* 2003, pp. 147-154

[30] G. Nachouki, M. Quafafou, M.P. Chastang, MDSManager: A System Based on Multidatasource Approach for Data Integration, in: 2005 IEEE / WIC /ACM International Conference on Web Intelligence (WI), *IEEE ComputerSociety*, 2005, pp. 438-441.

[31] G. Nachouki, A Method for Information Extraction from the Web, in: *Proceedings of the IEEE International Conference On Information and Communication Technologies (ICTTA*), 2006, pp. 517-521

[32] G. Nachouki, M. Quafafou, Multi-Data Source Fusion, in: *Information Fusion journal*, Special Issue on Web Information Fusion, Elsevier, V.9,N.4, 2008, pp. 523-537

[33] G. Nachouki, *Multi-Data Source Fusion in PDMS*, in: Sixth International Workshops, VLDB-DBISP2P 2008, pp. 68-80

[34] J. Peterson. *Petri Net Theory and the Modeling of systems*, Prentice Hall PTR, 1981

[35] RDF: Resource Description Framework http://www.w3.org/RDF/

[36] E. Rahm, P.A. Bernstein, A Survey of Approaches to Automatic Schema Matching, in: *Journal of the VLDB* 10(4), 2001, pp. 334-350

[37] D. Suciu, G. Vossen, Report on the International Workshop on the Web and Databases (WebDb), in: ACM SIGKDD, 2(1), 2000, pp. 80-83

[38] A.P. Sheth, J.A. Larson, Federated database systems for managing distributed, heterogeneous, and autonomous databases, in: *ACM Computing Surveys (CSUR),* 22(3),1990, pp. 183-236

[39] A. Tomasic, L. Raschid, P. Valduriez, Scaling heterogeneous databases and the design of Disco, in: *Proceedings of the Distributed Computing Systems Conference (DCSC),* 1996, pp. 449-459

[40] G. Wiederhold, Mediators in the architecture of future information systems, in: *IEEE Computer*, 25(3), 1992, pp. 38-49

[41] H. Wache, T. Vögele, U. Visser, H. Stuckenschmidt, G. Schuster, H. Neumann, and S. Hübner, Ontology-Based Integration of Information - A Survey of Existing Approaches, in: *Proceedings of the IJCAI-01 Workshop on Ontologies and Information Sharing*, 2001.
[42] xquery 1.0: An XML Query Language, http://www.w3.org/TR/xpathdatamodel
[43] XML : Extensible Markup Language, http://www.w3.org/TR/REC-xml

In: Data Management in the Semantic Web
Editor: Hal Jin, pp. 383-399

ISBN: 978-1-61122-862-5

Chapter 16

3D STAR COORDINATE-BASED VISUALIZATION OF RELATION CLUSTERS FROM OWL ONTOLOGIES

Cartik R. Kothari[1,*], Jahangheer S. Shaik[2], David J. Russomanno[3], and M. Yeasin[3]

[1]National Evolutionary Synthesis Center
Durham, NC, U. S.
[2]Department of Pathology and Immunology
School of Medicine, Washington University
St. Louis, MO, U. S.
[3]Department of Electrical and Computer Engineering
The University of Memphis
Memphis, TN, U. S.

Abstract

The recent proliferation of high-level and domain-specific ontologies has necessitated the development of prudent integration strategies. Visualization techniques are an important tool to support the data and knowledge integration initiative. This chapter reviews a methodology to visualize clusters of relations from ontologies specified using the Web Ontology Language (OWL). The relations, which in OWL are referred to as object properties, from various ontologies are organized into clusters based upon their intrinsic semantics. The intrinsic semantics of every relation from an input ontology is explicitly specified by a framework of 32 common elements; each element captures a specific aspect of the relationship between a relation's domain and range. Using this framework, each relation can be represented in a 32-dimensional "relation space." Relation clusters in 32 dimensions are projected to 3 dimensions using an automated 3-dimensional (3D) star coordinate-based visualization technique. Results from applying an algorithm to create and subsequently visualize relation clusters formed from the IEEE Suggested Upper Merged Ontology (SUMO) are presented in this chapter and discussed in the context of their potential utility for knowledge reuse and interoperability on the Semantic Web.

[*] E-mail address: cartik73@yahoo.com, Phone: +1 425 3511939

1. Introduction

Scientific research today is confronted by an unprecedented abundance of data across a variety of disciplines ranging from biology and the health sciences to astronomy [Boutell, 2008; NYT, 2008; Brunner et al., 2002; Hoelzer et al., 2006; Heus et al., 2008]. Such data is stored in a plethora of repositories, both open-access and access restricted, with widely varying architectures, logical schemas, access protocols, and user interfaces. Synergistic initiatives are necessary to harness this data, which promises to reveal the answers to some of the most pressing questions in science.

A. Ontologies and the Semantic Web

The Semantic Web initiative [Berners-Lee et al., 2001; Shadbolt et al., 2006] has been widely adopted by scientists and engineers from a wide variety of disciplines who seek the integration of distributed data for the advancement of the collective expertise in their respective domains of interest.

Semantic Web ontologies [Gruber, 1993], which can be understood as controlled vocabularies, wherein every term is defined using a rigorous logical framework, are crucial to the data integration initiative. Ontologies, such as the Unified Medical Language System (UMLS)[1], the Foundational Model of Anatomy (FMA)[2], the Geospatial Ontology[3], and the Astronomy Ontology[4] are being developed in various knowledge domains as part of the initiatives to share and integrate scientific data.

However, the creation of a universally accepted ontological representation of any knowledge domain is an impossible task given the lack of a universally applicable context within which the definitions can be framed. Furthermore, most ontologies seek to model a perfect world (canonical ontologies) and opinion is widely divided on what constitutes perfection. The idea of perfection in any knowledge domain is consistently redefined with evolving understanding of the requisite issues.

High-level ontologies, such as the Basic Formal Ontology (BFO)[5], the General Formal Ontology (GFO)[6], the Suggested Upper Merged Ontology (SUMO)[7], Cyc[8], and DOLCE[9], which contain generic concepts and relations that are pertinent to every knowledge domain are common today. In the same fashion, it is common to find more than one ontology in a specialized knowledge domain. Given this scenario, a pragmatic approach to this problem would be to contextualize ontological representations and rely on automated ontology mappings [Euzenat and Shvaiko, 2007; Kalfoglou and Schorlemmer, 2005; Maedche et al., 2002; Hasse and Motik, 2005] and visualization techniques [Katifori et al., 2007] to support re-use, integration, and interoperability of these knowledge and data repositories.

---

1 http://www.nlm.nih.gov/research/umls
2 http://sig.biostr.washington.edu/projects/fm/
3 http://www.w3.org/2005/Incubator/geo/XGR-geo-ont-20071023/
4 http://atlas.astro.umd.edu:8080/astro-onto/ontologies/astronomy.html
5 http://www.ifomis.org/bfo/
6 http://www.onto-med.de/ontologies/gfo
7 http://www.ontologyportal.org
8 http://www.cyc.com
9 http://www.loa-cnr.it/DOLCE.html

B. Relations in Semantic Web Ontologies

Ontological representations of knowledge domains contain mathematically grounded definitions of the relevant concepts and inter-concept relations. While most ontology mapping and visualization techniques focus on the integration of concepts within ontologies, the semantics concerning relations within the ontology are mostly ignored. Relations in ontologies are effectively second class entities, lacking explicit definitions of their intrinsic semantics. Relation semantics in ontologies, including those ontologies captured using OWL in which relations are expressed via object properties, are confined to narrow mathematical constructs for expressing the semantics of the relation, such as transitivity, symmetry, inversion, and relation hierarchies.

To capture the intrinsic semantics of every relation from an input ontology requires an enhanced ontology that leads to a high-dimensional relation space. The visualization of semantically rich relations may lead to a better understanding, re-use, and interoperability of ontologies in the context of the Semantic Web.

C. Visualizations of Relations

A simple idea is to use the expressive power of a 3D representation to provide visualization of relations for a knowledge engineer. Effective visualization techniques enable the user to observe and detect the underlying relation distributions, patterns, and similarities. One of the popular approaches to the visualization of complex, high-dimensional data is the use of a data projection method. The projected data, while providing enhanced understanding, should also preserve the local and global attributes of the data. To be pragmatic, projection techniques must be scalable, computationally efficient, and free of human intervention. This chapter reviews a novel, automated, 3D visualization algorithm to visualize relations that have been described with 32 elements to capture meta-knowledge about a set of relations from input OWL ontologies.

Projection methods attempt to take data from a high-dimensional space and map it onto a low-dimensional space with minimum error [Asimov, 1985; Bertin, 1981; Guyon, 2003; Inselberg, 1981]. A great deal of research is devoted to this subject and a number of useful methods have been reported in the literature with varying degrees of success [Asimov, 1985; Bertin, 1981; Inselberg, 1981; Ridder et al., 2003; Unsalan and Ercil, 2000; Wall et al., 2003; Kandogan, 2000; Kouropteva et al., 2003; Loftus, 1993; Beddow, 1990]. One of the popular methods in data projection and visualization is the star coordinate system [Kandogan, 2000] designed to project the high-dimensional data onto a 2D space. This chapter reviews an extension of the concept known as 3D star coordinate system [Shaik and Yeasin, 2006]. An initial application of 3D star coordinate system applied to the visualization of relation semantics was previously described by Shaik et al., 2006, and we summarize that technique and provide further context and elaboration in this chapter.

When using 3D star coordinates, each dimension is represented as a vector radiating from the center of the sphere to the circumference of the sphere. All the dimensions are normalized between [0 1]. Each data point (relation) has its dimensions (32 elements describing meta knowledge about the relation) lying along these vector axes radiating into 3D space. Objects lying on these axes are resolved into components along the *x, y,* and *z* coordinate axes, respectively. Individual contributions of objects pertaining to a data point along these axes are summed to obtain the points along these axes. Hence, a multi-dimensional data point is now represented in 3D. Initially, all the vectors are placed on a 3D sphere with equal weights given to all vectors. If no proper pattern emerges, the choices of the angles, as well as the lengths of the vectors are chosen randomly. In this iterative process, the vectors are rearranged in the 3D space at random angles and lengths. For each combination of angles and lengths, data is projected differently in 3D space. One or more of these combinations may produce a meaningful pattern. If a pattern emerges, depending on the orientation of the vectors and their length, one can infer the relationships between the dimensions and also their relative importance.

The remainder of this chapter is organized as follows: in Section II relation elements and their utility in representing the intrinsic nature of relations are discussed. Section III discusses the use of a framework of relation elements to cluster relations on the basis of their intrinsic semantics. The utility of these relation clusters to ontology reuse and interoperability are also presented in this section. Section IV reviews the 3D visualization technique used to reduce the multidimensional relational space into a human comprehensible format. Section V presents an analysis of the results. Comparison with related work is presented in Section VI. Conclusions and potential future areas of work are outlined in Section VII.

2. Elements and the Intrinsic Nature of Relations

Elements, or similar modeling constructs, have been defined and used by other researchers to explicitly describe the intrinsic nature of relations [Chaffin and Herman, 1987; Huhns and Stephens, 1989; Storey, 1993; DiMarco, 1994; Stephens and Chen, 1996]. For example, consider the relation instance *made-of* (*bicycle-tire*, *rubber*). Elements can be used to explicitly describe several aspects of the relationship between the domain and the range in a given relation. The *rubber* entity cannot be separated from the *bicycle-tire* entity in the *made-of* instance. In general, this aspect of the relationship between the domain and range of the relation *made-of* can be described by the *separable* element, which in this example is assigned a value *no* to denote "no, the entities in *made-of* cannot be separated from one another." Similarly, the fact that *rubber* is a component of the *bicycle-tire* can be specified by another element *meronymic*, which is assigned a value *yes* to describe this relation. The fact there is no temporal or time-based aspect to the relationship between the domain and range entities in the *made-of* relation, its semantics is further refined by a third element *temporal*, which is assigned *N/A*, or not applicable.

In this manner, different aspects of the relationship between the domain and range entities in a relation can be explicitly represented using elements, which take appropriate values from the value set {*yes*, *no*, *N/A*} to describe the intrinsic nature of relations. Elements provide a framework for better understanding of the intrinsic nature of relations, which can be utilized by knowledge modelers for fine-grained semantics specification in ontology development.

Influenced by prior work in specifying semantics of relations, Kothari and Russomanno [Kothari and Russomanno, 2005a] synthesized a two–tier taxonomy of elements that can be used to explicitly specify the intrinsic nature of relations in ontologies. Comprising 32 elements in all, this element taxonomy is shown in Figure 1. The relation element definitions are listed in Table I.

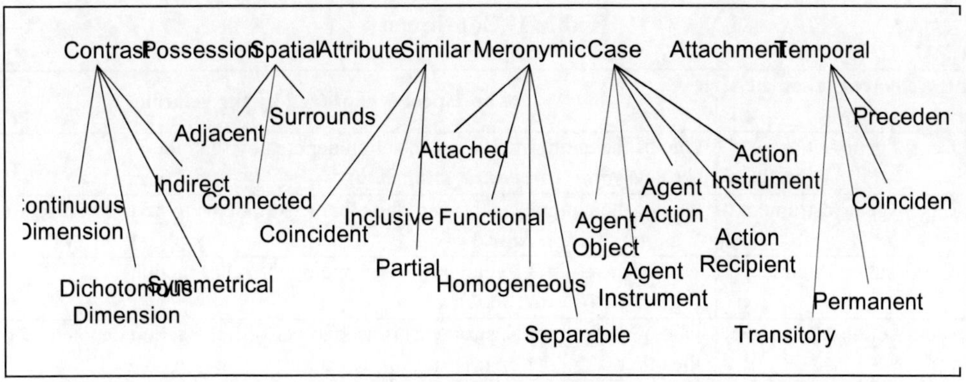

Figure 1. Two–tier taxonomy of elements to define relation semantics (RSEP elements).

Table 1. Definition of elements from the RSEP set (* from [Chaffin, 1987], † from [Storey, 1993])

If the element takes the value *yes*	The aspect is captured by the relation
1. Temporal	A temporal aspect of the relationship between the domain and range instances. E.g., *precedes* (*keynote-address*, *conference-session*)
1a. Temporal-Coincident	The domain and the range instances do not precede one another. They are temporally coincident. E.g., *co-occur* (*conference*, *workshop*)
1b. Temporal-Precedent	The domain and the range instances do not coincide temporally in terms of occurrence. E.g., *precedes* (*keynote-address*, *conference-session*)
1c. Temporal-Permanent	The relationship between the domain and range instances persists over time. E.g., *planet-of* (*earth*, *sun*)
1d. Temporal-Transitory	The relationship between the domain and range instances is transitory, does not persist over time. E.g., *associated-with* (*project*, *supplier*)
2. Spatial	A spatial aspect of the relationship between the domain and range instances. E.g., *located* (*lake*, *park*)
2a. Spatial-Surrounds	One of the instances spatially surrounds the other. E.g., *encloses* (*moat*, *fort*)
2b. Spatial-Adjacent	The instances are spatially adjacent to one another. E.g., *abuts* (*kitchen*, *pantry*)
2c. Spatial-Connected	The instances are both spatial and are connected to one another. E.g., *branch-of* (*river*, *tributary*)
3. Attribute	One of the instances is a descriptive attribute of the other. E.g., *color-of* (*sky*, *blue*)
4. Similar *	The two instances have some aspect of their intrinsic nature in common. This likeness can be of different extents. E.g., *like* (*rose*, *daisy*)
4a. Similar-Coincident	The intrinsic nature of the two instances coincide. E.g., *synonymous* (*car*, *automobile*)
4b. Similar-Inclusive	The intrinsic nature of one of the instances is included by the other (generalization relation). E.g., *kind-of* (*mammal*, *vertebrate*)
4c. Similar-Partial	The intrinsic nature of the two instances partially overlap. E.g., *like* (*movie*, *painting*)
5. Case * †	The two entities are related to one another through some action. E.g., *diagnoses* (*physician*, *disease*)
5a. Case-Agent Object	One of the entities (agent) performs an action that affects the other (object). E.g., *excises* (*surgeon*, *tumor*)

Table 1. Continued

If the element takes the value *yes*	The aspect is captured by the relation
5b. Case-Agent Action	One of the entities performs an action denoted by the other. E.g., *performs* (*orchestra, symphony*)
5c. Case-Agent Instrument	One of the entities (agent) uses the other (instrument) to perform an action. E.g., *uses* (*artist, canvas*)
5d. Case-Action Recipient	One of the entities (recipient) is affected by the other (action). E.g., *critic* (*review, book*)
5e. Case-Action Instrument	One of the entities (instrument) is used to perform the action denoted by the other. E.g., *action* (*incisor, bite*)
6. Contrast*	The two entities contrast or contradict one another on a common dimension. E.g., *opposites* (*chalk, cheese*)
6a. Contrast-Continuous Dimension	The common dimension is continuous. E.g., *not* (*hot, cool*)
6b. Contrast-Continuous Dimension Symmetrical	The intrinsic nature of the two entities is symmetrically placed on opposite ends of the continuous dimension. E.g., *antonym* (*hot, cold*)
6c.Contrast-Dichotomous Dimension	The common dimension is dichotomous. E.g., *opposite* (*dead, alive*)
6d. Contrast-Indirect	The connotation (indirect) of one of the entities contrasts the other. E.g., *unlike* (*extroverted, shy*)
7. Meronymic * †	One of the entities is a component (part) of the other (component-assembly or aggregation relation). E.g., *part-of* (*engine, car*)
7a. Meronymic-Attached	One of the entities (component) is attached to the other (assembly). E.g., *part-of* (*handle, kettle*)
7b. Meronymic-Separable	The component can be separated from the assembly without fundamentally altering the nature of the assembly. E.g., *part-of* (*slice, pie*)
7c. Meronymic-Functional	The position of the component is critical to the functioning of the assembly. E.g., *part-of* (*wheels, car*)
7d. Meronymic-Homogeneous	The component and the assembly are indistinguishable from one another. E.g., *part-of* (*pizza-slice, pizza*)
8. Attachment †	One of the entities is attached or connected to the other. E.g., *connected* (*subwoofer, audio-receiver*)
9. Possession †	One of the entities owns or possesses the other. E.g., *has* (*bird, wings*)

These elements are used by a knowledge elicitation system called the Relation Semantics Elicitation Prototype (RSEP) [Kothari et al., 2005] to elicit appropriate values from knowledge providers to describe relations extracted from input ontologies. The assignment of the element values is subjective in that the values are specified by the knowledge provider. Subsequently, these elicited values are appended to the input ontologies, where the intrinsic semantics of relations have not been previously specified. Because of their association with RSEP, these elements are called RSEP elements.

Figure 2 shows an example of the explicit specification of the intrinsic nature of a relation *ancestor* (*Organism, Organism*) from the IEEE Suggested Upper Merged Ontology (SUMO) [Niles and Pease, 2001] using RSEP elements.

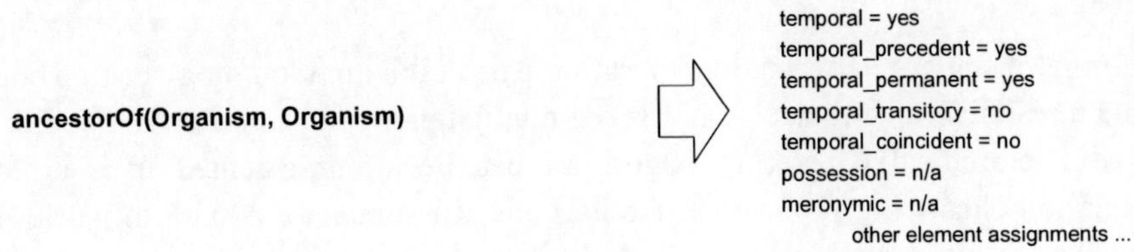

Figure 2. Example Element Specification.

3. Relational Clusters

Elements provide an organizational framework to capture additional semantics of relations, which can be used to quantify similarities and differences among relations. The organizational framework is illustrated by the development of relation clusters, which partition the "relation space" in an input ontology.

Given value assignments for the 32 RSEP elements for relations in an input ontology, each relation can be visualized as a point in a 32 dimensional "relation space." Differences in the intrinsic semantics of these relations can be quantified in the form of Hamming distances between them. Algorithm 1 [Kothari and Russomanno, 2005b] specifies how the relations in an input ontology can be clustered using Hamming distances.

Algorithm 1: Cluster Ontology Relations.

Input	A set of relations with element value assertions to describe each relation and a threshold value *T*
Step 1	For any given pair of relations, compare corresponding element values assigning a score of 0 if they are identical, +1 if both of them are either *yes* or *no* but not identical or +2 if they are not identical and one of them is *N/A*
Step 2	Sum up these scores to compute discrimination coefficient for the given pair of relations
Step 3	Perform Steps 1 and 2 for all pairs of relations in the input set and obtain discrimination coefficients for each pair
Step 4	Place every relation in the input set in its own cluster
Step 5	Given the set of discrimination coefficients, sort this list in ascending order keeping track of the relation pairs they correspond to
Step 6	For a given discrimination coefficient *D*, cluster two clusters together if $D \leq T$ and connect this new cluster to its children
Step 7	Repeat Step 6 until all the discrimination coefficients have been exhausted
Step 8	Repeat Steps 5 through 7 for increasing values of *T* until all the relations are in one cluster
Output	A tree of clusters

The Hamming distances between every relation pair in the input ontology can be coupled with a suitable threshold value to decide if a given relation pair can be clustered together. The Agglomerative Hierarchical Clustering Algorithm has been implemented in a prototype (called the Relation Clustering Prototype) [Kothari and Russomanno, 2005b] to partition the "relation space" of an input ontology into relation clusters.

The Relation Clustering Prototype outputs clusters of relations from an input OWL ontology in which the intrinsic semantics of relations have been explicitly specified by RSEP elements. Figure 3 displays a sample output from testing the Relation Clustering Module on the IEEE SUMO. The relations in each cluster share some common semantics. For example, in cluster one, the relations wife, spouse, husband, and holdsDuring from IEEE SUMO were clustered together. Note that the Relation Clustering Module outputs its results in textual format, detailing the clusters, the inter-cluster Hamming distances, and the relations in each cluster. A textual format was used because these clusters (and the relations in them) were expressed using 32 dimensions and cannot be easily rendered into a graphical display format.

```
Cluster 1:
1 wife
14 spouse
48 husband
51 holdsDuring
-------------

Cluster 3:
16 sister
18 sibling

Cluster 1 → Cluster 3 = 2
```

Figure 3. Example Element Specification.

4. 3D Star Coordinate Visualization Method

The 3D star coordinate visualization method has three major components. For the sake of clarity, the mathematical formulation of the method is presented first. Following this introduction, the 32-dimensional element representations of the relations from IEEE SUMO are projected onto a 3D format using the 3D star coordinate method. To obtain the relation clusters, the self-organizing map (SOM) algorithm is applied in the projected space. Finally, the quality of the clusters is obtained using the Dunn and Davies-Bouldin index [Davies and Bouldin, 1979] and is used as a measure to choose the optimum number of clusters. The subsequent subsections describe the development and formulation of the algorithm in detail.

A. 3D Star Coordinate Projection

The 3D star coordinate projection technique was presented in [Shaik and Yeasin, 2006]. It is summarized again here for completeness. The schematic diagram of the proposed 3D star coordinate based projection is shown in Figure 4. It is assumed that all the dimensions are radiating from the center of a hypothetical sphere at random angles in 3D space and are of random length. The attributes of individual data points are scaled and rotated.

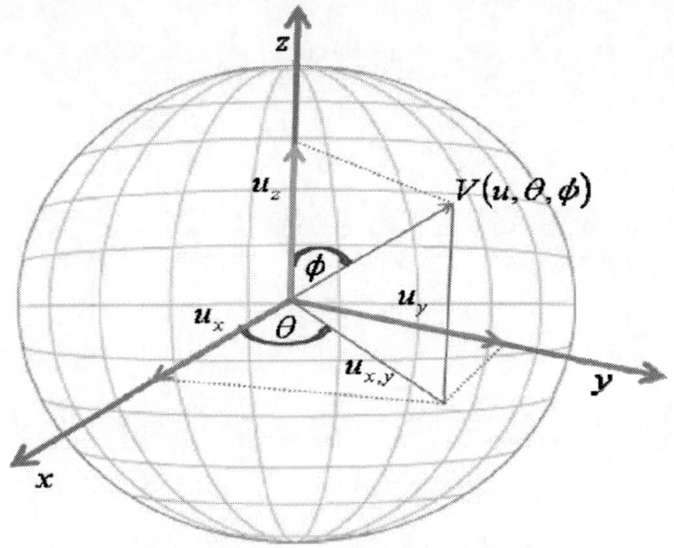

Figure 4. 3D Star Coordinate Projection.

For a given data point, each of its attributes (points along all dimensions of that data point) are multiplied with the component along a particular direction. Individual contributions are integrated along the direction to form a point projected in 3D space as shown in equation 6. Various stages and steps involved in the formation of 3D star coordinate system are summarized as follows:

Step I: Initialization:

1. Arrange the dimensional vectors on the sphere radiating into the 3D space.
2. Generate randomly the azimuthal and elevational angles among the vectors.
3. Map the star coordinate system to the Cartesian coordinate system by defining a point in the 3D space representing the origin and *n* 3-dimensional vectors representing the axes.
4. Generate randomly the lengths of the vectors. The lengths may vary between one unit vector and 5 times a unit vector.

Step II: Computation of Projection

The projection of the data point from n-dimensions to 3 dimensions is obtained by summing the unit vectors on each coordinate weighted by their respective attribute value. Let 'N' be the number of data points and 'n' be the number of attributes of each feature that needs to be visualized. The data matrix 'D' is of dimension N x n and its elements d_{ij} represent the components of 'n' dimensional data points. The components (u_x, u_y, u_z) and $\|u\|$ are given by Equations (1-4).

□

□

$$u_x = u\sin\phi\cos\theta \tag{1}$$

$$u_y = u\sin\phi\sin\theta \tag{2}$$

$$u_z = u\cos\phi \tag{3}$$

$$\|u\| = \sqrt{u_x^2 + u_y^2 + u_z^2} \tag{4}$$

The projection of each 'n' dimensional data point 'D_i' is given by $P_j(X,Y,Z) = (X_P, Y_P, Z_P)$ where,

$$\begin{bmatrix} X_p = O_x + \sum_{i=1}^{n} u_{xi}(d_{j,i} - \min(d_{i,.})), \\ Y_p = O_y + \sum_{i=1}^{n} u_{yi}(d_{j,i} - \min(d_{i,.})), \\ Z_p = O_z + \sum_{i=1}^{n} u_{zi}(d_{j,i} - \min(d_{i,.})). \end{bmatrix}. \tag{5}$$

Here, O_x, O_y and O_z are the coordinates defining the present origin of the system. The vectors in 'n' dimensional space are therefore projected into 3-D space given by $P(X,Y,Z)$. It is now easy to visualize various dimensions radiating at random angles in a pseudo sphere; more than one such combination provides insight into the underlying distribution.

Step III: Find the Best Projection Configuration

The current approaches reported in [Bertin, 1981; Kandogan, 2000] require human intervention to decide the best configuration of the projection from the high-dimensional space to the low-dimensional space. To alleviate this problem, an automated algorithm is developed to find the best projection for visualization of relation clusters. The IEEE SUMO is used later in the chapter as one test case to show the utility of the technique. The algorithm for choosing the best projection is summarized as follows:

Step1:

The values in data matrix 'D' are normalized by the largest value in the matrix. The length of the dimensional vectors is determined by the largest value in a particular dimension.

Step2:

Let 'δ_{NxN}' represent the inter-distances (pair-wise distances) between the data points in the high-dimensional space. Let '$d_{\max}$' be the maximum value and '$d_{\min}$' be the minimum value of matrix 'δ_{NxN}' respectively. The matrix 'δ_{NxN}' is transformed into 'δ_{theta}' as shown in (6):

$$\delta_{theta} = \frac{\delta_{NxN} - d_{\min}}{d_{\max} - d_{\min}} * 360 \tag{6}$$

The upper triangular matrix in 'δ_{theta}' are the Azimuthal angles at which the dimensional vectors are placed.

Step3:

Let 'ζ_{NxN}' represent the inter-distances between the data points in projected space, then, the measure of inter distance preservation is given as follows:

$$S = \left(\sum_{i,j=1}^{N} \left(\zeta_{ij} - (\delta_{ij})\right)^2 / \sum_{i,j=1}^{N} \delta_{ij}^{\;2} \right)^{0.5} . \tag{7}$$

Here, $S = 0$ represents a perfect fit. The Elevational angles are incremented randomly between -5 to 5 degrees for each iteration and 'ζ_{NxN}' are calculated.

Let S_1 be the value factor calculated for the first projection using Equation 7 and ξ be the value factor corresponding to the optimum projection, then, the algorithm to find the best projection is given as follows:

Begin Optimization
Begin Initialization
Randomize elevational angles
Calculate $S = S_1$
$\xi = S_1$
end Initialization
Begin Loop// Optimizes over all possible orientations of dimensional vectors
for p = 2 : k,
Step1: Randomize elevational angles
Calculate $S_p = S$ *using Equation 7;*
Step2: if $S_p < \xi$ then $\xi = S_p$;
If(ξ is negligible)
Exit loop
End if
end loop
end Optimization

5. Empirical Analysis

The objectives of the empirical analysis are as follows:

i) To reduce the dimensionality of 32 dimensional relational space into 3 dimensions ensuring the best projection without human intervention.
ii) To find the similarity among relations in the reduced dimensional space.

Since the length of the vectors and the azimuthal angles are selected based on the structure of the data, the automation algorithm takes a relatively smaller number of iterations to find the best configuration for projection. The number of iterations was set to 100 and the projection configuration corresponding to maximum inter-distance preservation is considered as the best projection. Figure 5 (a) and (b) show the intermediate results with some emergence of a pattern. While the results from Figures 5 (a) and (b) show some pattern, they fail to provide crisp boundaries between relation clusters. Nevertheless, this shows the evolution of the formation of relation clusters in this iterative process. The result in Figure 6 shows the best projection obtained using the proposed automated algorithm. A visual analysis of Figure 6 indicates the formation of crisper relation clusters.

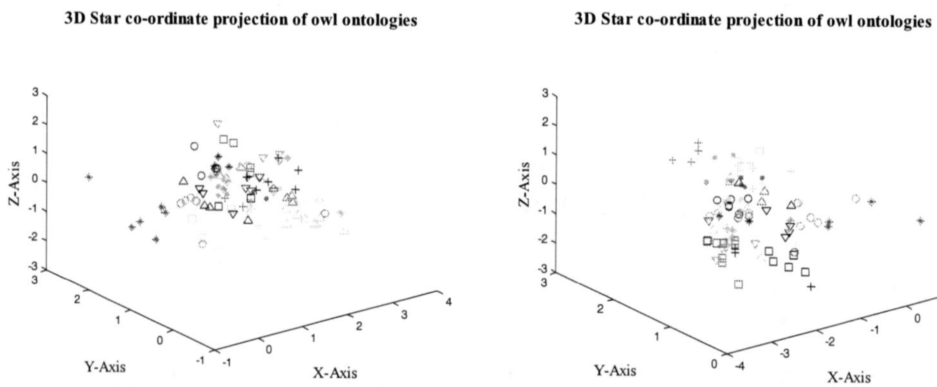

Figure 5. Evolution of relation clusters in 3D space showing intermediate results.

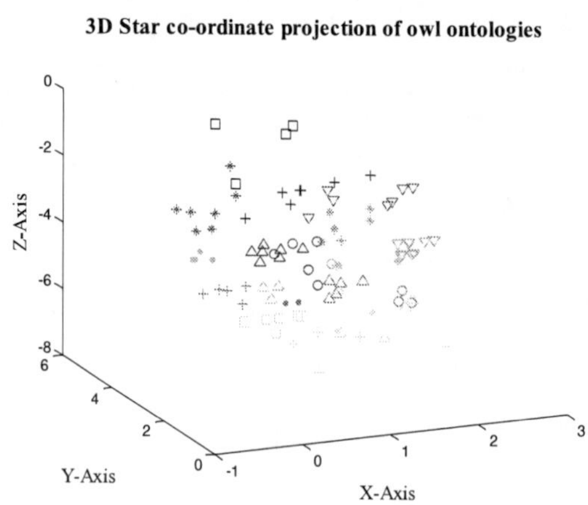

Figure 6. Best projection of relation clusters using the 3D visualization algorithm.

Table 2 shows the clustering of IEEE SUMO relations as obtained by SOM applied on top of the proposed 3D star coordinate projection algorithm. Improved quality clusters are obtained when the number of clusters is chosen to be 24 as specified by the Dunn index and Davies-Bouldin index, respectively [Davies and Bouldin, 1979]. Most of the relation objects that fell into a cluster have some similarity among them as shown in Table 2. For example, cluster 1 includes the IEEE SUMO relations wife, spouse, and husband while cluster 23 includes overlapsTemporally and beforeOrEqual.

Table 2. IEEE SUMO Relation Clusters Generated by the Proposed 3D Visualization Algorithm.

Cluster Number	Relations
1	wife, spouse, husband
2	wants, needs, holds during
3	property, measure, lineMeasure
4	height, expressedInLanguage
5	result, agent, frequency, causes
6	earlier, during, before, finishes
7	meetsTemporally, ancestor, developmentalForm, relatedInternalConcept
8	parallel, larger, identicalListItems, equivalentContentinstance, equivalentContentClass, equal
9	monetaryValue, hasPurpose, date
10	sister, sibling
11	desires, daughter, brother, parent
12	believes, considers attends
13	knows, instance, inScopeOfInterest, hasSkill, disjoint
14	properlyFills, fills
15	mother, father
16	faces, connected, angleOfFigure
17	inhabits, exploits, employs
18	uses, copy, coOccur
19	top, surface, side
20	wears, time, resource, leader, instrument, home
21	traverses, publishes, inhibits, grasps, experiencer, editor, authors
22	transactionAmount, successorAttribute, member, material, inList, hole, geometricPart, engineeringSubcomponent, element
23	overlapsTemporally, beforeOrEqual
24	temporalPart, stays, starts, refers, part

Information conveyed via visualization may be of utility to a knowledge engineer when performing the following tasks: i) assessing the semantics of a set of relations available in a given ontology; ii) determining whether the definition of a new relation as an extension of a given ontology is warranted based upon its similarity to already defined relations; iii) ontology integration in which similarities and differences of concepts and relations defined in two ontologies are compared for possible integration into a single, unified ontology; and iv) interoperability of agents using knowledge repositories that have committed to different ontologies.

6. Related Work

The RSEP elements discussed in this chapter are intended to capture the intrinsic semantics of binary relations. In a similar way, basic relations such as part-of and dependence proposed as part of the Descriptive Ontology for Linguistic and Cognitive Engineering (DOLCE) [Gangemi et al., 2002] may be used to describe the semantics of other relations in the same manner as RSEP elements. Comparing the capabilities of DOLCE with OWL Enhance, RSEP elements are broader in scope than DOLCE with respect to specifying relation semantics. There are no equivalents of the RSEP elements in DOLCE that can describe "similar," "contrast," "attachment" or "possession" relations. The strongest emphasis of DOLCE relations is in their ability to distinguish between short-term and long-term relations, i.e., relationships that hold over long periods of time and those that do not. For example, DOLCE relations can be used to distinguish between short-term and long-term meronymic relations. However, this capability can be emulated by combining the *temporal* and *meronymic* root elements from the RSEP set and appropriate combinations of the child elements of *temporal* viz. *temporal-permanent* and *temporal-transitory*.

The RSEP set of elements are also analogous to the properties of concept attributes proposed in the OntoClean methodology [Guarino and Welty, 2004]. The OntoClean methodology proposed properties such as "essence," "rigid," "identity" and "unity" that could be used to describe concept attributes and subsequently validate subsumptions between concepts in a concept hierarchy. RSEP elements promote deeper understanding of the semantics of relations in the same way that the OntoClean methodology enables a better understanding of concept attributes and concept subsumptions. However, RSEP elements promote a deeper understanding of all relations, not just subsumptions.

7. Conclusion

This chapter presented a validated and enhanced 3D visualization algorithm to uncover the intrinsic semantic relations in an ontology. An algorithm to choose the best configuration of the 3D projection was developed by using a number of cluster validation indices. In particular, the Dunn index and the Davies-Bouldin index are combined in a weighted fusion scheme to yield a unified score to assess the cluster quality. The utility of the proposed 3D algorithm was demonstrated by visualizing the relations clustered from the IEEE SUMO ontology. The relations, that is, OWL object properties, from any input OWL ontology could be used for clustering and visualization provided that the relations have values asserted for the 32 relation elements. The Relation Semantics Elicitation Prototype (RSEP), which was briefly described in this chapter, provides software for the knowledge engineer to enhance OWL ontologies with more precise semantics via the 32 relation elements. Empirical analysis indicated that the automated 3D visualization algorithm revealed the implicit semantic similarities among the relations within an ontology and enabled enhanced visualization of the relation definitions within an ontology.

Acknowledgments

The authors are grateful to the Herff College of Engineering Fellowship program and the National Science Foundation (Grant No. NSF-IIS 0746790) for partially funding the research described in this chapter. Any opinions, findings, and conclusions or recommendations expressed in this chapter are those of the authors and do not necessarily reflect the views of the National Science Foundation.

References

[Asimov, 1985] Asimov, D., "The grand tour: a tool for viewing multidimensional data," *SIAM Journal on Scientific and Statistical Computing*, Vol. 6, pp. 128–143, 1985.

[Beddow, 1990] Beddow, J., "Shape coding of multidimensional data on microcomputer display," In *Proceedings of 1st International Conference on Visualization*, San Francisco, CA, 1990.

[Berners-Lee et al., 2001] Berners-Lee, T., Hendler, J., and Lassila, O., “The Semantic Web,” *Scientific American*, 284(5), 34–43, 2001.

[Bertin, 1981] Bertin, J., *Graphics and Graphic Information Processing*: Walter de Gruyer & Co, Berlin, 1981.

[Boutell, 2008] Boutell, T., “WWW FAQ: How many Websites are there?” Available at: http://www.boutell.com/newfaq/sizeofweb.html, 2008 (accessed in March 2009).

[Brunner, 2002] Brunner, R, Djorgovski, S., Prince, T., and Szalay, S., “The National Virtual Observatory,” *Astronomical Society of the Pacific Conference Proceedings (ASP 2002)*, pp. 383 – 387, 2002.

[Chaffin and Hermann, 1987] R. Chaffin and D. Hermann, “Relation Element Theory: A New Account of the Representation and Process of Semantic Relations,” In D. Gorfein and R. Hoffman (Eds.), *Memory and Learning: The Ebbinghaus Centennial Conference*, Lawrence Erlbaum, Hillsdale, NJ, pp. 221–245, 1987.

[Davies and Bouldin, 1979] Davies, D.L. and Bouldin, D.W., "A cluster separation measure," *IEEE Transactions on Pattern Analysis and Machine Intelligence*, **1**(2), 224–227, 1979.

[DiMarco, 1994] iMarco, C., “The Nature of Near-Synonymic Relations,” In *Proceedings of the 15th International Conference on Computational Linguistics (COLING 1994)*, Kyoto, Japan, pp. 691–695, 1994.

[Euzenat and Shvaiko, 2007] Euzenat, J. and Shvaiko, P., *Ontology Matching*, Springer Verlag, 2007.

[Gangemi et al., 2002] Gangemi, A. et al., “Sweetening Ontologies with DOLCE,” In *Proceedings of the 13th International Conference on Knowledge Engineering and Knowledge Management (EKAW 2002),* Siguenza, Spain, pp. 166–181, 2002.

[Gruber, 1993] Gruber, T., “A Translational Approach to Portable Ontology Specifications,” *Knowledge Acquisition*, **5**(2), 199–220, 1993.

[Guarino and Welty, 2004] Guarino, N. and Welty, C., "An Overview of OntoClean," In Staab, S. and Studer, R. (Eds.), *Handbook on Ontologies,* Springer Verlag, Germany, pp. 151–159, 2004.

[Guyon, 2003] Guyon, I., "An Introduction of Variable and Feature Selection," *Journal of Machine Learning Research*, **3**(Mar), pp. 1157–1182, 2003.

[Haase and Motik, 2005] Haase, P. and Motik, B., "A Mapping System for the Integration of OWL-DL Ontologies," In *Proceedings of the ACM Workshop: Interoperability of Heterogeneous Information Systems (IHIS05)*, Bremen, Germany, pp. 9–16, 2005.

[Heus et al., 2008] Heus, H. et al., "A Semantic Web Management Model for Integrative Biomedical Informatics," *PLoS One*, **3**(8): e2946, 2008.

[Hoelzer et al., 2006] Hoelzer, S., Schweiger, R,K,, Rieger J., and Meyer M., "Dealing with Information Overload of Health Science Data: Structured Utilization of Libraries, Distributed Knowledge in Databases, and Web Content," *Studies in Health Technology and Informatics*, Volume 124, pp. 549–554, 2006.

[Huhns and Stephens, 1989] Huhns, M. and Stephens, L., "Plausible Inference using Extended Composition," In *Proceedings of the 11th International Joint Conference on Artificial Intelligence (IJCAI 1989)*, Detroit, MI, pp. 1420–1425, 1989.

[Inselberg, 1981] Inselberg, A., "N-dimensional graphics, part I-lines and hyperplanes," IBM Scientific Center, Los Angeles, CA, 1981.

[Kalfoglou and Schorlemmer, 2005] Kalfoglou, Y. and Schorlemmer, M., "Ontology Mapping: The State of the Art," In Kalfoglou, Y et al. (Eds.), *Semantic Interoperability and Integration*, IBFI, Germany, 2005.

[Kandogan, 2000] Kandogan, E., "Star Coordinates: A Multi-Dimensional Visualization Technique with Uniform Treatment of Dimensions," In *Proceedings of the IEEE Information Visualization Symposium*, 2000.

[Katifori et al., 2007] Katifori, A., Halatsis, C., Lepouras, G., Vassilakis, C., and Giannopoulou, E., "Ontology Visualization Methods: A Survey," *ACM Computing Surveys (CSUR)*, **39**(4), Article 10, 2007.

[Kothari and Russomanno, 2005a] Kothari, C. and Russomanno, D., "A Relation Semantics Elicitation Prototype for the Semantic Web," In *Proceedings of the 2005 International Conference on Artificial Intelligence (ICAI 2005)*, Las Vegas, NV, pp. 682–688, 2005.

[Kothari and Russomanno, 2005b] Kothari, C. and Russomanno, D., "Clustering Relations within OWL Ontologies," In *Proceedings of the 9th IASTED International Conf. on Software Engineering and Applications (SEA 2005)*, Phoenix, AZ, pp. 36–41, 2005.

[Kothari et al., 2005] Kothari, C., Russomanno, D., and Tran, P., "Interactive Elicitation of Relation Semantics for the Semantic Web," In *Proceedings of the International Conference on Systems, Computing Sciences and Software Engineering,* Bridgeport, CT, 2005.

[Kouropteva et al., 2003] Kouropteva, O., Okun, O., and Pietikainen, M., "Supervised locally linear embedding algorithm and support vector machine," In *ESANN'2003 Proceedings-European Symposium on Artificial Neural Networks*, pp. 229–234, 2003.

[Loftus, 1993] Loftus, G., "A picture is worth a thousand p values: On the irrelevance of hypothesis testing in the micro computer age, "*Behavior Research Methods, Instruments, and Computers*, **25**(2), pp. 250–256, 1993.

[Maedche et al., 2002] Maedche, A., Motik, B., Silva, N., and Volz, R., "MAFRA–A MApping FRAmework for Distributed Ontologies," In *Proceedings of the 13th*

International Conference on Knowledge Engineering and Knowledge Management (EKAW 2002), Siguenza, Spain, pp. 235–250, 2002.

[NYT, 2008] New York Times, "Is Information Overload a $650 Billion Drag on the Economy?" March 28, 2008.

[Niles and Pease, 2001]Niles, I. and Pease, A., "Towards a Standard Upper Ontology," In *Proceedings of the 2nd International Conference on Formal Ontology in Inference Systems (FOIS 2001)*, pp. 2–9, 2001.

[Ridder et al., 2003] Ridder, D., Kouropteva, O., Okun, O., Pietikainen, M., and Duin, R. P. W., "Supervised Locally Linear embedding," *ICANN*, pp. 333–341, 2003.

[Shadbolt et al., 2006] Shadbolt, N., Hall, W., and Berners-Lee, T., "The Semantic Web Revisited," *IEEE Intelligent Systems, 2006.*

[Shaik and Yeasin, 2006] Shaik, J. and Yeasin, M., "Functionally Classifying Genes from Microarray Data Using Linear and Non-linear Data Projection," In *Proceedings of the 4th ACS/IEEE International Conference on Computer Systems and Applications (AICCSA 06)*, 2006.

[Shaik et al., 2006] J. Shaik, C. Kothari, D.J. Russomanno and M. Yeasin (2006) "Visualization of Relation Clusters from OWL Ontologies," *Proceedings of the International Conference on Semantic Web and Web Services*, CSREA Press, Las Vegas, Nevada, pp. 17–23.

[Stephens and Chen, 1996] Stephens, L. and Chen Y., "Principles for Organizing Semantic Relations in Large Knowledge Bases," *IEEE Transactions in Knowledge and Data Engineering*, **8**(3), 492 – 496, 1996.

[Storey, 1993] V. Storey, "Understanding Semantic Relationships," *Very Large Databases Journal*, **2**(4), 455–488, 1993.

[Unsalan and Ercil, 2000] Unsalan, C., and Ercil, A., "Shapes of features and a modified measure for Linear Discriminant Analysis," *OCPR00*, Volume 2, pp. 410–413, 2000.

[Wall et al., 2003] Wall, E., Rechtsteiner, A., and Rocha, L. M., "Singular value decomposition and principal component analysis," *A Practical Approach to Microarray Data Analysis*, Kluwer: Norwell, MA, 2003.

Filename:	16-Kothari-PCCC.docx
Directory:	E:\Lucy_CORRECTIONS\203. Data Management in the Semantic We
Kothari-PCC	
Template:	C:\Documents and Settings\Owner\Application
Data\Microsoft\Templates\Normal.dotm	
Title:	Nova Layout [7x10]
Subject:	Cell Phone: 0040 721 269312
Author:	Marius Andronie, Romania
Keywords:	
Comments:	
Creation Date:	10/27/2011 3:06:00 PM
Change Number:	2
Last Saved On:	10/27/2011 3:06:00 PM
Last Saved By:	C84
Total Editing Time:	2 Minutes
Last Printed On:	10/27/2011 4:26:00 PM
As of Last Complete Printing	
Number of Pages:	17
Number of Words:	6,152 (approx.)
Number of Characters:	35,071 (approx.)

In: Data Management in the Semantic Web
Editor: Hal Jin, pp. 401-426
ISBN: 978-1-61122-862-5

Chapter 17

Annotating Semantics of Multidisciplinary Engineering Resources to Support Knowledge Sharing in Sustainable Manufacturing

Q.Z. Yang[1,] and X.Y. Zhang[2]*
[1] Singapore Institute of Manufacturing Technology, Singapore
[2] School of Information and Communications Technology, Republic Polytechnic, Singapore

Abstract

Semantic annotation of digital engineering resources is attributed as an enabling technology for knowledge sharing in sustainable manufacturing, where the economic, environmental and social objectives are incorporated into technical solutions to achieve competitive product advantages. The emerging needs for sustainability require seamless sharing of product lifecycle information and machine-understandable semantics across design and manufacturing networks. Towards this end, the chapter proposes an ontology-driven approach to semantic annotation of multidisciplinary engineering resources. The targeted application is for product knowledge sharing in sustainable manufacturing of consumer electronics. The proposed approach is based on two mechanisms: 1) ontology modeling – how to specify the meaning of annotations with ontological representations to enhance sharability of the annotation content; and 2) ontology implementation – how to effectively apply the meaning of annotations to heterogeneous computer-aided tools and lifecycle processes on the basis of ontology. These semantic knowledge sharing mechanisms are validated through annotation scenarios. Two use scenarios are illustrated in the chapter for semantics sharing based on annotations in sustainable manufacturing of consumer products.

Keywords: Semantic annotation, digital engineering resources, knowledge sharing, ontology, sustainable manufacturing

---

[*] E-mail address: qyang@simtech.a-star.edu.sg. Tel.: +65 6793 8348; fax: +65 6791 6377. (Corresponding author.)

Abbreviations

OWL	Web Ontology Language
XML	eXtensible Markup Language
RDF	Resource Description Framework
CAD	Computer Aided Design
mCAD	Mechanical CAD
eCAD	Electrical CAD
optCAD	Optical CAD
LCA	Life Cycle Assessment
LCC	Life Cycle Costing

1. Introduction

The concept of sustainable development has brought a global attention since the issue was raised in the 1987 Brundtland Commission report [1]. Specifically in product engineering and manufacturing, sustainability has been viewed as one of the two forces shaping the future of the manufacturing industry [2]. The emerging sustainability needs are challenging manufacturing to enable seamless sharing of product lifecycle information and machine-understandable semantics across heterogeneous design and manufacturing networks. Semantic annotation can be such an enabling technology for product knowledge sharing in sustainable manufacturing.

Annotating semantics of digital engineering resources is yet a common-practice currently. Instead, it is a vision in sustainable manufacturing, where multidisciplinary teams and computer-aided tools collaborate together to achieve innovative, environmentally friendly and safe products. This vision however has placed additional requirements on representation, transformation and sharing of product lifecycle information and sustainability knowledge. In particular, representing the product semantics [3] with formal and explicit specifications and sharing them across disparate sustainable design and manufacturing applications can be a challenge. Each such application has its own terminology system to specify the domain concepts, the data relationships, and the intended meanings of the data. These domain-specific terminologies and data schemas can be confusing, especially when these applications need to access multiple data sources. The difficulty is mainly from the issues in semantic, syntactic, structural and contextual interoperability [4] of these multidisciplinary applications and information resources. It has been acknowledged that the lack of ontologically-compatible semantics in digital engineering resources has caused great difficulties in mutual understanding and consistent sharing of product knowledge in sustainable manufacturing. Consequently, much of the rationale and implication of the domain-specific outcomes would be stripped away in the product information/knowledge communication process from one discipline to another. To improve the situation, there is clearly a need for technologies and methodologies to support semantic knowledge sharing across domain boundaries in multidisciplinary, sustainable manufacturing.

Seen in this light, this chapter intends to develop an ontology-driven approach to annotating semantics of digital engineering resources. The aim is to enhance product knowledge sharing through semantic annotations to support streamlined collaboration in sustainable consumer product development. Towards this end, annotation expressions are specified to explicitly capture the product characteristics implicated in disciplinary engineering resources. The concepts and relationships used in the annotation expressions are formalized with domain ontology. By populating the semantic annotation expressions with the product lifecycle information and sustainability knowledge explicated from the multidisciplinary engineering resources, the semantic annotations are generated. To seek better machine-interpretability, the annotations are also encoded in OWL/RDF format [10, 11]. As the semantics of the annotations have been specified by formal concept classes and logic axioms in domain ontology, these annotations can then support sharing of the meanings behind the annotated resource documents, drawings or data models. To validate the annotation mechanisms above, two use scenarios are discussed in the chapter for semantic knowledge sharing in multidisciplinary design and in sustainability assessment for consumer products.

2. Background and Related Work

2.1. Sustainable Manufacturing and Its Semantic Challenges

Manufacturing may have a broad definition, "encompassing from products and services, to processes sustaining their lifecycles, to companies and business models" [5]. In this chapter, *manufacturing* of consumer products is mainly concerned with product design and development activities and their associated computer-aided applications. Hence, *sustainable manufacturing* would be referred to the *manufacturing* technologies, processes and systems that create high-performing products cost-effectively with minimal environmental impact, while improving quality of life for social progress. Sustainable manufacturing is about incorporation of three sustainability issues in product design and development: economic, environmental and social issues – known as the triple bottom line [6] of sustainability.

Semantics sharing in sustainable manufacturing of consumer electronics has a few characteristics. First, sustainable design and development of consumer products involves multifunctional teams working with domain-specific engineering applications, such as CAD (computer aided design), PLM (product lifecycle management), LCA (life cycle assessment), LCC (life cycle costing) and EA (energy accounting) systems. Designers/engineers often create product information and associated semantics ad-hoc using their individual vocabularies, meanings of terms, proprietary representations, and on their preferred/available platforms. Second, they need to intensively use multidisciplinary information and knowledge from other teams and systems. Most possibly, the semantics of the needed information are represented in other domain-specific terminologies. This makes it difficult to interpret and understand the meanings of the data obtained. It thus hampers the effective cross-functional communications and workflows. Third, although the collaborating teams have common understanding of the shared product development goals, the individual team's information resources are often given additional meanings from its own contexts. The supplemented data semantics are often poorly documented. Background knowledge and specialized concepts are required for consistent understanding and sharing of such semantics.

Take the audio products development as an example. Teams of designers/engineers with a sufficient diversity of knowledge [7] are required in sustainable product development. This typically involves mechanical, electrical, and optical design teams, software engineers, sustainability analysts, manufacturing facilities, and outsourced engineering service suppliers. Each team excels at its particular engineering tasks for the common sustainable product goals. Domain-specific information models, tools and processes are used to generate, utilize and manage product lifecycle information in diverse engineering resources (e.g., CAD drawings, sustainable design guidelines, engineering databases and software executables). This results in efficiency and effectiveness in meeting the targets of the individual engineering functions, but often adds difficulties in integrating the total sustainable product solutions. The integrated product solutions highly rely on cross-functional interactions and meaningful communications of product semantics across multidisciplinary teams, systems and processes.

Traditionally the Mechanical CAD (mCAD), Electrical CAD (eCAD), Optical CAD (optCAD), and other computer applications used in the consumer product design and development lack the ability to understand, interpret and utilize semantics of the heterogeneous information from other systems. They do not necessarily share definitions of domain concepts. Instead, they are more tending to interpret and apply knowledge in the syntax of their own languages [8]. These characteristics have set the basic requirements to motivate our development of semantics sharing mechanisms for consumer products.

From these semantics sharing requirements and characteristics above, the key challenges in sustainable manufacturing of consumer products can be identified as follows.

- Semantic differences between the meanings of the terminologies used in domain concept definitions; and
- Incompatibility between the syntax (format) and semantics (meaning) of product lifecycle information/knowledge representations from different sustainable product design and development disciplines.

Using ontology engineering and industrial informatics technologies to address these semantic challenges is the focus of this chapter. Two mechanisms on ontology modeling and ontology implementation are therefore developed. They will be elaborated in Sections 3, 4 and 5 respectively.

2.2. Annotations in Product Engineering and Manufacturing

Annotations have been used in communicating technical illustrations and intentions in product engineering and manufacturing for decades. Specifically, the textual annotations [9, 12] have been widely accepted as a means to capture, add and comment the information contents of engineering resources. However, creating textual annotations from engineering resources has been tedious and difficult to maintain with engineering changes. It is even more challenging to describe the semantics of the engineering resources using the textual annotation techniques.

With the advent and proliferation of digitizing the product development process, a demand for digital annotations in design and manufacturing has emerged. Digital annotations associate the annotation contents with the annotated resources through links in a digital environment, so that the information contents of resources can be communicated more clearly and efficiently. Most of the leading commercial CAD systems, such as CATIA™ from Dassault System and NX™ from UGS, as well as some research prototypes [13 ~ 15] have been developed with digital CAD model annotation capabilities. These systems enable designers to capture, retrieve and utilize the shared design information through CAD annotations. Despite the fact that the digital annotation technology has brought the added benefits to designers, it does not provide sufficient solutions to the major challenges mentioned previously for sharing *semantics* of multidisciplinary engineering resources in sustainable manufacturing.

Semantic annotation provides a new way, beyond textual annotation and digital link annotation, to produce and utilize annotations for sharing product intent in digital environments. Semantic annotation makes the semantics embedded in design resources more formal and explicit through the use of a formal and structural language, e.g. OWL [10] or RDF [11]. The semantics of annotations are described in domain ontologies. As ontologies represent agreed upon views in product engineering and manufacturing, they help eliminate ambiguity in interpretation of annotations. It is therefore ensured that both annotator and annotation consumer to share the same meaning of the annotated resources.

2.3. Existing Semantic Annotation Methods and Applications

Semantic annotation is most commonly used in annotating Web resources (e.g. Web pages, images, audios, videos or Web Services) for search and discovery of Web contents. The basic idea is to annotate Web resources with semantic metadata schemas [32] provided by formal ontological models. The current practices in creating semantic annotations for Web resources, though varying across applications and techniques, generally follow three primary steps: Web entity identification, entity disambiguation and annotation [16]. Through these annotation steps, the identified entities in Web resources are directly matched with the concepts in the ontological models to generate annotations. There exist a number of semantic annotation frameworks, systems and tools for creating and maintaining semantic metadata (annotations) of Web resources. Uren et al. [17] analyzed 27 existing Web annotation systems in a recent report. More semantic annotation environments, services, platforms and techniques were summarized in Reeve's study [18].

The semantic annotation technology has also been applied to the product design and manufacturing domains. Kitamura et al. [19] proposed a functional ontology-based metadata schema for functional annotation of engineering designs in the Semantic Web. Their functional annotations can show designer's intentions behind the technical documents, thus to facilitate efficient retrieval of the documents. Lin et al. [20] developed a semantic annotation framework for annotating process models. Four perspectives are studied in this framework: profile annotation, meta-model annotation, process model annotation and goal annotation in order to achieve semantic interoperability in enterprise process management.

Several EU projects, such as SEVENPRO [21], ATHENA [22] and INTEROP-NoE [23] have developed semantic annotation methodologies and systems to improve engineering knowledge sharing in networked enterprises. In the SEVENPRO project (Semantic Virtual Engineering Environment for Product Design), a semi-automatic semantic annotation approach was developed [21]. By annotating multimedia design resources such as CAD, ERP and engineering documents, the project seeks to improve the product engineering and development process for acquisition, formalization and usage of product knowledge. The outcomes from the SEVENPRO project are being commercialized to promote semantic product design [24]. The ATHENA project (Advanced Technologies for Interoperability of Heterogeneous Enterprise Networks and their Applications) is another example. It has developed technologies for ontology-based semantic annotation and reconciliation methods, languages and tools [22]. The project outcomes would allow enterprises to enable seamless interoperation with others. Similarly, the INTEROP-NoE project (Interoperability Research for Networked Enterprises Applications and Software – Network of Excellence) has conducted detailed studies on semantic annotation of various perspectives of enterprise models. These include semantic annotation of information models, process models, strategical and business models, and decision models [23].

While each of the methods above is suitable for a specific type of semantic annotation applications, such as for enterprise model interoperation or for acquisition, formalization and utilization of product knowledge [21], some annotation principles presented in these projects can be applied to our multidisciplinary annotation applications in sustainable consumer product development. Next section proposes such a method.

2.4. Overview of Our Work

The proposed semantic annotation approach consists of the following annotation steps:

- Annotation expressions modeling to define annotation content using agreed common vocabulary;
- Formalization of annotation semantics in these expressions with OWL ontologies;
- Creation of semantic annotations by instantiating the annotation expressions with the semantic information explicated from the existing resources and/or enriched from external systems; and
- Neutral encoding of annotations to facilitate semantics sharing in heterogeneous sustainable manufacturing systems.

Fig. 1 shows an overview of the proposed semantic annotation approach. It also illustrates the information interactions between our approach and the selected sustainable manufacturing systems, as well as the involved multidisciplinary engineering resources.

The proposed approach is fundamentally different from the traditional design annotation methods as it specifies the meaning of annotations with product ontologies and it uses OWL/RDF to encode annotation semantics for meaningful communication across disciplines. The approach is also different from the existing methods for Web resources annotation. For example, unlike those Web annotation methods to directly match entities in resources with concepts in ontologies, our approach uses application-specific annotation expressions to define annotation contents. In this way, the requirements for semantic annotations from individual disciplines can be specifically addressed. Furthermore, the annotations (instances of the annotation expressions) can be stored in a semantic annotation repository and associated with product representation forms (geometry drawings, material/energy specifications, etc) accessible not only for information search and retrieval but also for product semantics sharing.

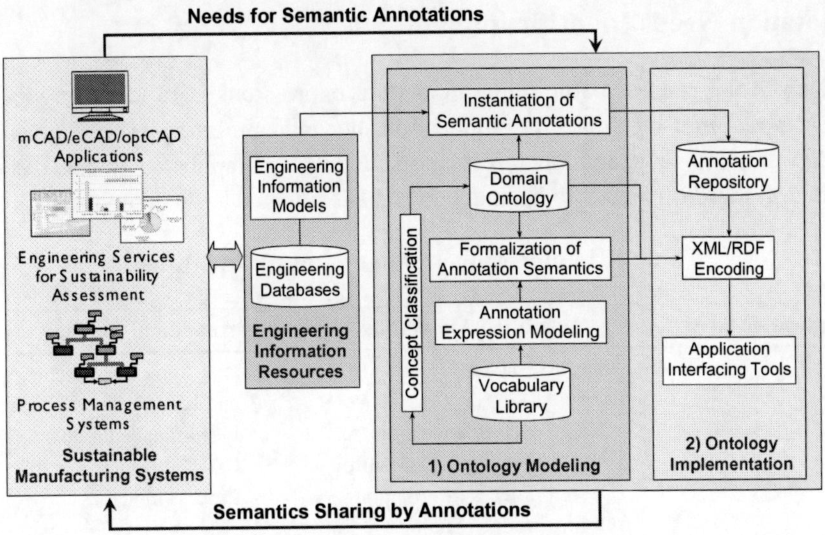

Figure 1. A semantic annotation approach.

3. Annotation Expression

An *annotation expression* is a representation of the annotation requirements from a particular engineering application, such as an optCAD application or a regulatory compliance simulation system. It explicitly specifies the annotation properties and value types that should be used for a selected engineering perspective to fulfill the required semantics need from that application. In our approach, we use the annotation expressions, instead of RDF [11] statements or the N3 [38] notations, to address the semantic needs of a given engineering application. The reason is twofold:

1) Simplicity. An annotation expression is a simple metadata schema that can be easily used by annotators/engineers who are unfamiliar with the technical details about semantic markup languages and ontologies; and
2) Flexibility. Annotation express is application-specific and adaptable to different annotation needs with different kinds of resource semantics to be described in tailored, pre-defined forms.

Annotation expressions are modeled with annotation attributes and contextual constraints (details in Section 3.2). Agreed common vocabularies are used to name the attributes of the annotation expressions. In this approach, an annotation expression does not play the role of an ontology. Instead, it provides annotators with a vocabulary backed by product ontologies to define a simple and flexible semantic structure, thus to specifically address an individual annotation need and to share the annotated semantics through an annotation repository. Annotation expressions are constructed in two steps: identifying annotation needs of sustainable manufacturing applications and defining the annotation expressions. They are discussed as follows.

3.1. Annotation Needs Identification

The first step in the process of defining annotation expressions is to identify what sharable information is required by a specific application, but either missing from a given resource (e.g. a CAD drawing or a domain information model), or implicated in the resource in a native format. It therefore needs to be added or to be explicated as an annotation.

Table 1. Engineering annotation needs identified

Application Area	Identified Annotation Need	Annotated Engineering Resource
mCAD eCAD optCAD	Cost assessment	Part / process / accounting databases and LCC systems
	Design performance indicator	Performance models
	Inter-part relationship control	CAD add-on executables
	Design process information	Process models
	Online product catalog	External data sources
Product Qualification Test	Sampling test constraint	Design rules database
	Testing plan input	CAD models and process models
Sustainability Assessment	Material selection	Intranet manuals, RoHS[†] and WEEE[‡] compliance rules
	Energy efficient process selection	Energy accounting databases
	Waste control and carbon footprint	Product and process specifications, LCA systems
Collaborative Design Process Management	Sourced design progress	Supplier's process model
	Sourced design quality	Client's design specifications

[†] RoHS: EU directive on the Restriction of the Use of certain Hazardous Substances in Electrical and Electronic Equipment.

[‡] WEEE: EU directive on Waste Electrical and Electronic Equipment.

As described in Section 2.1, multidisciplinary teams possessing different expertise and specialization are involved in sustainable consumer product development. Each has its own tools and processes to provide the discipline-specific information for product decisions. At the same time, it also depends on other collaborating disciplines to provide the relevant and reusable information. As the reused information is created away from its discipline-specific systems, the information contents are often in proprietary formats. To make them understandable and sharable among collaborating teams and systems, metadata constructed in an explicit, concise and structured manner play a key role. Engineering annotations are intended to serve as these metadata.

Through analyzing typical multidisciplinary collaboration scenarios in consumer product development, an initial set of annotation needs has been identified for the involved design and analysis applications, i.e., mCAD, eCAD, optCAD, product qualification test, sustainability assessment, and collaborative design process management. Table 1 presents exemplary results identified.

3.2. Annotation Expression Modeling

From the identified annotation needs above, the next step is to represent them in certain annotation expressions. A semantic annotation scheme is therefore defined for the provision of annotation expressions for the considered multidisciplinary engineering applications. The annotation scheme consists of attributes and contextual constraints:

- Attributes establish the meaning and information content of the annotation requirements. An attribute has an identifier and a type indicator. The identifier is taken from a controlled vocabulary and described with a concept class in product ontologies (in Section 4.2). Hence the identifier can specify the intended meaning of the attribute through semantic reference to the vocabulary and ontology. The type indicator indicates the stipulated data type of the attribute value.
- Contextual Constraints contain a set of methods and relationships to specify the validity of the attribute values, scopes and types that an application system can support.

The attributes and contextual constraints above are organized in a unified structure using the following grammar, in which a pair of brackets, [], indicates an optional instance; and a plus sign, +, indicates that there can be one or more instances of the definition. The annotation scheme is therefore represented as:

<Attribute.Identifier(Attribute.TypeIndicator[:ContextualConstraint]), + > (1)

Using the annotation scheme as a descriptive template, product engineering and manufacturing annotation expressions are defined. An annotation expression may contain any number of attributes and contextual constraints of Expression (1), depending on the need for semantic annotations from particular viewpoints. For example, the following annotation expression is instantiated from Expression (1) with five attributes and two contextual constraints. It is used to annotate the "inter-part relationship" and "online product catalog" in Table 1.

<BehaviorCategory(String), BehaviorName(String: Unique), Description(String), Value(String), ExeType(Enum: dvb, java, cc, html)> (2)

Similarly, another annotation expression may be instantiated using only four attributes and one contextual constraint as follows.

<PropertyName(String: Unique), Description(String), NominalValue(Real), Unit(String)> (3)

This expression is used to fulfill the annotation needs for the "collaborative design activity management" specified in Table 1. These may include those data describing the due date, resource use and progress of a design task, in a design process model.

As multi-domains, multi-views, and multi-resources are involved in creation and consumption of annotations, semantic issues are becoming critical. To make the annotation contents understandable and reusable among collaborating agents (both humans and computer systems), the start point is that any attribute identifiers in an annotation expression must be taken from controlled vocabularies. Moreover, the terminologies/concepts in the vocabularies must be described in a formal, explicit and semantically-sound way.

4. Formalization of Annotation Semantics with OWL Ontologies

4.1. Semantics Modeling Process

Modeling of annotation semantics involves a set of activities that concern domain knowledge acquisition, common vocabulary establishment, and domain ontology development, management and utilization. Different methodologies and frameworks have been proposed for the construction of lightweight engineering and manufacturing semantic models/ontologies. The most notable ones include the following as illustrated in Fig. 2:

- The Enterprise Ontology modeling methodology proposed by Uschold and King [33];
- The TOVE methodology from Grüninger and Fox [34];
- The Methontology methodology [35] and the On-To-Knowledge methodology [36];
- The DILIGENT methodology for distributed, loosely-controlled and evolving engineering process of ontologies [37].

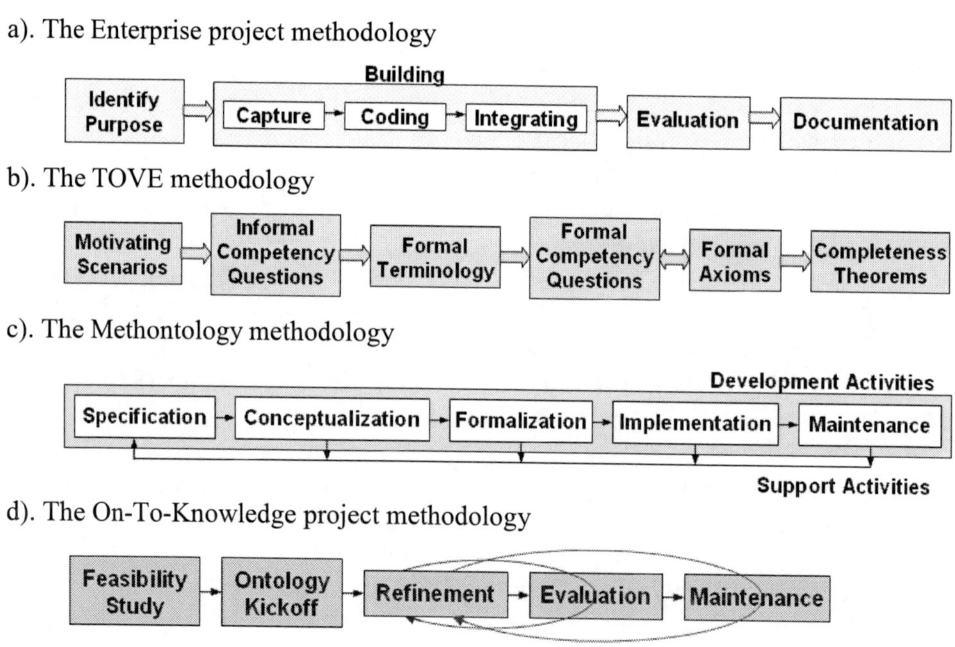

Figure 2. Examples of engineering/manufacturing ontology development methodologies.

From the methodologies in Fig. 2, some common ontology development activities and sequences can be identified: Most of them start the main ontology development process from the *specification* phase to identify the purpose and scope of ontologies. The modeling process goes through the *conceptualization* to structure the knowledge acquired as abstract conceptual models. It continues with the *formalization* to transform the conceptual models into formal machine-interpretable models. The process ends at the *implementation* phase to encode the formal models in some ontology languages. We use this generic ontology development process in the present study and enhance it with additional ontological engineering activities, such as ontology management and ontology utilization in sustainable manufacturing. Our semantics modeling process is depicted in Fig. 3.

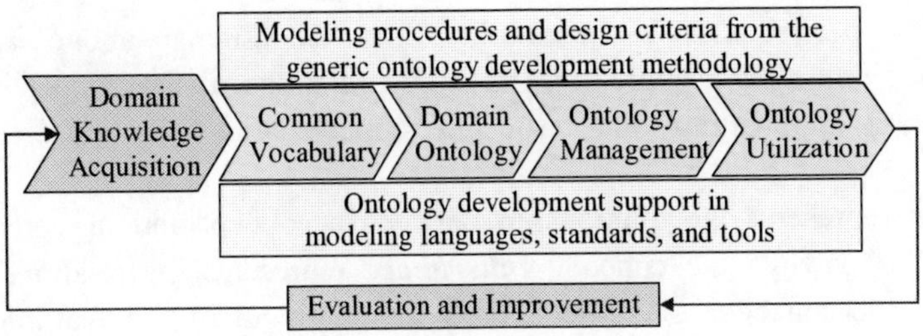

Figure 3. The semantics modeling process.

4.2. Taxonomy of Sustainability

The *taxonomy of sustainability* is a controlled vocabulary. It classifies and arranges sharable sustainable manufacturing concepts in a hierarchical structure with formally defined relationships between the concepts and with explicitly specified semantics for each vocabulary terminology. The concepts are mainly used in describing sustainability objectives along the three dimensions: economic, environmental and social aspects. The intention of the sustainability taxonomy is to remove ambiguity, mismatch and misunderstanding to the shared use of the concepts across multidisciplinary teams and applications. As sustainable manufacturing involves a wide range of knowledge concepts, what are focused here will be those concepts used in product sustainability assessment and in design reviews.

Table 2. Exemplary domain concepts

Domain Concept	Definition
Product quality	Capability of a product to satisfy given needs.
Development resource	Available resources for product development.
Customer satisfaction	A measure of how close a product meets customer expectations.
Process complexity	A measure of complexity of a manufacturing process.
Production automation	The automation level of production.
Environment and health cost	Indirect costs due to environment damages and health problems.
Profitability	The possibility to gain profit from the development of a product.
Solid waste	Non recyclable / renewable material wastes from a product.
Ecological risk	Possible damage imposed to ecological systems due to toxicity of pollutants emitted from the production, use and end-of-life treatment of a product.

The semantics modeling process in Fig. 3 has been applied to the development of the sustainability taxonomy. The knowledge items in the taxonomy are identified from the multidisciplinary design and analysis activities through process modeling. Another knowledge source is from the multidisciplinary engineering manuals, LCA/LCC domain expert interviews, and previous design documents. Through this identification process, an initial set of sustainability knowledge-items has been collected. The meaning of each knowledge item is specified explicitly and unambiguously, according to its multi-use conventions in the involved collaborative engineering systems. Table 2 gives examples of knowledge-items identified.

Relationships between the sustainability knowledge-items above are formulated according to the commonly-accepted and intended relations of the concepts in real-world design and analysis applications. The basic inter-concept relationships are aggregation and inheritance.

Aggregation represents the relationship between a concept and its constitute features. Each feature is a "part-of" the concept. *Inheritance* represents the relationship between a concept and its sub-concepts. A sub-concept can inherit all of the features of its super-concept, which defines an "is-a" hierarchy relationship in the taxonomy of sustainability. Fig. 4 shows an excerpt of the "is-a" hierarchy in Protégé [25] which is used as the modeling tool for the sustainability taxonomy.

4.3. Classification of Other Domain-Concepts Used in Annotation Expressions

Besides the sustainability concepts, other domain-concepts are also identified and organized in a commonly-agreed vocabulary for naming the attribute identifiers of annotation expressions in Section 3.2. This is done by the use of controlled vocabulary terminologies with their meanings and relationships being explicitly defined and agreed by all involved collaborating participants.

Figure 4. Example of "is-a" hierarchy relationships.

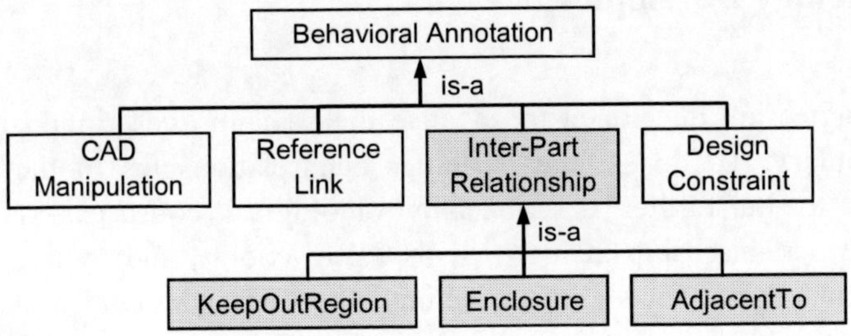

Figure 5. A partial classification hierarchy for behavioral annotation concepts.

The results from the annotation needs identification process in Section 3.1 are the main source to collect these controlled terminologies/concepts. For example, the identified annotation needs in the middle column of Table 1 express the additional metadata for semantic properties, CAD manipulations, reference links to external data sources, inter-part relationships and constraints, etc. These concepts are classified into two categories: property annotation concepts and behavioral annotation concepts. Property annotation concepts are used to enrich and explicate the *data semantics* of engineering resources through formal definitions of data meaning of the resources. Behavioral annotation concepts, on the other hand, are specified to enrich and explicate the *functional and executional semantics* related to the engineering resources. This is done by formal definitions of functionality elements (e.g. capabilities of a CAD manipulation, requirements of a testing constraint, etc). Fig. 5 depicts a partial classification hierarchy of the behavioral annotation concepts with a focus on the *Inter-Part Relationship* concepts needed in multidisciplinary consumer product design.

The identified domain concepts are organized in a common vocabulary library. Meanings of the concepts in the library are specified explicitly. The vocabulary library stores and manages these domain concepts together with their intended meanings and inter-relationships. Table 3 lists the semantics of the concepts shown in Fig. 5.

Table 3. Intended meanings of domain concepts

Concept	Semantics	Relationship
Behavioral Annotation	A Behavioral Annotation represents a type of design annotations used to enrich and explicate the functional and executional semantics related to the given design resources.	Supertype
Inter-Part Relationship	An Inter-Part Relationship is a subtype of Behavioral Annotation that identifies the relationship between two components designed by different disciplines.	Subtype of *Behavioral Annotation* with *is-a* relation
Keep out Region	It is a subtype of Inter-Part Relationship that specifies a reserved range box in a mechatronics design space for a certain purpose.	Subtype of *Inter-Part Relationship* with *is-a* relation
Enclosure	It stipulates an enclosure relationship between an enclosed component and an enclosing component.	Subtype of *Inter-Part Relationship* with *is-a* relation
Adjacent to	It stipulates that two components should be adjacent to each other.	Subtype of *Inter-Part Relationship* with *is-a* relation

4.3. OWL Ontology Development

OWL [10] ontologies are developed to enhance the semantic description capability of the annotation vocabulary. To do so, the meanings and relationships of the concepts in the vocabulary need to be further described by ontological constructs. For example, by formalizing the *is-a* relationship in Fig. 5 with OWL axioms, and by expanding the inter-concept relationships in the vocabulary to include other OWL ontological definitions, OWL-based ontologies have been defined for semantic annotation in multidisciplinary consumer product design and development. These ontologies have provided conceptual knowledge models for describing, understanding and sharing the semantics of design annotations across multiple CAD systems, sustainability assessment applications, and design process management systems in the current research.

Each domain concept in the annotation vocabulary is defined by an OWL class. For example, the ontological concept *Enclosure* in Fig. 5 is defined by an OWL class specification in Fig. 6 for its intended meanings and relationships with other domain concepts.

From Fig. 6, it can be seen that the *is-a* relationship between the sub-concept of *Enclosure* and its super-concept of *InterPartRelationship* (shown in Fig. 5) is formalized by the *rdfs:subClassOf* taxonomic constructor in OWL. Hence, both the asymmetric and transitive relations of *subClassOf* [26] should hold. By the transitivity, an *Enclosure* instance can inherit any attributes from its super-concept *InterPartRelationship.*

The concept *Enclosure* in Fig. 6 is defined with a synonym called *Inclusion*. The equivalence relationship between the two is modeled by *owl:equivalentClass* in Fig. 6. This implies that the *Enclosure* concept is semantically equivalent to the *Inclusion* concept in another ontology. The two concept classes should have exactly the same instances, so that the two domain concepts can be used alternatively across disciplines without ontological conflicts.

```
<owl:Class rdf:ID="Enclosure">
  <rdfs:subClassOf rdf:resource="#InterPartRelationship"/>
  <owl:equivalentClass rdf:resource="&onto2;Inclusion"/>
  <owl:disjointWith rdf:resource="#AdjacentWith"/>
  <owl:disjointWith rdf:resource="#KeepOutRegion"/>
  <rdfs:subClassOf>
    <owl:Restriction>
      <owl:onProperty rdf:resource="#hasEnclosingPart"/>
      <owl:cardinality rdf:datatype="&xsd;nonNegativeInteger">1</owl:cardinality>
    </owl:Restriction>
  </rdfs:subClassOf>
  <rdfs:subClassOf>
    <owl:Restriction>
      <owl:onProperty rdf:resource="#hasEnclosedPart"/>
      <owl:cardinality rdf:datatype="&xsd;nonNegativeInteger">1</owl:cardinality>
    </owl:Restriction>
  </rdfs:subClassOf>
</owl:Class>
```

Figure 6. Ontological definition for *Enclosure* concept.

The ontological definition for *Enclosure* in Fig. 6 also enhances its relationship definitions shown in Fig. 5. The purpose is to improve the query, matching and reasoning capabilities of the ontological concept class. For example, the specification of *owl:disjointWith* in Fig. 6 stipulates an exclusive one-of relation between three sub-concepts (*Enclosure, AdjacentTo, KeepOutRegion*) and their super-concept *InterPartRelationship* in Fig. 5. This will ensure that during concept instance matching, an individual can only be mapped to an instance of one sub-concept class among the three.

The sub-concept *Enclosure* inherits four attributes from its super-concept *InterPartRelationship*. Besides these, it also specifies two additional attributes (i.e. *hasEnclosingPart* and *hasEnclosedPart*) in Fig. 6. By using OWL property constructs of *owl:ObjectProperty* and *owl:DatatypeProperty*, all the six attributes of the *Enclosure* concept class can be fully specified as shown in Table 4.

Table 4. OWL properties of *Enclosure* concept

	Property	Domain	Range
At sub-concept level for *Enclosure*	owl:ObjectProperty hasEnclosingPart	*Enclosure*	*Part*
	owl:ObjectProperty hasEnclosedPart	*Enclosure*	*Part*
At super-concept level for *InterPartRelationship*	owl:DatatypeProperty hasName	*InterPartRelationship*	xsd: string
	owl:DatatypeProperty hasDescription	*InterPartRelationship*	xsd: string
	owl:DatatypeProperty hasValue	*InterPartRelationship*	xsd: string
	owl:ObjectProperty hasExeType	*InterPartRelationship*	*ExeType*

The Protégé toolkit [25] with an OWL plug-in is used to develop the domain ontologies in this research. These ontologies explicitly specify the formal and intended semantics for the identified domain concepts, their properties, and the relationships between the concepts. The concepts are mainly used in naming and searching the attribute identifiers of the design annotation expressions defined in Section 3.2. As ontologies represent a kind of semantic consensus of the concept definitions, the intended meanings of attribute values in design annotations can therefore be consistently interpreted and communicated among collaborating agents. On the other hand, the domain ontologies also enable reasoning, query, and mapping over ontological definitions and relationships of domain concepts across heterogeneous applications, so that the semantics of the engineering annotations can be shared among them.

5. Instantiation of Semantic Annotations

Semantic annotations are generated by instantiating the annotation expressions in Section 3 with the information extracted from the existing design resources, from the relevant external applications, or from user's inputs. The meanings of the information content in the instantiated annotations are specified by the domain ontologies in Section 4.

5.1. Two Types of Instantiations to Create Semantic Annotation Based on Annotation Expression

Instantiation is a process to generate engineering annotations according to the semantic requirements specified in annotation expressions. Instantiating these expressions with product semantics from a resource implies:

- To explicate the semantics of the resource data based on the concept definitions in domain ontologies; and/or
- To enrich the information meaning and information content from the resource with additional product semantics from other resources or from users.

The two types of instantiations need to be handled differently. If the product information models, database schemas of the existing engineering resources are unambiguous and semantically complete to fulfill the identified annotation needs, then the instantiation of annotation expressions will be a process to transfer the meaning of the same information in different representations in order to make the meaning more explicit. However in reality, there always are differences in what is required in an annotation expression and what can be offered in a given engineering resource. Certain information elements defined in the annotation expression and needed by collaborating applications do not have semantic equivalences in the existing resource. This would usually require humans and external systems to supply additional semantics to enrich the data meanings of the existing resource. The following two sections present two methods for explicating and enriching design semantics in the annotation instantiation process.

5.2. Explicating the Semantics of Resource Data

Based on the semantic requirements specified in annotation expressions, the semantic annotations can be instantiated from explicating the data meanings of the engineering resources. This is accomplished by finding the most appropriate semantic information from a resource for an attribute in an annotation expression. Domain ontologies are used in this matching process to regulate the interpretation of the meaning of the attribute through *Attribute.Identifier*. There are four possible situations arising from the matching process:

- There exists an exact match of meanings between an information element in the resource and an attribute in the annotation expression. The information element is therefore assigned to the attribute as its value.
- An information element in the resource is an equivalent value of an attribute in the annotation expression. The equivalence here refers to the same information content represented in different formats, units, etc.
- An information element in the resource consists of a part of the value of an attribute in the annotation expression.
- No information element is found in the resource that can be used as the value of an attribute in the annotation expression.

In the first two situations above, the instantiation of annotation expressions can be an automatic process. Once the mapping rules are defined, software tools will support the auto-matching process. One of our earlier projects has developed such a tool for explicating and extracting semantic information from collaborative product design (CDP) process models [27]. Fig. 7 shows an interface of the tool used in explicating CDP process data semantics to instantiate process annotations. The semantic structure of these process annotations is defined by an annotation expression given in Expression (3). Examples of the instantiated process annotations are given in Table 5.

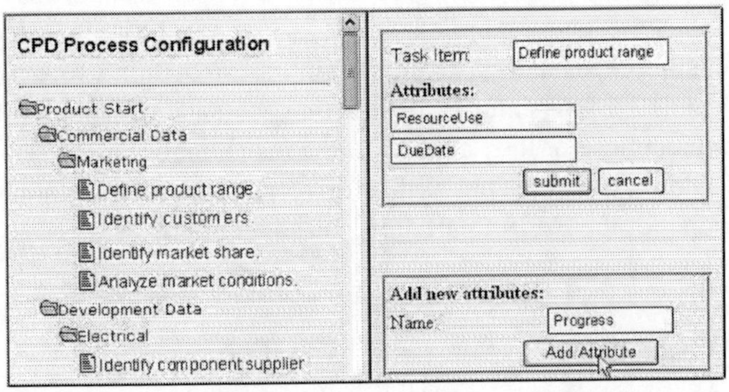

Figure 7. Explicating the process data semantics.

Table 5. Examples of process annotations

PropertyName (Unique)	Description	Value	Unit
Task	A composition of events or operations.	Assembly design for an optical disc drive	
DueDate	Due date of a task.	15 Oct 2010	
TaskOwner	Responsible person of a task.	Tom	
ResourceUse	Time resource used for a task.	36	hour
Progress	Completion percentage of a task.	70	percent

The property names in Table 5 are retrieved from the controlled vocabulary library in Section 4.2, with their meanings and relations specified in domain ontology in Section 4.3. As such, the semantics of the process annotations can be meaningfully communicated among humans. To make them also interpretable and reusable in heterogeneous computer applications, the semantic annotations should be represented in neutral, machine-readable formats as well. The details are given in Section 5.4.

5.3. Enriching the Semantics of Resource Data

The last two situations in the preceding list in Section 5.2 require enrichment of data semantics of engineering resources during the annotation instantiation process. In our current study, the semantics enrichment is a semi-automatic process. It is used for creating design annotations when a given resource can not completely fulfill the instantiation requirements of an annotation expression. Human's interactions are therefore needed to provide additional semantics. These interactions include: auto-invocation of external applications to generate the required supplementary information; auto-compilation of the generated information; user input; and manual-assignment of the information enrichment to an attribute in an annotation expression; etc. Some of these interactions highly depend on the experience and knowledge of annotators. Similar to the situations in Section 5.2, software tools can help this interactive instantiation process.

In our software implementation for semantics enrichment, the contextual constraints of the annotation expressions defined in Section 3.2 are implemented as constraint algorithms in add-on tools for CAD, sampling test, and design process management systems. These algorithms ensure that the auto-compiled and user-entered attribute values and types are compliant with the data scopes and types defined in the annotation expressions. Fig. 8 shows one of the add-on tools for enriching and extracting the data semantics from CAD models. The enriched data semantics are then applied to the instantiation of the semantic annotations for a mCAD part (*Base-A*) in an optical disc drive product. The instantiated property and behavioral annotations for the *Base-A* part are also shown in Fig. 8.

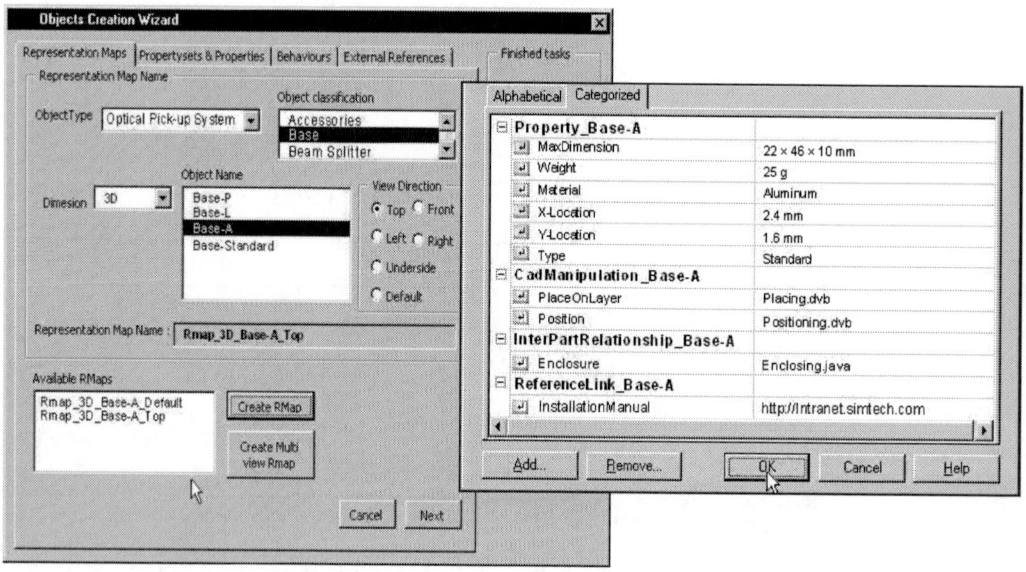

Figure 8. Semantics enrichment in instantiating annotations of a *Base-A* part.

5.4. OWL/RDF Encoding of Semantic Annotations

Annotations instantiated through the two methods above are readable and understandable to humans. They can also be embedded in CAD models to make them directly accessible and sharable among compatible CAD systems. However, as the annotations are in some CAD-proprietary formats as shown in Fig. 8, it would be difficult and impractical for non-CAD applications to make use of the embedded annotations without complex transformations. To leverage machine-readability of the semantic annotations for both CAD and non-CAD applications, neutral encoding in an application-independent, platform-independent and machine-interpretable language is necessary. In the current research, we select OWL/RDF to encode the semantic annotations, because our product ontologies are in OWL which is also compatible to RDF.

OWL/RDF encoding marks up the semantics in annotations according to the domain ontologies developed earlier. Through the encoding process, interpretive information elements in the annotations are organized in an XML-alike structure with semantic tags. The tags use commonly-agreed domain terminologies from the vocabulary library. Each tag has been semantically-specified by an OWL concept class in the domain ontology. Thus the intended meanings of the information elements of the annotations can be exactly captured in the resultant neutral representations. Take the CAD annotation "*Enclosure*" for the *Base-A* part in Fig. 8 as an example. According to the OWL ontological definitions of the *Enclosure* concept in Fig. 6 and in Table 4, the CAD annotation for the part "*Base-A*" can be encoded as follows.

```
<Enclosure rdf:ID="EnclosureAnnotation">
    <hasName rdf:datatype="&xsd;string">Enclosure_Base-A</hasName>
    <hasDescription rdf:datatype="&xsd;string">
        Laser driver circuit is enclosed in Base-A of the optical pickup unit
    </hasDescription>
    <hasValue rdf:datatype="&xsd;string">enclosing</hasValue>
    <hasExeType rdf:resource="#java"/>
    <hasEnclosedPart rdf:resource="#LaserDriverCircuit"/>
    <hasEnclosingPart rdf:resource="#Base-A"/>
</Enclosure>

<ECAD rdf:about="#LaserDriverCircuit">
  <rdf:type rdf:resource="&owl;Thing"/>
</ECAD>
<MCAD rdf:about="#Base-A">
  <rdf:type rdf:resource="&owl;Thing"/>
</MCAD>
```

Figure 9. OWL/RDF encoding for an *Enclosure* annotation.

With the neutral representation in Fig. 9, the CAD and non-CAD applications can understand the meanings of any tags in the annotation such as *Enclosure*, *hasName*, *hasEnclosedPart*, etc. That is because they interpret the tags following the same set of semantic definitions in the OWL ontology. Thus, different disciplines can reuse the annotation content in a semantically consistent way. This helps overcome the terminological ambiguity in utilization of semantic information across domains.

5.5. Associating Annotations with Annotated Engineering Resources

Given that the annotations and the annotated engineering resources are often from separate software platforms, digital associations between the two become critical. Two methods are developed to associate the annotations with the annotated target objects of engineering resources in the current study.

The first method is suitable for associating the semantic annotations with the CAD models (annotated target objects). A CAD link is established in a CAD modeling environment for this purpose. Many commercial CAD systems, such as the AutoCAD system, provide APIs (application programming interfaces) for constructing such CAD links. By using the APIs, the annotation contents are transformed into a format recognizable and processible by CAD systems. A CAD link relation is then constructed to associate an annotation with one or more CAD objects under annotation. This relation together with the annotation contents is embedded into the CAD model itself, retrievable and editable from the CAD modeling environment. This method is simple and effective for CAD annotations. However, as the native CAD APIs are involved, the application of the method is limited, only for compatible CAD systems to link CAD annotations with CAD objects.

The second method is more general. It is applicable to all kinds of annotations in OWL/RDF neutral format, for them to be associated with different types of annotated objects in engineering resources. The basic idea of the method is to virtually attach an annotation to an annotated object, by registering the annotation and the digital identifier of the object in an annotation repository of a collaboration server. The annotation can also be referred to multiple target objects, while the object can be associated with multiple annotations. A collaboration server is needed to implement this association mechanism. In our previous studies, a prototype of the collaboration server and other annotation interfacing toolkits have been developed. They will be used in the annotation application scenarios in the next section.

6. Semantic Annotation Scenarios in Sustainable Manufacturing

In sustainable manufacturing, a major application area of semantic annotations is for product semantics sharing rather for information search, browsing or indexing. This is one of the fundamental usage differences from the Web resources annotation. As such, this section provides two domain-specific use scenarios in sustainable manufacturing of consumer products. They highlight the capabilities of the proposed semantic annotation approach by demonstrating its potentials for:

- cross-functional communication of design intents over multiple CAD platforms; and
- semantic knowledge sharing in product sustainability assessment.

Multiple CAD and non-CAD teams/applications are involved in these annotation scenarios.

6.1. Multi-CAD Annotation for Design Intent Communication

One of the main motivations for annotating semantics in multidisciplinary resources is to allow the meaning of interpretative information in annotations to be shared by multi-CAD systems in the collaborative design process. Featuring extensive interactions between mCAD, eCAD, and optCAD teams with interdisciplinary coupling of constraints and relationships, this process requires unambiguous CAD semantics to enable close inter-discipline design collaboration. How can semantic annotations help? This will be illustrated in the following scenario for the collaborative design of an exemplary optical disc drive (ODD).

In the ODD design process, multiple CAD systems are used. Each discipline describes its design intent using own terminologies and CAD models. The ODD assembly design is in

Autodesk Inventor [28] DWG format. The assembly information needs to be shared by all the design disciplines for:

- mCAD modeling of part geometry, the dimension and location of mechanical fixtures, 3D obstacles, and enclosures, etc;
- eCAD modeling to decide the type, size and form of components, to place components on the board, to arrange multi-bus wiring, and to route traces based on the geometry restrictions given in the assembly design, followed by electrical circuit and component simulations;
- optCAD design to select off-the-shelf components, to design light path geometries, and to analyze the optical sub-system to meet the specifications and constraints set in the assembly design; and
- other design related activities and design iterations.

In the process above, semantic annotations are used to explicate and enrich the meaning and content of the ODD assembly drawings (created from an Inventor system). The purpose is for better sharability of the design intent and critical assembly information among the involved disciplines, especially for those CAD systems that are not compatible with the Inventor system. By using our collaborative design server and CAD add-on toolkit in Fig. 8, two types of semantic annotations are created for the ODD assembly drawings:

- Behavioral annotation for inter-part relationships between CAD models designed by different disciplines; and
- Property annotation for critical design parameters, such as component location coordinates, dimensions of keep-out regions, optics performing distance, and central spot power.

Among others, an inter-part relationship annotation for *Enclosure* is detailed below. The ontological concept for *Enclosure* is defined in Fig. 6 and Table 4. An instantiated *Enclosure* annotation is given in Fig. 9. The role of the annotation in support of consistent design intent communication across multi-CAD platforms can be explained as follows.

The annotation in Fig. 9 describes that the inter-part relationship between a mCAD model *Base-A* and an eCAD model *LaserDriverCircuit* would be an instance of the *Enclosure* concept. The relationship is built by referring to the *hasEnclosedPart* and *hasEnclosingPart* semantic tags in the annotation in Fig. 9. It further annotates the functional semantics of a design service – to conduct a check on validity of the *Enclosure* inter-part relationship between the two parts. The design service is specified through the *hasValue* and *hasExeType* semantic tags in Fig. 9.

When the annotation is communicated from a mCAD to an eCAD system, the eCAD add-on tool will interpret the meaning of the annotation according to the semantic definition for *Enclosure* specified in Fig. 6 and Table 4. Hence, the eCAD system is able to use the rich background knowledge specified in domain ontologies to understand the communicated design intents from the mCAD system. For example, by understanding the semantics of the *Enclosure* concept, then invoking the design service designated in the annotation, the eCAD system will ensure that the inter-part relationship holds. Thus, the functional semantics for checking the *Enclosure* relationship are unambiguously communicated across mCAD and eCAD systems to achieve the overall goal of the ODD design.

6.2. Ontology-Based Sustainability Knowledge Sharing

A proof-of-concept prototype has been developed to test our ontology implementation mechanism in sustainability assessment of consumer products [29]. The prototype is used for annotation of the LCA results and sharing the LCA semantics in ODD design reviews to recommend preferred design options.

This case study highlights the role of *Ecological Consequence* sustainability category under the criterion for *Environment Protection* in our sustainability taxonomy in Fig. 4. There are four sub-criteria in this category. They are global warming potential (GWP), acidification potential, ozone layer depletion potential, and solid waste. As sub-concepts of *Sustainability Criteria* in Fig. 4, the four sub-concepts inherit the same set of properties from their super-concept.

The four sub-concepts above illustrate four different environmental impacts. The impacts are quantified by environmental engineering specialists following an ISO standard methodology [30] for LCA. It involves the compilation of environmental intervention data, and the calculation of mass/energy flows and releases. In our study, the LCA calculation capability is provided by the GaBi LCA software package [31] and by an environmental engineering service provider. The LCA results need to be shared by multiple sustainable design disciplines in ODD sustainability evaluation and design reviews.

It is identified that sustainability annotations are needed for the following reasons:

- To explicate the LCA knowledge embedded in the LCA calculation results;
- To provide the ODD designers/reviewers with semantically rich, cross-domain information originated from external engineering service systems.

```
<CadModel rdf:about="#OpticalDiscDrive">
  <rdf:type rdf:resource="&owl;Thing"/>
</CadModel>
<EngineeringResources rdf:about="#GaBiSystem">
  <rdf:type rdf:resource="&owl;Thing"/>
</EngineeringResources>
<SustainabilityAssessment rdf:about="#DesignOption_3">
  <rdf:type rdf:resource="&owl;Thing"/>
</SustainabilityAssessment>
<CriteriaMeasures rdf:about="#kg CO2_equivalent">
  <rdf:type rdf:resource="&owl;Thing"/>
</CriteriaMeasures>

<GWP rdf:ID="GWP_Annotation">
  <hasName rdf:datatype="&xsd;string">GWP_ODD</hasName>
  <hasDescription rdf:datatype="&xsd;string">
   LCA annotation for global warming potential of optical disc drive
  </hasDescription>
  <hasCadModel rdf:resource="#OpticalDiscDrive"/>
  <hasWeightFactor rdf:datatype="&xsd;float">0.3275</hasWeightFactor>
  <hasCriterionValue rdf:datatype="&xsd;float">2.1732</hasCriterionValue>
  <hasMeasure rdf:resource="#kg CO2_equivalent"/>
  <isInstantiatedBy rdf:resource="#GaBiSystem"/>
  <isUsedBy rdf:resource="#DesignOption_3"/>
</GWP>
```

Figure 10. OWL encoding example of a *GlobalWarmingPotential* annotation.

In this way, the sustainability annotations would support LCA knowledge sharing among disciplines. Using the semantic annotation approach in the previous sections, the underlying LCA data are annotated. Fig. 10 shows an OWL encoding of a *GlobalWarmingPotential* annotation for the ODD product.

During design evaluation, the design review system receives the *GlobalWarmingPotential* annotation attached with the ODD design documents. It interprets the semantics of the annotated concepts, such as *kg CO2_equivalent* and *hasWeightFactor*, according to the ontological definitions specified in the sub-concept class for *GlobalWarmingPotential* and in its super-concept classes for *Ecological Consequence* and *Environment Protection* in a domain ontology. Using the markup in Fig. 10, the design review system would understand the semantics of the environmental sustainability knowledge from the environmental engineering domain. For example, based on the metadata of a "*DesignOption_3*" for an "*OpticalDiscDrive*" with a global warming potential of "*2.1732*" "*kg CO2_equivalent*" as the criterion value and "*0.3275*" as a weight factor, also based on other relevant knowledge, the design review system would compare and select an optimal ODD design with the minimal *GlobalWarmingPotential* impact. In this way, the annotation provides a means for ontology-based sharing of inter-disciplinary knowledge in selection of sustainable ODD design options.

7. Conclusion

Ontology-based semantic annotations are needed in sustainable manufacturing mainly for cross-domain semantics sharing. A novel annotation approach has been introduced in this chapter to serve this need in multidisciplinary, sustainable consumer product design and development. The approach takes advantage of sustainable manufacturing and Semantic Web technologies to achieve semantics-enabled capturing, formalization, annotation and sharing of product knowledge. The key idea is to have annotated metadata defined and described in such a way that their meanings can be explicitly interpreted and understood by multidisciplinary product development teams, processes and systems. Compared with the traditional annotation methods, the proposed approach provides more comprehensive solutions for product ontology modeling and ontology implementation. The main features of the approach include:

- Explicit specification of the semantic needs in annotation expressions;
- OWL ontology formalization of the concepts and relations used in the annotation expressions;
- Incorporation of sustainable manufacturing knowledge in the taxonomy of sustainability; OWL/RDF neutral encoding of annotation content for effective cross-functional communications; and
- Annotation prototyping toolkits to facilitate the generation and consumption of semantic annotations in sustainable consumer product realization.

It therefore contributes to the new development of the engineering annotation technologies to support sustainable manufacturing of consumer products.

The feature work will be focused on: enhancing the reasoning capability of the OWL domain ontologies with a semantic Web rule language such as SWRL [39]; developing new semantic transformation mechanisms; and applying the semantic annotation approach to more sustainable manufacturing applications.

References

[1] United Nations, Report of the World Commission on Environment and Development: *Our Common Future*, London, Oxford University Press, 1987.

[2] Manufacturing Engineering Laboratory of NIST, *Sustainable and lifecycle information-based manufacturing,* available at http://www.nist.gov/el/msid/dpg/slim.cfm (accessed on 8 Jun 2010).

[3] K. Krippendorff, *The semantic turn: a new foundation for design*, CRC Press, 2006.

[4] Q. Z. Yang and C. Y. Miao, Semantic enhancement and ontology for interoperability in integration of design information systems, *proceedings of the 12th IEEE international conference on emerging technologies and factory automation*, Patras, Greece, Sep 2007, pp. 169-176.

[5] F. Jovane, E. Westkämper, D. Williams, *The ManuFuture Road: towards competitive and sustainable high-adding-value manufacturing*, Springer, 2009.

[6] J. Elkington, *Cannibab with forks: the triple bottom line of 21st century business*, Cabriola Island: New Society Publishers, 1998.

[7] K. T. Ulrich and S. D. Eppinger, *Product design and development*, New York: McGraw-Hill, 1995.

[8] Q. Z. Yang, B. Song, Semantic knowledge management to support sustainable product design, *proceedings of the 2009 international conference on advanced management science,* Singapore, Apr 2009, pp. 407-411.

[9] 9F. M. Shipman III, R. J. McCall, *Integrating different perspectives on design rationale: supporting the emergence of design rationale from design communication.* Technical report CSDL 96-001, 1996, Texas A&M University, USA.

[10] M. Dean, G. Schreiber, *OWL Web ontology language reference*, W3C recommendation, available at http://www.w3.org/TR/2004/REC-owl-ref-20040210/ (accessed on 16 Jul 2010).

[11] D. Beckett, *RDF/XML syntax specification,* W3C recommendation, available at http://www.w3.org/TR/2004/REC-rdf-syntax-grammar-20040210/ (accessed on 16 Jul 2010).

[12] T. R. Gruber, J. M. Tenenbaum, J. C. Weber, Toward a knowledge medium for collaborative product development. In: J. S. Gero (ed) Artificial intelligence in design: *proceedings of the 2nd international conference on artificial intelligence in design,* Kluwer Academic Publishers, Boston, 1992.

[13] S. Aubry, S. Okawa, D. Lenne, I. Thouvenin, *Knowledge integration in annotation-based collaborative virtual environments, proceedings interaction 2005*, Tokyo, Japan, 2005.

[14] J. Olive, I. Thouvenin, D. Lenne, A new knowledge visualization and manipulation metaphor for collaborative and immersive environment, *proceedings of the 2nd international conference on enactive interfaces*, Genoa, Italy, 2005.

[15] E.Y.L. Do, VR sketchpad: create instant 3D worlds by sketching on a transparent window, *proceedings of the 9th international conference on computer-aided architectural design,* Eindhoven, The Netherlands, 2001, pp 161-172.

[16] M. Nagarajan, Semantic annotations in web services. In: Cardoso J, Sheth AP (eds) Semantic web services, processes and applications, pp35-61, Springer, 2006.

[17] V. Uren, P. Cimiano, J. Iria, S. Handschuh, M. Vargas-Vera, E. Motta, F. Ciravegna, Semantic annotation for knowledge management: requirements and a survey of the state of the art, *Journal of web semantics: science, services and agents on the World Wide Web* 4: 14–28, 2006.

[18] L. Reeve, H. Han, Survey of semantic annotation platforms, *proceedings of the ACM symposium on applied computing,* New Mexico, USA, 2005.

[19] Y. Kitamura, N. Washio, Y. Koji, R. Mizoguchi, Towards ontologies of functionality and semantic annotation for technical knowledge management, *in new frontiers in artificial intelligence: joint JSAI 2005 workshop post-proceedings,* pp 17-28, Springer-Verlag Berlin/Heidelberg, 2006

[20] Y. Lin, D. Strasunskas, S. Hakkarainen, J. Krogstie, A. Sølvberg, Semantic annotation framework to manage semantic heterogeneity of process models, *proceedings of the 18th conference on advanced information systems engineering,* pp 433-446, Springer-Verlag Berlin/Heidelberg, 2006.

[21] SEVENPRO project (FP6-027473), *SEVENPRO annual public report 2008*, available at http://www.sevenpro.org/ (accessed on 21 Oct 2009).

[22] ATHENA project (IST-507849), *ATHENA key results and ATHENA performance indicators,* in ATHENA project deliverables D.C1.1/D.C2.1 and D.C2.1, 2004.

[23] N. Boudjlida, N. Boudjlida, C. Dong, S. Baïna, H. Panetto, J. Krogstie, A. Hahn, K. Hausmann, J. V. Tomás, R. Poler, M. Á. Abián, M. J. Núñez, Zouggar, C. Diamantini, S. Tinella, *A practical experiment on semantic enrichment of enterprise models in a homogeneous environment*, INTEROP-NoE project deliverable DTG4.1, 2006.

[24] European Commission, *Semantic design cuts costs, saves time*, available at http://ec.europa.eu/research/headlines/news/article_09_05_14_en.html (accessed on 8 Jun 2010).

[25] Stanford University, Protégé release 3.4, available at http://protege.stanford.edu/ (accessed on 8 Jun 2010).

[26] C. Welty, M. K. Smith, D. L. McGuinness, *OWL Web Ontology Language Guide*, W3C recommendation, available at http://www.w3.org/TR/2004/REC-owl-guide-20040210/ (accessed on 16 Jul 2010).

[27] Q. Z. Yang, Y. Zhang, Semantic interoperability to support collaborative product development. In: Li WD, Ong SK, Nee AYC, McMahon C (eds) *Collaborative product design and manufacturing methodologies and applications,* pp 255-286, Springer, London, 2007.

[28] 28. Autodesk Inc., Autodesk Inventor, available at http://south-apac.autodesk.com/ (accessed on 9 Jul 2010).

[29] Q. Z. Yang and B. Song, Incorporating sustainability in the front end of design process, *proceedings of international conference on manufacturing automation*, Singapore, 2007, pp. 539-550.

[30] ISO, *Environmental management – Life cycle assessment – Principles and framework,* ISO 14040: 2006.

[31] PE International, GaBi - *Life cycle assessment software system*, available at http://www.gabi-software.com/ (accessed on 9 Jul 2010).
[32] T. Ruotsalo, L. Aroyo, G. Schreiber, Knowledge-based linguistic annotation of digital cultural heritage collections, *IEEE Intelligent Systems*, 24(2), pp. 64-75, IEEE Computer Society, 2009.
[33] M. Uschold, M. King, Towards a methodology for building ontologies, in Skuce D. (eds) *IJCAI'95 Workshop on basic ontological issues in knowledge sharing*, Montreal, Canada, pp 183.1-183.15, 1995.
[34] M. Grüninger, M. S. Fox, Methodology for the design and evaluation of ontologies, in Skuce D. (eds) *IJCAI'95 Workshop on basic ontological issues in knowledge sharing*, Montreal, Canada, pp 6.1-6.10, 1995.
[35] M. Fernández-López, A. Gómez-Pérez, N. Jristo, METHONTOLOGY: From ontological art towards ontological engineering, *Spring Symposium on ontological engineering of AAAI*, Stanford University, California, pp 33-40, 1997.
[36] Y. Sure, S. Staab, R. Studer, On-To-Knowledge methodology, in Staab S and Studer R(eds), *Handbook on Ontologies*, Springer, pp 117-132, 2004.
[37] H. S. Pinto, S. Staab, C. Tempich, DILIGENT: towards a fine-grained methodology for distributed, loosely-controlled and evolving engineering of ontologies. In: *European conference on Artificial Intelligence: 2004*; Valencia, Spain; 2004: 393-397.
[38] Tim Berners-Lee, *The specification of the Notation 3 (N3) language*, available at http://www.w3.org/DesignIssues/Notation3.html (accessed on 16 Jul 2010).
[39] I. Horrocks, P. F. Patel-Schneider, H. Boley, S. Tabet, B. Grosof, M. Dean, *SWRL: a semantic Web rule language combining OWL and RuleML*, available at http://www.w3.org/Submission/2004/SUBM-SWRL-20040521/ (accessed on 16 Jul 2010).

INDEX

A

B

C

D

E

F

G

H

I

J

K

L

M

N

O

P

Q

R

S

T

U

V